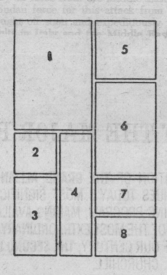

1 Roosevelt and Churchill seen during their historic meeting at sea in 1941. From this conference came the Atlantic Charter.

2 The United States tanker *P. B. Resor* in flames after being torpedoed in a surprise attack near the New Jersey shoreline.

3 Rudolph Hess, Nazi leader, said after his dramatic flight to Scotland in 1941 that Hitler "does not want to defeat England."

4 A photograph of a victim being hanged by the German Gestapo in the main square of Belgrade, Yugoslavia, in December 1941.

5 Ribbentrop reads note of the Foreign Office to Soviet government and to representatives of local and foreign press in 1941.

6 Field Marshall General Erwin Rommel, the famous Desert Fox, seen during an inspection of the Atlantic Wall installations.

7 On the eastern front Nazi troops proceed against the enemy, taking advantage of the cover provided by Soviet farm houses.

8 This photograph shows smiling British troops lined up on the waterfront awaiting evacuation by sea from Greece in 1941.

"ONE OF THE MAJOR PIECES

WITH THIS EDITION OF **THE GRAND ALLIANCE** BANTAM BOOKS CONTINUES TODAY'S MOST SIGNIFICANT PAPERBACK PUBLISHING PROGRAM, MAKING AVAILABLE, IN ITS ENTIRETY, ONE OF THE MOST EXTRAORDINARY HISTORICAL DOCUMENTS OF OUR CENTURY, **THE SECOND WORLD WAR**, BY WINSTON S. CHURCHILL.

IN THE THIRD VOLUME OF THIS NOBEL-PRIZE-WINNING SERIES, MR. CHURCHILL DESCRIBES THE BROADENING OF THE WAR TO A WORLD SCALE: THE GERMAN DRIVE TO THE EAST; THE BATTLE OF THE ATLANTIC; THE NORTH AFRICAN STRUGGLE; THE SPREAD OF THE WAR TO THE PACIFIC AND THE CEMENTING OF THE GRAND ALLIANCE WITH THE ENTRANCE OF RUSSIA INTO THE WAR.

THE FIRST TWO VOLUMES OF **THE SECOND WORLD WAR**, **THE GATHERING STORM** AND **THEIR FINEST HOUR**, HAVE

OF WRITING OF OUR TIME"

SATURDAY REVIEW OF LITERATURE

ALREADY BEEN PUBLISHED BY BANTAM BOOKS. THE REMAINING VOLUMES, ALL OF WHICH WILL APPEAR IN BANTAM EDITIONS, ARE **THE HINGE OF FATE, CLOSING THE RING** AND **TRIUMPH AND TRAGEDY.**

"CHURCHILL TREATS THESE EVENTS IN MASTERLY STYLE. A GREAT HISTORIAN, HE IS WRITING OF HISTORY IN WHICH HE WAS ONE OF THE MOST POWERFUL FIGURES."

"THE ACCOUNT IS SET FORTH IN THE FINEST CHURCHILLIAN PROSE. THE EVENTS AND DECISIONS ARE STIRRING; THE IMPACT IS IMMENSE..."

"YOU WILL NOT WANT TO MISS THIS THIRD AND MOST EXCITING VOLUME IN CHURCHILL'S STAGGERING HISTORY OF WORLD WAR II. HISTORY AT ITS FINEST! REVEALING, AWE-INSPIRING, MOMENTOUS!"

THE SECOND WORLD WAR
WINSTON S. CHURCHILL

★ ★ ★

THE GRAND ALLIANCE

BANTAM BOOKS
TORONTO · LONDON
NEW YORK

THE GRAND ALLIANCE

*A Bantam Book / published by arrangement with
Houghton Mifflin Company*

PRINTING HISTORY
Houghton Mifflin edition published April 1950

2nd printing	April 1950	4th printing	May 1956
3rd printing	April 1950	5th printing	November 1959

Book-of-the-Month Club edition published May 1950

Bantam edition / May 1962

2nd printing	December 1962	8th printing	August 1971
3rd printing	June 1964	9th printing	August 1973
4th printing	January 1965	10th printing	July 1974
5th printing	August 1966	11th printing	June 1975
6th printing	August 1967	12th printing	May 1976
7th printing	June 1969	13th printing	August 1977

The quotations from THE UNRELENTING STRUGGLE, *by William
S. Churchill, are reprinted by the courtesy of Cassell & Company, Ltd.*
The quotation from THE MEMOIRS OF CORDELL HULL *is reprinted by the courtesy of The Macmillan Company.*
Front cover photo: Wide World Photos, Inc.
*Inside front cover photos: 1, 4, 5, 6, and 8 from United Press
International; 2, 3,.and 7 from Wide World Photos, Inc.*
*Inside back cover photos: 1, 4, 6, and 7 from United Press
International; 8 from International News; 2, 3, and 5 from Wide
World Photos, Inc.*

ISBN 0-553-11311-9

Published simultaneously in the United States and Canada

*Bantam Books are published by Bantam Books, Inc. Its trademark, consisting of the words "Bantam Books" and the portrayal of a bantam, is registered in the United States Patent
Office and in other countries. Marca Registrada. Bantam
Books, Inc., 666 Fifth Avenue, New York, New York 10019.*

PRINTED IN THE UNITED STATES OF AMERICA

$\star$

Preface

THIS VOLUME, like the others, claims only to be a contribution to the history of the Second World War. The tale is told from the standpoint of the British Prime Minister, with special responsibility as Minister of Defence for military affairs. As these came directly to some extent into my hands, British operations are narrated in their scope and in some detail. At the same time it would be impossible to describe the struggles of our Allies except as a background. To do full justice these must be left to their own historians, or to later and more general British accounts. While recognising the impossibility of preserving proportion, I have tried to place our own story in its true setting.

The main thread is again the series of my directives, telegrams, and minutes upon the daily conduct of the war and of British affairs. These are all original documents composed by me as events unfolded. They therefore constitute a more authentic record and give, I believe, a better impression of what happened and how it seemed at the time than any account which I could write now that the course of events is known. Although they contain expressions of opinion and forecasts which did not come true, it is by them as a whole that I wish my own share in the conflict to be judged. Only in this way can the reader understand the actual problems we had to face as defined by the knowledge then in our possession.

Space would not allow, nor indeed in many cases have I the right, to print the replies, which very often took the form of lengthy departmental memoranda. I have therefore been careful to avoid, so far as I can, throwing blame on individuals. Where possible I have endeavoured to give a summary of replies to telegrams. In the main however the documents which are printed tell the tale.

We are again dealing with war on the giant scale, and the battle on the Russian front involved as many divisions on both sides as were engaged in the Battle of France. At every point along a far longer front the great masses engaged, with slaughter incomparable to anything which occurred elsewhere during the war. I cannot attempt to do more than refer to the struggle between the German and the Russian Armies as the background of the actions of Britain and the Western Allies. The Russian epic of 1941 and 1942 deserves a detailed and dispassionate study and record in the English language. Even though no facilities for foreigners to narrate the Russian agony and glory might be accorded, the effort should be made. Nor should this impulse be chilled by the fact that the Soviet Government have already claimed all the honour for themselves.

Hitler's invasion of Russia brought to an end the period of almost exactly a year during which Great Britain and her Empire stood alone, undismayed, and growing continually in strength. Six months later the United States, violently assaulted by Japan, became our ally for all purposes. The ground for our united action had been prepared beforehand by my correspondence with President Roosevelt, and it was possible to forecast not only the form of our operations but also their sequence. The effective combination of the whole English-speaking world in the waging of war and the creation of the Grand Alliance form the conclusion to this part of my account.

WINSTON S. CHURCHILL

CHARTWELL
January 1, 1950

☆

Acknowledgments

I MUST AGAIN ACKNOWLEDGE the assistance of those who helped me with the previous volume, namely, Lieutenant-General Sir Henry Pownall, Commodore G. R. G. Allen, Colonel F. W. Deakin, and Sir Edward Marsh, Mr. Denis Kelly and Mr. C. C. Wood. I have also to thank the very large number of others who have kindly read these pages and commented upon them.

Lord Ismay has continued to give me his aid, as have my other friends.

I record my obligation to His Majesty's Government for permission to reproduce the text of certain official documents of which the Crown Copyright is legally vested in the Controller of His Majesty's Stationery Office. At the request of His Majesty's Government on security grounds, I have paraphrased some of the telegrams published in this volume. These changes have not altered in any way the sense or substance of the telegrams.

Moral of the Work

In War: Resolution
In Defeat: Defiance
In Victory: Magnanimity
In Peace: Good Will

☆

Theme of the Volume

*How the British fought on
with Hardship their Garment
until
Soviet Russia and the United States
were drawn
into the Great Conflict*

Contents

Book One

GERMANY DRIVES EAST

Book Two

WAR COMES TO AMERICA

Maps and Diagrams

☆

Book One

GERMANY DRIVES EAST

1

The Desert and the Balkans

LOOKING BACK upon the unceasing tumult of the war, I cannot recall any period when its stresses and the onset of so many problems all at once or in rapid succession bore more directly on me and my colleagues than the first half of 1941. The scale of events grew larger every year; but the decisions required were not more difficult. Greater military disasters fell upon us in 1942, but by then we were no longer alone and our fortunes were mingled with those of the Grand Alliance. No part of our problem in 1941 could be solved without relation to all the rest. What was given to one theatre had to be taken from another. An effort here meant a risk there. Our physical resources were harshly limited. The attitude of a dozen Powers, friendly, opportunist, or potentially hostile, was unknowable. At home we must face the war against the U-boats, the invasion threat, and the continuing Blitz; we had to conduct the group of campaigns in the Middle East; and, thirdly, to try to make a front against Germany

3

in the Balkans. And we had to do all this for a long time alone. After shooting Niagara we had now to struggle in the rapids. One of the difficulties of this narrative is the disproportion between our single-handed efforts to keep our heads above water from day to day and do our duty, and the remorseless development of far larger events.

*   *   *

We had at any rate a solid foundation in Great Britain. I was sure that, provided we maintained the highest state of readiness at home and the necessary forces, a German attempt at invasion in 1941 would not be to our disadvantage. The German air strength in all theatres was very little greater than in 1940, whereas our air fighter force at home had grown from fifty-one to seventy-eight squadrons, and our bombers from twenty-seven to forty-five squadrons. The Germans had not won the air battle in 1940. They seemed to have little chance of winning it in 1941. Our army in the Island had grown far stronger. Between September, 1940, and September, 1941, it was raised from twenty-six active divisions to thirty-four, plus five armoured divisions. To this must be added the maturity of the troops and the enormous increase in their weapons. The Home Guard had risen from a million to a million and a half; and now all had firearms. Numbers, mobility, equipment, training, organisation, and defence works were vastly improved. Hitler, of course, had always a superabundance of soldiers for invasion. To conquer us he would have had to carry and supply across the Channel at least a million men. He could by 1941 have had a large though not a sufficient quantity of landing-craft. But with our dominant air force and naval power giving us the command of both elements we had no doubt of our ability to destroy or cripple his armada. All the arguments, therefore, on which we had relied in 1940 were now incomparably stronger. So long as there was no relaxation in vigilance or serious reduction in our own defence the War Cabinet and the Chiefs of the Staff felt no anxiety.

Although our American friends, some of whose generals visited us, took a more alarmist view of our position, and the world at large regarded the invasion of Britain as probable, we ourselves felt free to send overseas all the troops our available shipping could carry and to wage offensive war in the Middle East and the Mediterranean. Here was the hinge on which our ultimate victory turned, and it was in 1941 that the first significant events began. In war armies must fight. Africa was the only continent in which we could meet our foes on land. The defence of Egypt and of Malta were duties compulsive upon us, and the destruction of the Italian Empire the first prize we could gain. The British resistance in the Middle East to the triumphant Axis Powers and our attempt to rally the Balkans and Turkey against them are the theme and thread of our story now.

* * *

The Desert victories cheered the opening days of the year. Bardia, with more than forty thousand men, surrendered on January 5. Tobruk seemed certainly within our grasp, and was in fact taken, with nearly thirty thousand prisoners, in a fortnight. On the nineteenth we reoccupied Kassala, in the Sudan, and on the twentieth invaded the Italian colony of Eritrea, seizing the railhead at Biscia a few days later. On that same day the Emperor Haile Selassie re-entered Abyssinia. But all the while the reports accumulated of the German movements and preparations for a Balkan campaign. I drew up for the Chiefs of Staff an appreciation upon the war as a whole, with which I found them in general agreement.

Prime Minister to General Ismay, for C.O.S. Committee 6 Jan. 41

The speedy destruction of the Italian armed forces in Northeast Africa must be our prime major overseas objective in the opening months of 1941. Once the Italian army in Cyrenaica has been destroyed, the Army of the Nile becomes free for other tasks. We cannot yet tell what these will be.

2. The fall of Bardia should enable an advanced base to be established there for the capture of Tobruk. With Bardia and Tobruk in our hands it should be possible to drop the land communications with Alexandria almost entirely and to rely upon sea transport for our further westward advance. Every plan should be made now to use Tobruk to its utmost capacity.

3. The striking force to be maintained west of Bardia and Tobruk need not be large. The 2d and 7th British Armoured Divisions, the 6th Australian Division, the New Zealand brigade group, soon to become a division, with perhaps one or two British brigades, comprising not more than 40,000 to 45,000 men, should suffice to overpower the remaining Italian resistance and to take Benghazi. The distance from Tobruk to Benghazi by the coastal road is not much above 250 miles, compared with about 370 from Alexandria to Tobruk.[1] Thus, once Tobruk is established as the base and our land communications begin from there, no greater

[1] See map, page 54.

strain should be thrown upon the land transport than at present, and it should be possible to start afresh from Tobruk as if Tobruk were Alexandria, and to maintain the moderate but adequate striking force required. With the capture of Benghazi this phase of the Libyan campaign would be ended.

4. The question is, how long will this take? Having regard to the very heavy Italian losses in their best troops and in their vehicles and equipment, and to the fact that we have the command of the sea, the collapse in Cyrenaica might be very rapid. Indeed, all might go with a run at any time. The need for haste is obvious. It would, however, suffice for our general strategy if Benghazi and everything east of it were effectively in our possession and occupied as a military and naval base at any time during March.

5. The aforesaid Libyan operations need not, therefore, at all affect the simultaneous pushing of the campaign against the Italians in Abyssinia. General Wavell has already withdrawn the 4th Indian Division. The 5th Indian Division is also available, and it should be possible to carry out the Kassala operation and to spread the revolt in Abyssinia, while at the same time the Kenya forces press northward by Lake Rudolf. At any time we may receive armistice proposals from the cut-off Italian garrison in Abyssinia. This army must have been buoyed up with hopes of an Italian conquest of the Delta and of the Canal, enabling communications to be restored and supplies to reach them by the Nile and the Red Sea. These hopes are already dead. On the other hand, the vast size of Abyssinia, the lack of all communications, especially sea communications, and the impossibility of nourishing large forces may bring about an indefinite delay. It is, however, not an unreasonable hope that by the end of April the Italian army in Abyssinia will have submitted or been broken up.

6. The moment that this is apparent the northward movement of all the effective forces in Kenya, as well as those in the Sudan and Abyssinia, will become possible. These forces will thenceforward become a reserve available for operations in the Eastern Mediterranean. If we take the present total strength of the armies in the Middle East at about 370,000 (including convoys W.S. 5 and 6), it might be reasonably expected that the equivalent of ten divisions would stand in the Nile Valley, together with two additional divisions from home, a total of twelve, after providing the necessary garrisons and security troops for Abyssinia, Cyrenaica, Egypt, and Palestine. These twelve divisions should thus be free (apart from new distractions) by the end of April.

II

7. To invade and force a way through Spain to the Straits of Gibraltar against the will of the Spanish people and Government, especially at this season, is a most dangerous and questionable enterprise for Germany to undertake, and it is no wonder that Hitler, with so many sullen populations to hold down, has so far shrunk

from it. With the permission of the Spanish Government it would, of course, be a short and easy matter for the Germans to gain control of Lisbon and of the Algeciras and Ceuta batteries, together with appropriate airfields. According to Captain Hillgarth [our Naval Attaché in Madrid], who has lived long in Spain and is fresh from contact with our Ambassador, it is becoming increasingly unlikely that the Spanish Government will give Hitler passage or join the war against us. General Wavell's victories in Libya have played, and will play, an important part in Spanish opinion. If the Germans are refused permission it is most unlikely that they will try to force their way into and through Spain before the month of April. From every point of view this delay is helpful to us. We have the use of Gibraltar; we have the time for our strength in the Middle East to accomplish its task there and again to become free; above all, there is the possibility of events taking a favourable turn in France and at Vichy.

8. We must now be most careful not to precipitate matters in Spain, or set the Spanish Government against us more than it is already, or provoke Herr Hitler to a violent course towards Spain. All these matters are highly speculative. There can be no certainty about them. But the fact that Hitler has not acted through Spain as we feared, when conditions, both political and climatic, were more favourable to him, makes it on the whole a reasonable working assumption that any German adventure in Spain will at least wait for the spring.

III

9. The probabilities of delay in Spain until the spring give rise to the hope that the Vichy Government, under German pressure or actual German incursion, may either proceed to North Africa and resume the war from there, or authorise General Weygand to do so. If such an event could be brought about before the Straits of Gibraltar fell into German control, we should have a very good chance of resisting a German attempt against the Straits indefinitely. We could move troops into Morocco by the Atlantic ports; we should have the use of the French air bases in North Africa. The whole situation in the Mediterranean would be completely revolutionised in our favour. The position of any Italian forces remaining in Tripoli would become impossible. We might well be able to open the Mediterranean for supplies and reinforcements for the Middle East.

10. We have, therefore, thought it right to assure Marshal Pétain and General Weygand that we will assist them with up to six divisions, substantial air forces, and the necessary naval power from the moment they feel able to take the all-important step we so greatly desire. We have also impressed upon them the danger of delaying their action until the Germans have made their way through Spain and become masters of the Straits and of Northern Morocco. We can but wait and see what Vichy will do. Meanwhile

we enforce the blockade of France fitfully and as naval convenience offers, partly to assert the principle, partly to provide a "smoke-screen" of Anglo-French friction, and especially not to let the Vichy Government feel that if they do nothing life will be tolerable for them so far as we are concerned. It is greatly to our interest that events should develop rapidly in France. Presumably Herr Hitler realises this. Nevertheless the probabilities are that the French climax will come about before anything decisive happens in Spain.

IV

11. We must continually expect that Hitler will soon strike some heavy blow, and that he is now making preparations on a vast scale with customary German thoroughness. He can, of course, easily come down through Italy and establish an air power in Sicily. Perhaps this is already taking place.

The Chiefs of Staff Committee are requested to press on with their study of "Influx" [a scheme for the occupation of Sicily], which may conceivably require emergency treatment. It is not seen, however, how "Influx" can be accorded priority over the operations in Libya; certainly not, whatever happens, until Tobruk has been taken and a good forward base made there—if not farther west—to protect Egypt.

V

12. All the foregoing shows that nothing would suit our interest better than that any German advance in the Balkans should be delayed till the spring. For this very reason one must apprehend that it will begin earlier. The exploits of the Greek Army have been an enormous help to us. They have expressed themselves generously about the extremely modest aid in the air which was all we could give. But should their success be followed by a check or a deadlock, we must expect immediate demands for more aid. The only aid we can give quickly is four or five more squadrons from the Middle East, perhaps some artillery regiments, and some or all of the tanks of the 2d Armoured Division, now arrived and working up in leisurely fashion in Egypt.

"Furious" has reached Takoradi, and forty Hurricanes, etc., will soon raise Air Marshal Longmore's strength to well over a hundred Hurricane fighters. His losses in the offensive have been singularly small. His action in withdrawing squadrons from Aden and the Sudan has been vindicated. Tobruk may soon be in our hands, and thereafter it would seem that a strong reinforcement of air power for Greece should be provided. This should include Hurricane squadrons. Have the aerodromes in Greece been lengthened and adapted to them? Has the airfield in Crete yet been made suitable for their landing on passage? The call, when it comes, may be very urgent. Everything must be set in train now. We must know also how long it would take to move the 2d Armoured Division to the Piraeus, and what numbers are involved.

13. All accounts go to show that a Greek failure to take Valona will have very bad consequences. It may be possible for General Wavell, with no more than the forces he is now using in the Western Desert, and in spite of some reduction in his air force, to conquer the Cyrenaica province and establish himself at Benghazi; but it would not be right for the sake of Benghazi to lose the chance of the Greeks taking Valona, and thus to dispirit and anger them, and perhaps make them in the mood for a separate peace with Italy. Therefore, the prospect must be faced that after Tobruk the further westward advance of the Army of the Nile may be seriously cramped. It is quite clear to me that supporting Greece must have priority after the western flank of Egypt has been made secure.

VI

14. The attitude of Yugoslavia may well be determined by the support we give to Greece and by their fortunes before Valona. While it is impossible to dogmatise, it would be more natural for the Germans to push on through Rumania to the Black Sea and to press down through their old ally Bulgaria to Salonika, rather than to force their way through Yugoslavia. Many troop movements and many more rumours would seem to point to this. Evidently there is a great building-up of German strength, and improvement of German communications towards the southeast. We must so act as to make it certain that if the enemy enters Bulgaria, Turkey will come into the war. If Yugoslavia stands firm and is not molested, if the Greeks take Valona and maintain themselves in Albania, if Turkey becomes an active ally, the attitude of Russia may be affected favourably. Anyone can see how obnoxious, and indeed deadly, a German advance to the Black Sea or through Bulgaria to the Aegean must be to Russia. Fear only will restrain Russia from war, and perhaps a strong Allied front in the Balkans, with the growing prestige of the British Army and sea and air power, may lessen that fear. But we must not count on this.

VII

15. Last, but dominating all our war effort, is the threat of invasion, the air warfare and its effects on production, and the grievous pressure upon our western ports and northwestern communications. One cannot doubt that Herr Hitler's need to starve or crush Great Britain is stronger than it has ever been. A great campaign in the east of Europe, the defeat of Russia, the conquest of the Ukraine, and an advance from the Black Sea to the Caspian would none of them, separately nor all together, bring him victorious peace while the British air power grew ever stronger behind him and he had to hold down a whole continent of sullen,

starving peoples. Therefore, the task of preventing invasion, of feeding the Island, and of speeding our armament production must in no way be compromised for the sake of any other objective whatsoever.

*   *   *

Hitler also had his New Year thoughts, and it is interesting to compare his letter to Mussolini written a week earlier with my appreciation. Coincidence is evident about the attitude of General Franco and Spain.

31 Dec. 40

Duce,
    . . . In examining the general situation I reach the following conclusions:
    1. The war in the West is in itself won. A final violent effort is still necessary to crush England. In order to determine the manner of accomplishing this, we must weigh the factors which separate England from a complete collapse after the intensification of our air and submarine offensives will have produced their effect.
    In this battle, and after we have achieved the first stages of success, important German policies will be necessary for a final assault against the British Isles. The concentration of these forces—and particularly the enormous supply dumps—will require an anti-aircraft defence far superior to our original estimates.
    2. *France.* The French Government have dismissed Laval. The official reasons which have been communicated to me are false. I do not doubt for a moment that the real reason is that General Weygand is making demands from North Africa which amount to blackmail, and that the Vichy Government is not in a position to react without risking the loss of North Africa. I also consider it probable that there exists at Vichy itself a whole clique which approves of Weygand's policy, at least tacitly. I do not think that Pétain personally is disloyal. But one never knows. All this demands constant vigilance and a careful watching of events.
    3. *Spain.* Profoundly troubled by the situation, which Franco thinks has deteriorated, Spain has refused to collaborate with the Axis Powers. I fear that Franco may be about to make the biggest mistake of his life. I think that his idea of receiving from the democracies raw materials and wheat as a sort of recompense for his abstention from the conflict is extremely naïve. The democracies will keep him in suspense until he has consumed the last grain of wheat, and then they will unloose the fight against him.
    I deplore all this, for from our side we had completed our preparations for crossing the Spanish frontier on January 10, and to attack Gibraltar at the beginning of February. I think success would have been relatively rapid. The troops picked for this operation have been specially chosen and trained. The moment that

the Straits of Gibraltar fell into our hands the danger of a French change-over in North and West Africa would be definitely eliminated.

I am, therefore, very saddened by this decision of Franco, which is so little in accord with the aid which we, you, Duce, and myself, gave him when he found himself in difficulties. I still have the hope, the slight hope, that he will realise at the last minute the catastrophic consequences of his conduct, and that even tardily he will find his way to this battle front, where our victory will decide his own destiny.

4. *Bulgaria.* Bulgaria equally is reluctant to associate herself with the Tripartite Pact and to adopt a clear attitude in her international relations. The growing pressure exercised by Soviet Russia is the cause of this. If the King had adhered immediately to our pact, no one would have dared to put such pressure on him. The worst is that this influence poisons public opinion, which is not insensible to Communist infection.

5. Without doubt it is Hungary and Rumania who in this conflict have adopted the most clear-cut attitude. General Antonescu has recognised that the future of his régime, and even of his person, depends on our victory. From this he has drawn clear and direct conclusions which make him go up in my esteem.

The attitude of the Hungarians is no less loyal. Since December 18, German troops have been continually in transit in the direction of Rumania. Hungary and Rumania have put at my disposition their railway network, so that German divisions can be rapidly moved to the points of pressure. I cannot say any more yet of the operations which we are planning or which may become necessary, for these plans are being drawn up at this very moment. The strength of our forces will in any case be such that any threat of lateral counter-manoeuvre will be excluded.

It is simply necessary, Duce, that you stabilise your front in Albania so as to contain at least a part of the Greek and Anglo-Greek forces.

6. *Yugoslavia.* Yugoslavia is prudently gaining time. If circumstances are favourable it may be that she will conclude a non-aggression pact with us, but it seems now that she will not adhere in any case to the Tripartite Pact. I do not count on trying to obtain anything more until our military successes have improved the psychological climate.

7. *Russia.* Given the danger of seeing internal conflicts develop in a certain number of Balkan countries, it is necessary to foresee the extreme consequences and to have ready machinery capable of avoiding them. I do not envisage any Russian initiative against us so long as Stalin is alive, and we ourselves are not victims of serious setbacks. I consider it essential, Duce, as a premise of a satisfactory conclusion of this war that there should be in existence a German army sufficiently strong to deal with any eventuality in the East. The greater the strength of this army appears, the less

will be the probability that we shall have to employ it against an unforeseen danger. I should like to add to these general considerations that our present relations with the U.S.S.R. are very good. We are on the eve of concluding a trade treaty which will satisfy both parties, and there is considerable hope that we can resolve in a reasonable manner the remaining points at issue between us.

In fact, the only two questions which still divide us are Finland and Constantinople. In regard to Finland, I do not foresee fundamental difficulties, because we do not regard Finland as belonging essentially to our sphere of influence, and the only thing that interests us is that a second war should not break out in this area.

In contrast to this, it is not in our interest to abandon Constantinople to Russia and Bulgaria to Bolshevism. But even here it should be possible, with good intentions, to reach a solution which will avoid the worst and facilitate what we want. It will be easier to find a solution if Moscow is clear that nothing obliges us to accept an arrangement which is not satisfactory to us.

8. *Africa.* Duce, I do not think that in this theatre any counterattack on a large scale can be launched at the moment. The preparation of such an enterprise would take a minimum of three to five months. In the meantime we shall reach the season of the year in which the German armoured formations cannot successfully go into action. For unless they are equipped with special cooling devices even the armoured cars cannot be used in practice at such temperatures. In any case they cannot be used for tactical operations at long distances requiring a whole day.

The decisive solution in this sector seems to be to increase the number of anti-tank weapons, even if that means that in other sectors Italian formations must be deprived of these special guns.

Above all, as I stated recently, I believe nevertheless that we should try by all means to weaken the naval position of Great Britain in the Mediterranean with our air forces, because the employment of our ground troops in this sector cannot improve the situation.

For the rest, Duce, no decision of importance can be made before the month of March.

*   *   *

Mr. Eden was watching with close attention the darkening clouds in the East.

Foreign Minister to Prime Minister   6 Jan. 41

Salutations and congratulations upon the victory of Bardia! If I may debase a golden phrase, "Never has so much been surrendered by so many to so few."

The object of this minute, however, is to call attention to a less satisfactory sector of the international horizon, the Balkans. A mass of information has come to us over the last few days from divers sources, all of which tends to show that Germany is pressing forward her preparations in the Balkans with a view to an ultimate descent upon Greece. The date usually mentioned for such a descent is the beginning of March, but I feel confident that the Germans must be making every effort to antedate their move. Whether or not military operations are possible through Bulgaria against Salonika at this time of the year I am not qualified to say, but we may feel certain that Germany will seek to intervene by force to prevent complete Italian defeat in Albania. Already there are reports of increased enemy air forces operating against the Greeks, and General Papagos states that these are slowing down his advance. It would be in accordance with German methods to establish superiority in the air before making any move on land.

Politically the attitude of the Bulgarian Government causes me grave disquiet. They give the impression of men who have now little control of events. Their press is increasingly under German control, and is now little else but the mouthpiece of Axis propaganda. It is essential that our victories in North Africa should not result in any decrease of watchfulness on the part of the Turks and Yugoslavs, and we are doing what we can in the political sphere to ensure this. You may wish to have all these questions considered by the Defence Committee.

After reading this I issued the following minute:

Prime Minister to General Ismay, for C.O.S. Committee 6 Jan. 41

Pray see the attached from the Foreign Secretary. In spite of the evident need to pursue the Italians along the Libyan coast while the going is good, we shall have to consider the dispatch of four or five more squadrons of the Royal Air Force to Greece, and possibly the diversion of part of the 2d British Armoured Division.

I cannot look beyond Benghazi at the present time, and if Tobruk is taken there will be very few Italian troops, and by no means their best, east of Benghazi. . . .

Although perhaps by luck and daring we may collect comparatively easily most delectable prizes on the Libyan shore, the massive importance of the taking of Valona and keeping the Greek front in being must weigh hourly with us.

* * *

On January 8 the Defence Committee agreed that in view of the probability of an early German advance into Greece *through Bulgaria* it was of the first importance, from the political point of view, that we should do everything possible, by hook or by crook, to send at once to Greece the fullest support within our power. It was also agreed that a decision on the form and extent of our assistance to Greece should be taken within the next forty-eight hours. On this same day I received the following telegram from General Smuts. This was written quite independently of my minute two days earlier. I was fortified by his complete agreement with my view, endorsed as it was by the Chiefs of Staff and the Defence Committee.

General Smuts to Prime Minister   8 Jan. 41

Magnificent victories in the Middle East open up a field of speculation regarding our future course. Flowing tide will soon carry Wavell to Tobruk. Should he go farther? Tripoli is much too far. Even Benghazi is as far beyond the frontier as the frontier is from Alexandria. But there may be sound reasons, naval or other, for going so far as Benghazi. In the absence of good and special reasons Tobruk seems to me the terminus. Beyond it lie risks not necessary to detail. Leaving an adequate defensive force there in a fortified position, the rest of the army should be withdrawn to Egypt and the Middle East, where a strong army [of] manoeuvre will be required against possible attack through the Balkans.

2. I would however suggest that at such a stage liquidation of the Abyssinian situation should also be considered. Conquest of Abyssinia would mean a deadly blow at Mussolini's prestige and at the Fascist plunder. Italy may possibly be forced out of the war and the whole of the Mediterranean position transformed. Germany would once more be isolated, with prospect of certain defeat.

3. For an early liquidation of Abyssinia there is also the argument that the Italian morale there must be particularly low now, and early finish of the campaign would release large forces for reinforcing our front in the Middle East. If part of Wavell's Middle East army could be detailed shortly, reinforcing an attack on Abyssinia from the north, and a simultaneous attack is launched from Kenya, Italian resistance might rapidly disintegrate. I should think that an additional division in the north and another in Kenya would be sufficient if both attacks proceed simultaneously.

4. If such a plan for simultaneous attack is approved, I am prepared to supply the additional division for the south. Except for the deficiency in Bren guns, it is ready and could be moved as soon as shipping could be provided. Transport of such large forces both in the north and south must take some time, and if my suggestion is approved decision should be made as soon as possible. Attack from the south will rapidly push the fighting front away from Kenya, and so involve the scrapping of much of the plan now being worked on there. Plan of simultaneous attack from the north and south is required if unnecessary risk and a long campaign are to be avoided in so large an area as Eritrea and Abyssinia. For this [the] additional division in the north will be necessary, and probably sufficient. I hope it can be spared in spite of rumours of large German concentrations in Rumania and Hungary.

Question is whether Germany can afford to set the Balkans ablaze with Russia an incalculable factor and Turkey hostile. The Italian defeat in Africa and Greece, together with the failure of the German Air Force against Britain, have profoundly changed the position, and the German concentrations may only be intended to pacify the Italians, and to lure the British forces away from Britain, where the main attack is intended and has to be made. Whole situation is one for consideration of the General Staff, who have full facts before them. To me it would in the circumstances appear not to involve undue risk presently to detach one division with the necessary air force from the Middle East army in order to strengthen the Sudan force for this attack from the north. If the operation is brought off soon and expeditiously it might produce far-reaching results in Italy and the Middle East.

*   *   *

On January 10 the Chiefs of Staff warned the commanders in the Middle East that a German attack on Greece might start before the end of the month. It would come, they thought, through Bulgaria, and the probable line of advance would be down the Struma Valley against Salonika. Three divisions, supported by about two hundred dive-bombers, would be used, and three or four more divisions might be added after March. The Chiefs of Staff added that the decision of His Majesty's Government to give the greatest possible help to the Greeks meant that once Tobruk was taken all other operations in the Middle East must have second place, and they authorised the dispatch therefrom of mechanised and specialist units and air forces up to the following limits: one squadron of infantry tanks, one regiment of cruiser tanks,[2] ten regiments of artillery, and five squadrons of aircraft.

The Commanders-in-Chief in Cairo thought that the German concentration in Rumania, of which we had warned them, was merely a war of nerves, designed to induce us to disperse our forces in the Middle East and stop our advance in Libya. Wavell trusted that the Chiefs of Staff would "consider most urgently whether enemy's move is not bluff."

On reading this reply, which was far astray from the facts, I issued the following:

Prime Minister to General Ismay or Colonel Hollis,   10 Jan. 41
for C.O.S. Committee

Chiefs of Staff should meet tomorrow, Saturday morning, to consider the various telegrams from the Middle East H.Q., and

---

[2] The "infantry" tank was a heavy, slow, strongly armoured tank designed to accompany and support the infantry.

The "cruiser" tank was fast, better gunned than the infantry tank, but with lighter armour. It had a highly mobile fighting role.

The "light" tank was fast, with thin armour and only machine guns for armament. Used for reconnaissance.

they are authorised to dispatch the attached telegram which I have drafted to General Wavell and Air Marshal Longmore, unless they wish to make any communication to me upon it.

Prime Minister to General Wavell   10 Jan. 41

1. Our information contradicts idea that German concentration in Rumania is merely a "move in war of nerves" or a "bluff to cause dispersion of force." We have a mass of detail indicating that a large-scale movement through Bulgaria towards the Greek frontier, aimed presumably at Salonika, will begin before the end of the month. Hostile forces to be employed in the aforesaid invasion would not be large, but of deadly quality. One, perhaps two, armoured divisions, with one motorised division, about 180 dive-bombers, and some parachute troops, seems to be all that could cross the Bulgarian-Greek frontier up till the middle of February.

2. But this force, if not stopped, may play exactly the same part in Greece as the German Army's break-through at Sedan played in France. All Greek divisions in Albania will be fatally affected. These are the facts and implications which arise from our information, in which we have good reason to believe. But is this not also the very thing the Germans ought to do to harm us most? Destruction of Greece will eclipse victories you have gained in Libya, and may affect decisively Turkish attitude, especially if we have shown ourselves callous of fate of allies. You must now, therefore, conform your plans to larger interests at stake.

3. Nothing must hamper capture of Tobruk, but thereafter all operations in Libya are subordinated to aiding Greece, and all preparations must be made from the receipt of this telegram for the immediate succour of Greece up to the limits prescribed. These matters have been earnestly weighed by Defence Committee of Cabinet, and General Smuts has independently cabled almost identical views.

4. We expect and require prompt and active compliance with our decisions, for which we bear full responsibility. Your joint visit to Athens will enable you to contrive the best method of giving effect to the above decisions. It should not be delayed.

The Chiefs of Staff being in accord, this telegram was dispatched. It will be seen that our intentions at this time did not amount to the offer to Greece of an army, but only to special and technical units.

On these orders General Wavell and Air Chief Marshal Longmore flew to Athens for discussions with Generals Metaxas and Papagos. On January 15 they told us that the Greek Government were unwilling that any of our troops should land in Salonika until they could do so in sufficient numbers to act offensively. On receipt of this telegram the Chiefs of Staff telegraphed on January 17 that there could be no question of forcing our aid upon the Greeks. In consequence we modified our view of the immediate future, decided to push on to Benghazi, and meanwhile to build up the strongest strategic reserve possible in the Delta.

On January 21 the Chiefs of Staff accordingly proposed to Wavell that the capture of Benghazi was now of the highest importance. They considered that if it were made into a strongly fortified naval and air base the overland route might be dropped and both men and transport saved. They also urged him to seize the Dodecanese, and especially Rhodes, as soon as possible, in order to forestall the arrival of the German Air Force, with its consequent threat to our communications with Greece and Turkey, and to form a strategic reserve of four divisions to be ready to help these two countries.

Prime Minister to General Wavell   26 Jan. 41

The apparition of the German aircraft in the Central Mediterranean has forced me for the time being to abandon the hopes I had forced of opening and picketing the way through the Narrows, thus enabling troop convoys to pass regularly. Unless this situation can be rectified during the early months of this year, the lack of shipping and the distance round the Cape will undoubtedly affect the scale to which I had hoped to raise the Army of the Nile and the strength of your command. It pained me very much to find that the convoys sent at so much cost and risk round the Cape should so largely consist of rearward services and make so small an addition to our organised fighting units. I shall try my utmost to support you in every way, and I must ask in return that you convince me that every man in the Middle East is turned to the highest possible use and that the largest number of organised divisional or perhaps preferably brigade units are formed. The soldiers in the rearward services and establishments should play an effective part in internal security. . . .

The information reaching me from every quarter leaves me in no doubt that the Germans are now already establishing themselves upon the Bulgarian aerodromes and making every preparation for action against Greece. This infiltration may, indeed almost certainly will, attain decisive proportions before any clear-cut issue of invasion has been presented to the Turks, who will then be told to keep out or have Constantinople bombed. We must expect a series of very heavy, disastrous blows in the Balkans, and possibly a general submission there to German aims. The stronger the strategic reserve which you can build up in the Delta and the more advanced your preparations to transfer it to European shores, the better will be the chances of securing a favourable crystallisation.

I now replied to General Smuts:

Prime Minister to General Smuts   12 Jan. 41

Your message of the 8th arrived when we had reached certain definite conclusions after three or four days' thought. I read it myself to Defence Committee, three Chiefs of Staff, three Service Ministers, Attlee, and Eden. All struck by complete coincidence of view. Only point of difference is we think northward advance from Kenya with large forces would involve long delay through transport shortage. Rebellion making good headway; Emperor enters soon. Advance Kassala-Agordat cuts tap-root. Force you mention already on the way. Pressure from Kenya to be maintained at utmost, but we cannot carry too many troops on this line. Please send division at earliest. Perhaps by time it approaches can land it in Red Sea. Better keep as fluid as possible in view of imponderabilia. Come though, please, now.

Fully agreed to pay no heavy price beyond Tobruk, where very likely 25,000 Italians in net, and to go on while the going is good so as to make as far-thrown a western flank for Egypt as possible, meanwhile shifting all useful elements to impending war front, Bulgarian-Greek frontier. Naturally Wavell and Company heartset on chase, but Wavell is going Monday or Tuesday to Athens to concert reinforcements with Greeks. Cannot guarantee success; can only make what we think best arrangements. Weather, mountains, Danube crossing, fortified Greek-Bulgarian frontier, all helpful factors. Turkey, Yugoslavia, Russia, all perhaps favourably influenced by evidences of British support of Greece.

Whatever happens in Balkans Italian army in Abyssinia probably destroyable. If this should come off, everything useful from Kenya should go forward to Mediterranean. Hope Army of South African Union will be there for summer fighting. Very large reinforcements coming continually round Cape. Most grateful for all your help, and above all for your surefooted judgment, which marches with our laboriously reached conclusions.

2

The Widening War

More Intimate Contacts with President Roosevelt—Arrival of Harry Hopkins in London—A Precious Link with the President —Our Journey to Scapa—Mr. Wendell Willkie—"Sail On, O Ship of State!"—Politics and Strategy—Our Grim Alternatives—German Designs upon Rumania and Bulgaria—Soviet Concern— Ribbentrop's Explanations—My Telegram of January 31 to President Inönü—Our Offer of Military Help to Turkey—Turkish Lack of Modern Equipment—Vital Need to Form a Balkan Front.

W ITH THE NEW YEAR more intimate contacts developed with President Roosevelt. I had already sent him the compliments of the season.

Former Naval Person to President Roosevelt   1 Jan. 41

At this moment, when the New Year opens in storm, I feel it my duty on behalf of the British Government, and indeed of the whole British Empire, to tell you, Mr. President, how lively is our sense of gratitude and admiration for the memorable declaration which you made to the American people and to the lovers of freedom in all the continents on Sunday last.

We cannot tell what lies before us, but with this trumpet-call we march forward heartened and fortified, and with the confidence which you have expressed that in the end all will be well for the English-speaking peoples and those who share their ideals.

On January 10 a gentleman arrived to see me at Downing Street with the highest credentials. Telegrams had been received from Washington stating that he was the closest confidant and personal agent of the President. I therefore arranged that he should be met by Mr. Brendan Bracken on his arrival at Poole Airport, and that we should lunch together alone the next day. Thus I met Harry Hopkins, that extraor-

19

dinary man, who played, and was to play, a sometimes decisive part in the whole movement of the war. His was a soul that flamed out of a frail and failing body. He was a crumbling lighthouse from which there shone the beams that led great fleets to harbour. He had also a gift of sardonic humour. I always enjoyed his company, especially when things went ill. He could also be very disagreeable and say hard and sour things. My experiences were teaching me to be able to do this too, if need be.

At our first meeting we were about three hours together, and I soon comprehended his personal dynamism and the outstanding importance of his mission. This was the height of the London bombing, and many local worries imposed themselves upon us. But it was evident to me that here was an envoy from the President of supreme importance to our life. With gleaming eye and quiet, constrained passion he said:

"The President is determined that we shall win the war together. Make no mistake about it.

"He has sent me here to tell you that at all costs and by all means he will carry you through, no matter what happens to him—there is nothing that he will not do so far as he has human power."

Everyone who came in contact with Harry Hopkins in the long struggle will confirm what I have set down about his remarkable personality. And from this hour began a friendship between us which sailed serenely over all earthquakes and convulsions. He was the most faithful and perfect channel of communication between the President and me. But far more than that, he was for several years the main prop and animator of Roosevelt himself. Together these two men, the one a subordinate without public office, the other commanding the mighty Republic, were capable of taking decisions of the highest consequence over the whole area of the English-speaking world. Hopkins was, of course, jealous about his personal influence with his Chief and did not encourage American competitors. He therefore in some ways bore out the poet Gray's line, "A favourite has no friend." But this was not my affair. There he sat, slim, frail, ill, but absolutely glowing with refined comprehension of the Cause. It was to be the defeat, ruin, and slaughter of Hitler, to the exclusion of all other purposes, loyalties, or aims. In the history of the United States few brighter flames have burned.

Harry Hopkins always went to the root of the matter. I have been present at several great conferences, where twenty or more of the most important executive personages were gathered together. When the discussion flagged and all seemed baffled, it was on these occasions he would rap out the deadly question, "Surely, Mr. President, here is the point we have got to settle. Are we going to face it or not?" Faced it always was, and, being faced, was conquered. He was a true leader of men, and alike in ardour and in wisdom in times of crisis he has rarely been excelled. His love for the causes of the weak and poor was matched by his passion against tyranny, especially when tyranny was, for the time, triumphant.

*   *   *

In order to clothe the arrival of our new Ambassador, Lord Halifax, in the United States with every circumstance of importance, I arranged that our newest and strongest battleship, the *King George V*, with a proper escort of destroyers, should carry him and his wife across the ocean. I accompanied them north in my train and saw them off from Scapa Flow. I took advantage of the occasion to visit the Fleet, which I had not seen since I left the Admiralty. This fitted in with my plans for making much closer acquaintance with Harry Hopkins. We went together to the Fleet, inspecting ships and defences. My wife came with me, and excelled all others in nimbleness of skipping and scrambling from one destroyer to another. Hopkins nearly fell into the sea. I returned in my train to Glasgow. I was welcomed by very large crowds, saw all the local authorities, walked through a number of workshops, inspected the Defence, Fire, and Air Raid services, and made a number of impromptu speeches. We then went on to Tyneside, where the same thing happened. All the time I got to know this man—and to know about his Chief. Hopkins was about ten days with me, and in this time he put me into harmonious mental relations with the newly rechosen Master of the great Republic. Later on I took him to Dover to see our heavy batteries glaring across the Channel at the coast of France—for us Germany. He seemed to be keenly interested in all he saw.

Former Naval Person to President Roosevelt   13 Jan. 41

Hopkins and I spent the week-end together, and he is coming along with me on a short tour of Fleet bases, so we shall have plenty of time to cover all points at leisure. I am most grateful to you for sending so remarkable an envoy, who enjoys so high a measure of your intimacy and confidence.

Former Naval Person to President Roosevelt 19 Jan. 41

You probably know that Halifax will arrive at Annapolis in our new battleship H.M.S. *King George V.* She cannot of course stay more than twenty-four hours. I don't know whether you would be interested to see her. We should be proud to show her to you, or to any of your high naval authorities, if you could arrange that. She is due at entrance of Chesapeake Bay at 7 A.M. on January 24. If you will communicate to me any suggestions or wishes we will do our best to meet them.

* * *

Later on in the same month there arrived in England Mr. Wendell Willkie, the President's opponent in the recent election. He too brought recommendations of the highest character from the President, and as he was the accepted leader of the Republican Party every arrangement was made by us, with the assistance of the enemy, to let him see all he desired of London at bay. He also came to Chequers for a night, and I had a very long talk with this most able and forceful man, whose life was cut short so unexpectedly by illness three years later.

Former Naval Person to President Roosevelt 28 Jan. 41

I received Willkie yesterday, and was deeply moved by the verse of Longfellow's which you had quoted. I shall have it framed as a souvenir of these tremendous days, and as a mark of our friendly relations, which have been built up telegraphically but also telepathically under all the stresses.

All my information shows that the Germans are persevering in their preparations to invade this country, and we are getting ready to give them a reception worthy of the occasion. On the other hand, the news from the East shows that a large army and air force are being established in Rumania, and that the advance parties of the German Air Force have already to the extent of several thousands infiltrated themselves into Bulgarian aerodromes, with the full connivance of the Bulgarian Government. It would be natural for Hitler to make a strong threat against the British Isles in order to occupy us here and cover his Eastern designs. The forces at his disposal are, however, so large that he could carry out both offensives at the same time. You may be sure we shall do our best in both quarters.

I am most grateful to you for your splendid reception of Halifax and for all you are doing to secure us timely help. It has been a great pleasure to me to make friends with Hopkins, who has been a great comfort and encouragement to everyone he has met. One can easily see why he is so close to you. Colonel Donovan also has done fine work in the Middle East.

All my respects and kindest regards. I hope you are already better.

Here is the President's letter:

THE WHITE HOUSE
WASHINGTON

Jan. 20
1941

Dear Churchill

Wendell Wilkie will give you this — He is truly helping to keep politics out over here.

I think this verse applies to your people as it does to us:

"Sail on Oh Ship of State!
Sail on Oh Union strong and great.
Humanity with all its fears,
With all the hopes of future years
Is hanging breathless on Thy fate"

As ever yours
Franklin D. Roosevelt

THE WHITE HOUSE
WASHINGTON
JANUARY 20, 1941

DEAR CHURCHILL,

Wendell Willkie will give you this. He is truly helping to keep politics out over here.

I think this verse applies to your people as it does to us:

"Sail on, O ship of State!
Sail on, O Union, strong and great!

Humanity with all its fears,
With all the hopes of future years,
Is hanging breathless on thy fate!"

As ever yours,
FRANKLIN D. ROOSEVELT

These splendid lines from Longfellow's "Building of the Ship" were an inspiration.

*   *   *

It is not possible in a major war to divide military from political affairs. At the summit they are one. It is natural that soldiers should regard the military aspect as single and supreme, and even that they should speak of political considerations with a certain amount of disdain. Also the word "politics" has been confused, and even tarnished, by its association with party politics. Thus much of the literature of this tragic century is biased by the idea that in war only military considerations count and that soldiers are obstructed in their clear, professional view by the intrusion of politicians, who for personal or party advantage tilt the dread balances of battle. The extremely close, intimate contacts which prevailed between the War Cabinet, the Chiefs of Staff, and myself, and the total absence of party feeling in Britain at this time, reduced these discords to a minimum.

While the war with the Italians in Northeast Africa continued to prosper, and while the Greeks in Albania had good hopes of capturing Valona, all the news we got about the German movements and intentions proved every day more plainly that Hitler was about to intervene upon a large scale in the Balkans and the Mediterranean. From the beginning of January I had apprehended the arrival of German air power in Sicily, with the consequent menace to Malta and to all our hopes of resuming traffic through the Mediterranean. I also feared they would set up an air station on Pantelleria, with all the facilities this would give for a movement of German troops, presumably armoured, into Tripoli. They did not, as it turned out, think it necessary to occupy Pantelleria, but we could not doubt that their plans were progressing to establish a north-and-south passage through Italy to Africa, and at the same time and by the same measures to interrupt all our movements east and west in the Mediterranean.

On top of this now came the menace to the Balkan States, including Greece and Turkey, of being enticed or coerced into the Hitler empire, or conquered if they did not comply. Was the same hideous process we had witnessed in Norway, Denmark, Holland, Belgium, and France to be reproduced in Southeast Europe?· Were all the Balkan States, including heroic Greece, to be subjugated one by one, and Turkey, isolated, to be compelled to open for the German legions the road to Palestine, Egypt, Iraq, and Persia? Was there no chance of creating a Balkan unity and Balkan front which would make this new German aggression too costly to be worth while? Might not the fact of Balkan resistance to Germany produce serious and helpful reactions in Soviet Russia? Certainly this was a sphere in which the Balkan States were affected by interest, and even, so far as they allowed it to influence their calculations, by sentiment. Could we from our strained but growing resources find the extra outside contribution which might galvanise all these states, whose interests were largely the same, into action for a common cause? Or ought we, on the other hand, to mind our own business and make a success of our campaign in Northeast Africa, let Greece, the Balkans, and it might be Turkey and all else in the Middle East, slide to ruin?

There would have been much mental relief in such a clear-cut decision; and it has found its adherents in the books of various officers occupying subordinate positions who have given us their views. These writers certainly have the advantage of pointing to the misfortunes which we sustained, but they had not the knowledge to consider sufficiently what the results of the opposite policy might have been. If Hitler had been able, with hardly any fighting, to bring Greece to her knees and the whole of the Balkans into his system and then force Turkey to allow the passage of his armies to the south and east, might he not have made terms with the Soviets upon the conquest and partition of these vast regions and postponed his ultimate, inevitable quarrel with them to a later part of his programme? Or, as is more likely, would he not have been able to attack Russia in greater strength at an earlier date? The main question which the ensuing chapters will probe and expose is whether His Majesty's Government by their action influenced in a decisive, or even in an appreciable manner, Hitler's movements in Southeast Europe, and moreover whether that action did not produce consequences first upon the behaviour of Russia and next upon her fortunes.

*   *   *

We had, as is set forth in the previous volume, already given modest aid to Greece from the time when she was attacked by Italy, and four British air squadrons were operating with some success from Greek airfields. It is at this point worth while seeing what was actually in progress on the German side.

On January 7 Ribbentrop informed the heads of the German mission in Moscow:

Since early in January the movement of strong German troop formations to Rumania has been going on via Hungary. The movement of troops is being carried on with full concurrence of the Hungarian and Rumanian Governments. For the time being the troops will be quartered in the south of Rumania. The troop movements result from the fact that the necessity must be seriously contemplated of ejecting the English completely from the whole of Greece. German troops have been provided in such strength that they can easily cope with any military task in the Danubian region and with any eventualities from any side. The military measures being carried out by us are aimed exclusively against the British forces getting a foothold in Greece, and not against any Balkan country, including Turkey.

As for instructions for conversations, in general a reserved attitude is to be taken. In case of urgent official inquiries it is to be pointed out, depending on circumstances, that such inquiries are to be made in Berlin. In so far as conversation cannot be avoided an opinion in general terms is to be given. *In so doing our having reliable reports regarding larger and larger reinforcements of English troops of all kinds in Greece may be given as a plausible reason and the Salonika operation of the last World War may be recalled.*[1] Concerning the strength of the German troops, maintenance of the present vagueness is desired for the time being. Later on we shall presumably be interested in making known the full strength of the troops, and, beyond that, in stimulating exaggeration. The cue for that will be given at the proper time.

Also the same day to the German Ambassador in Japan:

I request that the Japanese Foreign Minister be personally and confidentially informed that at present rather strong German troop contingents are being transferred to Rumania. The movements are carried on with the full concurrence of the Hungarian and the Rumanian Governments. These troop shipments are being carried out as a security measure for an intervention that may become necessary in Greece if English military forces gain a foothold and necessitate such intervention there.

Schulenburg, the German Ambassador at Moscow, replied on January 8:

[1] My italics.—Author.

Numerous rumours are already circulating here concerning the sending of German troops to Rumania; the number of men in the movement is even estimated at two hundred thousand. Government circles here, the radio, and the Soviet press have not yet taken up the matter.

The Soviet Government will take the strongest interest in these troop movements, and will wish to know what purposes these troop concentrations serve, and particularly to what degree Bulgaria and Turkey [Straits] might possibly be affected by them. Please give me appropriate instructions.

The German Foreign Minister answered the same day.

Ribbentrop to Schulenburg   8 Jan. 41

I request you not to broach the question of increased German troop movements to Rumania with the Soviet Government.

Should you be approached regarding the matter by Herr Molotov or some other influential person in the Soviet Government, please say that according to your information the sending of German troops was exclusively a matter of precautionary military measures against England. The English already had military contingents on Greek soil, and it was to be expected that they would further increase those contingents in the immediate future. Germany would not under any circumstances tolerate England's gaining a foothold on Greek soil. Please do not go into greater detail until further notice.

* * *

By the middle of January the Russians were deeply perturbed, and raised the issue in Berlin. On January 17 the Russian Ambassador called at the German Foreign Office and communicated the substance of the following memorandum:

According to all reports, German troops in great numbers are in Rumania, and are now prepared to march into Bulgaria, having as their goal the occupation of Bulgaria, Greece, and the Straits. There can be no doubt that England will try to forestall the operations of German troops, to occupy the Straits, to start military operations against Bulgaria in alliance with Turkey, and turn Bulgaria into a theatre of operations. The Soviet Government has stated repeatedly to the German Government that it considers the territory of Bulgaria and of the Straits as the security zone of the U.S.S.R., and that it cannot be indifferent to events which threaten the security interests of the U.S.S.R. In view of all this the Soviet Government regards it as its duty to give warning that it will consider the appearance of any foreign armed forces on the territory of Bulgaria and of the Straits as a violation of the security interests of the U.S.S.R.

On January 21 the Russian Ambassador was called to the German Foreign Office and told that the Reich Government had not received any reports that England contemplated occupying the Straits. Nor did they believe that Turkey would permit English military forces to enter her territory. However, they were informed that England intended and was about to gain a foothold on Greek territory. It was their unalterable intention not to permit English military forces to establish themselves on Greek territory, which would mean a threat to vital interests of Germany in the Balkans. Certain troop concentrations in the Balkans, which had the sole purpose of preventing the British from gaining any foothold on Greek soil, were therefore in progress. The Reich Government believed that this action was also serving Soviet interests, which would be opposed to England's gaining a foothold in these regions.[2]

There for the moment the matter rested.

A few days later I addressed myself to the President of Turkey.

Prime Minister to President Inönü, Angora   31 Jan. 41

The rapidly growing danger to Turkey and to British interests leads me, Mr. President, to address you directly. I have sure information that the Germans are already establishing themselves upon Bulgarian aerodromes. Hutments are being prepared, and advance servicing personnel numbering several thousands have arrived. This has been done with the full connivance of the Royal Bulgarian Air Force and undoubtedly of the Bulgarian Government. Very soon, perhaps in a few weeks, the movement into Bulgaria of German troops and air squadrons will begin. The air squadrons will only have to fly from their stations in Rumania to the bases they are preparing in Bulgaria, and will immediately be able to come into action. Then, unless you promise the Germans not to march against Bulgaria or against their troops passing through Bulgaria, they will bomb Istanbul and Adrianople the same night, and also dive-bomb your troops in Thrace. No doubt they would hope either to reach Salonika unopposed or to compel the Greeks to make peace with Italy and yield them air bases in Greece and in the islands, thus endangering the communications between our armies in Egypt and the Turkish Army. They would deny the use of Smyrna to our Navy, they would completely control the exits from the Dardanelles, and thus complete the encirclement of Turkey in Europe on three sides. This would also facilitate their attacks upon Alexandria and Egypt generally.

Of course I know, Mr. President, that, confronted with these mortal dangers, Turkey would declare war. But why is it necessary to hand over to the enemy the enormous advantage of being able to secure the mastery of the Bulgarian airfields without a shot being fired or a word being said?

Germany is in fact preparing to repeat on the frontiers of

[2] *Nazi-Soviet Relations*, pp. 268, 271–72.

Turkey the same manoeuvre as she accomplished on the frontiers of France in April and May, 1940. But in this case, instead of hesitating and overawed neutrals like Denmark, Holland, and Belgium, she has in Bulgaria a confederate and former ally who has beyond all doubt abandoned the will, and never had the power, to resist. All this, I repeat, may fall upon us in February or in March, and all will be open to the Germans even without moving any large masses of troops from the moment when the Bulgarian airfields have been fitted to receive the German Air Force and are occupied by the advanced aircraft personnel and ground staff. Do we propose to sit still with folded hands and watch the steady preparation of this deadly stroke?

It seems to me that we should be held gravely blameworthy by our respective nations if we were to fail in ordinary prudence and foresight. Even now we have waited too long.

I therefore propose to you, Mr. President, that you and I should repeat in defence of Turkey the same kind of measures which the Germans are taking on the Bulgarian airfields. My Government wish to send to Turkey at the earliest moment when accommodation can be provided at least ten squadrons of fighter and bomber aircraft, apart from the five now in action in Greece. If Greece should surrender or be beaten down, we will transfer these other five air squadrons to Turkish airfields, and, further, we will fight the air war from Turkish bases with ever-increasing air forces of the highest quality. Thus we shall help to give the Turkish Army the additional air support which they need to sustain their famous military qualities.

But, more than that, we shall place Turkey in a position, once our squadrons are on the Turkish aerodromes, to threaten to bombard the Rumanian oilfields if any German advance is made into Bulgaria, or if the air personnel already in Bulgaria is not speedily withdrawn. We will undertake not to take such action from Turkish airfields except by agreement with you.

There is more to come. The attitude of Russia is uncertain, and it is our hope it may remain loyal and friendly. Nothing will more restrain Russia from aiding Germany, even indirectly, than the presence of powerful British bombing forces which could [from Turkey] attack the oilfields of Baku. Russia is dependent upon the supply from these oilfields for a very large part of her agriculture, and far-reaching famine would follow their destruction.

Thus Turkey, once defended by air power, would have the means perhaps of deterring Germany from overrunning Bulgaria and quelling Greece, and of counterbalancing the Russian fear of the German armies. If this decisive position is to be saved there is not an hour to lose, and on receipt of your assent His Majesty's Government will immediately give the necessary orders for our advanced personnel, either in uniform or in plain clothes, as you prefer, to start at once for Turkey.

Further, we are prepared to send you a hundred A.A. guns,

which are now either in or on their way to Egypt. These would be complete with personnel, either in uniform, if you so desire, or in the guise of instructors.

All other measures which have been discussed with Marshal Chakmak, and also the naval measures, will at the right moment be brought into operation.

The victories we have gained in Libya will enable us to give a far more direct and immediate measure of aid to Turkey in the event of our two countries becoming allied in war, and we will make common cause with you and use our growing strength to aid your valiant armies.

*   *   *

I also sent the following to the Chiefs of Staff:

Prime Minister to C.O.S. Committee   31 Jan. 41

We must not overlook the decision we conveyed to General Wavell, that once Tobruk was taken the Greek-Turkish situation must have priority. The advance to Benghazi is most desirable, and has been emphasised in later telegrams. Nevertheless, only forces which do not conflict with European needs can be employed. As the forecast is now that Benghazi cannot be captured till the end of February, it is necessary that this should be impressed upon General Wavell. For instance, the air support promised to Turkey cannot be delayed till then. It may, however, be possible to reconcile both objectives.

The Chiefs of Staff accordingly telegraphed to the Commanders-in-Chief in the Middle East inviting their attention to my message to President Inönü, and adding the following:

Steps to counter German infiltration into Bulgaria must now have the highest priority. Advantage of going on to Benghazi and thus securing Egypt and the fleet base in the Eastern Mediterranean are fully realised, provided that it can be done without prejudice to European interests. Its capture as soon as possible is, therefore, of the highest importance. Your wish to take "Mandibles" [Rhodes] is welcomed by us, and we have sent the three Glen ships to you at the cost of paralysing for some months similar operations in the Western Mediterranean. We did this in hope of preventing airborne German air occupation of "Mandibles," which would hamper our communications with Turkey. We have asked you to speed this operation as much as possible.

In conclusion we must repeat that the Graeco-Turkish situation predominates and should have first place in your thoughts.

I understood at this time how perilous the position of Turkey had become. It was obviously impossible to consider the treaty we had made with her before the war as binding upon

her in the altered circumstances. When war had broken out
in 1939, the Turks had mobilised their strong, good, brave
army. But this was all based upon the conditions of the First
Great War. The Turkish infantry were as fine as they had
ever been, and their field artillery was presentable. But they
had none of the modern weapons which from May, 1940,
were proved to be decisive. Aviation was lamentably weak
and primitive. They had no tanks or armoured cars, and
neither the workshops to make and maintain them nor the
trained men and staffs to handle them. They had hardly any
anti-aircraft or anti-tank artillery. Their signal service was
rudimentary. Radar was unknown to them. Nor did their
warlike qualities include any aptitude for all these modern
developments.

On the other hand, Bulgaria had been largely armed by
Germany out of the immense quantities of equipment of all
kinds taken from France and the Low Countries as a result
of the battles of 1940. The Germans had, therefore, plenty
of modern weapons with which to arm their allies. We, for our
part, having lost so much at Dunkirk, having to build up our
home army against invasion and to face all the continuous
pressure of the Blitz on our cities as well as maintain the war
in the Middle East, could only give very sparingly and at the
cost of other clamant needs. The Turkish army in Thrace was,
under these conditions, at a serious and almost hopeless disadvantage compared with the Bulgarians. If to this danger
were added even moderate detachments of German air and
armour, the weight upon Turkey might well prove insupport-
able.

The only policy or hope throughout this phase of the ever-
extending war was in an organised plan of uniting the forces
of Yugoslavia, Greece, and Turkey; and this we were now
trying to do. Our aid to Greece had been limited in the first
place to the few air squadrons which had been sent from
Egypt when Mussolini first attacked her. The next stage had
been the offer of the technical units set out in the Chiefs of
Staff telegram, which had been declined by the Greeks on
grounds which were by no means unreasonable. We now
reach the third phase, where it seemed possible to make a
safe and secure desert flank at and beyond Benghazi and concentrate the largest army of manoeuvre or strategic reserve
possible in Egypt.

In this condition we reached the month of February.

3

Blitz and Anti-Blitz, 1941: Hess

*The Blitz Continues—Need to Estimate the German Air Strength
—Differences Among the Departments—Mr. Justice Singleton's
Inquiry, December, 1940—His Report, January 21, 1941—Ger-
man Preparations to Invade Russia—And to Bomb and Starve Us
Out—Three Phases in the Blitz—Our Smoke-Screens and Decoy
Fires—The Luftwaffe Turns to the Ports, March and April,
1941—My Visit to Bristol, April 12—We Continue to Twist the
Enemy's Beams—Incendiary Attack on London, May 10—Fires
out of Control—The House of Commons Is Destroyed—The Ger-
man Air Fleet Moves to the East—We Investigate German
Radar Defence—The Battle of the Beams Postponed—A Week-
End at Ditchley—Unexpected and Fantastic News—Rudolf Hess
Lands in Scotland—A Guess at His Motives—The German Ex-
planation—Lord Simon's Interview with Him, June 10—A Vision
of Hitler's Mind—My Directions About His Treatment—I Tell
President Roosevelt—Stalin's Curiosity in 1944.*

A s THE END OF THE YEAR 1940 approached and the Blitz
continued to assail us, it seemed most necessary to peer
into the future and attempt to measure our ordeal. How much
longer and with what increase of severity must we expect the
night onslaughts on our factories and people to continue?
First we must form the most trustworthy estimate of the
German air strength, actual and relative, and of their programme for 1941.

Prime Minister to Secretary of State for Air and C.A.S. 2 Dec. 40
    One cannot doubt that the Germans will be making tremendous
efforts to increase their air force this winter, and that a far more
serious attempt must be expected against us in the spring. It is
most necessary to form the best opinion possible about the potential scale of the German increase (*a*) by March 31, (*b*) by June

30—these dates not being arbitrary if other dates are more convenient and equally illustrative. It is important not to exaggerate the German capacity, and therefore the limiting factors—for example, engines, special raw materials, pilot-training, effect of our bombing—are of special interest. On the other hand, full weight should be given to the German use of factories in the captive countries.

I should be glad if your Intelligence Branch would let me have a paper (not more than two or three sheets) upon this vital matter, and it would be convenient if they could keep in touch with Professor Lindemann while they are preparing this, so that we do not have to argue about the various bases of calculations adopted. While I want the report to be short, I want to be cognisant of the data and reasoning processes on which it has been built up. I am not sure to what extent the Ministry of Aircraft Production comes into this. It would be a comfort if an agreed view could be presented by the departments. Let me know how you will set about this. One week is all that can be spared.

*   *   *

With the aid of Professor Lindemann and his Statistical Branch I began to explore this obscure domain. We probed the Air Ministry statements. We confronted them with the quite separate figures and widely differing judgments of the Ministry of Economic Warfare and of the Air Ministry Intelligence, and with the views of the Ministry of Aircraft Production. I let the argument rip healthily between the departments. This is a very good way of finding out the truth. There was a great deal of friendship and accord between the less senior officers of these three departments, and I was very glad to convene them all together one afternoon at Chequers. Both sides produced their facts and figures, and each was tormented by doubt. The evidence was so conflicting, and all the witnesses so earnestly desirous of finding the truth, that I felt a judicial mind, a keen, clear, unhampered brain, should sift and weigh. Accordingly I persuaded all concerned to give their best to a factual inquiry by an eminent judge.

Prime Minister to Secretary of State for Air and C.A.S. 9 Dec. 40

I spent four hours on Saturday with the officers of the Air Ministry Intelligence Branch and those of the Ministry of Economic Warfare. I have not been able to reach a conclusion as to which are right. Probably the truth lies midway between them. The subject is of capital importance to the whole future picture we make to ourselves of the war. It would also influence the use we make of our forces in the meanwhile. I am most anxious that the two

branches mentioned, whose officers are in the most friendly relations, should sit together in an inquiry to sift the evidence and
ascertain the facts. There should be an impartial chairman accustomed to weigh evidence and to cross-examine, and I wondered
whether for this purpose Mr. Justice Singleton, who had war experience as a gunner and recently conducted an inquiry for me
into bomb-sights, would not be able to guide the discussions and
throw a valuable light on the obscurities of this all-important
scene. He would, of course, have to be given all the available information. Before taking any decision I should like to have your
views. Meanwhile I have set out a statement of what I learned in
our discussion on Saturday, as something for the departments to
bite on. Every fact in it is open to question, modification, or offset.
I have sent a copy to each branch, and it would form the staple of
the investigations I contemplate.

I composed this statement myself, and it took a good many
hours' concentration. As it is somewhat technical, I print it in
Appendix D where it should be read by those who wish to
probe the question at issue.[1]

Prime Minister to Secretary of State for Air   13 Dec. 40

Out of the estimated monthly German aircraft production of
1800 machines, the Intelligence Branch of the Air Ministry consider that only 400 are provided for training. This seems very few,
considering that the Air Ministry's view is that the Germans are
maintaining about two and a half times our strength in the front
lines. Alternatively, if the Air Ministry's requirement of trainers
is warranted, and if our trainers are not profusely and unthriftily
used, and [if] large numbers [are not] kept about the aerodromes
in an unserviceable state, the German front-line strength cannot
well be maintained on such a small proportion of trainers.

Mr. Justice Singleton is coming to lunch with me on Sunday,
and I will set him to work on the inquiry on which we are agreed.

*   *   *

Mr. Justice Singleton got on famously with the airmen and
other experts. On January 21 he presented me with his final
report. It was most difficult to compare British and German
air strengths in actual figures. Each side divided its air force
into authorised establishments, total aircraft, "operationally
fit," and "front line." These categories were different, arbitrary, and variable. Moreover, the Royal Air Force was divided between home and overseas, while at this moment the
Germans were all at home. I do not therefore baffle the reader
with disputable statistics. The Judge concluded that the

---

[1] See Appendix D, Book One.

strength of the German Air Force, compared with the British, might be taken as roughly four to three. Although the Air Ministry (Intelligence) still thought the Germans had more and the Ministry of Economic Warfare that they had less, there was a considerable measure of agreement, and the Singleton estimate became our working basis. I was encouraged by this report, which showed that we were steadily overhauling the Germans in the air. At the beginning of the Battle of France they were at least more than double. Now they were reported as only four to three. After the war we learnt that it was actually nearer three to two. This was a great improvement. We had not yet reached our full rate of expansion, nor had we received the great wave of American help which was on the way.

* * *

At the end of 1940, Hitler had realised that Britain could not be destroyed by direct air assault. The Battle of Britain had been his first defeat, and the malignant bombing of the cities had not cowed the nation or its Government. The preparations to invade Russia in the early summer of 1941 absorbed much of the German air power. The many very severe raids which we suffered till the end of May no longer represented the full strength of the enemy. To us they were most grievous, but they were no longer the prime thought cithcr of the German High Command or of the Fuehrer. To Hitler the continuance of the air attack on Great Britain was a necessary and convenient cover to the concentration against Russia. IIis optimistic time-table assumed that the Soviets, like the French, would be overthrown in a six-weeks campaign and that all German forces would then be free for the final overthrow of Britain in the autumn of 1941. Meanwhile the obstinate nation was to be worn down, first, by the combination of the U-boat blockade sustained by the long-range air, and secondly, by air attacks upon her cities and especially her ports. For the German Army "Sea Lion" (against Britain) was now replaced by "Barbarossa" (against Russia). The German Navy was instructed to concentrate on our Atlantic traffic and the German Air Force on our harbours and their approaches. This was a far more deadly plan than the indiscriminate bombing of London and the civil population, and it was fortunate for us that it was not pursued with all available forces and greater persistence.

* * *

Viewed in retrospect, the Blitz of 1941 falls into three phases. In the first, during January and February, the enemy were frustrated by bad weather, and, apart from attacks on Cardiff, Portsmouth, and Swansea, our Civil Defence Services gained a well-deserved breathing-space, by which they did not fail to profit. A system of Port Emergency Committees, representing all the main interests concerned in port organisation, had been set up long before the war by the Committee of Imperial Defence. Sharpened by the hard experience of the winter of 1940, and aided by the readiness of the Ministry of War Transport to decentralise, these bodies were now able to conduct the struggle very much more efficiently themselves, and could rely with confidence on outside assistance through the regional commissioners. Nor were more active methods of defence neglected. Smoke-screens, highly unpopular with the local inhabitants whose homes they contaminated, were prepared, and later proved their worth in protecting Midland industrial centres. Decoy fires, or "starfish," were made ready for the distraction of enemy bombers, and the whole defensive plan was knit together into one coherent system.

When better weather came, the Blitz started in earnest over again. The second phase, sometimes called "the Luftwaffe's tour of the ports," began in early March. It consisted of single or double attacks, which, though serious, failed to cripple our harbours. On the eighth and for three succeeding nights Portsmouth was heavily attacked and the dockyards damaged. Manchester and Salford were attacked on the eleventh. On the ensuing nights it was the turn of Merseyside. On the thirteenth and fourteenth the Luftwaffe fell for the first time heavily on the Clyde, killing or injuring over two thousand people and putting the shipyards out of action, some till June and others till November. At John Brown's Shipbuilding Works large fires caused stoppages, and normal production was only restored in April. This firm had been affected since March 6 by an extensive strike. Most of the strikers had been bombed out of their homes, but the raid sufferings and peril brought them back to eager duty. Merseyside, the Midlands, Essex, and London all had another dose before the month was out.

The heaviest blows did not fall till April. On the eighth the concentration was on Coventry, and in the rest of the country the sharpest impact was at Portsmouth. London had heavy attacks on the sixteenth and seventeenth; over twenty-three hundred people were killed, more than three thousand seriously injured. In this third and final phase the enemy went on trying to destroy most of our principal ports by attacks prolonged in some cases over a whole week. Plymouth was attacked from April 21 to 29, and though decoy fires helped to save the dockyard, this was only at the expense of the city. The climax came on May 1, when Liverpool and the Mersey were attacked for seven successive nights. Seventy-six thousand people were made homeless and three thousand killed or injured. Sixty-nine out of a hundred and forty-four berths were put out of action, and the tonnage landed for a while was cut to a quarter. Had the enemy persisted, the Battle of the Atlantic would have been even more closely run than it was. But as usual he turned away. For two nights he battered Hull heavily, where forty thousand people had their dwellings destroyed, the food stores were wrecked, and the marine engineering works were crippled for nearly two months. In that month he struck again at Belfast, already twice raided.

*   *   *

On April 12, as Chancellor of Bristol University, I conferred the honorary degree of Doctor of Laws on Mr. Winant, the United States Ambassador, on Dr. J. B. Conant, President of Harvard University, and on Mr. Menzies, Prime Minister of Australia. My wife came with me. Our train lay for the night in a siding in the open country, but we could see and hear the heavy air raid on the city of Bristol. We pulled into the station early in the morning and went straight to the hotel. There I met a number of dignitaries, and almost immediately started on a tour of the most stricken parts of the town. The Air Raid Services were feverishly at work and people were still being dug out of the ruins. The ordeal had been severe, but the spirit of the citizens was invincible. At one of the rest centres a number of old women whose homes had been wrecked and who still seemed stunned were sitting there, the picture of dejection. When I came in they wiped away their tears and cheered wildly for King and Country.

The ceremony went forward as planned. I spent an hour driving round the worst hit places, and then repaired to the University. Everything proceeded with strict formality, but the large building next to the University was still burning and the bright academic robes of some of the principal actors did not conceal the soaked and grimy uniforms of their night's toil. The whole scene was moving.

Many of those here today [I said] have been all night at their posts, and all have been under the fire of the enemy in heavy and protracted bombardment. That you should gather in this way is a mark of fortitude and phlegm, of a courage and detachment from material affairs, worthy of all that we have learned to believe of ancient Rome or of modern Greece.

I go about the country whenever I can escape for a few hours or for a day from my duty at headquarters, and I see the damage done by the enemy attacks; but I also see, side by side with the devastation and amid the ruins, quiet, confident, bright, and smiling eyes, beaming with a consciousness of being associated with a cause far higher and wider than any human or personal issue. I see the spirit of an unconquerable people. I see a spirit bred in freedom, nursed in a tradition which has come down to us through the centuries, and which will surely at this moment, this turning-point in the history of the world, enable us to bear our part in such a way that none of our race who come after us will have any reason to cast reproach upon their sires.

*   *   *

Meanwhile the Wizard War was unfolding in its own strange way. The forging of its first new weapons has already found mention in an earlier volume.[2] The plans for the air defence of Great Britain had, as early as the autumn of 1937, been rewritten round the assumption that the promises made by our scientists for the still unproven radar would be kept. The first five stations of the coastal radar chain, the five guarding the Thames Estuary, had watched Mr. Chamberlain's aeroplane go and come on its peace missions of September, 1938. Eighteen stations from Dundee to Portsmouth began in the spring of 1939 a twenty-four-hour watch, not to be interrupted in the next six years. These stations were the watchdogs of the air-raid warning service; they spared us alike grave losses in war production and intolerable burdens on our civil defence workers. They spared the anti-aircraft gun crews needless and tiring hours at action stations. They saved us from the exhaustion of man and machine that would have doomed our matchless but slender fighter force had it been compelled to maintain standing patrols. They could not give the accuracy required for night-time interception, but they enabled the day fighters to await their prey at the most favourable altitudes and aspects for attack. In their decisive contribution to victory in the day battles they were supported and supplemented by other stations of new technical design,[3]

[2] Volume I, Chapter 9.
[3] Called in our jargon C.H.L. and C.H.E.L.

which gave warning—all too brief, but invaluable—of the approach of the low fliers.

*   *   *

During 1941 we went on deflecting the German beams despite their various improvements. An example may be cited. On the night of May 8 the Germans planned two attacks, the first upon the Rolls-Royce Works at Derby and the second on Nottingham. Through our interference with their beams, which were set upon Derby, they bombed instead Nottingham, where small fires were still burning from the previous night. Their original error then carried their second attack to the Vale of Belvoir, about as far from Nottingham as Nottingham is from Derby. The German communiqué claimed the destruction of the Rolls-Royce Works at Derby, which they never got near. Two hundred and thirty high-explosive bombs and a large number of incendiaries were, however, unloaded in the open country. The total casualties there were two chickens.

The worst attack was the last. On May 10 the enemy returned to London with incendiary bombs. He lit more than two thousand fires, and, by the smashing of nearly a hundred and fifty water mains, coupled with the low tide in the Thames, he stopped us putting them out. At six o'clock next morning hundreds were reported as out of control, and four were still going on the night of the thirteenth. It was the most destructive attack of the whole night Blitz. Five docks and seventy-one keypoints, half of which were factories, had been hit. All but one of the main railway stations were blocked for weeks, and the through routes were not fully opened till early June. Over three thousand people were killed or injured. In other respects also it was historic. It destroyed the House of Commons. One single bomb created ruin for years. We were, however, thankful that the Chamber was empty. On the other hand, our batteries and night fighters destroyed sixteen enemy planes, the maximum we had yet attained in night fighting, and largely the fruits of our winter's toil in the Wizard War.

This, though we did not know it, was the enemy's parting fling. On May 22 Kesselring shifted the headquarters of his air fleet to Posen, and at the beginning of June the whole force was moved to the east. Nearly three years were to pass before our Civil Defence organisation in London had to deal with the "baby Blitz" of February, 1944, and the later onslaught of the rockets and the flying bombs. In the twelve months from June, 1940, to June, 1941, our civilian casualties were 43,381 killed and 50,856 seriously injured, a total of 94,237.

Except for their radar aids to anti-aircraft gunnery the enemy had hitherto concentrated on offensive devices like the beams, and 1941 was far spent before they felt the need of looking after themselves. In Britain, of course, we had trusted to our large and costly navigation schools for finding our targets, and thought of radar primarily for self-preservation. After the beams had been mastered and as things got better generally, we studied German radar for the purpose of removing obstacles to our hitting back. In February, 1941, we found and photographed for the first time a German radar station for detecting aircraft, and almost at once we picked up its transmissions. Having found this specimen near Cherbourg, we searched for others like it along the western coast-line of occupied Europe by photographic reconnaissance and secret agents. By the middle of 1941, the Royal Air Force was seeking to make heavy night attacks on Germany. To do this we had to know all about their defensive devices. These were likely to depend, as ours did, largely upon radar. From a study of German radar on the coast we gradually worked our way back to the German night-fighter defences. These stretched in a great belt running from Schleswig-Holstein through Northwest Germany and Holland to the Franco-Belgian frontier. But neither our new measures nor those of the enemy played a great part during the latter months of 1941. The German bomber force had been hopefully scheduled to begin its return from Russia six weeks after the invasion. Had it returned, it would have been supported in its attack on Britain by many new beam stations with more powerful transmitters along the Channel coast to help it bludgeon its way through the English jamming. It would have encountered many new transmitters on our side to distort and divert the new beams, as well as greatly improved radar on our night fighters. The ever-spreading character of the Russian entanglement prevented this new battle of the beams, and the great radio efforts on both sides remained for the time being unused.

*   *   *

On Sunday, May 11, I was spending the week-end at Ditchley. During the evening news kept coming in of the heavy air raid on London of the night before. There was nothing I could do about it, so I watched the Marx Brothers in a comic film which my hosts had arranged. I went out twice to inquire about the damage, and heard it was bad. The merry film clacked on, and I was glad of the diversion. Presently a secretary told me that somebody wanted to speak to me on the telephone on behalf of the Duke of Hamilton. The Duke was a personal friend of mine, and was commanding a fighter sector in the east of Scotland, but I could not think of any business he might have with me which could not wait till the morning. However, the caller pressed to speak with me, saying the matter was one of urgent Cabinet importance. I asked Mr. Bracken to hear what he had to say. After a few minutes Mr. Bracken told me that the Duke said he had an amazing piece of information to report. I therefore sent for him. On arrival he told me that a German prisoner, whom he had interviewed alone, said he was Rudolf Hess. "Hess in Scotland!" I thought this was fantastic. The report however was true. There was no doubt that Hess, the Deputy Fuehrer, Reich Minister without Portfolio, Member of the Ministerial Council for the Defence of the Reich, Member of the Secret Cabinet Council for Germany, and the Leader of the Nazi Party, had landed alone by parachute near the Duke of Hamilton's estate in the west of Scotland.

Piloting his own plane and dressed as a flight lieutenant of the Luftwaffe, he had flown from Augsburg and baled out. At first he gave his name as "Horn," and it was not till after his reception at a military hospital near Glasgow, where he had been brought for minor injuries caused by his drop, that it was learned who he was. He was soon removed by various stages to the Tower, and thence to other places of captivity in this country, and remained here till October 6, 1945, when in the cells of Nuremberg he rejoined such of his colleagues as had survived the war and were being tried for their lives by the conquerors.

I never attached any serious importance to this escapade. I knew it had no relation to the march of events. Throughout Britain, the United States, Russia, and above all Germany, there was a profound sensation, and books have been written about it all. I shall merely set down here what I believe to be the true story.

*   *   *

Rudolf Hess was a good-looking, youngish man to whom Hitler took a fancy, and who became an intimate member of his personal staff. He worshipped the Fuehrer, and felt passionately about the world issue at stake. He dined at Hitler's

table, often alone or with two or three. He knew and was
capable of understanding Hitler's inner mind—his hatred of
Soviet Russia, his lust to destroy Bolshevism, his admiration
for Britain and earnest wish to be friends with the British
Empire, his contempt for most other countries. No one knew
Hitler better or saw him more often in his unguarded moments. With the coming of actual war there was a change.
Hitler's meal-time company grew perforce. Generals, admirals, diplomats, high functionaries, were admitted from time
to time to this select circle of arbitrary power. The Deputy
Fuehrer found himself in eclipse. What were party demonstrations now? This was a time for deeds, not for antics.

We must discount to some extent the merits of his action
by a certain strain of jealousy which affected his nature at
finding that under war conditions he no longer played his old
part of friendly confidant with the beloved Fuehrer. Here, he
felt, are all these generals and others who must be admitted
to the Fuehrer's intimacy, and crowd his table. They have
their parts to play. But I, Rudolf, by a deed of superb devotion will surpass them all and bring to my Fuehrer a greater
treasure and easement than all of them put together. I will go
and make peace with Britain. My life is nothing. How glad I
am to have a life to cast away for such a hope! Such moods,
however naïve, were certainly neither wicked nor squalid.

Hess's idea of the European scene was that England had
been wrested from her true interests and policy of friendship
with Germany, and above all from alliance against Bolshevism,
by the warmongers, of whom Churchill was the superficial
manifestation. If only he, Rudolf, could get at the heart of
Britain and make its King believe how Hitler felt towards her,
the malign forces that now ruled in this ill-starred island and
had brought so many needless miseries upon it would be
swept away. How could Britain survive? France was gone.
The U-boats would soon destroy all sea communications; the
German air attack would overpower British industry and beat
down British cities.

But to whom should he turn? There was the Duke of
Hamilton who was known to the son of his political adviser,
Karl Haushofer.[4] He knew also that the Duke of Hamilton
was Lord Steward. A personage like that would probably be

[4] The Duke of Hamilton had first met Albrecht Haushofer, author of the
Nazi theory of *Geopolitik*, at the Olympic Games of 1936, at which time the
Duke was studying first the German and later the Russian Air Forces. Albrecht
Haushofer was executed by the Nazis for his suspected part in the plot against
Hitler.

dining every night with the King and have his private ear. Here was a channel of direct access.

* * *

"It seemed," said a German press notice a few days later, "that Party Member Hess lived in a state of hallucination, as a result of which he felt he would bring about an understanding between England and Germany. . . . The National Socialist Party regrets that this idealist fell a victim to his hallucination. This, however, will have no effect on the continuance of the war which has been forced on Germany." For Hitler the event was embarrassing. It was as if my trusted colleague, the Foreign Secretary, who was only a little younger than Hess, had parachuted from a stolen Spitfire into the grounds of Berchtesgaden. The Nazis no doubt found some relief in arresting Hess's adjutants.

Prime Minister to Foreign Secretary   13 May 41

On the whole it will be more convenient to treat him [Herr Hess] as a prisoner of war, under the War Office and not the Home Office; but also as one against whom grave political charges may be preferred. This man, like other Nazi leaders, is potentially a war criminal, and he and his confederates may well be declared outlaws at the close of the war. In this case his repentance would stand him in good stead.

2. In the meanwhile he should be strictly isolated in a convenient house not too far from London, and every endeavour should be made to study his mentality and get anything worth while out of him.

3. His health and comfort should be ensured, food, books, writing materials, and recreation being provided for him. He should not have any contacts with the outer world or visitors except as prescribed by the Foreign Office. Special guardians should be appointed. He should see no newspapers and hear no wireless. He should be treated with dignity, as if he were an important general who had fallen into our hands.

Prime Minister to Sir Alexander Cadogan   16 May 41

Please make now a fairly full digest of the conversational parts of Hess's three interviews, stressing particularly the points mentioned by me in the statement I prepared [for the House] but did not deliver. I will then send this to President Roosevelt with a covering telegram.

2. I approved the War Office proposal to bring Hess to the Tower by tonight pending his place of confinement being prepared at Aldershot.

Former Naval Person to President Roosevelt   17 May 41

Foreign Office representative has had three interviews with Hess.

At first interview, on night of May 11–12, Hess was extremely voluble, and made long statement with the aid of notes. First part recapitulated Anglo-German relations during past thirty years or so, and was designed to show that Germany had always been in the right and England in the wrong. Second part emphasised certainty of German victory, due to development in combination of submarine and air weapons, steadiness of German morale, and complete unity of German people behind Hitler. Third part outlined proposals for settlement. Hess said that the Fuehrer had never entertained any designs against the British Empire, which would be left intact save for the return of former German colonies, in exchange for a free hand for him in Europe. But condition was attached that Hitler would not negotiate with present Government in England. This is the old invitation to us to desert all our friends in order to save temporarily the greater part of our skin.

Foreign Office representative asked him whether when he spoke of Hitler having a free hand in Europe he included Russia in Europe or in Asia. He replied, "In Asia." He added, however, that Germany had certain demands to make of Russia which would have to be satisfied, but denied rumours that attack on Russia was being planned.

Impression created by Hess was that he had made up his mind that Germany must win the war, but saw that it would last a long time and involve much loss of life and destruction. He seemed to feel that if he could persuade people in this country that there was a basis for a settlement, that might bring the war to an end and avert unnecessary suffering.

At second interview, on fourteenth May, Hess made two further points:

(1) In any peace settlement Germany would have to support Rashid Ali and secure eviction of British from Iraq.

(2) U-boat war with air co-operation would be carried on till all supplies to these islands were cut off. Even if these islands capitulated and the Empire continued to fight, the blockade of Britain would continue, even if that meant that the last inhabitant of Britain died of starvation.

At third interview, on May 15, nothing much emerged save incidentally some rather disparaging remarks about your country and the degree of assistance that you will be able to furnish to us. I am afraid, in particular, he is not sufficiently impressed by what he thinks he knows of your aircraft types and production.

Hess seems in good health and not excited, and no ordinary signs of insanity can be detected. He declares that this escapade is his own idea and that Hitler was unaware of it beforehand. If he is to be believed, he expected to contact members of a "peace movement" in England, which he would help to oust the present Government. If he is honest and if he is sane this is an encouraging sign of ineptitude of German Intelligence Service. He will not be ill-treated, but it is desirable that the press should not romanticise him and his adventure. We must not forget that he shares responsibility for all Hitler's crimes and is a potential war criminal whose fate must ultimately depend upon the decision of the Allied Governments.

Mr. President, all the above is for your own information. Here we think it best to let the press have a good run for a bit and keep the Germans guessing. The German officer prisoners of war here were greatly perturbed by the news, and I cannot doubt that there will be deep misgivings in the German armed forces about what he may say.

Hess's own explanations to the doctors were hardly more illuminating. On May 22 his doctor reported as follows:

He said he was horrified at the heavy air raids on London in 1940, and loathed the thought of killing young children and their mothers. This feeling was intensified when he contemplated his own wife and son, and led to the idea of flying to Britain and arranging peace with the large anti-war faction which he thought existed in this country. He stressed that personal advantage played no part in this scheme—it was an increasing idealistic urge.[5]

It was with such thoughts in his mind that he was impressed on hearing Karl Haushofer express similar sentiments, and mention the Duke of Hamilton as a person of common sense, who must be horrified at this senseless slaughter. Haushofer had also remarked that he had seen Hess on three occasions in a dream piloting an aeroplane he knew not where. Hess took these remarks, coming from such a man, as a message to fly to this country as an emissary of peace, to seek the Duke of Hamilton, who would conduct him to King George. The British Government would be thrown out of office and a party desiring peace installed in its place. He was insistent that he would have no dealings with that "clique"—the ruling Administration—who would do all in their power to thwart him, but he was very vague as to what statesmen would replace them, and seemed to be extremely ill-informed as to the names and standing of our politicians. . . . He described how he approached Willi Messerschmidt and obtained facilities for long-distance flying inside Germany in training for the event, and how when he was prepared he set out on his voyage. He maintained that there were no confederates, and that he showed considerable skill in arranging his journey, working out the route himself, and flying with an accuracy which enabled him to land only some ten miles from his destination, Dungavel.[6]

*   *   *

[5] *The Case of Rudolf Hess*, edited by J. R. Rees, p. 2.
[6] *Ibid.*, pp. 18–19.

The Cabinet invited Lord Simon to interview him, and on June 10 a meeting took place. "When the Fuehrer," said Hess, "had come to the conclusion that common sense could not prevail in England, he acted just according to the rule of conduct of Admiral Lord Fisher: 'Moderation in war is folly. If you strike, strike hard and wherever you can.' But I can confirm that it was indeed always difficult for the Fuehrer to give orders for these [air and U-boat] attacks. It pained him deeply. He was constantly in full sympathy with the English people who were victims of this method of waging war. . . . He said that even if victorious one should not impose any severe conditions on a country with which it was desired to come to an agreement." Then, the keynote for Hess: "I thought that if England once knew of this fact it might be possible that England on her part would be ready for agreement." If only England knew how kind Hitler really was, surely she would meet his wishes!

*   *   *

Much learned medical investigation has been devoted to Hess's mental state. Certainly he was a neurotic, a split soul seeking peace in the pursuit of power and position and in the worship of a leader. But he was more than a medical case. He believed passionately in his vision of Hitler's mind. If only England could share it too, how much suffering could be saved and how easy it would be to agree! A free hand for Germany in Europe and for Britain in her own Empire! Other minor conditions were the return of the German colonies, the evacuation of Iraq, and an armistice and peace with Italy. As it was, England's position was hopeless. If she did not agree to these conditions, "sooner or later the day will come when she will be forced to accede to them." To this Lord Simon replied: "I do not think that that particular argument will be very good for the British Cabinet, because, you know, there is a good deal of courage in this country, and we are not very fond of threats!"

Considering how closely Hess was knit to Hitler, it is surprising that he did not know of, or that if he knew he did not disclose, the impending attack on Russia, for which such vast preparations were being made. The Soviet Government were deeply intrigued by the Hess episode, and they wove many distorted theories around it. Three years later, when I was in Moscow on my second visit, I realised the fascination which this topic had for Stalin. He asked me at the dinner table what

was the truth about the Hess mission. I said shortly what I
have written here. I had the feeling that he believed there had
been some deep negotiation or plot for Germany and Britain
to act together in the invasion of Russia which had mis-
carried. Remembering what a wise man he is, I was surprised
to find him silly on this point. When the interpreter made it
plain that he did not believe what I said, I replied through
my interpreter, "When I make a statement of facts within my
knowledge I expect it to be accepted." Stalin received this
somewhat abrupt response with a genial grin. "There are lots
of things that happen even here in Russia which our Secret
Service do not necessarily tell me about." I let it go at that.

*   *   *

Reflecting upon the whole of this story, I am glad not to be
responsible for the way in which Hess has been and is being
treated. Whatever may be the moral guilt of a German who
stood near to Hitler, Hess had, in my view, atoned for this by
his completely devoted and frantic deed of lunatic benevo-
lence. He came to us of his own free will, and, though without
authority, had something of the quality of an envoy. He was a
medical and not a criminal case, and should be so regarded.

4

The Mediterranean War

S INCE THE DAYS OF NELSON, Malta has stood a faithful British sentinel guarding the narrow and vital sea corridor through the Central Mediterranean. Its strategic importance was never higher than in this the latest war. The needs of the large armies we were building up in Egypt made the free passage of the Mediterranean for our convoys and the stopping of enemy reinforcements to Tripoli aims of the highest consequence. At the same time the new air weapon struck a deadly blow, not only at Malta but at the effective assertion of British sea power in these narrow waters. Without this modern danger our task would have been simple. We could have moved freely about the Mediterranean and stopped all other traffic. It was now impossible to base the main Fleet on Malta. The island itself was exposed to the threat of invasion from the Italian ports, as well as to constant and measureless air attack. Hostile air power also imposed almost prohibitive risks upon the passage of our convoys through the Narrows, condemning us to the long haul round the Cape. At the same time the superior air force of the enemy enabled them, by deterring our warships from acting fully in the Central Mediterranean except at much loss and hazard, to maintain a rivulet of troops and supplies into Tripoli.

About 140 miles from Malta, in the throat of the western Narrows between Sicily and Tunis, lay the Italian island of Pantelleria, reputed strongly fortified and with an invaluable airfield. This place was important to the enemy's route to Tunis and Tripoli, and in our hands would markedly expand the air cover we could give around Malta. In September, 1940, I had asked Admiral Keyes to make a plan for seizing Pantelleria with the newly formed commandos. The idea was to attach two or three troopships to the tail of one of our heavily guarded convoys. While the main body was engaging the enemy's attention these would drop off in the darkness and storm the island by surprise. The project, which was called "Workshop," gained increasing support from the Chiefs of Staff. Keyes was ardent, and claimed to lead the assault in person, waiving his rank as an Admiral of the Fleet.

In my circle we did not deem the actual capture too hard to try, but the difficulties of holding the prize while we were already hard pressed in Malta caused misgivings. Nevertheless, on December 28, 1940, I issued the following minute:

Prime Minister to General Ismay, for C.O.S. Committee

Constant reflection has made me feel the very high value of "Workshop," provided that a thoroughly good plan can be made and it is given a chance. The effect of "Workshop," if successful, would be electrifying, and would greatly increase our strategic hold upon the Central Mediterranean. It is also a most important step to opening the Narrows to the passage of trade and troop convoys, whereby so great an easement to our shipping could be obtained. Urgency is supplied by the danger that the Germans, if they take over Italy, will take over "Workshop" island and make it a very difficult proposition both for nuisance value and against assault.

The Chiefs of Staff set to work on the problem at once, and I returned to the charge in the New Year.

Prime Minister to General Ismay, for C.O.S. Committee 13 Jan. 41

The effective arrival of German aviation in Sicily may be the beginning of evil developments in the Central Mediterranean. The successful dive-bombing attacks upon *Illustrious* and the two cruisers show the need for having these ships fitted with aerial minethrowers. I do not know why *Illustrious* could not have had a couple. The improved naval pattern of aerial mine should be pressed on with to the utmost. The need for high-speed aircraft to catch dive-bombers out at sea seems very great. Surely we ought to try to put half a dozen Grummans on *Formidable* before she goes into the Mediterranean.

2. I am very apprehensive of the Germans establishing themselves in Pantelleria, in which case with a strong force of dive-bombers they will close the Narrows. I fear this may be another example of the adage "A stitch in time saves nine."

3. It is necessary now that "Workshop" should be reviewed. It has become far more urgent, and also at the same time more difficult, and once the Germans are installed there it will become more difficult still. I should be glad if revised and perfected plans could be ready by today week. Plans should also be made to find an opportunity at the earliest moment. The question of whether to try it or not can only be settled after these matters of method and timing have been satisfactorily disposed of.

4. I remain completely of opinion that "Workshop" is cardinal.

All agreements were obtained, but with our other affairs we could not meet the date at the end of January at which we had aimed. At a conference at Chequers on the morning of January 18, I agreed with the First Sea Lord and the other Chiefs of Staff to put it off for a month. I think I could have turned the decision the other way, but, like the others, I was constrained by the pressure of larger business, and also by talk about the commandos not being yet fully trained. Keyes, who was not present, was bitterly disappointed. The delay proved fatal to the plan. Long before the month had passed, the German Air Force arrived in Sicily, and all wore a very different complexion. There is no doubt about the value of the prize we did not gain. Had we been in occupation of Pantelleria in 1942 many fine ships that were lost in our convoys, which we then fought through to Malta, might have been saved, and the enemy communications with Tripoli still further impaired. On the other hand, we might well have been overpowered by German air attack, lost our vantage, and complicated our defence of Malta in the interval.

I felt acutely the need of Pantelleria. But our hour had passed. Too much was upon us from many quarters. It was not till May, 1943, after the destruction of the German and Italian armies in Tunis, that, under a heavy bombardment, Pantelleria was taken by a British landing force at the order of General Eisenhower. We were then all-powerful in this theatre, and though the task was deemed very serious beforehand there was no loss.

* * *

Our first serious naval encounter with the German Air Force occurred on January 10. The Fleet was engaged in covering a series of important movements, including the passage of a convoy through the Central Mediterranean from the west, the replenishment of Malta from the east, and various minor shipping movements to Greece. Early that morning the destroyer *Gallant* was mined in the Malta Channel while attending on the battle fleet. Presently shadowing aircraft appeared, and in the afternoon the severe attack of the German bombers began. Their efforts were concentrated on the new carrier *Illustrious*, under Captain Boyd, and in three attacks she was hit six times with big bombs. Heavily damaged and on fire, with eighty-three killed and sixty seriously wounded, she successfully fought back, thanks to her armoured deck, and her aircraft destroyed at least five assailants. That night, under increasing air attack, and with disabled steering gear, Captain Boyd brought the *Illustrious* into Malta.

During the night Admiral Cunningham with the battle fleet escorted the east-bound convoy south of Malta unmolested. The next day the cruisers *Southampton* and *Gloucester*, by then well to the east of Malta, were hit by dive-bombers approaching unobserved down sun. The *Gloucester* was only slightly damaged by a bomb which failed to explode, but the *Southampton* was struck in the engine-room. A fire started which could not be controlled, and the ship had to be abandoned and was sunk. Thus, although the convoys passed on safely to their destinations the cost to the Fleet was heavy.

The Germans realised the desperate position of the wounded *Illustrious* in Malta, and made determined efforts to destroy her. However, our air power in the island had already grown, and nineteen enemy planes were shot down in a single day during the contest. In spite of further hits while in the dockyard, the *Illustrious* was made capable of sailing on the evening of January 23. The enemy, seeing she was gone, tried hard to find her, but she reached Alexandria safely two days later.

By this time no fewer than two hundred and fifty German aircraft were working from Sicily. Malta was attacked fifty-eight times in January, and thereafter till the end of May three or four times daily with only brief respites. But our resources mounted. Between April and June, 1941, Admiral Somerville's Force H ferried six considerable flights to within flying distance of Malta, and two hundred and twenty-four Hurricanes, together with a few of other kinds, reached the battle scene from the west. Supplies and reinforcements also got through from the east. By June the first fierce onslaught had been repulsed, and by the skin of its teeth the island survived. Its main ordeal was reserved for 1942.

In General Dobbie Malta found a governor of outstanding character who inspired all ranks and classes, military and civil, with his own determination. He was a soldier who in fighting leadership and religious zeal recalled memories of General Gordon, and, looking farther back, of the Ironsides and Covenanters of the past.

Prime Minister to General Dobbie, Malta   21 Jan. 41

I send you, on behalf of the War Cabinet, our heartfelt congratulations upon the magnificent and ever-memorable defence which your heroic garrison and citizens, aided by the Navy and above all by the Royal Air Force, are making against Italian and German attacks. The eyes of all Britain, and indeed of the whole British Empire, are watching Malta in her struggle day by day, and we are sure that success as well as glory will reward your efforts.

*   *   *

Amid the stresses of the ever-expanding scale of events in the Mediterranean we tried to find means of bringing the war to the Italian mainland. The morale of the Italian people was said to be low, and a blow here would depress them still more and bring closer the collapse which we desired. On February 9, Admiral Somerville carried out a daring and successful raid on the port of Genoa. Force H, comprising the *Renown, Malaya,* and *Sheffield,* appeared off the town and subjected it to heavy bombardment for half an hour. At the same time aircraft from the *Ark Royal* bombed Leghorn and Pisa and laid mines off Spezia. Complete surprise was achieved, and the only opposition from the shore batteries at Genoa was slight and wholly ineffective. Much damage was done to port installations and shipping. Aided by low clouds, Admiral Somerville's ships withdrew, successfully evading interference from the enemy fleet, which was searching for them west of Sardinia.

The reinforcement of Malta, now that the Germans were taking an interest in the Mediterranean, was urgent.

Prime Minister to General Ismay, for C.O.S. Committee 6 Feb. 41

Although of course the difficulties of [the enemy] assaulting Malta are enormously increased by the British fuelling base in Suda Bay, nevertheless I shall be glad to see a second battalion sent there at the earliest opportunity, making seven British battalions in all. Considering that in view of the Italian rout there should be no great difficulty in sparing this seventh battalion from Egypt, and that the trouble is carrying them there by the Fleet, one must ask whether it is not as easy to carry two as it is to carry one. It seems a pity to let the baker's cart go with only one loaf, when the journey is so expensive and the load available, and it might as easily carry two. Pray consider this. But no delay.

* * *

By the beginning of April we were able to intensify our attacks on enemy shipping feeding Rommel's forces in Libya. In this British submarines operating from Malta played a leading part, and the scale of their activities and successes mounted steadily. In this sphere Lieutenant-Commander Malcolm Wanklyn was outstanding, and his exploits later earned him the Victoria Cross. The following year he was lost with his ship, the *Upholder*, but his example lived among those who carried on his work.

On April 10 a striking force of four destroyers under Captain Mack in the *Jervis* was sent to Malta to operate against enemy convoys. Within a week they achieved a spectacular success. On a night of bright moonlight they encountered a convoy of five southbound ships with an escort of three destroyers. All were annihilated in a general scrimmage at close range. Our destroyer *Mohawk* was also torpedoed and had to be sunk, but her captain and most of her crew were saved. In this action alone 14,000 tons of enemy shipping fully loaded with vital war materials was destroyed.

* * *

Good news continued to reach us from the Desert. On February 6 Benghazi was entered, three weeks ahead of the expected date, by the 6th Australian Division. By daybreak on February 5 the 7th British Armoured Division (now at a tank strength of one brigade), had reached Msus after much rough

THE ADVANCE FROM TOBRUK

going. The division was directed to cut the coastal road. That evening an enemy column of about five hundred ran into the road block at Beda Fomm and promptly surrendered. Early on February 6 the enemy main columns started to come down the road, and there was severe fighting throughout the day with successive groups, including a considerable number of tanks. By nightfall the enemy were in a desperate plight, with a confused mass of vehicles almost twenty miles in length, blocked in front and attacked in flank. Soon after dawn on February 7 they made a final attack with thirty tanks. When this, too, failed General Berganzoli surrendered with his army.

Thus, in two months the Army of the Nile had advanced five hundred miles, had destroyed an Italian army of more than nine divisions, and had captured 130,000 prisoners, 400 tanks, and 1290 guns. The conquest of Cyrenaica was complete.

*   *   *

In spite of these victories, so grave and complex were the issues, both diplomatic and military, which were at stake in the Middle East, and General Wavell had so much on his hands, that at the meeting of the Defence Committee on February 11 it was proposed to send the Foreign Secretary and General Dill, the Chief of the Imperial General Staff, to join him in Cairo.

Prime Minister to General Wavell   12 Feb. 41

Accept my heartfelt congratulations on this latest admirable victory, and on the unexpected speed with which Cyrenaica has been conquered. I have carried out your wishes in mentioning Generals O'Connor and Creagh.

2. Defence Committee considered whole situation last night, comprising, first, the extremely favourable developments in United States supplies; second, increasingly menacing attitude of Japan and plain possibility she may attack us in the near future; third, undoubted serious probability of attempt at invasion here. In this general setting we must settle Mediterranean plans.

3. We should have been content with making a safe flank for Egypt at Tobruk, and we told you that thereafter Greece and/or Turkey must have priority, but that if you could get Benghazi easily and without prejudice to European calls so much the better. We are delighted that you have got this prize three weeks ahead of expectation, but this does not alter, indeed it rather confirms, our previous directive, namely, that your major effort must now be to aid Greece and/or Turkey. This rules out any serious effort against Tripoli, although minor demonstrations thitherwards would be a useful feint. You should, therefore, make yourself secure in Benghazi and concentrate all available forces in the Delta in preparation for movement to Europe.

4. Both Greece and Turkey have hitherto refused our offers of technical units, because they say these are too small to solve their main problem, but conspicuous enough to provoke German intervention. However, this intervention becomes more certain and imminent every day, and may begin at any time now. If Turkey and Yugoslavia would tell Bulgaria they will attack her unless she joins them in resisting a German advance southward, this might create a barrier requiring much larger German forces than are now available in Rumania. But I fear they will not do this, and will fool away their chances of combined resistance, as was done in the Low Countries.

5. Our first thoughts must be for our ally Greece, who is actually fighting so well. If Greece is trampled down or forced to make a separate peace with Italy, yielding also air and naval strategic points against us to Germany, effect on Turkey will be very bad. But if Greece, with British aid, can hold up for some months German advance, chances of Turkish intervention will be favoured. Therefore, it would seem that we should try to get in a position to offer the Greeks the transfer to Greece of the fighting portion of the army which has hitherto defended Egypt, and make every plan for sending and reinforcing it to the limit with men and material.

6. We do not know what Greece will say to a great offer of this

kind. We do not know what are her means of resisting an invasion from Bulgaria by German forces. It is reasonable to assume that they have a plan to move troops from Albania to hold the passes and the lines of defence already built along or near the Bulgarian frontier. They cannot surely have pursued their advantage in Albania without any thought of this mortal danger to their right and almost rear. If they have a good plan it would be worth our while to back it with all our strength and fight the Germans in Greece, hoping thereby to draw in both Turks and Yugoslavs. You should begin forthwith plans and time-tables, as well as any preparatory movements of shipping.

7. It is not intended that you should delay [the capture of] Rhodes, which we regard as most urgent.

8. In order to give the very best chance to concerting all possible measures, both diplomatic and military, against the Germans in the Balkans, we are sending the Foreign Secretary and General Dill to join you in Cairo. They will leave on February 12, and should reach you 14th or 15th February. Having surveyed the whole position in Cairo and got all preparatory measures on the move, you will no doubt go to Athens with them, and thereafter, if convenient, to Angora. It is hoped that at least four divisions, including one armoured division, and whatever additional air forces the Greek airfields are ready for, together with all available munitions, may be offered in the best possible way and in the shortest time.

9. We can form no opinion here as to what ports of Greece we should use or what front we should try to hold or try to get them to hold. That can only be settled on the spot with the Greek Command.

10. In the event of its proving impossible to reach any good agreement with the Greeks and work out a practical military plan, then we must try to save as much from the wreck as possible. We must at all costs keep Crete and take any Greek islands which are of use as air bases. We could also reconsider the advance on Tripoli. But these will only be consolation prizes after the classic race has been lost. There will always remain the support of Turkey.

General Wavell replied on February 12, returning me compliments for my congratulations. He had naturally been considering the problem of assistance to Greece and Turkey for some time. He hoped he might be able to improve on his earlier estimate of available reserves, especially if the Australian Government would give him a certain latitude. He had already spoken to Mr. Menzies, the Prime Minister of Australia, who was in Cairo on his way to London, about this, and found him very ready to agree to what he suggested. He welcomed the visit of the Foreign Secretary and General Dill.

"We will do our best," he said, "to frustrate German plans in the Balkans, but Greek and Turkish hesitations and Yugoslav timidity have made our task very difficult. Owing to difficulties of shipping and ports our arrival is bound to be somewhat piecemeal."

* * *

I drafted and obtained formal Cabinet approval for the instructions to the Foreign Secretary on his mission.

12 Feb. 41

During his visit to the Mediterranean theatre the Foreign Secretary will represent His Majesty's Government in all matters diplomatic and military. He will report whenever necessary to the War Cabinet through the Prime Minister.

2. His principal object will be the sending of speedy succour to Greece. For this purpose he will initiate any action he may think necessary with the Commander-in-Chief of the Middle East, with the Egyptian Government, and with the Governments of Greece, Yugoslavia, and Turkey. He will of course keep the Foreign Office informed, and he will himself be informed by the Foreign Office or the Prime Minister of all changes of plan or view occurring at home.

3. The C.I.G.S. will advise on the military aspect, and the Foreign Secretary will make sure that in case of any difference his views are also placed before His Majesty's Government.

4. The following points require particular attention: (a) What is the minimum garrison that can hold the western frontier of Libya and Benghazi, and what measures should be taken to make Benghazi a principal garrison and air base? The extreme importance is emphasised of dropping the overland communications at the earliest moment. (b) The régime and policy to be enforced in Cyrenaica, having regard to our desire to separate the Italian nation from the Mussolini system. (c) The execution of the operation "Mandibles" [Rhodes] at the earliest moment, including, if necessary, repacking of the commandos at Capetown [for an opposed landing], having regard, however, to its not becoming an impediment to the main issue. (d) The formation in the Delta of the strongest and best-equipped force in divisional or brigade organisations which can be dispatched to Greece at the earliest moment. (e) The drain to be made upon our resources for the purpose of finishing up in Eritrea and breaking down the Italian positions in Abyssinia. The former is urgent; the latter, though desirable, most not conflict with major issues. It may be necessary to leave it to rot by itself. (f) The great mass of troops, over 70,-000, now engaged in the Kenya theatre must be severely scrutinised in order particularly to liberate the South African divisions for service in Egypt. Any communication with General Smuts had

better pass through the Prime Minister. A further conference between the Foreign Secretary and General Smuts might well be
convenient. (g) The Foreign Secretary, when visiting Athens with
the C.I.G.S., General Wavell, and any other officers, is fully empowered to formulate with the Greek Government the best arrangements possible in the circumstances. He will at the same time
try to keep H.M.G. informed, or seek their aid as far as possible.
In an emergency he must act as he thinks best. (h) He will communicate direct with the Governments of Yugoslavia and Turkey,
duplicating his messages to the Foreign Office. The object will be
to make them both fight at the same time or do the best they can.
For this purpose he should summon the Minister at Belgrade or
the Ambassador in Turkey to meet him as may be convenient. He
will bear in mind that while it is our duty to fight, and if need be,
suffer with Greece, the interests of Turkey in the second stage are
no less important to us than those of Greece. It should be possible
to reconcile the Greek and Turkish claims for air and munitions
support. (i) The Foreign Secretary will address himself to the
problem of securing the highest form of war economy in the
armies and air forces of the Middle East for all the above purposes, and to making sure that the many valuable military units
in that theatre all fit into a coherent scheme and are immediately
pulling their weight. (j) He should advise H.M.G. through the
Prime Minister upon the selection of commanders for all the different purposes in view. In this he will no doubt consult with
General Wavell, who enjoys so large a measure of the confidence
of H.M.G. The selection of the general who commands in Greece
is of the highest consequence, and it is hoped that an agreed recommendation may be made on this point. (k) Air Chief Marshal
Longmore will be required to give effect to the wishes and decisions of the Foreign Secretary in accordance with the general scope
of the policy here set out. But here again in the event of any difference the Foreign Secretary will transmit the Air Chief Marshal's
views to the War Cabinet through the Prime Minister. The duty
of the air force in the Middle East is to provide the maximum air
effort in Greece and Turkey compatible with the nourishing of
operations in the Sudan and Abyssinia and the maintenance of
Benghazi. (l) The Foreign Secretary will consult with Admiral
Cunningham upon naval operations necessary for all the above
purposes, and will ask H.M.G. for any further support, either by
transports or warships, which may seem necessary. (m) He will
propose to H.M.G. any policy concerning Iraq, Palestine, or
Arabia which may harmonise with the above purposes. He may
communicate direct with these countries and with the Government
of India, though not in a mandatory sense. The India Office must
be kept informed. (n) He will report upon the whole position at
Gibraltar, Malta, and, if possible, on return, at Takoradi. (o) In
short, he is to gather together all the threads, and propose continuously the best solutions for our difficulties, and not be deterred

from acting upon his own authority if the urgency is too great to allow reference home.

* * *

I thought that Smuts should know of Eden's mission, and hoped that he might be able to go to Cairo himself.

Prime Minister to General Smuts   15 Feb. 41

Joyful acceleration capture Benghazi, Cyrenaica, gives us secure flank for Egypt. Kismayu is also good. We must now try to help Greeks and spur Turks to resist forthcoming German offensive towards Aegean. Cannot guarantee good results on mainland of Europe, but we must do our best and save what islands we can from the wreck should our utmost efforts prove vain. We have therefore sent Foreign Secretary and C.I.G.S. to Cairo, thereafter visiting Athens and Angora, in order to concert strongest possible front. They will probably be three weeks in Middle East. Pray consider whether you could meet them. Please duplicate to me through United Kingdom High Commissioner any messages you send to them.

During Mr. Eden's absence I took charge of the Foreign Office. This was, of course, a heavy addition to my work. I had, however, been accustomed to read all the top-level daily telegrams and special reports since I became Prime Minister, and in my correspondence with President Roosevelt and other heads of Governments I had drafted many of the most important outgoing messages. Except in special cases I left the interviews with foreign Ambassadors to the Permanent Under-Secretary, Sir Alexander Cadogan, and to Mr. Butler, the Parliamentary Under-Secretary. The whole story of foreign affairs and war strategy was at this time fused into one single theme, and this I had in any case to comprehend, and as far as possible shape.

Prime Minister to Mr. Eden, Cairo   20 Feb. 41

Thankful you have arrived safely. I was making great exertions to carry 50th Division to you, and had wrung additional shipping from Shipping Ministry, with generous contribution by Admiralty. Am baffled by reply. Clearly H.Q. Middle East is not accurately informed about composition of convoys. . . . Hope you will be able to clear all this up. Essential that exact details of convoys and field states should be known at both ends. My impression is one of enormous jumbles of ration-strength troops in Middle East with many half-baked tactical formations. The 6th British Division and 7th Australian Division both seem likely to be imperfect for some time. Find out what we can send to make these effective

fighting units. Some local improvisation by transfer from other
half-baked units should surely be possible. Establishments are not
sacrosanct if practical results obtainable on different basis. Latest
Middle East ration-strength return shows increase of nearly 50,000
between December 31 and January 31. Does nothing emerge in
the shape of fighting units from this reinforcement? If fighting
formations are so few compared with ration strength, and in addition movement of these few formations to another theatre is so
lengthy and nothing can be done to improve matters, we must
recognise limits of our power to act on mainland, and indeed
whole Middle East proposition must be relegated to secondary
sphere.

2. Am concerned at check developing at Keren. Abyssinia might
be left, but we had hopes Eritrea would be cleaned up. Try to
include this in your disposition of air and other forces.

3. Do not consider yourselves obligated to a Greek enterprise
if in your hearts you feel it will only be another Norwegian fiasco.
If no good plan can be made please say so. But of course you
know how valuable success would be.

This crossed telegrams from Mr. Eden, which gave a clear
picture of the convictions of the men on the spot, and included
the conclusions of the conference in Cairo between him and
Dill with three Commanders-in-Chief.

We are agreed we should do everything in our power to bring
the fullest measure of help to Greeks at earliest possible moment.
If the help we can offer is accepted by the Greeks we believe that
there is a fair chance of halting a German advance and preventing
Greece from being overrun. Limitation of our resources, however,
especially in the air, will not allow of help being given to Turkey
at the [same] time if Greece is to be supported on an effective
scale.

After explaining that the scantiness of our air resources
made it doubtful whether a line so advanced as to cover
Salonika could be held, he continued:

General Wavell proposes the following military dispositions:
Cyrenaica will be garrisoned by one of the less trained and
equipped Australian divisions, Indian Motor Brigade, at present
under training, and one armoured brigade group, which represents
all remaining at present of the 7th Armoured Division. You will
remember that this armoured division was never at full strength.
Further complication reported by Commander-in-Chief Mediterranean is that troops at Benghazi cannot at present be maintained
by sea owing to destruction of port. Supply must, therefore, be by
road from Tobruk. The 6th Division is being formed, and will be
used for Rhodes. Forces committed to operations in Eritrea can-

not be reduced until operations there have been successfully completed. Keren is proving a tough nut to crack. On the other hand, it is agreed that forces in Kenya can be reduced, and warning orders have been issued for withdrawal of South African division with a view to its movement to Egypt when shipping can be made available. I hope to see Smuts on this and other matters before I return home.

General Wavell has therefore the following forces available for Greece in the immediate and near future: firstly, one armoured brigade and the New Zealand division, now raised to three infantry brigades, ready to sail; to be followed by Polish Brigade, an Australian division, a second armoured brigade, if required, and a second Australian division, in that order. Dispatch of this force will inevitably strain administrative resources to the utmost and must involve much improvisation.

Timings cannot yet be given, as these depend on discussion with the Greeks and shipping. It is estimated that to move the above forces at least fifty-three ships will be required. These can, of course, only be obtained by holding ships of convoys arriving in the Middle East, with all that that implies. Additional to present anxiety is the menace of mines to the Suez Canal. Energetic measures are being taken to deal with this, but until they are fully organised and material arrives from home there is always a risk that the Canal may be closed for from five to seven days.

My own conclusion, which General Dill and Commanders-in-Chief share, is that in the immediate future assistance to the Greeks, who are fighting and are threatened, must have first call on resources. Extent of help which we can later give Turks must depend upon volume of air reinforcements that can reach the Middle East and war wastage in African operations.

My present intention is to tell the Greeks of the help we are prepared to give them now, and to *urge* them to accept it as fast as it can be shipped to them. If they will accept this help and brave any risk it may entail of involving them in early hostilities with Germany there is a fair chance that we can hold a line in Greece. If we now split our small resources, especially in the air, we can effectively help neither Greece nor Turkey.

The word "urge," which I have italicised, in this telegram must not be misunderstood. Mr. Eden meant it to apply, not to the principle of acceptance by the Greeks of British help, but to the timing of their acceptance, if that was their resolve.

I replied:

Prime Minister to Mr. Eden, Cairo   21 Feb. 41

I have always felt it essential you should see Greeks before Angora, otherwise commitments might have been made to Angora which would tie your hands about Greeks, who are actually fighting. Therefore, am in complete agreement with procedure you propose.

And to General Smuts:

21 Feb. 41

I share your misgivings that Russian attitude has undermined Turks, and it may be that they will do no more than maintain an honest neutrality. Whole Greek position must be considered now by our envoys at Cairo. Will keep you informed.

On the same day Mr. Eden sent another telegram from Cairo:

As regards the general prospects of a Greek campaign, it is, of course, a gamble to send forces to the mainland of Europe to fight Germans at this time. No one can give a guarantee of success, but when we discussed this matter in London we were prepared to run the risk of failure, thinking it better to suffer with the Greeks than to make no attempt to help them. This is the conviction we all hold here. Moreover, though campaign is a daring venture, we are not without hope that it might succeed to the extent of halting the Germans before they overrun all Greece.

It has to be remembered that the stakes are big. If we fail to help the Greeks there is no hope of action by Yugoslavia, and the future of Turkey may easily be compromised. Though, therefore, none of us can guarantee that we may not have to play trump cards, we believe that this attempt to help Greece should be made. It is, of course, quite possible that when we see the Greeks tomorrow they may not wish us to come.

We have discussed the question of command. Dill, Wavell, and I are all agreed that we must select a figure who will command respect with the Greeks and exercise authority over the Greek officers with whom he will have to work. It is also necessary to choose a first-class tactical soldier. We have, therefore, decided that the command should be given to Wilson, who will be replaced in the military governorship of Cyrenaica by Neame, at present commanding in Palestine. . . . Wilson has a very high reputation here among the general public, as well as among the soldiers, and his appointment to lead the forces in Greece will be a guarantee to the Greeks that we are giving of our best.

*   *   *

On February 22, Mr. Eden, with General Wavell, Sir John Dill, and other officers, flew to Athens, to confer with the Greek King and Government. When Mr. Eden arrived in the evening for the first contacts with the Greeks he was taken to the Royal Palace at Tatoi. The King at once asked him if he would receive his Prime Minister alone. He explained to the

King his reluctance to do this, because he wished the discussions to be on an entirely military basis. If we were to send assistance to Greece it should be because of military reasons, and he did not want political considerations to play an undue part. However, the King persevered in his request, and he consented. At the meeting the Prime Minister, M. Korysis, read him a statement setting forth the outcome of the Greek Cabinet discussions in the past day or two.

As this statement forms the basis of our action, I set it forth in full.

Mr. Eden to Prime Minister   22 Feb. 41

Following is summary of written declaration given to me by President of the Council at outset of our meeting today:

"I desire to repeat most categorically that Greece, as a faithful ally, is determined to go on fighting with all her forces until final victory. This determination is not limited to the case of Italy, but will apply to any German aggression.

"2. Greece has only three divisions in Macedonia on the Bulgarian frontier. Consequently, a purely military problem arises of what reinforcements should be sent to enable the Greek army to resist the German. While more or less accurate information is available about German forces in Rumania and about forces mobilised in Bulgaria, the Greek Government, for their part, so far only know what British help might be given to them within a period of a month's time. Moreover, they do not know what are the intentions of Turkey and Yugoslavia. In these circumstances, Your Excellency's arrival in the Middle East is of the greatest help, not only for the purpose of clarifying the situation, but also of turning it to the common advantage of Great Britain and Greece.

"3. I desire to repeat once again that, whatever the outcome and whether Greece has or has not any hope of repulsing the enemy in Macedonia, she will defend her national territory, even if she can only count on her own forces."

The Greek Government wished us to understand that their decision had been taken before they knew whether we could give them any help or not. The King had wished Mr. Eden to know this *before* the military conversations opened, and this was the basis upon which they took place.

After military conferences and staff meetings held all night and the next day, Mr. Eden sent us the following most important telegram, dated the twenty-fourth:

Foreign Secretary to Prime Minister   24 Feb. 41

Agreement was reached today [23d] with the Greek Government on all points.

When at the end of discussions I asked whether the Greek Government would welcome the arrival in Greece of British troops in numbers and on conditions we proposed, President of Council stated formally that the Greek Government accepted our offer with gratitude and approved all detailed arrangements reached between the two General Staffs.

2. On arrival here this afternoon we met with the King of Greece, the President of Council and General Papagos. I gave an account of the international situation as we see it and dealt in detail with German designs upon the Balkans. I then explained that the conclusion had been reached by Ministers and Chiefs of Staff in London, with which Commanders-in-Chief here are in full agreement, that we should give maximum help to Greece at the earliest possible moment. We then gave details of the forces which we should be able to make available for Greece, explaining that this was all we could do at the moment. What we should be able to do in future depended on the development of the general war situation and the state of our resources. All I could say was that the troops we offered were well equipped and well trained and we were confident that they would acquit themselves well.

3. The President of Council, after reaffirming the determination of Greece to defend herself against Germany, reiterated the misgivings of the Greek Government lest insufficient British help should merely precipitate German attack, and stated that it was essential to determine whether available Greek forces and forces which we could provide would suffice to constitute efficacious resistance to the Germans, taking into account the doubtful attitude of Turkey and Yugoslavia. Before the Greek Government committed themselves, the President of the Council, therefore, wished the military experts to consider the situation in the light of the British offer. I made plain the logical conclusion of the attitude taken up by the President of Council. If we were to delay action for fear of provoking the Germans, such action must inevitably be too late.

4. From the ensuing discussion between General Dill, Commander-in-Chief Middle East, and the Air Officer Commanding on the one hand, and General Papagos on the other hand, it emerged that in view of the doubtful attitude of Yugoslavia the only line that could be held and would give time for withdrawal of troops from Albania would be a line west of the Vadar, Olympus-Veria-Edessa-Kajmakcalan. If we could be sure of Yugoslav moves it should be possible to hold a line farther north from the mouth of the Nestos to Beles, covering Salonika. It would be impracticable, unless Yugoslavia came in, to hold a line covering Salonika in view of exposure of Greek left flank to German attack.

He then described the detailed arrangements which had been agreed:

The discussions lasted some ten hours, and covered the main points of political and military co-operation. . . . We were all impressed by frankness and fair dealing of Greek representatives on all subjects discussed. I am quite sure that it is their determination to resist to the utmost of their strength, and that His Majesty's Government have no alternative but to back them whatever the ultimate consequences. While recognizing the risks, we must accept them.

In a further message he said:

We are all convinced that we have chosen the right course and as the eleventh hour has already struck felt sure that you would not wish us to delay for detailed reference home.

The risks are great, but there is a chance of success. We are accepting difficulties which will make a heavy demand upon our resources, more particularly of fighter aircraft. . . .

On these messages, which carried with them the assent of both Dill and Wavell, it was decided in the Cabinet to give full approval to the proposals.

Prime Minister to Mr. Eden, Cairo   24 Feb. 41

The Chiefs of Staff having endorsed action on lines proposed in your telegrams from Cairo and from Athens, I brought whole question before War Cabinet this evening, Mr. Menzies being present. Decision was unanimous in the sense you desire, but of course Mr. Menzies must telegraph home. Presume, also, you have settled with New Zealand Government about their troops. No need anticipate difficulties in either quarter. Therefore, while being under no illusions, we all send you the order, "Full steam ahead."

*   *   *

So far we had not taken any steps which went beyond gathering the largest possible strategic reserve in the Delta and making plans and shipping preparations to transport an army to Greece. If the situation changed through a reversal of Greek policy or any other event, we should be in the best position to deal with it. It was agreeable, after being so hard pressed, to be able to wind up satisfactorily the campaigns in Abyssinia, Somaliland, and Eritrea and bring substantial forces into our "mass of manoeuvre" in Egypt. While neither the intentions of the enemy nor the reactions of friends and neutrals could be divined or forecast, we seemed to have various important options open. The future remained inscrutable, but not a division had yet been launched, and meanwhile not a day was being lost in preparation.

5

Conquest of the Italian Empire

Origin and Growth of the Italian Empire in Africa—The Disaster of Adowa, 1896—The Italian Descent on Tripoli in 1911—Mussolini's Ambitions—Remarkable Development of the Italian Colonies—Imposing Fortifications and Military Power—"The Chance of Five Thousand Years"—Wavell's New Plan—Operations to Clear the Sudan—The Hard Core of Keren—Wingate Raises Rebellion—The Emperor Returns to Abyssinia—Unused Forces in Kenya—Smuts Points to Kismayu—Cunningham Calls a Halt— We Press for Action—Kismayu Taken—A Lightning Campaign in Italian Somaliland—All British Somaliland Regained—Attack on French Somaliland and Blockade of Jibuti—President Roosevelt's Concern for the Italian Civil Population in Abyssinia— The Struggle for Keren—Tribute to the Indian Troops—The Italian Navy Eliminated from the Red Sea—Pursuit of the Italians—The Emperor Reenters his Capital—Surrender of the Duke of Aosta—The End in Abyssinia.

WHEN MUSSOLINI DECLARED WAR on Great Britain at the moment of the fall of France in 1940, the Italian Empire in North and East Africa presented a majestic appearance. The kingdom of Italy had been a late-comer among the nation states of nineteenth-century Europe. Weak in industrial strength, and thus in military power, but thrust forward by her expanding population, she entered the race for Africa under a serious handicap. With the opening of the Suez Canal in 1869, Italian eyes had turned increasingly to African expansion. Sixteen years later Massawa was occupied and the Colony of Eritrea was formally established as Italian sovereign territory. The colony of Italian Somaliland, with its access to the Indian Ocean, also slowly grew. In between these two early settlements lay the ancient kingdom of Ethiopia. Upon this wild land Signor Crispi marched with the imperialist movement of the nineties, and hoped thereby to gain for Italy the prestige of a major Power in European affairs. The frightful disaster at Adowa in 1896, when the Italian army invading Abyssinia was annihilated, caused his fall and a halt to Italian adventures in Africa.

This tragic episode bit deep into Italian memories. When the Balkan States attacked Turkey in 1911, in the advent of the First World War, the Italian Government shocked and alarmed the sedate world of those days by leaping across to Tripoli and beginning its conquest. The need of France and Great Britain to gain Italy against the darkening German menace and the Turkish defeat in the Balkan fighting enabled a tenuous Italian foothold to be established on the North African coast. The fact that Italy was on the winning side in the first great struggle ratified her acquisition of Tripoli and Cyrenaica, which reviving Roman memories, was presently re-christened Libya. The rebellion of the Senussi remained a continuing challenge to the industrious occupation and colonisation of Arab deserts by the teeming population of Italy.

Such was the position when Mussolini came to power on the flowing Fascist tide against Bolshevism. The years which followed saw the planned expansion of Italy as an African colonial Power. The North African territories were subjugated under the stern military rule of General Graziani. Rebellions were ruthlessly quelled; the settlers multiplied; the desert was reclaimed; forts and acrodromes were built; roads and railways spread along the Mediterranean shore. Behind all this heavy but by no means ineffective expenditure of Italian resources lurked the national desire to avenge the defeat and shame of Adowa. My first volume has described the manner in which Mussolini's resolve and audacity overcame the timid, half-hearted resistance of Britain through the League of Nations and reduced to failure the authority of "fifty nations led by one." We have also seen how all this conflict and the conquest of Abyssinia played its part in the advent of the Second World War.

In June, 1940, when the British Empire seemed to Fascist eyes reeling to ruin, and France was almost prostrate, the Italian Empire in Africa spread far and wide. Libya, Eritrea, Abyssinia, Somaliland, nourished by Italian taxation, comprised a vast region in which nearly a quarter of a million Italian colonists toiled, and began to thrive, under the protection of more than four hundred thousand Italian and native troops. All the ports on the Red Sea and the Mediterranean were fortified. The British Intelligence readily accepted the Italian statements of their scale of armament, and classed them as naval bases of a high order. If the British Empire fell, as then seemed to Mussolini certain, Egypt, British Somaliland, and British East Africa, added to the existing possessions of Italy, would form indeed an immense area of the earth's surface under Italian sovereignty, the like of which had not been seen since the days of the Caesars. Here was what the ill-starred Ciano had called "the chance of five thousand years." It was this gleaming vision which was now to be abruptly extinguished.

*   *   *

Up till December, 1940, our attitude towards the Italians throughout the east of Africa had been purely defensive. General Wavell held a conference in Cairo on December 2 at which he laid down a new policy. He did not yet contemplate any deep penetration by Regular troops into Abyssinia, but the Italians, who had occupied Kassala and Galabat in the Sudan on July 4, 1940, were to be ejected. When these minor offensives were completed, Wavell originally intended to withdraw the majority of the troops for operations in the Middle East, leaving to the patriot movement, fostered and nourished by British officers, arms, and money, the task of making the Italian position within Abyssinia impossible, and eventually of reconquering the country.

The operations to clear the Sudan began in January under General Platt. The opening phase met with easy success. Platt had the 5th British-Indian Division, which was reinforced in January by the 4th British-Indian Division, brought over from the Western Desert, where it had played its part in the victorious battles of December. The force was supported by six air squadrons. Two Italian divisions evacuated Kassala on January 19 under the threat of attack and after a bombardment from the air. Soon after they also withdrew from Galabat, and quitted the Sudan. Our pursuit from Kassala was carried on without serious check until it came up to the very strong mountain position at Keren. At this point the enemy's two metropolitan divisions were firmly installed and holding tenaciously. Several attacks in early February could make no progress, and Platt decided that to force such a position he must accept the administrative delays involved in staging a fully prepared assault.

Meanwhile the work of raising rebellion in Abyssinia progressed. A small force under Brigadier Sanford of one Sudanese battalion and a number of selected British officers and N.C.O.'s, of whom Colonel Wingate was afterwards to gain high distinction, formed the core of the rising. As their successes grew they received help from increasing numbers of patriots. The Emperor re-entered his kingdom on January 20, and a large part of the western district of Gojjam was steadily cleared of the enemy.

* * *

Readers of the previous volume will be aware of my discontent with the large numbers of troops which had so long stood motionless in Kenya. Smuts had visited Kenya in November, 1940, and urged that we should assume the offensive, aiming at the Italian port of Kismayu.

He had telegraphed to me as follows:

5 Nov. 40

In Kenya I visited most of the fronts and studied plans with General Cunningham and his staff. There too the morale is good and the general position favourable, but there too prolonged inactivity in and by the desert will present danger to us. Best objective to go for in the near future is Kismayu, which is serious present threat to Mombasa, our essential base. Once Kismayu is captured and well held the bulk of our forces could be moved from that forbidding desert area towards the north so as to threaten Addis Ababa. For the Kismayu move Cunningham requires larger force than at first contemplated, and I shall send another infantry brigade from the Union as soon as sea transport is available. Additional Bren [guns] are badly wanted, and further transport for water and supply purposes will be provided. With serious internal unrest in Abyssinia and an attack both from the south and north, the Italians may crack in the summer, and considerable forces may thus be released for the more important theatre farther north.

This was in the fullest accord with my views. The brigade was sent from the Cape, and I understood that all preparations were moving for an advance in January before the rains set in. I was therefore shocked to see the following telegram:

General Wavell to C.I.G.S. 23 Nov. 40

Cunningham has decided not possible to carry out bold operations this winter. He proposes to carry out series of minor operations in Northern Kenya about middle of December, and requires both West African brigades for these. . . .

The High Commissioner for South Africa told us that General Smuts had expressed disappointment that the expedition against Kismayu, which he had hoped would be in January, was apparently being postponed till May in spite of the dispatch of the 3d Union Brigade. At the meeting of the Defence Committee on November 25, 1940, I inquired why the projected operation against Kismayu had been postponed until May. Sir John Dill said that he had received a telegram from General Wavell saying that he would shortly be holding a conference of commanders, including General Cunningham, to consider plans for the next six months.

We were none of us satisfied with this, and the Committee invited the Chiefs of Staff to call for a full explanation of the matter from General Wavell, and to report further to the Prime Minister.

I minuted as follows to the Secretary of State for War and the C.I.G.S.:

26 Nov. 40

I understand we are to receive from you a full account of the reasons now alleged to prevent the operation against Kismayu before May, and that you will make a strenuous effort not to succumb to these reasons. If it should be decided that nothing can be done till May, the West African brigade must go with the first set of empty transports to the West Coast, relieving the battalion now at Freetown.

The proposal to keep the brigade and not to fight is most depressing.

As a result of Wavell's conference on December 2, it was decided to attack the Italians in Kassala and to stimulate the rebellion in Abyssinia by all possible means. But the attempt to capture Kismayu was still to be postponed till after the spring rains, which meant May or June.

                       *   *   *

I continued to gird at the numbers and the inaction of troops in Kenya.

Prime Minister to General Wavell   26 Jan. 41

I was perplexed by your telegram of the twenty-first. I thought you wanted to have a large strategic reserve in the Delta, and this is in accordance with the directions we have given from here. Certainly there is no need to send another South African division to swell the 70,000 troops of various kinds who are now virtually out of action in Kenya. I asked General Smuts, and he has agreed, to keep the destination of the new division fluid, as I thought that by the time transport, etc., could be arranged he might be willing for them to come north to join the Army of the Nile. How can you expect me to face the tremendous strain upon our shipping, affecting as it does all our food and import of munitions, in order to carry more divisions from this country to the Middle East, when you seem opposed to taking a South African division, which would only have less than half the distance to come? I hope indeed that both the South African divisions now in Kenya will in a few months be moved to the Delta, and that the West African brigade will be sent, as promised, back to Freetown. On no account must General Smuts be discouraged from his bold and sound policy of gradually working South African forces into the main theatre.

Under the strong pressure from home Wavell eventually decided to make the effort before the rains. He animated the Kenya Command, and we were presently informed that the Nairobi forces hoped to carry out Operation "Canvas" (as the attack on Kismayu was called) between February 10 and 16. This signified a real movement in the East African theatre. I was much relieved to get Wavell's telegram of February 2, 1941, in which he said:

In Kenya I have approved the proposal to attempt capture of Kismayu about the middle of February. Enemy has strong positions and supply situation limits our force, but think attempt has reasonable chance of success. . . . Generally I have given instructions to both Platt and Cunningham for the maximum effort they can make against Italian East Africa in the next two months.

Thus we achieved the forward movement. The results showed how unduly the commanders on the spot had magnified the difficulties and how right we were at home to press them to speedy action.

February marked the beginning of General Cunningham's attack in strength. An Italian force of six brigades and six groups of local levies held the river Juba, near the mouth of which lies the port of Kismayu. Against them General Cunningham deployed, on February 10, four brigade groups. Kismayu was taken without opposition on the fourteenth. North of the port, beyond the river, stood the main enemy position at Jelib. That was attacked on the twenty-second, from both flanks and from the rear. A considerable success was gained. The enemy was completely routed, over thirty thousand being killed, captured, or dispersed into the bush. The enemy air had been roughly handled by the South African airplanes and took no part in the battle. Nothing now remained to hinder the advance to Mogadishu, the major seaport

of Italian Somaliland, two hundred miles farther north. Our
motorised troops entered it on the twenty-fifth, to find great
quantities of material and stores and over four hundred thousand gallons of precious petrol. On its airfield lay twenty-one
destroyed aircraft. General Cunningham rightly judged that
there was no enemy to oppose his next move. He had sufficient
troops, even though the 1st South African Division, except
for one brigade, was held back for operations elsewhere. Distance was the only problem. Transport and supply were the
decisive factors. Cunningham got permission from General
Wavell to make his next objective Jijiga, no less than 740 miles
from Mogadishu. After pausing only three days the advance
was renewed on March 1, and, brushing aside only light opposition, and meeting little interference from the enemy air
force, whose airfields were subjected to frequent attacks,
reached Jijiga on March 17. These were fine operations.

Prime Minister to General Wavell   1 March 41

Hearty congratulations on the brilliant result of the campaign
in Italian Somaliland. Will you convey to General Cunningham
the thanks and appreciation of His Majesty's Government for the
vigorous, daring, and highly successful operations which he has
conducted in command of his ardent, well-trained, well-organised
army. Will you ask him to convey this message to his troops. Publish as you find convenient.

You will no doubt discuss future operations with General Smuts
on the seventh. As you know, I have always wanted the South
African divisions to come forward to the Mediterranean shore.

General Wavell to Prime Minister   2 March 41

Your congratulations are very much appreciated. I have conveyed your message to General Cunningham.

2. Cunningham is pushing light forces on to Ferfer [about two
hundred miles north of Mogadishu and Dolo], which will complete occupation of Italian Somaliland. Owing to situation as regards supplies and transport, he does not think he can advance on
Harrar before March 21. He is coming to Cairo March 7, and we
will discuss future plans and moves of South African divisions.

3. Have already instructed Aden to reconnoitre Berbera with
view to reoccupation if possible.

*   *   *

At this point our troops from Aden could help. Our four air
squadrons there had, apart from their duties over the Red Sea,
been supporting from their central position both Cunningham's and Platt's campaigns by attacking the enemy air bases.
On March 16 two of our battalions were landed at Berbera.

The enemy garrison of a brigade melted away, leaving two hundred prisoners in our hands. All British Somaliland was now quickly regained, and through the port of Berbera General Cunningham's further advance could now be more readily sustained. He resumed his advance to Harrar, which surrendered on March 26, and on March 29 he entered Diredawa. This brought us to the railway from French Somaliland. Had the port of Jibuti been opened to us by the Vichy French, it would have greatly eased supply. That, however, was not to be. At Diredawa General Cunningham collected his resources for the final bound to Addis Ababa. During the month of March he had traversed eight hundred and fifty miles from Mogadishu with the 11th African Division and the 1st South African Brigade. Since the crossing of the river Juba his troops had accounted for more than fifty thousand of the enemy, killed, prisoners, or dispersed, at a cost of under five hundred casualties.

As a result of these successes various complications arose. General Wavell feared that the policy of strict blockade of Jibuti favoured by Generals de Gaulle and Le Gentilhomme would merely stiffen its resistance. He proposed instead making an offer to admit sufficient supplies, such as milk for children, to prevent distress, to allow any troops wishing to join the Free French to do so and to evacuate the rest to some other French colony, and to negotiate for the use of the railway for supplying his own forces. But at home we took a different view.

Prime Minister to General Wavell   1 April 41

We consider that you should follow policy laid down in Chiefs of Staff telegram of March 25 as closely as possible, subject to any modification which may seem desirable after your discussions with General de Gaulle. In particular, the initial approach to French Somaliland should be made by Free French authorities, and there should be no hesitation in using the blockade weapon to the full. Do not worry about the susceptibilities of Weygand and Vichy. We will look after them at this end.

2. I hope that on this and similar matters you will feel able to give full weight to the views of General de Gaulle, to whom His Majesty's Government have given solemn engagements, and who has their full backing as leader of the Free French Movement.

*   *   *

President Roosevelt was concerned about the Italian civil population in Abyssinia.

Former Naval Person to President Roosevelt   4 April 41

Count Sforza's suggestion [about Italian noncombatants] has been most attentively considered here. I beg you to realise our difficulties. Duke of Aosta might indeed be ready to yield Addis Ababa and march off into the mountains to carry on the war for some weeks, or even months, while leaving us with the whole responsibility for the health and safety of the civilian population, numbering scores of thousands. We have no means of discharging such a task until the organised fighting ends. We do not even hold port Jibuti, the railway line is broken, every ounce of transport we possess is sustaining our troops in their long advance. Result might well be a lamentable breakdown, whole burden of which would be cast on us, like the concentration camps in the old South African War. The moment the Duke brings the fighting to an end we will strain every nerve, and there might be prospects of success. Any prolongation of Italian resistance in Ethiopia delays our reinforcement of Libya, and you can see how urgent that has become. It is not merely a case of giving the enemy an immense military advantage, but undertaking a task in which we should fail.

Prime Minister to General Wavell   30 May 41

It will be convenient to have [Jibuti] in the near future, and I shall be glad if you will consider what forces would be necessary to break the French resistance, and whether they could be found without prejudice to other needs. The time to strike depends, of course, upon events in Syria, which may lead to a breach with Vichy, or alternatively to co-operation between the French army in Syria and the Free French. Either way the seizure of Jibuti might be fitted in. Meanwhile the blockade should be maintained with the utmost strictness, and any preparatory concentrations on the Jibuti frontier which you think helpful may be made. In this way actual fighting may be avoided, as is greatly to be desired. The moment for action can only be fixed in consultation with us.

*   *   *

Meanwhile the campaign in Abyssinia had progressed. Keren resisted obstinately. The flanks of this position could not be turned; only direct frontal attack was possible. To build up his resources for this effort and to deploy both his divisions Platt had but a single road, which lay in full view of the enemy. Railhead was a hundred and fifty miles away, so that not only did his preparations take several weeks, but surprise was out of the question. The air forces, including those from Aden, now played an invaluable part. In the first phase of this campaign Italian pilots had shown considerable initiative, but after the arrival of Hurricanes for the South African fighter squadron superiority was soon achieved. During the preparatory stages of the final Keren battle the Italian army was constantly harried on the ground and in the air. Soon the enemy ceased to interfere with troop movements, and when the battle opened support from the air did much to pave the way for our advance and to break enemy morale. The battle proved stubborn and cost us three thousand casualties. After the first three days, March 15 to 17, there was a pause for regrouping. On the twentieth General Wavell telegraphed that the fighting had been severe. The enemy had been counter-attacking fiercely and repeatedly, and although their losses had been extremely heavy and they had achieved only one success, there were no immediate signs of a crack. The Italians were evidently making desperate efforts to save this stronghold, and their air force was active. From London it looked rather evenly balanced, and we raised the question of reinforcements. These, however, were not needed. The attack was renewed on March 25, and two days later the Italian defence broke and Keren fell. Pursuit was rapid. Asmara fell on April 1, and Massawa, with ten thousand prisoners, surrendered on April 8.

The victory at Keren was mainly gained by the 4th and 5th British Indian Divisions. I paid them the tribute that their prowess deserved.

Prime Minister to Viceroy of India   7 April 41

The whole Empire has been stirred by the achievement of the Indian forces in Eritrea. For me the story of the ardour and perseverance with which they scaled and finally conquered the precipitous heights of Keren recalls memories of the North-West Frontier of long years ago, and it is as one who has had the honour to serve in the field with Indian soldiers from all parts of Hindustan, as well as in the name of His Majesty's Government, that I ask Your Excellency to convey to them and to the whole Indian Army the pride and admiration with which we have followed their heroic exploits.

I hastened to send Generals Cunningham and Platt and their gallant armies my heartfelt congratulations and those of His Majesty's Government upon "this timely and brilliant culmination of your memorable and strenuous campaign."

Other clearances were also effected. On entering the war Italy had a force of nine destroyers, eight submarines, and a number of minor vessels in the Red Sea. All these had now been accounted for by the Royal Navy and the Fleet air arm. By April 11 President Roosevelt was able to declare that the Red Sea and Gulf of Aden were no longer "combat zones" and were therefore open to American ships.

What remained of the Italian army in Eritrea retreated two hundred and thirty miles south through the mountains and fortified itself on the position of Amba Alagi. General Platt followed in their tracks. The 4th Indian Division and the majority of the supporting air squadrons were now diverted to Egypt, as a part of events presently to be narrated. With what remained Platt closed with the enemy. General Cunningham had reached Addis Ababa on April 6, where remnants of the Italian Air Force lay in wreckage on the airfield. He thrust the South African brigade northward through Dessie, and it came upon the rear of the Italians at Amba Alagi. With their retreat thus cut off, with General Platt attacking from the north, harassed by patriots, machine-gunned and bombed from the air, the Italian resistance could not last long. In early April Wingate's Sudanese battalion and local units, together with the irregulars who had come over to the Emperor, drove twelve thousand of the enemy in Gojjam into Debra Markos. Half of them were taken; the rest fled north to Gondar. The Emperor re-entered his capital on May 5.

*   *   *

When we look back upon the part played by Mussolini in the European crisis and the events leading to the war arising out of his attack on Abyssinia, and remember how he had successfully defied the League of Nations—"Fifty nations led by one"—we can see how easily firmness and action might have cleared this complication from the darkening European scene. Now, at any rate, among all our stresses and dangers we had made a good job of it. It was not without emotion springing from past thoughts and experience that I was able to offer my salutations to Haile Selassie.

Prime Minister to the Emperor of Ethiopia   9 May 41
It is with deep and universal pleasure that the British nation and Empire have learned of Your Imperial Majesty's welcome home to your capital at Addis Ababa. Your Majesty was the first of the lawful sovereigns to be driven from his throne and country by the Fascist-Nazi criminals, and you are now the first to return in triumph. Your Majesty's thanks will be duly conveyed to the commanders, officers, and men of the British and Empire forces who have aided the Ethiopian patriots in the total and final destruction of the Italian military usurpation. His Majesty's Government look forward to a long period of peace and progress in Ethiopia after the forces of evil have been finally overthrown.

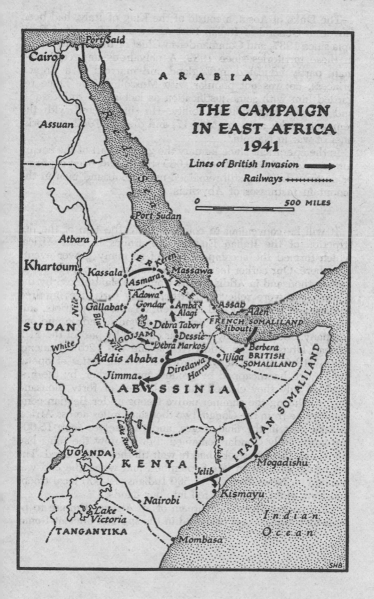

THE CAMPAIGN
IN EAST AFRICA
1941

Lines of British Invasion ➡
Railways ┄┄┄┄┄

0 ‖‖‖‖‖ 500 MILES

The Duke of Aosta, a cousin of the King of Italy, had been Governor-General of Italian East Africa and Viceroy of Ethiopia since 1937, and Commander-in-Chief of the Italian armies in these territories since 1939. A chivalrous and cultivated man, partly educated in England and married to a French princess, he was not popular with Mussolini. The Duce regarded him with some justification as lacking in ruthlessness and commanding military ability. He surrendered with the remnants of his army on May 17, and died in 1942 as a prisoner of war in Nairobi.

In the operations since January the greater part of the enemy forces, originally more than 220,000 strong, had been captured or destroyed. There still remained many thousand men in the mountain fastnesses of Abyssinia.

*   *   *

It will be convenient to complete here the tale of the destruction of the Italian Empire and armies in East Africa, which formed the accompaniment of so many graver events elsewhere. Our earlier fears that the Italian civil population of twenty thousand in Addis Ababa would be slaughtered by the Abyssinians were relieved. Farther north forty-five hundred Italians and levies, pressed into Debra Tabor by patriots, surrendered on July 2 to a British force of one squadron and one company. Southwest Abyssinia was cleared by part of the 11th African Division from Addis Ababa and the 12th advancing northward from the Kenya border. In a long series of operations much handicapped by ground and weather, by the first week of July they cleared the whole area of forty thousand enemy. During the summer native troops under Belgian command came from the Congo, two thousand miles across Africa, to take part in the final stages, and themselves took 15,000 prisoners. Only Gondar remained. But by now the rains had come, and this last stroke had to wait till they had passed. The net began to close in late September, and when the end was reached on November 27, 11,500 Italians, 12,000 local troops and forty-eight field guns fell into our hands.

Thus ended Mussolini's dream of an African Empire to be built by conquest and colonised in the spirit of ancient Rome.

6

Decision to Aid Greece

*A Strategic Reserve in the Delta—The Moment of Resolve—Our
Freedom to Withdraw—Hopes of a Balkan Front—Admiral
Cunningham on the Naval Risks to Be Run—My Telegram to
General Smuts of February 28—Mr. Eden's Discussions with the
Turks, February 28—My Comment Thereon—Yugoslavia the
Key—The German Army Moves into Bulgaria—Changed and
Disturbing Situation at Athens—Views of the Chiefs of Staff—
My Reflections upon It and My Message to Mr. Eden, March 6
—Distress of Our Ambassador at Athens—To Help or to Aban-
don Greece?—A Measured Reply from Mr. Eden—Smuts and
the Commanders in Chief Advise Us to Go On—A Short Cabi-
net and a Final Decision, March 7—Response from New Zealand—And from the Poles—My Telegram to Mr. Eden of March
14—My Message to President Roosevelt of March 10.*

HITHERTO we had not committed ourselves to the Greek
adventure, except by continuous large-scale preparations in Egypt, and by the discussions and agreements at
Athens which have been described. The preparations could
be arrested by a single order, and anyhow the assembly of a
strategic reserve of four divisions in the Delta was good in itself. The Greeks had departed in so many ways from the terms
of the Athens Agreement that we could, had we so wished,
have asked for release from it. Dangers approached from every
quarter, but up to the early days of March I felt fairly comfortable and in essentials free, with a "mass of manoeuvre" in
hand.

Now the moment had come when the irrevocable decision
must be taken whether or not to send the Army of the Nile to
Greece. This grave step was required, not only to help Greece
in her peril and torment, but to form against the impending

German attack a Balkan Front comprising Yugoslavia, Greece, and Turkey, with effects upon Soviet Russia which could not be measured by us. These would certainly have been all-important if the Soviet leaders had realised what was coming upon them. It was not what we could send ourselves that could decide the Balkan issue. Our limited hope was to stir and organise united action. If at the wave of our wand Yugoslavia, Greece, and Turkey would all act together, it seemed to us that Hitler might either let the Balkans off for the time being or become so heavily engaged with our combined forces as to create a major front in that theatre. We did not then know that he was already deeply set upon his gigantic invasion of Russia. If we had, we should have felt more confidence in the success of our policy. We should have seen that he risked falling between two stools, and might easily impair his supreme undertaking for the sake of a Balkan preliminary. This is what actually happened, but we could not know at the time. Some may think we builded rightly; at least we builded better than we knew. It was our aim to animate and combine Yugoslavia, Greece, and Turkey. Our duty so far as possible was to aid the Greeks. For all these purposes our four divisions in the Delta were well placed.

*   *   *

On March 4 Admiral Cunningham left us in no doubt as to the considerable naval risks in the Mediteranean which were involved in the move of the Army and the Royal Air Force to Greece. This meant continuous convoys of men, stores, and vehicles for the next two months. Destroyers in particular would have to be very heavily worked, and fighter and anti-aircraft defence would be weak for some time to come. If the Germans started an air offensive from Bulgaria we must expect losses in the convoys both at sea and at their ports of disembarkation. Nor could we rule out surface action by the Italian Fleet. This could be met by our battleships based on Suda Bay in Crete, but only at the expense of weakening the destroyer escort for the convoys and leaving the supply line to Cyrenaica practically unprotected. All this in its turn would increase the strain on Malta. The vulnerability of the Suez Canal to magnetic and acoustic mines gave cause for much anxiety just when these big movements of troops and convoys were starting. All offensive plans, including the combined operations against Rhodes, must, the Admiral said, be postponed. His resources would be taxed to the limit, but he was convinced that our policy was right and that the risks should be faced. The shelving of Rhodes was to us all a serious disappointment. We recognised its commanding importance. Rhodes, and also Scarpanto, with their invaluable airfields so near to Crete, were key points. Many times in the years that followed did we plan to assault Rhodes. Never could we fit it in to the main course of events.

* * *

I now learned that General Smuts was going to Cairo at Mr. Eden's earnest request, and I cabled to him:

28 Feb. 41

I am so glad you are going to meet Eden and Dill. We have taken a grave and hazardous decision to sustain the Greeks and try to make a Balkan Front. I look forward to receiving your personal views upon this after your conference. This decision makes it most necessary to reinforce Egypt and Libya, and I hope you will arrange with Wavell and Dill to bring "Acanthus" [the 1st South African Division] forward to the Mediterranean at the earliest moment, asking me about shipping difficulties, which are great. Our affairs are helped by rapid successes gained in East Africa. It is only a few weeks ago they were telling us they could not move on Kismayu till May. Now we have Mogadishu and the whole place in our hands.

* * *

Mr. Eden's account of his discussions with the Turks was not encouraging. They realised their own dangers as acutely as we did, but they, like the Greeks, were convinced that the forces we could offer would not be sufficient to make any real difference to an actual battle.

Mr. Eden to Prime Minister 28 Feb. 41

C.I.G.S. and I this morning had discussion on extremely frank and friendly basis with President of the Council, Minister for Foreign Affairs, and Marshal Chakmak.

Our decision to send Greece the maximum assistance at the earliest possible moment was well received. They reiterated Turkey's determination to fight if attacked by Germany, and stated their conviction that German attack on Greece meant that Turkey's turn would come next. But since Turkey's forces at present had no offensive power they considered the common cause would be better served by Turkey remaining out of the war until her deficiencies had been remedied and she could be employed with the maximum effect.

If attacked, Turks felt confident that they could hold the Germans for a time, though they would hope that we should be able immediately to come to their assistance. . . . They stated their readiness to concert action with Yugoslav Government, from whom, however, they had so far only received an evasive reply to [their] approach made at our instance. They felt concerned lest Russians should attack [them] if Turkey became involved in war with Germany.

The upshot of these discussions is that Turkey undertakes in any event to enter the war at some stage. She will, of course, do so immediately she is attacked. But if she is given time by Germans to re-equip herself she will take advantage of it, and will then make war at a moment favourable to the common cause, when her weight can be used with real effect.

To this I replied:

Prime Minister to Mr. Eden, Athens   1 March 41

Obvious German move is to overrun Bulgaria, further to intimidate Turkey by threat of air attacks, force Greece out of the war, and then turn on Yugoslavia, compelling her to obey; after which Turkey can be attacked or not, at their hostile convenience.

Your main appeal should now be made to Yugoslavia. *A sudden move south by Yugoslavia would produce an Italian disaster of the first magnitude, possibly decisive on whole Balkan situation.*[1] If at the same moment Turkey declared war the enemy could not gather sufficient forces for many months, during which our air strength will grow. I am absolutely ready to go in on a serious hazard if there is reasonable chance of success, at any rate for a few months, and all preparations should go forward at fullest speed. But I should like you so to handle matters in Greece that if upon final consideration of all the factors, including Rhodes possibilities, you feel that there is not even a reasonable hope, you should still retain power to liberate Greeks from any bargain and at the same time liberate ourselves. Evidently you and we have a few days in which to make our final decision. Meanwhile all should proceed as arranged.

*   *   *

Our efforts to warn the Yugoslavian Government must now be described. The whole defence of Salonika depended on their coming in, and it was vital to know what they would do. On March 2 Mr. Campbell, our Ambassador at Belgrade, met Mr. Eden in Athens. He said that the Yugoslavs were frightened of Germany and unsettled internally by political difficulties. There was a chance, however, that if they knew our plans for aiding Greece they might be ready to help. Mr. Eden and the Greeks feared lest the enemy should find out. On the

[1] My subsequent italics.—Author.

fifth the Foreign Secretary sent Mr. Campbell back to Belgrade
with a confidential letter to the Regent. In this he portrayed
Yugoslavia's fate at German hands, and said that Greece and
Turkey intended to fight if attacked. In such a case Yugoslavia
must join us. The Regent was to be told verbally that the British had decided to help Greece with land and air forces as
strongly and quickly as possible, and that if a Yugoslav staff
officer could be sent to Athens we would include him in our
discussions. The defence of Salonika would depend on Yugoslavia's attitude. If she gave way to Germany the consequences
would be obvious. She was urged instead to join us and have a
British army to fight by her side. Our effort in Greece would
be a vigorous one, and we had a good chance of holding a line.

On March 1 the German Army began to move into Bulgaria.
The Bulgarian Army mobilised and took up positions along
the Greek frontier. A general southward movement of the German forces was in progress, aided in every way by the Bulgarians. On the following day Mr. Eden and General Dill
returned to Athens from Angora and military conversations
were resumed. As the result of these Mr. Eden sent a very
serious message.

Mr. Eden and C.I.G.S. to Prime Minister   5 March 41

On arrival here we found a changed and disturbing situation
and the atmosphere quite different from that of our last visit.

2. General Papagos had on the last occasion insisted strongly
that the withdrawal of all troops in Macedonia to the Aliakhmon
line was the only sound military solution. We had expected that
this withdrawal to the Aliakhmon line had already begun. Instead
we found that no movement had in fact commenced, Papagos
alleging that it had been agreed that the decision taken at our
last meeting was dependent on the receipt of an answer from
Yugoslavia as to their attitude. . . .

3. Papagos now proposed to hold the line of fortifications near
the Macedonian frontier with four divisions, although he thought
they could not hold out for long, and also simply to remain where
he was on the Albanian front. This seemed an admission of de-
spair, as he himself practically admitted.

4. He proposed that British troops should, as they arrived, be
moved up piecemeal to the Macedonian frontier line, although it
was unlikely that they could arrive in time. We naturally refused
to accept this proposal, which was so entirely different from the
conditions under which we had agreed to send our forces. We
telegraphed to the Commander-in-Chief Middle East to come to
Athens for discussion. He arrived March 3, and discussions have
been practically continuous. As attitude of Papagos was unac-

commodating, we had to enlist the aid of the King, who was throughout the very trying discussions which followed calm, determined, and helpful.

5. We were finally offered three Greek divisions. . . .

6. We were thus faced with following alternatives: (a) To accept the plan of Papagos, to which he constantly returned, of attempting to dribble our forces piecemeal up to Macedonian frontier. (b) To accept three Greek divisions offered for Aliakhmon line, the equivalent of about sixteen to twenty-three battalions, instead of thirty-five we had been led to expect on our previous visit, and to build up our concentration behind this. (c) To withdraw our offer of military support altogether.

7. We were agreed that course (a) could only lead to military wavering, while course (c) seemed equally disastrous. . . .

8. We therefore agreed, after some misgivings, to solution (b), but with the proviso that the command and organisation of the whole Aliakhmon line was entrusted to General Wilson as soon as he was in a position to take it over. This was agreed to.

9. Our military advisers did not consider it by any means a hopeless proposition to check and hold the German advance on this line, which is naturally strong, with few approaches. At the worst it should always be possible to make fighting withdrawal from this line through country eminently suitable for rearguard action. . . .

14. We are all sure that we have in a very difficult situation arrived at correct decision. These two days have been indescribably anxious, but now that decision has been taken there is a marked improvement in the general atmosphere on Greek side. The hard fact remains that our forces, including Dominions contingents, will be engaged in an operation more hazardous than it seemed a week ago. You will no doubt decide on any communications to be made to the Dominions Governments. . . .

*   *   *

A marked change now came over our views in London. The Chiefs of Staff recorded the various factors developing unfavourably against our Balkan policy, and particularly against sending an army to Greece. They first emphasised the main changes in the situation: the depression of the Greek Commander-in-Chief; the omission of the Greeks to carry out their undertaking of twelve days earlier to withdraw their troops to the line we should have to hold if Yugoslavia did not come in; the fact that thirty-five Greek battalions were to have helped us hold this line, and that now there were to be only twenty-three at most, all newly formed, untried in battle, and lacking in artillery. In addition it had been expected that the Greeks would be able to withdraw some divisions from their Albanian front. "General Papagos now says that this cannot be done, as they are exhausted and outnumbered."

Turning to our own difficulties, the Chiefs of Staff pointed out that they had always expected that Rhodes would be captured before, or simultaneously with, the move to Greece; instead, this could not now be done till the move was over. This would mean that instead of our being able to concentrate our air forces against the German advance we should now have to conduct "considerable" air operations against Rhodes in order to protect our lines of communication to Greece. Finally, the Suez Canal was for the moment completely blocked by mines, and was not expected to be cleared until March 11. Half the ships carrying motor transport were north of the Canal and all the personnel ships south of it. Time, moreover, was running short. The Chiefs of Staff estimated that the Germans could concentrate two divisions on the Aliakhmon line by March 15 and three more by the twenty-second. One of these would be armoured. Assuming that the Greeks could only delay them in front of this line for a short time, the best we could hope for would be to have one armoured and one New Zealand brigade against the first two German divisions.

"The hazards of the enterprise," they concluded, "have considerably increased." They did not, however, feel that they could as yet question the military advice of those on the spot, who described the position as not by any means hopeless.

*   *   *

After reflecting alone at Chequers on the Sunday night upon the Chiefs of Staff paper and the trend of discussion in the War Cabinet that morning I sent the following message to Mr. Eden, who had now left Athens for Cairo. This certainly struck a different note on my part. But I take full responsibility for the eventual decision, because I am sure I could have stopped it all if I had been convinced. It is so much easier to stop than to do.

Prime Minister to Mr. Eden, Cairo   6 March 41

Situation has indeed changed for worse. Chiefs of Staff have presented serious commentary, which follows in my next. Failure of Papagos to act as agreed with you on February 22, obvious difficulty of his extricating his army from contact in Albania, and time-table of our possible movements furnished by Wavell, together with other adverse factors recited by Chiefs of Staff—for example, postponement of Rhodes and closing of Canal—make it difficult for Cabinet to believe that we now have any power to

avert fate of Greece unless Turkey and/or Yugoslavia come in,
which seems most improbable. We have done our best to promote Balkan combination against Germany. We must be careful
not to urge Greece against her better judgment into a hopeless
resistance alone when we have only handfuls of troops which can
reach scene in time. Grave Imperial issues are raised by committing New Zealand and Australian troops to an enterprise which,
as you say, has become even more hazardous. We are bound to
lay before the Dominions Governments your and Chiefs of Staff
appreciation. Cannot forecast their assent to operation. We do not
see any reasons for expecting success, except that, of course, we
attach great weight to opinions of Dill and Wavell.

We must liberate Greeks from feeling bound to reject a German ultimatum. If on their own they resolve to fight, we must to
some extent share their ordeal. But rapid German advance will
probably prevent any appreciable British Imperial forces from
being engaged.

Loss of Greece and Balkans is by no means a major catastrophe
for us, provided Turkey remains honest neutral. We could take
Rhodes and consider plans for "Influx" [descent on Sicily] or
Tripoli. We are advised from many quarters that our ignominious
ejection from Greece would do us more harm in Spain and Vichy
than the fact of submission of Balkans, which with our scanty
forces alone we have never been expected to prevent.

I send you this to prepare your mind for what, in the absence
of facts very different from those now before us, will probably be
expressed in Cabinet decision tomorrow.

Attached to this was the grave commentary, summarised
above, of the Chiefs of Staff.

*   *   *

As soon as my warning telegram was read by Sir Michael
Palairet in Athens he showed lively distress, and telegraphed
to the Foreign Secretary, who had now reached Cairo, as
follows:

6 March 41

I have just read the Prime Minister's message to you. I need
not emphasise to you the effect of our now withdrawing from the
agreement actually signed between Chief of the Imperial General
Staff and Greek Commander-in-Chief and now in process of execution here by General Wilson himself. How can we possibly
abandon the King of Greece after the assurances given him by
the Commander-in-Chief and Chief of the Imperial General Staff
as to reasonable chances of success? This seems to me quite unthinkable. We shall be pilloried by the Greeks and the world in
general as going back on our word.

2. There is no question of "liberating the Greeks from feeling

bound to reject the ultimatum." They have decided to fight Germany alone if necessary. The question is whether we help or abandon them.

And again to Mr. Eden later in the day:

King of Greece spoke today to Air Attaché with deep appreciation of your visit and absolute determination to carry out agreed plan of action against German attack. He has every confidence in the chances for success, and is satisfied that this confidence is shared by General Papagos and his Government. He emphasised the great importance of speed, and particularly of adequate air forces here, in order to break up the German air attack, which is their customary opening offensive. Initial German defeat in the air would, more than anything else, do away with the myth of German invincibility and give the whole country the same confidence which he has in prospects for success. I have not yet seen him myself since you left.

And still later:

General Wilson has had a most satisfactory talk with General Papagos this morning. He is greatly encouraged by the marked improvement in the latter's attitude. He found him most helpful and anxious to co-operate in every possible way.

Prime Minister to Mr. Eden (Cairo)   6 March 41
War Cabinet are taking no decision until we receive your reply.

Mr. Eden to Prime Minister   6 March 41
Chief of Imperial General Staff and I, in consultation with the three Commanders-in-Chief, have this afternoon re-examined the question. We are unanimously agreed that, despite the heavy commitments and grave risks which are undoubtedly involved, especially in view of our limited naval and air resources, the right decision was taken in Athens. Palairet's telegrams to Cairo show the position from Greek angle.

2. This is merely to indicate to you how our minds are working while we await Cabinet view.

And later:

Mr. Eden to Prime Minister   6 March 41
We have had further discussion this evening with General Smuts and Commanders-in-Chief, and further detailed appreciation follows tomorrow morning.

Prime Minister to Mr. Eden, Cairo   7 March 41
I will bring your measured and deliberate reply before the Cabinet today. Meanwhile all preparations and movements should go forward at utmost speed.

2. I am deeply impressed with steadfast attitude maintained by you and your military advisers, Dill, Wavell, and, I presume, Wilson, on the broad merits, after full knowledge of local and technical situation and in view of the memorandum by the C.O.S. Committee.

3. Two points are dominant. First, we must not take on our shoulders responsibility of urging Greeks against their better judgment to fight a hopeless battle and involve their country in probable speedy ruin. If, however, knowing how little we can send at particular dates, they resolve to fight to the death, obviously we must, as I have already said, share their ordeal. It must not be said, and on your showing it cannot be said, that, having so little to give, we dragged them in by overpersuasion. I take it, from your attitude and Athens telegrams, that you are sure on this point.

4. Second point. It happens that most of the troops to be devoted to this solemn duty are the New Zealand Division and after March the Australians. We must be able to tell the New Zealand and Australian Governments faithfully that this hazard, from which they will not shrink, is undertaken, not because of any commitment entered into by a British Cabinet Minister at Athens and signed by the Chief of the Imperial General Staff, but because Dill, Wavell, and other Commanders-in-Chief are convinced that there is a reasonable fighting chance. This I regard as implied by your positive reactions to our questioning telegrams.

5. Please remember in your stresses that, so far, you have given us few facts or reasons on their authority which can be presented to these Dominions as justifying the operation on any grounds but *noblesse oblige*. A precise military appreciation is indispensable.

6. You know how our hearts are with you and your great officers.

On the seventh the promised fuller statement of the case reached us in London.

Mr. Eden to Prime Minister   7 March 41

Following are the views of your envoys:

Whole position again fully reviewed with the Commanders-in-Chief and Smuts. While we are all conscious of the gravity of the decision, we can find no reason to vary our previous judgment.

2. There has been no question of urging Greece against her better judgment. At our first meeting at Tatoi Greek Prime Minister handed me at the outset of the proceedings written statement announcing Greece's determination to resist an attack by Italy or Germany, if necessary alone. The Greek Government have consistently maintained this attitude, with varying degrees of confidence as to the outcome. The Greeks appreciate that there is no honourable peace open to them with Italy and Germany

menacing their frontiers. The Greeks can only share the fate of Rumania, or continue the struggle whatever the odds.

3. We have already undertaken commitments towards Greece. Eight squadrons of the R.A.F., ground defences and anti-aircraft personnel, have been operating there for months past.

4. Collapse of Greece without further effort on our part to save her by intervention on land, after the Libyan victories had, as all the world knows, made forces available, would be the greatest calamity. Yugoslavia would then certainly be lost; nor can we feel confident that even Turkey would have the strength to remain steadfast if the Germans and Italians were established in Greece without effort on our part to resist them. No doubt our prestige will suffer if we are ignominiously ejected, but in any event to have fought and suffered in Greece would be less damaging to us than to have left Greece to her fate. . . .

In the existing situation we are all agreed that the course advocated should be followed and help given to Greece.

We devoutly trust, therefore, that no difficulties will arise with regard to the dispatch of Dominions forces as arranged. At the same time, if the operation is to have a fair chance of success, it is vital to find means of supplementing the very serious gap in our forces, particularly in the air. As we have already many times emphasised since our arrival, weakness in the air is our chief anxiety in this theatre of war. Germans, working on interior lines, are increasing their weight of attack from Sicily and Tripoli, from the Balkans and the Dodecanese. We are making no corresponding increase in our own reinforcements, and drastic reduction in the promised allotment of Tomahawks has come as a grievous blow. Royal Air Force here are daily engaged with the Italian Metropolitan Air Force in Albania, and with an ever-increasing proportion of German Air Force in other areas.

The struggle in the air in this theatre will be a stern one. Longmore requires all the help that can be given. If he can hold his own most of the dangers and difficulties of this enterprise will disappear.

Accompanied by the Chiefs of Staff, I brought the issue before the War Cabinet, who were fully apprised of everything as it happened, for final decision. In spite of the fact that we could not send more aircraft than were already ordered and on the way, there was no hesitation or division among us. Personally I felt that the men on the spot had been searchingly tested. There was no doubt that their hands had not been forced in any way by political pressure from home. Smuts, with all his wisdom, and from his separate angle of thought and fresh eye, had concurred. Nor could anyone suggest that we had thrust ourselves upon Greece against her wishes. No one had been overpersuaded. Certainly we had with us the highest expert authority, acting in full freedom and with all knowledge of the men and the scene. My colleagues, who were toughened by the many risks we had run successfully, had independently reached the same conclusions. Mr. Menzies, on whom a special burden rested, was full of courage. There was a strong glow for action. The Cabinet was short; the decision final.

Prime Minister to Mr. Eden, Cairo   7 March 41

Cabinet this morning considered project in light of your telegrams from Athens and Cairo, and my telegrams. Chiefs of Staff advised that, in view of steadfastly expressed opinion of Commanders-in-Chief on the spot, of the Chief of the Imperial General Staff, and commanders of the forces to be employed, it would be right to go on. Cabinet decided to authorise you to proceed with the operation, *and by so doing Cabinet accepts for itself the fullest responsibility.*[2] We will communicate with Australian and New Zealand Governments accordingly.

In a more personal strain I telegraphed two days later:

Prime Minister to Mr. Eden, Cairo   9 March 41

I entirely agree with all your handling of the Balkan telegrams. There seems still a chance of Yugoslavia coming in, and more than a chance of her keeping the door shut.

2. While you are on the spot you should deal faithfully with Egyptian Prime Minister, Farouk, and anyone else about our security requirements. It is intolerable that Rumanian Legation should become a nest of Hun spies, or that the Canal Zone should be infested by enemy agents. I am relying on you to put a stop to all this ill-usage we are receiving at the hands of those we have saved.

3. Will you tell Smuts how glad I should be if now he is so near he could come and do a month's work in the War Cabinet as of old.

4. Do not overlook those parts of your instructions dealing with the economy of the Middle East armies. Am relying on you to clean this up, and to make sure that every man pulls his weight. A few days might well be devoted to this.

Meanwhile New Zealand made a fine response to our request for her division.

Prime Minister to Prime Minister of New Zealand   12 March 41

We are deeply moved by your reply, which, whatever the fortunes of war may be, will shine in the history of New Zealand and be admired by future generations of free men in every quarter of the globe.

[2] My subsequent italics.—Author.

To make good the request and assumption at the end of your message shall be our faithful, unremitting endeavour.

Prime Minister to Mr. Eden, Cairo   14 March 41

I have come to the conclusion that it is better for you to stay in Middle East until the opening phase of this crisis has matured. Your instructions give you the means of concerting the political and military action of all the factors involved. The attitude of Yugoslavia is still by no means hopeless, and a situation may at any moment arise which would enable you to go there. Turkey requires stimulus and guidance as events develop. No one but you can combine and concert the momentous policy which you have pressed upon us and which we have adopted. The War Cabinet needs a representative on the spot, and I need you there very much indeed.

2. I saw Sikorski this morning and asked for the Polish Brigade. He agreed in the most manly fashion, but he asked that this Brigade, which was one of the few remaining embodiments of Polish nationality, should not be lightly cast away or left to its fate. I promised full equipment and no greater risks than would be run by own flesh and blood. He said, "You have millions of soldiers; we have only these few units." I hope you appreciate what we are asking of these valiant strangers, and that General Wavell will have this in his mind always.

3. I feel very much the fact that we are not using a single British division. I am arranging to send the 50th Division with Convoy W.S. 8, leaving April 22. A special convoy would only have saved a week, and we cannot afford the extra escort.

4. We have not been told by Wavell whether Glens [3] got through Canal, but presume this will be regarded as urgent in the highest degree. A source of which you are aware shows that preparations are being made to withdraw German personnel from Rhodes in expectation of its British occupation. You ought not to be easily contented with delaying Rhodes indefinitely. We need to take it at earliest moment, and thereafter we need the 6th British Division, whether things go well or ill. We must not be reproached with hazarding only other people's troops. You ought to press hard and long for taking Rhodes before the end of this month.

5. Can you tell me why Papagos does not draw three or four divisions from Albania to strengthen his right front? Recent check which Italians are said to have received and fact that German advance has not yet begun may still give time for this. Present strategic layout of Greek Army looks to me most dangerous. Papagos must have good reasons, and if you have learned them pray let me know.

6. Of course, if Yugoslavia came in this would justify Greek strength in Albania. But this is not yet known. Presume you and Dill have studied carefully possibilities of a Yugoslav attack on

[3] This refers to three fast transports specially prepared for military operations. See Volume II, page 396.

Italians in Albania. Here they might win victory of the first order, and at the same time gain the vast mass of the equipment they need to preserve their independence and can never find elsewhere in time.

7. Do not let Lemnos be picked up by the Germans as an air base for nothing.

8. It seems right to obtain a decision at Keren before withdrawing air squadrons you have thereabouts.

9. Your message containing Longmore's complaints overlooks what is on the way.

After giving the details of these air reinforcements I added:

The fact that Longmore thinks you ought to come home via Lagos, in which view Portal concurs, is final reason for my wish for you and Dill to remain on scene. For otherwise, apart from larger considerations in my paragraph 1, you will both be out of action at either end during a most critical seven days. Everything is going quietly here, and we have begun to claw the Huns down in the moonlight to some purpose. God bless you all.

I thought it right to inform President Roosevelt of our plans in a message which may well end this anxious chapter.

Former Naval Person to President Roosevelt   10 March 41

I must now tell you what we have resolved about Greece. Although it was no doubt tempting to try to push on from Benghazi to Tripoli, and we may still use considerable forces in this direction, we have felt it our duty to stand with the Greeks, who have declared to us their resolve, even alone, to resist the German invader. Our Generals Wavell and Dill, who accompanied Mr. Eden to Cairo, after heart-searching discussions with us, believe we have a good fighting chance. We are therefore sending the greater part of the Army of the Nile to Greece, and are reinforcing to the utmost possible in the air. Smuts is sending the South Africans to the Delta. Mr. President, you can judge these hazards for yourself.

At this juncture the action of Yugoslavia is cardinal. No country ever had such a military chance. If they will fall on the Italian rear in Albania there is no measuring what might happen in a few weeks. The whole situation might be transformed, and the action of Turkey also decided in our favour. One has the feeling that Russia, though actuated mainly by fear, might at least give some reassurance to Turkey about not pressing her in the Caucasus or turning against her in the Black Sea. I need scarcely say that the concerted influence of your Ambassadors in Turkey, Russia, and above all in Yugoslavia, would be of enormous value at the moment, and indeed might possibly turn the scales.

In this connection I must thank you for magnificent work done by Donovan in his prolonged tour of Balkans and Middle East. He has carried with him throughout an animating, heart-warming flame.

7

The Battle of the Atlantic, 1941

The Western Approaches

A Supreme Anxiety—Combination of U-Boats and Aircraft—Strain on the Western Approaches—Our Counter-Measures—A Struggle to Breathe—Landed Cargoes Drop by Half—Damage to Shipping and Congestion at the Ports—Formation of the Import Executive, January—The Work of the Lord President's Committee— My Minute of January 28—And of February 22—Move of the Command of the Western Approaches from Plymouth to Liverpool, February 17—Storm Havoc Among Our Older Ships— Hitler's Menace of January 30—The Admiralty Salvage Organisation—Sorties by German Cruisers—The "Scheer" in the South Atlantic—The "Scharnhorst" and "Gneisenau" Break Out— Eighty Thousand Tons of Shipping Sunk in Two Days, March 15-16—Raiders Take Refuge in Brest, March 22—Hitler's Error— The Battle of the Atlantic—The Battle of the Atlantic Committee —My Directive of March 6—The U-Boats in "Wolf-Packs"— Tactical Problems—Help from the United States, March 11— Passing of the Lend-Lease Bill—The Imports Budget, March 26 —Close Relations with the United States—The "Dunkerque" Incident—Pressure by President Roosevelt on Vichy.

AMID THE TORRENT of violent events one anxiety reigned supreme. Battles might be won or lost, enterprises might succeed or miscarry, territories might be gained or quitted, but dominating all our power to carry on the war, or even keep ourselves alive, lay our mastery of the ocean routes and the free approach and entry to our ports. I have described in the previous volume the perils which the German occupation of the coast of Europe from the North Cape to the Pyrenees brought upon us. From any port or inlet along this enormous front the hostile U-boats, constantly improving in speed, endurance, and radius, could sally forth to destroy our sea-borne food and trade. Their numbers grew steadily. In the first quarter of 1941 production of new craft was at the rate of ten a month—soon afterward increased to eighteen a month. These included the so-called 500-ton and 740-ton types, the first with a cruising range of 11,000 miles and the latter of 15,000 miles.

To the U-boat scourge was now added air attack far out on the ocean by long-range aircraft. Of these the Focke-Wulf 200, known as the Condor, was the most formidable, though happily at the beginning there were few of them. They could start from Brest or Bordeaux, fly right round the British Island, refuel in Norway, and then make a return journey next day. On their way they would see far below them the very large convoys of forty or fifty ships to which scarcity of escort had forced us to resort, moving inward or outward on their voyages. They could attack these convoys, or individual ships, with destructive bombs, or they could signal the positions to which the waiting U-boats should be directed in order to make interceptions. Already in December we had begun preparations for the desperate expedient of an underwater dynamite carpet from the mouths of the Mersey and the Clyde to the hundred-fathom line northwest of Ireland.[1]

Meanwhile we had ordered the expansion and redeployment of the Air Coastal Command, giving it high priority in pilots and machines. We planned to increase this command by fifteen squadrons by June, 1941, and these reinforcements were to include all the fifty-seven American long-range Catalinas which we expected to receive by the end of April. The denial to us of all facilities in Southern Ireland again exerted its baleful influence on our plans. We pressed forward with the construction of new airfields in Ulster as well as in Scotland and the Hebrides.

The evil conditions thus described continued, some in an aggravated form. The stranglehold of the magnetic mine was only loosened and kept from closing by triumphs of British science and ingenuity, carried into effect by the ceaseless toil of twenty thousand devoted men in a thousand small craft with many strange varieties of apparatus. All our traffic along the east coast of Britain was under constant menace from German light bombers or fighter aircraft, and was in consequence severely restricted and reduced. The port of London, which

[1] A proposed mine barrier which was never laid. See Volume II, Book II, Chapter 30, page 516.

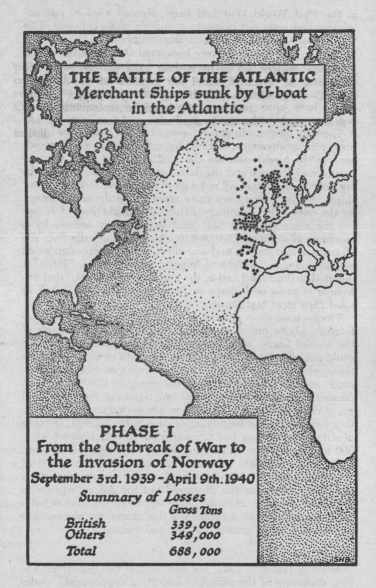

THE BATTLE OF THE ATLANTIC
Merchant Ships sunk by U-boat
in the Atlantic

PHASE I
From the Outbreak of War to
the Invasion of Norway
September 3rd. 1939 – April 9th. 1940
Summary of Losses

	Gross Tons
British	339,000
Others	349,000
Total	688,000

in the First World War had been deemed vital to our existence, had been cut down to a quarter of its capacity. The Channel was an actual war area. Bombing raids on the Mersey, the Clyde, and Bristol gravely hampered these sole remaining major commercial ports. The Irish and Bristol Channels were closed or grievously obstructed. Every expert authority, if presented a year earlier with the conditions now prevailing, would have pronounced our plight hopeless beforehand. It was a struggle to breathe.

The very magnitude and refinement of our protective measures—convoy, diversion, degaussing, mine-clearance, the avoidance of the Mediterranean—the lengthening of most voyages in time and distance and the delays at the ports through bombing and the black-out, all reduced the operative fertility of our shipping to an extent even more serious than the actual losses. At the outset the Admiralty naturally thought first of bringing the ships safely to port, and judged their success by a minimum of sinkings. But now this was no longer the test. We all realised that the life and war effort of the country depended equally upon the weight of imports safely landed. *"I see,"* I minuted to the First Lord in the middle of February, *"that entrances of ships with cargo in January were less than half of what they were last January."*

The pressure grew unceasingly, and our shipping losses were fearfully above our new construction. The vast resources of the United States were only slowly coming into action. We could not expect any further large windfalls of vessels such as those which had followed the overrunning of Norway, Denmark, and the Low Countries in the spring of 1940. Moreover, damaged shipping far exceeded our repairing resources, and every week our ports became more congested and we fell further behind. At the beginning of March over 2,600,000 tons of damaged shipping had accumulated, of which about 930,-000 tons were ships undergoing repair while loading cargoes, and nearly 1,700,000 tons were immobilised by the need of repairs. Indeed, it was to me almost a relief to turn from these deadly undertides to the ill-starred but spirited enterprises in the military sphere. How willingly would I have exchanged a full-scale attempt at invasion for this shapeless, measureless peril, expressed in charts, curves, and statistics!

*   *   *

Early in January, 1941, we had formed the Import Executive, consisting of the principal importing departments, under the chairmanship of the Minister of Supply, and the parallel body, the Production Executive, under the Minister of Labour. The principal object of the first of these bodies was to grapple with the import situation, to improve the organisation of shipping and transport, and to solve the many intricate problems of labour and organisation arising at the ports. I now worked closely with these powerful bodies, which often sat together, and I sought to concert their action.

Prime Minister to Minister of Shipping   4 Jan. 41

The Import Executive will explore the whole of this situation, the development of which was one of the reasons for calling the said Executive into being. I shall myself keep in the closest touch with the Import Executive, and will endeavour to give the necessary decisions. It is hoped that by the more efficient use of our shipping, its turn-round, port and labour resources, the tonnage available may be increased beyond the 33,000,000 tons which is all you can at present foresee. The Ministry of Shipping and the Ministry of Transport, together with the Ministry of Labour, will cooperate actively with the Import Executive, and their work will be effectively concerted by that Executive. In addition to this, the Admiralty will be asked to concentrate more effort upon the repair of ships, even to some extent to the detriment of new merchant shipbuilding. We hope American aid will be forthcoming, and that greater security will be achieved by our convoys as the nights shorten and our main reinforcements of escorting craft come into service.

Prime Minister to Import Executive   23 Jan. 41

I request that you will not consider yourselves bound by the estimate of losses put forward by the Ministry of Shipping, or take that as the foundation for future calculations. The Ministry of Shipping have reached a total of 5,250,000 tons per annum by taking as their basis the period since the collapse of France, including the quite exceptional losses of the Norwegian and French evacuations. A better alternative method of calculation would be to take the monthly rate for the whole year 1940, which is 4,250,000 tons; or, again, for the whole war, which is between 3,750,000 and 4,000,000 tons, provided the extraordinary evacuation losses are deducted.

2. It is probably prudent to assume that this rate will continue. It does not follow, however, that it will not be reduced as our improved methods come into play and the additional destroyers reach the Fleet. Bearing this in mind, I think it would be safe to work on the monthly average since the beginning of the war.

My estimate was fully justified by events in the year 1941.

* * *

At the beginning of the year, I asked Sir John Anderson, the Lord President of the Council, to make it his particular task to grip and drive forward the plans for harnessing to our war-making machine the full economic resources of the nation.

Prime Minister to Lord President of the Council   28 Jan. 41

While the Import and Production Executives necessarily are concerned with the practical handling of the business committed to them, it is essential that the larger issues of economic policy should be dealt with by your committee, and primarily by you. This is in accordance with the drift of well-informed public opinion. You should, therefore, not hesitate to take the initiative over the whole field. You should summon economists like Keynes to give their views to you personally. You should ask for any assistance or staff you require, utilising, of course, the Statistical Department. Professor Lindemann and his branch will assist you in any way you wish, and will also act as liaison between you and me. I wish you to take the lead prominently and vigorously in this committee, and it should certainly meet at least once a week, if not more often.

Will you consult with Sir Edward Bridges on the above, and let me know how you propose to implement it.

Anderson bent to this task his energy, mature judgment, and skill in administration. His long experience as a civil servant at home, and as Governor of Bengal, had given him a wide knowledge of Government departments and of the official machine. He soon gained the confidence of his Ministerial colleagues, and shaped the Lord President's committee into a powerful instrument for concerting departmental plans over the whole range of wartime economic policy. As time went on this committee came to exercise on behalf of the War Cabinet a large measure of authority and power of decision in this and other spheres. Its sure control over economic policy and Home Front problems helped to free me for the military field.

*   *   *

Prime Minister to Sir Andrew Duncan,   22 Feb. 41
Minister of Supply

The Prime Minister would be glad if you would bring the attached notes and diagrams to the attention of the Import Executive. They have been prepared under the Prime Minister's personal direction by Professor Lindemann. They disclose a most grave and as yet unexplained tendency, which, if it is not corrected, will hazard the life of Britain and paralyse her war effort.

The Prime Minister does not understand how it is that, when the sinkings are less (although very serious) and the volume of tonnage (apart from its routing) very little diminished, there should be such a frightful fall in imports.

He is very glad to see that there is a sharp recovery in the last two weeks, and he hopes this may be the first fruits of the Import Executive.

The Prime Minister will be glad to see the Import Executive Committee at 5 P.M. on Tuesday, with a view to learning from them whether they have any further measures to propose to avert a potentially mortal danger.

* * *

As early as August 4, 1940, I had asked the Admiralty to move the controlling centre of the western approaches from Plymouth to the Clyde.[2] This proposal had encountered resistance, and it was not until February, 1941, that the increasing pressure of events produced Admiralty compliance. The move to the north was agreed. The Mersey was rightly chosen instead of the Clyde, and on February 17 Admiral Noble was installed at Liverpool as Commander-in-Chief of the western approaches. Air Chief Marshal Bowhill, commanding the Coastal Command, worked with him in the closest intimacy. The new joint headquarters was soon operating, and from April 15 the two commands were forged into a single highly tempered weapon under the operational control of the Admiralty.

* * *

The new year opened with violent and almost continuous storms, causing much havoc among the older ships which, despite their age and infirmity, we had been compelled to use on the ocean routes. Presently, in Berlin, on January 30, 1941, Hitler made a speech threatening us with ruin and pointing with confidence to that combination of air and sea power lapping us about on all sides by which he hoped to bring about our starvation and surrender. "In the spring," he said, "our U-boat war will begin at sea, and they will notice that we have not been sleeping [shouts and cheers]. And the air force will play its part, and the entire armed forces will force a decision by hook or by crook."

* * *

Prime Minister to Import Executive   25 Feb. 41

I learn that the Admiralty salvage organisation has recently made as great a contribution to the maintenance of our shipping capac-
[2] Volume II, Book II, Chapter 30, page 510.

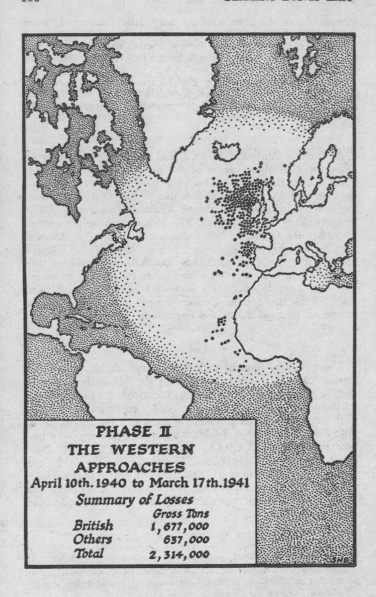

PHASE II
THE WESTERN
APPROACHES
April 10th. 1940 to March 17th. 1941
Summary of Losses
                    Gross Tons
British   1,677,000
Others   637,000
Total   2,314,000

ity as new construction, about 370,000 gross tons having been salved in the last five months of 1940, as against 340,000 tons built, while the number of ships being dealt with by the salvage organisation has increased very rapidly, from ten in August to about thirty now.

They are to be congratulated on this, and I feel sure that if anything can be done to assist in the expansion of their equipment and finding of suitable officers your Executive will see that such measures are taken.

Meanwhile we cannot take full advantage of these results owing to shortage of repairing capacity. I have no doubt that your Executive is planning an increase of this capacity, and meanwhile is making use of facilities overseas in the case of all vessels capable of doing one more voyage before repair.

*   *   *

Apart from the U-boat war upon us, we were at this time seriously affected by the sorties of powerful German cruisers. The attack on a convoy by the *Scheer* in November, 1940, when she sank the noble *Jervis Bay*, has already been recorded. In January she was in the South Atlantic, moving towards the Indian Ocean. In three months she destroyed ten ships, of sixty thousand tons in all, and then succeeded in making her way back to Germany, where she arrived on April 1, 1941. We had not been able to deploy against her the powerful forces which a year before had tracked down the *Graf Spee*. The cruiser *Hipper*, which had broken into the Atlantic at the beginning of December, 1940, was sheltering in Brest. At the end of January the battle-cruisers *Scharnhorst* and *Gneisenau*, having at length repaired the damage inflicted upon them in Norway, were ordered to make a sortie into the North Atlantic, while the *Hipper* raided the route from Sierra Leone. In their first attempt to break out, these battle-cruisers, under the command of Admiral Lutjens, narrowly escaped destruction by the Home Fleet. They were saved by persistent fogs, and on February 3 successfully passed through the Denmark Strait unobserved. At the same time the *Hipper* had left Brest for the southward.

On February 8 the two German battle-cruisers, astride the Halifax route, sighted an approaching British convoy. The German ships separated so as to attack from different angles. Suddenly, to their surprise, they perceived that the convoy was escorted by the battleship *Ramillies*. Admiral Lutjens at once broke off the engagement. In his basic instructions he had been ordered to avoid action with an equal opponent, which he was to interpret as meaning any one British fifteen-inch-gun battleship. His prudence was rewarded, and on February 22, he sank five ships, dispersed from an outward-bound convoy. Fearing our reactions, he then moved to an area farther south, and on March 8 he met a convoy from Freetown. But here again he found a battleship, the *Malaya*, in company, and he could do no more than call for U-boats to converge and attack. The U-boats sank five ships. Having shown himself in this area, he once more returned to the West Atlantic, where he now achieved his biggest success. On March 15 he intercepted six empty tankers, dispersed from an outward-bound convoy, and sank or captured them all. The next day he sank ten more ships, mostly from the same convoy. Thus in these two days alone he destroyed or captured over eighty thousand tons of shipping.

But the *Rodney*, escorting a Halifax convoy, was drawing near. Admiral Lutjens had run risks enough and had much to show. Early on March 22 he entered Brest. During their cruise of two months the *Scharnhorst* and *Gneisenau* had sunk or captured twenty-two ships, amounting to 115,000 tons. Meanwhile the *Hipper* had fallen upon a homeward-bound Sierra Leone convoy near the Azores which had not yet been joined by an escort. In a savage attack lasting an hour she destroyed seven out of nineteen ships, making no attempt to rescue survivors, and regained Brest two days later. These were heavy losses for us, additional to the toll of the U-boat war. Moreover, the presence of these strong hostile vessels compelled the employment on convoy duty of nearly every available British capital ship. At one period the Commander-in-Chief of the Home Fleet had only one battleship in hand.

The *Bismarck* was not yet on the active list. The German Admiralty should have waited for her completion and for that of her consort, the *Tirpitz*. In no way could Hitler have used his two giant battleships more effectively than by keeping them both in full readiness in the Baltic and allow rumours of an impending sortie to leak out from time to time. We should thus have been compelled to keep concentrated at Scapa Flow or thereabouts practically every new ship we had, and he would have had all the advantages of a selected moment without the strain of being always ready. As ships have to go for periodic refits, it would have been almost beyond our power to maintain a reasonable margin of superiority. Any serious accident would have destroyed that power.

*   *   *

My thought had rested day and night upon this awe-striking problem. At this time my sole and sure hope of victory depended upon our ability to wage a long and indefinite war until overwhelming air superiority was gained and probably other Great Powers were drawn in on our side. But this mortal danger to our life-lines gnawed my bowels. Early in March exceptionally heavy sinkings were reported by Admiral Pound to the War Cabinet. I had already seen the figures, and after our meeting, which was in the Prime Minister's room at the House of Commons, I said to Pound, "We have got to lift this business to the highest plane, over everything else. I am going to proclaim 'the Battle of the Atlantic.'" This, like featuring "the Battle of Britain" nine months earlier, was a signal intended to concentrate all minds and all departments concerned upon the U-boat war.

In order to follow this matter with the closest personal attention, and to give timely directions which would clear away difficulties and obstructions and force action upon the great number of departments and branches involved, I brought into being the Battle of the Atlantic Committee. The meetings of this committee were held weekly, and were attended by all Ministers and high functionaries concerned, both from the fighting services and from the civil side. They usually lasted not less than two and a half hours. The whole field was gone over and everything thrashed out; nothing was held up for want of decision. An illustration of the tempo of the Battle of the Atlantic in 1941 is afforded by the meetings of this committee. It met weekly without fail during the period March 19 to May 8. It then met fortnightly for a spell, and finally much less frequently. The last meeting was on October 22.

Throughout the wide circles of our war machine, embracing thousands of able, devoted men, a new proportion was set, and from a hundred angles the gaze of searching eyes was concentrated. March 6, as the preceding chapter may have shown, was an exacting day, when the decision about sending the Army to Greece hung in the balance. Nevertheless, before it ended my directive entitled "The Battle of the Atlantic" was achieved. I read this to the House in the Secret Session of June 25, 1941, but it is necessary to the story to reprint it here.

THE BATTLE OF THE ATLANTIC

Directive by the Minister of Defence, March 6, 1941

In view of various German statements, we must assume that the Battle of the Atlantic has begun.

The next four months should enable us to defeat the attempt to strangle our food supplies and our connection with the United States. For this purpose—

1. We must take the offensive against the U-boat and the Focke-Wulf wherever we can and whenever we can. The U-boat at sea must be hunted, the U-boat in the building yard or in dock must be bombed. The Focke-Wulf and other bombers employed against our shipping must be attacked in the air and in their nests.

2. Extreme priority will be given to fitting out ships to catapult or otherwise launch fighter aircraft against bombers attacking our shipping. Proposals should be made within a week.

3. All the measures approved and now in train for the concentration of the main strength of the Coastal Command upon the northwestern approaches, and their assistance on the East Coast by Fighter and Bomber Commands, will be pressed forward. It may be hoped that, with the growing daylight and the new routes to be followed, the U-boat menace will soon be reduced. All the more important is it that the Focke-Wulf, and, if it comes, the Junkers 88, should be effectively grappled with.

4. In view of the great need for larger numbers of escorting destroyers, it is for consideration whether the American destroyers now in service should go into dock for their second scale of improvements until the critical period of this new battle has been passed.

5. The Admiralty will re-examine, in conjunction with the Ministry of Shipping, the question of liberating from convoys ships between thirteen and twelve knots, and also whether this might not be tried experimentally for a while.

6. The Admiralty will have the first claim on all the short-range A.A. guns and other weapons that they can mount upon suitable merchant ships plying in the danger zone. Already two hundred Bofors or their equivalents have been ordered to be made available by Air Defence Great Britain and the factories. But these should be followed by a constant flow of guns, together with crews or nucleus crews, as and when they can be taken over by the Admiralty. A programme for three months should be made.

7. We must be ready to meet concentrated air attacks on the ports on which we specially rely (Mersey, Clyde, and Bristol Channel). They must, therefore, be provided with a maximum defence. A report of what is being done should be made in a week.

8. A concerted attack by all departments involved must be made upon the immense mass of damaged shipping now accumulated in our ports. By the end of June this mass must be reduced by not less than 400,000 tons net. For this purpose a short view may for the time being be taken both on merchant and naval shipbuilding. Labour should be transferred from new merchant shipbuilding which cannot finish before September, 1941, to repairs. The Admiralty have undertaken to provide from long-distance projects of warship building or warship repairs up to five thousand

men at the earliest moment, and another five thousand should be transferred from long-distance merchant shipbuilding.

9. Every form of simplification and acceleration of repairs and degaussing, even at some risk, must be applied in order to reduce the terrible slowness of the turn-round of ships in British ports. A saving of fifteen days in this process would in itself be equivalent to 5,000,000 tons of imports, or a tonnage [equal to] 1,250,000 of the importing fleet saved. The Admiralty have already instructed their officers in all ports to aid this process, in which is involved the process of repairs, to the utmost. Further injunctions should be given from time to time, and the port officers should be asked to report what they have done and whether they have any recommendations to make. It might be desirable to have a conference of port officers, where all difficulties could be exposed and ideas interchanged.

10. The Minister of Labour has achieved agreement in his conference with employers and employed about the interchangeability of labour at the ports. This should result in a substantially effective addition to the total labour force. In one way or another, at least another forty thousand men must be drawn into ship-repairing, shipbuilding, and dock labour at the earliest moment. Strong propaganda should be run locally at the ports and yards, in order that all engaged may realise the vital consequences of their work. At the same time, it is not desirable that the press or the broadcast should be used unduly, since this would only encourage the enemy to further exertions.

11. The Ministry of Transport will ensure that there is no congestion at the quays, and that all goods landed are immediately removed. For this purpose the Minister will ask the Chairman of the Import Executive for any further assistance required. He should also report weekly to the Import Executive upon the progress made in improving the ports on which we specially rely by transference of cranes, etc., from other ports. He should also report on the progress made in preparing new facilities at minor ports, and whether further use can be made of lighterage to have more rapid loading or unloading.

12. A Standing Committee has been set up of representatives from the Admiralty Transport Department, the Ministry of Shipping, and the Ministry of Transport, which will meet daily and report all hitches or difficulties encountered to the Chairman of the Import Executive. The Import Executive will concert the whole of these measures and report upon them to me every week, in order that I may seek Cabinet authority for any further steps.

13. In addition to what is being done at home, every effort must be made to ensure a rapid turn-round at ports abroad. All concerned should receive special instructions on this point, and should be asked to report on the measures which they are taking to implement these instructions, and on any difficulties that may be encountered.

* * *

On this same busy March 6 I also produced a memorandum on the strength of the Army in the light of all I had learnt about the import situation. This will be found among the Appendices.[3]

* * *

The U-boats now began to use new methods, which became known as "wolf-pack" tactics. These consisted of attacks from different directions by several U-boats working together. Attacks were at this time usually made by night, the U-boats operating on the surface at full speed unless detected in the approach. Under these conditions only the destroyers could rapidly overhaul them.

These tactics, which formed the keynote of the conflict for the next year or more, presented us with two problems. First, how to defend our convoys against this high-speed night attack, in which the Asdic was virtually impotent. The solution lay not only in the multiplication of fast escorts, but still more in the development of effective radar. Moreover, a prompt answer here was imperative or our losses would soon become unbearable. The small scale of the earlier onslaughts of the U-boats, against which we had been relatively successful, had created an undue sense of security. Now, when the full fury of the storm broke, we lacked the scientific equipment equal to our needs. We addressed ourselves vigorously to this problem, and by the unsparing efforts of the scientists, supported by the solid teamwork of sailors and airmen, good progress was made. The results came slowly, and meanwhile grave anxiety and heavy losses continued.

The second need was to exploit the vulnerability to air attack of the surfaced U-boat. Only when we could afford to court attack in the knowledge that we were masters would the long-drawn battle be won. For this we needed an air weapon which would kill, and also time to train both our sea and air forces in its use. When eventually both these problems were solved the U-boat was once more driven back to the submerged attack, in which it could be dealt with by the older and well-tried methods. This vital relief was not achieved for another two years.

Meanwhile the new "wolf-pack" tactics, inspired by Admiral Doenitz, the head of the U-boat service, and himself a U-boat captain of the previous war, were vigorously applied by the redoubtable Prien and the other tiptop U-boat commanders.

[3] See Appendix D, Book One.

Swift retribution followed. On March 8 Prien's U-47 was sunk with himself and all hands by the destroyer *Wolverine*, and nine days later U-99 and U-100 were sunk while engaged in a combined attack on a convoy. Both were commanded by outstanding officers, and the elimination of these three able men had a marked effect on the progress of the struggle. Few U-boat commanders who followed them were their equals in ruthless ability and daring. Five U-boats were sunk in March in the western approaches, and though we suffered grievous losses, amounting to 243,000 tons, by U-boat, and a further 113,000 tons by air attack, the first round in the Battle of the Atlantic may be said to have ended in a draw.

*   *   *

An all-important event now impended upon the other side of the Atlantic. I was in close touch with Hopkins in these days. After thanking him for the "packet of 250,000 rifles and ammunition, which has safely arrived," I cabled on February 28:

I am, however, increasingly anxious about the high rate of shipping losses in northwestern approaches and the shrinkage in tonnage entering Britain. This has darkened since I saw you. Let me know when the [Lend-Lease] Bill will be through. The strain is growing here.

Presently came good tidings from the United States. The Lend-Lease Bill had passed Congress, and on March 11 received the eager assent of the President. Hopkins sent me the earliest intimation. This was at once a comfort and a spur. The stuff was coming. It was for us to get it over.

Prime Minister to Mr. Hopkins   9 March 41
Thank God for your news. Strain is serious. Kindest regards.
To President Roosevelt from Former Naval Person   9 March 41
Our blessings from the whole British Empire go out to you and the American nation for this very present help in time of trouble.

In my broadcast of February 9 I had already said, "Give us the tools and we will finish the job." This could only be an interim pronouncement. Far more was needed, but we did our best.

*   *   *

We had now to make our budget of imports for the U-boat year 1941, exactly like a Chancellor of the Exchequer in finance. By the end of March all the studies and discussions of our ways and means were completed, and I could submit to the War Cabinet my final proposals for the size and character of the three branches of the fighting services, and also the quantity and character of the imports for which we should strive.

THE IMPORT PROGRAMMES

Memorandum by the Prime Minister, March 26, 1941

We should assume an import of not less than 31,000,000 tons in 1941. On this basis food cannot be cut lower than 15,000,000 tons, and 1,000,000 is required for the Board of Trade. This leaves 15,000,000 for the Ministry of Supply, as against 19,000,000 to which they were working on the 35,000,000 programme. A cut of 4,000,000 has therefore to be made by the Ministry of Supply, for which a revised programme should be framed. Ferrous metals, timber, and pulp seem to offer the main field of reduction. As we can now buy steel freely in the United States, the keeping in being of the whole of the existing steel industry cannot be accepted as an indispensable factor. We must try to import in the most concentrated forms and over the shortest routes. This principle must also influence food imports.

2. Should our total imports fall below 31,000,000, the deficit should for the present be met by the Ministry of Food and the Ministry of Supply on the basis of one ton cut in food to two tons in supply. Should the imports exceed 31,000,000, the benefit will be shared in the same proportion. The position will be reviewed in the autumn, when this year's harvest is known.

3. I have received from the War Office a reply to my notes about Army Scales, which they have had under consideration for three weeks.[4] My notes do not look farther ahead than 1942, and must be subject to review in the light of events. My figure of "about two millions" may be interpreted as desired by the War Office at "2,195,000 [men]," for which the arrangements are completed. The War Office proposal to substitute for my figure of fifteen armoured divisions twelve armoured divisions and nine army tank brigades may be approved, and the target figure for the grand total of the Imperial Army in March, 1942, of fifty-nine and one third "equivalent divisions" may be accepted. The resultant saving on man-power intake from now to the end of 1942 is about 475,000. This saving, and the increase in armoured forces at the expense of infantry and artillery, should afford an important relief to the Ministry of Supply in hutments, clothing, and projectiles.

4. The Purvis Programme, which was submitted to President Roosevelt in January to give him the general scale, may now be more precisely defined as the Ministry of Supply desire, and in so

[4] See Appendix F, Book One.

doing, if convenient, the adjustment may be made to cover the change in the proportion of armoured forces. However, it is important that no diminution should be made in anything we need and are likely to get from the United States; in particular, the equipment for the ten extra divisions should stand.

5. The Naval Programme is the subject of a separate note,[5] but the following principles which have a bearing on imports may be stated here.

The remaining three *King George V* class battleships must be completed at full speed. The construction of *Vanguard,* which is the only capital ship which can reach us in 1943 and before 1945, is most desirable. One new monitor is also needed. No other heavy ships can be proceeded with at present, and no more armour-plate can be provided for other naval purposes for the next six months; nor should new armour-plate factories be laid down. This position will be reviewed on September 1 in the light of (*a*) the Battle of the Atlantic, (*b*) the relationship of the United States to the war.

The requirements of the Admiralty for armour-plate must not exceed the 16,500 tons provided for 1941, nor the 25,000 tons for 1942. If these limits are observed, the Ministry of Supply should be able to execute the increased tank programme.

6. The Ministries of Food and Agriculture should, upon the basis of 15,000,000 tons import in 1941, concert an eighteen months' programme, drawing as may be necessary upon our meat reserves on the hoof to cover the next six months, but endeavouring to provide by concentrated imports the most varied dietary possible for the nation at war. By taking a period as long as eighteen months it should be possible to avoid hurried changes in policy, to use reserves as balancing factors, and to make the best use of the assigned tonnage.

7. The British air power will continue to be developed to the utmost within the above limits and with the present priorities and assignments.

When these precise instructions received the assent of the War Cabinet they were obeyed without demur by all concerned.

*   *   *

From the time of the passing of the Lend-Lease Bill our relations with the United States grew steadily closer. Under our pressures we adopted a stronger attitude towards Vichy France. The recent depredations of the German battle-cruisers had shown the mischief of these powerful ships, soon to be reinforced by the *Bismarck.* There was also the fear that the Germans might gain control over the French Fleet and bring the fast battleship *Dunkerque* into their service.

[5] See Appendix G, Book Two.

I cabled to President Roosevelt:

Former Naval Person to President Roosevelt   2 April 41

We have entirely trustworthy information that Vichy Government received "permission" from Armistice Commission to transfer the battleship *Dunkerque*, with escort protection of the whole *Strasbourg* group, from Oran to Toulon for "disarmament."

2. It seems certain that object of transfer is to effect repairs, and we must, of course, assume it is being done on German orders.

3. I do not need to point out to you the grave danger to which this exposes us. The menace from German surface raiders is already great enough. The addition of such a vessel to the raiding fleet would set us a hard problem indeed. If any value were to be attached to Admiral Darlan's word, it might be hoped that he would in the last resort order out of French metropolitan ports naval units ready for sea. But if *Dunkerque* is docked and immobilised for repairs, that gives the Germans time to swoop and gain possession of her.

4. I fear this is a sinister confirmation of our worst suspicions of Darlan.

5. You have already, through your Ambassador in Vichy, indicated to the French Government that negotiations for the supply of grain to unoccupied France would be greatly facilitated if French warships in metropolitan ports were gradually transferred to North African Atlantic ports. Here we have Darlan not merely failing to comply with your wishes, but deliberately flying in the face of them.

6. I earnestly hope that you may at once indicate to Marshal Pétain that if Darlan persists in this action he will be cutting off relief from his country and finally forfeiting American sympathy. We ourselves in this situation could, of course, lend no assistance to the revictualling of France. There may be just a chance that Marshal Pétain may deter him from this action, but if not the matter for us is so vital that we may, even in spite of all the dangerous implications, have to make an effort to intercept and sink this vessel. I should like to hear from you that you would understand the necessity for such a step.

7. It is, of course, of first importance that neither the French nor their masters should be made aware that we might take the drastic action mentioned in paragraph 6.

Urgent as was the matter, I would not take action till I knew what the President felt and wished.

Prime Minister to First Lord   3 April 41

No attack should be made upon the *Dunkerque* unless or until an answer is received from President Roosevelt which expresses no objection. Absence of any reference to the topic in his answer may be taken as consent.

2. On this reply being received, the First Lord should, if possible, consult the Lord Privy Seal in my absence, and decide.

3. Personally, my bias is strongly in favour of making the attack. Alas, we cannot be sure of success. Perhaps it is ten to one against a successful attack on a ship properly escorted by destroyers.

4. The reaction on Vichy would not, in my opinion, be serious. They would know they were found out doing a pro-Hun trick. So far as the French people are concerned, nothing would be easier than by repeated broadcasts to explain that this ship was being delivered over in a helpless condition into the German power, as in the event of a German descent she could not get away from the dock at Toulon like the mobile units of the French Fleet.

* * *

The next days we learned from the President that there would be at least a pause, because the *Dunkerque* would not be leaving Oran within the next ten days. On April 6 he told us that Mr. Matthews, the American Counsellor at Vichy, had asked Marshal Pétain for an urgent appointment. This was granted, but as soon as Matthews told Pétain that he wished to discuss the *Dunkerque* the Marshal, who was obviously not informed upon the situation, sent for Darlan. Darlan arrived and said that, of course, this information came from the English, and complained that they wanted theirs to be the only fleet in the Mediterranean. He admitted that he was bringing the battleship to Toulon because he could not have it repaired at Oran, and anyway he was not going to leave it there. The Marshal and he had pledged their word of honour that French ships would not fall into German hands, and he repeated this assurance. The *Dunkerque* would not be moved immediately, and would not be ready for ten days or more. The American Embassy at Vichy believed that this was true, and thought that even if the ship were brought to Toulon she could not be put into service before the end of August. Darlan had then made a series of anti-British statements, and the Marshal had promised Mr. Matthews a formal reply. The President said that Pétain apparently grasped the written word better than he trusted his memory, and might upon closer study give us the promise for which we asked.

I expressed my thanks and continuing concern.

Former Naval Person to President Roosevelt   6 April 41

Most grateful for your spirited intervention about *Dunkerque*. It is quite true that Toulon could not repair her for from three to six months, but why do we want that hanging over our head anyway? Darlan's honour about her never falling into German hands is rooted in dishonour. A ship in dry dock or under heavy repair could not possibly get away before the Germans could lay hold of Toulon. Their officers and agents are on the spot all the time, and remember how easy we found it to cop the French ships at Portsmouth and Plymouth. We ought to stick to our settled policy of resisting all transfers of French ships from African to German-controlled or potentially German-controlled French ports, and encourage all movement the other way. If Darlan gets *Dunkerque* to Toulon, why should he not ask for *Jean Bart* from Casablanca or *Richelieu* from Dakar? Therefore, I urge strong and stern continuance of utmost pressure you can exert. Evidently this is most powerful, as we have certain knowledge that they were to sail morning fourth and all preparations made. Pétain does not know half what this dirty Darlan does. It would be far better if your pressure deterred Darlan, as it has already, than that we should have to take rough action, with all its dangers.

2. Question is whether timely publicity might not help deter. Do you mind if I say something like this on Wednesday in Commons: "There was always the risk that Darlan might bring *Dunkerque* from Oran to Toulon in order to prepare her for war purposes. Such an act would affect the balances of naval power throughout the world, and would affect American interests besides our own. Representations have been made to Marshal Pétain by the United States Government which should have shown Vichy Government how undesirable this step would be from the point of view of French interests. His Majesty's Government would certainly be bound to regard it as a menacing act done at Hitler's instigation and as a step in Admiral Darlan's schemes for gaining personal control of France as the Germans' trusted agent. In these circumstances His Majesty's Government would hold themselves free to take any action which was suitable against this ship, either in passage or while under repair in Toulon Harbour. They would greatly regret if such a situation arose, as they have no wish or policy towards France other than her liberation from the German yoke and the maintenance of the integrity of the French Empire." Please let me know what you think of this, or whether you can get the matter settled behind the scenes.

On April 9 I used these words to the House of Commons, and the *Dunkerque* incident was finally settled by the submission of the Vichy Government to President Roosevelt's pressure.

President Roosevelt to Former Naval Person   11 April 41

I have received the following [note] from Vichy, dated April 8:
"By memorandum handed to Marshal Pétain on April 4, the American Chargé d'Affaires called attention to a report according to which the French Government, 'authorised by the Wiesbaden Armistice Commission,' was preparing to transfer the *Dunkerque*

from Oran to Toulon, at the very moment when the Government of the United States was expressing its interest in an opposite movement of naval forces. 'Should such a transfer take place,' adds the memorandum, 'the Government of the United States could no longer envisage the continuation of the policy which it desired to pursue for the supplying, as far as possible, of its indispensable aid to unoccupied France, to say nothing of the other acts of co-operation envisaged.'

"The Marshal's Government loyally admits without any embarrassment that it had in fact intended to have the *Dunkerque* made ready for transfer to Toulon in the near future. But this measure had been envisaged with full sovereignty, without any foreign pressure whatsoever, and solely for technical reasons.

"The Government of the United States is fully aware that the *Dunkerque* was severely damaged in the month of July, 1940, as the result of an odious assault in which numerous Frenchmen were killed.

"The ship is today in condition to move; but its final repairs require a stay in dry dock, which can only be made in Toulon, the only arsenal of either North Africa or the unoccupied zone able to accommodate it. This is the sole reason why the transfer of the *Dunkerque* was envisaged and remains necessary. Nevertheless, in view of the political significance which the Government of the United States seems disposed to attach to this transfer, the French Government agrees to delay the preparation of the ship until the conclusion of an agreement on this subject. It desires thus to show the Federal Government its will to pursue loyally, for its part, as far as its means will permit, the policy undertaken with a view to assuring the supplying of French Africa and the unoccupied zone.

"But by postponing putting into final shape one of its most precious war vessels the French Government is making a heavy sacrifice of self-respect and interest which affects its possibilities of defending its Empire as well as its means of protecting French maritime traffic.

"The French Government thus expects the American Government to use its good offices in London in order to obtain from the British Government the guarantee that as long as the *Dunkerque* remains in North Africa no further capture will be exercised against our legitimate commercial traffic between the French colonies, French Africa, and the unoccupied zone. It is evident in fact that a country as threatened with famine as France is cannot be asked to renounce the utilisation of all its means of defence if the commercial maritime traffic for the protection of which guarantees have been offered continues to be pursued and attacked."

Of course no such guarantee was given by us, and the powerful intervention of President Roosevelt at this time enabled our relations with Vichy France to become somewhat less hostile.

8

The Battle of the Atlantic: 1941

The American Intervention

IMPORTANT CHANGES now took place in the U-boat war. The
elimination of the three German "aces" in March and the
improvement in our defense measures had their effect on
U-boat tactics. Finding the western approaches too hot, they
moved farther west into waters where, since the Southern Irish
ports were denied us, only a few of our flotilla escorts could
reach them and where air protection was impossible. From

our bases in the United Kingdom our escorts could only provide effective protection to our convoys over about a quarter of the route to Halifax. Early in April a wolf-pack struck a convoy in longitude 28° West before the escort had joined it. In a protracted action ten ships were sunk out of a total of twenty-two, one U-boat also being destroyed. Somehow we had to contrive to extend our reach or our days would be numbered.

Hitherto help from across the ocean had been confined to supplies; but now in this growing tension the President, acting with all the powers accorded to him as Commander-in-Chief of the armed forces and enshrined in the American Constitution, began to give us armed aid. He resolved not to allow the German U-boat and raider war to come near the American coast, and to make sure that the munitions he was sending Britain at least got nearly halfway across. As early as July, 1940, he had sent a naval and military mission to England for "exploratory conversations." Admiral Ghormley, the United States Naval Observer, was soon satisfied that Britain was inflexibly resolved, and could hold out against any immediate threat. His task, in collaboration with the Admiralty, was to determine how the power of the United States could best be brought to bear, first under the existing policy of "all aid short of war," and secondly in conjunction with the British armed forces if and when the United States should be drawn into war.

From these early beginnings sprang the broad design for the joint defence of the Atlantic Ocean by the two English-speaking Powers. In January, 1941, secret Staff discussions began in Washington covering the whole scene, and framing a combined world strategy. The United States war chiefs agreed that should the war spread to America and to the Pacific the Atlantic and European theatre should be regarded as decisive. Hitler must be defeated first, and on this conception American aid in the Battle of the Atlantic was planned. Preparations were started to meet the needs of joint ocean convoy in the Atlantic. In March, 1941, American officers visited Great Britain to select bases for their naval escorts and air forces. Work on these was at once begun. Meanwhile the development of American bases in British territory in the West Atlantic, which had begun in 1940, was proceeding rapidly. The most important for the North Atlantic convoys was Argentia, in Newfoundland. With this and with harbours in the United Kingdom American forces could play their fullest permissible part in the battle, or so it seemed when these measures were planned.

Between Canada and Great Britain are the islands of Newfoundland, Greenland, and Iceland. All these lie near the flank of the shortest, or great-circle, track between Halifax and Scotland. Forces based on these "stepping-stones" could control the whole route by sectors. Greenland was entirely devoid of resources, but the other two islands could be quickly turned to good account. It has been said, "Whoever possesses Iceland holds a pistol firmly pointed at England, America, and Canada." It was upon this thought that, with the concurrence of its people, we had occupied Iceland when Denmark was overrun in 1940. Now we could use it against the U-boats, and in April, 1941, we established bases there for the use of our escort groups and aircraft. Iceland became a separate command, and thence we extended the range of the surface escorts to 35° West. Even so there remained an ominous gap to the westward which for the time being could not be bridged. In May a Halifax convoy was heavily attacked in 41° West and lost nine ships before our anti-U-boat escort could join it.

Meanwhile the strength of the Royal Canadian Navy was increasing, and their new corvettes were beginning to emerge in good numbers from the building yards. At this crucial moment Canada was ready to play a conspicuous part in the deadly struggle. The losses in the Halifax convoy made it quite clear that nothing less than end-to-end escort from Canada to Britain would suffice, and on May 23 the Admiralty invited the Governments of Canada and Newfoundland to use St. John's, Newfoundland, as an advanced base for our joint escort forces. The response was immediate, and by the end of the month continuous escort over the whole route was at last a reality. Thereafter the Royal Canadian Navy accepted responsibility for the protection, out of its own resources, of convoys on the western section of the ocean route. From Great Britain and from Iceland we were able to give protection over the remainder of the passage. Even so the strength available remained perilously small for the task to be performed. Meanwhile our losses had been mounting steeply. In the three months ending with May U-boats alone sank 142 ships, of 818,000 tons. Of these, 99 ships, of about 600,000 tons, were British. To achieve these results the Germans maintained continuously about a dozen U-boats in the North Atlantic, and in addition endeavoured to spread-eagle our defence by determined attacks in the Freetown area, where six U-boats in May alone sank thirty-two ships.

* * *

In the United States the President was moving step by step ever more closely with us, and his powerful intervention soon became decisive. As we had found it necessary to develop bases in Iceland, so he in the same month took steps to establish an air base for his own use in Greenland. It was known that the Germans had already installed weather-reporting stations on the Greenland east coast and opposite Iceland. The President's action was therefore timely. Furthermore, by other decisions not only our merchant ships but our warships, damaged in the heavy fighting in the Mediterranean and elsewhere, could be repaired in American shipyards, thus giving instant and much-needed relief to our heavily strained resources at home. The President confirmed this in a telegram of April 4, which also stated that he had allotted funds to build another fifty-eight launching yards and two hundred more ships.

Former Naval Person to President Roosevelt   4 April 41

I am most grateful for your message just received through the Ambassador about the shipping.

2. During the last few weeks we have been able to strengthen our escorts in home northwestern approaches, and in consequence have hit the U-boats hard. They have now moved farther west, and this morning (April 3) sank four ships on the twenty-ninth meridian one day before our escort could meet them. Beating the U-boat is simply a question of destroyers and escorts, but we are so strained that to fill one gap is to open another. If we could get your ten cutters taken over and manned we would base them on Iceland, where their good radius would give protection to convoys right up to where they meet our British-based escorts. Another important factor in northwestern approaches is long-distance aircraft. These are now coming in. Meanwhile, though our losses are increasingly serious, I hope we shall lessen the air menace when in a month or six weeks' time we have a good number of Hurricane fighters flying off merchant ships patrolling or escorting in the danger zone.

Great news arrived a week later. The President cabled me on April 11 that the United States Government proposed to extend their so-called security zone and patrol areas, which had been in effect since very early in the war, to a line covering all North Atlantic waters west of about West Longitude 26°. For this purpose the President proposed to use aircraft

**PHASE III
THE OCEAN**
Up to the Entry of the United States
into the War March 18 th. 1941
to Dec. 6 th. 1941
Summary of Losses

	Gross Tons
British	1,134,000
Others	430,000
Total	1,564,000

SHB.

and naval vessels working from Greenland, Newfoundland, Nova Scotia, the United States, Bermuda, and the West Indies, with possibly a later extension to Brazil. He invited us to notify him in great secrecy of the movement of our convoys, "so that our patrol units can seek out any ships or planes of aggressor nations operating west of the new line of the security zones." The Americans for their part would immediately publish the position of possible aggressor ships or planes when located in the American patrol area. "It is not certain," the President ended, "that I would make a specific announcement. I may decide to issue the necessary naval operative orders and let time bring out the existence of the new patrol area."

I transmitted this telegram to the Admiralty with a deep sense of relief.

Former Naval Person to President Roosevelt   16 April 41

I had intended to cable you more fully on your momentous message about the Atlantic. Admiralty received the news with the greatest relief and satisfaction, and have prepared a technical paper. They wonder whether, since Admiral Ghormley arrives here in about two days, it would be better to discuss this with him before dispatch. I do not know whether he is apprised or not. The matter is certainly of highest urgency and consequence. There are about fifteen U-boats now operating on the thirtieth meridian, and of course United States flying-boats working from Greenland would be a most useful immediate measure.

Two days later, on April 18, the United States Government announced the line of demarcation between the Eastern and Western Hemispheres to which the President had referred in his message of April 11. This line, drawn along the meridian of 26° West, became thereafter the virtual sea frontier of the United States. It included within the United States' sphere all British territory in or near the American continent, Greenland, and the Azores, and was soon afterward extended eastward to include Iceland. Under this declaration United States warships would patrol the waters of the Western Hemisphere, and would incidentally keep us informed of any enemy activities therein. The United States, however, remained nonbelligerent and could not at this stage provide direct protection for our convoys. This remained solely a British responsibility over the whole route.

Both the British and American naval chiefs were at this time anxious about the Azores. We strongly suspected that the enemy were planning to seize them as a base for U-boats and aircraft. These islands, lying near the centre of the North

Atlantic, would in enemy hands have proved as great a menace to our shipping movements in the south as Iceland in the north. The British Government for its part could not tolerate such a situation arising, and in response to urgent calls from the Portuguese Government, who were fully alive to the danger to their own country, we planned and prepared an expedition to forestall such a German move. We had also made plans to occupy Grand Canary and the Cape Verde Islands, should Hitler move into Spain. The urgency of these expeditions vanished once it became clear that Hitler had shifted his eyes towards Russia.

Former Naval Person to President Roosevelt   24 April 41

I now reply in detail to your message of April 11. The delay has been caused by waiting for Admiral Ghormley, whose arrival was uncertain. The First Sea Lord has had long discussions with Ghormley, as the result of which I am advised as follows:

2. In the Battle of the Atlantic we have two main problems to deal with in addition to the menace from aircraft round our coast. These problems are those of the U-boats and the raiders.

3. As regards the U-boats, we have had considerable success in dealing with these pests when they were working somewhere in the longitude of 22° West in the northwestern approaches. Whether it was because of our success or for some other reason, they are now working in about 30° West.

4. We have, however, been able gradually to strengthen our escorting forces, thanks to the United States destroyers which were sent us, and by the use of Iceland as a refuelling base for the escorts.

5. It may be expected that the enemy's reaction to this will be to send his U-boats still farther west, and as most of them are based on either L'Orient or Bordeaux they can do this without operating farther from their bases than they are at the present time.

6. It is quite likely therefore that the area to the westward of 35° West and to the southward of Greenland will be the next danger area, and it is one which it is difficult for us to deal with. Aerial reconnaissance which could be carried out from Greenland to cover this area would therefore be of the greatest value, as if a U-boat were located we should be able to reroute our convoys by signal so as to pass clear of the danger.

7. Another area in which we are having considerable trouble is that from Freetown up through the Cape Verdes to the Azores. We cannot route our convoys very far to the west owing to the [limited] endurance of the vessels on this run. In fact, it is only by reducing their cargo and taking in extra fuel that they can make the passage. We are providing such escort for these convoys as we are able, but it is quite inadequate, and it would be of the greatest help if air reconnaissance by one of the United States carriers

would cover the water some distance in advance of the convoys.

8. There will be no difficulty in giving the American naval authorities notification of the movements of convoys.

9. As regards raiders, one great danger point is off Newfoundland, as we have a very large amount of shipping proceeding independently through this area. This was the area in which the *Scharnhorst* and *Gneisenau* made such a bag. Any additional long-range air reconnaissance which could be carried out from Newfoundland or Nova Scotia would be of the greatest assistance.

10. We hope to station a powerful capital ship in either Nova Scotia or Newfoundland, which would be able to take advantage of any information which we receive regarding the activities of raiders.

11. There are various areas on our trade routes in which the enemy is liable to operate and which are west of the longitude 26° West. There are also certain areas in the North and South Atlantic off the trade routes in which the enemy maintain their supply ships and where they go to refuel. Up to the present time we have been unable to search out these seas, as we have not had the ships to do it with. If we knew that reconnaissance was going to take place over any given area we would endeavour to have in the vicinity a force which would be capable of dealing with any raider which was located. Apart from any information which your ships were able to broadcast, the mere fact of air reconnaissance taking place over these areas would give the enemy a great feeling of uneasiness.

12. It is understood that arrangements have already been made for secret intercommunication between British and United States warships.

13. For yourself alone. There is another matter closely connected with the above which is causing me and the Naval Staff increasing anxiety. The capacity of Spain and Portugal to resist the increasing German pressure may at any time collapse, and the anchorage at Gibraltar be rendered unusable. To effect this the Germans would not need to move a large army through Spain, but merely to get hold of the batteries which may molest the anchorage, for which a few thousand artillerists and technicians might be sufficient. They have already done some of their usual preliminary penetration into Tangier, and thus both sides of the Straits might quickly pass into the hands of expert hostile gunners.

14. Of course, the moment Spain gives way or is attacked we shall dispatch two expeditions which we have long been holding in readiness, one from Britain to one of the islands in the Azores, and subsequently to a second island, and the second expedition to do the same in the Cape Verdes. But these operations will take eight days from the signal being given, and one can never tell that the Germans may not have forestalling plans on foot. With our other naval burdens we have not the forces to maintain a continuous watch. It would be a very great advantage if you could send an American squadron for a friendly cruise in these regions at the

earliest moment. This would probably warn Nazi raiders off, and would keep the place warm for us as well as giving us invaluable information.

15. I have had long talks with Mr. Forrestal, and am taking him and Harriman with me tomorrow night to study the position in the Mersey area, so important to the northwestern approaches.

*   *   *

Meanwhile, as a result of the Admiralty talks with Admiral Ghormley, a detailed plan for helping us in the Atlantic had been arranged with the United States.

Former Naval Person to President Roosevelt   24 April 41

Greatly cheered by the news about "Navy Western Hemisphere Defence Plan No. 2." It almost entirely covers the points made in my cable to you, which crossed the official communication. We are deeply impressed by the rapidity with which it is being brought into play. We have just received a report which indicates that a surface raider is operating in a position about three hundred miles southeast of Bermuda. Everything will be done to tell the Commander-in-Chief of the United States Fleet about our convoys and other matters. Admiral Ghormley is in closest touch with the Admiralty, and the necessary Staff arrangements will be perfected.

2. The route taken by British shipping to and from the Cape is dependent on the areas in which U-boats are suspected, but a route west of 26° West is being used at the present time, and will be used whenever possible.

3. We welcome the energetic steps the United States Navy are taking to prepare the bases in the northwestern approaches. . . . The action you have taken may well decide the Battle of the Atlantic in a favourable sense.

We are, of course, observing the strictest secrecy. You will, I am sure, however, realise that if it were possible for you to make any kind of disclosure or declaration on these lines, it might powerfully influence the attitude both of Turkey and Spain at a cardinal moment.

The effects of the President's policy were far-reaching, and we continued our struggle with important parts of our load taken off our backs by the Royal Canadian and the United States Navies. The United States was moving ever nearer to war, and this world-tide was still further speeded by the irruption of the *Bismarck* into the Atlantic towards the end of May. This episode will be described in due course. In a broadcast on May 27, the very day that the *Bismarck* was sunk, the President declared, "The war is approaching the brink of the Western Hemisphere itself. . . . The Battle of the Atlantic now extends from the icy waters of the North Pole to the frozen continent of the Antarctic." He went on, "It would be

suicide to wait until they [the enemy] are in our front yard.
. . . We have accordingly extended our patrols in North and
South Atlantic waters." At the conclusion of this speech the
President declared an "Unlimited National Emergency."

*   *   *

There is ample evidence to show that the Germans were
greatly disturbed at this extension of American activity, and
Admirals Raeder and Doenitz besought the Fuehrer to grant
greater latitude to the U-boats and permit them to operate
towards the American coast as well as against American ships
if convoyed or if proceeding without lights. Hitler, however,
remained adamant. He always dreaded the consequences of
war with the United States, and insisted that German forces
should avoid provocative action against her.

*   *   *

The expansion of the enemy's efforts also brought its own
correctives. By June he had, apart from those training, about
thirty-five U-boats at sea, but the manning of the numbers of
new craft now coming forward outstripped his resources in
highly trained crews, and above all in experienced captains.
The "diluted" crews of the new U-boats, largely composed of
young and unpractised men, showed a decline in pertinacity
and skill. Furthermore, the extension of the battle into the
remoter expanses of the ocean disrupted the dangerous combination of the U-boats and the air. German aircraft in large
numbers had not been equipped or trained for operations over
the sea. None the less, in the same three months of March,
April, and May 179 ships, of 545,000 tons, were sunk by air
attack, mainly in the coastal regions. Of this total 40,000 tons
were destroyed, as has been described in an earlier chapter, in
two fierce attacks on the Liverpool docks early in May. I was
thankful the Germans did not persevere on this tormented
target. All the while the stealthy, insidious menace of the
magnetic mine had continued around our coasts, with varying
success; but our counter-measures remained dominant, and by
1941 sinkings by mines were greatly diminishing.

By June the steady growth of our defence measures both in
home waters and in the Atlantic, aided by Canada and
America, began once more to gain the upper hand. The utmost exertions were being made both to improve the organisation of our convoy escorts and to develop new weapons and
devices to aid them in their task. The chief needs were for

more and faster escorts with greater fuel endurance, for more
long-range aircraft, and above all for good radar. Shore-based
aircraft alone were not enough, and every convoy needed
ship-borne airplanes to detect any U-boat within striking
distance in daylight, and by forcing it to dive prevent it making contact, or making a report which would draw others to
the scene. Even so, the value of the air arm at this stage was
still chiefly for reconnaissance. Aircraft could observe U-boats
and force them down, but the power to kill was not yet developed, and at night their value was greatly limited. The
lethal power of the air in U-boat warfare was yet to come.

Against the Focke-Wulf assailant, however, the air weapon
could be quickly turned to good account. By the use of fighter
aircraft discharged from catapults mounted in ordinary merchant ships, as well as in converted ships manned by the
Royal Navy, we soon met this thrust. The fighter pilot, having
been tossed like a falcon against his prey, had at first to rely
for his life on being retrieved from the sea by one of the
escorts.

The Focke-Wulf, being challenged itself in the air, was no
longer able to give the same assistance to the U-boats, and
gradually became the hunted rather than the hunter.

                    *   *   *

Our losses from enemy action during the fateful months
show the stresses of this life-and-death struggle:

	Gross Tons		Gross Tons
January	320,000	April	654,000
February	402,000	May	500,000
March	537,000	June	431,000

The April figures, of course, include the exceptional losses
in the fighting around Greece.

                    *   *   *

I watched the process with constant attention.

Prime Minister to Minister of Information   14 April 41

The publication of the weekly sinkings is to be discontinued
henceforward—that is, no more, no publication next Tuesday.
When the press ask why have the week's figures not come out, the
answer will be they are to be published monthly instead of weekly.
When the comment is made that we are afraid to publish weekly
because, as you say, we "desire to cover up the size of our most
recent shipping losses," the answer should be, "Well, that is what
we are going to do anyway." Friends and enemies will no doubt

put on their own interpretation. But only the facts will decide. We shall have a lot of worse things than that to put up with in the near future.

I will answer any questions on the subject myself in the House.

Prime Minister to Sir Edward Bridges, General Ismay, 28 April 41 *and other members of Atlantic Committee concerned*

It is not intended to use the catapult ships as ordinary freighters, nor can a number like two hundred, which has been mentioned, be at any time contemplated.

2. There are at present five catapult patrol vessels working like the *Pegasus*. These should be joined at the earliest moment by the first ten catapult-fitted merchant ships, and from these fifteen vessels there must be found a regular patrol covering or accompanying the convoys in the Focke-Wulf zone.

3. As some of these vessels are probably heavier, faster, and more valuable merchant vessels than are required for this patrolling service, they are to be replaced at earliest by other smaller vessels which the Ministry of Shipping can better spare. The large ones already fitted, having been relieved, may ply on the Freetown-Britain route, as they will have the opportunity of going through two danger zones in each voyage, and the catapult Hurricanes will thus have adequate opportunities of fighting.

4. If the fifteen ships devoted to the northwestern approaches patrol are proved to be a success and it is thought necessary to increase their numbers, a proposal should be put forward. At the same time the Beaufighter aircraft now employed on patrol duties should be returned to Fighter Command, where they are most urgently needed for night fighting.

* * *

We developed and expanded our bases in Canada and Iceland with all possible speed, and planned our convoys accordingly. We increased the fuel capacity of our older destroyers and their consequent radius. The newly formed Combined Headquarters at Liverpool threw itself heart and soul into the struggle. As more escorts came into service and the personnel gained experience, Admiral Noble formed them into permanent groups under group commanders. Thus the essential team spirit was fostered and men became accustomed to working in unison with a clear understanding of their commander's methods. These escort groups became ever more efficient, and as their power grew that of the U-boats declined.

* * *

Meanwhile in June President Roosevelt made an important move. He decided to establish a base in Iceland. It was agreed that United States forces should relieve the British garrison.

They reached Iceland on July 7, and this island was included in the defence system of the Western Hemisphere. Thereafter American convoys escorted by American warships ran regularly to Reykjavik, and although the United States were still not at war they admitted foreign ships to the protection of their convoys.

Throughout these critical months the two German battle-cruisers remained poised in Brest. At any moment it seemed that they might again break out, to cause further havoc in the Atlantic. It was due to the Royal Air Force that they continued inactive. Repeated air attacks were made on them in port, with such good effect that they remained idle through the year. The enemy's concern soon became to get them home; but even this they were unable to do until 1942. Hitler's plan for the invasion of Russia soon brought us much-needed respite in the air. For this new enterprise the German Air Force had to be re-deployed in strength; and thus from May onward the scale of air attack against our shipping fell.

* * *

It is worth while at this point to anticipate some of the results which were gained in the Battle of the Atlantic by the intensive study which we made of all the knowable factors at work. It was a great advantage that the whole process of our many decisions could be passed continuously through a single mind, and that, as Prime Minister, I received in so full a measure from my colleagues the authority necessary to give a unified direction throughout this vast administrative sphere. The war machine over which I presided as Minister of Defence was capable of enforcing all decisions with precision.

At the end of June I reported, on the authority of the Admiralty, to the House of Commons a decisive decline in British losses by aircraft attack in the North Atlantic:

February	86,000 tons
March	69,000
April	59,000
May	21,000
June (to date)	18,000 [1]

[1] The total losses in the undermentioned five months in 1941 from air attack, including Allied and neutral shipping, and the losses in Greece, are now known to be as follows:

Month	British	Allied	Neutral	Total
February	51,865	34,243	3,197	89,305
March	70,266	36,780	5,731	112,777
April	122,503	164,006	9,909	296,418
May	115,131	21,004	125	136,260
June	39,301	18,449	3,664	61,414
Totals	399,066	274,482	22,626	696,174

In my directive of March 6 I had aimed at reducing the 1,700,000 tons of shipping immobilised by the need for repairs by 400,000 tons by July 1. Later on we became more ambitious and set ourselves as a target a reduction of 750,000 tons by the same date. Actually we achieved a reduction of 700,000 tons. This was accomplished in the teeth of the air attacks made on the Mersey and the Clyde at the beginning of May. The welcome addition of a large number of ships, hitherto given up as hopeless, which were rescued by our splendid Salvage Service and added to the repair list, was another gain. A substantial saving in the turn-round of ships was also effected by various processes, and every day's saving in the turn-round was worth a quarter of a million tons in effective imports during a year.

There were many complications in all this. We could not always arrange to discharge a ship at the most convenient port. One carrying a mixed cargo might have to visit several ports during the process of discharge, with added risk of destruction by air or mine during coastal passages; and all the time the ports themselves, particularly those on the East Coast, were subject to attack which might temporarily paralyse them. London, by far our main port, was largely immobilised owing to the risk of sending large vessels round to the East Coast in the face of attacks by air, by E-boats, and by mines. Thus the East Coast ports could not take their full share of the load, and the greater burden fell upon the ports in the west—Liverpool, the Clyde, and the Bristol Channel. None the less, by intense efforts London, the Humber, and the more northerly ports on the East Coast remained open to coastal and a certain amount of ocean-going traffic throughout these harassing times.

* * *

At the height of this struggle I made one of the most important and fortunate appointments of my war administration. In 1930, when I was out of office, I accepted for the first and only time in my life a directorship. It was in one of the subsidiary companies of Lord Inchcape's far-spreading organisation of the Peninsular and Oriental shipping lines. For eight years I regularly attended the monthly board meetings and discharged my duties with care. At these meetings I gradually became aware of a very remarkable man. He presided over thirty or forty companies, of which the one with which I was connected was a small unit. I soon perceived that Frederick

Leathers was the central brain and controlling power of this combination. He knew everything and commanded absolute confidence. Year after year I watched him from my small position at close quarters. I said to myself, "If ever there is another war, here is a man who will play the same kind of part as the great business leaders who served under me at the Ministry of Munitions in 1917 and 1918."

Leathers volunteered his services to the Ministry of Shipping on the outbreak in 1939. We did not come much into contact while I was at the Admiralty, because his functions were specialised and subordinate. But now in 1941, in the stresses of the Battle of the Atlantic, and with the need for combining the management of our shipping with all the movements of our supplies by rail and road from our harried ports, he came more and more into my mind. On May 8 I turned to him. After much discussion I remodelled the Ministries of Shipping and Transport into one integral machine. I placed Leathers at its head. To give him the necessary authority I created the office of Minister of War Transport. I was always shy of bringing people into high Ministerial positions in the House of Commons if they had not been brought up there for a good many years. Experienced Members out of office may badger the newcomer, and he will always be unduly worried by the speeches he has to prepare and deliver. I therefore made a submission to the Crown that a peerage should be conferred upon the new Minister.

Henceforward to the end of the war Lord Leathers remained in complete control of the Ministry of War Transport, and his reputation grew with every one of the four years that passed. He won the confidence of the Chiefs of Staff and of all departments at home, and established intimate and excellent relations with the leading Americans in this vital sphere. With none was he more closely in harmony than with Mr. Lewis Douglas, of the United States Shipping Board, and later Ambassador in London. Leathers was an immense help to me in the conduct of the war. It was very rarely that he was unable to accomplish the hard tasks I set. Several times when all staff and departmental processes had failed to solve the problems of moving an extra division or transshipping it from British to American ships, or of meeting some other need, I made a personal appeal to him, and the difficulties seemed to disappear as if by magic.

*   *   *

I was able to tell the House in secret session on June 25 some encouraging facts about the clearance of goods from our ports.

I have never allowed the excuse to be pleaded of congestion at our ports, because, in spite of all our difficulties, we are in fact only handling and budgeting to handle about half the prewar traffic. Nonetheless, a great effort is being made. Inland sorting depots which enable the goods to be got away quickly from the air-raided quaysides into the country are recommended by the Select Committee. Six of these are in process of construction to serve our West Coast ports. The first will come into partial operation in September. To get the best out of the South Wales ports we are quadrupling the railway line from Newport to the Severn Tunnel; part of the quadrupled line is already in operation. Some of the transport bottlenecks are found at inland junctions on the western side of the Island, because a greater strain is being cast upon them than they were constructed to bear. These are being opened up. A considerable development of overside discharge at suitable anchorages has been organised, not only as a relief but as an alternative in case of very heavy attack.

A large expansion in our crane facilities is on foot, both to equip new emergency ports and to make existing port facilities more flexible under attack. In May alone a hundred and fifty mobile cranes were delivered from British factories and from the United States, as compared with the previous average of fifty in the last four months.

On all this I felt able to ask the House to approve stopping, as already ordered, the weekly publication of our tonnage losses, which had been of so much assistance to the enemy, but to which the press and Parliament attached fictitious importance. As has been mentioned, I had already given directions to this effect in April. "I have no doubt," I now said, "there will be a howl, not only from the Germans, but from some well-meaning patriots of this Island. Let them howl. We have got to think of our sailors and merchant seamen, the lives of our countrymen and of the life of our country, now quivering in the balance of mortal peril."

The House seemed greatly reassured by all this account, and gave me a full measure of support.

If we can resist [I said] or deter actual invasion this autumn, we ought to be able, on the present undertaking of the United States, to come through the year 1941. In 1942 we hope to be possessed of very definite air ascendancy, and to be able not only to carry our offensive bombing very heavily into Germany, but to redress to some extent the frightful strategic disadvantages we suffer from the present German control of the Atlantic seaports of Europe. If we can deny to the enemy or at least markedly neutralise the enemy-held Atlantic ports and airfields, there is no reason why the year 1942, in which the enormous American new building comes to hand, should not present us with less anxious ordeals than those we must now endure and come through.

I ended thus:

I will add only one other word. Let us not forget that the enemy has difficulties of his own; that some of these difficulties are obvious; that there may be others which are more apparent to him than to us; and that all the great struggles of history have been won by superior will-power wresting victory in the teeth of odds or upon the narrowest of margins.

9

Yugoslavia

*Peril of Yugoslavia—The German Net Closes—Colonel Donovan's
Mission to Belgrade, January, 1941—Pressure on the Regent—
Hitler's offer of February 14—Bulgaria Adheres to the Tripartite
Pact—Prince Paul at Berchtesgaden, March 5—Yugoslavian
Opposition Attempts to Rally the Yugoslavs—Secret Pact with
Germany, March 25—My Telegram of March 26—A Bloodless
Revolution in Belgrade, March 27—Prince Paul Forced to Resign
—Popular Enthusiasm—Hitler's Rage—His Decision to Crush
Yugoslavia—Orders the Destruction of Belgrade—His Telegram
to Mussolini—Dislocation of the German Plans—No Balkan Bloc
—Hitler's Threat to Hungary—Treachery of the Chief of the
Hungarian General Staff—Mr. Eden's Warning—Suicide of Count
Teleki, April 2—My Hopes for Yugoslavia—And for Turkey—
My Message to Mr. Eden, March 28—New Significance of Our
Aid to Greece—My Telegram to Australia, March 30—The
Yugoslav Opportunity in Albania—Dill's Mission to Belgrade—
Confusion and Paralysis—Dill's Report of April 4—My Appeal
and Warning—The Soviet Gesture—Operation "Punishment,"
April 6–8—The Uncomprehending Bear.*

T HE MURDER of King Alexander of Yugoslavia in October,
1934, at Marseilles, which has already been mentioned,
opened a period of disintegration for the Yugoslav State, and
thereafter its independent position in Europe declined. The
political hostility of Fascist Italy and the economic advance of
Hitlerite Germany into Southeast Europe had speeded this
process. The decay of internal stability, the antagonism between Serb and Croat, sapped the strength of this Southern
Slav State. Under the regency of Prince Paul, an amiable,
artistic personage, the prestige of the monarchy waned. Doctor Machek, the leader of the Peasant Party of Croatia, pur-

sued obstinately a policy of non-co-operation with the Government of Belgrade. Extremist Croats, protected by Italy and Hungary, worked from bases abroad for the detachment of Croatia from Yugoslavia. The Belgrade Government turned away from co-operation with the Little Entente of Balkan Powers to follow a "realist" line of understanding with the Axis. The champion of this policy was M. Stoyadinovic, who signed the Italo-Yugoslav Pact of March 25, 1937. This attitude seemed to be justified by what happened at Munich the year after. Weakened internally by an alliance between the Croat Peasant Party and the Serb opposition, who were suspicious of the closer relations with Italy and Germany, Stoyadinovic was defeated in the elections, and in February, 1939, was forced to retire.

The new Prime Minister, Cvetkovic, and his Minister for Foreign Affairs, Markovic, sought to appease the swelling Axis power. In August, 1939, agreement with the Croats was reached and Machek entered the Belgrade Government. In the same month came the news of the Soviet-German Pact. In spite of ideological differences, the Serbs had always felt drawn by Slav instincts towards Russia. The Soviet attitude at the time of Munich had encouraged them to hope that the unity of Eastern Europe might still be maintained. Now the signing of the fateful pact seemed to deliver the Balkans at a stroke into Axis hands. The fall of France in June, 1940, deprived the Southern Slavs of their traditional friend and protector. The Russians revealed their intentions about Rumania and occupied Bessarabia and Bukovina. At Vienna in August, 1940, Transylvania was awarded to Hungary by Germany and Italy. The net around Yugoslavia was closing. In November, 1940, Markovic first trod in secrecy the road to Berchtesgaden. He escaped without formally committing his country to the Axis side, but on December 12 a pact of amity was signed with the minor Axis partner, Hungary.

*   *   *

As these impressions grew they caused us concern. In this atmosphere Prince Paul carried the policy of neutrality to its limits. He feared particularly that any move by Yugoslavia or her neighbours might provoke the Germans into a southward advance into the Balkans.

Prime Minister to Foreign Secretary   14 Jan. 41
The Cabinet today should consider these telegrams from Belgrade about Prince Paul's views. They leave me unchanged. It is

for the Greeks to say whether they want Wavell to visit Athens or not. It is the Greeks who must be the judges of the German reactions.

Secondly, if the Germans are coming south they will not require pretexts. They are, it would seem, already acting in pursuance of a carefully thought-out plan which one can hardly assume will be hurried or delayed in consequence of any minor movements of ours. The evidence in our possession of the German movements seems overwhelming. In the face of it Prince Paul's attitude looks like that of an unfortunate man in the cage with a tiger, hoping not to provoke him while steadily dinner-time approaches.

At the end of January, 1941, in these days of growing anxiety, Colonel Donovan, a friend of President Roosevelt, came to Belgrade on a mission from the American Government to sound opinion in Southeastern Europe. Fear reigned. The Ministers and the leading politicians did not dare to speak their minds. Prince Paul declined a proposed visit from Mr. Eden. There was one exception. An air force general named Simovic represented the nationalist elements among the officer corps of the armed forces. Since December his office in the air force headquarters across the river from Belgrade at Zemun had become a clandestine centre of opposition to German penetration into the Balkans and to the inertia of the Yugoslav Government.

On February 14 Cvetkovic and Markovic obeyed a summons to Berchtesgaden. Together they listened to Hitler's account of the might of victorious Germany and to his emphasis on the close relations between Berlin and Moscow. If Yugoslavia would adhere to the Tripartite Pact, Hitler offered, in the event of operations against Greece, not to march through Yugoslavia, but only to use its roads and railways for military supplies. The Ministers returned to Belgrade in sombre mood. To join the Axis might infuriate Serbia. To fight Germany might cause conflict of loyalty in Croatia. Greece, the only possible Balkan ally, was heavily engaged with Italian armies of more than two hundred thousand men, and was under the menace of imminent German attack. English help seemed doubtful, and at the best symbolic. In order to help the Yugoslav Government to reach a satisfactory decision, Hitler proceeded with the strategic encirclement of their country. On March 1 Bulgaria adhered to the Tripartite Pact, and the same evening German motorised elements reached the Serbian frontiers. Meanwhile, to avoid provocation, the Yugoslav Army remained unmobilised. The hour of choice had now struck.

On March 4 Prince Paul left Belgrade on a secret visit to Berchtesgaden, and under dire pressure undertook verbally that Yugoslavia would follow the example of Bulgaria. On his return, at a meeting of the Royal Council and in separate discussion with political and military leaders, he found opposing views. Debate was violent, but the German ultimatum was real. General Simovic, when summoned to the White Palace, Prince Paul's residence on the hills above Belgrade, was firm against capitulation. Serbia would not accept such a decision, and the dynasty would be endangered. But Prince Paul had already in effect committed his country.

*   *   *

From London I did what I could to rally the Yugoslavs against Germany, and on March 22 I telegraphed to Doctor Cvetkovic, the Yugoslav Premier.

22 March 41

Your Excellency: The eventual total defeat of Hitler and Mussolini is certain. No prudent and farseeing man can doubt this in view of the respective declared resolves of the British and American democracies. There are only 65,000,000 malignant Huns, most of whom are already engaged in holding down Austrians, Czechs, Poles, and many other ancient races they now bully and pillage. The peoples of the British Empire and of the United States number nearly 200,000,000 in their homelands and British Dominions alone. We possess the unchallengeable command of the oceans, and with American help will soon obtain decisive superiority in the air. The British Empire and the United States have more wealth and more technical resources and they make more steel than the whole of the rest of the world put together. They are determined that the cause of freedom shall not be trampled down nor the tide of world progress turned backwards by the criminal dictators, one of whom has already been irretrievably punctured. We know that the hearts of all true Serbs, Croats, and Slovenes beat for the freedom, integrity, and independence of their country, and that they share the forward outlook of the English-speaking world. If Yugoslavia were at this time to stoop to the fate of Rumania, or commit the crime of Bulgaria, and become an accomplice in an attempted assassination of Greece, her ruin will be certain and irreparable. She will not escape, but only postpone, the ordeal of war, and her brave armies will then fight alone after being surrounded and cut off from hope and succour. On the other hand, the history of war has seldom shown a finer opportunity than is open to the Yugoslav armies if they seize it while time remains. If Yugoslavia and Turkey stand together with Greece, and with all the aid which the British Empire can give, the German curse will be stayed and final

victory will be won as surely and decisively as it was last time.
I trust Your Excellency may rise to the height of world events.

But during the night of March 20, at a Cabinet meeting,
the Yugoslav Government decided to adhere to the Tripartite
Pact. Three Ministers however resigned on this issue. On
March 24 Cvetkovic and Markovic crept out of Belgrade from
a suburban railway station on the Vienna train. Next day they
signed the Pact with Hitler in Vienna, and the ceremony was
broadcast over the Belgrade radio. Rumours of imminent disaster swept through the cafés and conclaves of the Yugoslav
capital.

I now sent instructions to Mr. Campbell, our Minister in
Belgrade.

26 March 41

Do not let any gap grow up between you and Prince Paul or
Ministers. Continue to pester, nag, and bite. Demand audiences.
Don't take *NO* for an answer. Cling on to them, pointing out Germans are already taking the subjugation of the country for granted.
This is no time for reproaches or dignified farewells. Meanwhile,
at the same time, do not neglect any alternative to which we may
have to resort if we find present Government have gone beyond
recall. Greatly admire all you have done so far. Keep it up by
every means that occur to you.

* * *

Direct action, if the Government capitulated to Germany,
had been discussed for some months in the small circle of
officers around Simovic. A revolutionary stroke had been
carefully planned. The leader of the projected rising was
General Bora Mirkovic, commander of the Yugoslav Air
Force, aided, among many hundreds of patriots, by Major
Knezevic, an army officer, and his brother, a professor, who
established political contacts through his position in the Serb
Democrat Party. Knowledge of the plan was confined to a
small number of trustworthy officers, nearly all below the rank
of colonel. The network extended from Belgrade to the main
garrisons in the country, Zagreb, Skoplje, and Sarajevo. The
forces at the disposal of the conspirators in Belgrade comprised two regiments of the Royal Guard, with the exception
of their colonels, one battalion of the Belgrade garrison, a
company of gendarmes on duty at the Royal Palace, part of
the anti-aircraft division stationed in the capital, the air force
headquarters at Zemun, where Simovic was chief, and the

cadet schools for officers and non-commissioned officers, together with certain artillery and sapper units.

When during March 26 the news of the return from Vienna of the Yugoslav Ministers began to circulate in Belgrade, the conspirators decided to act. The signal was given to seize key points in Belgrade, and the royal residence, together with the person of the young King, Peter II, by dawn on March 27. While troops, under the command of resolute officers, were sealing off the Royal Palace on the outskirts of the capital, Prince Paul, knowing nothing or too much of what was afoot, was in the train bound for Zagreb. Few revolutions have gone more smoothly. There was no bloodshed. Certain senior officers were placed under arrest. Cvetkovic was brought by the police to Simovic's headquarters and obliged to sign a letter of resignation. Machine guns and artillery were placed at suitable points in the capital. Prince Paul on arrival in Zagreb was informed that Simovic had taken over the Government in the name of the young King, Peter II, and that the Council of Regency had been dissolved. The military commander of Zagreb requested the Prince to return at once to the capital. As soon as he reached Belgrade, Prince Paul was escorted to the office of General Simovic. Together with the other two regents, he then signed the act of abdication. He was allowed a few hours to collect his effects, and, together with his family, he left the country that night for Greece.

The plan had been made and executed by a close band of Serb nationalist officers who had identified themselves with the true public mood. Their action let loose an outburst of popular enthusiasm. The streets of Belgrade were soon thronged with Serbs, chanting, "Rather war than the pact; rather death than slavery." There was dancing in the squares; English and French flags appeared everywhere; the Serb national anthem was sung with wild defiance by valiant, helpless multitudes. On March 28 the young King, who by climbing down a rainpipe had made his own escape from Regency tutelage, attended divine service in Belgrade Cathedral amid fervent acclamation. The German Minister was publicly insulted, and the crowd spat on his car. The military exploit had roused a surge of national vitality. A people paralyzed in action, hitherto ill-governed and ill-led, long haunted by the sense of being ensnared, flung their reckless, heroic defiance at the tyrant and conqueror in the moment of his greatest power.

*   *   *

Hitler was stung to the quick. He had a burst of that convulsive anger which momentarily blotted out thought and sometimes impelled him on his most dire adventures. In a cooler mood, a month later, conversing with Schulenburg, he said, "The Yugoslav *coup* came suddenly out of the blue. When the news was brought to me on the morning of the twenty-seventh I thought it was a joke." But now in a passion he summoned the German High Command. Goering, Keitel, and Jodl were present, and Ribbentrop arrived later. The minutes of the meeting are found in the Nuremberg records. Hitler described the Yugoslav situation after the upheaval. He said that Yugoslavia was an uncertain factor in the coming action against Greece ("Marita"), and even more in the "Barbarossa" undertaking against Russia later on. He deemed it fortunate that the Yugoslavs had revealed their temper before "Barbarossa" was launched.

The Fuehrer is determined, without waiting for possible loyalty declarations of the new Government, to make all preparations in order *to destroy Yugoslavia militarily and as a national unit.* No diplomatic inquiries will be made nor ultimatums presented. Assurances of the Yugoslav Government, which cannot be trusted anyhow in the future, will be "taken note of." The attack will start as soon as the means and troops suitable for it are ready.

Actual military support against Yugoslavia is to be requested of Italy, Hungary, and in certain respects of Bulgaria too. Rumania's main task is the protection against Russia. The Hungarian and Bulgarian Ambassadors have already been notified. During the day a message will be addressed to the Duce.

Politically it is especially important that the blow against Yugosalvia is *carried out with unmerciful harshness* and that the military destruction is done in a lightning-like undertaking. In this way Turkey would become sufficiently frightened and the campaign against Greece later on would be influenced in a favourable way. It can be assumed that the Croats will come to our side when we attack. A corresponding political treatment (autonomy later on) will be assured to them. The war against Yugoslavia should be very popular in Italy, Hungary, and Bulgaria, as territorial acquisitions are to be promised to these States: the Adriatic coast for Italy, the Banat for Hungary, and Macedonia for Bulgaria. This plan assumes that we speed up the schedule of all preparations and use such strong forces that the Yugoslav collapse will take place within the shortest time. . . . The main task of the air force is to start as early as possible with the destruction of the Yugoslav Air Force ground installations and to destroy the capital, Belgrade, in attacks by waves.

On the same day the Fuehrer signed "Directive No. 25":

My intention is to invade Yugoslavia by powerful thrusts from
the area of Fiume and Sofia in the general direction of Belgrade
and farther to the south, with the objective of inflicting on the
Yugoslav Army a decisive defeat, as well as to cut off the southern
part of Yugoslavia from the rest of the country and to turn it into
a base for further operations of German-Italian forces against
Greece.

In detail I order the following:

(a) As soon as the concentration of sufficient forces is concluded
and meteorological conditions permit, all Yugoslav surface installations and Belgrade must be destroyed by continuous day and night
air attacks.

(b) If possible simultaneously, but under no circumstances
sooner, Operation "Marita" must be started, with the primary
limited objective of seizing the harbour of Salonika and the Dios
Mountains.

He now telegraphed to Mussolini:

Duce, events force me to give you, by this, the quickest means,
my estimate of the situation and the consequences which may
result from it.

From the beginning I have regarded Yugoslavia as a dangerous factor in the controversy with Greece. Considered from the
purely military point of view, German intervention in the war in
Thrace would not be at all justified as long as the attitude of
Yugoslavia remained ambiguous and she could threaten the left
flank of the advancing columns on our enormous front.

2. For this reason I have done everything and have honestly
endeavoured to bring Yugoslavia into our community bound together by mutual interests. Unfortunately these attempts did not
meet with success, or they were begun too late to produce any
definite result. Today's reports leave no doubt of the imminent
turn in the foreign policy of Yugoslavia.

3. I do not consider this situation as being catastrophic, but
nevertheless it is a difficult one, and we on our part must avoid
any mistake if we do not want, in the end, to endanger our whole
position.

4. Now I would cordially request you, Duce, not to undertake
any further operations in Albania in the course of the next few
days.

Hitler saw as clearly as we did the one chance of the Yugoslavs to strike a deadly blow.

I consider it necessary that you should cover and screen the
most important passes from Yugoslavia into Albania with all available forces. These measures should not be considered as designed

for a long period of time, but as auxiliary measures to prevent for at least fourteen days to three weeks a crisis arising.

I also consider it necessary, Duce, that you should reinforce your forces on the Italian-Yugoslav front with all available means and with the utmost speed.

. . . If silence is maintained, Duce, on these measures I have no doubt we shall both witness a success that will not be less than that of Norway. This is my granite conviction.

The night was spent by the generals in drafting the operation orders. Keitel in his evidence confirms our view that the greatest danger to Germany was "an attack upon the Italian Army from the rear." Jodl testified as follows: "I worked all night at the Reich Chancellery [which also shows the surprise nature of the case]. At 4 A.M. on the twenty-eighth I put an *aide-mémoire* into the hands of General von Rintelen, our liaison officer with the Italian General Staff." Keitel records: "The decision to attack Yugoslavia meant completely upsetting all military movements and arrangements made up to that time. 'Marita' had to be completely readjusted. New forces had to be brought through Hungary from the north. All had to be improvised."

* * *

From the time of Munich, Hungary had attempted to extend her post-1920 frontiers in the wake of the German diplomatic victories at the expense of Czechoslovakia and Rumania, while at the same time trying to maintain a neutral position in the international sphere. Hungarian diplomacy sought to avoid precise commitments to the Axis about becoming an ally in the war. Hungary adhered at Vienna to the Tripartite Pact, but, like Rumania, undertook no definite obligations. Neither Hitler nor Mussolini desired a quarrel between the Balkan countries. They hoped to get control of them all at the same time. For this reason they had imposed a settlement upon Hungary and Rumania about Transylvania. Mussolini's attack on Greece, which Hitler did not favour, brought with it the prospect of British intervention in Southeastern Europe. Pressure was therefore brought upon Yugoslavia to follow the example of Hungary and Rumania in joining the Axis bloc. When the Yugoslav Ministers had been summoned to Vienna for this purpose everything seemed settled. The dramatic events of March 27 in Belgrade upset all hope of a united Balkan group adhering to the Axis.

Hungary was directly and immediately affected. Although

the main German thrust against the recalcitrant Yugoslavs would clearly come through Rumania, all lines of communication led through Hungarian territory. Almost the first reaction of the German Government to the events in Belgrade was to send the Hungarian Minister in Berlin by air to Budapest with an urgent message to the Hungarian Regent, Admiral Horthy:

Yugoslavia will be annihilated, for she has just renounced publicly the policy of understanding with the Axis. The greater part of the German armed forces must pass through Hungary. But the principal attack will not be made on the Hungarian sector. Here the Hungarian Army should intervene, and, in return for its cooperation, Hungary will be able to reoccupy all those former territories which she had been forced at one time to cede to Yugoslavia. The matter is urgent. An immediate and affirmative reply is requested.[1]

Hungary was bound by a pact of friendship to Yugoslavia signed only in December, 1940. But open opposition to the German demands could only lead to the German occupation of Hungary in the course of the imminent military operations. There was also the temptation of reoccupying the territories on her southern frontiers which Hungary had lost to Yugoslavia by the Treaty of Trianon. The Hungarian Premier, Count Teleki, had been working consistently to maintain some liberty of action for his country. He was by no means convinced that Germany would win the war. At the time of signing the Tripartite Pact he had little confidence in the independence of Italy as an Axis partner. Hitler's ultimatum required the breach of his own Hungarian agreement with Yugoslavia. The initiative was, however, wrested from him by the Hungarian General Staff, whose chief, General Werth, himself of German origin, made his own arrangements with the German High Command behind the back of the Hungarian Government. Details regarding the passage of troops were being arranged on this basis.

Teleki at once denounced Werth's action as treasonable. On the evening of April 2, 1941, he received a telegram from the Hungarian Minister in London that the British Foreign Office had stated formally to him that if Hungary took part in any German move against Yugoslavia she must expect a declaration of war upon her by Great Britain. Thus the choice for Hungary was either a vain resistance to the passage of German troops or ranging herself openly against the Allies and betraying Yugoslavia. In this cruel position Count Teleki saw

[1] Ullein Reviczy, *Guerre Allemande: Paix Russe,* page 89.

but one means of saving his personal honour. Shortly after nine o'clock he left the Hungarian Ministry of Foreign Affairs and retired to his apartments in the Sandor Palace. There he received a telephone call. It is believed that this message stated that the German armies had already crossed the Hungarian frontier. Shortly afterward he shot himself. His suicide was a sacrifice to absolve himself and his people from guilt in the German attack upon Yugoslavia. It clears his name before history. It could not stop the march of the German armies nor the consequences.

* * *

The news of the revolution in Belgrade naturally gave us great satisfaction. Here at least was one tangible result of our desperate efforts to form an Allied front in the Balkans and prevent all falling piecemeal into Hitler's power. I received the earliest telegrams only half an hour before I had to address the Conservative Central Council for the first time as leader of the party. I ended as follows:

Here at this moment I have great news for you and the whole country. Early this morning the Yugoslav nation found its soul. A revolution has taken place in Belgrade, and the Ministers who but yesterday signed away the honour and freedom of the country are reported to be under arrest. This patriotic movement arises from the wrath of a valiant and warlike race at the betrayal of their country by the weakness of their rulers and the foul intrigues of the Axis Powers.

We may, therefore, cherish the hope—I speak, of course, only on information which has reached me—that a Yugoslav Government will be formed worthy to defend the freedom and integrity of their country. Such a Government in its brave endeavour will receive from the British Empire, and, I doubt not, in its own way, from the United States, all possible aid and succour. The British Empire and its Allies will make common cause with the Yugoslav nation, and we shall continue to march and strive together until complete victory is won.

* * *

Mr. Eden had reached Malta on his way home, but on the news of the Belgrade revolution I thought he should change his plans and be upon the spot with Generals Dill and Wavell.

Prime Minister to Mr. Eden 27 March 41

In view of *coup d'état* in Serbia it would surely be well for you both to be on the spot in Cairo so as to concert events. Now surely is the chance to bring in Turkey and form a joint front in the Balkans. Can you not get a meeting in Cyprus or Athens of all concerned? When you know the situation, ought you not to go to Belgrade? Meanwhile we are doing all possible and carrying on.

I telegraphed to the President of Turkey:

27 March 41

Your Excellency: The dramatic events which are occurring in Belgrade and throughout Yugoslavia may offer the best chance of preventing the German invasion of the Balkan Peninsula. Surely now is the time to make a common front which Germany will hardly dare assail. I have cabled to President Roosevelt to ask him for American supplies to be extended to all Powers resisting German aggression in the East. I am asking Mr. Eden and General Dill to concert all possible measures of common safety.

During the day I drafted the following message to Mr. Eden who had already reached Athens.

28 March 41

Let us visualise clearly what we want in the Balkans and from Turkey, and work towards it as events serve.

2. Together Yugoslavia, Greece, Turkey, and ourselves have seventy divisions mobilised in this theatre. Germans have not yet got more than thirty. Therefore, the seventy could say to the thirty, "If you attack any of us you will be at war with all." The Germans would either attack in mountainous regions and with poor communications at heavy odds, or alternatively they would have to bring large reinforcements from Germany. But even this does not cure their difficulties, because, first, it will take some months to bring the reinforcements to the theatre, and, secondly, the theatre itself, and indeed the communications leading to it, are not strong enough to carry much larger forces without a prolonged process of improving the communications. Therefore, it is very likely that a triple note by the three Balkan Powers would lead to the maintenance of peace, or to a lengthy delay in the German advance. Perhaps the advance could not be made for many months, and then they miss the season. Meanwhile British reinforcements and British and American supplies will vastly increase resisting power of the Allied armies. There is, therefore, a good prospect if the three Allies could be brought into line that no invasion southwards would be tried by the enemy. Here is what the Turks want.

3. This is Turkey's best chance of avoiding war. For look at the alternative. If all three remain disunited the Germans may feel that it will be better to leave Greece and Yugoslavia alone and turn their whole striking force rapidly against Turkey in Thrace. There have been suggestions of this in various telegrams.

Thus, by doing nothing Turkey runs the greatest danger of having everything concentrated upon her. One can hardly doubt that the mass of Turkish troops gathered in Thrace would soon be driven back in confusion upon the Chatalja [lines] and the Bosporus, without any obligation or opportunity on the part of Yugoslavia or Greece to take the pressure off by counter-attack, or by lengthening the fighting front.

4. The proper order for anyone to give who had the power would be (a) the diplomatic declaration of unity and demand to be let alone as set forth above, and (b) a simultaneous withdrawal of the bulk of the Turkish Army to Chatalja and the Asiatic shore, leaving only strong covering troops and rear guards in Thrace. Such a policy of firm, united declaration, coupled with sound strategic withdrawal, would prevent the Germans from gaining a decisive victory in Thrace, would not require any offensive from Turkey, and would, unless the Germans shied off, expose them to a stalemate front from, say, the lines of Chatalja through the Rupel-Nestor sector right up along the northern Serbian front. Even this could not develop for a long time. But what a dangerous and uninviting prospect for an enemy for whom quick successes are especially important! Surely this is the true Turkish interest, if it can be brought about, and we ought to try to make them see it, however unresponsive they may be. The Turks' greatest danger is to be taken on alone jammed up in Thrace.

5. How does this above square with British interests? If Germany, not withstanding the objections, attacks in the Balkans, we must play our part there with our full available strength. If, on the other hand, she pretends that she never wished to bring war into the Balkans, and leaves Greece, Yugoslavia, and Turkey alone, then we might turn our forces to a strong summer and autumn campaign in the Central Mediterranean, including Tripoli, Sicily, and the Italian toe. We should have a good pad in our right hand to protect our Middle Eastern interests, and take smart action in a medium scale with our left in the Central Mediterranean.

6. Is it not possible that if a united front were formed in the Balkan Peninsula Germany might think it better business to take it out of Russia, observing that we have had many reports of heavy concentrations in Poland and intrigues in Sweden and Finland?

7. Pray consider these opinions for what they are worth.

I also cabled to Mr. Fadden, the Acting Prime Minister of the Commonwealth of Australia.

30 March 41

When a month ago we decided upon sending an army to Greece it looked rather a blank military adventure dictated by *noblesse oblige*. Thursday's events in Belgrade show the far-reaching effects of this and other measures we have taken on whole Balkan situation. German plans have been upset, and we may cherish renewed hopes of forming a Balkan front with Turkey, comprising about seventy Allied divisions from the four Powers concerned. This is, of course, by no means certain yet. But even now it puts "Lustre" [the expedition to Greece] in its true setting, not as an isolated military act, but as a prime move in a large design. Whatever the outcome may be, everything that has happened since our decision was taken justifies it. Delay will also enable full concentration to be made on the Greek front instead of piecemeal engagements of our forces. Result unknowable, but prize has increased and risks have somewhat lessened. Am in closest touch with Menzies. Wish I could talk it over with you.

*   *   *

It was settled that Eden should remain in Athens to deal with Turkey and that General Dill should proceed to Belgrade. Anyone could see that the position of Yugoslavia was forlorn unless a common front was immediately presented by all the Powers concerned. There was, however, open to Yugoslavia the chance already mentioned of striking a deadly blow at the naked rear of the disorganised Italian armies in Albania. If they acted promptly they might bring about a major military event, and while their own country was being ravaged from the north might possess themselves of the masses of munitions and equipment which would give them the power of conducting the guerrilla in their mountains which was now their only hope. It would have been a grand stroke, and would have reacted upon the whole Balkan scene. In our circle in London we all saw this together. The diagram below shows the movement which was deemed feasible.

General Dill was now in Belgrade, and I sent him this message:

1 April 41

A variety of details shows rapid regrouping against Yugoslavia. To gain time against Germans is to lose it against Italians. Nothing should stop Yugo developing full strength against latter at earliest. By this alone can they gain far-reaching initial success and masses of equipment in good time.

The mistakes of years cannot be remedied in hours. When the general excitement had subsided, everyone in Belgrade realised that disaster and death approached them and that there was little they could do to avert their fate. The High Command thought themselves forced to garrison Slovenia and Croatia, to maintain a fictitious internal cohesion. They could now at last mobilise their armies. But there was no strategic plan. Dill found only confusion and paralysis in Belgrade. "In

The BALKANS

Italian forces in Albania
Greek forces
Lines of entry for Yugoslav forces into Albania

spite of my best endeavours," he reported to Mr. Eden on
April 1, "I was unable to persuade President of the Council
to agree to visit by you in the immediate future. He made it
plain that the Yugoslav Government, mainly for fear of the
effect on the internal situation, were determined to take no
step which might be considered provocative to Germany." At
this moment all the might of Germany within reach was descending like an avalanche upon them.

On April 4 General Dill sent a full account of his mission
to Belgrade, which shows how utterly remote from their immediate peril were the minds of the Yugoslav Ministers. One
would have thought from their mood and outlook that they
had months in which to take their decision about peace or
war with Germany. Actually they had only seventy-two hours
before the onslaught fell upon them. Dill wrote:

Final result of Belgrade visit was disappointing in many ways,
but it was impossible to get [General] Simovic to sign any sort of
agreement. Nevertheless, I was impressed with offensive spirit of
Yugoslav leaders, who will fight if Yugoslavia is attacked or if Germany attacks Salonika. Staff discussions today should have useful
results in exchange of views, and, I hope, in agreement on best
plans to meet various eventualities. None of these plans will be

binding on either side, but there is reasonable prospect that when time comes Yugoslavs will be prepared to carry them out.

Fact is that Simovic, though a leader and able, is in no sense dictator. He had difficult task in keeping Cabinet together, and dare not propose to them any form of agreement with us. Nor can he effect such agreement without knowledge and consent of Cabinet. But he and War Minister Ilic, who is tougher but less intelligent, seem determined to fight. . . .

Yugoslavs' forces are not yet ready for war, and Simovic wants to gain time to complete mobilisation and concentration. For internal political reasons he cannot take first step in hostilities, but must await German move. He expects Germany to attack Southern Yugoslavia from Bulgaria and leave Greece alone at the moment. . . . Yugoslavs will aid in Albania, but will not attack even there until Germany attacks them or their vital interests.

Simultaneously with this I made the following appeal:

Prime Minister to General Simovic   4 April 41

From every quarter my information shows rapid heavy concentration and advance towards your country by German ground and air forces. Large movements of air forces are reported to us from France by our agents there. Bombers have even been withdrawn from Tripoli, according to our African Army Intelligence. I cannot understand argument that you are gaining time. The one supreme stroke for victory and safety is to win a decisive forestalling victory in Albania, and collect the masses of equipment that would fall into your hands. When the four German mountain divisions reported by your General Staff as entraining in the Tyrol reach Albania, a very different resistance will confront you than could be offered by rear of the demoralised Italians. As this is the first time I have had the honour to address Your Excellency, I send my heartiest good wishes for the success of your Administration and for the safety and independence of the brave nation whose fortunes you guide.

*   *   *

We have now to chronicle the only occasion when a dash of sentiment was allowed to mingle in the calculations of the Kremlin oligarchy.

The national movement in Belgrade had been a spontaneous revolt entirely divorced from the activities of the small illegal but Soviet-sponsored Yugoslav Communist Party. After waiting a week Stalin decided to make a gesture. His officials were negotiating with M. Gavrilovic, the Yugoslav Minister in Moscow, and with a mission sent from Belgrade after the revolution. Little progress had been made. During the night of April 5–6 the Yugoslavs were summoned abruptly to the

Kremlin. They were confronted with Stalin in person, who presented them with a pact in draft, ready for signature. The work was speedily done. Russia agreed to respect "the independence, sovereign rights, and territorial integrity of Yugoslavia," and in the event of that country being attacked Russia would adopt an attitude of good will "based on friendly relations." This was at any rate an amicable grimace. Gavrilovic stayed alone till morning discussing with Stalin the question of military supplies. As their conversations came to an end the Germans struck.

* * *

On the morning of April 6 German bombers appeared over Belgrade. Flying in relays from occupied airfields in Rumania, they delivered a methodical attack lasting three days upon the Yugoslav capital. From rooftop height, without fear of resistance, they blasted the city without mercy. This was called Operation "Punishment." When silence came at last on April 8 over seventeen thousand citizens of Belgrade lay dead in the streets or under the débris. Out of the nightmare of smoke and fire came the maddened animals released from their shattered cages in the zoological garden. A stricken stork hobbled past the main hotel, which was a mass of flames. A bear, dazed and uncomprehending, shuffled through the inferno with slow and awkward gait down towards the Danube. He was not the only bear who did not understand. Operation "Punishment" had been performed.

10

The Japanese Envoy

THE NEW YEAR had brought disturbing news from the Far East. The Japanese Navy was increasingly active off the coasts of Southern Indo-China. Japanese warships were reported in Saigon Harbor and the Gulf of Siam. On January 31 the Japanese Government negotiated an armistice between the Vichy French and Siam. Rumours spread that this settlement of a frontier dispute in Southeast Asia was to be the prelude to the entry of Japan into the war. The Germans were at the same time bringing increased pressure to bear upon Japan to attack the British at Singapore. "I tried," said Ribbentrop at his Nuremberg trial, "to induce Japan to attack Singapore because it was impossible to make peace with England, and I did not know what military measures we could take to achieve this end—in any case, the Fuehrer directed me to do everything I could through diplomatic channels to weaken England's position and thus achieve peace. We believed that this could best be done through an attack by Japan on England's strong position in East Asia." [1]

* * *

About this time several telegrams arrived from our Commander-in-Chief in the Far East urging the reinforcement of Hong Kong. I did not agree with his views.

Prime Minister to General Ismay   7 Jan. 41

This is all wrong. If Japan goes to war with us there is not the slightest chance of holding Hong Kong or relieving it. It is most unwise to increase the loss we shall suffer there. Instead of increasing the garrison it ought to be reduced to a symbolical scale. Any trouble arising there must be dealt with at the Peace conference after the war. We must avoid frittering away our resources on untenable positions. Japan will think long before declaring war on the British Empire, and whether there are two or six battalions at Hong Kong will make no difference to her choice. I wish we had fewer troops there, but to move any would be noticeable and dangerous.

Later on it will be seen that I allowed myself to be drawn from this position, and that two Canadian battalions were sent as reinforcements.

* * *

In the second week of February I became conscious of a stir and flutter in the Japanese Embassy and colony in London. They were evidently in a high state of excitement, and they chattered to one another with much indiscretion. In these days we kept our eyes and ears open. Various reports were laid before me which certainly gave the impression that they had received news from home which required them to pack up without a moment's delay. This agitation among people usually so reserved made me feel that a sudden act of war upon us by Japan might be imminent, and I thought it well to impart my misgivings to President Roosevelt.

Former Naval Person to President Roosevelt   15 Feb. 41

Many drifting straws seem to indicate Japanese intention to make war on us or do something that would force us to make war on them in the next few weeks or months. I am not myself convinced that this is not a war of nerves designed to cover Japanese encroachments in Siam and Indo-China. However, I think I ought to let you know that the weight of the Japanese Navy, if thrown

[1] *Nuremberg Documents,* Part X, page 200.

against us, would confront us with situations beyond the scope of our naval resources. I do not myself think that the Japanese would be likely to send the large military expedition necessary to lay siege to Singapore. The Japanese would no doubt occupy whatever strategic points and oilfields in the Dutch East Indies and thereabouts they covet, and thus get into a far better position for a full-scale attack on Singapore later on. They would also raid Australian and New Zealand ports and coasts, causing deep anxiety in those Dominions, which have already sent all their best-trained fighting men to the Middle East. But the attack which I fear the most would be by raiders, including possibly battle-cruisers, upon our trade routes and communications across the Pacific and Indian Oceans.

We could by courting disaster elsewhere send a few strong ships into these vast waters, but all the trade would have to go into convoy and escorts would be few and far between. Not only would this be a most grievous additional restriction and derangement of our whole war economy, but it would bring altogether to an end all reinforcements of the armies we had planned to build up in the Middle East from Australian and Indian sources. Any threat of a major invasion of Australia or New Zealand would, of course, force us to withdraw our Fleet from the Eastern Mediterranean, with disastrous military possibilities there, and the certainty that Turkey would have to make some accommodation for reopening of the German trade and oil supplies from the Black Sea.

You will therefore see, Mr. President, the awful enfeeblement of our war effort that would result merely from the sending out by Japan of her battle-cruisers and her twelve eight-inch-gun cruisers into the Eastern oceans, and still more from any serious invasion threat against the two Australian democracies in the Southern Pacific.

Some believe that Japan in her present mood would not hesitate to court or attempt to wage war both against Great Britain and the United States. Personally I think the odds are definitely against that, but no one can tell. Everything that you can do to inspire the Japanese with the fear of a double war may avert the danger. If, however, they come in against us and we are alone, the grave character of the consequences cannot easily be overstated.

The agitation among the Japanese in London subsided as quickly as it had begun. Silence and Oriental decorum reigned once more.

Former Naval Person to President Roosevelt   20 Feb. 41

I have better news about Japan. Apparently Matsuoka is visiting Berlin, Rome, and Moscow in the near future. This may well be a diplomatic sop to cover absence of action against Great Britain. If Japanese attack which seemed imminent is now postponed, this is largely due to fear of United States. The more these fears can be played upon the better, but I understand thoroughly your difficulties pending passage of [Lend-Lease] Bill on which our hopes depend. Appreciation given in my last "Personal and Secret" of naval consequences following Japanese aggression against Great Britain holds good in all circumstances.

*   *   *

On February 24 Mr. Shigemitsu, the Japanese Ambassador, came to see me. A record was kept of the meeting.

I dwelt upon the long and friendly relations of the two countries, my own feelings ever since the Japanese Alliance of 1902, and the great desire that we all felt here not to sunder the relations between the two countries. Japan could not expect us to view with approval what was going on in China; but we had maintained a correct attitude of neutrality, and indeed a very different kind of neutrality to that which we had shown when we had helped them in their war against Russia. We had not the slightest intention of attacking Japan, and had no wish to see her other than prosperous and peaceful, and I said what a pity it would be if at this stage, when she already had China on her hands, she got into a war with Great Britain and the United States.

The Ambassador said that Japan had no intention of attacking us or the United States, and had no desire to become involved in a war with either Power. They would not attempt to attack Singapore or Australia, and he repeated several times that they would not attempt to gain a footing or make encroachments in the Dutch East Indies. The only complaint which Japan had, he said, was our attitude to China, which was encouraging China and adding to their difficulties. . . . I felt bound to remind him of the Triple Pact which they had made with the Axis Powers, and that this naturally was ever in our minds. One could not believe that a pact so much in favour of Germany and so little in favour of Japan had not got some secret provisions, and at any rate Japan had left us in doubt as to what interpretation she would put upon it in certain eventualities. The Ambassador said they had made explanations at the time, and that their object was to limit the conflict, etc. I told him the Axis Pact had been a very great mistake for Japan. Nothing had done them more harm in their relations with the United States, and nothing had brought Great Britain and the United States closer together.

I then renewed my friendly assurances. His whole attitude throughout was most friendly and deprecatory, and we have no doubt where he stands in these matters.

On March 4, after he could certainly have reported to Tokyo, I recorded in a minute a second visit from Mr. Shigemitsu.

The Japanese Ambassador called upon me today and spoke in agreeable terms of the great desire in Japan not to be involved in war and not to have a rupture with Great Britain. He described the Tripartite Pact as a pact of peace, and said it arose only out of the desire of Japan to limit the conflict. I asked him specifically whether the pact left Japan the full right of interpreting any given situation, and I put it to him that nothing in the pact obliged her to go to war. He did not dissent from this; in fact, he tacitly assented. I received all his assurances with cordiality, and asked him to convey my thanks to the Foreign Minister of Japan. I do not think Japan is likely to attack us unless and until she is sure we are going to be defeated. I doubt very much whether she would come into the war on the side of the Axis Powers if the United States joined us. She would certainly be very foolish to do so. It would be more sensible for her to come in if the United States did not join us.

This was for very different reasons also the German view. Germany and Japan were both eager to despoil and divide the British Empire. But they approached the target from different angles. The German High Command argued that the Japanese ought to commit their armed forces in Malaya and the Dutch East Indies without worrying about the American Pacific bases, and the main fleet which lay on their flank. Throughout February and March they urged the Japanese Government to strike without delay at Malaya and Singapore and not to bother about the United States. Hitler had already enough on his shoulders without drawing them in. Indeed, we have seen how many American actions he put up with, any one of which would have provided ample grounds for war. Hitler and Ribbentrop were above all things anxious that Japan should attack what they called "England"—the name still lingers—and not on any account embroil themselves with the United States. They assured Tokyo that if Japan acted with vigour against Malaya and the Dutch East Indies the Americans would not dare to move. The Japanese naval and military leaders were by no means convinced by this reasoning, or that it was disinterested. In their view an operation in Southeast Asia was out of the question unless either a prior assault was made on the American bases or a diplomatic settlement reached with the United States.

Behind the complex political scene in Japan three decisions seem to emerge at this time. The first was to send the Foreign Secretary, Matsuoka, to Europe to find out for himself about the German mastery of Europe, and especially when the invasion of Britain was really going to begin. Were the British forces so far tied up in naval defence that Britain could not afford to reinforce her Eastern possessions if Japan attacked them? Although he had been educated in the United States, Matsuoka was bitterly anti-American. He was deeply impressed by the Nazi movement and the might of embattled Germany. He was under the Hitler spell. Perhaps even there were moments when he saw himself playing a similar part in Japan. Secondly, the Japanese Government decided that their navy and army command should have a free hand *to plan* operations against the American base at Pearl Harbour and against the Philippines, the Dutch East Indies, and Malaya. Thirdly, a "liberal" statesman, Admiral Nomura, was to be sent to Washington to explore the chances of a general settlement with the United States in the Pacific. This not only served as a camouflage, but might lead to a peaceful solution. Thus agreement between conflicting opinions was reached in the Japanese Cabinet.

* * *

Matsuoka set out on his mission on March 12. On the twenty-fifth, passing through Moscow, he had a two hours' interview with Stalin and Molotov, and he assured the German Ambassador, Schulenburg, that he would repeat to Ribbentrop personally all details of the conversation.

The captured documents published by the American State Department throw a searching light on Matsuoka's mission and upon the whole German mood and mind. On March 27 the Japanese envoy was cordially welcomed in Berlin as a kindred spirit by Ribbentrop. The Reich Foreign Minister dilated upon the might of his country.

Germany [he said] was in the final phase of her battle against England. During the past winter the Fuehrer had made all necessary preparations so that Germany stood completely ready today to meet England anywhere. The Fuehrer had at his disposal perhaps the strongest military power that had ever existed. Germany had 240 combat divisions, of which 186 were first-class assault divisions and 24 were Panzer divisions. The Luftwaffe had grown greatly and had introduced new models, so that it was not only a match for England and America in this field, but definitely superior to them.

The German Navy at the outbreak of the war had had only a relatively small number of battleships. Nevertheless, the battleships under construction had been completed, so that the last of them would shortly be put into service. In contrast to the First World War, the German Navy this time did not stay in port, but from the first day of the war had been employed against the foe. Matsuoka had probably gathered from the reports of the past few weeks that large German battle units had interrupted the supply lines between England and America with extraordinary success.[2]

The number of submarines heretofore employed was very small. There had been at most eight or nine boats in service against the enemy at any one time. Nevertheless, even these few U-boats, in conjunction with the Luftwaffe, had sunk 750,000 tons per month in January and February, and Germany could furnish accurate proof of this at any time. This number, moreover, did not include the great additional losses that England had sustained through floating and magnetic mines. At the beginning of April the number of submarines would increase eight- to tenfold, so that sixty to eighty U-boats, could then be continually employed against the enemy. The Fuehrer had pursued the tactics of at first employing only a few U-boats, and using the rest to train the personnel necessary for a larger fleet, in order then to proceed to a knock-out blow against the enemy. Therefore, the tonnage sunk by the German U-boats could be expected in the future greatly to exceed what had already been accomplished. In these circumstances the U-boat alone could be designated as absolutely deadly.

On the continent of Europe Germany had practically no foe of any consequence other than the small British forces that remained in Greece. Germany would fight off any attempt of England to land on the Continent or entrench herself there. She would not, therefore, tolerate England's staying in Greece. The Greek question was of secondary importance, but by the thrust towards Greece, which would probably be necessary, dominant positions in the Eastern Mediterranean would be won for further operations.

In Africa the Italians had had bad luck in recent months, because the Italian troops there were not familiar with modern tank warfare and were not prepared with anti-tank defence, so that it was relatively easy for the British armoured divisions to capture the not very important Italian positions. Any further advance of the British had been definitely blocked. The Fuehrer had dispatched one of the most able of German officers, General Rommel, to Tripoli with sufficient German forces. The hope that General Wavell would attack had unfortunately not been realised. The British had come upon the Germans in some skirmishes at an outpost, and had thereupon abandoned any further intention of attacking. Should they by chance attempt another attack upon Tripoli [tania] they would court annihilating defeat. Here too the tables would be turned some day, and the British would disappear from North Africa, perhaps even more quickly than they had come.

In the Mediterranean the German Luftwaffe had been doing good work for two months and had inflicted heavy shipping losses on the British, who were holding on tenaciously. The Suez Canal had been blocked for a long time, and would be blocked again.

[2] This refers to the sortie by the *Scharnhorst* and the *Gneisenau* into the Atlantic in February and March.

It was no longer any fun for the British to hold out in the Mediterranean.

If, then, we summed up the military situation in Europe we should come to the conclusion that in the military sphere the Axis was completely master of Continental Europe. A huge army, practically idle, was at Germany's command, and could be employed at any time and at any place the Fuehrer considered necessary.

Leaving the military for the political scene, Ribbentrop said:

Confidentially, he could inform Matsuoka that present relations with Russia were correct, to be sure, but not very friendly. After Molotov's visit, during which accession to the Three-Power Pact was offered, Russia had made conditions that were unacceptable. They involved the sacrifice of German interests in Finland, the granting of bases on the Dardanelles, and a strong [Soviet] influence on conditions in the Balkans, particularly in Bulgaria. The Fuehrer had not concurred, because he had been of the opinion that Germany could not permanently subscribe to such a Russian policy. Germany needed the Balkan Peninsula above all for her own economy, and had not been inclined to let it come under Russian domination. For this reason she had given Rumania a guarantee. It was this latter action particularly that the Russians had taken amiss. Germany had further been obliged to enter into a closer relationship with Bulgaria in order to obtain a vantage point from which to expel the British from Greece. Germany had had to decide on this course because this campaign would otherwise not have been possible. This too the Russians had not liked at all.

In these circumstances relations with Russia were externally normal and correct. The Russians, however, had for some time demonstrated their unfriendliness to Germany whenever they could. The declaration made to Turkey within the last few days was an example of this. Germany felt plainly that since Sir Stafford Cripps became Ambassador to Moscow . . . ties between Russia and England were being cultivated in secret and even relatively openly. Germany was watching these proceedings carefully.

Ribbentrop continued:

He knew Stalin personally, and did not assume that the latter was inclined towards adventure; but it was impossible to be sure. The German armies in the East were prepared at any time. *Should Russia some day take a stand that could be interpreted as a threat to Germany the Fuehrer would crush Russia. Germany was certain that a campaign against Russia would end in the absolute victory of German arms and the total crushing of the Russian Army and the Russian State. The Fuehrer was convinced that in case of action against the Soviet Union there would in a few months be no more Great Power of Russia. In any case, the Fuehrer was not* counting on the treaties with Russia alone, but was relying first of all on his *Wehrmacht*.

It must also not be overlooked that the Soviet Union, in spite of all protestations to the contrary, was still carrying on Communistic propaganda abroad. It was attempting not only in Germany, but also in the occupied areas of France, Holland, and Belgium, to continue its misleading propagandist activity. For Germany this propaganda naturally constituted no danger. But what it had unfortunately led to in other countries Matsuoka well knew. As an example, the Reich Foreign Minister cited the Baltic States, in which today, one year after the occupation by the Russians, the entire intelligentsia had been wiped out and really terrible conditions prevailed. Germany was on guard, and would never suffer the slightest danger from Russia.

Further, there was the fact that Germany had to be protected in the rear for her final battle against England. She would therefore not put up with any threat from Russia if such a threat should some day be considered serious. Germany wanted to conquer England as rapidly as possible, and would not let anything deter her from doing so.

These were grave words for the Reich Foreign Minister to use on such an occasion, and Matsuoka could certainly not complain that he had not been kept well informed. Ribbentrop then reiterated that

the war had already been definitely won for the Axis. It could in any case no longer be lost. It was now only a question of time until England would admit having lost the war. When, he could, of course, not predict. It might be very soon. It would depend upon events of the next three or four months. It was highly probable, however, that England would capitulate in the course of this year.

Finally he spoke of America.

There was no doubt that the British would long since have abandoned the war if Roosevelt had not always given Churchill new hope. It was difficult to say what Roosevelt's intention was in the long run. It would be a long time before the American aid in munitions for England would really be effective, and even then the quality of airplane deliveries was doubtful. A country far from the war could not turn out the highest quality aircraft. What the German fliers had thus far encountered they described as "junk."

The Three-Power Pact [he said] had above all the goal of frightening and keeping America out of the war. The principal enemy of the New Order was England, who was as much the enemy of Japan as of the Axis Powers.

Ribbentrop then stated that

the Fuehrer, after careful consideration, believed that it would be advantageous if Japan would decide as soon as possible to take an active part in the war upon England. A quick attack upon Singapore, for instance, would be a decisive factor in the speedy overthrow of England. If today in a war against England Japan were to succeed with one decisive stroke on Singapore Roosevelt would be in a very difficult position. If he declared war upon Japan he must expect that the Philippine question would be resolved in favour of Japan. He would probably reflect for a long time before incurring such a serious loss of prestige. Japan, on the other hand, through the conquest of Singapore would gain an absolutely dominant position in that part of East Asia. She would in fact "cut the Gordian knot."

*   *   *

After an interval for luncheon, Matsuoka was received by Hitler. The Fuehrer dwelt in his own words upon German military triumphs. Since the war began sixty Polish, six Norwegian, eighteen Dutch, twenty-two Belgian, and one hundred and thirty-eight French divisions had been eliminated, and twelve or thirteen British divisions had been driven from the Continent. Resistance to the will of the Axis Powers had become impossible. Hitler went on to speak of the British losses in tonnage. The real U-boat warfare was just beginning. In the present and coming months England would be damaged to an extent far surpassing her present rate of losses. In the air Germany had absolute supremacy, in spite of all the claims of the English to success. The attacks of the Luftwaffe in the coming months would actually grow much stronger. The effectiveness of the German blockade had made rationing more severe in England than in Germany. Meanwhile the war would go on in preparation for the final stroke against England.

Matsuoka listened to this harangue. He expressed his thanks for the frankness with which he had been treated. He said that on the whole he agreed with the view of the Fuehrer. There were in Japan, as in other countries, certain intellectual circles which only a powerful individual could hold firmly under control. *Japan would take action in a decisive form if she had the feeling that otherwise she would lose a chance which could only occur once in a thousand years.* He had explained to the two princes of the Japanese Imperial Family that preparation could not always be complete and perfect. Risks must be run. It was only a question of time when Japan would attack. The hesitant politicians in Japan would always delay, and act partly from a pro-British or pro-American attitude. Personally he wished the attack to come as soon as possible. Unfortunately he did not control Japan, but had to bring those who were in control round to his point of view. He would certainly be successful some day, but at the present moment and under these circumstances he could make no pledge on behalf of the Japanese Empire that it would take action. He would give his closest attention to these matters on his return. He could make no definite commitment, but he personally would do his utmost. These were considerable reservations.

He then referred to his conference with Stalin when he had passed through Moscow. He had at first wanted only to make a courtesy call on Molotov, but the Russian Government had proposed a meeting between him, Stalin, and Molotov. He had conversed with Molotov, taking into account the necessary translations, for perhaps ten minutes, and with Stalin for twenty-five minutes. He had told Stalin that the Japanese were *moral* Communists, though he did not believe in political and economic Communism. This Japanese ideal of moral Communism had been overthrown by the liberalism, individualism, and egoism produced in the West. The ideological struggle in Japan was extremely bitter, but those who were fighting for the restoration of the old ideals were convinced they would finally win. The Anglo-Saxons represented the greatest hindrance to the establishment of the New Order. He had told Stalin that after the collapse of the British Empire the differences between Japan and Russia would be eliminated. The Anglo-Saxons were the common foe of Japan, Germany, and Soviet Russia. After some reflection Stalin had stated that Soviet Russia had never got along well with Great Britain and never would.

*   *   *

The conversations in Berlin were continued throughout March 28 and 29 without altering the essential features: first, the Germans strove hard to persuade Japan to attack the British Empire; secondly, they admitted that their relations with Russia were uncertain; and, thirdly, they made it plain that Hitler hoped earnestly to avoid a conflict with the United States.

To neither of the important questions whether Germany still intended, as before, to effect a landing in Britain and how German-Soviet relations were now viewed did Matsuoka ob-

tain a clear answer. To his question as to whether, on his return journey through Moscow, he should touch on political
questions lightly or go into them more deeply, Ribbentrop
answered through his interpreter: "You had better treat your
visit as a mere formality." [3]

* * *

Without, of course, knowing the substance or character of
these secret Berlin parleys, but deeply impressed with their
importance, I thought I would use the Japanese Ambassador,
whom Matsuoka had summoned to meet him on the Continent, to convey to his chief a few counter-considerations. Mr.
Shigemitsu, who, if he was hostile to Britain and the United
States and working for war against us, must have been a very
good deceiver, accepted with a courtly gesture the task of
delivering my message. In the end he did not travel, and the
letter was telegraphed to our Ambassador in Moscow, to be
given to Mr. Matsuoka on his return journey by the Siberian
Railway.

Mr. Churchill to M. Yosuke Matsuoka   2 April 41

I venture to suggest a few questions which it seems to me deserve the attention of the Imperial Japanese Government and
people.

Will Germany, without the command of the sea or the command of the British daylight air, be able to invade and conquer
Great Britain in the spring, summer, or autumn of 1941? Will
Germany try to do so? Would it not be in the interests of Japan
to wait until these questions have answered themselves?

2. Will the German attack on British shipping be strong enough
to prevent American aid from reaching British shores, with Great
Britain and the United States transforming their whole industry
to war purposes?

3. Did Japan's accession to the Triple Pact make it more likely
or less likely that the United States would come into the present
war?

4. If the United States entered the war at the side of Great
Britain, and Japan ranged herself with the Axis Powers, would
not the naval superiority of the two English-speaking nations enable them to dispose of the Axis Powers in Europe before turning
their united strength upon Japan?

5. Is Italy a strength or a burden to Germany? Is the Italian
Fleet as good at sea as on paper? Is it as good on paper as it used
to be?

6. Will the British Air Force be stronger than the German Air

[3] Kordt, *Wahn und Wirklichkeit*, page 303.

Force before the end of 1941, and far stronger before the end of 1942?

7. Will the many countries which are being held down by the German Army and Gestapo learn to like the Germans more or will they like them less as the years pass by?

8. Is it true that the production of steel in the United States during 1941 will be 75,000,000 tons, and in Great Britain about 12,500,000 making a total of nearly 90,000,000 tons? If Germany should happen to be defeated, as she was last time, would not the 7,000,000 tons steel production of Japan be inadequate for a single-handed war?

From the answers to these questions may spring the avoidance by Japan of a serious catastrophe, and a marked improvement in the relations between Japan and the two great sea Powers of the West.

I was rather pleased with this when I wrote it, and I don't mind the look of it now.

* * *

Matsuoka meanwhile went to Rome, where he saw Mussolini and the Pope. We now have the German account of what he said to Hitler on April 4, when he returned to Berlin. The Duce, he said, had informed him about the war in Greece, Yugoslavia, and North Africa, and of the part which Italy herself had in these events. Finally he had spoken of Soviet Russia and America. The Duce had said that one must have a clear notion of the importance of one's opponents. The enemy Number 1 was America and Soviet Russia came only in the second place. By these remarks the Duce had given him to understand that America as enemy Number 1 would have to be very carefully watched, but should not be provoked. On the other hand one must be thoroughly prepared for all eventualities. Matsuoka had agreed with this line of thought.

* * *

Before his homeward journey by the Trans-Siberian Railway Matsuoka tarried for a week in Moscow. He had several long conversations both with Stalin and Molotov. The only account we have of these is from the German Ambassador Schulenburg, who of course was only told what the Russians and Japanese wished him to know. It seemed that all the declarations, true or boastful, of German might had by no means convinced the Japanese envoy. The guarded attitude of the German leaders towards a collision with the United States had made a dint in Matsuoka's mind. At the same time he was aware, from Ribbentrop's language, of the menacing, widening gulf between Germany and Russia. How much he told his new hosts about this we cannot tell. But certainly, surveying the scene with peculiar advantages, and after receiving from Sir Stafford Cripps the telegraphed version of my letter with its questions, it would appear that Matsuoka found himself closer to Molotov than to Ribbentrop. In this doom-balance of mighty nations Japan was asked by Germany to take the irrevocable step of declaring war on Britain, and potentially on the English-speaking world. By Russia she was only asked to mark time, to wait and see. Evidently he did not believe that Britain was finished. He could not be sure what would happen between Germany and Russia. He was not inclined, or perhaps he had not the power, to commit his country to decisive action. He greatly preferred a neutrality pact, which at least gave time for unpredictable events to unfold, as they must do soon.

Accordingly, when Matsuoka visited Schulenburg in Moscow on April 13 to make his farewell call, he mentioned with incongruous preciseness that a Japanese-Soviet Neutrality Pact had been arranged at the last moment, and "in all likelihood would be signed this afternoon at 2 P.M. local time." Both sides had made concessions about the disputed island of Sakhalin. This new agreement, he assured the German Ambassador, in no way affected the Three-Power Pact. He added that the American and English journalists who had reported that his journey to Moscow had been a complete failure would be compelled now to acknowledge that the Japanese policy had achieved a great success, which could not fail to have its effect on England and America.

Schulenburg has recorded the demonstration of unity and comradeship arranged by Stalin at the railway station on Matsuoka's departure for Japan. The train was delayed for an hour for salutes and ceremonies, apparently unexpected by both the Japanese and Germans. Stalin and Molotov appeared, and greeted Matsuoka and the Japanese in a remarkably friendly manner and wished them a pleasant journey. Then Stalin publicly asked for the German Ambassador. "And when he found me," said Schulenburg, "he came up and threw his arm around my shoulder. 'We must remain friends. You must now do everything to that end.'" Later Stalin turned to the German Military Attaché, first having made sure that he had got the right man, and said to him, "We will remain friends with you in any event." "Stalin," adds Schulenburg, "doubt-

less brought about this greeting of Colonel Krebs and myself
intentionally, and thereby he consciously attracted the attention of the numerous persons who were present."

These embraces were a vain pretence. Stalin should surely
have known from his own reports the enormous deployment
of German strength which now began to be visible to British
Intelligence all along the Russian frontier. It was only ten
weeks before Hitler's terrific onslaught on Russia began. It
would have been only five weeks but for the delay caused by
the fighting in Greece and Yugoslavia.

* * *

Matsuoka returned to Tokyo from his European visit at the
end of April. He was met at the airport by the Prime Minister,
Prince Konoye, who informed him that on that very day the
Japanese had been considering the possibilities of an understanding in the Pacific with the United States. This was contrary to Matsuoka's theme. Though beset by doubts, he was
still on the whole a believer in ultimate German victory.
Backed by the prestige of the Tripartite Pact and the neutrality treaty with Russia, he saw no special need to conciliate
the Americans, who, in his opinion, would never face simultaneous war in the Atlantic against Germany and in the Pacific
against Japan. The Foreign Minister, therefore, found himself
confronted with a mood in Government circles widely different from his own. In spite of his vehement protests the Japanese resolved to continue the negotiations at Washington,
and also to conceal them from the Germans. On May 4 Matsuoka took it upon himself to acquaint the German Ambassador with the text of an American Note to Japan offering to
reach a general Pacific settlement, beginning with American
mediation between Japan and China. The main obstacle to
this proposal was the American requirement that Japan should
first evacuate China.

* * *

While in Moscow Mr. Matsuoka had received my message,
and on his return journey in the train across Siberia he wrote
a barren reply, which was dispatched on his arrival in Tokyo.

Mr. Matsuoka to Mr. Winston Churchill   22 April 1941
Your Excellency,

I have just come back from my trip, and hasten to acknowledge
the receipt of a paper handed to me at Moscow on the evening of

the twelfth instant by Sir Stafford Cripps with a remark that it was a copy in substance of a letter addressed to me, dated London, the second April, 1941, and forwarded to Tokyo.

I wish to express my appreciation for the facilities with which your Government made efforts to provide our Ambassador when he wanted to meet me on the Continent. I was deeply disappointed when I learned that he could not come. Your Excellency may rest assured that the foreign policy of Japan is determined upon after an unbiased examination of all the facts and a very careful weighing of all the elements of the situation she confronts, always holding steadfastly in view the great racial aim and ambition of finally bringing about the conditions envisaged in what she calls Hakko-ichiu, the Japanese conception of a universal peace under which there would be no conquest, no oppression, no exploitation of any and all peoples. And, once determined, I need hardly tell Your Excellency that it will be carried out with resolution but with utmost circumspection, taking in every detail of changing circumstances.

> I am, believe me,
> Your Excellency's obedient servant,
> YOSUKE MATSUOKA

*   *   *

Matsuoka and his colleagues in the Japanese Government were soon to confront a situation which required such an "unbiased examination." On June 28, a week after Hitler's invasion of Russia, a meeting of the Japanese Cabinet and officials of the Imperial Household was held. Matsuoka found his position irremediably weakened. He had "lost face" because he had not known of Hitler's intention to attack Russia. He spoke in favour of joining Germany, but the majority opinion was overwhelmingly against him. The Government decided to adopt a compromise policy. Armament preparations were to be augmented. Article 5 of the Tripartite Pact was invoked, which stated that the instrument was not valid against Russia. Germany was to be informed confidentially that Japan would fight "Bolshevism in Asia," and the Neutrality Treaty with Russia was cited to justify non-intervention in the German-Russian War. On the other hand, it was agreed to go ahead in the Southern seas and to complete the occupation of South Indo-China. These decisions were not agreeable to Matsuoka. In order to stir up agitation for entering the war on Germany's side, he had one of his speeches printed as a pamphlet for wide distribution. The copies were suppressed by the Japanese Government. On July 16 he disappeared from office.

But while the Japanese Cabinet were not prepared to follow in the wake of German policy, their policy did not represent a triumph for the moderates in Japanese public life. The strengthening of the Japanese armed forces was pressed forward, and bases were to be established in South Indo-China. This was a prelude to attack on the British and Dutch colonies in Southeast Asia. It seems, from the evidence up till now available, that the leaders of Japanese policy did not expect from the United States or Great Britain any vigorous counter-measures to this projected southward advance.

Thus we see as this world drama marches on how all these three coldly calculating empires made at this moment mistakes disastrous alike to their ambitions and their safety. Hitler was resolved on the war with Russia, which played a decisive part in his ruin. Stalin remained, to Russia's bitter cost, in ignorance or underestimation of the blow about to fall on him. Japan certainly missed the best chance—for what it was ever worth—of realising her dreams.

11

The Desert Flank: Rommel: Tobruk

*The Vital Desert Flank—Wavell's Dispositions—His Estimate of the
Situation of March 2—Rommel's Arrival in Tripoli, February 12
—His Determination to Attack—A Great General—The Gateway
at Agheila—Our Inadequate Resources—Personal Inspection by
Wavell and Dill, March 17—My Telegram to Wavell of March
26—His Reply—The Position in Cyrenaica—Rommel's Attack
upon Agheila, March 31—Failure of Our Armoured Forces—My
Telegram of April 2—Unexpected German Strength—Evacuation
of Benghazi—Capture of Generals Neame and O'Connor—Importance of Holding Tobruk—Wavell's Decision—German Mastery of the Air—My Directive of April 14—My Telegram to
President Roosevelt, April 16—Wavell's Explanation.*

ALL OUR EFFORTS to form a front in the Balkans were
founded upon the sure maintenance of the Desert flank
in North Africa. This might have been fixed at Tobruk; but
Wavell's rapid westward advance and the capture of Benghazi had given us all Cyrenaica. To this the sea corner at
Agheila was the gateway. It was common ground between all
authorities in London and Cairo that this must be held at all
costs and in priority over every other venture. The utter destruction of the Italian forces in Cyrenaica and the long road
distances to be traversed before the enemy could gather a
fresh army led Wavell to believe that for some time to come
he could afford to hold this vital western flank with moderate
forces and to relieve his tried troops with others less well
trained. The Desert flank was the peg on which all else hung,
and there was no idea in any quarter of losing or risking that
for the sake of Greece or anything in the Balkans.

At the end of February the 7th British Armoured Division
had been withdrawn to Egypt to rest and refit. This famous

unit had rendered the highest service. Its tanks had travelled far and were largely used up. Its numbers had shrunk by fighting and wear and tear. Still there was a core of the most experienced, hard-bitten, desert-worthy fighting men, the like of whom could not be found by us. It was a pity not to keep in being the nucleus of this unique organisation and rebuild its strength by drafts of officers and men arriving trained, fresh, and keen from England, and to send up to them the pick of whatever new tanks or spare parts could be found. Thus the 7th Armoured Division would have preserved a continuity of life and been resuscitated in strength.

It was only after some weeks, marked by serious decisions, that I realised that the 7th Armoured Division did not exist as a factor in the protection of our vital Desert flank. The place of the 7th Armoured Division was taken by an armoured brigade and part of the support group of the 2d Armoured Division. The 6th Australian Division was also relieved by the 9th. Neither of these new formations was fully trained, and, to make matters worse, they were stripped of much equipment and transport to bring up to full scale the divisions soon to go to Greece. The shortage of transport was severely felt and affected the dispositions of the troops and their mobility. Because of maintenance difficulties farther forward, one Australian brigade was held back in Tobruk, where also was a brigade of motorised Indian cavalry recently formed and under training.

*   *   *

Our Intelligence reports now began to cause the Chiefs of Staff some concern. On February 27 they sent a warning telegram to General Wavell:

In view of arrival of German armoured formations and aircraft in Tripolitania the question of defence commitments in Egypt and Cyrenaica has been considered here. Would be grateful if you would telegraph a short appreciation.

This drew an important considered reply which included the following:

2 March 41

Latest information indicates recent reinforcements to Tripolitania comprise two Italian infantry divisions, two Italian motorised artillery regiments, and German armoured troops estimated at maximum of one armoured brigade group. No evidence of additional mechanical transport landed, and enemy must still be short of transport. Latest air reconnaissance, however, shows considerable increase in mechanical transport on Tripoli-Sirte road.

2. Tripoli to Agheila is 471 miles and to Benghazi 646 miles. There is only one road, and water is inadequate over 410 miles of the distance; these factors, together with lack of transport, limit the present enemy threat. He can probably maintain up to one infantry division and armoured brigade along the coast road in about three weeks, and possibly at the same time employ a second armoured brigade, if he has one available, across the desert via Hon and Marada against our flank.

3. He may test us at Agheila by offensive patrolling, and if he finds us weak push on to Agedabia in order to move up his advanced landing grounds. I do not think that with this force he will attempt to recover Benghazi.

4. Eventually two German divisions might be employed in a large-scale attack. This, with one or two infantry divisions, would be the maximum maintainable via Tripoli. Shipping risks, difficulty of communications, and the approach of hot weather make it unlikely that such an attack could develop before the end of the summer. Effective interference by sea with convoys and by air with Tripoli might extend this period.

The Italian air threat to Cyrenaica is at present almost negligible. On the other hand, the Germans are well established in Central Mediterranean. . . . German parachute troops might be landed on our lines of communication in combination with armoured forces. I do not anticipate that parachutists will be used with the scale of attack likely to be developed in near future, but they are a possible accompaniment of a large-scale attack at later date.

*   *   *

But now a new figure sprang upon the world stage—a German warrior who will hold his place in their military annals. Erwin Rommel was born in Heidenheim, in Württemberg, in November, 1891. He was a delicate boy, and was educated at home till, at the age of nine, he joined the local Government school, of which his father was headmaster. In 1910 he was an officer cadet in the Württemberg Regiment. When he did his training at the military school at Danzig his instructors reported that he was physically small, but strong. Mentally he was not remarkable. He fought in the First World War in the Argonne, in Rumania, and in Italy, being twice wounded and awarded the highest classes of the Iron Cross and of the order Pour le Mérite. Between the two wars he served as a regimental officer and on the Staff. On the outbreak of the Second World War he was appointed commandant of the Fuehrer's field headquarters in the Polish campaign, and was then given command of the 7th Panzer Division of the Fif-

teenth Corps. This division, nicknamed "the Phantoms,"
formed the spearhead of the German break-through across the
Meuse. He narrowly escaped capture when the British counter-
attacked at Arras on May 21, 1940. Thereafter he led his division through La Bassée towards Lille. If this thrust had had
a little more success, or perhaps not been restrained by orders
from the High Command, it might have cut off a large part of
the British Army, including the 3d Division, commanded by
General Montgomery. His was the spearhead which crossed
the Somme and advanced on the Seine in the direction of
Rouen, rolling up the French left wing and capturing numerous French and British forces around Saint-Valery. His
division was the first to reach the Channel, and entered Cherbourg just after our final evacuation where Rommel took the
surrender of the port and thirty thousand French prisoners.

These many services and distinctions led to his appointment
early in 1941 to command the German troops sent to Libya.
On February 12 he arrived with his personal staff at Tripoli to
campaign with the ally against whom he had formerly won
distinction. At that time Italian hopes were limited to holding
Tripolitania, and Rommel took charge of the growing German
contingent under Italian command. He strove immediately to
enforce an offensive campaign. When early in April the Italian Commander-in-Chief tried to persuade him that the German Afrika Corps should not advance without his permission,
Rommel protested that "as a German general he had to issue
orders in accordance with what the situation demanded." Any
reservations because of the supply problem were, he declared,
"unfounded." He demanded and obtained complete freedom
of action.

Throughout the African campaign Rommel proved himself
a master in handling mobile formations, especially in regrouping rapidly after an operation and following up success. He
was a splendid military gambler, dominating the problems of
supply and scornful of opposition. At first the German High
Command, having let him loose, were astonished by his successes, and were inclined to hold him back. His ardour and
daring inflicted grievous disasters upon us, but he deserves the
salute which I made him—and not without some reproaches
from the public—in the House of Commons in January, 1942,
when I said of him, "We have a very daring and skilful opponent against us, and, may I say across the havoc of war, a
great general." He also deserves our respect because, although
a loyal German soldier, he came to hate Hitler and all his

works, and took part in the conspiracy of 1944 to rescue Germany by displacing the maniac and tyrant. For this he paid the forfeit of his life. In the sombre wars of modern democracy chivalry finds no place. Dull butcheries on a gigantic scale and mass effects overwhelm all detached sentiment. Still, I do not regret or retract the tribute I paid to Rommel, unfashionable though it was judged.

* * *

In London we accepted Wavell's telegram of March 2, as the basis of our action. The Agheila defile was the kernel of the situation. If the enemy broke through to Agedabia, Benghazi and everything west of Tobruk were imperilled. They could choose between taking the good coast road to Benghazi and beyond or using the tracks leading straight to Mechili and Tobruk, which cut off the bulge of desert, two hundred miles long by a hundred miles broad. Taking this latter route in February, we had nipped and captured many thousands of Italians retiring through Benghazi. It should not have been a matter of surprise to us if Rommel also took the desert route to play the same trick on us. However, so long as we held the gateway at Agheila the enemy was denied the opportunity of bemusing us in this fashion. There are good positions there, but partly owing to the extra strain on transport from Tobruk, through the port of Benghazi not being judged usable, they were not adequately defended.

All this depended upon a knowledge not only of the ground, but of the conditions of desert warfare. So rapid had been our advance, so easy and complete our victories, that these strategic facts were not effectively grasped at this stage. However, a superiority in armour and in quality rather than numbers, and a reasonable parity in the air, would have enabled the better and more lively force to win in a rough-and-tumble in the desert, even if the gateway had been lost. None of these conditions were established by the arrangements which were made. We were inferior in the air; and our armour, for reasons which will be explained later, was utterly inadequate, as was also the training and equipment of the troops west of Tobruk.

On March 17 Generals Wavell and Dill visited Cyrenaica and made a personal inspection. They motored through Antelat to Agheila, and Dill was immediately struck by the difficulty of defending the large stretches of desert between Agheila and Benghazi. In a telegram on March 18 from Cairo to his deputy at home he said that the outstanding fact was that between the salt-pans east of Agheila and Benghazi the desert was so open and so suitable for armoured vehicles that, other things being equal, the stronger fleet would win. There were no infantry positions on which to fight. Of course, the maintenance problem over these vast distances of desert remained and entirely favoured defence. Wavell, he said, had this difficult defence problem well in hand.

In a conversation with the Australian Staff of General Morshead, whom he met on the way, the C.I.G.S. is said to have expressed the opinion that the force looked like getting "a bloody nose" in the near future, adding, "This will not be the only place either." [1] This latter opinion was not in harmony with any statement he made to us.

*   *   *

There had been during March increasing evidence of the arrival of German troops from Tripoli towards Agheila, and on March 20 Wavell reported that an attack on a limited scale seemed to be in preparation and that the situation on the Cyrenaica frontier was causing him some anxiety. If our advanced troops were driven from their present positions there would be no good blocking points south of Benghazi, as the country was dead-level plain. Administrative problems should, however, preclude anything but a limited advance by the enemy.

I telegraphed:

Prime Minister to General Wavell   26 March 41

We are naturally concerned at rapid German advance to Agheila. It is their habit to push on whenever they are not resisted. I presume you are only waiting for the tortoise to stick his head out far enough before chopping it off. It seems extremely important to give them an early taste of our quality. What is the state and location of 7th Armoured Division? Pray give me your appreciation. I cordially approve your request to General Smuts for a brigade of 1st South African Division. Everything must be done to accelerate movement of 2d South African Division. The 50th British Division starts twenty-second. . . .

Wavell replied to this at once as follows:

27 March 41

No evidence yet that there are many Germans at Agheila; probably mainly Italian, with small stiffening of Germans.

2. I have to admit to having taken considerable risk in Cyrenaica after capture of Benghazi in order to provide maximum support

[1] Major-General R. J. Collins, *Lord Wavell,* page 355.

for Greece. My estimate at that time was that Italians in Tripolitania could be disregarded and that Germans were unlikely to accept the risk of sending large bodies of armoured troops to Africa in view of the inefficiency of the Italian Navy. I, therefore, made arrangements to leave only small armoured force and one partly trained Australian division in Cyrenaica.

3. After we had accepted Greek liability evidence began to accumulate of German reinforcements to Tripoli, which were coupled with attacks on Malta which prevented bombing of Tripoli from there, on which I had counted. German air attacks on Benghazi, which prevented supply ships using harbour, also increased our difficulties.

4. Result is I am weak in Cyrenaica at present and no reinforcements of armoured trops, which are chief requirement, are at present available. I have one brigade of 2d Armoured Division in Cyrenaica, one in Greece. The 7th Armoured Division is returning [to Cairo], and as no reserve tanks were available is dependent on repair, which takes time. Next month or two will be anxious, but enemy has extremely difficult problem and am sure his numbers have been much exaggerated. I cannot, however, at present afford to use my small armoured force as boldly as I should like.

Steps to reinforce Cyrenaica are in hand. . . . My own chief difficulty is transport.

He added what may well remind us of his many cares:

Have just come back from Keren front. Capture was very fine achievement by Indian divisions, and their tails are high in spite of fairly heavy casualties. Platt will push on towards Asmara as quickly as he can, and I have authorised Cunningham to continue towards Addis Ababa from Harrar, which surrendered yesterday.

*   *   *

Rommel's attack upon Agheila began on March 31. General Neame had been ordered, if pressed, to fight a delaying action back to near Benghazi, and to cover that port as long as possible. He was given permission to evacuate it if necessary after making demolitions. Our armoured division at Agheila, which had in fact only one armoured brigade and its support group, therefore, withdrew slowly during the next two days. In the air the enemy proved greatly superior. The Italian Air Force still counted for little, but there were about a hundred German fighters and a hundred bombers and dive-bombers. On April 2 General Wavell reported that the forward troops in Cyrenaica were being attacked by a German colonial armoured division.

Some forward posts were overrun yesterday and losses occurred. Losses not serious at present, but the mechanical condition of the

armoured brigade is causing Neame much concern, and there seem
to be many breakdowns. As I can produce no more armoured units
for at least three or four weeks, I have warned him to keep three
brigades in being, even if it involves considerable withdrawal,
possibly even from Benghazi.

I was still under the impression, derived from Wavell's previous estimates, of the enemy's limited potential strength.

Prime Minister to General Wavell   2 April 41
   It seems most desirable to chop the German advance against
Cyrenaica. Any rebuff to the Germans would have far-reaching
prestige effects. It would be all right to give up ground for the
purposes of manoeuvre, but any serious withdrawal from Benghazi
would appear most melancholy. I cannot understand how the
enemy can have developed any considerable force at the end of
this long, waterless coast road, and I cannot feel that there is at
this moment a persistent weight behind his attack in Cyrenaica. If
this blob which has come forward against you could be cut off you
might have a prolonged easement. Of course, if they succeed in
wandering onward they will gradually destroy the effect of your
victories. Have you got a man like O'Connor or Creagh dealing
with this frontier problem?

   On April 2 the support group of our 2d Armoured Division
was driven out of Agedabia by fifty enemy tanks, and retreated to the Antelat area, thirty-five miles to the northeast.
The division was ordered to withdraw to the neighbourhood of
Benghazi. Our armoured forces under the German attack became disorganised and there were serious losses. The message
ended,*"Orders have been given for demolitions in Benghazi."*
General Wavell flew to the front on the third, and reported on
his return that a large part of the armoured brigade had been
overrun and disorganised by superior German armour. This
would uncover the left flank of the 9th Australian Division east
and northeast of Benghazi. *"Their withdrawal may be necessary."* In consequence of the enemy's strength in Libya he
said the 7th Australian Division could not go to Greece, but
must move to the Western Desert instead. The 6th British
Division, still incomplete, must become the reserve. *"This will
involve the postponement of the attack on Rhodes."* Thus at a
single stroke, and almost in a day, the desert flank upon which
all our decisions had depended had crumpled and the expedition to Greece, already slender, was heavily reduced. The
seizure of Rhodes, which was an essential part of our air plans
in the Aegean, became impossible.
   The evacuation of Benghazi was ordered. The support group

was sent northward to cover the withdrawal of the 9th Australian Division, which began early on April 4. At the same time the 3d Armoured Brigade were to move on Mechili to block any attempt on the part of the enemy to interfere with the withdrawal. To reinforce them there two regiments of the Indian Motorised Cavalry Brigade were ordered up from Tobruk.

* * *

I was disturbed by this new and unexpected situation, and cabled the same day to Mr. Eden, who was still in Athens.

Prime Minister to Mr. Eden   3 April 41

Evacuation Benghazi serious, as Germans, once established in aerodromes thereabouts, will probably deny us use of Tobruk. Find out what is strategic and tactical plan to chop the enemy. Let me know to what point retirement is ordered. How does 9th Australian Division get back, and how far? Remember that in his telegram of March 2, Wavell gave many cogent arguments for believing his western flank secure.

2. Far more important than the loss of ground is the idea that we cannot face the Germans and that their appearance is enough to drive us back many scores of miles. This may react most evilly throughout Balkans and Turkey. Pray go back to Cairo and go into all this. Sooner or later we shall have to fight the Huns. By all means make the best plan of manoeuvre, but anyhow fight. Can nothing be done to cut the coastal road by a seaborne descent behind them, even if it means putting off Rhodes?

Mr. Eden replied from Cairo:

        5 April 41

Dill and I arrived safely this evening, and have had full discussion with Wavell and Tedder in Longmore's absence in the Sudan.

The general conclusion to which we have all come is that the Italian-German effort in Cyrenaica is a major diversion well timed to precede the German attack in the Balkans. This judgment in no way diminishes the seriousness of the indirect threat to Egypt, for quite clearly the enemy must be expected to press any advantage he gains. Unfortunately, his first moves attained a greater measure of success than had been expected, and he is following up his initial success. . . .

* * *

Wavell had gone to the Desert front with the intention of putting O'Connor in command. That officer, who was not well at the moment, had represented to the Commander-in-Chief that it would be better if he did not actually take over

command from Neame in the middle of the battle, but that he
should be at hand to help him with his expert local knowledge. Wavell agreed. The arrangement did not work well or
last long. On the night of the sixth the retreat from Benghazi
was in full progress. The 9th Australian Division was withdrawing eastward along the coastal road, and in order to avoid
the traffic General Neame took General O'Connor in his car,
and without escort of any kind motored along a by-road. In
the darkness they were suddenly stopped, and the pistols of a
German patrol presented through the car windows left them
no choice but personal surrender. The loss of these two gallant
lieutenant-generals, Neame a V.C., and O'Connor on the whole
our most experienced and successful desert commander, was
grievous.

In the afternoon of April 6, at a conference in Cairo at which
Wavell, Eden, Dill, Longmore, and Cunningham were present,
the question of where to make a stand was discussed. Wavell
decided to hold Tobruk if possible, and with his usual personal mobility flew thither on the morning of the eighth with
the Australian General Laverack, whom he placed in temporary command. Eden and Dill started on their homeward
journey, and the War Cabinet anxiously awaited their return
with all the knowledge they had gathered in Athens and Cairo.

Wavell reported that the withdrawal of the 9th Australian
Division seemed to be proceeding without interference though
twenty-four hundred Italian prisoners had to be left at Barce.
But later the same day he telegraphed that the position in the
Western Desert had greatly deteriorated. The enemy had
moved on Mechili by the desert route, and there were further
vehicle losses in the 2d Armoured Division by mechanical
breakdowns and air bombing. The 3d Armoured Brigade had
little or no fighting value.

Meanwhile I sent the following message to General Wavell:

7 April 41

You should surely be able to hold Tobruk, with its permanent
Italian defences, at least until or unless the enemy brings up strong
artillery forces. It seems difficult to believe that he can do this for
some weeks. He would run great risks in masking Tobruk and advancing upon Egypt, observing that we can reinforce from the sea
and would menace his communications. Tobruk, therefore, seems
to be a place to be held to the death without thought of retirement. I should be glad to hear of your intentions.

Wavell flew to Tobruk on April 8 and gave orders for the
defence of the fortress. He started back for Cairo as night fell.

The engine failed and they made a forced landing in the dark. The aircraft was smashed and they stepped out onto the open desert, they knew not where. The Commander-in-Chief decided to burn his secret papers. After a long wait the lights of a vehicle were seen. Fortunately it proved to be a British patrol, who approached in menacing fashion. For six hours the Staff in Cairo were alarmed, not without reason, at Wavell's disappearance.

On his return to Cairo the Commander-in-Chief replied. After giving a detailed statement of the troop positions, he said:

Although first enemy effort seems to have exhausted itself, I do not feel we shall have long respite and am still very anxious. Tobruk is not good defensive position; long line of communication behind is hardly protected at all and is unorganised.

As the last sentence of this message seemed to leave the question of Tobruk in doubt, I drafted the following message in conclave with the Chiefs of Staff:

Prime Minister and Chiefs of Staff to General Wavell   10 April 41

We await your full appreciation. Meanwhile you should know how the problem looks to us. From here it seems unthinkable that the fortress of Tobruk should be abandoned without offering the most prolonged resistance. We have a secure sealine of communications. The enemy's line is long and should be vulnerable, provided he is not given time to organise at leisure. So long as Tobruk is held and its garrison includes even a few armoured vehicles which can lick out at his communications, nothing but a raid dare go past Tobruk. If you leave Tobruk and go 260 miles back to Mersa Matruh may you not find yourself faced with something like the same problem? We are convinced you should fight it out at Tobruk.

But before the meeting broke up we learned of Wavell's final decision to hold Tobruk.

I propose [he said] to hold Tobruk, to place a force in Bardia-Sollum area with as much mobility as possible to protect communications and act against flank or rear of enemy attacking Tobruk, and to build up old plan of defence in Mersa Matruh area. Distribution of force so as to gain time without risking defeat in detail will be difficult calculation. My resources are very limited, especially of mobile and armoured troops and of anti-tank and anti-aircraft weapons. It will be a race against time.

Our message was therefore not sent. Instead:

Prime Minister to General Wavell   10 April 41

We all cordially endorse your decision to hold Tobruk, and will do all in our power to bring you aid.

* * *

The retreat to Tobruk was carried out successfully along the coast road. But inland only the headquarters of the 2d Armoured Division arrived at Mechili, on April 6, having lost all touch with its subordinate formations. On April 7 this headquarters and the two Indian motorised regiments found themselves surrounded. Attacks were repulsed, and two ultimatums to surrender, one signed by Rommel, were rejected. A number of men fought their way out, bringing in a hundred German prisoners, but the great majority were forced back into the camp, and there surrendered. The missing 3d Armoured Brigade, now reduced to a dozen tanks, moved on Derna, reputedly because of shortage of petrol, and near that place was ambushed and destroyed on the night of April 6. Throughout the operations the German Air Force had had complete air superiority. This contributed in no small degree to the enemy success. On the night of the eighth the Australians reached Tobruk, which had by then been reinforced by sea with a brigade of the 7th Australian Division from Egypt. The enemy, whose forward troops included parts of the 5th (Light) Panzer Division, one Italian armoured and one infantry division, took Bardia on April 12, but made no effort to penetrate the frontier defences of Egypt.

The enemy pushed on very quickly round Tobruk and towards Bardia and Sollum, with heavy armoured cars and motorised infantry. Other troops attacked the Tobruk defences. The garrison, consisting of the 9th Australian Division, one brigade group of the 7th Australian Division, and a small armoured force, beat off two attacks, destroying a number of enemy tanks. In view of the changed situation and loss of the generals, Wavell had to reorganise the system of command as follows: Tobruk fortress, General Morshead; Western Desert, General Beresford-Peirse; troops in Egypt, General Marshall-Cornwall; Palestine, General Godwin-Austen.

If I get time [said the Commander-in-Chief] to put the above organisation into effect we shall be back to something resembling situation of last autumn, with additional excrescence of Tobruk. But we shall be much harder pressed on ground, and shall not

escape with ineffective air attack that Italians made last year. I
can see no hope of being able to relieve Tobruk for at least several
months. . . . The possible attitude of Egypt is obviously going to
be matter of great anxiety. The next few months will be very difficult, quite apart from what happens in Greece.

Former Naval Person to President Roosevelt   13 April 41

We are, of course, going all out to fight for the Nile Valley. No
other conclusion is physically possible. We have half a million men
there or on the way and mountains of stores. All questions of cutting the loss are ruled out. Tobruk must be held, not as a defensive position, but as an invaluable bridgehead on the flank of any
serious by-pass advance on Egypt. Our Air and Navy must cut or
impede enemy communications across Central Mediterranean. Matter has to be fought out, and must in any case take some time.
Enemy's difficulties in land communication, over eight hundred
miles long, must make attack in heavy force a matter of months.
Even if Tobruk had to be evacuated from the sea, which we command, there are other strong fighting positions already organised.
I personally feel that this situation is not only manageable, but
hopeful. Dill and Eden, who have just come back, concur.

Good news now arrived from Tobruk, where the audacious
and persistent enemy met their first definite rebuff.

General Wavell to War Office   14 April 41

Libya. Between two hundred and three hundred German p.o.w.,
captured at Tobruk morning April 14, stated they were badly
shaken by our artillery fire and were very short of food and water.
These troops wept when their attack was driven off, and their
morale is definitely low.

Perhaps it was because their morale and expectations had
been so high that they wept!

Prime Minister to General Wavell   14 April 41

Convey heartiest congratulations from War Cabinet to all engaged in most successful fight. Bravo Tobruk! We feel it vital that
Tobruk should be regarded as sally-port and not, please, as an
"excrescence." Can you not find good troops who are without
transport to help hold perimeter, thus freeing at least one, if not
two, Australian brigade groups to act as General Fortress Reserve
and potential striking force?

*   *   *

After considering the whole situation at this moment when
a temporary stabilisation on the Egyptian frontier and at Tobruk seemed to have been achieved, I issued the following to
the Chiefs of Staff:

DIRECTIVE BY THE PRIME MINISTER AND MINISTER OF DEFENCE
The War in the Mediterranean

April 14, 1941

If the Germans can continue to nourish their invasion of Cyrenaica and Egypt through the port of Tripoli and along the coastal
road, they can certainly bring superior armoured forces to bear
upon us, with consequences of the most serious character. If, on
the other hand, their communications from Italy and Sicily with
Tripoli are cut, and those along the coastal road between Tripoli
and Agheila constantly harassed, there is no reason why they
should not themselves sustain a major defeat.

2. It becames the prime duty of the British Mediterranean Fleet
under Admiral Cunningham to stop all seaborne traffic between
Italy and Africa by the fullest use of surface craft, aided so far as
possible by aircraft and submarines. For this all-important objective heavy losses in battleships, cruisers, and destroyers must if
necessary be accepted. The harbour at Tripoli must be rendered
unusable by recurrent bombardment, and/or by blocking and mining, care being taken that the mining does not impede the blocking or bombardments. Enemy convoys passing to and from Africa
must be attacked by our cruisers, destroyers, and submarines,
aided by the Fleet Air Arm and the Royal Air Force. Every convoy which gets through must be considered a serious naval failure.
The reputation of the Royal Navy is engaged in stopping this
traffic.

3. Admiral Cunningham's fleet must be strengthened for the
above purposes to whatever extent is necessary. The *Nelson* and
Rodney, with their heavily armoured decks, are especially suitable
for resisting attacks from the German dive-bombers, of which undue fears must not be entertained. Other reinforcements of cruisers, minelayers, and destroyers must be sent from the west as opportunity serves. The use of the *Centurion* as a blockship should
be studied, but the effectual blocking of Tripoli Harbour would be
well worth a battleship upon the active list.

4. When Admiral Cunningham's fleet has been reinforced he
should be able to form two bombarding squadrons, which may in
turn at intervals bombard the port of Tripoli, especially when
shipping or convoys are known to be in the harbour.

5. In order to control the sea communications across the Mediterranean, sufficient suitable naval forces must be based on Malta,
and protection must be afforded to these naval forces by the air
force at Malta, which must be kept at the highest strength in fighters of the latest and best quality that the Malta aerodromes can
contain. The duty of affording fighter protection to the naval
forces holding Malta should have priority over the use of the aerodromes by bombers engaged in attacking Tripoli.

6. Every endeavour should be made to defend Malta Harbour
by the U.P. weapon [rockets] in its various developments, espe-

cially by the F.A.M. [Fast Aerial Mine], fired by the improved naval method.

7. Next in importance after the port at Tripoli comes the 400-mile coastal road between Tripoli and Agheila. This road should be subjected to continuous harassing attacks by forces landed from the Glen ships in the special landing-craft. The commandos and other forces gathered in Egypt should be freely used for this purpose. The seizure of particular points from the sea should be studied, and the best ones chosen for prompt action. Here again losses must be faced, but small forces may be used in this harassing warfare, being withdrawn, if possible, after a while. If even a few light or medium tanks could be landed, these could rip along the road, destroying very quickly convoys far exceeding their own value. Every feasible method of harassing constantly this section of the route is to be attempted, the necessary losses being faced.

8. In all the above paragraphs the urgency is extreme, because the enemy will grow continually stronger in the air than he is now, especially should his attack on Greece and Yugoslavia be successful, as may be apprehended. Admiral Cunningham should not, therefore, await the arrival of battleship reinforcements, nor should the use of the Glen ships be withheld for the sake of Rhodes.

9. It has been decided that Tobruk is to be defended with all possible strength. But [holding] Tobruk must not be regarded as a defensive operation, but rather as an invaluable bridgehead or sally-port on the communications of the enemy. It should be reinforced as may be necessary both with infantry and by armoured fighting vehicles, to enable active and continuous raiding of the enemy's flanks and rear. If part of the defences of the perimeter can be taken over by troops unprovided with transport, this should permit the organisation of a mobile force both for the fortress reserve and for striking at the enemy. It would be a great advantage should the enemy be drawn into anything like a siege of Tobruk and compelled to transport and feed the heavy artillery forces for that purpose.

10. It is above all necessary that General Wavell should regain unit ascendancy over the enemy and destroy his small raiding parties, instead of our being harassed and hunted by them. Enemy patrols must be attacked on every occasion, and our own patrols should be used with audacity. Small British parties in armoured cars, or mounted on motor-cycles, or, if occasion offers, infantry, should not hesitate to attack individual tanks with bombs and bombards, as is planned for the defence of Britain. It is important to engage the enemy even in small affairs in order to make him fire off his gun ammunition, of which the supply must be very difficult.

11. The use of the Royal Air Force against the enemy's communications, or concentrations of fighting vehicles, is sufficiently obvious not to require mention.

All this was easier to say than do.

* * *

I kept President Roosevelt fully informed.

Former Naval Person to President Roosevelt   16 April 41

I cannot tell what will happen in Greece, and we have never underrated the enormous power of the German military machine on the mainland of Europe.

I am personally not unduly anxious about the Libyan-Egyptian position. We estimate Germans have one colonial armoured division and perhaps the whole of one ordinary armoured division, comprising, say, 600 to 650 tanks, of which a good many have already been destroyed or have broken down. There are no German infantry yet in Cyrenaica, except the few battalions comprised in the German armoured divisions. Difficulties of supply of petrol, food, water, and ammunition must be severe, and we know from prisoners of the strain under which these audacious formations are working. We are naturally trying to bring our own armoured forces, which were largely refitting at the time of the attack, into action, and are reinforcing Egypt from all parts of the Middle East, where we have nearly half a million men. Tobruk I regard as an invaluable bridgehead or sally-port. We do not feel at all outmatched at present in the air, and are growing stronger constantly. The whole power of the Mediterranean Fleet, which is being strongly reinforced, will be used to cut the sea and coastal communications. There are, of course, Italian forces besides the Germans, and we believe the Germans are now sending, or trying to send, a third armoured division from Sicily.

The repulse of the German attacks on Tobruk on the 14th/15th seems to me important, as this small, fierce fight, in which the enemy lost prisoners, killed, and tanks, together with aircraft, out of all proportion to our losses, is the first time they have tasted defeat, and they are working on very small margins. Meanwhile our efforts to turn off the tap have met with a noteworthy success in the Central Mediterranean. Four destroyers from Malta in the early hours of this morning, sixteenth, caught a German-Italian convoy of five large ships loaded with ammunition and mechanical transport and escorted by three Italian destroyers. The whole convoy and all its escort were sunk. We lost one destroyer in the fight. We are keeping the strength of our forces secret for the present.

* * *

The beating-in of our Desert flank while we were full-spread in the Greek adventure was, however, a disaster of the first magnitude. I was for some time completely mystified about its cause, and as soon as there was a momentary lull I felt bound to ask General Wavell for some explanation of what had happened. It was not till April 24 that I burdened him with this request.

We still await news of the actions at Agheila and Mechili which resulted in the loss of the 3d Armoured Brigade and the best part of a motorised cavalry brigade. Evidently there was a severe defeat, and it is essential to our comprehension of your difficulties, as well as of our own, that we should know broadly what happened, and why. Were the troops outnumbered, outmanoeuvred, or outfought, or was there some mistake, as is alleged, about premature destruction of petrol store? Surely the reports of the survivors should have made it possible to give us a coherent story of this key action. I cannot help you if you do not tell me. . . .

Wavell replied on the twenty-fifth. He pointed out that as practically all the senior officers concerned were missing and could give no account of their actions or motives care must be taken not to prejudice them unfairly. Characteristically he took the responsibility upon himself. His summary followed the same day. In this he said that he had been aware that the headquarters of the 2d Armoured Division and 3d Armoured Brigade would take some time to become skilful in desert conditions and desert warfare. He had hoped that they would have a period of minor skirmishing on the frontier for at least a month or so before a serious attack developed, and that this would give them time to adapt themselves. Actually the attack took place before they had settled down, and was launched at least a fortnight before his Staff had calculated on a time and space basis that it was possible, but in approximately the strength he had anticipated. He had expected a limited advance to Agedabia, and captured documents and prisoners' statements had since confirmed that this was the enemy's intention. The subsequent exploitation by the enemy of his initial success, which, it is now known, came as a complete surprise to him,[2] was made possible only through the early and unfortunate disappearance of the 3d Armoured Brigade as a fighting force. There was complete evidence to prove that the enemy's advance from Agedabia was hastily improvised in eight small columns consisting of both German and Italian units, several of which outran their own maintenance and had to be supplied by aircraft.

Our 3d Armoured Brigade was an improvised organisation containing one regiment of cruiser tanks in poor mechanical

[2] That Rommel's early attack, with its frightful consequences, was as great a surprise to his own superiors as to us is explained by Desmond Young in his book *Rommel*.

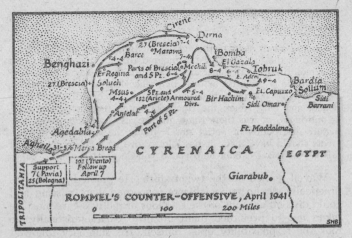

ROMMEL'S COUNTER-OFFENSIVE, April 1941

condition, one regiment of light tanks, and one regiment armed
with captured Italian medium tanks. In view of the state of the
armoured fighting vehicles at the end of the Cyrenaican campaign, it was the best he could produce if any armoured force
was to accompany the troops to Greece. If it had been at full
strength and had had more time to settle down as a fighting
formation, it should have been capable of dealing with the
opposition expected.

I did not become aware till just before the German attack of the
bad mechanical state of the cruiser regiment, on which we chiefly
relied. A proportion of these tanks broke down before reaching
the front, and many others became casualties from mechanical
defects during the early fighting. The same seems to have occurred
with the other cruiser regiment of the 2d Armoured Division,
which went to Greece. Our light tank was powerless against German tanks, which were all armed with guns. Regiment armed with
[captured] Italian tanks had not had time to get accustomed to
them.

Instructions to armoured division were to withdraw gradually
if attacked by superior strength, so as to maintain force in being
until difficulties of supply weakened enemy and gave opportunity
for counter-stroke. These were my instructions.

As matters turned out, this was mistaken policy. Immediate
counter-stroke would at least have inflicted serious losses on enemy
and delayed him considerably. It might have stopped him altogether. As it was, 3d Armoured Brigade practically melted away
from mechanical and administrative breakdowns during the retreat,
without much fighting, while the unpractised headquarters of the

2d Armoured Division seems to have lost control. This was partly due to inexperience of signal personnel. . . .

When I visited the front after the first day's action, I felt need of a commander experienced in desert warfare, and telegraphed for O'Connor to come and assist Neame. Both these generals were captured during the withdrawal by patrol from the enemy column which penetrated to Derna.

Such is the outline of disastrous episode, for which main responsibility is mine. Obviously mistakes were made in the handling of the headquarters 2d Armoured Division and 3d Armoured Brigade during the withdrawal, but I hope that judgment on this will be reserved until those mainly concerned can give full account and reasons for actions. Their difficulties were considerable.

Fighting spirit of troops even in retreat and disorganisation seems to have been excellent, and there were many instances of cool and determined action.

I replied:

Prime Minister to General Wavell   28 April 41

Thank you very much for your general outline of what occurred on the western frontier. We seem to have had rather bad luck. I expect we shall get this back later. Every good wish.

12

The Greek Campaign

Naval Victory off Matapan, March 28—Our Expedition to Greece —Disappointing News from General Papagos—The R.A.F. Outnumbered—The Germans Attack—Shattering Blow at the Piraeus, April 6—Yugoslavia Overrun—And Capitulates—Danger to Our Left Flank—General Papagos Suggests Evacuation—The Retreat to Thermopylae—My Telegram to Wavell of April 17—Suicide of the Greek Prime Minister—My Directive of April 18—The Enemy Kept at Bay—Hope of a Stand at Thermopylae—Decision to Evacuate, April 21—Final Greek Surrender, April 24— Namsos Over Again—Disaster at Nauplion—Achievement of the Royal Navy—Four-Fifths of Our Forces Rescued—Greek Martial Honour Undimmed—President Roosevelt's Gracious Appreciation —My Reply to Him of May 4—My Broadcast, May 3.

TOWARDS THE END of March it was evident that a major movement of the Italian Fleet, probably towards the Aegean, was impending. Admiral Cunningham decided temporarily to move our convoys out of the way, and himself left Alexandria after dark on March 27 in the *Warspite* with the *Valiant* and *Barham*, the carrier *Formidable*, and nine destroyers. Light forces, comprising four cruisers and four destroyers, under Vice-Admiral Pridham-Wippell, then at Crete, were ordered to join the Commander-in-Chief next day south of the island. At dawn on the twenty-eighth an aircraft from the *Formidable* reported four enemy cruisers and six destroyers on a southeasterly course. At 7.45 A.M. these same ships were in sight from the cruiser flagship, *Orion*. The Italian force included three eight-inch-gun cruisers, whereas all the British were six-inch-gun ships. But after half an hour's inconclusive action the enemy retired, and the British cruisers turned in pursuit. Two hours later the *Orion* sighted an enemy battleship

184

—the *Vittorio Veneto*—which opened fire on her at a range of sixteen miles. Once more the rôles changed, and the *Orion* and her cruisers again retired towards the British battle fleet, then approaching at full speed and about seventy miles away. An air striking force launched by the *Formidable* now arrived on the scene and attacked the Italian battleship, which at once withdrew to the northwest.

Meanwhile our air patrols sighted another enemy force of five cruisers and five destroyers to the northward about a hundred miles from the advancing British fleet. After further air attacks from the *Formidable*, and also from shore bases in Greece and Crete, it became clear that the *Vittorio Veneto* was damaged and could not make more than fifteen knots. In the evening a third air attack from the *Formidable* found all the enemy ships protecting the injured battleship with their A.A. batteries. Our planes did not seek to penetrate the barrage, but hit the heavy cruiser *Pola*, which was seen to haul out of line and stop. As darkness fell, Admiral Cunningham decided to make a destroyer attack, and also to accept the uncertainties of a night action with his battle fleet, in the hope of destroying the crippled battleship and cruiser before they could gain the cover of their own shore-based aircraft. On the way in the darkness he surprised two Italian cruisers, the eight-inch-gun *Fiume* and *Zara*, which were going to the *Pola's* aid. At close range the *Fiume* was immediately overwhelmed and sunk by fifteen-inch broadsides from the *Warspite* and *Valiant*. The *Zara*, engaged by all three battleships, was soon reduced to a blazing wreck.

Admiral Cunningham then withdrew the fleet to avoid mistaking friends for foes, and left his destroyers to deal with the damaged ship and with the two destroyers which had been with her. They also found and sank the crippled *Pola*. In this fortunate night encounter, with all its chances, the British fleet suffered no loss of any kind. In the morning, as our aircraft could not find the *Vittorio Veneto*, our fleet returned to Alexandria. This timely and welcome victory off Cape Matapan disposed of all challenge to British naval mastery in the Eastern Mediterranean at this critical time.

*   *   *

The expedition to Greece, in its order of embarkation, comprised the British 1st Armoured Brigade, the New Zealand Division, and the 6th Australian Division. These were all fully equipped at the expense of other formations in the Middle

East. They were to be followed by the Polish Brigade and the
7th Australian Division. The movement began on March 5.
The plan was to hold the Aliakhmon line, which ran from the
mouth of the river of that name through Veria and Edessa to
the Yugoslav frontier. Our forces were to join the Greek forces
deployed on this front, namely, the 12th and 20th Greek Divisions, each of six battalions and three or four batteries, the
19th (Motorised) Division, weak in numbers and training,
and about six battalions from Thrace. This army, nominally the
equivalent of seven divisions, was to come under the command of General Wilson.

The Greek troops were far less than the five good divisions
General Papagos had originally promised.[1] The great majority
of the Greek Army, about fifteen divisions, was in Albania,
facing Berat and Valona, which they had not been able to capture. They repulsed an Italian offensive launched on March 9.
The rest of the Greek Army, three divisions and frontier defence troops, was in Macedonia, whence Papagos declined to
withdraw them, and where, after four days' fighting, when the
Germans attacked, they ceased to be a military force. The
19th Greek (Motorised) Division, which joined them, was also
destroyed or dispersed.

Our air force in Greece in March numbered only seven
squadrons (eighty operational aircraft), and was badly handicapped by the scarcity of landing grounds and inadequate signal communications. Although some small reinforcements were
sent in April, the R.A.F. were overwhelmingly outnumbered
by the enemy. Two of our squadrons fought on the Albanian
front. The remaining five, supported by two Wellington squadrons from Egypt for night operations, had to meet all other
needs. They were matched against a German air strength of
over eight hundred operational aircraft.

The attack on Southern Yugoslavia and Greece was entrusted to the German Twelfth Army, of fifteen divisions, of
which four were armoured. Of these, five divisions, including
three armoured, took part in the southward drive towards
Athens. The weakness of the Aliakhmon position lay on its
left flank, which could be turned by a German advance
through Southern Yugoslavia. There had been little contact
with the Yugoslav General Staff, whose plan of defence and
degree of preparedness were not known to the Greeks or our-

---

[1] Papagos has since claimed that his first agreement to the holding of the
Aliakhmon line was contingent on a clarification of the situation with the Government of Yugoslavia, which never was reached.

selves. It was hoped, however, that in the difficult country which the enemy would have to cross the Yugoslavs would at least be able to impose considerable delay on them. This hope was to prove ill-founded. General Papagos did not consider that withdrawal from Albania to meet such a turning movement was a feasible operation. Not only would it severely affect morale, but the Greek Army was so ill-equipped with transport and communications were so bad that a general withdrawal in the face of the enemy was impossible. He had certainly left the decision till too late. It was in these circumstances that our 1st Armoured Brigade reached the forward area on March 27, where it was joined a few days later by the New Zealand Division.

*   *   *

In the early morning of April 6, German armies invaded both Greece and Yugoslavia. Intensive air attacks were at the same time launched on the Pireaus, where our expeditionary convoys were discharging. That night the port was almost completely wrecked by the blowing-up of the British ship *Clan Fraser* alongside the quay with two hundred tons of T.N.T. on board. Here was a misfortune which made it necessary to divert supplies to other and minor ports. This attack alone cost us and the Greeks eleven ships, aggregating forty-three thousand tons.

Henceforward the maintenance of the Allied armies by sea continued against an increasing scale of air attack, to which no effective counter could be made. The key to the problem at sea was to overcome the enemy's air bases in Rhodes, but no adequate forces were available for such a task, and meanwhile heavy shipping losses were certain. It was fortunate that the recent Battle of Matapan had, as Admiral Cunningham stated in his dispatch, taught the Italian Fleet a lesson which kept them out of action for the rest of the year. Their active intervention during this period would have made the Navy's task in Greece impossible.

Simultaneously with the ferocious bombardment of Belgrade the converging German armies already poised on the frontiers invaded Yugoslavia from several directions. The Yugoslav General Staff did not attempt to strike their one deadly blow at the Italian rear. They conceived themselves bound not to abandon Croatia and Slovenia, and were therefore forced to attempt the defence of the whole frontier line. The four Yugoslav army corps in the north were rapidly and irresistibly bent inward by the German armoured columns, supported by Hungarian troops which crossed the Danube and by German and Italian forces advancing towards Zagreb. The main Yugoslav forces were thus driven in confusion southward, and on April 13 German troops entered Belgrade. Meanwhile General List's Twelfth German Army, assembled in Bulgaria, had swung into Serbia and Macedonia. They had entered Monastir and Yannina on the tenth, and thus prevented any contact between the Yugoslavs and Greeks and broken up the Yugoslav forces in the south.

*   *   *

Confronted by the collapse of Yugoslav resistance, Mr. Campbell, the British Minister in Belgrade, had left the capital with its garrison. He now sought instructions, which I sent him as follows:

Prime Minister to British Minister in Yugoslavia   13 April 41

It will not be possible at any time to send British surface warships, or British or American merchant ships or transports, up the Adriatic north of Valona. The reason for this is the air, which did not exist effectively in the last war. The ships would only be sunk, and that would help no one. All the aircraft we can allot to the Yugoslav theatre is already at the service of the Yugoslav General Staff through Air Marshal D'Albianc. There are no more at present. You must remember Yugoslavs have given us no chance to help them and refused to make a common plan, but there is no use in recriminations, and you must use your own judgment how much of this bad news you impart to them.

2. We do not see why the King or Government should leave the country, which is vast, mountainous, and full of armed men. German tanks can no doubt move along the roads and tracks, but to conquer the Serbian armies they must bring up infantry. Then will be the chance to kill them. Surely the young King and the Ministers should play their part in this. However, if at any time the King and a few personal attendants are forced to leave the country and no aeroplanes can be provided, a British submarine could be sent to Kotor or some other neighbouring place.

3. Apart from the successful defence of mountain regions, the only way in which any portion of the Serbian Army can get in touch with our supplies by land is through establishing contact with Greeks in Albania and through Monastir. They could then share in the defence of Greece and in the common pool of supplies, and if all fails every effort will be made to evacuate as many fighting men as possible to islands or to Egypt.

4. You should continue to do your utmost to uphold the fighting spirit of the Yugoslav Government and Army, reminding them how the war in Serbia ebbed and flowed back and forth last time.

But the days of the Yugoslav guerrillas were still to come. On April 17 Yugoslavia capitulated.[2]

*   *   *

This sudden collapse destroyed the main hope of the Greeks. It was another example of "One at a time." We had done our utmost to procure concerted action, but through no fault of ours we had failed. A grim prospect now gaped upon us all.

At the moment of the German advance into Greece the 1st British Armoured Brigade was forward on the river Vardar. The New Zealand Division lay on the river Aliakhmon. On their left were the 12th and 20th Greek Divisions. The leading troops of the 6th Australian Division were also arriving. By April 8 it was clear that Yugoslav resistance in the south was breaking down and that the left flank of the Aliakhmon position would shortly be threatened. To meet this an Australian brigade group, later joined by the 1st Armoured Brigade, was posted to block the approach from Monastir. The enemy advance was delayed by demolitions and some effective bombing by the Royal Air Force, but on April 10 the attack on our flank guard began. It was arrested during two days of stiff fighting in severe weather.

Farther west there was only one Greek cavalry division keeping touch with the forces in Albania, and General Wilson decided that his hard-pressed left flank must be pulled back on Kozani and Gravena. This move was completed on April 13, but in the process the 12th and 20th Greek Divisions began to disintegrate, and could no longer play an effective part. Henceforward our Expeditionary Force was alone. By April 14 the New Zealand Division had also withdrawn to guard the important mountain pass north of Mount Olympus. One of its brigades was covering the main road to Larissa. The enemy made strong attacks, which were held. But Wilson, still menaced upon his left flank, decided to withdraw to Ther-

---

[2] King Peter was evacuated from Kotor in an R.A.F. Sunderland flying-boat. Mr. Ronald Campbell had made his way to the Adriatic coast. On April 18 he and his staff fell into Italian hands. An attempt was made to rescue him and his staff, and a week later the British submarine *Regent* was sent to the Bay of Kotor. She found the Italians in possession. An Italian officer was taken on board as a hostage, while an officer from the submarine parleyed with the Italians for the release of the British diplomatic party. Meanwhile three Stukas arrived and bombed and machine-gunned the *Regent*, wounding the captain and members of the crew. She had to put to sea under fire from the shore batteries and escape through the minefields. The British diplomats and staff were moved to Italy and interned. In June they were repatriated to England in accordance with international usage after negotiations with the Italian Government.

mopylae. He put this to Papagos, who approved, and who himself at this stage suggested British evacuation from Greece.

Prime Minister to General Wilson, Athens   13 April 41

I am glad to see the movement of 20th Greek and Cavalry Division to close the gap between the Greek western army and your army. It is glaringly obvious that a German advance southward through this gap will not only turn your Aliakhmon position, but far more decisively round up the whole of the Greek Army in Albania. It is impossible for me to understand why the Greek western army does not make sure of its retreat into Greece. The Chief of the Imperial General Staff states that these points have been put vainly time after time. All good wishes to you in this memorable hour.

I am also glad to hear that King is not leaving Greece at present. He has a great opportunity of leaving a name in history. If, however, he or any part of the Greek Army is forced to leave Greece every facility will be afforded them in Cyprus, and we will do our best to carry them there. The garrisoning of Crete by a strong Greek force would also be highly beneficial, observing that Crete can be fed by sea.

The next few days were decisive. Wavell telegraphed on the sixteenth that General Wilson had had a conversation with Papagos, who described the Greek Army as being severely pressed and getting into administrative difficulties owing to air action. He agreed to a withdrawal to the Thermopylae position. The first moves were already made. Papagos also repeated his suggestion that we should re-embark the British troops and spare Greece from devastation. Wilson considered that this course should commence with the occupation of the new position and that evacuation should be arranged forthwith. Wavell's instructions to Wilson were to continue the fighting in co-operation with the Greeks so long as they were able to resist, but authorised any further withdrawal judged necessary. Orders had been given for all ships on the way to Greece to be turned back, for no more ships to be loaded, and for those already loading or loaded to be emptied. He presumed that a formal request to this effect from the Greek Government should be obtained before our actual re-embarkation. He assumed Crete would be held.

To this grave but not unexpected news I replied at once.

Prime Minister to General Wavell   17 April 41

We have no news from you of what has happened on Imperial front in Greece.

2. We cannot remain in Greece against wish of Greek Com-

mander-in-Chief, and thus expose country to devastation. Wilson or Palairet should obtain endorsement by Greek Government of Papagos's request. Consequent upon this assent, evacuation should proceed, without, however, prejudicing any withdrawal to Thermopylae position in co-operation with the Greek Army. You will naturally try to save as much material as possible.

3. Crete must be held in force, and you should provide for this in the redistribution of your forces. It is important that strong elements of Greek Army should establish themselves in Crete, together with King and Government. We shall aid and maintain defence of Crete to the utmost.

On the seventeenth General Wilson motored from Thebes to the palace at Tatoi, and there met the King, General Papagos, and our Ambassador. It was accepted that withdrawal to the Thermopylae line had been the only possible plan. General Wilson was confident that he could hold that line for a while. The main discussion was the method and order of evacuation. The Greek Government would not leave for at least another week.

The Greek Prime Minister, M. Korysis, has already been mentioned. He had been chosen to fill the gap when Metaxas died. He had no claim to public office except a blameless private life and clear, resolute convictions. He could not survive the ruin, as it seemed, of his country or bear longer his own responsibilities. Like M. Teleki in Hungary, he resolved to pay the forfeit of his life. On the eighteenth he committed suicide. His memory should be respected.

* * *

It was necessary in this convulsive scene to try to assign proportions and priorities as far as possible. Air Marshal Longmore appealed for guidance in the use of his overstrained air power. I therefore sent a directive to the Chiefs of Staff, which they endorsed and telegraphed textually to the Middle East commanders.

Chiefs of Staff to Commanders-in-Chief   18 April 41

Following directive has been issued by the P.M. and Minister of Defence:

It is not possible to lay down precise sequence and priority between interests none of which can be wholly ignored, but the following may be a guide. The extrication of New Zealand, Australian, and British troops from Greece affects the whole Empire.

2. It ought to be possible to arrange shipping in and out of Tobruk either before or after the evacuation crisis, observing that Tobruk has two months' supplies.

3. You must divide between protecting evacuation and sustaining battle in Libya. But if these clash, which may not be avoidable, emphasis must be given to victory in Libya.

4. Don't worry about Iraq for the present. It looks to be going smoothly.

5. Crete will at first only be a receptacle of whatever can get there from Greece. Its fuller defence must be organised later. In the meanwhile all forces there must protect themselves from air bombing by dispersion and use their bayonets against parachutists or airborne intruders if any.

6. Subject to the above general remarks, victory in Libya counts first, evacuation of troops from Greece second. Tobruk shipping, unless indispensable to victory, must be fitted in as convenient. Iraq can be ignored and Crete be worked up later.

*   *   *

The retreat to Thermopylae was a difficult manoeuvre, since, while the enemy was kept at bay in the Tempe Gorge, the Olympus Pass, and at other points, our whole force had to pass through the bottleneck of Larissa. Wilson expected the most dangerous threat on his western flank, and placed a brigade group at Kalabaka to deal with it. But the crisis came on the east, at the Tempe Gorge and the Olympus Pass. The pass was sternly defended for the necessary three days by the 5th New Zealand Brigade. The Tempe Gorge was even more critical, as it was for the Germans the shortest approach to Larissa. It was defended at first only by the 21st New Zealand battalion, later reinforced by an Australian brigade. This was held for the three days needed for all our troops to pass through the Larissa bottleneck.

Until April 13 bad weather had prevented the full use of the enemy's tenfold superiority in the air, but on the fifteenth a heavy dawn attack on the airfield near Larissa destroyed many of our remaining aircraft. The rest were ordered back to Athens, there being no intermediate landing grounds. The weather was again bad on the sixteenth and seventeenth, but then it cleared, and the German Air Force came out in strength and harassed continually the stream of troops making for Thermopylae. They were not unresisted, for in a raid near Athens twenty-two of the enemy machines were brought down for a loss of five Hurricanes.

These stubborn and skilful rear-guard actions checked the impetuous German advance at all points, inflicting severe losses. By April 20 the occupation of the Thermopylae position was complete. Frontally it was strong, but with the need to guard the coast road, to watch for possible intrusion from

Euboea, and above all to prevent a move on Delphi, our forces
were strained. But the Germans made slow progress and the
position was never severely tested. On this same day the Greek
armies on the Albania front surrendered.

I did not, however, give up hope of a final stand at Thermopylae. The intervening ages fell away. Why not one more
undying feat of arms?

Prime Minister to Foreign Secretary   20 April 41

I am increasingly of the opinion that if the generals on the spot
think they can hold on in the Thermopylae position for a fortnight
or three weeks, and can keep the Greek Army fighting, or enough
of it, we should certainly support them, if the Dominions will
agree. I do not believe the difficulty of evacuation will increase if
the enemy suffers heavy losses. On the other hand, every day the
German Air Force is detained in Greece enables the Libyan situation to be stabilised, and may enable us to bring in the extra tanks
[to Tobruk]. If this is accomplished safely and the Tobruk position holds, we might even feel strong enough to reinforce from
Egypt. I am most reluctant to see us quit, and if the troops were
British only and the matter could be decided on military grounds
alone, I would urge Wilson to fight if he thought it possible. Anyhow, before we commit ourselves to evacuation the case must be
put squarely to the Dominions after tomorrow's Cabinet. Of course,
I do not know the conditions in which our retreating forces will
reach the new key position.

On the twenty-first General Wavell asked the King about
the state of the Greek Army and whether it could give immediate and effective aid to the left flank of the Thermopylae
position. His Majesty said that time rendered it impossible for
any organised Greek force to support the British left flank
before the enemy could attack. General Wavell replied that in
that case he felt that it was his duty to take immediate steps
for re-embarkation of such portion of his army as he could
extricate. The King entirely agreed, and seemed to have expected this. He spoke with deep regret of having been the
means of placing the British forces in such a position. General
Wavell then impressed on His Majesty the need for absolute
secrecy and for all measures to be taken that would make the
re-embarkation possible—for instance, that order should be preserved in Athens and that the departure of the King and Government for Crete should be delayed as long as possible; also
that the Greek army in Epirus should stand firm and prevent
any chance of an enemy advance from the west along the
north shores of the Gulf of Corinth. The King promised what

help he could. But all was vain. The final surrender of Greece to overwhelming German might was made on April 24.

*   *   *

We were now confronted with another of those evacuations by sea which we had endured in 1940. The organised withdrawals of over fifty thousand men from Greece under the conditions prevailing might well have seemed an almost hopeless task. It was, however, accomplished by the Royal Navy under the direction of Vice-Admiral Pridham-Wippell afloat and Rear-Admiral Baillie-Grohman with Army Headquarters ashore. At Dunkirk on the whole we had air mastery. In Greece the Germans were in complete and undisputed control of the air and could maintain an almost continuous attack on the ports and on the retreating army. It was obvious that embarkation could only take place by night, and, moreover, that troops must avoid being seen near the beaches in daylight. This was Namsos over again, and on ten times the scale.

Admiral Cunningham threw nearly the whole of his light forces, including six cruisers and nineteen destroyers, into the task. Working from the small ports and beaches in Southern Greece, these ships, together with eleven transports and assault ships and many smaller craft, began the work of rescue on the night of April 24.

For five successive nights the work continued. On the twenty-sixth the enemy captured the vital bridge over the Corinth Canal by parachute attack, and thereafter German troops poured into the Peloponnese, harrying our hard-pressed soldiers as they strove to reach the southern beaches. During the nights of the twenty-fourth and twenty-fifth 17,000 men were brought out, with the loss of two transports. On the following night about 19,500 were got away from five embarkation points. At Nauplion there was disaster. The transport *Slamat* in a gallant but misguided effort to embark the maximum stayed too long in the anchorage. Soon after dawn, when clearing the land, she was attacked and sunk by dive-bombers. The destroyers *Diamond* and *Wryneck*, who rescued most of the seven hundred men on board, were both in turn sunk by air attack a few hours later. There were only fifty survivors from all three ships.

On the twenty-eighth and twenty-ninth efforts were made by two cruisers and six destroyers to rescue 8000 troops and 1400 Yugoslav refugees from the beaches near Kalamata. A destroyer sent on ahead to arrange the embarkation found the

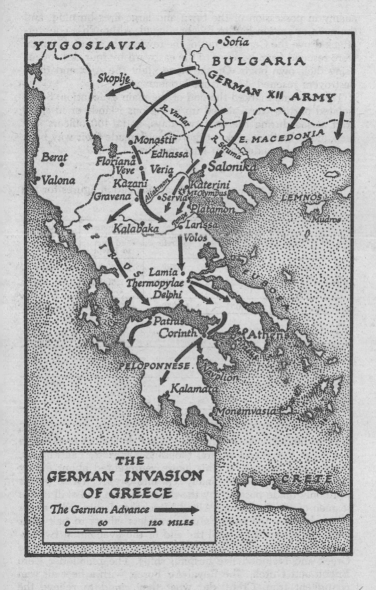

THE
GERMAN INVASION
OF GREECE

The German Advance ⟶

0   60   120 MILES

enemy in possession of the town and large fires burning, and the main operation had to be abandoned. Although a counter-attack drove the Germans out of the town, only about 450 men were rescued from beaches to the eastward by four destroyers, using their own boats. On the same night the *Ajax* and three destroyers rescued 4300 from Monemvasia.

These events marked the end of the main evacuation. Small isolated parties were picked up in various islands or in small craft at sea during the next two days, and 1400 officers and men, aided by the Greeks at mortal peril, made their way back to Egypt independently in later months.

*   *   *

The following table gives the final evacuation figures for the Army:

Forces	In Country at Time of Attack	Evacuated to Crete	Evacuated to Crete and later to Egypt	Direct to Egypt (Including Wounded)
United Kingdom troops	19,206	5,299	3,200	4,101
Australian	17,125	6,451	2,500	5,206
New Zealand	16,720	7,100	1,300	6,054
Totals	53,051	18,850	7,000	15,361

The losses were:

Forces	Losses	Percentage of Total Losses
United Kingdom troops	6,606	55.8
Australian	2,968	25.1
New Zealand	2,266	19.1
Totals	11,840	100

In all 50,662 were safely brought out, including men of the Royal Air Force and several thousand Cypriots, Palestinians, Greeks, and Yugoslavs. This figure represented about eighty per cent of the forces originally sent into Greece. These results were only made possible by the determination and skill of the seamen of the Royal and Allied Merchant Navies, who never faltered under the enemy's most ruthless efforts to halt their work. From April 21 until the end of the evacuation twenty-six ships were lost by air attack. Twenty-one of these were Greek and included five hospital ships. The remainder were British and Dutch. The Royal Air Force, with a fleet air arm contingent from Crete, did what they could to relieve the

situation, but they were overwhelmed by numbers. Nevertheless, from November onward the few squadrons sent to Greece
had done fine service. They inflicted on the enemy confirmed
losses of 231 planes and had dropped 500 tons of bombs. Their
own losses of 209 machines, of which 72 were in combat, were
severe, their record exemplary.

The small but efficient Greek Navy now passed under British control. A cruiser, six modern destroyers, and four submarines escaped to Alexandria, where they arrived on April 25.
Thereafter the Greek Navy was represented with distinction
in many of our operations in the Mediterranean.

*   *   *

If in telling this tale of tragedy the impression is given that
the Imperial and British forces received no effective military
assistance from their Greek allies, it must be remembered that
these three weeks of April fighting at desperate odds were for
the Greeks the culmination of the hard five months' struggle
against Italy in which they had expended almost the whole
life-strength of their country. Attacked in October without
warning by at least twice their numbers, they had first repulsed
the invaders and then in counter-attack had beaten them back
forty miles into Albania. Throughout the bitter winter in the
mountains they had been at close grips with a more numerous
and better-equipped foe. The Greek Army of the Northwest
had neither the transport nor the roads for a rapid manoeuvre
to meet at the last moment the new overpowering German attack cutting in behind its flank and rear. Its strength had
already been strained almost to the limit in a long and gallant
defence of the homeland.

There were no recriminations. The friendliness and aid
which the Greeks had so faithfully shown to our troops endured nobly to the end. The people of Athens and at other
points of evacuation seemed more concerned for the safety of
their would-be rescuers than with their own fate. Greek martial
honour stands undimmed.

*   *   *

I have now set forth in narrative the outstanding facts of
our adventure in Greece. After things are over, it is easy to
choose the fine mental and moral positions which one should
adopt. In this account I have recorded events as they occurred
and action as it was taken. Later on these can be judged in the
glare of consequences; and finally, when our lives have faded,

History will pronounce its cool, detached, and shadowy verdict.

There is no doubt that the Mussolini-Hitler crime of overrunning Greece, and our effort to stand against tyranny and save what we could from its claws, appealed profoundly to the people of the United States, and above all to the great man who led them. I had at this moment a moving interchange of telegrams with the President.

. . . My thoughts [he said] in regard to the Eastern Mediterranean are: You have done not only heroic but very useful work in Greece, and the territorial loss is more than compensated for by the necessity for an enormous German concentration and resulting enormous German losses in men and material.

Having sent all men and equipment to Greece you could possibly spare, you have fought a wholly justified delaying action, and will continue to do so in other parts of the Eastern Mediterranean, including North Africa and the Near East. Furthermore, if additional withdrawals become necessary, they will all be a part of the plan which at this stage of the war shortens British lines, greatly extends the Axis lines, and compels the enemy to expend great quantities of men and equipment. I am satisfied that both here and in Britain public opinion is growing to realise that even if you have to withdraw farther in the Eastern Mediterranean, you will not allow any great *débâcle* or surrender, and that in the last analysis the naval control of the Indian Ocean and the Atlantic Ocean will in time win the war.

My reply may be thought less responsive than this generous message deserved. I felt myself held in such harsh duress by events and was also so conscious of the sentiment alive in the United States, that I sought to make claims on the future.

Former Naval Person to President Roosevelt   4 May 41

Your friendly message assures me that no temporary reverses, however heavy, can shake your resolution to support us until we gain the final victory. . . .

We must not be too sure that the consequences of the loss of Egypt and the Middle East would not be grave. It would seriously increase the hazards of the Atlantic and the Pacific, and could hardly fail to prolong the war, with all the suffering and military dangers that this would entail. We shall fight on whatever happens, but please remember that the attitude of Spain, Vichy, Turkey, and Japan may be finally determined by the outcome of the struggle in this theatre of war. I cannot take the view that the loss of Egypt and the Middle East would be a mere preliminary to the successful maintenance of a prolonged oceanic war. If all Europe, the greater part of Asia and Africa, became, either by conquest or agreement under duress, a part of the Axis system, a war maintained by the British Isles, United States, Canada, and Australasia against this mighty agglomeration would be a hard, long, and bleak proposition. Therefore, if you cannot take more advanced positions now, or very soon, the vast balances may be tilted heavily to our disadvantage. Mr. President, I am sure that you will not misunderstand me if I speak to you exactly what is in my mind. The one decisive counterweight I can see to balance the growing pessimism in Turkey, the Near East, and in Spain would be if United States were immediately to range herself with us as a belligerent Power. If this were possible I have little doubt that we could hold the situation in the Mediterranean until the weight of your munitions gained the day.

We are determined to fight to the last inch and ounce for Egypt, including its outposts of Tobruk and Crete. Very considerable risks are being run by us for that, and personally I think we shall win, in spite of the physical difficulties of reinforcing by tanks and air. But I adjure you, Mr. President, not to underrate the gravity of the consequences which may follow from a Middle-Eastern collapse. In this war every post is a winning-post, and how many more are we going to lose?

With regard to Vichy, we are more than willing that you should take the lead, and work out how to get the best from them by threats or favours. *You alone can forestall the Germans in Morocco.*[3] If they are once installed, it will not be necessary for them to go overland; they will soon get airborne troops to Dakar.

I shall await with deep anxiety the new broadcast which you contemplate. It may be the supreme turning-point.

Let me thank you for the splendid help in shipping and tankers which we owe to your action, and for all your generous and bold assistance to us and to the common cause.

*   *   *

In my broadcast the night before I had tried not only to express the feelings of the English-speaking world, but to state the dominant facts which ruled our fate.

While we naturally view with sorrow and anxiety much that is happening in Europe and in Africa, and may happen in Asia, we must not lose our sense of proportion and thus become discouraged or alarmed. When we face with a steady eye the difficulties which lie before us, we may derive new confidence from remembering those we have already overcome. Nothing that is happening now is comparable in gravity with the dangers through which we passed last year. Nothing that can happen in the East is comparable with what is happening in the West.

Last time I spoke to you I quoted the line of Longfellow which President Roosevelt had written out for me in his hand. I have

---

[3] My subsequent italics.—Author.

some other lines which are less well known but which seem apt and appropriate to our fortunes tonight, and I believe they will be so judged wherever the English language is spoken or the flag of freedom flies:

> For while the tired waves, vainly breaking,
>   Seem here no painful inch to gain,
> Far back, through creeks and inlets making,
>   Comes silent, flooding in, the main.
>
> And not by eastern windows only,
>   When daylight comes, comes in the light;
> In front the sun climbs slow, how slowly!
>   But westward, look, the land is bright.

13

Tripoli and "Tiger"

From Desert Sand to Salt Water—Admiral Cunningham's Anxieties—Our Need to Strike at Tripoli—The Hard Alternative to Bombardment—Drastic Proposal by the First Sea Lord—Admiral Cunningham's Reply—A Successful and Bloodless Operation, April 21—Admiral Cunningham's Strong View—Credit for All— My Explanations to Admiral Cunningham—The American Aid— Disquieting News from Wavell—My Minute of April 21—The Defence Committee Agree to Send Three Hundred Tanks Through the Mediterranean—A Severe Comment on Tobruk, April 22—Reinforcements for Rommel—Operation "Tiger" Arrives—A Brilliant Success—Tanks for Crete—My Wish to Repeat Operation "Tiger"—Wavell Does Not Press.

DISASTER on our Desert flank had produced the consequences in Africa which have been described. It also meant the failure to take Rhodes which impaired our communications with Greece. It severely injured that already hazardous enterprise, though this would have foundered by itself. We must now add to the tale of what happened in the desert sand the simultaneous events upon salt water. Anyone can see how great was the strain which the Greek expedition had put upon our Eastern Mediterranean Fleet. But this was only one of the demands made upon them at this chaotic time. As early as April 10, Admiral Cunningham felt himself seriously affected by the sudden leap forward of Rommel's triumphant armoured forces.

If [he warned us] the Germans can get sufficient forces across in the next month, they will probably gain control up to Mersa Matruh at least, and if they do this, it will be questionable if Alexandria will be usable for the Fleet against attack by fighter-escorted aircraft. The German prospects of achiev-

ing this are good unless Tripoli is destroyed. I do not think it
feasible to do this by bombardment. It is not only a question
of the risk to the battle fleet, but of lasting effects being sufficient to make it justifiable. I feel continuous air attack is
solution. . . . I consider, therefore, that it is essential that
long-range bombers should be flown out immediately to Egypt
for this work and that nothing should stand in way of this. It
may well be a matter of days, and the results will decide
whether we are going to be able to hold the Eastern Mediterranean. I would again emphasise the time factor, which is vital.

There could, alas, be no question of building up in Egypt
within a few weeks a long-range bomber force capable of having any appreciable effect on Tripoli. Bombardment from the
sea, besides being far more effective and economical in effort,
was the only practical measure within our power, and I felt
that the Fleet might perhaps make a vital contribution to the
defence of Egypt in this way, notwithstanding the heavy
strain it was then bearing in the Greek campaign.

*   *   *

The need to strike at Tripoli led to vehement discussion
between the Admiralty and Admiral Cunningham, in which
the First Sea Lord, strong in the consciousness of the American aid accorded by the President, confronted the Commander-in-Chief in the Mediterranean with a hard alternative
to risking his fleet by a bombardment in a most dangerous
area. The incident is unusual in our naval records.

Admiralty to Commander-in-Chief, Mediterranean   15 April 41

It is evident that drastic measures are necessary to stabilise the
position in the Middle East. After thorough investigation it is considered that air action alone against Tripoli will not sufficiently
interrupt the flow of reinforcements which are entering Libya
chiefly through that port.

It is essential, therefore, to do something at Tripoli which may
interrupt their communications drastically and for a considerable
time. We are of opinion that heavy and consistent mining of the
harbour and approaches would have a considerable effect, but we
cannot wait until this is proved. It is essential, therefore, to take
other measures at the earliest moment.

There are two alternatives: (*a*) bombardment of the harbour,
(*b*) attempting to block it.

Their Lordships are in agreement with you that the result of
bombardment is uncertain and could not be expected drastically
to reduce the rate of reinforcement even temporarily. It has been

decided, therefore, that an attempt must be made to carry out a combined blocking and bombardment, the latter being carried out by the blocking ships at point-blank range as they approach the harbour.

After carefully considering the types of ship which can be used, it has been decided that *Barham* and a "C" Class cruiser should be used for the purpose.

The use of *Barham* for this purpose will no doubt fill you with the deepest regret, but it is considered far preferable to sacrifice one ship entirely with the chance of achieving something really worth while than to get several ships damaged in bombardment the result of which might be most disappointing.

This order was intended to convince the gallant Cunningham of the scale of events as we saw them in Whitehall, and of the almost desperate risks that should be run at this crisis. Admiral Cunningham vehemently protested against the suggestion that he should sacrifice a first-class battleship like the *Barham*.

Commander-in-Chief Mediterranean to Admiralty   15 April 41

I fully realise the grave consideration which must have been given to the matter before their Lordships and H.M. Government came to the decision to make the sacrifice entailed by this operation, but I would submit that such a price is only justified if first of all success is reasonably assured, and, secondly, if, having been successful, the result will be efficacious. I do not consider either condition would be fulfilled. As regards success, it seems to me doubtful if there is one chance in ten of getting this large ship into the right position.

Even if we are successful, we shall have lost a first-class fighting unit whose passing is liable to give an inestimable fillip to Italian naval morale, and by this very effort shall give the enemy the measure of how desperate we consider Cyrenaican situation to be.

If operation fails or is only partially successful, these aspects will be intensified. We shall furthermore have to replace the ship by taking another unit away from the Battle of the Atlantic.

In return for all this at best we shall make the actual harbour unusable, but unloading will still be possible, and alternative French harbours are available.

Nor in these considerations have I taken into account the certain loss of nearly a thousand officers and men from the two ships, who will have to be sent recklessly into the operation, unaware of what they are in for, and whom I see no prospect of being able to bring away.[1]

Rather than send in *Barham* without support and with such

---

[1] A ship to be sacrificed as a blockship or a fireship requires, after being brought near the objective, only a skeleton crew.

slender chances of success, I would prefer to attack with the whole
battle fleet and to accept the risks.

For the above reasons I have seen fit to query their Lordships'
decision, and most earnestly request that reconsideration be given
in light of these remarks.

It was not without relief that we received the news that the
Fleet would bombard Tripoli, and the Admiralty hastened to
concur and share from a distance the burden of responsibility.
At daylight on April 21, Cunningham appeared off Tripoli
with the battleships *Warspite*, *Barham* and *Valiant*, the cruiser
Gloucester, and destroyers, and bombarded the town for forty
minutes. To the astonishment of all, complete surprise was
achieved; the coastal batteries did not reply for twenty minutes, nor was there any opposition from the air. Much damage
was done to shipping in the harbour, as well as to quays and
to port installations. Large fires were started in a fuel depot
and the buildings surrounding it. The British fleet withdrew
without loss. Not a ship was even hit.

Tripoli [reported Admiral Cunningham] was bombarded for 42
minutes at 5 A.M. today, Monday, at a range of between 14,000
and 11,000 yards. To my astonishment, surprise was achieved,
probably owing to the preoccupation of the German Air Force in
the other zones. . . . My remarks on the policy of this bombardment will follow in due course.

The Commander-in-Chief pursued this signal with another,
in which he expressed his feelings strongly.

C.-in-C. Mediterranean to Admiralty   23 April 41

We are finding our present commitments rather more than we
can deal with efficiently.

I wish to make it quite clear that I remain strongly opposed to
this policy of bombardment of Tripoli by Mediterranean Fleet.
We have got away with it once, but only because the German Air
Force were engaged elsewhere. Thus we achieved surprise. It has
taken the whole Mediterranean Fleet five days to accomplish what
a heavy flight squadron working from Egypt could probably carry
out in a few hours. The fleet has also run considerable, and in my
opinion unjustifiable, risks in this operation, which has been at
the expense of all other commitments, and at a time when these
commitments were most pressing. . . .

I cannot see how *Nelson* and *Rodney* can be spared [from the
Atlantic] to join Mediterranean Fleet.

To me it appears that the Air Ministry are trying to lay their
responsibilities on Navy's shoulders and are not helping us out
here on naval side of the war as they should.

In my opinion this story reflects credit upon both the high Admirals concerned, and illustrates for the benefit of future naval readers the extraordinary pressures under which we were all acting in this crisis. It may well be that the Admiralty, with my cordial agreement, forced their Commander-in-Chief to run an unnecessary risk; and the fact that no loss was sustained is no absolute proof that they were right on the merits. On the other hand, we at home alone could measure the proportion of world events, and final responsibility lay with us. While remaining wholly convinced of the vigour and correctness of the First Sea Lord's action, I thought it necessary to offer the Commander-in-Chief the fullest explanation, and a wider view of the war scene than was possible from Alexandria.

Prime Minister to Commander-in-Chief, Mediterranean
24 April 41

There can be no departure from the principle that it is the prime responsibility of the Mediterranean Fleet to sever all communication between Italy and Africa.

2. I am sorry that the haze caused by the aircraft attack hampered your firing at Tripoli. We ought to have foreseen this, but it is no use repining, and after all results were substantial and achieved without casualties in ships or men. Personally, I was not surprised at this immunity, and certainly the fact that the main batteries of the principal enemy base in Africa, although under German control, were at twenty minutes' notice shows that the enemy cannot be always ready everywhere at the same time. I suppose there is no doubt that the blocking plan would, in these circumstances, have come off.

3. About your air support: you should obtain accurate information, because no judgment can be formed without it. The Chief of the Air Staff tells me that the same weight of bombs as you fired of shells into Tripoli in 42 minutes, namely, 530 tons, might have been dropped: (*a*) by one Wellington squadron from Malta in 10½ weeks, or (*b*) by one Stirling squadron from Egypt in about 30 weeks. . . .

5. The main disposition of forces between the various theatres rests with the Defence Committee, over which I preside, and not with the Air Ministry, who execute our decisions. Ever since November I have tried by every method and every route to pump aircraft into the Middle East. Great risks have been run and sacrifices made, especially when two-thirds of one whole fighter squadron were drowned in trying to fly to Malta, and when *Furious* was taken off her Atlantic duties to make three voyages to Takoradi. I always try hard here to sustain you in every way and acclaim your repeated successes, and I earnestly hope you

will also believe that we at the centre try to make sound and bold decisions amid our many difficulties. . . .

7. You wonder how I could have suggested that *Nelson* and *Rodney* should be spared from the Atlantic to join the Mediterranean Fleet. I thought they were specially suitable because of their deck armour and the apprehensions entertained of the dive-bomber attacks. Whether they could be spared or not depends upon the situation in the Atlantic. About this, in view of your high position, I will now inform you. I have been for a long time in constant intimate communication with President Roosevelt. He has now begun to take over a great part of the patrolling west of the twenty-sixth meridian West. The whole American Atlantic Fleet, with numerous flying-boats, entered into action in the first phase of this plan at midnight of April 24. United States warships will cruise along our convoy routes, shadow—or, as they call it, "trail"—all raiders or U-boats observed, and broadcast their positions in plain language to the world at four-hourly intervals, or oftener if needed. It is desired that this shall not be announced suddenly, but become apparent as it develops. The matter is, therefore, confided to you in the highest secrecy. The easement and advantage of it to the Admiralty is enormous, and, of course, it may easily produce even more decisive events. Therefore, you do not need at this moment to be unduly concerned about the Atlantic, and can devote your resources, which we are increasing in so many ways, to the cutting-off of enemy communication with Africa, whether by Tripoli or Cyrenaica. On this depends the Battle of Egypt.

8. I have taken the pains to give you this full account out of my admiration for the successes you have achieved, your many cares, my sympathy for you in the many risks your fleet has to run, and because of the commanding importance of the duty you have to discharge.

*   *   *

My supreme object continued to be a victory in the Western Desert to destroy Rommel's army before he became too strong and before the dreaded new armoured division reached him in full strength. This would at any rate save our position in Egypt from the wreck. I must, therefore, recount an episode for which I took a more direct measure of responsibility than usual. The disaster which Wavell had sustained on his Desert flank had stripped him almost entirely of his armour. On Sunday, April 20, I was spending the week-end at Ditchley and working in bed, when I received a telegram from General Wavell to the C.I.G.S. which disclosed his plight in all its gravity.

Though the situation in Cyrenaica has improved [he said], the future outlook will cause anxiety for some time, owing to my weakness in tanks, especially cruiser tanks. As you realise, this desert warfare depends very largely upon armoured strength. . . . The enemy has probably at least a hundred and fifty tanks, of which about half are medium, in the fighting line in Cyrenaica. Most of these are now in the Bardia-Sollum area, and the enemy may be preparing further forward movements, if he can arrange supply. I have one weak unit in Tobruk of mixed cruiser, infantry, and light tanks, and in the Matruh area one squadron of cruisers. . . . The best I can hope for by the end of the month is one cruiser regiment less one squadron, and one infantry tank regiment less one squadron, to assist defence of Matruh. During May I may get another thirty or forty cruisers out of the workshops to make another weak unit, and some infantry tanks which will probably be required for the close defence of Alexandria against possible raids. I cannot count on getting any tanks back from Greece, and no more are in sight for some time.

He added the following:

Stop press. I have just received disquieting intelligence. I was expecting another German colonial division, which disembarked at Tripoli early this month, to appear in the fighting line about the end of the month. Certain units have already been identified. I have just been informed that latest evidence indicates this is not a colonial but an *armoured* division. If so, the situation is indeed serious, since an armoured division contains over 400 tanks,[2] of which 138 are medium. If the enemy can arrange supply, it will take a lot of stopping. I will cable again when I have digested this unwelcome news.

In a separate telegram of the same date General Wavell described his tank position in detail.

It will be seen [he said] that there are only two regiments of cruiser tanks in sight for Egypt by the end of May, and no reserves to replace casualties, *whereas there are now in Egypt, trained, an excellent personnel for six tank regiments.* I consider the provision of cruiser tanks vital, in addition to infantry tanks, which lack speed and radius of action for desert operations. C.I.G.S., please give your personal assistance.

On reading these alarming messages I resolved not to be governed any longer by the Admiralty reluctance, but to send a convoy through the Mediterranean direct to Alexandria carrying all the tanks which General Wavell needed. We had a convoy containing large armoured reinforcements starting immediately round the Cape. I decided that the fast tank-carrying ships in this convoy should turn off at Gibraltar and take the short cut, thus saving nearly forty days. General

[2] This proved an excessive estimate.

Ismay, who was staying near by, came over at noon to see me. I prepared the following personal minute to him for the Chiefs of Staff. I asked him to go to London with it at once and make it clear that I attached supreme importance to this step being taken.

Prime Minister to General Ismay, for Chiefs of Staff   20 April 41

See General Wavell's latest telegrams. The fate of the war in the Middle East, the loss of the Suez Canal, the frustration or confusion of the enormous forces we have built up in Egypt, the closing of all prospects of American co-operation through the Red Sea—all may turn on a few hundred armoured vehicles. They must if possible be carried there at all costs.

2. I will preside at noon tomorrow (Monday), the twenty-first, at a meeting of C.O.S. and Service Ministers, and any necessary action or collection of information must proceed forthwith.

3. The only way in which this great purpose can be achieved is by sending the fast mechanical transport ships of the fast section of [Convoy] W.S. 7 *through the Mediterranean.* General Wavell's telegram shows that machines, not men, are needed. The risk of losing the vehicles, or part of them, must be accepted. Even if half got through, the situation would be restored. The five M.T. ships carry 250 tanks, all but fourteen of which are "I" tanks. Every endeavour should be made to increase the numbers of cruiser tanks in this consignment. I am told twenty more can be loaded at a delay of perhaps twenty-four hours—that is, M.T. convoy would sail on the morning of April 23.

4. The personnel will go by the Cape, subject to any modifications which the C.I.G.S. may desire.

5. I have asked the Ministry of Shipping to try to find two other M.T. ships of equal speed, without regard to other interests, by the date mentioned. If these are found, an additional hundred cruiser tanks should be taken from the best armoured division at home, assuming that they are fitted for tropical warfare, apart altogether from the special "desert-worthy" fittings.

6. The Admiralty and Air Ministry will consider and prepare *this day* a plan for carrying this vital convoy through the Mediterranean. Of course, we must accept the risk, and no guarantee can be expected. Malta, however, should have been reinforced by then. The Mountbatten destroyers and other naval reinforcements should have reached there (or else be with the convoy). The enemy's dive-bombers have many other objectives, and they will not know what the convoy contains.

7. Speed is vital. Every day's delay must be avoided. Let me have a time-table of what is possible, observing that at sixteen knots the distance is only about eight days—say, ten—from the date of sailing, namely, April 23. This would give General Wavell effective support during the first week in May. Secrecy is of the highest importance, and no one outside the highest circles need

know of the intention to turn off at Gibraltar. Everyone on board the convoys must think they are going round the Cape.

The Chiefs of Staff were assembled by the time Ismay reached London, and they discussed my minute until late into the night. Their first reactions to the proposals were unfavourable. The chances of getting the M.T. ships through the Central Mediterranean unscathed were not rated very high, since on the day before entering the Narrows and on the morning after passing Malta they would be subjected to dive-bombing attacks out of range of our own shore-based fighters. The view was also expressed that we were dangerously weak in tanks at home, and that if we now suffered heavy losses in tanks abroad there would be demands for their replacement, and consequently a further diversion of tanks from the home forces.

However, when the Defence Committee met the next day Admiral Pound, to my great satisfaction, stood by me and agreed to pass the convoy through the Mediterranean. The Chief of the Air Staff, Air Marshal Portal, said he would try to arrange for a Beaufighter squadron to give additional protection from Malta. I then asked the committee to consider sending a hundred additional cruiser tanks with the convoy. I was willing to accept two days' delay in sailing. General Dill opposed the dispatch of these additional tanks *in view of the shortage for home defence*. Considering what he had agreed to ten months before, when we sent half our few tanks round the Cape to the Middle East in July, 1940, I could not feel that this reason was at this time valid. As the reader is aware, I did not regard invasion as a serious danger in April, 1941, since proper preparations had been made against it. We now know that this view was correct. It was settled that this operation, which I called "Tiger," should proceed, and that a sixth ship should be added to the convoy to include sixty-seven Mark VI (cruiser) tanks. This ship could not, however, be loaded in time to sail with the convoy, though every effort was made.

* * *

I made haste to tell Wavell the good news.

Prime Minister to General Wavell 22 April 41

I have been working hard for you in the last few days, and you will, I am sure, be glad to know that we are sending 307 of our best tanks through the Mediterranean, hoping they will reach you around May 10. Of these, 99 are cruisers, Mark IV and Mark VI, with the necessary spare parts for the latter, and 180 "I" tanks.

2. In your telegram of April 18 you said you had the trained personnel for six regiments. We are, therefore, sending only the vehicles to you by the short cut. The men go round the Cape as already arranged, subject to some adjustments.

3. You will receive through the regular channels (a) full details of the tanks which are being sent and of the spare parts, which fit in with what you have got already, and (b) directions as to various fittings you have to make for desert service. I hope you will immediately set to work on all preparations so that a real evolution can be made of this job, and the famous 7th Armoured Division, whose absence was so unexpected to us, will resume under Creagh its victorious career.

4. On the receipt of the detailed information you should furnish us with your plan for bringing these vehicles into action at the very earliest moment. If this consignment gets through the hazards of the passage, which, of course, cannot be guaranteed, the boot will be on the other leg and no German should remain in Cyrenaica by the end of the month of June.

5. In making your preparations for bringing these vehicles into action you should pretend that they are coming round the Cape, as secrecy is most important, and very few here have been told. Thus, when you get them the chance of surprise may be offered. All good wishes.

* * *

While all this was on the move Tobruk lay heavily upon our minds. General Wavell reported on the twenty-fourth that the air fighter situation was serious. All Hurricanes in Greece had been lost, and as a result of recent enemy air attacks on Tobruk a large proportion of the Hurricanes there had been destroyed or damaged. Air Marshal Longmore considered that any further attempt to maintain a fighter squadron inside Tobruk would only result in heavy loss to no purpose. Thus the enemy would have complete air superiority over Tobruk until a fresh fighter force could be built up. However, the garrison had beaten off an attack that morning, causing the enemy heavy casualties and taking one hundred and fifty prisoners.

There was much anxiety at this time, and some pessimism. I could not refrain from a severe comment.

Prime Minister to C.I.G.S.   22 April 41

We must not forget that the besieged are four or five times as strong as the besiegers. There is no objection to their making themselves comfortable, but they must be very careful not to let themselves be ringed in by a smaller force, and consequently lose their offensive power upon the enemy's communications. Twenty-five thousand men with one hundred guns and ample supplies are expected to be able to hold a highly fortified zone against forty-five hundred men at the end of seven hundred miles of communications, even though those men be Germans; in this case some of them are not. The figures which I have used are those which have been furnished to me by the War Office. We must not put our standards too low in relation to the enemy.

* * *

Soon General Wavell sent us more disquieting information about Rommel's approaching reinforcements. The disembarkation of the 15th German Armoured Division, less its losses in crossing the Mediterranean, would probably be completed by April 21. Several units had already been identified opposite Tobruk or in the Capuzzo area. Prisoners of war stated that the division was still short of supply transport. From our observation of shipping arriving in Tripoli, it seemed that twenty-one shipments, averaging five thousand or six thousand tons, were still required to complete the division. The question of its maintenance eastward depended on the use of Benghazi and other small ports in Cyrenaica. There were signs that Benghazi was being regularly used. At least fifteen days would be required for the gathering of supplies. On this assumption the 15th Armoured Division, the 5th Light Motorised Division, and the Ariete and Trento divisions would be able to move forward after the middle of June, instead of only from July onward—an acceleration of a fortnight upon the previous estimate.

Wavell added that he must confess that German performance so often exceeded calculations that he was not confident that they would not improve on his estimate of their abilities. They had, for instance, begun an advance the previous evening from the Sollum area which would not be justified by what was believed to be their supply situation.

It seemed very unsatisfactory to us at home that Benghazi, which we had failed to make a useful base, was already playing so important a part now that it had passed into German hands.

* * *

During the next fortnight my keen attention and anxieties were riveted upon the fortunes of operation "Tiger." I did not underrate the risks which the First Sea Lord had been willing to accept, and I knew that there were many misgivings in the Admiralty. The convoy, consisting of five fifteen-knot ships, escorted by Admiral Somerville's Force H (*Renown, Malaya, Ark Royal,* and *Sheffield*), passed Gibraltar on May 6. With it also were the reinforcements for the Mediterranean Fleet, comprising the *Queen Elizabeth* and the cruisers *Naiad* and *Fiji.* Air attacks on May 8 were beaten off without damage, seven enemy aircraft being destroyed. During that night, however, two ships of the convoy struck mines when approaching the Narrows. One, the *Empire Song,* caught fire and sank after an explosion; the other, the *New Zealand Star,* was able to continue with the convoy. On reaching the entrance to the Skerki Channel, Admiral Somerville parted company and returned to Gibraltar. He detached six of his destroyers, with the cruiser *Gloucester,* to reinforce the convoy escort. In the afternoon of the ninth Admiral Cunningham, having seized the opportunity to pass a convoy into Malta, met the "Tiger" convoy with the fleet fifty miles south of Malta. All his forces then shaped their course for Alexandria, which they reached without further loss or damage. The opportunity was also taken during these operations to carry out two night bombardments of Benghazi with light naval forces on May 7 and 10.

I was delighted to learn that this vital convoy, on which my hopes were set, had come safely through the Narrows and was now protected by the whole strength of the reinforced Mediterranean Fleet. While this hung in the balance, my thoughts turned to Crete, upon which we were now sure a heavy airborne attack impended. It seemed to me that if the Germans could seize and use the airfields on the island, they would have the power of reinforcing almost indefinitely, and that even a dozen "I" tanks might play a decisive part in preventing their doing so. I, therefore, asked the Chiefs of Staff to consider turning one ship of "Tiger" to unload a few "I" tanks in Crete on their way through. My expert colleagues, while agreeing that tanks would be of special value for the purpose I had in mind, deemed it inadvisable to endanger the rest of the ship's valuable cargo by such a diversion. Accordingly, I suggested to them on May 9 that if it were "thought too dangerous to take the *Clan Lamont* into Suda, she should take twelve tanks, or some other ship should take them, immediately after she has discharged her cargo at Alexandria." Orders were sent accordingly. Wavell replied on May 10 that he "had already arranged to send six infantry tanks and fifteen light tanks to Crete," and that they "should arrive within next few days if all goes well."

*   *   *

Naturally I was eager to repeat the brilliant success of "Tiger." I had not perhaps realised what a strain it had been on all concerned, although clearly I had borne the main responsibility. I considered my judgment about the dangers of the Mediterranean passage was at last vindicated. My naval friends, on the other hand, declared we had enjoyed a stroke of good luck and weather which might never recur. The Admiralty certainly did not wish to be led into a succession of these hazardous operations, and I encountered resistance which I found serious. I should not have been deterred from seeking and obtaining a Cabinet decision upon the issue but for the fact that General Wavell himself did not press the point, and indeed took the other side. This cut the ground from under my feet. Accordingly fifty cruiser and fifty infantry tanks went round the Cape in a later convoy, which did not anchor off Suez till July 15.

Many things had happened by then. However, not all were bad.

14

The Revolt in Iraq

The Anglo-Iraqi Treaty of 1930—"The Golden Square"—Rein-
forcements from India—The Attack upon Habbaniya—Spirited
Assistance from the Flying School—Wavell's Reluctance—His
Many Cares—Firm Attitude at Home—Better News from Hab-
baniya—Collapse and Flight of the Iraqi Army—My Telegram
to Wavell of May 9—His Reply—Arrival of the "Habforce"—
Hitler's Belated Directive, May 23—The Advance on Baghdad—
Flight of Rashid Ali—Iraq Effectively Occupied—The Regent
Returns to Baghdad—Serious Dangers Narrowly Averted at
Small Cost—Divergence Between London and Cairo.

THE ANGLO-IRAQI TREATY of 1930 provided that in time
of peace we should, among other things, maintain air
bases near Basra and at Habbaniya, and have the right of
transit for military forces and supplies at all times. The treaty
also provided that in war we should have all possible facilities, including the use of railways, rivers, ports, and airfields,
for the passage of our armed forces. When war came Iraq
broke off diplomatic relations with Germany, but did not declare war; and when Italy came into the war, the Iraq Government did not even sever relations. Thus the Italian Legation in Baghdad became the chief centre for Axis propaganda
and for fomenting anti-British feeling. In this they were aided
by the Mufti of Jerusalem, who had fled from Palestine shortly
before the outbreak of war and later received asylum in Baghdad.

With the collapse of France and the arrival of the Axis
Armistice Commission in Syria, British prestige sank very low
and the situation gave us much anxiety. But with our preoccupations elsewhere military action was out of the question,
and we had to carry on as best we could. In March, 1941,

there was a turn for the worse. Rashid Ali, who was working with the Germans, became Prime Minister, and began a conspiracy with three prominent Iraqi officers, who were styled "the Golden Square." At the end of March the pro-British Regent, Emir Abdul-Ilah, fled from Baghdad.

It was now more than ever important to make sure of Basra, the main port of Iraq on the Persian Gulf, and I minuted to the Secretary of State for India:

Prime Minister to Secretary of State for India   8 April 41

Some time ago you suggested that you might be able to spare another division taken from the frontier troops for the Middle East. The situation in Iraq has turned sour. We must make sure of Basra, as the Americans are increasingly keen on a great air assembling base being formed there to which they could deliver direct. This plan seems of high importance in view of the undoubted Eastern trend of the war.

I am telling the Chiefs of Staff that you will look into these possibilities. General Auchinleck also had ideas that an additional force could be spared.

Mr. Amery telegraphed in this sense to the Viceroy on the same day, and Lord Linlithgow and the Commander-in-Chief, General Auchinleck, promptly offered to divert to Basra an infantry brigade and a regiment of field artillery, most of which was already on board ship for Malaya. Other troops were to follow as quickly as possible. The brigade group disembarked without opposition at Basra on April 18, under cover of an airborne British battalion which had alighted at Shaiba the day before. The Government of India was requested to follow them up, as quickly as possible with two more brigades also assigned to Malaya.

Prime Minister to General Ismay, for C.O.S. Committee,
and all concerned   20 April 41

Troops should be sent to Basra as fast as possible. At least the three brigades originally promised should be hurried there.

And also:

Prime Minister to Foreign Secretary   20 April 41

It should be made clear to Sir Kinahan Cornwallis[1] that our chief interest in sending troops to Iraq is the covering and establishment of a great assembly base at Basra, and that what happens up-country, except at Habbaniya, is at the present time on an altogether lower priority. Our rights under the treaty were invoked to cover this disembarkation and to avoid bloodshed, but force would have been used to the utmost limit to secure the disem-

[1] The British Ambassador in Baghdad.

barkation, if necessary. Our position at Basra, therefore, does not
rest solely on the treaty, but also on a new event arising out of
the war. No undertakings can be given that troops will be sent
to Baghdad or moved through to Palestine, and the right to require such undertakings should not be recognised in respect of a
Government which has in itself usurped power by a *coup d'état,*
or in a country where our treaty rights have so long been frustrated in the spirit. Sir Kinahan Cornwallis should not, however,
entangle himself by explanations.

When accordingly Rashid Ali was informed by our Ambassador that more transports would reach Basra on the thirtieth,
he said that he could not give permission for any fresh landings until the troops already at Basra had passed through the
port. General Auchinleck was told that the landings should
go forward none the less, and Rashid Ali, who had been
counting on the assistance of German aircraft, and even of
German airborne troops, was forced into action.

His first hostile move was towards Habbaniya, our air force
training base in the Iraqi Desert. On April 29, 230 British
women and children had been flown to Habbaniya from Baghdad. The total number in the cantonment was just over 2200
fighting men, with no fewer than 9000 civilians. The Flying
School thus became a point of grave importance. Air Vice-
Marshal Smart, who commanded there, took bold and timely
precautions to meet the mounting crisis. The Flying School
had previously held only obsolescent or training types, but a
few Gladiator fighters had arrived from Egypt, and eighty-
two aircraft of all sorts were improvised into four squadrons.
A British battalion flown from India, had arrived on the
twenty-ninth. The ground defence of the seven miles perimeter, with its solitary wire fence, was indeed scanty. On the
thirtieth Iraqi troops from Baghdad appeared barely a mile
away on the plateau overlooking both the airfield and the
camp. They were soon reinforced from Baghdad, until they
numbered about nine thousand men, with fifty guns. The next
two days were spent in fruitless parleys, and at dawn on May
2 fighting began.

*   *   *

From the outset of this new danger General Wavell showed
himself most reluctant to assume more burdens. He said he
would make preparations and do what he could to create the
impression of a large force being prepared for action from
Palestine, which might have some effect on the Iraqi Government. The force he could make available would in his opinion

be both inadequate and too late. It would be at least a week before it could start. Its departure would leave Palestine most dangerously weak, and incitement to rebellion there was already taking place. "I have consistently warned you," he said, "that no assistance could be given to Iraq from Palestine in present circumstances, and have always advised that a commitment in Iraq should be avoided. . . . My forces are stretched to the limit everywhere, and I simply cannot afford to risk part of them on what cannot produce any effect."

In Syria resources were equally strained. The Commanders-in-Chief Middle East had said that the maximum force that could be spared for Syria until the Australians were re-equipped was one mechanised cavalry brigade, one regiment of artillery, and one infantry battalion, *subject to no Iraq commitment*. This force could not be expected to deal with the number of troops which the Germans would be able to send to Syria, and should not be sent unless the Vichy French were actively resisting. If it was decided to send troops into Syria it would certainly be better to send British in the first instance and not Free French, whose intervention would be bitterly resented.

On May 4 we sent General Wavell our decisions about Iraq:

A commitment in Iraq was inevitable. We had to establish a base at Basra, and control that port to safeguard Persian oil in case of need.

The line of communication to Turkey through Iraq has also assumed greater importance owing to German air superiority in the Aegean Sea. . . . Had we sent no forces to Basra the present situation at Habbaniya might still have arisen under Axis direction, and we should also have had to face an opposed landing at Basra later on instead of being able to secure a bridgehead there without opposition. . . . There can be no question of accepting the Turkish offer of mediation. We can make no concessions. The security of Egypt remains paramount. But it is essential to do all in our power to save Habbaniya and to control the pipeline to the Mediterranean.

General Auchinleck continued to offer reinforcements up to five infantry brigades and ancillary troops by June 10 if shipping could be provided. We were gratified by his forward mood. General Wavell only obeyed under protest. "Your message," he said on the fifth, "takes little account of realities. You must face facts." He doubted whether the forces he himself was gathering were strong enough to relieve Habbaniya, or whether Habbaniya could hold out till they might arrive on the twelfth. "I feel it my duty to warn you in the gravest possible terms," he said, "that I consider the prolongation of fighting in Iraq will seriously endanger the defence of Palestine and Egypt. The political repercussions will be incalculable, and may result in what I have spent nearly two years trying to avoid, namely, serious internal trouble in our bases. I, therefore, urge again most strongly that a settlement should be negotiated as early as possible."

I was not content with this.

Prime Minister to General Ismay, for C.O.S. Committee   6 May 41

The telegrams from Generals Wavell and Auchinleck should be considered forthwith, and a report made to me at the House of Commons before luncheon today.

The following points require attention: (1) Why should the force mentioned, which seems considerable, be deemed insufficient to deal with the Iraq Army? What do you say about this? Fancy having kept the cavalry division in Palestine all this time without having the rudiments of a mobile column organised! (2) Why should the troops at Habbaniya give in before May 12? Their losses have been nominal as so far reported. Their infantry made a successful sortie last night, and we are told that the bombardment stops whenever our aircraft appear. Great efforts should be made by the air force to aid and encourage Habbaniya. Surely some additional infantry can be flown there as reinforcements from Egypt? The most strenuous orders should be given to the officer commanding to hold out.

How can a settlement be negotiated, as General Wavell suggests? Suppose the Iraqis, under German instigation, insist upon our evacuating Basra, or moving in small detachments at their mercy across the country to Palestine. The opinion of the senior naval officer at Basra is that a collapse or surrender there would be disastrous. This is also the opinion of the Government of India. I am deeply disturbed at General Wavell's attitude. He seems to have been taken as much by surprise on his eastern as he was on his western flank, and in spite of the enormous number of men at his disposal, and the great convoys reaching him, he seems to be hard up for battalions and companies. He gives me the impression of being tired out.

The proposals of C.-in-C. India for reinforcing Basra seem to deserve most favourable consideration.

*   *   *

Supported by the Chiefs of Staff, I brought all this to an issue before the Defence Committee when it met at noon. There was a resolute temper. The following orders were sent at their direction:

Chiefs of Staff to General Wavell and others concerned 6 May 41

Your telegram of yesterday has been considered by Defence Committee. Settlement by negotiation cannot be entertained except on the basis of a climb down by Iraqis, with safeguard against future Axis designs on Iraq. Realities of the situation are that Rashid Ali has all along been hand-in-glove with Axis Powers, and was merely waiting until they could support him before exposing his hand. Our arrival at Basra forced him to go off at half-cock before the Axis was ready. Thus there is an excellent chance of restoring the situation by bold action, if it is not delayed.

Chiefs of Staff have, therefore, advised Defence Committee that they are prepared to accept responsibility for dispatch of the force specified in your telegram at the earliest possible moment. Defence Committee direct that Air Vice-Marshal Smart should be informed that he will be given assistance, and that in the meanwhile it is his duty to defend Habbaniya to the last. Subject to the security of Egypt being maintained, maximum air support possible should be given operations in Iraq.

* * *

Meanwhile at Habbaniya the squadrons of the Flying School, together with Wellington bombers from Shaiba, at the head of the Persian Gulf, attacked the Iraqi troops on the plateau. They replied by shelling the cantonment, their aircraft joining in with bombs and machine guns. Over forty of our men were killed or wounded that day, and twenty-two aircraft destroyed or disabled. Despite the difficulty of taking off under close artillery fire, our airmen continued their attacks. No enemy infantry assault developed, and gradually their batteries were mastered. It was found that the enemy gunners would not stand to their pieces under air attack or even if our aircraft were to be seen overhead. Full advantage was taken of their nervousness, and it was possible from the second day to turn a proportion of our air effort to dealing with the Iraqi Air Force and their bases. On the nights of May 3 and 4, offensive land patrols from Habbaniya moved out to raid the enemy lines, and by the fifth, after four days of attack from the Royal Air Force, the enemy had had enough. That night they withdrew from the plateau. They were followed up, and a very successful action yielded four hundred prisoners, a dozen guns, sixty machine guns, and ten armoured cars. A reinforcing column from Falluja was caught on the road and destroyed by forty of our aircraft dispatched from Habbaniya for the purpose. By May 7, therefore, the siege of Habbaniya was over. The defenders had been reinforced by fighter aircraft from Egypt; British women and children had all been evacuated by air to Basra; the Iraqi Air Force of about sixty planes had been virtually destroyed. This good news only reached us late and bit by bit.

Prime Minister to Air Vice-Marshal Smart   7 May 41

Your vigorous and splendid action has largely restored the situation. We are all watching the grand fight you are making. All possible aid will be sent. Keep it up.

       *   *   *

Prime Minister to General Wavell   7 May 41

It would seem that the Habbaniya show has greatly improved, and audacious action now against the Iraqis may crush the revolt before the Germans arrive. They can, of course, fly there direct in heavy bombers, but these would only have what they stand up in and could not operate long. We must forestall the moral effect of their arrival by a stunning blow. I presume that, if Rutba and Habbaniya are clear, [our] column will take possession of Baghdad or otherwise exploit success to the full. Other telegrams are being sent to you about rousing the tribes and about Government policy.

General Wavell replied to the Chiefs of Staff direct:

8 May 41

I think you should appreciate the limits of military action in Iraq during next few months without a favourable political situation. Forces from India can secure Basra, but cannot, in my opinion, advance northward unless the co-operation of the local population and tribes is fully secured. Force from Palestine can relieve Habbaniya and hold approaches from Baghdad to prevent farther advance on Habbaniya; but it is not capable of entering Baghdad against opposition or maintaining itself there. . . . In order, therefore, to avoid a heavy military commitment in a non-vital area, I still recommend that a political solution be sought by all available means.

Although I realised his cares and his devotion, I continued to press General Wavell hard.

Prime Minister to General Wavell   9 May 41

The Defence Committee have considered your telegram of May 8 about Iraq. Our information is that Rashid Ali and his partisans are in desperate straits. However this may be, you are to fight hard against them. The mobile column being prepared in Palestine should advance as you propose, or earlier if possible, and actively engage the enemy, whether at Rutba or Habbaniya. Having joined the Habbaniya forces, you should exploit the situation to the utmost, not hesitating to try to break into Baghdad even with quite small forces, and running the same kind of risks as the Germans are accustomed to run and profit by.

2. There can be no question of negotiation with Rashid Ali unless he immediately accepts the terms in C.O.S. telegram. Such negotiation would only lead to delay, during which the German Air Force will arrive. We do not think that any ground forces you may be able to divert to Iraq will affect your immediate problem in the Western Desert. The air force must do its best to cover both situations. Only in the event of your being actually engaged or about to engage in an offensive in the Western Desert should Tedder deny the necessary air support to the Iraq operations.

I tried to reassure General Wavell that we had no extensive operation in view and were only seeking to cope with the immediate need.

You do not need to bother too much about the long future in Iraq. Your immediate task is to get a friendly Government set up in Baghdad, and to beat down Rashid Ali's forces with the utmost vigour. We do not wish to be involved at present in any large-scale advance up the river from Basra, nor have we prescribed the occupation of Kirkuk or Mosul. We do not seek any change in the independent status of Iraq, and full instructions have been given in accordance with your own ideas upon this point. But what matters is action; namely, the swift advance of the mobile column to establish effective contact between Baghdad and Palestine. Every day counts, for the Germans may not be long. We hoped that the column would be ready to move on the tenth, and would reach Habbaniya on the twelfth, assuming Habbaniya could hold out, which they have done, and a good deal more. We trust these dates have been kept, and that you will do your utmost to accelerate movement.

Wavell responded gallantly to the many cumulative calls made upon him.

Without waiting for "Tiger" [he reported on the thirteenth] I ordered all available tanks to join Gott's force and attack the enemy in the Sollum area. . . . If things go well in the Western Desert I will try to move additional troops to Palestine for action towards Iraq. . . . We will try to liquidate this tiresome Iraq business quickly. . . . I am doing my best to strengthen Crete against impending attack. I discussed the question of Syria with Catroux this afternoon.

* * *

By this time "Tiger" had begun to arrive safely at Alexandria, and I cherished many hopes of good results in Crete, in the Western Desert, and in Syria. Varied fortunes attended these interrelated ventures.

Prime Minister to General Auchinleck   14 May 41

1. I am very glad you are going to meet Wavell at Basra. He will tell you about "Tiger" and "Scorcher" [defence of Crete]. A victory in Libya would alter all values in Iraq, both in German and Iraqi minds.

2. We are most grateful to you for the energetic efforts you have made about Basra. The stronger the forces India can assemble there the better. But we have not yet felt able to commit ourselves to any advance (except with small parties when the going is good) northward towards Baghdad, and still less to occupation in force of Kirkuk and/or Mosul. This cannot be contemplated until we see what happens about "Tiger" and "Scorcher." We are, therefore, confined at the moment to trying to get a friendly Government installed in Baghdad and building up the largest possible bridgehead at Basra. Even less can we attempt to dominate Syria at the present time, though the Free French may be allowed to do their best there. The defeat of the Germans in Libya is the commanding event, and larger and longer views cannot be taken till that is achieved. Everything will be much easier then.

*   *   *

It will be well to complete the Iraq story before the impact of more sanguinary events, though not graver dangers, fell upon us in Crete.

The advance guard of the relieving "Habforce," a motorised brigade group from Palestine, arrived at Habbaniya on May 18 to resume the attack on the enemy, now holding the bridge across the Euphrates at Falluja. By this time the Iraqis were not the only enemy. The first German aircraft were established on Mosul airfield on May 13, and thenceforward our air force had as a principal task to attack them and prevent their being supplied by railway from Syria. The attack on Falluja by the advance guard of "Habforce" and the land elements of the Habbaniya garrison took place on May 19. Inundations hampered direct approach from the west, and small columns were, therefore, dispatched over a flying bridge upstream from the town to cut off the retreat of the defenders; another party made an air landing to block the road to Baghdad. It had been expected that this action, together with air bombardment, would make the enemy, about a brigade strong, surrender or disperse. But in the end ground attack was needed. A small force on the west bank whose task had been to prevent by rifle fire the demolition of the vital bridge was ordered to rush it; they did so successfully and without casualties. The enemy gave way; three hundred prisoners were taken. A counter-attack three days later was beaten off.

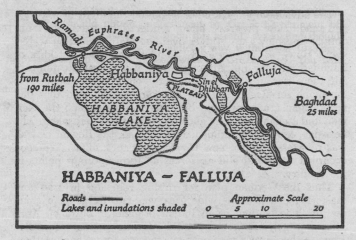

HABBANIYA – FALLUJA

Roads ————
Lakes and inundations shaded

Approximate Scale
0   5   10   20

Some days were spent in making preparations for the final advance on Baghdad, during which our air action against the German Air Force on the northern airfields of Iraq finally crushed their effort. Later an Italian fighter squadron appeared, but accomplished nothing. The German officer charged with co-ordinating the action of the Axis air squadrons with the Iraqi forces, a son of Field Marshal Blomberg, landed at Baghdad with a bullet in his head, thanks to misjudged firing by his allies. His successor, General Felmy, though more fortunate in his landing, could do nothing. His vigorous instructions from Hitler were dated May 23, by which time all chance of useful Axis intervention had passed.

HITLER'S DIRECTIVE No. 30. MIDDLE EAST

Field Headquarters: May 23, 1941

The Arab Freedom Movement is, in the Middle East, our natural ally against England. In this connection the raising of rebellion in Iraq is of special importance. Such rebellion will extend across the Iraq frontiers to strengthen the forces which are hostile to England in the Middle East, interrupt the British lines of communication, and tie down both English troops and English shipping space at the expense of other theatres of war. For these reasons I have decided to push the development of operations in the Middle East through the medium of going to the support of Iraq. Whether and in what way it may later be possible to wreck finally the English position between the Mediterranean and the Persian Gulf, in conjunction with an offensive against the Suez Canal, is still in the lap of the gods. . . .

The advance upon Baghdad began on the night of May 27, and made slow progress, being hindered by extensive inundations and blown-up bridges over the many irrigation waterways. However, our forward troops reached the outskirts of Baghdad on May 30. Although they were weak in numbers and there was an Iraqi division in the city, their presence was too much for Rashid Ali and his companions, who that day fled to Persia, accompanied by other troublemakers, the German and Italian Ministers and the ex-Mufti of Jerusalem. The next day, May 31, an armistice was signed, the Regent of Iraq was reinstated, and a new Government took office. We soon occupied with land and air forces all the important points in the country.

Thus the German plan for raising rebellion in Iraq and mastering cheaply this wide area was frustrated on a small margin. The landing of an Indian brigade at Basra on April 18 was timely. It forced Rashid Ali into premature action. Even so there was a race with our meagre forces against time. The spirited defence of Habbaniya by the Flying School was a prime factor in our success. The Germans had, of course, at their disposal an airborne force which would have given them at this time Syria, Iraq, and Persia, with their precious oilfields. Hitler's hand might have reached out very far towards India, and beckoned to Japan. He had chosen, however, as we shall soon see, to employ and expend his prime air organism in another direction. We often hear military experts incul-

SYRIA AND IRAQ

cate the doctrine of giving priority to the decisive theatre.
There is a lot in this. But in war this principle, like all others,
is governed by facts and circumstances; otherwise strategy
would be too easy. It would become a drill-book and not an
art; it would depend upon rules and not on an instructed and
fortunate judgment of the proportions of an ever-changing
scene. Hitler certainly cast away the opportunity of taking a
great prize for little cost in the Middle East. We in Britain,
although pressed to the extreme, managed with scanty forces
to save ourselves from far-reaching or lasting injury.

It must be remembered that the revolt in Iraq was but one
small sector of the immense emergency in the Middle East
which lapped General Wavell on all sides simultaneously.
This comprised the impending German onslaught upon Crete,
our plans to attack Rommel in the Western Desert, the campaigns in Abyssinia and Eritrea, and the bitter need to forestall the Germans in Syria. In the same way the whole Mediterranean scene, as viewed from London, was but a secondary
part of our world problem, in which the invasion menace, the
U-boat war, and the attitude of Japan were dominant features. Only the strength and cohesion of the War Cabinet, the
relations of mutual respect and harmony of outlook between
political and military chiefs, and the smooth working of our
war machine enabled us to surmount, though sorely mauled,
these trials and perils.

The reader will be conscious of the tension which grew
between the British War Cabinet and Chiefs of Staff and their
overstrained but gallantly struggling Commander-in-Chief in
Cairo. The authorities at home, over whom I presided, directly overruled from Whitehall the judgment of the man on
the spot. They took the issue out of his hands and assumed the
responsibility themselves for ordering the relief of Habbaniya
and for rejecting all ideas of negotiation with Rashid Ali or
accepting Turkish mediation, which at one time was mentioned. The result was crowned with swift and complete success. Although no one was more pleased and relieved than
Wavell himself, the episode could not pass without leaving
impressions in his mind and in ours. At the same time General
Auchinleck's forthcoming attitude in sending, at our desire,
and with the Viceroy's cordial assent, the Indian division to
Basra so promptly, and the readiness with which Indian
reinforcements were supplied, gave us the feeling of a fresh
mind and a hitherto untaxed personal energy. The consequences of these impressions will be seen as the story unfolds.

15

Crete: The Advent

*The Situation in Crete—Weak and Inadequate Defences—The
Overloaded Administration in Cairo—Agreement at Home and
on the Spot About Defending Crete—Our Precise Intelligence
—Wavell's Visit, April 30—Bernard Freyberg in Command—My
Telegram to Admiral Cunningham of May 1—Efforts to Rein-
force Our Air—Wavell and Freyberg Under No Illusions—Frey-
berg's Telegrams to Wavell and to the New Zealand Govern-
ment—Wavell's Telegram of May 2—Anxiety in New Zealand—
My Message to Mr. Fraser, May 3—Freyberg Undaunted—Ger-
man Blockade of Crete from the Air—Our Pitiful Air Resources
—The German Plan of Attack—"Colorado" and "Scorcher"—A
Breathless Pause—Wavell's Humour—I Keep Smuts Informed—
On the Verge.*

THE STRATEGIC IMPORTANCE of Crete in all our Mediterranean affairs has already been explained by argument
and events. British warships based on Suda Bay or able to
refuel there could give an all-important protection to Malta.
If our base in Crete was well defended against air attack the
whole process of superior sea power would come into play
and ward off any seaborne expedition. But only a hundred
miles away lay the Italian fortress of Rhodes, with its ample
airfields and well-established installations. The capture and
occupation of Rhodes had been our aim since the beginning
of the year, and the Mobile Naval Base Defence Organisation,
a splendid body of men, most carefully trained and fitted together, fifty-three hundred strong, had been sent from England either for Rhodes or Suda Bay as circumstances might
require. Besides this the commando force, over two thousand
strong, under Colonel Laycock, had also come round the
Cape, and with the British 6th Division, which was being

formed in Egypt, would have made an assaulting force capable of taking Rhodes. The pressure of events had forced us to postpone this enterprise, and meanwhile Crete was vulnerable in a high degree should German aircraft be sent to Rhodes. The Mobile Naval Defence Organisation was kept in hand at Alexandria for emergencies instead of helping either to take and hold Rhodes or to work up and man the defences of Suda Bay.

Locally in Crete everything had proceeded in a halting manner. The reader has seen my repeated injunctions to have Suda Bay fortified. I had even used the expression "a second Scapa." The island had been in our possession for nearly six months, but it would only have been possible to equip the harbour with a more powerful outfit of anti-aircraft guns at the expense of other still more urgent needs; nor was the Middle East Command able to find the labour, locally or otherwise, to develop the airfields. There could be no question of sending a large garrison to Crete or of basing strong air forces upon its airfields while Greece was still in Allied hands. But all should have been in readiness to receive reinforcements should they become available and should the need arise. There had been, however, neither plan nor drive. Six successive commanders were appointed in as many months. The Middle East Command should have made a more careful study of the conditions under which Crete might have to be defended from air or sea attack. The need of providing if not a harbour at least landing facilities on the southern side of the island at Sphakia or Timbaki and the making of a road therefrom to Suda Bay and the airfields by which Western Crete could have been reinforced from Egypt was not foreseen. The responsibility for the defective study of the problem and for the feeble execution of the direction given must be shared between Cairo and Whitehall.

It was only after the disasters had occurred in Cyrenaica, in Crete, and in the desert that I realised how overloaded and undersustained General Wavell's organisation was. Wavell tried his best; but the handling machine at his disposal was too weak to enable him to cope with the vast mass of business which four or five simultaneous campaigns imposed upon him.

* * *

With the German conquest of Greece, Crete became the last foothold for the Greek King and Government, and an important repository for evacuated troops of all kinds. We could be sure that German eyes were glaring upon it. To us it seemed a vital outpost both of Egypt and Malta. Even in this welter of failure and wreckage in which we were now plunged there were no disagreements between the authorities, either at home or on the spot, about holding Crete. "I am assuming," telegraphed Wavell (April 16), "that Crete will be held." And the next day, "We are making preparations for evacuation [of Greece] and for holding Crete."

*   *   *

We had known for a long time the efforts Goering had made to create and develop a powerful airborne force, capable of a large-scale descent from the air. This had appealed to the ardent and devoted Nazi youth of Germany. The German Parachute Division was a *corps d'élite* which had played its part in our thoughts about home defence against invasion. All such plans, however, require at least the temporary command of the daylight air. This the Germans had failed to gain in Britain. Crete was a different tale. Ample and, as it seemed, long-lasting air superiority both in the Balkans and in the Aegean Sea was now the enemy's master weapon.

At no moment in the war was our Intelligence so truly and precisely informed. In the exultant confusion of their seizure of Athens the German staffs preserved less than their usual secrecy, and our agents in Greece were active and daring. In the last week of April we obtained from trustworthy sources good information about the next German stroke. The movements and excitement of the German XIth Air Corps, and also the frantic collection of small craft in Greek harbours, could not be concealed from attentive eyes and ears. All pointed to an impending attack on Crete, both by air and sea. In no operation did I take more personal pains to study and weigh the evidence or to make sure that the magnitude of the impending onslaught was impressed upon the Commanders-in-Chief and imparted to the general on the actual scene.

Our Joint Intelligence Committee in London made an appreciation on April 28 of the scale and character of the hostile design against Crete in which they expressed their belief that simultaneous airborne and seaborne attack was imminent. They thought that the enemy could gather in the Balkans for all purposes 315 long-range bombers, 60 twin-engine fighters, 240 dive-bombers, and 270 single-engine fighters; that he might drop 3000 to 4000 parachutists or airborne troops in the first sortie, and that he might make two or three sorties per day from Greece and three or four from Rhodes, all with fighter escort. There would be heavy bombing attacks prior to the arrival of the airborne and seaborne troops, and no lack of troops or shipping for the seaborne attack.

This was immediately telegraphed to the Cairo headquarters, and I emphasised it the same day by a personal message to General Wavell.

Prime Minister to General Wavell   28 April 41

It seems clear from our information that a heavy airborne attack by German troops and bombers will soon be made on Crete. Let me know what forces you have in the island and what your plans are. It ought to be a fine opportunity for killing the parachute troops. The island must be stubbornly defended.

Although General Wavell did not at first wholly accept our view that Crete was the target, and thought that the Germans might be deliberately letting rumours circulate to cover their real plans, he acted at once with his customary energy and mobility and flew to the island. His answers show the situation.

General Wavell to Prime Minister and C.O.S.   29 April 41

Crete was warned of possibility of airborne attack on April 18. Besides original permanent garrison of three infantry battalions, two heavy A.A. batteries, three light A.A. batteries, and coast defence artillery, Crete now contains at least 30,000 personnel evacuated from Greece. These are being organised for the defence of the vital places on the island: Suda Bay, Canea, Retimo, and Heraklion. Morale reported good. Arms mainly rifles, with low proportion light machine guns. In addition certain units of Greek recruits have been organised for defence of aerodromes and [guarding] prisoners of war.

2. The Mobile Naval Base Defence Organisation is due to reach the island during first fortnight in May.

3. Propose visiting Crete tomorrow, and will report on return.

4. It is just possible that plan for attack on Crete may be cover for attack on Syria or Cyprus, and that real plan will only be disclosed even to [their] own troops at last moment. This would be consistent with German practice.

I had suggested to the C.I.G.S. that General Freyberg should be placed in command of Crete, and he proposed this to Wavell, who had immediately agreed. Bernard Freyberg and I had been friends for many years. When as a young volunteer from New Zealand in the First World War he had made his way through many difficulties to England, he had an introduction to me, and met me one day in the Admiralty in September, 1914, and asked for a commission. I was at that time forming the Royal Naval Division, and I soon made the necessary recommendations. In a few days he became a sub-lieutenant in the "Hood" Battalion. Here is no place to describe the long succession of glorious deeds of valour by which he rose in four years of front-line war to the command of a brigade, and in the crisis of the German summer offensive of 1918 was placed in command of all the troops, amounting almost to a corps, which held the gap in front of Bailleul. The Victoria Cross and the D.S.O. with two bars marked his unsurpassed service.

Freyberg, like his only equal, Carton de Wiart, deserved the title with which I acclaimed them of "Salamander." Both thrived in the fire, and were literally shot to pieces without being affected physically or in spirit. One day in the nineteen-twenties, when I was staying at a country house with Bernard Freyberg, I asked him to show me his wounds. He stripped himself, and I counted twenty-seven separate scars and gashes. To these he was to add in the Second World War another three. But of course, as he explained, "You nearly always get two wounds for every bullet or splinter, because mostly they have to go out as well as go in." At the outset of the new war no man was more fitted to command the New Zealand Division, for which he was eagerly chosen. In September, 1940, I had toyed with the idea of giving him a far greater scope. Now at length this decisive personal command had come to him. Freyberg is so made that he will fight for King and Country with an unconquerable heart anywhere he is ordered, and with whatever forces he is given by superior authorities, and he imparts his own invincible firmness of mind to all around him.

At home we did our utmost to help our hard-pressed commanders and troops.

Prime Minister to Admiral Cunningham   1 May 41

We are making extreme exertions to reinforce you from the air. It has been decided to repeat as soon as possible and on a much larger scale the recent operations [for air reinforcement]. *Ark Royal, Argus, Furious,* and *Victorious* will all be used to carry up to 140 additional Hurricanes, as well as 18 Fulmars, with pilots. We hope that 64 Hurricanes and 9 Fulmars will arrive in Middle East by May 25. Meanwhile, 25 fighter pilots leave May 23 for Takoradi to hasten ferrying of Hurricanes and Tomahawks. Capacity of route to Egypt via Takoradi freed by above use of carriers will be employed to increase the flow of Tomahawks and Hurricanes. Greatest possible shipment of Blenheims will be made at the same time. I may have more to signal about bomber reinforcements later.

2. I also congratulate you upon the brilliant and highly successful manner in which the Navy have once again succoured the Army and brought off four-fifths of the entire force.

3. It is now necessary to fight hard for Crete, which seems soon to be attacked heavily, and [also] for Malta as a base for flotilla action against the enemy's communications with Libya. Constantly improving attitude of United States and their naval co-operation justifies risks involved. Your plans for "Tiger" are excellent and give good chances.

4. But above all we look to you to cut off seaborne supplies from the Cyrenaican ports and to beat them up to the utmost. It causes grief here whenever we learn of the arrival of precious aviation spirit in one ship after another. This great battle for Egypt is what the Duke of Wellington called "a close-run thing," but if we can reinforce you and Wavell as proposed by Operations "Tiger" and "Jaguar" [air reinforcements], and you can cut off the tap of inflow, our immense armies in the Middle East will soon resume their ascendancy. All good wishes.

*   *   *

Freyberg and Wavell were under no illusions.

General Freyberg to General Wavell   1 May 41

Forces at my disposal are totally inadequate to meet attack envisaged. Unless fighter aircraft are greatly increased and naval forces made available to deal with seaborne attack, I cannot hope to hold out with land forces alone, which as result of campaign in Greece are now devoid of any artillery, have insufficient tools for digging, very little transport, and inadequate war reserves of equipment and ammunition. Force here can and will fight, but without full support from Navy and air force cannot hope to repel invasion. If for other reasons these cannot be made available at once, urge that question of holding Crete should be reconsidered. I feel that under terms of my charter it is my duty to inform New Zealand Government of situation in which greater part of my division is now placed.

He also informed his own Government:

1 May 41

Feel it is my duty to report military situation in Crete. Decision taken in London that Crete must be held at all costs. Have received appreciation scale of attack from War Office. In my opinion Crete can only be held with full support from Navy and air force. There is no evidence of naval forces capable of guaranteeing us against seaborne invasion, and air forces in island consist of six Hurricanes and seventeen obsolete aircraft. Troops can and will fight, but as result of campaign in Greece are devoid of any artillery and have insufficient tools for digging, little transport, and inadequate war reserves of equipment and ammunition. Would strongly represent to your Government grave situation in which bulk of New Zealand Division is placed, and recommend you bring pressure to bear on highest plane in London either to supply us with sufficient means to defend island or to review decision Crete must be held. I have, of course, made my official representation on this matter to C.-in-C. Middle East.

General Wavell to C.I.G.S.   2 May 41

Defence of Crete will present difficult problem for all three services, mainly on account of enemy air superiority. Ports and aerodromes, being in north of island, involve greater exposure of aircraft and shipping. Only good road in island (and that none too good) runs east and west along north coast, and also exposed.

2. There are no good roads north and south or harbours on south coast, though with time it may be possible to develop them. There is a great shortage of transport in island.

3. Food for civil population will have to be imported in considerable quantities. If towns heavily bombed and we are unable to provide fighter protection we may be faced with political problem.

4. To garrison island effectively at least three brigade groups required and considerable number of A.A. units. Present garrison three British Regular battalions, six New Zealand battalions, one Australian battalion, and two composite battalions of details evacuated from Greece. Those from Greece are weak in numbers and equipment. There is no artillery. Scale of A.A. defence inadequate, but is being reinforced.

5. As regards air force, there are at present no modern aircraft in island.

6. Greek troops at present are mostly untrained and unarmed.

7. Difficulties are being dealt with, and will be overcome if we get time, but air defence will always be difficult problem.

The Government of New Zealand were not unnaturally anxious about their division. I explained the position to them and to Mr. Fraser, their Prime Minister, who had just arrived in Cairo on his journey to England.

Prime Minister to Prime Minister of New Zealand   3 May 41

I am very glad that the exigencies of evacuation should have carried the New Zealand Division, after its brilliant fighting in Greece, in such good order to Crete. Naturally, every effort will be made to re-equip them, and in particular artillery, in which General Wavell is already strong, is being sent. The successful defence of Crete is one of the most important factors in the defence of Egypt. I am very glad that General Wavell has accepted my suggestion to put Freyberg in command of the whole island. You may be sure we shall sustain him in every way possible.

2. Our information points to an airborne attack being delivered in the near future, with possibly an attempt at seaborne attack. The Navy will certainly do their utmost to prevent the latter, and it is unlikely to succeed on any large scale. So far as airborne attack is concerned, this ought to suit the New Zealanders down to the ground, for they will be able to come to close quarters, man to man, with the enemy, who will not have the advantage of tanks and artillery, on which he so largely relies. Should the enemy get a landing in Crete that will be the beginning, and not the end, of embarrassments for him. The island is mountainous and wooded, giving peculiar scope to the qualities of your troops. We can reinforce it far more easily than the enemy, and there are over thirty thousand men there already.

3. It may be, however, that the enemy is only feinting at Crete, and will be going farther east. We have to consider all contingencies in the employment of our scanty and overpressed air force. Why is it scanty and overpressed? Not because we do not possess ever-growing resources and reserves here. Not because we have not done everything in human power to reinforce the Middle East with air. It is simply because of the physical difficulties of getting aircraft and their servicing personnel to the spot by the various routes and methods open to us. You may be sure we shall try our best to reinforce our air power, and we are at this moment making very far-reaching but hazardous efforts. The disposition between competing needs of such air forces as are in the East must be left to the Commanders-in-Chief. I am not without hope that things will be better in the Middle East in a month or so.

4. Everyone here admires the dignity and stoicism of New Zealand in enduring the agonising suspense of the evacuation. Its successful conclusion, after inflicting so much loss upon the enemy and paying our debt of honour to Greece, is an inexpressible relief to the Empire.

Freyberg was undaunted. He did not readily believe the scale of air attack would be so gigantic. His fear was of powerful organised invasion from the sea. This we hoped the Navy would prevent in spite of our air weakness.

General Freyberg to Prime Minister, England   5 May 41

Cannot understand nervousness; am not in the least anxious about airborne attack; have made my dispositions and feel can cope adequately with the troops at my disposal. Combination of seaborne and airborne attack is different. If that comes before I can get the guns and transport here the situation will be difficult. Even so, provided Navy can help, trust all will be well.

When we get our equipment and transport, and with a few extra fighter aircraft, it should be possible to hold Crete. Meanwhile there will be a period here during which we shall be vulnerable.

Everybody in great form and most anxious to renew battle with our enemy, whom we hammered whenever we met him in Greece.

All New Zealanders greatly and justly incensed at not being mentioned adequately in B.B.C. and press accounts of the vital and gallant part played by them in Greek rear-guard action.

I immediately did my best to remedy the sense of injustice from which the New Zealanders were suffering.

Prime Minister to General Wavell   7 May 41

Please pass following to General Freyberg, unless you disagree:

Everyone in Britain has watched with gratitude and admiration the grand fighting deeds of the New Zealand Division upon the ever-famous battlefields of Greece. It is only gradually that we have learned and are learning the full tale, and the more the accounts come in the more we realise the vital part you played in a task of honour and a deed of fame. Throughout the whole Empire and the English-speaking world the name of New Zealand is saluted. Our thoughts are with you now. God bless you all.

*   *   *

The geography of Crete indeed made its defence problem difficult. There was but a single road running along the north coast, upon which were strung all the vulnerable points of the island. Each of these had to be self-supporting. There could be no central reserve free to move to a threatened point once this road was cut and firmly held by the enemy. Only tracks unfit for motor transport ran from the south coast to the north from Sphakia and Timbaki. As the impending danger began to dominate directing minds strong efforts were made to carry reinforcements and supplies of weapons, especially artillery, to the island, but it was then too late. During the second week in May the German Air Force from its bases in Greece and in the Aegean established a virtual daylight blockade of Crete, and took their toll of all traffic, especially on the northern side, where alone the harbours lay. Out of twenty-seven thousand tons of vital munitions sent in the first three weeks of May to Crete, under three thousand could be landed, and the rest had to turn back with the loss of over three thousand tons. Our strength in A.A. weapons was sixteen heavy A.A. guns (3.7-inch mobile), thirty-six light A.A. guns (Bofors), and twenty-four A.A. searchlights. There were only nine part-worn in-

fantry tanks, distributed at the airfields, and sixteen light
tanks. On May 9 a part of the Mobile Naval Base Organisation arrived, including one heavy and one light A.A. battery,
which were deployed for the better protection of Suda Bay.
Altogether about two thousand men of this organisation landed
in Crete, but over three thousand were held back in Egypt,
though they might have got there. Six thousand Italian prisoners of war were an additional burden to the defence.

Our defending forces were distributed principally to protect
the landing grounds. At Heraklion were two British and three
Greek battalions; about Retimo the 19th Australian Brigade
and six Greek battalions; in the neighbourhood of Suda two
Australian and two Greek battalions; at Maleme a New
Zealand brigade near the airfield and a second brigade in
support farther east. Some parties of riflemen were added to
these garrisons, consisting of temporary units of men evacuated from Greece. The Greek battalions were weak in numbers, armed with a mixed assortment of rifles and little ammunition. The total of Imperial troops that took part in the
defence amounted to about 28,600.

But of course it was only our weakness in the air that rendered the German attack possible. The R.A.F. strength early
in May was twelve Blenheims, six Hurricanes, twelve Gladi-
ators, and six Fulmars and Brewsters of the Fleet air arm, of
which only one-half were serviceable. These were distributed
between the Retimo landing-strip, the Maleme airfield, for
fighters only, and the Heraklion airfield, which accepted all
types. This was but a trifle compared with the overwhelming
air forces about to be hurled upon the island. Our inferiority
in the air was fully realised by all concerned, and on May 19,
the day before the attack, all remaining aircraft were evacuated to Egypt. It was known to the War Cabinet, the Chiefs
of Staff, and the Commanders-in-Chief in the Middle East that
the only choice lay between fighting under this fearful
disadvantage or hurrying out of the island, as might have
been possible in the early days of May. But there was no
difference of opinion between any of us, about facing the
attack; and when we see in the light and knowledge of the
after-time how nearly, in spite of all our shortcomings, we
won, and how far-reaching were the advantages even of our
failure, we must be well content with the risks we ran and the
price we paid.

*   *   *

We may now set out the German plan of attack, which we have learnt since the war. It was confided to the XIth Air Corps, comprising the 7th Air Division and the 5th Mountain Division, with the 6th Mountain Division held in support. Nearly sixteen thousand men, mostly paratroops, were to be landed from the air, and seven thousand by sea. Additional air support was to be given by the Eighth Air Corps. The number of aircraft made available was: bombers, 280; dive-bombers, 150; fighter (M.E. 109 and M.E. 110), 180; reconnaissance, 40; gliders, 100; Ju. 52's (transport aircraft), 530; total, 1280.

The seaborne troops and a quantity of supplies were to be carried in two organised convoys of Greek caiques.[1] They had no protection except from the German Air Force. We shall see presently what was their fate.

The air attack was planned on three areas: in the east Heraklion; in the centre Retimo, Suda, Canea; and of course most important, Maleme, in the west. The immediate preparation for the attack was in general an hour's concentrated bombing of the ground and anti-aircraft defences with bombs of up to a thousand pounds weight. This was to be followed by the arrival of the leading troops in gliders and/or by parachute descents. These again were to be followed by reinforcements in transport aircraft. It was vital to the whole conception that Maleme airfield should be secured. Mere landings of parachute troops in the countryside several miles away would not have enabled the troop-carrying airplanes to land the 6th Mountain Division by forties and fifties and then return for further instalments. The Germans would have to have effective and undisturbed possession of the airfield, not only for landing but for taking off again. Only by repeated journeys could they bring the numbers which were the foundation of their whole enterprise.

*   *   *

We adopted the code name "Colorado" for Crete and "Scorcher" for the German onslaught as we imagined it.

The breathless days slipped by. They were only rendered endurable by other cares. The hour drew near.

Prime Minister to General Wavell   12 May 41

Will you consider whether at least another dozen "I" tanks with skilled personnel should not go to help [against] "Scorcher."

[1] Caique: a type of schooner, now usually motor-driven.

Prime Minister to General Wavell   14 May 41

All my information points to "Scorcher" any day after seventeenth. Everything seems to be moving in concert for that and with great elaboration. Hope you have got enough in "Colorado," and that those there have the needful in cannon, machine guns, and armoured fighting vehicles. It may well be that in so large and complicated a plan zero date will be delayed. Therefore, reinforcements sent now might well arrive in time, and certainly for the second round, should enemy gain a footing. I should particularly welcome chance for our high-class troops to come to close grips with those people under conditions where enemy has not got his usual mechanical advantages, and where we can surely reinforce much easier than he can. I suppose Admiral is with you in every detail of this, and that you and Tedder have concerted the best possible air plan, having regard to other tasks. All good wishes.

Prime Minister to General Wavell   15 May 41

I am increasingly impressed with the weight of the attack impending upon "Colorado," especially from the air. Trust all possible reinforcements have been sent.

Wavell's good-humour did not desert him in these moments.

General Wavell to Prime Minister   15 May 41

Have done best to equip "Colorado" against beetle pest. Recent reinforcements include six "I" tanks, sixteen light tanks, eighteen A.A. guns, seventeen field guns, one battalion. Am preparing small force, one or two battalions, with some tanks, to land south side "Colorado" as reserve. Propose also holding Polish Brigade as possible reinforcement. But problem landing reinforcements is difficult.

2. Cunningham, Tedder, and I discussed "Colorado" May 12, followed by inter-Service staff meeting. We have concerted plans as far as possible.

3. "Colorado" is not easy commitment, and German blitzes usually take some stopping. But we have stout-hearted troops, keen and ready to fight, under resolute commander, and I hope enemy will find their "Scorcher" red-hot proposition.

General Wavell to Prime Minister   16 May 41

Have just received following from Freyberg:

"Have completed plan for defence of Crete and have just returned from final tour of defences. I feel greatly encouraged by my visit. Everywhere all ranks are fit and morale is high. All defences have been extended, and positions wired as much as possible. We have forty-five field guns placed, with adequate ammunition dumped. Two infantry tanks are at each aerodrome. Carriers and transport still being unloaded and delivered. 2nd

Leicesters have arrived, and will make Heraklion stronger. I do not wish to be overconfident, but I feel that at least we will give excellent account of ourselves. With help of Royal Navy I trust Crete will be held."

Prime Minister to Commander-in-Chief Mediterranean   18 May 41

Our success in "Scorcher" would, of course, affect whole world situation. May you have God's blessing in this memorable and fateful operation, which will react in every theatre of the war.

Prime Minister to General Freyberg   18 May 41

We are glad to hear of the strong dispositions which you have made, and that reinforcements have reached you. All our thoughts are with you in these fateful days. We are sure that you and your brave men will perform a deed of lasting fame. The Royal Navy will do its utmost. Victory where you are would powerfully affect world situation.

I exposed my general view at this time fully to Smuts, who was in constant contact.

Prime Minister to General Smuts   16 May 41

I am, as usual, in close sympathy and agreement with your military outlook. I recently had measures taken to reinforce Wavell where he was weakest, and I have hopes that we shall be successful in heavy offensive fighting in the Western Desert during the next few weeks. We also expect a strong attack by the enemy on Crete almost immediately, and have made all possible preparations for it. If favourable decisions are obtained at these two points our problems in Syria and Iraq should be simplified. We are also reinforcing Middle East most powerfully from the air by every conceivable method. I have good hopes that we shall win the campaign in the Eastern Mediterranean this summer, and maintain our hold upon the Nile Valley and the Suez Canal. President Roosevelt is pushing United States supplies towards Suez to the utmost. The South African Army will be very welcome on the Mediterranean shore.

2. The western end of the Mediterranean is more doubtful, but Spain has hitherto stood up well to German pressure. We shall let Darlan know at the proper time that if Vichy aircraft bomb Gibraltar we shall not bomb France, but the Vichy skunks wherever they may hide out. We have not overlooked the possibility of Gibraltar Harbour becoming unusable, and have made the best preparations open to us. Perhaps the United States may be willing to come more closely into the West African business, especially at Dakar.

3. Finally, the Battle of the Atlantic is going fairly well. Instead of Hitler reaching a climax of blockade in May as he expected, we have just finished the best six weeks of convoys for

many months. We shall certainly get increasing American help in the Atlantic, and personally I feel confident our position will be strengthened in all essentials before the year is out. The Americans are making very great provision to replace shipping losses in 1942, and I feel they are being drawn nearer and nearer to their great decision. It is better, however, not to count too much on this.

4. It looks as if Hitler is massing against Russia. A ceaseless movement of troops, armoured forces, and aircraft northward from the Balkans and eastward from France and Germany is in progress. I should myself suppose his best chance was to attack the Ukraine and Caucasus, thus making sure of corn and oil. Nobody can stop him doing this, but we hope to blast the Fatherland behind him pretty thoroughly as the year marches on. I am sure that with God's help we shall beat the life out of the Nazi régime.

5. The King tells me he is going to send you a special message for your birthday on May 24, so I will send my heartfelt good wishes now.

Thus we reached the verge.

16

Crete: The Battle

The German Air Corps—The Attack Begins, May 20—Retimo and Heraklion Held—But Maleme Lost, May 23—The Navy Joins In —Destruction of German Convoys—Costly Days for the Navy, but Admiral Cunningham Throws Everything into the Scale— Loss of the "Gloucester" and the "Fiji"—"Kelly" and "Kashmir" Sunk—A Grave Telegram from Admiral Cunningham—And a Serious Report from General Freyberg—All Hope of Success Gone—We Decide to Evacuate, May 26—A Bitter and Dismal Task—Tragedy of the Heraklion Rescue—Admiral Cunningham's Decision to Continue the Evacuation—German Severities on the Island Population—The Price Paid—A Pyrrhic Victory.

IN MANY OF ITS ASPECTS at the time it was fought the Battle of Crete [1] was unique. Nothing like it had ever been seen before. It was the first large-scale airborne attack in the annals of war. The German Air Corps represented the flame of the Hitler Youth Movement and was an ardent embodiment of the Teutonic spirit of revenge for the defeat of 1918. The flower of German manhood was expressed in these valiant, highly trained, and completely devoted Nazi parachute troops. To lay down their lives on the altar of German glory and world-power was their passionate resolve. They were destined to encounter proud soldiers many of whom had come all the way from the other side of the world to fight as volunteers for the Motherland and what they deemed the cause of right and freedom. Here was the collision of which this chapter tells the tale.

The Germans used the whole strength they could command.

[1] See map, page 255.

240

This was to be Goering's prodigious air achievement. It might have been launched upon England in 1940 if British air power had been broken. But this expectation had not been fulfilled. It might have fallen on Malta. But this stroke was spared us. The German Air Corps had waited for more than seven months to strike their blow and prove their mettle. Now at length Goering could give them the long-awaited signal. When the battle joined we did not know what were the total resources of Germany in parachute troops. The XIth Air Corps might have been only one of half a dozen such units. It was not till many months afterwards that we were sure it was the only one. It was in fact the spear-point of the German lance. And this is the story of how it triumphed and was broken.

*   *   *

The battle began on the morning of May 20, and never was a more reckless, ruthless attack launched by the Germans. Their first and main aim was the Maleme airfield. For an hour the surrounding positions were subjected to the heaviest bombing and machine-gunning hitherto experienced from the air. The bulk of our A.A. artillery was put out of action practically at once. Before the bombardment was over, gliders began to land west of the airfield. At 8 A.M. parachutists were dropped in large numbers from heights varying from three hundred to six hundred feet, in the area between Maleme and Canea. One German regiment of four battalions in the morning, and a second in the afternoon, were thrown in by a continuous stream of aircraft, utterly regardless of losses to men and machines. They were resolutely encountered on and near the airfield by a battalion of the 5th New Zealand Brigade, with the rest of the brigade in support to the eastward. Wherever our troops were noticed, they were subjected to tremendous bombardment, bombs of five hundred and even a thousand pounds being used in profusion. Counter-attacks were impossible in daylight. A counter-attack with only two "I" tanks proved a failure. Gliders or troop-carriers landed or crashed on the beaches and in the scrub or on the fire-swept airfield. In all, around and between Maleme and Canea over five thousand Germans reached the ground on the first day. They suffered very heavy losses from the fire and fierce hand-to-hand fighting of the New Zealanders. In our defended area practically all who alighted were accounted for, most being killed. At the end of the day we were still in possession of the airfield, but that evening the few who were left of the battalion fell back on its supports. Two companies sent up to reinforce were too late to make a counter-attack for the airfield, which was still, however, under our artillery fire.

Retimo and Heraklion were both treated to a heavy air bombardment on that morning, followed by parachute drops in the afternoon of two and four battalions respectively. Heavy fighting followed, but at nightfall we remained in firm possession of both airfields. At Retimo and Heraklion there were also descents on a smaller scale, with hard fighting and heavy German casualties. The result of this first day's fighting was, therefore, fairly satisfactory, except at Maleme; but in every sector bands of well-armed men were now at large. The strength of the attacks far exceeded the expectations of the British command, and the fury of our resistance astonished the enemy.

This was the report we got:

General Freyberg to General Wavell   10 P.M. 20 May 41
Today has been a hard one. We have been hard pressed. So far, I believe, we hold aerodromes at Retimo, Heraklion, and Maleme, and the two harbours. Margin by which we hold them is a bare one, and it would be wrong of me to paint optimistic picture. Fighting has been heavy and we have killed large numbers of Germans. Communications are most difficult. Scale of air attacks upon Canea has been severe. Everybody here realises vital issue and we will fight it out.

The onslaught continued on the second day, when troop-carrying aircraft again appeared. Although Maleme airfield remained under our close artillery and mortar fire, troop-carriers continued to land upon it and in the rough ground to the west. The German High Command seemed indifferent to losses, and at least a hundred planes were wrecked by crash-landing in this area. Nevertheless, the build-up continued. A counter-attack made that night reached the edge of the airfield, but with daylight the German Air Force reappeared and the gains could not be held.

On the third day Maleme became an effective operational airfield for the enemy. Troop-carriers continued to arrive at a rate of more than twenty an hour. Even more decisive was the fact that they could also return for reinforcements. Altogether it was estimated that in these and the ensuing days more than six hundred troop-carriers landed or crashed more or less successfully on the airfield. Under the increasing pressure of these growing forces the plan for a major counter-attack had finally to be abandoned, and the 5th New Zealand Brigade gradually gave way until they were nearly ten miles from Maleme. At Canea and Suda there was no change, and at Retimo the situation was well in hand. At Heraklion the enemy were landing east of the airfield, and an effective hostile lodgment there began and grew. After the opening attacks on May 20 the German High Command switched off Retimo and Heraklion and concentrated mainly on the Suda Bay area.

* * *

Air reconnaissance having reported the presence of caiques in the Aegean, Admiral Cunningham had on the twentieth dispatched a light force to the northwest of Crete. It consisted of the cruisers *Naiad* and *Perth*, and the destroyers *Kandahar*, *Nubian*, *Kingston*, and *Juno*, under the command of Rear-Admiral King.

A powerful force under Rear-Admiral Rawlings, consisting of the battleships *Warspite* and *Valiant*, screened by eight destroyers, lay to the west of Crete on the lookout for the expected intervention by the Italian Fleet. Throughout the twenty-first our ships were subjected to heavy air attacks. The destroyer *Juno* was hit, and sank in two minutes with heavy loss of life. The cruisers *Ajax* and *Orion* were also damaged, but continued in action.

That night our weary troops saw to the northward the whole skyline alive with flashes and knew the Royal Navy was at work. The first German seaborne convoy had started on its desperate mission. In the afternoon groups of small craft were reported approaching Crete, and Admiral Cunningham ordered his light forces into the Aegean to prevent landings during the darkness. At 11.30 P.M., eighteen miles north of Canea, Rear-Admiral Glennie, with the cruisers *Dido*, *Orion*, and *Ajax* and four destroyers, caught the German troop convoy, composed chiefly of caiques escorted by torpedo boats. For two and a half hours the British ships hunted their prey, sinking not less than a dozen caiques and three steamers, all crowded with German troops. It was estimated that about four thousand men were drowned that night.

* * *

Meanwhile Rear-Admiral King, with the cruisers *Naiad*, *Perth*, *Calcutta*, and *Carlisle* and three destroyers, spent the night of the twenty-first patrolling off Heraklion, and at daylight on the twenty-second began to sweep northward. A single caique loaded with troops was destroyed, and by ten o'clock the squadron was approaching the island of Melos. A few minutes later an enemy destroyer with five small craft was sighted to the northward, and was at once engaged. Another destroyer was then seen laying a smoke-screen, and behind the smoke were a large number of caiques. We had in fact intercepted another important convoy crammed with soldiers. Our air reconnaissance had reported this fact to Admiral Cunningham, but it took more than an hour for this news to be confirmed to Rear-Admiral King. His ships had been under incessant air attack since daylight, and although they had hitherto suffered no damage all were running short of A.A. ammunition. Their combine speed was also reduced, as the *Carlisle* could steam no more than twenty-one knots. The Rear-Admiral, not fully realising the prize which was almost within his grasp, felt that to go farther north would jeopardise his whole force, and ordered a withdrawal to the west. As soon as this signal was read by the Commander-in-Chief, he sent the following order:

Stick it out. Keep in visual signalling touch. Must not let Army down in Crete. It is essential no seaborne enemy force land in Crete.

*   *   *

It was now too late to destroy the convoy, which had turned back and scattered in all directions among the numerous islands. Thus at least five thousand German soldiers escaped the fate of their comrades. The audacity of the German authorities in ordering these practically defenceless convoys of troops across waters of which they did not possess the naval command as well as that of the air is a sample of what might have happened on a gigantic scale in the North Sea and the English Channel in September, 1940. It shows the German lack of comprehension of sea power against invading forces, and also the price which may be exacted in human life as the penalty for this kind of ignorance.

*   *   *

The Rear-Admiral's retirement did not save his squadron from the air attack. He probably suffered as much loss in his withdrawal as he would have done in destroying the convoy. For the next three and a half hours his ships were bombed

continuously. His flagship, the *Naiad,* and the *Carlisle,* whose
commander, Captain T. C. Hampton, was killed, were both
damaged. At 1.10 P.M. they were met by the battleships
Warspite and *Valiant,* with the cruisers *Gloucester* and *Fiji*
and seven destroyers under Rear-Admiral Rawlings, who were
hastening through the Cythera Strait from the westward to
support them. Almost at the moment when the *Warspite*
arrived, she was hit by a bomb which wrecked her starboard
four-inch and six-inch batteries and reduced her speed, and as
the enemy had now escaped, the combined British squadrons
drew off to the southwestward. Inflexibly resolved, whatever
the cost, to destroy all seaborne invaders, Admiral Cunningham had indeed thrown everything into the scale. It is clear
that throughout these operations he did not hesitate for this
purpose to hazard not only his most precious ships, but the
whole naval command of the Eastern Mediterranean. His
conduct on this issue was highly approved by the Admiralty.
In this grim battle the German command was not alone in
playing the highest stakes. The events of these forty-eight
hours of sea-fighting convinced the enemy, and no further
attempts at seaborne landings were attempted until the fate
of Crete had been decided.

*   *   *

May 22 and 23 were costly days for the Navy. The destroyer *Greyhound* in Rear-Admiral Rawlings's squadron was
bombed and sunk. Rear-Admiral King, senior officer of the
now combined forces, ordered two other destroyers to rescue
survivors and the cruisers *Gloucester* and *Fiji* to protect them
against air attack, which was incessant and increasing. This
delayed the whole fleet and greatly prolonged the air attack
upon them. At 2.57 P.M. on the twenty-second, Rear-Admiral
King, informed that their A.A. ammunition was running short,
told the two cruisers to withdraw at discretion. At 3.30 P.M.
the *Gloucester* and *Fiji* were reported approaching the fleet
from astern at high speed under heavy aircraft attack. Twenty
minutes later the *Gloucester,* hit by several bombs, was
brought to a full stop, badly on fire, and with her upper deck
a shambles. The *Fiji* had no choice but to leave her, and,
having lost contact with the Fleet and being short of fuel,
she steered more directly towards Alexandria with her two destroyers. Three hours later, after surviving nearly twenty attacks by formations of bombers and having fired all her heavy
A.A. ammunition, she fell a victim to an M.E. 109 which

approached unseen through the clouds. There was a heavy
explosion. The ship took a list, but still made seventeen knots,
until another attack came and three more bombs struck home.
At 8.15 P.M. she capsized and sank, but 523 out of her company of 780 were picked up from the water by her two
destroyers, which returned after dark.

*   *   *

Meanwhile the Fleet, twenty miles to the westward, had
been subjected to recurrent air attacks, during which the
Valiant was hit, but not seriously damaged. At 4 P.M. Captain
Lord Louis Mountbatten, in the *Kelly*, with four other destroyers of the latest type, with which flotilla we had just
reinforced the Central Mediterranean, arrived from Malta and
joined the Fleet. After dark his destroyers were sent back to
search for survivors from the *Gloucester* and *Fiji*. But this
work of mercy was brushed aside by the Commander-in-Chief
in favour of patrolling the north coast of Crete during the
dark hours. Here again was a right decision, however painful.
All the night of the twenty-second Mountbatten's destroyers
patrolled off Canea, while Captain Mack in the *Jervis* and
three others scoured the approaches to Heraklion. One caique
crowded with troops fell to the *Kelly*, another was set on fire,
and at dawn the destroyers withdrew to the southward.

During the night Admiral Cunningham learned the general
situation and of the loss of the *Gloucester* and *Fiji*. Owing to
a clerical error in the signal distribution office at Alexandria it
appeared to him as if not only the cruisers, but the battleships
also, had expended nearly all their A.A. ammunition. At 4
A.M., therefore, he ordered all forces to retire to the eastward.
In fact the battleships had ample ammunition, and Cunningham has stated since that had he known this he would not
have withdrawn them. Their presence the following morning
might possibly have prevented another disaster which must
now be recorded.

At dawn on the twenty-third the *Kelly* and *Kashmir* were
retiring at full speed round the west of Crete. After surviving
two heavy air attacks they were overtaken at 7.55 A.M. by
a formation of twenty-four dive bombers. Both ships were
quickly sunk, with a loss of 210 lives. Fortunately the destroyer *Kipling* was near by, and, despite continuous bombing,
rescued from the sea 279 officers and men, including Lord
Louis Mountbatten, while she herself remained unscathed.
Next morning, while still fifty miles away from Alexandria,

and crowded from stem to stern with men, she ran completely
out of fuel, but was safely met and towed in.

*   *   *

Thus, in the fighting of May 22 and 23 the Navy had lost
two cruisers and three destroyers sunk, one battleship, the
Warspite, put out of action for a long time, and the *Valiant*
and many other units considerably damaged. Nevertheless,
the sea-guard of Crete had been maintained. The Navy had
not failed. Not a single German landed in Crete from the sea
until the battle for the island was ended.

The Commander-in-Chief did not know as yet how well he
had succeeded.

The operations of the last four days [he signalled on the
twenty-third] have been nothing short of a trial of strength between the Mediterranean Fleet and the German Air Force. . . .
I am afraid that in the coastal area we have to admit defeat and
accept the fact that losses are too great to justify us in trying to
prevent seaborne attacks on Crete. This is a melancholy conclusion, but it must be faced. As I have always feared, enemy command of air, unchallenged by our own air force, and in these
restricted waters, with Mediterranean weather, is too great odds
for us to take on except by seizing opportunities of surprise and
using utmost circumspection. . . .
It is perhaps fortunate that H.M.S. *Formidable* [aircraft carrier]
was immobilised, as I doubt if she would now be afloat.

To this the Admiralty replied at once:

If it were only a duel between the Mediterranean Fleet and the
German Air Force, it would probably be necessary to accept the
restrictions on the movements of the Fleet which you suggest.
There is, however, in addition the battle for Crete. If the Fleet
can prevent seaborne reinforcements and supplies reaching the
enemy until the Army has had time to deal successfully with all
airborne troops, the Army may then be able to deal with seaborne
attacks. It is vitally important therefore to prevent a seaborne
expedition reaching the island during the next day or two, even if
this results in further losses to the Fleet. Their Lordships most
fully appreciate the heavy strain under which your fleet is
working.

As the agony in Crete approached its climax, I telegraphed
to President Roosevelt:

23 May 41
Battle in Crete is severe, because, having no airfields within
effective range, we cannot bring any air force into action either

to aid the defence or protect our patrolling squadrons. Two of our cruisers and two destroyers were sunk today. We are destroying many of the highest class German troops, and have sunk at least one convoy.

And to Wavell:

23 May 41

Crete battle must be won. Even if enemy secure good lodgments fighting must be maintained indefinitely in the island, thus keeping enemy main striking force tied down to the task. This will at least give you time to mobilise "Tiger Cubs" and dominate situation Western Desert. While it lasts it also protects Cyprus. Hope you will reinforce Crete every night to fullest extent. Is it not possible to send more tanks and thus reconquer any captured aerodrome? Enemy's exertions and losses in highest class troops must be very severe. He cannot keep it up for ever. Following for General Freyberg from me: "The whole world is watching your splendid battle, on which great events turn."

The Chiefs of Staff were in full accord, and telegraphed to the Commanders-in-Chief:

24 May 41

Our difficulties in Crete are great, but from all the information we have so are those of enemy. If we stick it out enemy's effort may peter out. It seems to us imperative that reinforcements in greatest strength possible should be sent as soon as possible to island to ensure the destruction of the enemy already landed before they can be seriously reinforced. The vital importance of this battle is well known to you, and great risks must be accepted to ensure our success.

Admiral Cunningham replied to the Admiralty message of the twenty-third:

C.-in-C. Mediterranean to Admiralty   26 May 41

Their Lordships may rest assured that determining factor in operating in Aegean is not fear of sustaining losses, but need to avoid loss which, without commensurate advantage to ourselves, will cripple Fleet out here. So far as I am aware, enemy has not yet succeeded in getting any considerable reinforcements to Crete by sea, if indeed he has sent any at all, though I agree this may soon be appreciable.

2. Surely we have already sufficient experience of what losses are likely to be. In three days two cruisers and four destroyers were sunk, one battleship is out of action for several months, and two other cruisers and four destroyers sustained considerable damage. We cannot afford another such experience and retain sea control in Eastern Mediterranean.

3. In point of fact, supply by sea has not yet come much into picture, as, despite loss and turning back to his convoys, enemy is so prolific in air that for the moment he is able to reinforce and keep his forces supplied by air at will. This process is quite unchecked by air action on our part, and sight of constant unhindered procession of Ju. 52's flying into Crete is among factors likely to affect morale of our forces.

4. I feel that their Lordships should know that effect of recent operations on personnel is cumulative. Our light craft, officers, men, and machinery alike are nearing exhaustion. Since "Lustre" [Greece] started, at end of February, they have been kept running almost to limit of endurance, and now, when work is redoubled, they are faced with an air concentration beside which, I am assured, that in Norway was child's play. It is inadvisable to drive men beyond a certain point.

5. I have been able to do rather more than was foreshadowed. Each night destroyers and cruisers sweep north coast of Crete, we have bombarded Maleme, and this morning attacked Scarpanto. Melos is also receiving attention from a submarine. . . . I have not, however, yet received reinforcements of reconnaissance aircraft which I so earnestly requested.

6. Since writing above I learn H.M.S. *Formidable* and H.M.S. *Nubian* have been hit by bombs and are returning to harbour. I have no details.

Still heavier trials lay before this resolute Commander-in-Chief, to which he proved himself more than equal.

* * *

But now late on the twenty-sixth grave news reached Wavell from Freyberg.

I regret to have to report [said Freyberg] that in my opinion the limit of endurance has been reached by the troops under my command here at Suda Bay. No matter what decision is taken by the Commanders-in-Chief from a military point of view, our position here is hopeless. A small ill-equipped and immobile force such as ours cannot stand up against the concentrated bombing that we have been faced with during the last seven days. I feel I should tell you that from an administrative point of view the difficulties of extricating this force in full are insuperable. Provided a decision is reached at once, a certain proportion of the force might be embarked. Once this section has been reduced the reduction of Retimo and Heraklion by the same methods will only be a matter of time. The troops we have, with the exception of the Welsh Regiment and the commandos, are past any offensive action. If you decide, in view of the whole Middle-East position, that hours will help we will carry on. I would have to consider how this would be best achieved. Suda Bay may be under fire within twenty-four hours. Further casualties have been heavy, and we have lost the majority of our immobile guns.

To Freyberg I telegraphed:

27 May 41

Your glorious defence commands admiration in every land. We know enemy is hard pressed. All aid in our power is being sent.

Prime Minister to Commanders-in-Chief Middle East   27 May 41

Victory in Crete essential at this turning-point in the war. Keep hurling in all aid you can.

   *   *   *

But that night we learned that all hope of success was gone.

General Wavell to Prime Minister   27 May 41

Fear that situation in Crete most serious. Canea front has collapsed and Suda Bay only likely to be covered for another twenty-four hours, if as long. There is no possibility of hurling in reinforcements. . . .

2. On the island itself our troops, majority of whom had most severe trial in Greece from overwhelming air attack, have been subjected to same conditions on steadily increasing scale in Crete. Such continuous and unopposed air attack must drive stoutest troops from positions sooner or later and makes administration practically impossible.

3. Telegram just received from Freyberg states only chance of survival of force in Suda area is to withdraw to beaches in south of island, hiding by day and moving by night. Force at Retimo reported cut off and short of supplies. Force at Heraklion also apparently almost surrounded.

4. Fear we must recognise that Crete is no longer tenable and that troops must be withdrawn as far as possible. It has been impossible to withstand weight of enemy air attack, which has been on unprecedented scale and has been through force of circumstances practically unopposed.

   *   *   *

On the fourth day of the land battle General Freyberg had formed a new line in the Maleme-Canea sector. Thanks to the free use of the airfield, the Germans' strength grew continually. May 26 was the decisive day. Our troops forced back in the neighbourhood of Canea had been under ever-growing pressure for six days. Finally they could stand it no more. The front was broken on the landward side and the enemy reached Suda Bay. Communication with Freyberg's headquarters failed, and retirement southward across the island to Sphakia began on his delegated authority. Late that night the decision to evacuate Crete was taken. There was much confusion on the trek across the mountains. Fortunately two commandos, about seven hundred and fifty men, under Colonel Laycock, had been landed at Suda by the minelayer *Abdiel* on the night of the twenty-sixth. These comparatively fresh forces, with the remains of the 5th New Zealand Brigade and the 7th and 8th Australian battalions, fought a strong rear-guard action, which enabled almost the whole of our forces in the Suda-Canea-Maleme area that still survived to make their way to the southern shore.

At Retimo the position was firmly held, although the troops were completely surrounded on the landward side and food and ammunition ran low. They received some rations by motor craft, but no orders to break for the south coast could reach them. Steadily the enemy closed in, until on the thirtieth, with their food exhausted, the survivors surrendered, having killed at least three hundred Germans. About one hundred and forty individuals contrived their escape.

At Heraklion the German strength east of the airfield grew daily. The garrison had been reinforced by part of the Argyll and Sutherland Highlanders, who had landed at Timbaki and fought their way through to join them. The Navy now came to the rescue, just in time.

*   *   *

We had to face once again the bitter and dismal task of an evacuation and the certainty of heavy losses. The harassed, overstrained Fleet had to undertake the embarking of about twenty-two thousand men, mostly from the open beach at Sphakia, across three hundred and fifty miles of sea dominated by hostile air forces. The Royal Air Force had done their best from Egypt with the few aircraft which had the necessary range. The principal target was the enemy-held Maleme airfield, which received a number of bombing attacks both by day and night. While these operations threw a heavy strain on the crews, their necessarily small scale could not have any appreciable effect. Air Marshal Tedder promised to provide some fighter cover for the ships, but this, he warned us, would be meagre and spasmodic. Sphakia, a small fishing village on the south coast, lies at the foot of a steep cliff five hundred feet high traversed only by a precipitous goat track. It was necessary for the troops to hide near the edge until called

forward for embarkation. Four destroyers, under Captain
Arliss, arrived on the night of the twenty-eighth and embarked seven hundred men, besides bringing food for the very
large numbers now gathering. Fighter protection was available for the return voyage, which was made with only minor
damage to one destroyer. At least fifteen thousand men lay
concealed in the broken ground near Sphakia, and Freyberg's
rear guard was in constant action.

A tragedy awaited the simultaneous expedition by Rear-
Admiral Rawlings, which, with the cruisers *Orion*, *Ajax*, and
Dido and six destroyers, went to rescue the Heraklion garrison. His force was under severe air attack from Scarpanto
from 5 P.M. till dark. The *Ajax* and the destroyer *Imperial*
were near-missed, and the former had to return. Arriving at
Heraklion before midnight, the destroyers ferried the troops
to the cruisers waiting outside. By 3.20 A.M. the work was
complete. Four thousand men had been embarked and the
return voyage began. Half an hour later the steering gear of
the damaged *Imperial* suddenly failed, and collision with the
cruisers was narrowly averted. It was imperative that the
whole force should be as far as possible to the south by daylight. Rear-Admiral Rawlings nevertheless decided to order the
destroyer *Hotspur* to return, take off all the *Imperial's* troops
and crew, and sink her. He himself reduced speed to fifteen
knots, and the *Hotspur*, carrying nine hundred soldiers, rejoined him just before daylight. He was now an hour and a
half late on his time-table, and it was not until sunrise that he
turned south to pass through the Kaso Strait. Fighter protection had been arranged, but partly through the change in
times the aircraft did not find the ships. The dreaded bombing
began at 6 A.M., and continued until 3 P.M. when the squadron was within a hundred miles of Alexandria.

The *Hereward* was the first casualty. At 6.25 A.M. she was
hit by a bomb and could no longer keep up with the convoy.
The Admiral rightly decided that he must leave the stricken
ship to her fate. She was last seen approaching the coast of
Crete. The majority of those on board survived, though as
prisoners of war. Worse was to follow. During the next four
hours the cruisers *Dido* and *Orion* and the destroyer *Decoy*
were all hit. The speed of the squadron fell to twenty-one
knots, but all kept their southerly course in company. In the
Orion conditions were appalling. Besides her own crew, she
had 1100 troops on board. On her crowded mess-decks about
260 men were killed and 280 wounded by a bomb which

penetrated the bridge. Her commander, Captain G. R. B. Back, was also killed, the ship heavily damaged and set on fire. At noon two Fulmars of the Fleet air arm appeared, and thereafter afforded a measure of relief. The fighters of the Royal Air Force, despite all efforts, could not find the tortured squadron, though they fought several engagements and destroyed at least two aircraft. When the squadron reached Alexandria at 8 P.M. on the twenty-ninth it was found that one-fifth of the garrison rescued from Heraklion had been killed, wounded, or captured.

* * *

We have seen how hard the Commanders-in-Chief in Cairo were pressed from home both by the political and military authorities, and much of this pressure was passed on to our forces in contact with the enemy, who responded nobly. But after the experiences of the twenty-ninth, General Wavell and his colleagues had to decide how far the effort to bring our troops off from Crete should be pursued. The Army was in mortal peril, the Air could do little, and again the task fell upon the wearied and bomb-torn Navy. To Admiral Cunningham it was against all tradition to abandon the Army in such a crisis. He declared, "It takes the Navy three years to build a new ship. It will take three hundred years to build a new tradition. The evacuation [that is, rescue] will continue." But it was only after much heart-searching and after consultation both with the Admiralty and General Wavell that the decision was taken to persevere. By the morning of the twenty-ninth nearly five thousand men had been brought off, but very large numbers were holding out and sheltering on all the approaches to Sphakia, and were bombed whenever they showed themselves by day. The decision to risk unlimited further naval losses was justified, not only in its impulse but by the results.

On the evening of the twenty-eighth, Rear-Admiral King had sailed, with the *Phoebe*, *Perth*, *Calcutta*, *Coventry*, the assault-ship *Glengyle*, and three destroyers, for Sphakia. On the night of the twenty-ninth about six thousand men were embarked there without interference, the *Glengyle's* landing-craft greatly helping the work. By 3.20 A.M. the whole body was on its way back, and, though attacked three times during the thirtieth, reached Alexandria safely. Only the cruiser *Perth* was damaged, by a hit in a boiler-room. This good luck was due to the R.A.F. fighters, who, few though they were, broke up more than one attack before they struck home. It was thought that the night of the twenty-ninth–thirtieth would be the last for trying, but during the twenty-ninth it was felt that the situation was less desperate than it had seemed. Accordingly, on the morning of the thirtieth, Captain Arliss once more sailed for Sphakia, with four destroyers. Two of these had to return, but he continued with the *Napier* and *Nizam* (a destroyer given to us by the Prince and people of Hyderabad), and successfully embarked over fifteen hundred troops. Both ships were damaged by near-misses on the return voyage, but reached Alexandria safely. The King of Greece, after many perils, had been brought off with the British Minister a few days earlier. That night also General Freyberg was evacuated by air on instructions from the Commanders-in-Chief.

On May 30 a final effort was ordered to bring out the remaining troops. It was thought that the numbers at Sphakia did not now exceed three thousand men, but later information showed that there were more than double that number. Rear-Admiral King sailed again on the morning of the thirty-first, with the *Phoebe*, *Abdiel*, and three destroyers. They could not hope to carry all, but Admiral Cunningham ordered the ships to be filled to the utmost. At the same time the Admiralty were told that this would be the last night of evacuation. The embarkation went well, and the ships sailed again at 3 A.M. on June 1, carrying nearly four thousand troops safely to Alexandria. The cruiser *Calcutta*, sent out to help them in, was bombed and sunk within a hundred miles of Alexandria.

Upward of five thousand British and Imperial troops were left somewhere in Crete, and were authorised by General Wavell to capitulate. Many individuals, however, dispersed in the mountainous island, which is a hundred and sixty miles long. They and the Greek soldiers were succoured by the villagers and country folk, who were mercilessly punished whenever detected. Barbarous reprisals were made upon innocent or valiant peasants, who were shot by twenties and thirties. It was for this reason that I proposed to the Supreme War Council three years later, in 1944, that local crimes should be locally judged, and the accused persons sent back for trial on the spot. This principle was accepted, and some of the outstanding debts were paid.

❊   ❊   ❊

Sixteen thousand five hundred men were brought safely back to Egypt. These were almost entirely British and Imperial troops. Nearly a thousand more were helped to escape later by various commando enterprises. Our losses were about thirteen thousand killed, wounded, and taken prisoners. To these must be added nearly two thousand naval casualties. Since the war more than four thousand German graves have been counted in the area of Maleme and Suda Bay; another thousand at Retimo and Heraklion. Besides these were the very large but unknown numbers drowned at sea, and those who later died of wounds in Greece. In all, the enemy must have suffered casualties in killed and wounded of well over fifteen thousand. About a hundred and seventy troop-carrying aircraft were lost or heavily damaged. But the price they paid for their victory cannot be measured by the slaughter.

* * *

The Battle of Crete is an example of the decisive results that may emerge from hard and well-sustained fighting apart from manoeuvring for strategic positions. We did not know how many parachute divisions the Germans had. Indeed, as the result of what happened in Crete, we made preparations, as will presently be described, for home defence against four or five of these audacious airborne divisions; and later still we and the Americans reproduced them ourselves on an even larger scale. But in fact the 7th Airborne Division was the only one which Goering had. This division was destroyed in the Battle of Crete. Upward of five thousand of his bravest

men were killed, and the whole structure of this organisation
was irretrievably broken. It never appeared again in any effective form. The New Zealanders and other British, Imperial,
and Greek troops who fought in the confused, disheartening,
and vain struggle for Crete may feel that they played a definite
part in an event which brought us far-reaching relief at a
hingeing moment.

The German losses of their highest class fighting men removed a formidable air and parachute weapon from all further
part in immediate events in the Middle East. Goering gained
only a Pyrrhic victory in Crete; for the forces he expended
there might easily have given him Cyprus, Iraq, Syria, and
even perhaps Persia. These troops were the very kind needed
to overrun large wavering regions where no serious resistance
would have been encountered. He was foolish to cast away
such almost measureless opportunities and irreplaceable
forces in a mortal struggle, often hand-to-hand, with the
warriors of the British Empire.

We now have in our possession the "battle report" of the
XIth Air Corps, of which the 7th Airborne Division was a
part. When we recall the severe criticism and self-criticism to
which our arrangements were subjected, it is interesting to
read the other side.

British land forces in Crete [said the Germans] were about
three times the strength which had been assumed. The area of
operations on the island had been prepared for defence with the
greatest care and by every possible means. . . . All works were
camouflaged with great skill. . . . The failure, owing to lack of
information, to appreciate correctly the enemy situation endangered the attack of the XIth Air Corps and resulted in exceptionally high and bloody losses.

In the German report of their examination of our prisoners
of war the following note occurs, which, in my gratitude to
those unknown friends, I venture to quote:

As regards the spirit and morale of the British troops, it is
worth mentioning that in spite of the many setbacks to the conduct of the war there remains, generally, absolute confidence in
Churchill.

*   *   *

The naval position in the Mediterranean was, on paper at
least, gravely affected by our losses in the battle and evacuation of Crete. The Battle of Matapan on March 28 had for the

time being driven the Italian Fleet into its harbours. But now new, heavy losses had fallen upon our Fleet. On the morrow of Crete Admiral Cunningham had ready for service only two battleships, three cruisers, and seventeen destroyers. Nine other cruisers and destroyers were under repair in Egypt, but the battleships *Warspite* and *Barham* and his only aircraft-carrier, the *Formidable*, besides several other vessels, would have to leave Alexandria for repair elsewhere. Three cruisers and six destroyers had been lost. Reinforcements must be sent without delay to restore the balance. But, as will presently be recorded, still further misfortunes were in store. The period which we now had to face offered to the Italians their best chance of challenging our dubious control of the Eastern Mediterranean, with all that this involved. We could not tell they would not seize it.

17

The Fate of the "Bismarck"

*Danger in the Atlantic—The "Bismarck" and "Prinz Eugen" at
Sea, May 20—The Denmark Strait—The Destruction of the
"Hood," May 24—The "Bismarck" Turns South—Suspense at
Chequers—The "Prinz Eugen" Escapes—Torpedo Hit on "Bis-
marck" at Midnight—Contact Lost on May 25—But Regained
on the Twenty-Sixth—Shortage of Fuel—The "Sheffield" and the
"Ark Royal"—The "Bismarck" Out of Control—Captain Vian's
Destroyers—"Rodney" Strikes, May 27—My Report to the House
—Credit for All—My Telegram to President Roosevelt.*

AFTER THE GREEK COLLAPSE, while all was uncertain in the
Western Desert, and the desperate battle in Crete was
turning heavily against us, a naval episode of the highest consequence supervened in the Atlantic.

Besides the constant struggle with the U-boats, surface
raiders had already cost us over three-quarters of a million
tons of shipping. The two enemy battle-cruisers *Scharnhorst*
and *Gneisenau* and the cruiser *Hipper* remained poised at
Brest under the protection of their powerful A.A. batteries,
and no one could tell when they would again molest our trade
routes. By the middle of May there were signs that the new
battleship *Bismarck*, possibly accompanied by the new eight-
inch-gun cruiser *Prinz Eugen*, would soon be thrown into the
fight. A combination of all these fast, powerful vessels in the
great spaces of the Atlantic Ocean would subject our naval
strength to a trial of the first magnitude. The *Bismarck*,
mounting eight fifteen-inch guns, and built regardless of treaty
limitations, was the most heavily armoured ship afloat. Her
displacement exceeded that of our newest battleships by nearly
ten thousand tons, and she was at least their equal in speed.

"You are the pride of the Navy," said Hitler when he visited her in May.

To meet this impending menace the Commander-in-Chief, Admiral Tovey, had at Scapa our new battleships, *King George V* and *Prince of Wales,* and the battle-cruiser *Hood.* At Gibraltar lay Admiral Somerville with the *Renown* and *Ark Royal.* The *Repulse* and the new carrier *Victorious* were at this moment about to sail with a convoy of more than twenty thousand men for the Middle East. The *Rodney* and *Ramillies,* which the *Bismarck* could probably have sunk had she met either of them singly, were on convoy escort in the Atlantic, and the *Revenge* was at Halifax ready to sail. In all at this time eleven convoys, including a precious troop convoy, with its risk of fearful loss of life, were at sea or about to sail. Cruiser patrols covered the exits from the North Sea and vigilant air reconnaissance watched the Norwegian coast. The naval situation was both obscure and tense, and the Admiralty, with whom I was in constant touch, became conscious of something coming, and also, acutely, of our full-spread target of merchant shipping.

In the early hours of May 21 we learned that two large warships had been seen leaving the Kattegat with a strong escort, and later the same day both the *Bismarck* and the *Prinz Eugen* were identified in Bergen Fiord. Clearly some important operation impended, and instantly our whole Atlantic control apparatus flashed into intense activity. The Admiralty pursued the sound and orthodox principle of concentrating upon the raiders and running risks with the convoys, including even the troop convoy. The *Hood,* with the *Prince of Wales* and six destroyers, left Scapa soon after midnight on the twenty-second to cover the cruisers *Norfolk* and *Suffolk,* already on patrol in the dreary, ice-bound stretch of water between Greenland and Iceland known as the Denmark Strait. The cruisers *Manchester* and *Birmingham* were ordered to guard the channel between Iceland and the Faroes. The *Repulse* and *Victorious* were placed at the disposal of the Commander-in-Chief, and the troop convoy was allowed to sail naked, except for destroyer escorts, from the Clyde.

Thursday, May 22, was a day of uncertainty and suspense. In the North Sea all was unbroken cloud and rain. In spite of these conditions a naval aircraft from Hatston (Orkney) penetrated into Bergen Fiord and forced home a determined reconnaissance in the teeth of heavy fire. The two enemy warships were no longer there! When at 8 P.M. this news reached

Admiral Tovey he at once set forth in the *King George V*, with the *Victorious*, four cruisers, and seven destroyers, to take up a central position to the westward so as to support his cruiser patrols whichever side of Iceland the enemy might choose. The *Repulse* joined him at sea the following morning. The Admiralty judged it probable that the enemy would pass through the Denmark Strait. That evening, within a few minutes of receiving the report, I telegraphed to President Roosevelt:

Former Naval Person to President Roosevelt   23 May 41

Yesterday, twenty-first, *Bismarck, Prinz Eugen,* and eight merchant ships located in Bergen. Low clouds prevented air attack. Tonight [we find] they have sailed. We have reason to believe that a formidable Atlantic raid is intended. Should we fail to catch them going out, your Navy should surely be able to mark them down for us. *King George V, Prince of Wales, Hood, Repulse,* and aircraft-carrier *Victorious,* with ancillary vessels, will be on their track. Give us the news and we will finish the job.

The *Bismarck* and the *Prinz Eugen* had in fact left Bergen nearly twenty-four hours before, and were now to the northeast of Iceland, heading for the Denmark Strait. Here the pack-ice had narrowed the strait to only eighty miles, mostly shrouded in dense mist. Towards evening on the twenty-third first the *Suffolk* and then the *Norfolk* sighted two ships approaching from the north, skirting the edge of the ice in a patch of clear weather. The *Norfolk's* sighting report was received first in the Admiralty, and was at once broadcast in secret code to all concerned. The hunt was on; the quarry was in view; and all our forces moved accordingly. The Commander-in-Chief turned to the westward and increased his speed. The *Hood* and the *Prince of Wales* shaped their course to intercept the enemy at daylight the next morning west of Iceland. The Admiralty called Admiral Somerville, with Force H (*Renown, Ark Royal,* and the cruiser *Sheffield*), northward at high speed to protect the troop convoy, now more than halfway down the Irish coast, or join in the battle. Admiral Somerville's ships, already under steam, left Gibraltar at 2 A.M. on the twenty-fourth. They carried with them, as it turned out, the *Bismarck's* fate.

*   *   *

I went to Chequers on Friday afternoon (May 23). Averell Harriman and Generals Ismay and Pownall were to be with me till Monday. With the Battle of Crete at its height it was likely to be an anxious week-end. I had, of course, a most complete service of secretaries in the house, and also direct telephone connections with the duty captain at the Admiralty and other key departments. The Admiralty expected the *Bismarck* and the *Prinz Eugen* to come through the Denmark Strait in the early dawn, and that the *Prince of Wales* and the *Hood*, with two or three cruisers, would bring them to battle. All our ships were moving towards the scene in accordance with the general plan. We spent an anxious evening, and did not go to bed until two or three o'clock.

At about seven I was awakened to hear formidable news. The *Hood*, our largest and also our fastest capital ship, had blown up. Although somewhat lightly constructed, she carried eight fifteen-inch guns, and was one of our most cherished naval possessions. Her loss was a bitter grief, but knowing of all the ships that were converging towards the *Bismarck* I felt sure we should get her before long, unless she turned north and went home. I went straight to Harriman's room at the end of the corridor, and, according to him, said, "The *Hood* has blown up, but we have got the *Bismarck* for certain." I then returned to my room, and was so well tired out that I went to sleep again. At about half-past eight my principal private secretary, Martin, came into the room in his dressing-gown with a strained look on his ascetic, clear-cut face. "Have we got her?" I asked. "No, and the *Prince of*

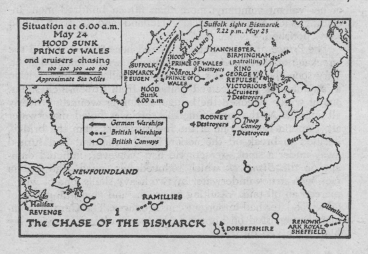

Situation at 6.00 a.m.
May 24
HOOD SUNK
PRINCE OF WALES
and cruisers chasing
0 100 200 300 400 500
Approximate Sea Miles

Suffolk sights Bismarck
7.22 p.m. May 23

ICELAND

MANCHESTER
BIRMINGHAM
(patrolling)   SCAPA

SUFFOLK   HOOD
BISMARCK   PRINCE OF WALES
P. EUGEN   NORFOLK Destroyers   KING
           PRINCE OF   GEORGE V.
           WALES   REPULSE
HOOD   VICTORIOUS
Sunk   4 Cruisers
6.00 a.m   7 Destroyers

RODNEY   Troop
4 Destroyers Convoy
              7 Destroyers

Brest

German Warships
British Warships
British Convoys

NEWFOUNDLAND

RAMILLIES

Halifax
REVENGE   1

The CHASE OF THE BISMARCK   DORSETSHIRE   RENOWN
                                              ARK ROYAL
                                              SHEFFIELD

Gibraltar

Wales has broken off the action." This was a sharp disappointment. Had then the *Bismarck* turned north and gone home? Here was my great fear. We now know what happened.

* * *

All that night (May 23–24), amidst driving rain and snow, the *Norfolk* and *Suffolk* with great skill shadowed the enemy, despite the weather and his efforts to shake them off, and all through the night their signals showed the exact positions of friend and foe. As the Arctic twilight grew into day the *Bismarck* could be seen twelve miles to the south on a southerly course. Soon there was smoke on the *Norfolk's* port bow. The *Hood* and *Prince of Wales* were in sight, and mortal conflict was at hand. In the *Hood* as day was dawning the enemy was discerned seventeen miles to the northwest. The British ships turned to engage, and the *Hood* opened fire at 5.52 A.M. at a range of about twenty-five thousand yards. The *Bismarck* replied, and almost at once the *Hood* suffered a hit which started a fire in the four-inch battery. The fire spread with alarming speed, until it engulfed the whole midship part. All the ships were now in full action, and the *Bismarck* too was hit. Suddenly came disaster. At 6 o'clock, after the *Bismarck* had fired her fifth salvo, the *Hood* was rent in twain by a mighty explosion. A few minutes later she had vanished beneath the waves amidst a vast pall of smoke. All but three of her valiant company, more than fifteen hundred men, including Vice-Admiral Lancelot Holland and Captain Ralph Kerr, perished.

The *Prince of Wales* quickly altered her course to avoid the wreckage of the *Hood* and continued the now unequal fight. Very soon the *Bismarck's* fire began to tell upon her. Within a few minutes she received four hits from fifteen-inch shells, one of which wrecked the bridge, killing or wounding nearly all upon it. At the same time the ship was holed underwater aft. Captain Leach, one of the few survivors from the bridge, decided to break off the action for the moment and turned away under a smoke-screen. He had, however, inflicted damage on the *Bismarck* which reduced her speed. She had in fact been struck underwater by two heavy shells, one of which pierced an oil tank, resulting in serious and continuing loss of oil which later had important consequences. The German commander persisted on his course to the southwest, leaving behind a marked oil trace.

The command now passed to Rear-Admiral Wake-Walker on his bridge in the cruiser *Norfolk*. It was for him to decide whether to renew the fight at once or hold on to the enemy till the Commander-in-Chief should arrive with the *King George V* and the aircraft-carrier *Victorious*. A dominant factor was the state of the *Prince of Wales*. This ship had only recently been commissioned, and scarcely a week had passed since Captain Leach had been able to report her "fit for battle." She had been severely mauled, and two of her ten fourteen-inch guns were unserviceable. It was highly doubtful whether in this condition she was a match for the *Bismarck*. Admiral Wake-Walker, therefore, decided not to renew the action, but to hold the enemy under observation. In this he was indisputably right.

*   *   *

The *Bismarck* would indeed have been wise to rest content with what amounted by itself to a resounding triumph. She had destroyed in a few minutes one of the finest ships in the Royal Navy, and could go home to Germany with a major success. Her prestige and potential striking power would rise immensely, in circumstances difficult for us to measure or explain.

Moreover, as we now know, she had been seriously injured by the *Prince of Wales*, and oil was leaking from her heavily. How then could she hope to discharge her mission of commerce destruction in the Atlantic? She had the choice of returning home victorious, with all the options of further enterprises open, or of going to almost certain destruction. Only the extreme exaltation of her Admiral or the imperious orders by which he was bound can explain the desperate decision which he took. When I saw my American friend at about ten o'clock, I had already learned that the *Bismarck* was steaming southward, and I was, therefore, able to speak with renewed confidence about the final result.

I had to read for very long hours each day to keep abreast of the ceaseless flow of military, Foreign Office, and Secret Service telegrams, which streamed in by private telephone and dispatch-riders. This was a great comfort, because as long as one is doing something the mind is saturated and cannot worry. Nevertheless, only one scene riveted my background thoughts: this tremendous *Bismarck*, forty-five thousand tons, perhaps almost invulnerable to gunfire, rushing southward towards our convoys, with the *Prinz Eugen* as her scout. Then

I thought of these convoys. Their battleships had left during the hunt. There was the troop convoy, with all its precious men on board, now well to the south of Ireland, with Admiral Somerville closing it at full speed, and presently to be between it and peril. I questioned the duty captain about times and distances. His reports were reassuring. Although the convoy only made about twelve knots and the *Bismarck* could, so far as we knew, do twenty-five, there was a lot of salt water between them. Besides, as long as we could hold fast to the *Bismarck* we could dog her to her doom. But what if we lost touch in the night? Which way would she go? She had a wide choice, and we were vulnerable almost everywhere.

The House of Commons, too, might be in no good temper when we met on Tuesday. They had been blown out of their Chamber on May 10 and were now crammed into the Church House, not far away. This was indeed a port in a storm, but there were no conveniences. Writing-rooms, smoking-rooms, dining-rooms, all the customary facilities, were improvised and primitive. The air-raid alarms were frequent and means for Members getting about scarce. How would they like to be told on Tuesday when they met that the *Hood* was unavenged, that several of our convoys had been cut up or even massacred, and that the *Bismarck* had got home to Germany or to a French-occupied port, that Crete was lost, and evacuation without heavy casualties doubtful? I had great confidence in their pluck and fidelity if once they could be convinced that their business was not being muddled. But could they be? My American guest thought I was gay, but it costs nothing to grin.

*   *   *

All through the twenty-fourth the British cruisers and the *Prince of Wales* continued to dog the *Bismarck* and her consort. Admiral Tovey, in the *King George V*, was still a long way off, but signalled that he hoped to engage by 9 A.M. on the twenty-fifth. The Admiralty summoned all forces. The *Rodney*, five hundred miles away to the southeast, was ordered to steer a closing course. The *Ramillies* was ordered to quit her homeward-bound convoy and place herself to the westward of the enemy; and the *Revenge*, from Halifax, was also directed to the scene. Cruisers were posted to guard against a break-back by the enemy to the north and east, while all the time Admiral Somerville's force was pressing northward from

Gibraltar. Subject to all the uncertainties of the sea, the net was drawing tighter.

That evening about 6.40 the *Bismarck* suddenly turned to engage her pursuers, and there was a brief encounter. We now know that this movement was made to cover the escape of the *Prinz Eugen*, which then made off at high speed to the south, and after refuelling at sea reached Brest unchallenged ten days later. Admiral Tovey had sent the *Victorious* ahead to make an air attack in the hope of reducing the enemy's speed. The *Victorious* was newly commissioned, and some of her air crews had little fighting experience. At 10 P.M., covered by four cruisers, she released her nine Swordfish torpedo-aircraft on a hundred-and-twenty-mile flight against a strong head wind with rain and low cloud. Led by Lieutenant-Commander Esmonde and guided by the *Norfolk's* wireless, the aircraft two hours later [1] found the *Bismarck*, and attacked with great gallantry against intense fire. They scored a torpedo hit under the bridge. On board the *Victorious* the question of the recovery of the air squadron was causing acute anxiety. By now it was pitch-dark, with a high wind and blinding showers of rain, and the pilots had had little practice in deck-landing even in daylight. Furthermore, the homing beacon, by which alone they could be safely guided to the ship, had failed. Despite any prowling U-boats, searchlights and signal lamps were used to help the pilots in their approach. It is pleasant to record that their splendid efforts were rewarded. All succeeded in landing safely in the darkness amidst general rejoicing and relief.

Once more everything seemed to be set for a morning climax, and once more the Admiralty hopes were dashed. Soon after 3 A.M. on the twenty-fifth the *Suffolk* suddenly and unexpectedly lost contact with the *Bismarck*. She had been shadowing by radar with skill from a position on the enemy's port quarter. All ships were now zigzagging as they moved south into waters infested by U-boats, and it was this which brought about the misfortune. At the end of each outward leg of her zigzag course the *Suffolk* lost radar contact, but regained it on the inward leg. Perhaps she was overconfident after such prolonged and successful shadowing. But now

[1] The British ships were keeping double British Summer Time (two hours in advance of Greenwich). Furthermore, they were by now a long way to the west of the meridian of Greenwich, and therefore their clock time was about four hours ahead of the sun. Thus the attack took place about 8 P.M. by sun time.

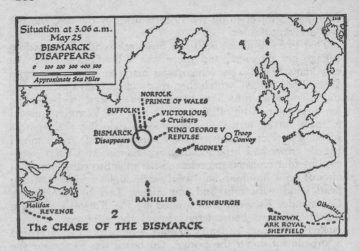

Situation at 3.06 a.m.
May 25
BISMARCK
DISAPPEARS

0   100 200 300 400 500
Approximate Sea Miles

NORFOLK
PRINCE OF WALES
SUFFOLK
VICTORIOUS,
4 Cruisers
BISMARCK
Disappears
KING GEORGE V
REPULSE
Troop
Convoy
RODNEY

RAMILLIES   EDINBURGH

Halifax
REVENGE   RENOWN,
                               ARK ROYAL,
                               SHEFFIELD
        2
The CHASE OF THE BISMARCK

when she turned once more to the westward the enemy was
no longer on the presumed course. Had he turned west or
doubled back to the north and east? This caused the utmost
anxiety and rendered all concentration futile. After making
a cast to the westward at daylight the *King George V* turned
eastward in the belief that the *Bismarck* was making towards
the North Sea, and the whole British pursuit now trended in
this direction. At the Admiralty there was a growing opinion
that the *Bismarck* was steering for Brest, but it was not until
six o'clock that this hardened. The Admiralty forthwith deflected all our forces towards the more southerly route. But
meanwhile the confusion and delay arising from the loss of
contact had enabled the *Bismarck* to slip through the cordon
and gain a commanding lead in her race for safety. By 11
P.M. she was already well to the eastward of the British flagship. She was short of oil through the leakage. The *Rodney*,
with her sixteen-inch guns, still lay between her and home,
but she too was moving to the northeastward and crossed
ahead of the *Bismarck* during the afternoon. The day which
had begun so full of promise ended in disappointment and
frustration. Happily, from the south, breasting the heavy
Atlantic seas, the *Renown*, the *Ark Royal*, and the cruiser
Sheffield were steadily approaching on an intercepting course.

By the morning of May 26 the problem of fuel for all our
widely scattered ships, which had now been steaming hard for
four days, began to clamour for attention. Already several of

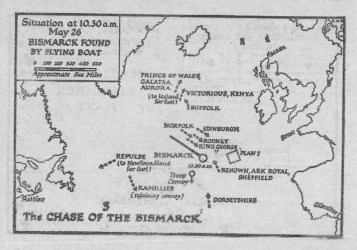

the pursuers had had to reduce speed. It was clear that in
these wide expanses all our efforts might soon be vain. However, at 10.30 A.M., just as hopes were beginning to fade, the
Bismarck was found again. The Admiralty and Coastal Command were searching with Catalina aircraft working from
Lough Erne in Ireland. One of these now located the fugitive
steering towards Brest and still about seven hundred miles
from home. The *Bismarck* damaged the aircraft and contact
was lost. But within an hour two Swordfish from the *Ark
Royal* spotted her once more. She was still well to the westward of the *Renown* and not yet within the German air cover
radiating powerfully from Brest. The *Renown*, however,
could not face her single-handed. It was necessary to await
the arrival of the *King George V* and *Rodney*, both still far
behind the chase. But now Captain Vian, of *Altmark* fame,
still in the *Cossack*, with four other destroyers which had
been escorting the troop convoy and had been ordered to
leave it, received a signal from a Catalina aircraft which gave
him the *Bismarck's* position. Without waiting for further
orders he at once turned towards the enemy.

Further confusion was in store in this clutching and grab-
bing scene. Admiral Somerville, hastening northward, sent
on the *Sheffield* to close and shadow the enemy. The *Ark
Royal* was not informed of this movement, and when she
launched her air striking force their radar led them to the
Sheffield, which they attacked but did not hit. The *Sheffield*,

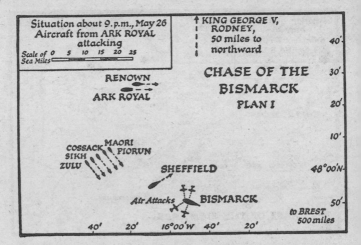

Situation about 9 p.m., May 26
Aircraft from ARK ROYAL
attacking
Scale of Sea Miles: 0 5 10 15 20 25

↑ KING GEORGE V,
   RODNEY,
   50 miles to
   northward

CHASE OF THE
BISMARCK
PLAN I

RENOWN
ARK ROYAL

COSSACK MAORI
SIKH   PIORUN
ZULU

SHEFFIELD

Air Attacks BISMARCK

to BREST
500 miles

40'   20'   16°00'W   40'   20'

understanding the mistake, dodged successfully and did not
fire.[2] The airplanes, penitent, returned to the *Ark Royal,* and
the *Sheffield* gained contact with the *Bismarck* and henceforth
held her for sure. Fifteen Swordfish again left the *Ark Royal*
a little after 7 P.M. The enemy was now less than forty miles
away, and this time there was no mistake. Directed on their
prey by the forgiving *Sheffield,* they pressed home their attack with determination. By 9.30 their work was done. Two
torpedoes had certainly hit, and possibly a third. A shadowing
aircraft reported that the *Bismarck* had been seen to make
two complete circles, and it seemed she was out of control.
Captain Vian's destroyers were now approaching, and
throughout the night they surrounded the stricken ship,
attacking with torpedoes whenever the chance came.

*   *   *

On this Monday night I went to the Admiralty and watched
the scene on the charts in the War Room, where the news
streamed in every few minutes. "What are you doing here?"
I said to the Controller, Admiral Fraser. "I am waiting to see
what I have got to repair," he said. Four hours passed quickly
away, and when I left I could see that Admiral Pound and his
select company of experts were sure the *Bismarck* was
doomed.

The German commander, Admiral Lutjens, had no illu-

[2] One aircraft signalled to the *Sheffield,* "Sorry for the kipper!"

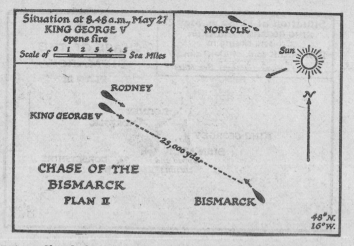

Situation at 8.48 a.m., May 27
KING GEORGE V
opens fire
Scale of 0 1 2 3 4 5 Sea Miles

NORFOLK

Sun

RODNEY

KING GEORGE V

N

25,000 yards

CHASE OF THE
BISMARCK
PLAN II

BISMARCK

48°N.
16°W.

sions. Shortly before midnight he reported, "Ship unmanoeu-
vrable. We shall fight to the last shell. Long live the Fuehrer!"
The *Bismarck* was still four hundred miles from Brest, and no
longer even able to steer thither. Strong German bomber
forces were now sent forward to the rescue, and U-boats hastened to the scene, one of which, *having already expended her
torpedoes,* reported that the *Ark Royal* had passed her within
easy striking distance. Meanwhile the *King George V* and the
Rodney were drawing near. Fuel was a grave anxiety, and
Admiral Tovey had decided that unless the *Bismarck's* speed
could be greatly reduced he would have to abandon the chase
at midnight. At my suggestion the First Sea Lord told him to
go on even if he had to be towed home. But by now it was
known that the *Bismarck* was actually steaming in the wrong
direction. Her main armament was uninjured, and Admiral
Tovey decided to bring her to battle in the morning.

A northwesterly gale was blowing when daylight came on
the twenty-seventh. The *Rodney* opened fire at 8.47 A.M., followed a minute later by the *King George V.* The British ships
quickly began to hit, and after a pause the *Bismarck* too
opened fire. For a short time her shooting was good, although
the crew, after four gruelling days, were utterly exhausted and
falling asleep at their posts. With her third salvo she straddled
the *Rodney,* but thereafter the weight of the British attack
was overwhelming, and within half an hour most of her guns
were silent. A fire was blazing amidships, and she had a heavy

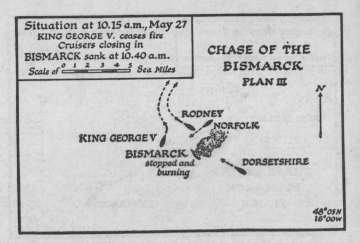

Situation at 10.15 a.m., May 27
KING GEORGE V. ceases fire
Cruisers closing in
BISMARCK sank at 10.40 a.m.
Scale of 0 1 2 3 4 5 Sea Miles

CHASE OF THE
BISMARCK
PLAN III

N

RODNEY
NORFOLK
KING GEORGE V
BISMARCK
stopped and
burning
DORSETSHIRE

48°05N
16°00W

list to port. The *Rodney* now turned across her bow, pouring in a heavy fire from a range of no more than four thousand yards. By 10.15 all the *Bismarck's* guns were silent and her mast was shot away. The ship lay wallowing in the heavy seas, a flaming and smoking ruin; yet even then she did not sink.

*   *   *

At eleven o'clock I had to report to the House of Commons, meeting in the Church House, both about the battle of Crete and the drama of the *Bismarck*.

This morning [I said], shortly after daylight the *Bismarck*, virtually at a standstill, far from help, was attacked by the British pursuing battleships. I do not know what were the results of the bombardment. It appears, however, that the *Bismarck* was not sunk by gunfire, and she will now be dispatched by torpedo. It is thought that this is now proceeding, and it is also thought that there cannot be any lengthy delay in disposing of this vessel. Great as is our loss in the *Hood*, the *Bismarck* must be regarded as the most powerful, as she is the newest, battleship in the world.

I had just sat down when a slip of paper was passed to me which led me to rise again. I asked the indulgence of the House and said, "I have just received news that the *Bismarck* is sunk." They seemed content.

It was the cruiser *Dorsetshire* that delivered the final blow with torpedoes, and at 10.40 the great ship turned over and foundered. With her perished nearly two thousand Germans and their Fleet Commander, Admiral Lutjens. One hundred and ten survivors, exhausted but sullen, were rescued by us. The work of mercy was interrupted by the appearance of a U-boat and the British ships were compelled to withdraw. Five other Germans were picked up by a U-boat and a ship engaged in weather reporting, but the Spanish cruiser *Canarias*, which arrived on the scene later, found only floating bodies.

* * *

This episode brings into relief many important points relating to sea warfare, and illustrates both the enormous structural strength of the German ship and the immense difficulties and dangers with which her sortie had confronted our very numerous forces. Had she escaped, the moral effects of her continuing existence as much as the material damage she might have inflicted on our shipping would have been calamitous. Many misgivings would have arisen regarding our capacity to control the oceans, and these would have been trumpeted round the world to our great detriment and discomfort. All branches rightly claimed their share in the successful outcome. The pursuit began with the cruisers, which led to the first disastrous action. Then when the enemy was lost it was aircraft that found him and guided the cruisers back to the chase. Thereafter it was a cruiser which directed the seaborne aircraft who struck the decisive blows, and finally it was the destroyers who harassed and held him through a long night and led the battleships to the last scene of destruction. While credit is due to all, we must not forget that the long-drawn battle turned on the first injury inflicted on the *Bismarck* by the guns of the *Prince of Wales*. Thus the battleship and the gun were dominant both at the beginning and at the end.

The traffic in the Atlantic continued unmolested.

To President Roosevelt I telegraphed on the twenty-eighth:

Former Naval Person to President Roosevelt   28 May 41

I will send you later the inside story of the fighting with the *Bismarck*. She was a terrific ship, and a masterpiece of naval construction. Her removal eases our battleship situation, as we should have had to keep *King George V, Prince of Wales*, and the two *Nelsons* practically tied to Scapa Flow to guard against a sortie of *Bismarck* and *Tirpitz*, as they could choose their moment and we should have to allow for one of our ships refitting. Now it is a different story. The effect upon the Japanese will be highly beneficial. I expect they are doing all their sums again.

18

Syria

S<small>YRIA</small> was one of the many overseas territories of the French
Empire which on the collapse of France considered themselves bound by the surrender of the French Government, and
the Vichy authorities did their utmost to prevent anybody in
the French Army of the Levant from crossing into Palestine
to join us. The Polish Brigade marched over, but very few
Frenchmen. In August, 1940, the Italian Armistice Commission appeared, and German agents, who had been interned on
the outbreak of war, were released and became active. By the
end of the year many more Germans had arrived, and, with
ample funds, proceeded to arouse anti-British and anti-Zionist
feeling among the Arab peoples of the Levant. By the end of
March, 1941, Syria forced itself on our attention. The Luftwaffe were already attacking the Suez Canal from bases in
the Dodecanese, and they could obviously, if they chose,
operate against Syria, especially with airborne troops. With
the Germans in control of Syria, Egypt, the vital Canal
Zone, and the oil refineries at Abadan would come under the

direct threat of continuous air attack. Our land communications between Palestine and Iraq would be in danger. There might well be political repercussions in Egypt, and our diplomatic position in Turkey and throughout the Middle East would be gravely weakened.

On May 2, Rashid Ali appealed to the Fuehrer for armed support against us in Iraq, and the following day the German Embassy in Paris was instructed to obtain permission from the French Government for the transit of planes and war materials across Syria to Rashid Ali's forces. Admiral Darlan negotiated a preliminary agreement with the Germans on May 5 and 6 by which three-quarters of the war material assembled in Syria under the control of the Italian Armistice Commission was to be transported to Iraq and the German Air Force granted landing facilities in Syria. General Dentz, the Vichy High Commissioner and Commander-in-Chief, received instructions to this effect, and between May 9 and the end of the month about a hundred German and twenty Italian aircraft landed on Syrian airfields.

At this time, as we have seen, the Middle East Command was strained to the limit. The defence of Egypt was dominant; Greece had been evacuated; Crete had to be defended; Malta pleaded for reinforcement; the conquest of Abyssinia was not yet complete; troops had to be provided for Iraq. All that was available for the defence of Palestine from the north was the 1st Cavalry Division, of excellent quality, but stripped for other needs of its artillery and ancillary services. General de Gaulle pressed for prompt military action by the Free French forces, if necessary unsupported by British troops. But, with the experience of Dakar behind us, it was felt, both by General Wavell on the spot and by all of us in London, that it was inadvisable to use the Free French alone, even to resist a German advance through Syria. It might, however, be inevitable.

Nevertheless, we could not let Syria go without doing our utmost with anything that could be scraped up. Reluctant as we were to add to Wavell's burdens, it was necessary to press him to do what he could to help the Free French. On April 28 he replied that all he could manage was a single brigade group. On this telegram I minuted: "It seems most necessary that General Wavell should prepare the brigade group and mobile group [he mentions] as far as he can, and have it in readiness on the Palestine border." Accordingly the Chiefs of Staff sent instructions to Wavell that no definite offer of

help should be made to General Dentz, but that if he resisted
a German landing, by sea or air, all available British help
would be given to him at once. General Wavell was also told
that immediate air action should be taken against any German
descent.

The outlook was threatening, and on May 8 I minuted to
the Chiefs of Staff:

General Ismay for C.O.S. Committee

I must have the advice of the Staffs upon the Syrian business
available for Cabinet this morning. A supreme effort must be
made to prevent the Germans getting a footing in Syria with
small forces and then using Syria as a jumping-off ground for the
air domination of Iraq and Persia. It is no use General Wavell
being vexed at this disturbance on his eastern flanks. . . . We
ought to help in every way without minding what happens at
Vichy.

I shall be most grateful if the Staff will see what is the most
that can be done.

On May 9, with the approval of the Defence Committee, I
telegraphed to General Wavell:

You will no doubt realise the grievous danger of Syria being
captured by a few thousand Germans transported by air. Our information leads us to believe that Admiral Darlan has probably
made some bargains to help the Germans to get in there. In face
of your evident feeling of lack of resources we can see no other
course open than to furnish General Catroux with the necessary
transport and let him and his Free French do their best at the
moment they deem suitable, the R.A.F. acting against German
landings. Any improvement you can make on this would be
welcome.

On May 14 the Royal Air Force was authorised to act
against German aircraft in Syria and on French Airfields. On
the seventeenth General Wavell telegraphed that in view of
the dispatch of troops from Palestine to Iraq the Syrian affair
would involve either using Free French alone or bringing
troops from Egypt. He felt strongly that the Free French
would be ineffective and likely to aggravate the situation; and
he concluded by saying that he hoped he would not be burdened with a Syrian commitment unless is was absolutely
essential. The Chiefs of Staff replied that there was no option
but to improvise the largest force that he could provide without prejudice to the security of the Western Desert, and that
he should prepare himself to move into Syria at the earliest

possible date. The composition of that force would be left to him.

On May 21—at the moment of the German attack on Crete —Wavell ordered the 7th Australian Division, less the brigade at Tobruk, to be ready to move to Palestine, and instructed General Maitland Wilson, who early in the month on his return from Greece had assumed command of Palestine and Transjordan, to prepare a plan for an advance into Syria.

*   *   *

At this time a misunderstanding arose between us at home and General Wavell, through his deriving the impression from a telegram of the Chiefs of Staff that we were relying on the advice of the Free French leaders rather than upon his own. He, therefore, telegraphed to the C.I.G.S. that if this was so he would prefer to be relieved of his command. I hastened to reassure him on the point, but at the same time I felt it necessary to make it clear that we were determined upon the Syrian adventure and to assume the full burden of responsibility for what was, after all, hardly a military proposition.

Prime Minister to General Wavell   21 May 41

Nothing in Syria must detract at this moment from winning the Battle of Crete or in the Western Desert. . . .

There is no objection to your mingling British troops with the Free French who are to enter Syria; but, as you have clearly shown, you have not the means to mount a regular military operation, and, as you were instructed yesterday, all that can be done at present is to give the best possible chance to the kind of armed political inroad described in Chiefs of Staff message of twentieth.

You are wrong in supposing that policy described in this message arose out of any representations made by the Free French leaders. It arises entirely from the view taken here by those who have the supreme direction of war and policy in all theatres. Our view is that if the Germans can pick up Syria and Iraq with petty air forces, tourists, and local revolts, we must not shrink from running equal small-scale military risks and facing the possible aggravation of political dangers from failure. For this decision we, of course, take full responsibility, and should you find yourself unwilling to give effect to it arrangements will be made to meet any wish you may express to be relieved of your command.

Wavell showed by his reply that he fully understood. He explained that the proved inaccuracy of Free French information about the position in Syria made him unwilling to commit himself to military action at a time when Crete, Iraq, and the Western Desert required all available resources.

General Wavell to Prime Minister   22 May 41

This Syrian business is disquieting, since German Air Force
established in Syria are closer to the Canal and Suez than they
would be at Mersa Matruh. The [Vichy] French seem now wholly
committed to the Germans. I am moving reinforcements to Palestine, after full discussion with Cunningham, Tedder, and Blamey,
because we feel we must be prepared for action against Syria, and
weak action is useless. The whole position in Middle East is at
present governed mainly by air power and air bases. Enemy air
bases in Greece make our hold of Crete precarious, and enemy air
bases in Cyrenaica, Crete, Cyprus, and Syria would make our hold
on Egypt difficult. The object of the Army must be to force the
enemy in Cyrenaica as far west as possible, to try to keep him
from establishing himself in Syria, and to hang on to Crete and
Cyprus. It will not be so easy, with our resources and those of the
air force. I know you realise all this and are making every effort
to provide requirements, and we are doing our best to secure
Middle East. We have some difficult months ahead, but will not
lose heart.

I replied on the following day:

Prime Minister to General Wavell   23 May 41

Many thanks for your telegram. These are very hard times, and
we must all do our best to help each other. . . .

Syria. It is your views that weigh with us, and not those of Free
French. You had better have de Gaulle close to you. Let me
know if I can help you with him. *We cannot have Crète battle
spoiled for the sake of Syria.* Therefore, inferior methods may be
the only ones open at the moment. . . .

Iraq. We hope Habforce will soon enter Baghdad, establishing
Regent there.

As the hopes of holding Crete diminished, the possible
German threat to Syria commanded increasing attention. On
May 25 General Wavell telegraphed his outline plan for
"Exporter," the code name now allotted to the Syrian operation. General Wilson was preparing to advance northward
with a force consisting of the 7th Australian Division, the
Free French troops, part of the 1st Cavalry Division, now
motorised, and certain other units. Wavell estimated that the
earliest date by which he could move would be the first week
of June. Although the danger of the establishment of German
air bases in the Levant was most serious in its possible consequences, particularly if it synchronised with German land
operations through Turkey—a possibility which could not be
ignored—priority must be given to the attempt to obtain a
successful military decision in the Western Desert Operation
"Battleaxe."

On the night of May 27 the Defence Committee of the Cabinet was summoned to consider the general situation throughout the Middle East, and I embodied their conclusions in a telegram to General Wavell.

Prime Minister to General Wavell   28 May 41

. . . Our immediate action in the Middle East is dictated by the following facts: (1) Possession of Crete will enable enemy to establish direct line of communication to Cyrenaica via west coast of Greece and Crete. Unless we can establish air forces in Cyrenaica we can neither interrupt this line nor can we easily maintain Malta and continue interruption of Tripoli line of communication. (2) Attack through Turkey and/or through Syria cannot develop in real strength for a good many weeks.

Our first object must be to gain a decisive military success in the Western Desert and to destroy the enemy armed forces in a battle fought with our whole available strength.

Meanwhile, it is important to establish ourselves in Syria before the Germans have recovered from the immense drain on their air power which the vigorous resistance of Freyberg's army has produced. Accordingly, the general plan outlined in your telegram of May 25 is approved.

Preparations for the occupation of Syria, therefore, went forward amid anxieties about the fall of Crete and prior concentration on the Western Desert.

On June 3 I telegraphed to General Wavell:

Prime Minister to General Wavell   3 June 41

Please telegraph exactly what ground and air forces you are using for Syria. What are you doing with the Poles? It seems important to use and demonstrate as much air power as possible at the very outset, and even the older machines may play their part, as they did so well in Iraq.

2. There is a storm of criticism about Crete, and I am being pressed for explanations on many points. Do not worry about this at all now. Simply keep your eye on Syria, and above all "Battleaxe." These alone can supply the answers to criticisms, just or unjust. The air superiority available for "Battleaxe" far exceeds anything you are likely to have for many months. As Napoleon said, "La bataille répondra." All good wishes.

Wavell replied on the fifth informing us of the forces he would use. Fighting would be avoided as far as possible, progress being at first by propaganda, leaflets, and display of force. If resistance was encountered, the utmost force would be used. He said he had always estimated the strength required for the occupation of Syria as two divisions and one armoured division, or at least [some] armoured brigades. He must, therefore, regard success as at least problematical, and dependent on the attitude of the French garrison and local population.

*   *   *

Remembering the baffling and confused nature of the problems which confronted de Gaulle, I now sent on the eve of our joint expedition into Syria the following telegram of good will:

Prime Minister to General de Gaulle   6 June 41

I wish to send you my best wishes for success of our joint enterprise in the Levant. I hope you are satisfied that everything possible is being done to provide support to the arms of Free France. You will, I am sure, agree that this action, and indeed our whole future policy in the Middle East, must be conceived in terms of mutual trust and collaboration. Our policies towards the Arabs must run on parallel lines. You know that we have sought no special advantages in the French Empire, and have no intention of exploiting the tragic position of France for our own gain.

I welcome, therefore, your decision to promise independence to Syria and the Lebanon, and, as you know, I think it essential that we should lend to this promise the full weight of our guarantee. I agree that we must not in any settlement of the Syrian question endanger the stability of the Middle East. But subject to this we must both do everything possible to meet Arab aspirations and susceptibilities. You will, I am sure, bear in mind the importance of this.

All our thoughts are with you and the soldiers of Free France. At this hour, when Vichy touches fresh depths of ignominy, the loyalty and courage of the Free French save the glory of France.

I must ask you in this grave hour not to insist on declaring Catroux High Commissioner for Syria.

As usual, I kept President Roosevelt fully informed.

Former Naval Person to President Roosevelt   7 June 41

We enter Syria in some force tomorrow morning in order to prevent further German penetration. Success depends largely upon attitude of local French troops. De Gaulle's Free French outfit will be prominent, but not in the van. He is issuing a proclamation to the Arabs offering in the name of France complete independence and opportunity to form either three or one or three-in-one free Arab States. Relations of these States with France will be fixed by treaty safeguarding established interests somewhat on the Anglo-Egyptian model. General Catroux is not to be called High Commissioner, but French Delegate and Plenipotentiary.

2. I cannot tell how Vichy will react to what may happen. I do not myself think they will do much worse than they are now doing, but of course they may retaliate on Gibraltar or Freetown. I should be most grateful if you would keep up your pressure

upon them. We have no political interests at all in Syria except to
win the war.

* * *

All Wavell could muster for the advance was the 7th
Australian Division, part of the 1st Cavalry Division, the 5th
Indian Infantry Brigade, recently returned from Eritrea, and
the Free French force under General Le Gentilhomme, comprising six battalions, one battery, and a company of tanks.
Air support was limited at first to about seventy aircraft in all.
The Crete battle had priority with both sides. Two cruisers
and ten destroyers, besides smaller craft, were spared for the
Syrian effort. The Vichy forces, under General Dentz, comprised eighteen battalions, with a hundred and twenty guns
and ninety tanks, thirty-five thousand men in all, an air force
amounting to ninety aircraft, and a naval force of two destroyers and three submarines based on Beirut.

The task assigned to the Allied army was to capture Damascus, Rayak, and Beirut as a preliminary to the occupation of
the whole country. The advance began on June 8, and at first
met little opposition. No one could tell how much Vichy would
fight. Although our attack could hardly achieve a surprise, it
was thought by some that the enemy would offer only a token
resistance. But when the enemy realised how weak we were
they took heart and reacted vigorously, if only for the honour
of their arms. The Free French were held ten miles short of
Damascus, and a counter-movement round their eastern flank
threatened their line of communications. The Australians, on
the coast road, made slow progress over difficult ground. A
British battalion was overwhelmed at Kuneitra by a counter-
attack of two battalions with tanks. At sea contact was made
with the Vichy destroyers, but they fled with superior speed.
On the ninth a brief encounter took place at sea, in which the
destroyer *Janus* was severely hit. On the fifteenth, while
bombarding Sidon, two British destroyers were damaged by
air attack, but a Vichy destroyer approaching the coast from
the west was sunk by the Fleet air arm.

As a result of the first week's fighting, it was clear to Wavell
that reinforcements were necessary. He was able to collect
transport for one brigade of the 6th British Division, which
was now partly formed, followed at the end of June by a second brigade. He also arranged for a brigade group of the 1st
Cavalry Division, "Habforce," which had taken part in the
capture of Baghdad, to advance on Palmyra through the
deserts from the south; and two brigades of the 10th Indian

Division in Iraq were ordered to move up the Euphrates on Aleppo. This enlargement of the campaign began to take effect from June 20. Damascus was captured by the Australians on the twenty-first, after three days of severe fighting. Their advance was aided by a daring raid by Number 11 Commando, which was landed from the sea behind the enemy lines. In this devoted stroke the Commando lost their leader, Colonel Pedder, and all its other officers were either killed or wounded, together with nearly a hundred and twenty other ranks, or one quarter of its total strength.

The operations of the first week of July brought the Vichy collapse into sight. General Dentz realised that his limit was reached. He still had about 24,000 men, but he could not hope to offer continued resistance. Barely one-fifth of his air force remained. At 8.30 A.M. on July 12, Vichy envoys arrived to sue for an armistice. This was granted, a convention was signed, and Syria passed into Allied occupation. Our casualties in killed and wounded were over 4600; those of the enemy about 6500. One distasteful incident remained. British prisoners taken during the fighting had been hurriedly shipped off to Vichy France, whence they would certainly have passed into German keeping. When this was discovered and no redress was offered, General Dentz and other highly placed

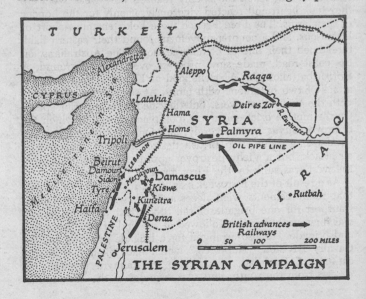

THE SYRIAN CAMPAIGN

officers were taken into custody as hostages. This had the desired effect, and our men were returned.

*   *   *

The successful campaign in Syria greatly improved our strategical position in the Middle East. It closed the door to any further attempt at enemy penetration eastward from the Mediterranean, moved our defence of the Suez Canal northward by two hundred and fifty miles, and relieved Turkey of anxiety for her southern frontier. She could now be assured of aid from a friendly Power if she were attacked. Although, for the sake of the narrative, it has been necessary to divide the four sets of operations in Iraq, Crete, Syria, and the Western Desert from one another, it must not be forgotten that they were all running together, and reacted upon each other to produce a sensation of crisis and complexity combined. Nevertheless, it may be claimed that the final result constituted in effect, though not in appearance, an undoubted and important victory for the British and Imperial armies in the Middle East, the credit of which may be shared between our authorities in London and Cairo.

The battle in Crete, which cost us so dear, ruined the striking power of the German airborne corps. The Iraq revolt was finally crushed, and with pitifully small and improvised forces we regained mastery of the wide regions involved. The occupation and conquest of Syria, which was undertaken to meet a desperate need, ended, as it proved for ever, the German advance towards the Persian Gulf and India. If under all the temptations of prudence, the War Cabinet and Chiefs of Staff had not made every post a winning-post, and imposed their will on all commanders, we should have been left only with the losses sustained in Crete, without gathering the rewards which followed from the hard and glorious fighting there. If General Wavell, though exhausted, had broken under the intense strain to which he was subjected by events and by our orders, the whole future of the war and of Turkey might have been fatefully altered. There is always much to be said for not attempting more than you can do and for making a certainty of what you try. But this principle, like others in life and war, has its exceptions.

One more operation, the battle in the Western Desert, which ranked first with me and the Chiefs of Staff, has still to be described. And this, though denied success, brought Rommel to a standstill for nearly five months.

19

General Wavell's Final Effort: "Battleaxe"

The Need to Defeat Rommel—Wavell's Determination—The Attack on Sollum and Capuzzo, May 15–16—A Limited Success——"Tiger Cubs'" Teething Troubles—Arrival of the Fifteenth Panzer Division—Halfaya Lost, May 26—Preparations for "Battleaxe"—Enemy Strength Underestimated—Our Attack Starts, June 15—All Goes Wrong, June 17—Rommel Does Not Pursue—The Willing Horse—My Telegrams of June 21—General Auchinleck Relieves General Wavell—Need for Devolution at Cairo—An Intendant-General—A Telegram—Captain Oliver Lyttelton—His Appointment as Minister of State in the Middle East—My Telegram to President Roosevelt of July 4.

ALL OUR HEARTS AT HOME had throughout been set on beating Rommel in the Western Desert. There was no difference of any kind between us, soldiers or civilians, in the supreme consequence we assigned to this. The tragedy of the evacuation of Greece, the distractions in Iraq and Syria, the dire struggle in Crete, all paled before the gleam of hope which we attached, and rightly, to victory in the Western Desert. One did not have to argue this matter in London.

Wavell, of course, had all the other troubles leaping upon him from day to day. He was, however, firmly with us in thought that the crushing of Rommel's venturous offensive and the consequent relief of Tobruk would make amends for all. Moreover, he realised what risks we had run to give him back the armour which he had lost when the desert flank crumpled. He had loyalty to Operation "Tiger." He knew what this effort of sending nearly three hundred tanks to him through the Mediterranean had meant. His spirit was buoyant, and he did not overlook the broad principle that in war as in life everything is relative. Our united strategic conception may be claimed to be correct. At this time we had a spy in close touch with Rommel's headquarters, who gave us accurate information of the fearful difficulties of Rommel's assertive but precarious position. We knew how narrow was the margin on which he hoped to maintain himself, and also the strong and strict injunctions of the German High Command that he was not to cast away his victories by asking too much of fortune.

Prime Minister to General Wavell   7 May 41

You and your generals alone can judge the tactical possibilities whether at Sollum or Tobruk. But if "Tiger" comes through it will be a moment to do and dare. I am asking for a rapid transfer from Malta of Hurricanes to your command once the "Tiger's" tail is clear. Those Hun people are far less dangerous once they lose the initiative. All our thoughts are with you.

Wavell, who had all our information, tried on his own initiative, even in the imminent advent of Crete, to claw down Rommel before the dreaded 15th Panzer Division arrived in full strength over the long road from Tripoli, and before Benghazi was effectively opened as a short cut for enemy supply. He, therefore, wished to strike at Rommel's force even before the tanks delivered by "Tiger"—"Tiger Cubs," as Wavell and I called them in our correspondence—could be brought into action. The armoured force in the Western Desert at the beginning of May consisted of only two squadrons of cruisers and two squadrons of infantry tanks, stationed southeast of Matruh. Wavell hoped to build this up into an adequate striking force by early June. He thought he saw an opportunity for a blow before the Tiger Cubs could be ready. He hoped to catch the enemy unawares before they could be reinforced by the 15th Panzer Division.

General Wavell to Prime Minister   9 May 41

I have ordered all available tanks to be placed at disposal of Gott's force for offensive action in Sollum area. This is now in active preparation and should take place soon. I shall only cancel it if complete disaster overtakes "Tiger." . . .

General Wavell to Prime Minister   13 May 41

Without waiting for "Tiger" I ordered available tanks to join Gott's force to attack enemy Sollum area. Action should take place in next day or two, and I think Gott should be able to deal with forward enemy troops. If successful, will consider immediate combined action by Gott's force and Tobruk garrison to drive enemy west of Tobruk. It may be necessary to wait for some of

"Tiger" to do this, but am anxious to act as quickly as possible before enemy can be reinforced.

I had full and active agreement from the Chiefs of Staff. What a relief it was to have no differences at home!

Chief of the Air Staff to Air Marshal Tedder   14 May 41

After Chiefs of Staff had today expressed general agreement with your appreciation the Prime Minister discussed it fully with me. He was much pleased with the general lay-out, and felt glad that you had the handling of the important and complicated air operations impending.

2. Following general observations on time-table and relative emphasis may assist without fettering your freedom of action.

3. Victory in Libya comes first in time and importance. Results would dominate Iraq situation in German and Iraqi minds.

4. Our object in Iraq is to get back a friendly Government in Baghdad, and you should do all you can to help in this, but nothing must prejudice victory in Western Desert.

5. From here it seems probable that "Scorcher" [the attack on Crete] will happen after smaller operations in Libya, and before larger, which depend on "Tiger Cubs." You should allow for, but not rely on, "Colorado" [Crete] being attacked later than expected owing to complexity of operations.

6. One clear-cut result is worth a dozen wise precautions. Longer views about Iraq, Syria, and preparations in Palestine can be taken later. Prime importance of Desert operations would justify accepting necessary risks elsewhere.

*   *   *

A force under General Gott, consisting of the 7th Armoured Brigade, mustering about fifty-five tanks, and the 22d Guards Brigade, now advanced northwestward along the top of the escarpment, and on May 15 captured Sollum and Capuzzo, the armoured brigade on the left moving on to Sidi Azeiz. The enemy were quick to counter-attack, and retook Capuzzo the same afternoon, inflicting heavy casualties on the Durham Light Infantry, who had taken it. This enforced the withdrawal of the 7th Armoured Brigade from Sidi Azeiz. The enemy, employing about seventy tanks, showed greater strength than had been expected. Although we still held Sollum that night, it was decided to withdraw the whole force next day, the 16th, leaving garrisons on the pass over the escarpment at Halfaya and at Sidi Suleiman.

Wavell's report of this action was not sanguine. He said that after a preliminary advance which cleared the enemy from the Sollum-Bardia area, an enemy counter-attack with tanks had forced our troops back to Halfaya. We were able to maintain forward posts in Sollum, and a sortie by the Tobruk garrison achieved a local success. We had inflicted significant casualties. At home we were pleased.

Prime Minister to General Wavell   17 May 41

Results of action seem to us satisfactory. Without using Tiger Cubs, you have taken the offensive, have advanced thirty miles, have captured Halfaya and Sollum, have taken five hundred German prisoners, and inflicted heavy losses in men and tanks upon the enemy. For this twenty "I" tanks and one thousand or one thousand five hundred casualties do not seem to be at all too heavy a cost.

2. News from Tobruk is also good, especially as enemy's loss is greater than ours. Enemy is certainly anxious about Tobruk, and reports with apparent satisfaction when it is quiet. It seems of the utmost importance to keep on fighting at Tobruk.

3. Enemy is bringing up reinforcements and is seeking to re-establish the situation. We should surely welcome this, as he may not be in a condition to stand severe continuous fighting. Dill and I both feel confident of good results of sustained pressure, because the extremely worried state of the enemy is known to us. We feel sure you should keep at it both at Sollum and Tobruk. He cannot possibly fill the gap as you can. Presume you are using your powerful mechanised field artillery to the full at both places, compelling him to fire off ammunition, of which we know he is short. We should also be grateful if, without burdening yourself personally, you could have some officer on your staff send a fuller report of the events and position as known at your headquarters each evening. This is all the more desirable when operations of such outstanding importance for the world situation as those of the Western Desert are in progress.

4. What are your dates for bringing Tiger Cubs into action?

General Wavell to Prime Minister   18 May 41

Enemy proved rather stronger than we thought, and has forced us back on defensive till Tiger Cubs come into action. This will not be before end of month, and it would be better if they could be given more time to settle down, but this must depend on situation. Enemy is collecting strength in forward area and may try further advance.

You will have heard of Aosta's surrender, which practically completes East African campaign.

*   *   *

On May 20 Wavell reported that a tank battalion of the 15th Panzer Division was believed to have arrived in the forward area. Thus the opportunity of defeating Rommel before he could be reinforced had passed. Despite preparations made in advance, the delays in unloading, refitting, and making desert-worthy the Tiger Cubs proved severe. The mechanical condition of many of the "I" tanks was found on arrival to be indifferent.

General Wavell to Prime Minister   25 May 41

Many thanks for your message. We realise that our burdens and responsibilities here, though heavy, are nothing to those you shoulder so gallantly. . . .

Weaning of Tiger Cubs proceeding satisfactorily, but even tigers have teething troubles.

"I remember," says my wife, "terrible anxiety and even anger at Chequers on several Sundays because the newly arrived tanks could only come into action so slowly."

*   *   *

But trouble soon descended. During the ensuing week considerable movement of enemy armoured vehicles was observed. From documents captured later it was learnt that Rommel was expecting a serious attack to relieve Tobruk, and was determined to recapture and hold Halfaya in order to make such an attempt more difficult. He deployed the greater part of the newly arrived 15th Panzer Division, which, except for a small reconnaissance force thrown out to the south, he concentrated on the frontier between Capuzzo and Sidi Omar. Halfaya was held by a battalion group composed of the 3d Battalion Coldstream Guards, a regiment of field artillery, and two squadrons of tanks. The remainder of our frontier troops, except for observation patrols to the south, had been withdrawn considerable distances to the rear. The enemy advanced on Halfaya on May 26, and that evening captured a feature north of the pass which gave good observation over the whole position held by the Coldstream. A counter-attack to regain the feature was unsuccessful, and next morning after heavy shelling a concerted attack by at least two battalions and sixty tanks placed our small force in great jeopardy. Reserves were too distant to be able to intervene, and it remained only to extricate the force without more ado. This was accomplished, but losses were severe; only two of our tanks remained effective, and the Coldstream Guards lost eight officers and a hundred and sixty-five men. The enemy had gained his objective, and proceeded to install himself firmly at Halfaya. As he had hoped, his occupation of this position was to prove a considerable hindrance to us three weeks later.

*   *   *

Preparations for "Battleaxe" continued actively; but there was a darker side.

General Wavell to C.I.G.S.   28 May 41

All available armoured strength, which will be deciding factor, is being put into "Battleaxe." Various difficulties are delaying reconstitution 7th Armoured Division. Earliest date for beginning of forward move from Matruh will be June 7, and may be later.

2. I think it right to inform you that the measure of success which will attend this operation is in my opinion doubtful. I hope that it will succeed in driving enemy west of Tobruk and reestablishing land communications with Tobruk. If possible we will exploit success further. But recent operations have disclosed some disquieting features. Our armoured cars are too lightly armoured to resist the fire of enemy fighter aircraft, and, having no gun, are powerless against the German eight-wheeled armoured cars, which have guns and are faster. This makes reconnaissance difficult. Our infantry tanks are really too slow for a battle in the desert, and have been suffering considerable casualties from the fire of the powerful enemy anti-tank guns. Our cruisers have little advantage in power or speed over German medium tanks. Technical breakdowns are still too numerous. We shall not be able to accept battle with perfect confidence in spite of numerical inferiority, as we could against Italians. Above factors may limit our success. They also make it imperative that adequate flow of armoured reinforcements and reserves should be maintained.

On May 31 General Wavell reported the technical difficulties which he was having with the re-formation of the 7th Armoured Division. The earliest date at which he was able to launch "Battleaxe" would be June 15. While he realised the dangers of postponement, with the risk of enemy air reinforcements and a heavy attack on Tobruk, he felt that, as the forthcoming battle would be primarily a tank engagement, he must give the armoured division every chance, and the extra days gained by waiting should "double the possibilities of success."

I now awaited in keen hope and fear our attack in the Desert, from which results might be gained which might change in our favour the whole course of the campaign. The extra fortnight that had passed before the Tiger Cubs could be assimilated by the 7th Armoured Division made me fear that the 15th Panzers would all have reached Rommel.

According to our Intelligence there were now known to be in, or approaching, Eastern Cyrenaica the German 5th (Light) Panzer and the 15th Panzer Divisions, with the

Italian Ariete Armoured Division, the Trento Motorised Division, and the Brescia Infantry Division. Another Italian infantry division was in reserve at Derna. In disquieting contrast with our own performances earlier in the year, the Germans had brought Benghazi rapidly into use, and the bulk of their forces was probably already being maintained to a large extent through that port.

In his dispatch Wavell states that the bulk of the enemy lay before Tobruk with about one hundred and thirty medium and seventy light tanks. In the forward area it was estimated that there were only one hundred medium tanks, with the equivalent of seven German and nine Italian battalions. Two-thirds of the enemy's tank strength was, therefore, believed to be seventy miles back from the frontier. If Tobruk by a sortie could hold for a while the enemy around it, we should have at the outset a superiority in armour on the frontier of one hundred and eighty to one hundred tanks. Wavell comments that these estimates were wrong. So far as now can be established, Italian tanks were not used at all in the frontier battle. The Germans had succeeded in concentrating forward a large part of their own armour without our becoming aware of it. Actually they brought rather more than two hundred tanks into action against our one hundred and eighty.

*   *   *

"Battleaxe" started early on June 15. General Creagh commanded our armour, and General Messervy the 4th Indian Division and the 22d Guards Brigade. The whole force comprising about twenty-five thousand men, was under General Beresford-Peirse. At first things went reasonably well. Although the enemy defence about Halfaya held out against the combined attack from north and south, the Guards Brigade took Capuzzo in the afternoon with several hundred prisoners. A part of this brigade also moved on against the western defences of Sollum, but there they were stopped. The 7th Armoured Brigade, moving in protection of the outer flank, reached a position west of Capuzzo without encountering enemy tanks. On June 16 no progress was made. Halfaya and Sollum held firm against us, and in the afternoon strong forces of enemy tanks appeared, moving with the clear intention of outflanking our attack from the west. The 7th Armoured Division, both the brigade and the support group, moved to deal with this threat. They engaged the enemy near Sidi Omar, but were outnumbered and forced to withdraw. The flank of the main attack, which it was their task to protect, was thereby imperilled.

Next day, June 17, everything went wrong. In the morning the Guards Brigade were still in Capuzzo and facing Sollum. Capuzzo was taken from them by a considerable force, with tanks reported to be one hundred strong. The 7th Armoured Brigade, with only about twenty cruiser tanks now in action, had spent the night near Sidi Suleiman. The enemy force, which had forced them back overnight from Sidi Omar, made towards Halfaya and threatened to cut off the Guards Brigade. To deal with this threat Creagh proposed an attack with the 7th Armoured Brigade from the south, while the 4th Armoured Brigade, to be relieved of its task of co-operating with the Guards Brigade, attacked from the north. But as soon as the 4th Brigade started to move off yet another enemy armoured column coming in from the west threatened the Guards' flank. The armoured brigade held this attack off, but the enemy pressure continued, and Messervy informed Creagh that he could not part with the brigade lest his infantry be cut off.

At this decisive moment General Wavell flew to General Beresford-Peirse's battle headquarters. He still hoped to turn the scale by Creagh's armoured attack. He got into his airplane and flew to the 7th Armoured Division. He had no sooner reached it than he learned that General Messervy had independently decided that with the double threat against his flank and rear, which he now estimated as at least two hundred tanks, he must immediately retreat to avoid being surrounded. He had given orders accordingly. Wavell, out on the desert flank with Creagh, was confronted with this fact and concurred in the decision. Our stroke had failed. The withdrawal of the whole force was carried out in good order, protected by our fighter aircraft. The enemy did not press the pursuit, partly no doubt because his armour was heavily attacked by R.A.F. bombers. There was probably, however, another reason. As we now know, Rommel's orders were to act purely on the defensive and to build up resources for operations in the autumn. To have embroiled himself in a strong pursuit across the frontier, and suffered losses thereby, would have been in direct contravention of orders.

The policy of close protection of our troops by fighter aircraft, though effective, led to dispersion and a relatively high rate of air casualties. When, on the second day, the enemy air effort intensified, it was decided to modify the policy and,

while continuing a degree of protection, to operate offensively
in large units and farther afield. When the withdrawal began,
on the seventeenth, our fighters not only fended off three out
of four considerable air attacks on our troops, but also co-
operated with the bombers, often at low level, against enemy
columns. These attacks undoubtedly impeded the enemy's
movement and inflicted considerable casualties. Our airmen
rendered good service to the withdrawing troops, but they
were hampered by the difficulty of distinguishing between our
own and enemy forces.

Our casualties in the three days' battle were just over one
thousand, of which a hundred and fifty were killed and two
hundred and fifty missing. Twenty-nine cruisers and fifty-
eight "I" tanks were lost, the cruisers mainly from enemy
action. A considerable portion of the losses in "I" tanks were
due to mechanical breakdowns, there being no transporters to
bring them back. The best part of one hundred enemy tanks
were claimed as accounted for; five hundred and seventy
prisoners were taken and many enemy corpses buried.

*　　*　　*

Although this action may seem small compared with the
scale of the Mediterranean war in all its various campaigns,

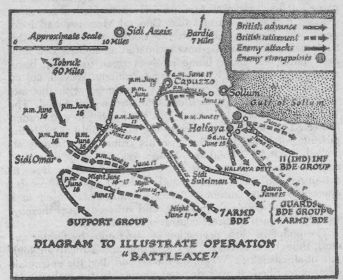

DIAGRAM TO ILLUSTRATE OPERATION
"BATTLEAXE"

GENERAL WAVELL'S FINAL EFFORT: "BATTLEAXE"   291

its failure was to me a most bitter blow. Success in the Desert
would have meant the destruction of Rommel's audacious
force. Tobruk would have been relieved, and the enemy's
retreat might well have carried him back beyond Benghazi
as fast as he had come. It was for this supreme object, as I
judged it, that all the perils of "Tiger" had been dared. No
news had reached me of the events of the seventeenth, and,
knowing that the result must soon come in, I went down to
Chartwell, which was all shut up, wishing to be alone. Here I
got the reports of what had happened. I wandered about the
valley disconsolately for some hours.

*   *   *

The reader who has followed the exchange of telegrams
between General Wavell and me and with the Chiefs of Staff
will be prepared in his mind for the decision which I took in
the last ten days of June, 1941. At home we had the feeling
that Wavell was a tired man. It might well be said that we had
ridden the willing horse to a standstill. The extraordinary
convergence of five or six different theatres, with their ups and
downs, especially downs, upon a single Commander-in-Chief
constituted a strain to which few soldiers have been subjected.
I was discontented with Wavell's provision for the defence of
Crete, and especially that a few more tanks had not been sent.
The Chiefs of Staff had overruled him in favour of the small
but most fortunate plunge into Iraq which had resulted in the
relief of Habbaniya and complete local success. One of their
telegrams had provoked from him an offer of resignation which
was not pressed, but which I did not refuse. Finally, there was
"Battleaxe," which Wavell had undertaken in loyalty to the
risks I had successfully run in sending out the Tiger Cubs. I
was dissatisfied with the arrangements made by the Middle
East Headquarters Staff for the reception of the Tiger Cubs,
carried to his aid through the deadly Mediterranean at so
much hazard and with so much luck. I admired the spirit with
which he had fought this small battle, which might have been
so important, and his extreme disregard of all personal risks
in flying to and fro on the wide, confused field of fighting.
But, as has been described, the operation seemed ill-concerted,
especially from the failure to make a sortie from the Tobruk
sally-port as an indispensable preliminary and concomitant.
Above all this there hung the fact of the beating-in of the
desert flank by Rommel, which had undermined and overthrown all the Greek projects on which we had embarked,

with all their sullen dangers and glittering prizes in what was
for us the supreme sphere of the Balkan War. General Ismay,
who was so close to me every day, has recorded the following:
"All of us at the centre, including Wavell's particular friends
and advisers, got the impression that he had been tremen-
dously affected by the breach of his desert flank. His Intelligence had been at fault, and the sudden pounce came as a
complete surprise. I seem to remember Eden saying that
Wavell had 'aged ten years in the night.'" I am reminded of
having commented: "Rommel has torn the new-won laurels
from Wavell's brow and thrown them in the sand." This was
not a true thought, but only a passing pang. Judgment upon
all this can only be made in relation to the authentic documents written at the time which this volume contains, and no
doubt also upon much other valuable evidence which time
will disclose. The fact remains that after "Battleaxe" I came
to the conclusion that there should be a change.

General Auchinleck was now Commander-in-Chief in India.
I had not altogether liked his attitude in the Norwegian campaign at Narvik. He had seemed to be inclined to play too
much for safety and certainty, neither of which exists in war,
and to be content to subordinate everything to the satisfaction of what he estimated as minimum requirements. However, I had been much impressed with his personal qualities,
his presence and high character. When after Narvik he had
taken over the Southern Command I received from many
quarters, official and private, testimony to the vigour and
structure which he had given to that important region. His
appointment as Commander-in-Chief in India had been generally acclaimed. We have seen how forthcoming he had been
about sending the Indian forces to Basra, and the ardour with
which he had addressed himself to the suppression of the
revolt in Iraq. I had the conviction that in Auchinleck I should
bring a new, fresh figure to bear the multiple strains of the
Middle East, and that Wavell, on the other hand, would find
in the great Indian command time to regain his strength before the new but impending challenges and opportunities
arrived. I found that these views of mine encountered no
resistance in our Ministerial and military circles in London.
The reader must not forget that I never wielded autocratic
powers, and always had to move with and focus political and
professional opinion. Accordingly I sent the following telegrams:

Prime Minister to General Wavell   21 June 41

I have come to the conclusion that the public interest will best be served by the appointment of General Auchinleck to relieve you in the command of the armies of the Middle East. I have greatly admired your command and conduct of these armies both in success and adversity, and the victories which are associated with your name will be famous in the story of the British Army, and are an important contribution to our final success in this obstinate war. I feel, however, that after the long strain you have borne a new eye and a new hand are required in this most seriously menaced theatre. I am sure that you are incomparably the best man and most distinguished officer to fill the vacancy of Commander-in-Chief in India. I have consulted the Viceroy upon the subject, and he assures me that your assumption of this great office and task will be warmly welcomed in India, and adds that he himself will be proud to work with one who bears, in his own words, "so shining a record." I propose, therefore, to submit your name to His Majesty accordingly.

2. General Auchinleck is being ordered to proceed at once to Cairo, where you will make him acquainted with the whole situation and concert with him the future measures which you and he will take in common to meet the German drive to the East now clearly impending. I trust he may arrive by air within the next four or five days at latest. After you have settled everything up with him you should proceed at your earliest convenience to India. No announcement will be made, and the matter must be kept strictly secret until you are both at your posts.

Prime Minister to Viceroy of India   21 June 41

Will you kindly convey the following to General Auchinleck. I have already telegraphed to General Wavell.

After very careful consideration of all the circumstances I have decided to submit your name to the King for the command of His Majesty's armies in the Middle East. You should proceed forthwith to Cairo and relieve General Wavell. General Wavell will succeed you as Commander-in-Chief in India. You should confer with him upon the whole situation, and should also concert with him the measures you will take in common to arrest the eastward movement of the German armies which is clearly impending. Pray let me know when you will arrive. The change is to be kept absolutely secret until you are installed in your new post.

Wavell received the decision with poise and dignity. He was at that time about to undertake a flight to Abyssinia which proved extremely dangerous. His biographer records that on reading my message he said, "The Prime Minister is quite right. There ought to be a new eye and a new hand in this theatre." In regard to the new command, he placed himself entirely at the disposal of His Majesty's Government.

                              *   *   *

I had for several months past been extremely distressed by the apparent inadequacy of the Cairo Staff, and I increasingly realised the undue burdens of so many different kinds cast upon our struggling Commander-in-Chief. He had himself, together with other Commanders-in-Chief, as early as April 18 asked for some relief and assistance. His view was endorsed by his two professional colleagues. "We consider it necessary for some authority to be established here to deal, inside the broad lines of policy laid down by His Majesty's Government, with the political aspects of issues affecting more than one department or territory. This will, of course, entail his being directly responsible to the War Cabinet and not to any one department." The Commanders-in-Chief had felt the convenience of having high political authority close at hand during Mr. Eden's visit. They were conscious of a vacuum after his departure.

I had already by June 4 appointed General Haining to the unusual office, which I created, of "Intendant-General." This officer had deputised for the C.I.G.S. during his absence abroad, and was consequently familiar with War Cabinet procedure and the wider aspects of the war. I hoped he would be able to relieve Wavell of all the business of supply and technical administration. I meant him to overhaul the whole rearward administrative machine, paying particular attention to the great tank and aircraft repairing establishments, as well as to the ever-growing railway, road, and port development which was now in progress. Thus the commanders would be freed from a mass of detail, and need think only of the fighting.

My son Randolph, who had gone out with the commandos, now to some extent dispersed, was at this time serving in the Desert. He was a Member of Parliament and had considerable contacts. I did not hear much or often from him, but on June 7 I had received through the Foreign Office the following telegram which he had sent from Cairo with the knowledge and encouragement of our Ambassador, Sir Miles Lampson:

Personal and Secret. From Randolph Churchill to Prime Minister

Do not see how we can start winning war out here until we have a competent civilian on the spot to provide day-to-day political and strategic direction. Why not send a member of the War Cabinet here to preside over whole war effort? Apart from small personal staff, he would need two outstanding men to co-ordinate supply and direct censorship, intelligence, and propaganda. Most thoughtful people here realise need for radical reform along these lines. No mere shunting of personnel will suffice, and the present time seems particularly ripe and favourable for a change of system. Please forgive me troubling you, but consider present situation deplorable and urgent action vital to any prospects of success.

It is the fact that this clinched matters in my mind. "I have been thinking," I replied to him a fortnight later, "a good deal for some time on the lines of your helpful and well-conceived telegram." And thereupon I took action.

I had brought Captain Oliver Lyttelton into the Government as President of the Board of Trade in October, 1940. I had known him from his childhood. His father, Alfred Lyttelton, had been Mr. Balfour's Secretary of State for the Colonies in 1904, and had before the Home Rule split been a youthful private secretary to Mr. Gladstone. He was for many years a distinguished member of the House of Commons. His son was thus brought up in a political atmosphere. He served in the Grenadiers through the hardest fighting of the First World War, being wounded and decorated several times. I remember going to see him in hospital in 1918 after he had had the good luck to be wounded by a poison-gas shell, which burst at his feet and burned him all over, instead of being killed, as he would have been, by a more orthodox and humane high-explosive projectile. After leaving the Army he had entered business and became the managing director of a large metal firm. Knowing his remarkable personal qualities, I did not hesitate to bring him into Parliament and high office. As President of the Board of Trade his administration had won respect from all parties in our National Government. I had not liked his proposals of 1941 for clothing coupons, but I found these were received with favour by the Cabinet and the House of Commons, and there is no doubt they were necessary at the time. My unusual choice had been vindicated by the results, although he had still much to learn as a newcomer in the House of Commons. He was an all-round man of action, and I now felt that he was in every way fitted for this new and novel post of a War Cabinet Minister resident in the Middle East. This would take another large slice of business off the shoulders of the military chiefs. I found this idea most readily acceptable to my colleagues of all parties. Accordingly:

Prime Minister to General Wavell   29 June 41

The King has been pleased to appoint Captain Oliver Lyttelton, formerly President of the Board of Trade, to be Minister of State in the War Cabinet, vice Lord Beaverbrook, who becomes Minister of Supply. Captain Lyttelton leaves by air on the thirtieth, and should reach Cairo July 3, with a small nucleus secretariat. He will represent the War Cabinet in the Middle East, and his prime duty will be to relieve the High Command of all extraneous burdens, and to settle promptly on the spot in accordance with the policy of H.M.G. many questions affecting several departments or authorities which hitherto have required reference home. This is largely in accordance with your telegram of April 18, but goes a good deal further. The instructions I am giving to Captain Lyttelton follow in my next.

Please inform General Auchinleck when he arrives and Sir Miles Lampson. Complete secrecy should be observed about Captain Lyttelton's journey and mission till he has arrived.

⁂   ⁂   ⁂

All these new arrangements, with their consequential ad-ministerial reactions, fitted in with, and were appropriate to, the change in the command in the Middle East. I cannot better sum them up than by the telegram which I sent to President Roosevelt, who was now giving us most important material aid in this theatre.

Former Naval Person to President Roosevelt   4 July 41

Following are considerations which weighed with us in deciding upon change in command in the Middle East. Wavell has a glorious record, having completely destroyed the Italian Army and conquered the Italian Empire in Africa. He has also borne up well against German attacks and has conducted war and policy in three or four directions simultaneously since the beginning of the struggle. I must regard him as our most distinguished General. Nevertheless, though this should not be stated publicly, we felt that, after the long strain he had borne, he was tired, and a fresh eye and an unstrained hand were needed in this most seriously menaced theatre. Incomparably the best and most distinguished officer to take his place was General Auchinleck, the Commander-in-Chief in India. We feel sure that Auchinleck will infuse a new energy and precision into the defence of the Nile Valley, while Wavell will make an admirable Commander-in-Chief in India who will aid him in the whole of the great sphere which India is now assuming, as our flank moves eastward. As Commander-in-Chief India Wavell will have operations in Iraq under his control.

Wavell has accepted this decision gracefully, saying that he thinks us wise to make the change and get new ideas and action on the many problems in the Middle East. The Viceroy has assured me that his shining achievements will secure him a very warm welcome in India from the Army and public opinion.

The present lull in the German offensive in the Middle East has provided a convenient opportunity for change-over. It coincides also with the appointment of Oliver Lyttelton as Minister of State to represent the War Cabinet in that theatre and relieve the Commanders-in-Chief of many non-operational functions which have hitherto greatly increased their burdens, such as relations with the Free French, relations with the Emperor of Abyssinia, the administration of occupied enemy territory, propaganda, and economic warfare. The Minister of State will also exercise general supervision over the activities of the Intendant-General (another innovation), including all matters locally connected with supplies from the United States.

The Intendant-General (General Haining) will relieve the Army Commander-in-Chief of detailed control of rearward administrative services and supply arrangements.

All these changes will, I hope, result in a greatly increased vigour and drive in our effort in the Middle East, and ensure that the fullest use is made of the formidable resources steadily accumulating there from the United Kingdom, the overseas Empire, and the United States. Harriman will doubtless be reporting upon them. He is being asked to await Lyttelton's arrival in Cairo (now expected on July 5), so as to pool all information and settle arrangements for the reception of American supplies.

20

The Soviet Nemesis

Nemesis personifies "the Goddess of Retribution, who
brings down all immoderate good fortune, checks the
presumption that attends it . . . and is the punisher of extraordinary crimes." [1] We must now lay bare the error and
vanity of cold-blooded calculation of the Soviet Government
and enormous Communist machine, and their amazing ignorance about where they stood themselves. They had shown
a total indifference to the fate of the Western Powers, although this meant the destruction of that "Second Front" for
which they were soon to clamour. They seemed to have no
inkling that Hitler had for more than six months resolved to
destroy them. If their Intelligence Service informed them of
the vast German deployment towards the East, which was
now increasing every day, they omitted many needful steps
to meet it. Thus they had allowed the whole of the Balkans
to be overrun by Germany. They hated and despised the
democracies of the West; but the four countries, Turkey,
Rumania, Bulgaria, and Yugoslavia, which were of vital

[1] Oxford English Dictionary.

interest to them and their own safety, could all have been combined by the Soviet Government in January with active British aid to form a Balkan front against Hitler. They let them all break into confusion, and all but Turkey were mopped up one by one. War is mainly a catalogue of blunders, but it may be doubted whether any mistake in history has equalled that of which Stalin and the Communist chiefs were guilty when they cast away all possibilities in the Balkans and supinely awaited, or were incapable of realising, the fearful onslaught which impended upon Russia. We have hitherto rated them as selfish calculators. In this period they were proved simpletons as well. The force, the mass, the bravery and endurance of Mother Russia had still to be thrown into the scales. But so far as strategy, policy, foresight, competence are arbiters, Stalin and his commissars showed themselves at this moment the most completely outwitted bunglers of the Second World War.

* * *

Hitler's "Barbarossa" directive of December 18, 1940, had laid down the general grouping and primary tasks of the forces to be concentrated against Russia. At that date the total German strength on the Eastern Front was thirty-four divisions. To multiply that figure more than thrice was an immense process both of planning and preparation, and it fully occupied the early months of 1941. In January and February the Balkan adventure into which the Fuehrer allowed himself to be drawn caused a drain-away from the East to the South of five divisions, of which three were armoured. In May the German deployment in the East grew to eighty-seven divisions, and there were no less than twenty-five of their divisions absorbed in the Balkans. Considering the magnitude and hazard of the invasion of Russia, it was improvident to disturb the concentration to the East by so serious a diversion. We shall now see how a delay of five weeks was imposed upon the supreme operation as the result of our resistance in the Balkans, and especially of the Yugoslav revolution. No one can measure exactly what consequences this had before winter set in upon the fortunes of the German-Russian campaign. It is reasonable to believe that Moscow was saved thereby. During May and the beginning of June many of the best-trained German divisions and all the armour were moved from the Balkans to the Eastern Front, and at the moment of their assault the Germans attacked with a hundred and twenty divisions, seventeen of which were armoured and twelve motorised. Six Rumanian divisions were also included in their Southern Army Group. In general reserve a further twenty-six divisions were assembled or assembling; so that by early June the German High Command could count on at least a hundred and fifty divisions, supported by the main striking power of their air force, about twenty-seven hundred aircraft.

*   *   *

Up till the end of March I was not convinced that Hitler was resolved upon mortal war with Russia, nor how near it was. Our Intelligence reports revealed in much detail the extensive German troop movements towards and into the Balkan States which had marked the first three months of 1941. Our agents could move with a good deal of freedom in these quasi-neutral countries, and were able to keep us accurately posted about the heavy German forces gathering by rail and road to the southeast. But none of these necessarily involved the invasion of Russia, and all were readily explainable by German interests and policy in Rumania and Bulgaria, by her designs on Greece and arrangements with Yugoslavia and Hungary. Our information about the immense movement taking place through Germany towards the main Russian front, stretching from Rumania to the Baltic, was far more difficult to acquire. That Germany should at this stage, and before clearing the Balkan scene, open another major war with Russia seemed to me too good to be true.

We did not know the tenor of the conversations of November, 1940, between Molotov, Hitler, and Ribbentrop at Berlin, nor of the negotiations and proposed pacts which had followed them. There was no sign of lessening German strength opposite us across the Channel. The German air raids on Britain continued with intensity. The manner in which the German troop concentrations in Rumania and Bulgaria had been glozed over and apparently accepted by the Soviet Government, the evidence we had of large and invaluable supplies being sent to Germany from Russia, the obvious community of interest between the two countries in overrunning and dividing the British Empire in the East, all made it seem more likely that Hitler and Stalin would make a bargain at our expense rather than a war upon each other. This bargain we now know was within wide limits Stalin's aim.

These impressions were shared by our Joint Intelligence

Committee. On April 7 they stated that there were a number of reports circulating in Europe of a German plan to attack Russia. Although Germany, they said, had considerable forces available in the East, and expected to fight Russia some time or other, it was unlikely that she would choose to make another major war front yet. Her main object in 1941 would, according to them, remain the defeat of the United Kingdom. As late as May 23 this committee from the three services reported that rumors of impending attack on Russia had died down, and that there were reports that a new agreement between the two countries was impending. This they considered likely, since German economy would require strengthening to meet the needs of a long war. The necessary assistance could be obtained by Germany from Russia either by force or agreement. They thought the latter would be the German choice, although a threat of force would help to bring it about. This threat was now building up. There was plenty of evidence of the construction of roads and railway sidings in German Poland, of the preparation of aerodromes and of large-scale troop concentrations, including troops and air units from the Balkans.

Our Chiefs of Staff were ahead of their advisers; and more definite. "We have firm indications," they warned the Middle East Command on May 31, "that the Germans are now concentrating large army and air forces against Russia. Under this threat they will probably demand concessions most injurious to us. If the Russians refuse, the Germans will march."

It was not till June 5 that the Joint Intelligence Committee reported that the scale of German military preparations in Eastern Europe seemed to indicate that an issue more vital than an economic agreement was at stake. It was possible that Germany desired to remove from her eastern frontier the potential threat of increasingly powerful Soviet forces. They considered it as yet impossible to say whether war or agreement would result. On June 10 they stated, "The latter half of June will see either war or agreement." And finally on June 12 they reported, "Fresh evidence is now at hand that Hitler has made up his mind to have done with Soviet obstruction, and to attack."

*   *   *

I had not been content with this form of collective wisdom, and preferred to see the originals myself. I had arranged, therefore, as far back as the summer of 1940, for Major Desmond Morton to make a daily selection of titbits, which I always read, thus forming my own opinion, sometimes at much earlier dates.[2]

It was thus with relief and excitement that towards the end of March, 1941, I read an Intelligence report from one of our most trusted sources of the movement and counter-movement of German armour on the railway from Bucharest to Cracow. This showed that as soon as the Yugoslav Ministers made their submission in Vienna, three out of the five Panzer divisions which had moved through Rumania southward towards Greece and Yugoslavia had been sent northward to Cracow, and secondly, that the whole of this transportation had been reversed after the Belgrade revolution and the three Panzer divisions sent back to Rumania. This shuffling and reversal of about sixty trains could not be concealed from our agents on the spot.

To me it illuminated the whole Eastern scene like a lightning flash. The sudden movement to Cracow of so much armour needed in the Balkan sphere could only mean Hitler's intention to invade Russia in May. This seemed to me henceforward certainly his major purpose. The fact that the Belgrade revolution had required their return to Rumania involved perhaps a delay from May to June. I sent the momentous news at once to Mr. Eden in Athens.

Prime Minister to Mr. Eden, Athens   30 March 41

My reading of the Intelligence is that the bad man concentrated very large armoured forces, etc., to overawe Yugoslavia and Greece, and hoped to get former or both without fighting. The moment he was sure Yugoslavia was in the Axis he moved three of the five Panzers towards the Bear, believing that what was left would be enough to finish the Greek affair. However, the Belgrade revolution upset this picture and caused the northward move to be arrested in transit. This can only mean, in my opinion, the intention to attack Yugoslavia at earliest, or alternatively [to] act against the Turk. It looks as if heavy forces will be used in Balkan Peninsula and that Bear will be kept waiting a bit. Furthermore, these orders and counter-orders in their relation to the Belgrade *coup* seem to reveal magnitude of design both towards southeast and east. This is the clearest indication we have had so far. Let me know in guarded terms whether you and Dill agree with my impressions.

[2] *Prime Minister to General Ismay*   5 Aug. 40
I do not wish such reports as are received to be sifted and digested by the various Intelligence authorities. For the present Major Morton will inspect them for me and submit what he considers of major importance. He is to be shown everything, and submit authentic documents to me in their original form.

I also cast about for some means of warning Stalin, and, by arousing him to his danger, establishing contacts with him like those I had made with President Roosevelt. I made the message short and cryptic, hoping that this very fact, and that it was the first message I had sent him since my formal telegram of June 25, 1940, commending Sir Stafford Cripps as Ambassador, would arrest his attention and make him ponder.

Prime Minister to Sir Stafford Cripps   3 April 41
Following from me to M. Stalin, *provided it can be personally delivered by you:*
I have sure information from a trusted agent that when the Germans thought they had got Yugoslavia in the net—that is to say, after March 20—they began to move three out of the five Panzer divisions from Rumania to Southern Poland. The moment they heard of the Serbian revolution this movement was countermanded. Your Excellency will readily appreciate the significance of these facts.

The Foreign Secretary, who had by this time returned from Cairo, added some comments:

If your reception gives you opportunity of developing the argument, you might point out that this change in German military dispositions surely implies that Hitler, through the action of Yugoslavia, has now postponed his previous plans for threatening Soviet Government. If so, it should be possible for Soviet Government to use this opportunity to strengthen their own position. This delay shows that the enemy forces are not unlimited, and illustrates the advantage that will follow anything like a united front.
2. Obvious way of Soviet Government strengthening its own position would be to furnish material help to Turkey and Greece, and through latter to Yugoslavia. This help might so increase German difficulties in Balkans as still further to delay the German attack on Soviet Union, of which there are so many signs. If, however, opportunity is not now taken to put every possible spoke in the German wheel danger might revive in a few months' time.
3. You would not, of course, imply that we ourselves required any assistance from Soviet Government or that they would be acting in any interests but their own. What we want them to realise, however, is that Hitler intends to attack them sooner or later if he can; that the fact that he is in conflict with us is not in itself sufficient to prevent him doing so if he is not also involved in some special embarrassment, such as now confronts him in Balkans, and that it is consequently in Soviet interests to take every possible step to ensure that he does not settle his Balkan problem in the way he wants.

The British Ambassador did not reply till April 12, when he said that just before my telegram had been received he had himself addressed to Vyshinsky a long personal letter reviewing the succession of failures of the Soviet Government to counteract German encroachments in the Balkans, and urging in the strongest terms that the U.S.S.R. in her own interest must now decide on an immediate vigorous policy of co-operation with countries still opposing the Axis in that area if she was not to miss the last chance of defending her own frontiers in alliance with others.

Were I now [he said] to convey through Molotov the Prime Minister's message, which expresses the same thesis in very much shorter and less emphatic form, I fear that the only effect would be probably to weaken impression already made by my letter to Vyshinsky. Soviet Government would not, I feel sure, understand why so short and fragmentary a commentary on facts of which they are certainly well aware, without any definite request for explanation of Soviet Government's attitude or suggestion for action by them, should be conveyed in so formal a manner.

I have felt bound to put these considerations before you, as I greatly fear that delivery of Prime Minister's message would be not merely ineffectual but a serious tactical mistake. If, however, you are unable to share this view, I will, of course, endeavour to arrange urgently for an interview with Molotov.

On this the Foreign Secretary minuted to me:

In this new situation I think there may be some force in Sir Stafford Cripps' arguments against the delivery of your message. If you agree I would propose to tell him that he need not now deliver the message, but that if Vyshinsky responds favourably to his letter he should give the latter the facts contained in your message. Meanwhile I should ask him to telegraph to us as soon as possible a summary of the letter which he has sent to Vyshinsky and to send us the text by the next opportunity.

I was vexed at this and at the delay which had occurred. This was the only message before the attack that I sent Stalin direct. Its brevity, the exceptional character of the communication, the fact that it came from the head of the Government and was to be delivered personally to the head of the Russian Government by the Ambassador, were all intended to give it special significance and arrest Stalin's attention.

Prime Minister to Foreign Secretary   16 April 41

I set special importance on the delivery of this personal message from me to Stalin. I cannot understand why it should be resisted.

The Ambassador is not alive to the military significance of the facts. Pray oblige me.

And again:

Prime Minister to Foreign Secretary   18 April 41
Has Sir Stafford Cripps yet delivered my personal message of warning about the German danger to Stalin? I am very much surprised that so much delay should have occurred, considering the importance I attach to this extremely pregnant piece of information.

The Foreign Secretary, therefore, telegraphed on the eighteenth to the Ambassador instructing him to deliver my message. As no answer was received from Sir Stafford, I asked what had happened.

Prime Minister to Foreign Secretary   30 April 41
When did Sir Stafford Cripps deliver my message to Mr. Stalin? Will you very kindly ask him to report.

Foreign Secretary to Prime Minister   30 April 41
Sir Stafford Cripps sent the message to M. Vyshinsky on April 19, and M. Vyshinsky informed him in writing on April 23 that it had been conveyed to M. Stalin.
I very much regret that, owing to an error, the telegrams reporting this were not sent to you at the time. I attach copies.

These were the enclosures:

Sir Stafford Cripps, Moscow, to Foreign Secretary   19 April 41
I have today sent text of message to Vyshinsky, asking him to convey it to Stalin. It was not clear from your telegram whether commentary was to be incorporated in message or added as from myself, and consequently, in view of my letter to Vyshinsky of April 11 and my interview with him yesterday, I felt it preferable to abstain from adding any commentary, which could only have been repetition.

Sir Stafford Cripps, Moscow, to Foreign Secretary   22 April 41
Vyshinsky informed me in writing today that message had been conveyed to Stalin.

I cannot form any final judgment upon whether my message, if delivered with all the promptness and ceremony prescribed, would have altered the course of events. Nevertheless, I still regret that my instructions were not carried out effectively. If I had had any direct contact with Stalin I might perhaps have prevented him from having so much of his air force destroyed on the ground.

* * *

We know now that Hitler's directive of December 18 had prescribed May 15 as the date for invading Russia, and that in his fury at the revolution in Belgrade this date had on March 27 been postponed for a month, and later till June 22. Until the middle of March the troop movements in the north on the main Russian front were not of a character to require special German measures of concealment. On March 13, however, orders were issued by Berlin to terminate the work of the Russian commissions working in German territory and to send them home. The presence of Russians in this part of Germany could only be permitted up to March 25. In the northern sector strong German formations were already being assembled. From March 20 onward an even heavier massing would take place.[3]

On April 22 the Soviet complained to the German Foreign Office about continuing and increasing violations of the U.S.S.R. boundary by German planes. From March 27 to April 18 eighty such cases had occurred. "It is very likely," added the Russian note, "that serious incidents are to be expected if German planes continue to fly across the Soviet border."

The German reply was a series of counter-complaints against Soviet planes.

* * *

During this time the one hundred and twenty German divisions of the highest quality were assembling in their three army groups along the Russian front. The Southern Group, under Rundstedt, was, for the reasons explained, far from well found in armour. Its Panzer divisions had only recently returned from Greece and Yugoslavia. Despite the postponement of the date till June 22, they badly needed rest and overhaul after their mechanical wear and tear in the Balkans.

On April 13 Schulenburg came from Moscow to Berlin. Hitler received him on April 28, and treated his Ambassador to a tirade on the Russian gesture towards Yugoslavia. Schulenburg, according to his minute of this conversation, strove to excuse the Soviet behavior. He related that "Russia was alarmed by the rumours predicting a German attack. He could

[3] Nazi-Soviet Relations, 1939–1941, published by the State Department of the United States, 1948, page 279.

not believe that Russia would ever attack Germany. Hitler
said that he had been forewarned by events in Serbia. What
had happened there was to him an example of the political
unreliability of states." But Schulenburg adhered to the theme
which had governed all his reports from Moscow. "I am convinced that Stalin is prepared to make even further concessions to us. It has already been indicated to our economic ne-
gotiators that (if we applied in due time) Russia could supply
us with up to five million tons of grain a year." [4]

Schulenburg returned to Moscow on April 30, profoundly
disillusioned by his interview with Hitler. He had a clear
impression that Hitler was bent on war. It seems that he had
even tried to warn the Russian Ambassador in Berlin, Dekanosov, in this sense. And he fought persistently in the last
hours of his policy of Russo-German understanding.

Weizsäcker, the official head of the German Foreign Office,
was a highly competent civil servant of the type to be found
in the Government departments of many countries. He was not
a politician with executive power, and would not, according
to British custom, be held accountable for State policy. He is
now undergoing seven years' penal servitude by the decree of
the courts set up by the conquerors. Although he is, therefore, classified as a war criminal, he certainly wrote good advice to his superiors, which we may be glad they did not
take. He commented as follows upon this interview:

Weizsäcker to Ribbentrop   Berlin, April 28, 1941

I can summarise in one sentence my views on a German-Russian
conflict. If every Russian city reduced to ashes were as valuable
to us as a sunken British warship, I should advocate the German-
Russian war for this summer; but I believe that we should be
victors over Russia only in a military sense, and should, on the
other hand, lose in an economic sense.

It might perhaps be considered an alluring prospect to give the
Communist system its death-blow, and it might also be said that it
was inherent in the logic of things to muster the Eurasian continent against Anglo-Saxondom and its following. But the sole
decisive factor is whether this project will hasten the fall of
England.

We must distinguish between two possibilities:

(a) England is close to collapse. If we accept this assumption
we shall encourage England by taking on a new opponent. Russia
is no potential ally of the English. England can expect nothing
good from Russia. Hope in Russia is not postponing England's
collapse. With Russia we do not destroy any English hopes.

[4] *Ibid.*, page 332.

(b) If we do not believe in the imminent collapse of England, then the thought might suggest itself that by the use of force we must feed ourselves from Soviet territory. I take it as a matter of course that we shall advance victoriously to Moscow and beyond that. I doubt very much, however, whether we shall be able to turn to account what we have won in the face of the well-known passive resistance of the Slavs. I do not see in the Russian State any effective opposition capable of succeeding the Communist system and uniting with us and being of service to us. We should, therefore, probably have to reckon with a continuation of the Stalin system in Eastern Russia and in Siberia and with a renewed outbreak of hostilities in the spring of 1942. The window to the Pacific Ocean would remain shut.

A German attack on Russia would only give the British new moral strength. It would be interpreted there as German uncertainty about the success of our fight against England. We should thereby not only be admitting that the war was going to last a long time yet, but we might actually prolong it in this way, instead of shortening it.

On May 7 Schulenburg hopefully reported that Stalin had taken over the chairmanship of the Council of People's Commissars in place of Molotov, and had thereby become head of the Government of the Soviet Union.

The reason for this may be sought in the recent mistakes in foreign policy which led to a cooling-off of the cordiality of German-Soviet relations, for the creation and preservation of which Stalin had consciously striven.

In his new capacity Stalin assumes responsibility for all acts of the Government, in both the domestic and foreign fields. . . . I am convinced that Stalin will use his new position in order to take part personally in the maintenance and development of good relations between the Soviets and Germany.

The German Naval Attaché, reporting from Moscow, expressed the same point in these words: "Stalin is the pivot of German-Soviet collaboration." Examples of Russian appeasement of Germany increased. On May 3 Russia had officially recognised the pro-German Government of Rashid Ali in Iraq. On May 7 the diplomatic representatives of Belgium and Norway were expelled from Russia. Even the Yugoslav Minister was flung out. At the beginning of June the Greek Legation was banished from Moscow. As General Thomas, the head of the economic section of the German War Ministry, later wrote in his paper on the war economy of the Reich: "The Russians executed their deliveries up to the eve of the attack, and in the last days the transport of rubber from the Far East was expedited by express trains."

We had not, of course, full information about the Moscow moods, but the German purpose seemed plain and comprehensible. On May 16 I cabled to General Smuts: "It looks as if Hitler is massing against Russia. A ceaseless movement of troops, armoured forces, and aircraft northward from the Balkans and eastward from France and Germany is in progress." Stalin must have tried very hard to preserve his illusions about Hitler's policy. After another month of intense German troop movement and deployment, Schulenburg could telegraph to the German Foreign Office on June 13:

People's Commissar Molotov has just given me the following text of a Tass dispatch which will be broadcast tonight and published in the papers tomorrow:

Even before the return of the English Ambassador Cripps to London, but especially since his return, there have been widespread rumours of an impending war between the U.S.S.R. and Germany in the English and foreign press. These allege:

That Germany supposedly has made various territorial and economic demands on the U.S.S.R., and negotiations are impending between Germany and the U.S.S.R. for a new and closer agreement.

2. That the Soviet Union is supposed to have declined these demands, and that as a result Germany has begun to concentrate her troops on the frontier of the Soviet Union in order to attack the Soviet Union.

3. That on its side the Soviet Union is supposed to have begun intensive preparations for war with Germany and to have concentrated its troops on the German border.

Despite the obvious absurdity of these rumours, responsible circles in Moscow have thought it necessary to state that they are a clumsy propaganda manoeuvre of the forces arrayed against the Soviet Union and Germany, which are interested in a spread and intensification of the war.

Hitler had every right to be content with the success of his measures of deception and concealment, and with his victim's state of mind.

Molotov's final fatuity is worth recording.

Schulenburg to the German   Moscow, June 22, 1941, 1.17 A.M.
Foreign Office

Molotov summoned me to his office this evening at 9.30 P.M. After he had mentioned the alleged repeated border violations by German aircraft, with the remark that Dekanosov had been in-

structed to call on the Reich Foreign Minister in this matter,
Molotov stated as follows:

There were a number of indications that the German Government was dissatisfied with the Soviet Government. Rumours were
even current that a war was impending between Germany and the
Soviet Union. They found sustenance in the fact that there was no
reaction whatsoever on the part of Germany to the Tass report of
June 15; that it was not even published in Germany. The Soviet
Government was unable to understand the reasons for Germany's
dissatisfaction. If the Yugoslav question had at the time given rise
to such dissatisfaction, he—Molotov—believed that by means of
his earlier communications he had cleared up this question, which,
moreover, was a thing of the past. He would appreciate it if I
could tell him what had brought about the present situation in
German-Soviet Russian relations.

I replied that I could not answer his question, as I lacked the
pertinent information; that I would, however, transmit his communication to Berlin.

*   *   *

But the hour had now struck.

Ribbentrop to Schulenburg   Berlin, June 21, 1941

Upon receipt of this telegram all of the cipher material still
there is to be destroyed. The radio set is to be put out of commission.

2. Please inform Herr Molotov at once that you have an urgent
communication to make to him and would, therefore, like to call
on him immediately. Then please make the following declaration
to him:

". . . The Government of the Reich declares that the Soviet
Government, contrary to the obligations it assumed, (1) has not
only continued, but even intensified, its attempts to undermine
Germany and Europe; (2) has adopted a more and more anti-
German foreign policy; (3) has concentrated all its forces in
readiness at the German border.

"Thereby the Soviet Government has broken its treaties with
Germany and is about to attack Germany from the rear, in its
struggle for life. The Fuehrer has, therefore, ordered the German
armed forces to oppose this threat with all the means at their
disposal."

Please do not enter into any discussion of this communication.
It is incumbent upon the Government of Soviet Russia to safeguard the security of the Embassy personnel.

At 4 A.M. on June 22 Ribbentrop delivered a formal declaration of war to the Russian Ambassador in Berlin. At daybreak Schulenburg presented himself to Molotov in the
Kremlin. The latter listened in silence to the statement read

by the German Ambassador, and then commented, "It is war. Your aircraft have just bombarded some ten open villages. *Do you believe that we deserved that?*" [5]

In the face of the Tass broadcast it had been vain for us to add to the various warnings which Eden had given to the Soviet Ambassador in London or for me to make a renewed personal effort to arouse Stalin to his peril. Even more precise information had been constantly sent to the Soviet Government by the United States. Nothing that any of us could do pierced the purblind prejudice and fixed ideas which Stalin had raised between himself and the terrible truth. Although on German estimates 186 Russian divisions were massed behind the Soviet boundaries, of which 119 faced the German front, the Russian armies to a large extent were taken by surprise. The Germans found no signs of offensive preparations in the forward zone, and the Russian covering troops were swiftly overpowered. Something like the disaster which had befallen the Polish Air Force on September 1, 1939, was now to be repeated on a far larger scale on the Russian airfields, and many hundreds of Russian planes were caught at daybreak and destroyed before they could get into the air. Thus the ravings of hatred against Britain and the United States which the Soviet propaganda machine cast upon the midnight air were overwhelmed at dawn by the German cannonade. The wicked are not always clever, nor are dictators always right.

* * *

It is impossible to complete this account without referring to a terrible decision of policy adopted by Hitler towards his new foes, and enforced under all the pressure of the mortal struggle in vast barren or ruined lands and winter horrors. Verbal orders were given by him at a conference on June 14, 1941, which to a large extent governed the conduct of the German Army towards the Russian troops and people, and led to many ruthless and barbarous deeds. According to the Nuremberg documents, General Halder testified:

Prior to the attack on Russia the Fuehrer called a conference of all the commanders and persons connected with the Supreme

[5] This was the last act of Count Schulenburg's diplomatic career. Late in 1943 his name appears in the secret circles of conspiracy against Hitler in Germany as possible Foreign Minister of a Government to succeed the Nazi régime in view of his special qualifications to negotiate a separate peace with Stalin. He was arrested by the Nazis after the attempted assassination of Hitler in July, 1944, and imprisoned in the Gestapo cells. On November 10 he was executed.

Command on the question of the forthcoming attack on Russia. I cannot recall the exact date of this conference. . . . At this conference the Fuehrer stated that the methods used in the war against the Russians would have to be different from those used against the West. . . . He said that the struggle between Russia and Germany was a Russian struggle. He stated that since the Russians were not signatories of the Hague Convention the treatment of their prisoners of war did not have to follow the Articles of the Convention. . . . He [also] said that the so-called Commissars should not be considered prisoners of war.[6]

And according to Keitel:

Hitler's main theme was that this was the decisive battle between the two ideologies and that this fact made it impossible to use in this war [with Russia] methods, as we soldiers knew them, which were considered to be the only correct ones under international law.[7]

On the evening of Friday, June 20, I drove down to Chequers alone. I knew that the German onslaught upon Russia was a matter of days, or it might be hours. I had arranged to deliver a broadcast on Saturday night dealing with this event. It would, of course, have to be in guarded terms. Moreover, at this time the Soviet Government, at once haughty and purblind, regarded every warning we gave as a mere attempt of beaten men to drag others into ruin. As the result of my reflections in the car, I put off the broadcast till Sunday night, when I thought all would be clear. Thus Saturday passed with its usual toil.

Five days earlier, on the fifteenth, I had cabled to President Roosevelt as follows:

Former Naval Person to President Roosevelt   15 June 41

From every source at my disposal, including some most trustworthy, it looks as if a vast German onslaught on Russia was imminent. Not only are the main German armies deployed from Finland to Rumania, but the final arrivals of air and armoured forces are being completed. The pocket-battleship *Lutzow,* which put her nose out of the Skaggerak yesterday and was promptly torpedoed by our coastal aircraft, was very likely going north to give naval strength on the Arctic flank. Should this new war break out, we shall, of course, give all encouragement and any help we can spare to the Russians, following the principle that Hitler is the foe we have to beat. I do not expect any class political reactions here, and trust a German-Russian conflict will not cause you any embarrassment.

[6] *Nuremberg Documents,* Part VI, page 310.
[7] *Ibid.,* Part XI, page 16.

The American Ambassador, who was my guest at the weekend, brought me the President's answer to my message. He promised that if the Germans struck at Russia he would immediately support publicly "any announcement that the Prime Minister might make welcoming Russia as an ally." Mr. Winant delivered this important reassurance verbally.

    *   *   *

When I awoke on the morning of Sunday, June 22, the news was brought to me of Hitler's invasion of Russia. This changed conviction into certainty. I had not the slightest doubt where our duty and our policy lay. Nor indeed what to say. There only remained the task of composing it. I asked that notice should immediately be given that I would broadcast at nine o'clock that night. Presently General Dill, who had hastened down from London, came into my bedroom with detailed news. The Germans had invaded Russia on an enormous front, had surprised a large portion of the Soviet Air Force grounded on the airfields, and seemed to be driving forward with great rapidity and violence. The Chief of the Imperial General Staff added, "I suppose they will be rounded up in hordes."

I spent the day composing my statement. There was not time to consult the War Cabinet; nor was it necessary. I knew that we all felt the same on this issue. Mr. Eden, Lord Beaverbrook, and Sir Stafford Cripps—he had left Moscow on the tenth—were also with me during the day.

    *   *   *

The following account of this Sunday at Chequers by my private secretary, Mr. Colville, who was on duty this weekend, may be of interest:

On Saturday, June 21, I went down to Chequers just before dinner. Mr. and Mrs. Winant, Mr. and Mrs. Eden, and Edward Bridges were staying. During dinner Mr. Churchill said that a German attack on Russia was now certain, and he thought that Hitler was counting on enlisting capitalist and Right Wing sympathies in this country and the U.S.A. Hitler was, however, wrong and we should go all out to help Russia. Winant said the same would be true of the U.S.A.

After dinner, when I was walking on the croquet lawn with Mr. Churchill, he reverted to this theme, and I asked whether for him, the arch anti-Communist, this was [not] bowing down in the House of Rimmon. Mr. Churchill replied, "Not at all. I have only one purpose, the destruction of Hitler, and my life is much simplified thereby. If Hitler invaded Hell I would make at least a favourable reference to the Devil in the House of Commons."

2. I was awoken at 4 A.M. the following morning by a telephone message from the F.O. to the effect that Germany had attacked Russia. The P.M. had always said that he was never to be woken up for anything but invasion [of England]. I therefore postponed telling him till 8 A.M. His only comment was, "Tell the B.B.C. I will broadcast at nine tonight." He began to prepare the speech at 11 A.M., and except for luncheon, at which Sir Stafford Cripps, Lord Cranborne, and Lord Beaverbrook were present, he devoted the whole day to it. . . . The speech was only ready at twenty minutes to nine.

In this broadcast I said:

The Nazi régime is indistinguishable from the worst features of Communism. It is devoid of all theme and principle except appetite and racial domination. It excels all forms of human wickedness in the efficiency of its cruelty and ferocious aggression. No one has been a more consistent opponent of Communism than I have for the last twenty-five years. I will unsay no word that I have spoken about it. But all this fades away before the spectacle which is now unfolding. The past, with its crimes, its follies, and its tragedies, flashes away. I see the Russian soldiers standing on the threshold of their native land, guarding the fields which their fathers have tilled from time immemorial. I see them guarding their homes where mothers and wives pray—ah, yes, for there are times when all pray—for the safety of their loved ones, the return of the bread-winner, of their champion, of their protector. I see the ten thousand villages of Russia where the means of existence is wrung so hardly from the soil, but where there are still primordial human joys, where maidens laugh and children play. I see advancing upon all this in hideous onslaught the Nazi war machine, with its clanking, heel-clicking, dandified Prussian officers, its crafty expert agents fresh from the cowing and tying-down of a dozen countries. I see also the dull, drilled, docile, brutish masses of the Hun soldiery plodding on like a swarm of crawling locusts. I see the German bombers and fighters in the sky, still smarting from many a British whipping, delighted to find what they believe is an easier and a safer prey.

Behind all this glare, behind all this storm, I see that small group of villainous men who plan, organise, and launch this cataract of horrors upon mankind. . . .

I have to declare the decision of His Majesty's Government— and I feel sure it is a decision in which the great Dominions will in due course concur—for we must speak out now at once, without a day's delay. I have to make the declaration, but can you doubt what our policy will be? We have but one aim and one single, irrevocable purpose. We are resolved to destroy Hitler and every vestige of the Nazi régime. From this nothing will turn us —nothing. We will never parley, we will never negotiate with Hitler or any of his gang. We shall fight him by land, we shall fight him by sea, we shall fight him in the air, until, with God's help, we have rid the earth of his shadow and liberated its peoples from his yoke. Any man or state who fights on against Nazidom will have our aid. Any man or state who marches with Hitler is our foe. . . . That is our policy and that is our declaration. It follows, therefore, that we shall give whatever help we can to Russia and the Russian people. We shall appeal to all our friends and allies in every part of the world to take the same course and pursue it, as we shall faithfully and steadfastly to the end. . . .

This is no class war, but a war in which the whole British Empire and Commonwealth of Nations is engaged, without distinction of race, creed, or party. It is not for me to speak of the action of the United States, but this I will say, if Hitler imagines that his attack on Soviet Russia will cause the slightest divergence of aims or slackening of effort in the great democracies who are resolved upon his doom, he is woefully mistaken. On the contrary, we shall be fortified and encouraged in our efforts to rescue mankind from his tyranny. We shall be strengthened and not weakened in determination and in resources.

This is no time to moralise on the follies of countries and Governments which have allowed themselves to be struck down one by one, when by united action they could have saved themselves and saved the world from this catastrophe. But when I spoke a few minutes ago of Hitler's blood-lust and the hateful appetites which have impelled or lured him on his Russian adventure, I said there was one deeper motive behind his outrage. He wishes to destroy the Russian power because he hopes that if he succeeds in this he will be able to bring back the main strength of his army and air force from the East and hurl it upon this island, which he knows he must conquer or suffer the penalty of his crimes. His invasion of Russia is no more than a prelude to an attempted invasion of the British Isles. He hopes, no doubt, that all this may be accomplished before the winter comes, and that he can overwhelm Great Britain before the Fleet and air power of the United States may intervene. He hopes that he may once again repeat, upon a greater scale than ever before, that process of destroying his enemies one by one by which he has so long thrived and prospered, and that then the scene will be clear for the final act, without which all his conquests would be in vain—namely, the subjugation of the Western Hemisphere to his will and to his system.

The Russian danger is, therefore, our danger, and the danger of the United States, just as the cause of any Russian fighting for his hearth and home is the cause of free men and free peoples in every quarter of the globe. Let us learn the lessons already taught by such cruel experience. Let us redouble our exertions, and strike with united strength while life and power remain.

END OF BOOK ONE

☆

Book Two

War Comes to America

PART TWO

The Crown on America

1

Our Soviet Ally

Hitler's Plan for the Invasion of Russia—Soviet Demands on Britain—"Second Front Now"—Russian Ignorance of Amphibious War—I Address Stalin—A Military Mission Goes to Moscow—Naval Contacts—A War Alliance Proposed—Stalin Presses for the Second Front—Our Reasoned Reply—Our Efforts to Supply the Russian Army—Ten Thousand Tons of Rubber Fruitless Attempts to Establish Friendly Relations with Stalin—The German Attack Develops—Russia's Attitude to Poland—Our View—Russia a Burden upon Us at First.

HITLER'S INVASION OF RUSSIA altered the values and relationships of the war. The Soviet prejudices had blinded them to many of the steps which comprehension and prudence would have dictated for their own safety. On the other hand, by indifference to the fate of others they had gained time, and when their hour of trial struck on June 22, 1941, they were far stronger than Hitler imagined. Perhaps not only he but his generals had been misled by their poor performance against the Finns. Nevertheless, it was the Russians who were taken by surprise, and tremendous initial disasters fell upon them. It will not be possible in this account to do more than place before the reader the salient features of the new colossal struggle of armies and populations which now began.

The German line of battle was drawn up along the whole frontier from the Baltic to the Black Sea. The Northern Army Group, under von Leeb, with twenty-nine divisions, including three armoured and three motorised, was to advance from East Prussia upon Leningrad. The Central Army Group, under von Bock, consisting of fifty divisions, including nine armoured and six motorised, was to move from Northern Poland on Smolensk. The Southern Army Group of von Rundstedt, with forty-one divisions, including five armoured and three motorised, was to drive from Southern Poland to the lower Dnieper. A further twenty-six divisions were held, or would shortly be available, as the General Reserve. Over twenty-seven hundred aircraft supported the attack. In the North twelve Finnish divisions were to advance on Leningrad to support the main attack. In the South eleven divisions of the Rumanian Army were to stand on the defensive along the river Pruth, and six to join in the advance of Army Group South. In all one hundred and sixty-four divisions rolled eastward.

The invaders, according to the best accounts available, were confronted by a hundred and nineteen Russian divisions and at least five thousand aircraft. Sixty-seven more divisions were available in Finland, the Caucasus, and in Central Russia. Although nearly equal in numbers to the German armies, the Russians were at once swept back by deep-plunging armoured thrusts, and their air force suffered severe losses. Other countries had been surprised and overrun. Only vast Russia had the supreme advantage of depth; and this was once again to prove her salvation. In the first month the Germans bit and tore their way three hundred miles into Russia. Smolensk was taken after stern fighting in which the Russians had counter-attacked heavily. But Leningrad was not attained, and Kiev was still in Russian hands.

* * *

Up to the moment when the Soviet Government was set upon by Hitler they seemed to care for no one but themselves. Afterwards this mood naturally became more marked. Hitherto they had watched with stony composure the destruction of the front in France in 1940, and our vain efforts in 1941 to create a front in the Balkans. They had given important economic aid to Nazi Germany and had helped them in more minor ways. Now, having been deceived and taken by surprise, they were themselves under the flaming German sword. Their first impulse and lasting policy was to demand all possible succour from Great Britain and her Empire, the possible partition of which between Stalin and Hitler had for the last eight months beguiled Soviet minds from the progress of German concentration in the East. They did not hesitate to appeal in urgent and strident terms to harassed and struggling Britain to send them the munitions of which her armies were so short. They urged the United States to divert to them the largest quantities of the supplies on which we were counting, and above all, even in the summer of 1941 they clamoured for British landings in Europe, regardless of risk and cost, to establish a second front. The British Communists, who had hitherto done their worst, which was not much, in our factories, and had denounced "the capitalist and imperialist war," turned about again overnight and began to scrawl the slogan, "Second Front Now," upon the walls and hoardings.

We did not allow these somewhat sorry and ignominious facts to disturb our thought, and fixed our gaze upon the heroic sacrifices of the Russian people under the calamities which their Government had brought upon them, and their passionate defence of their native soil. This, while the struggle lasted, made amends for all.

* * *

The Russians never understood in the smallest degree the nature of the amphibious operation necessary to disembark and maintain a great army upon a well-defended hostile coast. Even the Americans were at this time largely unaware of the difficulties. Not only sea but air superiority at the invasion point was indispensable. Moreover, there was a third vital factor. A vast armada of specially constructed landing-craft, above all tank landing-craft in numerous varieties, was the foundation of any successful heavily opposed landing. For the creation of this armada, as has been and will be seen, I had long done my best. It could not be ready even on a minor scale before the summer of 1943, and its power, as is now widely recognised, could not be developed on a sufficient scale till 1944. At the period we have now reached, in the autumn of 1941, we had no mastery of the enemy air over Europe, except in the Pas de Calais, where the strongest German fortifications existed. The landing-craft were only a-building. We had not even got an army in Britain as large, as well trained, as well equipped, as the one we should have to meet on French soil. Yet Niagaras of folly and misstatement still pour out on this question of the Second Front. There was certainly no hope of convincing the Soviet Government at this or any other time. Stalin even suggested to me on one occasion later on that if the British were afraid he would be willing to send round three or four Russian army corps to do the job. It was not in my power, through lack of shipping and other physical facts, to take him at his word.

* * *

There was no response from the Soviet Government to my broadcast to Russia and the world on the day of the German attack, except that parts of it were printed in *Pravda* and other Russian Government organs, and that we were asked to receive a Russian Military Mission. The silence on the top level was oppressive, and I thought it my duty to break the ice. I quite understood that they might feel shy, considering all that had passed since the outbreak of the war between the Soviets and the Western Allies, and remembering what had happened twenty years before between me and the Bolshevik Revolutionary Government. I therefore addressed myself to Stalin and expressed our intention to bring all aid in our power to the Russian people.

Prime Minister to Monsieur Stalin   7 July 41

We are all very glad here that the Russian armies are making such strong and spirited resistance to the utterly unprovoked and merciless invasion of the Nazis. There is general admiration of the bravery and tenacity of the soldiers and people. We shall do everything to help you that time, geography, and our growing resources allow. The longer the war lasts, the more help we can give. We are making very heavy attacks both by day and night with our air force upon all German-occupied territory and all Germany within our reach. About four hundred daylight sorties were made overseas yesterday On Saturday night over two hundred heavy bombers attacked German towns, some carrying three tons apiece, and last night nearly two hundred and fifty heavy bombers were operating. This will go on. Thus we hope to force Hitler to bring back some of his air power to the West and gradually take some of the strain off you. Besides this the Admiralty have at my desire prepared a serious operation to come off in the near future in the Arctic, after which I hope contact will be established between the British and Russian Navies. Meanwhile by sweeps along the Norwegian coast we have intercepted various supply ships which were moving north against you.

We welcome arrival of Russian Military Mission in order to concert future plans.

We have only got to go on fighting to beat the life out of these villains.

The first step was clearly to make such contact as was permitted by the Soviet authorities with the Russian Military Command. Accordingly, after obtaining the necessary consent from our new allies, a powerful Military Mission was at once dispatched to Moscow. It was also urgent to create relations between the two navies. On July 10 I sent the following minute to the Admiralty:

Prime Minister to First Lord and First Sea Lord   10 July 41

It seems absolutely necessary to send a small mixed squadron of British ships to the Arctic to form contact and operate with the Russian naval forces. This should be done in advance of the particular operation we have in hand. The effect upon the Russian Navy and upon the general resistance of the Russian Army of the arrival of what would be called a British fleet in the Arctic might be of enormous value and spare a lot of English blood.

The advantage we should reap if the Russians could keep the field and go on with the war, at any rate until the winter closes in, is measureless. A premature peace by Russia would be a terrible disappointment to great masses of people in our country. As long as they go on it does not matter so much where the front lies. These people have shown themselves worth backing, and we must make sacrifices and take risks, even at inconvenience, which I realise, to maintain their morale. . . . The squadron would no doubt go to Archangel.

Pray let me know about this at your earliest.

* * *

We also hoped at this early stage to establish the general basis of a war alliance between the two countries.

Prime Minister to Sir Stafford Cripps   10 July 41

Please immediately convey following message from Prime Minister to M. Stalin:

Ambassador Cripps having reported his talk with you and having stated the terms of a proposed Anglo-Russian agreed declaration under two heads, namely, (1) mutual help without any precision as to quantity or quality, and (2) neither country to conclude a separate peace, I have immediately convened the War Cabinet, including Mr. Fraser, Prime Minister of the Dominion of New Zealand, who is with us now. It will be necessary for us to consult with the Dominions of Canada, Australia, and South Africa, but in the meanwhile I should like to assure you that we are wholly in favour of the agreed declaration you propose. We think it should be signed as soon as we have heard from the Dominions, and published to the world immediately thereafter.

2. For your own information, what we have in mind is a declaration in the following terms: H.M. Government in the United Kingdom and the Government of the U.S.S.R. have agreed and declare as follows: (1) The two Governments mutually undertake to render each other assistance of all kinds in the present war against Germany. (2) They further undertake that during this war they will neither negotiate nor conclude an armistice or treaty of peace except by mutual agreement.

3. As Dominions Governments have to be consulted, you should not yet communicate actual text to Stalin. But it will help to

show you what we mean and to give him any explanations he may require.

Official communications passed between the two Foreign Offices, but it was not until July 19 that I received the first direct communication from M. Stalin. On that day M. Maisky, the Soviet Ambassador in London, called on me to deliver the following message:

M. Stalin to the Prime Minister   18 July 41

Let me express my gratitude for the two personal messages which you have addressed to me.

Your messages were the starting-point of developments which subsequently resulted in agreement between our two Governments. Now, as you said with full justification, the Soviet Union and Great Britain have become fighting allies in the struggle against Hitlerite Germany. I have no doubt that in spite of the difficulties our two States will be strong enough to crush our common enemy.

Perhaps it is not out of place to mention that the position of the Soviet forces at the front remains tense. The consequences of the unexpected breach of the Non-Aggression Pact by Hitler, as well as of the sudden attack against the Soviet Union—both facts bringing advantages to the German troops—still remain to be felt by the Soviet armies.

It is easy to imagine that the position of the German forces would have been many times more favourable had the Soviet troops had to face the attack of the German forces, not in the regions of Kishinev, Lwow, Brest, Kaunas, and Viborg, but in the region of Odessa, Kamenets Podolski, Minsk, and the environs of Leningrad.

It seems to me therefore that the military situation of the Soviet Union, as well as of Great Britain, would be considerably improved if there could be established a front against Hitler in the West—Northern France, and in the North—the Arctic.

A front in Northern France could not only divert Hitler's forces from the East, but at the same time would make it impossible for Hitler to invade Great Britain. The establishment of the front just mentioned would be popular with the British Army, as well as with the whole population of Southern England.

I fully realise the difficulties involved in the establishment of such a front. I believe however that in spite of the difficulties it should be formed, not only in the interests of our common cause, but also in the interests of Great Britain herself. This is the most propitious moment for the establishment of such a front, because now Hitler's forces are diverted to the East and he has not yet had the chance to consolidate the position occupied by him in the East.

It is still easier to establish a front in the North. Here, on the part of Great Britain, would be necessary only naval and air operations, without the landing of troops or artillery. The Soviet mili-

tary, naval, and air forces would take part in such an operation.
We would welcome it if Great Britain could transfer to this theatre
of war something like one light division or more of the Norwegian
volunteers, who could be used in Northern Norway to organise
rebellion against the Germans.

Thus the Russian pressure for the establishment of a Second
Front was initiated at the very beginning of our correspondence, and this theme was to recur throughout our subsequent
relations with monotonous disregard, except in the Far North,
for physical facts. This, my first telegram from Stalin, contained the only sign of compunction I ever perceived in the
Soviet attitude. In this he volunteered a defence of the Soviet
change of side, and of his agreement with Hitler before the
outbreak of the war, and dwelt, as I have already done in my
first volume, on the Russians' strategic need to hold a German
deployment as far as possible to the west in Poland in order
to gain time for the fullest development of Russian far-drawn
military strength. I have never underrated this argument, and
could well afford to reply in comprehending terms upon it.

Prime Minister to Monsieur Stalin   20 July 41
I am very glad to get your message, and to learn from many
sources of the valiant fight and the many vigorous counter-attacks
with which the Russian armies are defending their native soil. I
fully realise the military advantage you have gained by forcing
the enemy to deploy and engage on a forward westerly front, thus
exhausting some of the force of his initial effort.
2. Anything sensible and effective that we can do to help will
be done. I beg you however to realise limitations imposed upon
us by our resources and geographical position. From the first day
of the German attack upon Russia we have examined possibilities of
attacking Occupied France and the Low Countries. The Chiefs
of Staff do not see any way of doing anything on a scale likely to
be of the slightest use to you. The Germans have forty divisions in
France alone, and the whole coast has been fortified with German
diligence for more than a year, and bristles with cannon, wire, pill-
boxes, and beach-mines. The only part where we could have even
temporary air superiority and air-fighter protection is from Dunkirk to Boulogne. This is one mass of fortifications, with scores of
heavy guns commanding the sea approaches, many of which can
fire right across the Straits. There is less than five hours' darkness,
and even then the whole area is illuminated by searchlights. To
attempt a landing in force would be to encounter a bloody repulse,
and petty raids would only lead to fiascos doing far more harm
than good to both of us. It would be all over without their having
to move or before they could move a single unit from your front.
3. You must remember that we have been fighting alone for

more than a year, and that, though our resources are growing and will grow fast from now on, we are at the utmost strain both at home and in the Middle East by land and air, and also that the Battle of the Atlantic, on which our life depends, and the movement of all our convoys in the teeth of the U-boat and Focke-Wulf blockade, strains our naval resources, great though they be, to the utmost limit.

4. It is therefore to the North we must look for any speedy help we can give. The Naval Staff have been preparing for three weeks past an operation by seaborne aircraft upon German shipping in the north of Norway and Finland, hoping thereby to destroy enemy power of transporting troops by sea to attack your Arctic flank. We have asked your Staffs to keep a certain area clear of Russian vessels between July 28 and August 2, when we shall hope to strike. Secondly, we are sending forthwith some cruisers and destroyers to Spitzbergen, whence they will be able to raid enemy shipping in concert with your naval forces. Thirdly, we are sending a flotilla of submarines to intercept German traffic on the Arctic coast, although owing to perpetual daylight this service is particularly dangerous. Fourthly, we are sending a minelayer with various supplies to Archangel.

This is the most we can do at the moment. I wish it were more. Pray let the most extreme secrecy be kept until the moment when we tell you publicity will not be harmful.

5. There is no Norwegian Light Division in existence, and it would be impossible to land troops, either British or Russian, on German-occupied territory in perpetual daylight without having first obtained reasonable fighter air cover. We had bitter experiences at Namsos last year, and in Crete this year, of trying such enterprises.

6. We are also studying as a further development the basing of some British fighter air squadrons on Murmansk. This would require first of all a consignment of anti-aircraft guns, then the arrival of the aircraft, some of which could be flown off carriers and others crated. When these were established our Spitzbergen squadron could come to Murmansk and act with your naval forces. We have reason to believe that the Germans have sent a strong group of dive-bombers, which they are keeping for our benefit should we arrive, and it is therefore necessary to proceed step by step. All this however will take weeks.

7. Do not hesitate to suggest anything else that occurs to you, and we will also be searching earnestly for other ways of striking at the common foe.

From the first moment I did my utmost to help with munitions and supplies, both by consenting to severe diversions from the United States and by direct British sacrifices. Early in September the equivalent of two Hurricane squadrons were dispatched in H.M.S. *Argus* to Murmansk, to assist in the

defence of the naval base and to co-operate with Russian
forces in that area. By September 11 the squadrons were in
action, and they fought valiantly for three months. I was well
aware that in the early days of our alliance there was little we
could do, and I tried to fill the void by civilities.

Prime Minister to Monsieur Stalin   25 July 41

I am glad to inform you that the War Cabinet have decided, in
spite of the fact that this will seriously deplete our fighter aircraft
resources, to send to Russia as soon as possible two hundred Toma-
hawk fighter airplanes. One hundred and forty of these will be sent
from here to Archangel, and sixty from our supplies in the United
States of America. Details as to spare parts and American personnel
to erect the machines have still to be arranged with the American
Government.

2. Up to two to three million pairs of ankle boots should shortly
be available in this country for shipment. We are also arranging to
provide during the present year large quantities of rubber, tin, wool
and woollen cloth, jute, lead, and shellac. All your other requirements from raw materials are receiving careful consideration.
Where supplies are impossible or limited from here, we are discussing with the United States of America.

Details will of course be communicated to the usual official
channels.

3. We are watching with admiration and emotion Russia's magnificent fight, and all our information shows the heavy losses and
concern of the enemy. Our air attack on Germany will continue
with increasing strength.

Rubber was scarce and precious, and the Russian demand
for it was on the largest scale. I even broke into our modest
reserves.

Prime Minister to Monsieur Stalin   28 July 41

Rubber. We will deliver the goods from here or United States
by the best and quickest route. Please say exactly what kind of
rubber, and which way you wish it to come. Preliminary orders are
already given. . . .

3. The grand resistance of the Russian Army in defence of their
soil unites us all. A terrible winter of bombing lies before Germany. No one has yet had what they are going to get. The naval
operations mentioned in my last telegram to you are in progress.
Thank you very much for your comprehension in the midst of your
great fight of our difficulties in doing more. We will do our utmost.

Prime Minister to Monsieur Stalin   31 July 41

Following my personal intervention, arrangements are now complete for the dispatch of ten thousand tons of rubber from this
country to one of your northern ports.

In view of the urgency of your requirements, we are taking the risk of depleting to this extent our metropolitan stocks, which are none too large and will take time to replace. British ships carrying this rubber, and certain other supplies, will be loaded within a week, or at most ten days, and will sail to one of your northern ports as soon as the Admiralty can arrange convoy. This new amount of ten thousand tons is additional to the ten thousand tons of rubber already allotted from Malaya.

*   *   *

I tried my best to build up by frequent personal telegrams the same kind of happy relations which I had developed with President Roosevelt. In this long Moscow series I received many rebuffs and only rarely a kind word. In many cases the telegrams were left unanswered altogether or for many days.

The Soviet Government had the impression that they were conferring a great favour on us by fighting in their own country for their own lives. The more they fought, the heavier our debt became. This was not a balanced view. Two or three times in this long correspondence I had to protest in blunt language, but especially against the ill-usage of our sailors, who carried at so much peril the supplies to Murmansk and Archangel. Almost invariably however I bore hectoring and reproaches with "a patient shrug; for sufferance is the badge" of all who have to deal with the Kremlin. Moreover, I made constant allowances for the pressures under which Stalin and his dauntless Russian nation lay.

*   *   *

The German armies in Russia had driven deep into the country, but at the end of July there arose a fundamental clash of opinion between Hitler and Brauchitsch, Commander-in-Chief. Brauchitsch held that Timoshenko's Army Group, which lay in front of Moscow, constituted the main Russian strength and must first be defeated. This was orthodox doctrine. Thereafter, Brauchitsch contended, Moscow, the main military, political, and industrial nerve centre of all Russia, should be taken. Hitler forcefully disagreed. He wished to gain territory and destroy Russian armies on the broadest front. In the North he demanded the capture of Leningrad, and in the South of the industrial Donetz Basin, the Crimea, and the entry to Russia's Caucasian oil supplies. Meanwhile Moscow could wait.

After vehement discussion Hitler overruled his Army chiefs.

THE
GERMAN
ATTACK
ON
RUSSIA

The Northern Army Group, reinforced from the centre, was ordered to press operations against Leningrad. The German Centre Group was relegated to the defensive. They were directed to send a Panzer group southward to take in flank the Russians who were being pursued across the Dnieper by Rundstedt. In this action the Germans prospered. By early September a vast pocket of Russian forces was forming in the triangle Konotop-Kremenchug-Kiev, and over half a million men were killed or captured in the desperate fighting which lasted all that month. In the North no such success could be claimed. Leningrad was encircled but not taken. Hitler's decision had not been right. He now turned his mind and will-power back to the centre. The besiegers of Leningrad were ordered to detach mobile forces and part of their supporting air force to reinforce a renewed drive on Moscow. The Panzer group which had been sent south to von Rundstedt came back again to join in the assault. At the end of September the stage was reset for the formerly discarded central thrust, while the southern armies drove on eastward to the lower Don, whence the Caucasus would lie open to them.

*   *   *

The attitude of Russia to Poland lay at the root of our early relations with the Soviets.

The German attack on Russia did not come as a surprise to Polish circles abroad. Since March, 1941, reports from the Polish underground upon German troop concentrations on the western frontiers of Russia had been reaching their Government in London. In the event of war a fundamental change in the relations between Soviet Russia and the Polish Government in exile would be inevitable. The first problem would be how far the provisions of the Nazi-Soviet Pact of August, 1939, relating to Poland could be reversed without endangering the unity of a combined Anglo-Russian war alliance. When the news of the German attack on Russia broke upon the world, the re-establishment of Polish-Russian relations, which had been broken off in 1939, became important. The conversations between the two Governments began in London under British auspices on July 5. Poland was represented by the Prime Minister of her exiled Government, General Sikorski, and Russia by the Soviet Ambassador, M. Maisky. The Poles had two aims—the recognition by the Soviet Government that the partition of Poland agreed to by Germany and Russia in 1939 was now null and void, and the liberation by Russia of all Polish prisoners of war and civilians deported to the Soviet Union after the Russian occupation of the eastern areas of Poland.

Throughout the month of July these negotiations continued in a frigid atmosphere. The Russians were obstinate in their refusal to make any precise commitment in conformity with Polish wishes. Russia regarded the question of her western frontiers as not open to discussion. Could she be trusted to behave fairly in this matter in the possible distant future, when hostilities would come to an end in Europe? The British Government were in a dilemma from the beginning. We had gone to war with Germany as the direct result of our guarantee to Poland. We had a strong obligation to support the interest of our first ally. At this stage in the struggle we could not admit the legality of the Russian occupation of Polish territory in 1939. In this summer of 1941, less than two weeks after the appearance of Russia on our side in the struggle against Germany, we could not force our new and sorely threatened ally to abandon, even on paper, regions on her frontiers which she had regarded for generations as vital to her security. There was no way out. The issue of the territorial future of Poland must be postponed until easier times. We had the invidious responsibility of recommending General Sikorski to rely on Soviet good faith in the future settlement of Russian-Polish relations, and not to insist at this moment on any written guarantees for the future. I sincerely hoped for my part that with the deepening experience of comradeship in arms against Hitler the major Allies would be able to resolve the territorial problems in amicable discussion at the conference table. In the clash of battle at this vital point in the war, all must be subordinated to strengthening the common military effort. And in this struggle a resurgent Polish army based on the many thousands of Poles now held in Russia would play a noble part. On this point the Russians were prepared to agree in a guarded fashion.

On July 30, after many bitter discussions, agreement was reached between the Polish and Russian Governments. Diplomatic relations were restored, and a Polish army was to be formed on Russian soil and subordinated to the supreme command of the Soviet Government. There was no mention of frontiers, except a general statement that the Soviet-German treaties of 1939 about territorial changes in Poland "have lost their validity." In an official Note of July 30 to the Polish Government the Foreign Secretary stated our view:

On the occasion of the signature of the Soviet-Polish Agreement of today I desire to take this opportunity of informing you that in conformity with the provisions of the agreement for mutual assistance between the United Kingdom and Poland of the 25th of August, 1939, His Majesty's Government in the United Kingdom have entered into no undertaking towards the Union of Socialist Soviet Republics which affects relations between that country and Poland. I also desire to assure you that His Majesty's Government do not recognise any territorial changes which have been effected in Poland since August, 1939.

Mr. Eden quoted this Note in the House of Commons on the same day, and added:

It is stated in paragraph 1 of the Soviet-Polish Agreement that the Soviet Government recognise the Soviet-German treaties of 1939 concerning territorial changes in Poland as having lost their validity. The attitude of His Majesty's Government in these matters was stated in general terms by the Prime Minister in the House of Commons on September 5, 1940, when he said that His Majesty's Government did not propose to recognise any territorial changes which took place without the free consent and good-will of the parties concerned. This holds good with the territorial changes which have been effected in Poland since August, 1939, and I informed the Polish Government accordingly in my official Note.

And in reply to a question Mr. Eden concluded: "The exchange of Notes which I have just read to the House does not involve any guarantee of frontiers by His Majesty's Government."

There the matter rested, and during the autumn the Poles were occupied in the grim task of collecting those of their nationals who had survived captivity in the prison camps of the Soviet Union.

*   *   *

The entry of Russia into the war was welcome but not immediately helpful to us. The German armies were so strong that it seemed that for many months they could maintain the invasion threat against England while at the same time plunging into Russia. Almost all responsible military opinion held that the Russian armies would soon be defeated and largely destroyed. The fact that the Soviet Air Force was allowed by its Government to be surprised on its landing grounds and that the Russian military preparations were far from being complete gave them a bad start. Frightful injuries were sustained by the Russian armies. In spite of heroic resistance,

competent despotic war direction, total disregard of human
life, and the opening of a ruthless guerrilla warfare in the rear
of the German advance, a general retirement took place on
the whole twelve-hundred-mile Russian front south of Leningrad for about four or five hundred miles. The strength of the
Soviet Government, the fortitude of the Russian people, their
immeasurable reserves of man-power, the vast size of their
country, the rigours of the Russian winter, were the factors
which ultimately ruined Hitler's armies. But none of these
made themselves apparent in 1941. President Roosevelt was
considered very bold when he proclaimed in September, 1941,
that the Russian front would hold and that Moscow would not
be taken. The glorious strength and patriotism of the Russian
people vindicated this opinion.

Even in August, 1942, after my visit to Moscow and the
conferences there, General Brooke, who had accompanied me,
adhered to the opinion that the Caucasus Mountains would
be traversed and the basin of the Caspian dominated by
German forces, and we prepared accordingly on the largest
possible scale for a defensive campaign in Syria and Persia.
Throughout I took a more sanguine view than my military
advisers of the Russian powers of resistance. I rested with
confidence upon Premier Stalin's assurance, given to me at
Moscow, that he would hold the line of the Caucasus and
that the Germans would not reach the Caspian in any
strength. But we were vouchsafed so little information about
Soviet resources and intentions that all opinions either way
were hardly more than guesses.

It is true that the Russian entry into the war diverted the
German air attack from Great Britain, and diminished the
threat of invasion. It gave us important relief in the Mediterranean. On the other hand, it imposed upon us most heavy
sacrifices and drains. At last we were beginning to be well
equipped. At last our munitions factories were pouring
out their supplies of every kind. Our armies in Egypt
and Libya were in heavy action and clamouring for the latest
weapons, above all tanks and aeroplanes. The British armies
at home were eagerly awaiting the long-promised modern
equipment which in all its ever-widening complications was
flowing at last towards them. At this moment we were compelled to make very large diversions of our weapons and vital
supplies of all kinds, including rubber and oil. On us fell the
burden of organising the convoys of British and still more of
United States supplies and carrying them to Murmansk and

Archangel through all the dangers and rigours of this Arctic passage. All the American supplies were a deduction from what had in fact been, or was to be, successfully ferried across the Atlantic for ourselves. In order to make this immense diversion and to forgo the growing flood of American aid without crippling our campaign in the Western Desert, we had to cramp all preparations which prudence urged for the defence of the Malay Peninsula and our Eastern Empire and possessions against the ever-growing menace of Japan.

Without in the slightest degree challenging the conclusion which History will affirm that the Russian resistance broke the power of the German armies and inflicted mortal injury upon the life-energies of the German nation, it is right to make it clear that for more than a year after Russia was involved in the war she presented herself to our minds as a burden and not as a help. None the less we rejoiced to have this mighty nation in the battle with us, and we all felt that even if the Soviet armies were driven back to the Ural Mountains, Russia would still exert an immense and, if she persevered in the war, an ultimately decisive force.

2

An African Pause: Tobruk

General Auchinleck Takes Command, July 2—Need for an Offensive in the Western Desert—My Telegram of July 6—Auchinleck's Prohibitive Requirement—"British" Divisions—Four and a Half Months' Delay—Unjustified Concern for the Northern Flank—The Chiefs of Staff Telegram of July 19—My Telegram of the Same Date—Auchinleck's Stiff Reply, July 23—His Visit to London—I Am Not Convinced, but Agree—The German View of Rommel's Situation and the Prospects in North Africa—Mr. Menzies' Return Home—Our Divergence on the Structure of the War Cabinet—Fall of Mr. Menzies—My Telegram to Him—Relations with Mr. Fadden's Government—Demand for the Withdrawal of the Australian Division from Tobruk—Relief of One Australian Brigade—Australian Insistence on Full Relief—My Telegram to General Auchinleck of September 17—He Threatens Resignation—Further Appeals to Mr. Fadden—Refusals—Defeat of Mr. Fadden's Government—Mr. Curtin's Labour Party Assumes Power—New Appeal Concerning Tobruk—Further Refusals—We Comply with Australian Demands—Appreciable Losses in the Relief—Work of the Royal Navy in the Defence of Tobruk.

GENERAL AUCHINLECK assumed effective command of the Middle East on July 2, and formally on July 5. I started my relations with our new Commander-in-Chief in high hopes.

Prime Minister to General Auchinleck   1 July 41

You take up your great command at a period of crisis. After all the facts have been laid before you it will be for you to decide whether to renew the offensive in the Western Desert, and if so when. You should have regard especially to the situation at Tobruk, the process of enemy reinforcement of Libya, and the temporary German preoccupation in their invasion of Russia. You should also consider the vexatious dangers of the operations in Syria flagging and the need for a decision on one or both of these fronts. You will decide whether and how these operations can be fitted in together. The urgency of these issues will naturally impress itself upon you. We shall be glad to hear from you at your earliest convenience.

And again on the following day:

Prime Minister to General Auchinleck   2 July 41

Once Syria is cleared up we hope you will consider Wilson for the Western Desert, but of course that decision rests with you.

It is much to be regretted that this advice, subsequently repeated, was not taken.

On July 4 General Auchinleck replied to my first message. He agreed that as soon as Syria had been secured, and with it our position in Iraq re-established, the offensive in the Western Desert could be contemplated. Adequate armoured forces were however essential to success. He reckoned that two and probably three armoured divisions, together with a motor division, would be required. The advance, which aimed at driving the enemy from North Africa, would for administrative reasons have to be conducted by stages. The first objective would be the reoccupation, also by stages, of Cyrenaica. The General stated in conclusion that a simultaneous action in the Western Desert and Syria would "invite failure on both fronts."

I thought it wise to set out the position as we saw it fully:

Prime Minister to General Auchinleck   6 July 41

I agree about finishing off Syria, and here we have always thought that holding Syria is the necessary foundation for holding or retaking Cyprus. One hopes that Syria may not be long now and that you will not be forestalled in Cyprus. The priority of both these operations over offensive action in Western Desert after what has happened is fully recognised.

2. Nevertheless, Western Desert remains decisive theatre this autumn for defense of Nile Valley. Only by reconquering the lost airfields of Eastern Cyrenaica can Fleet and Air Force resume effective action against enemy seaborne supplies.

3. In General Wavell's message of April 18 he stated that he had six regiments of trained armoured personnel awaiting tanks. This was a main element in decision to send "Tiger." Besides this, personnel for three additional tank regiments are now approaching round the Cape. Your need for armoured vehicles is therefore fully realised, in spite of the stress which Wavell and you both lay upon further training for these already-trained armoured units. We make out that you should have by end of July five hundred cruiser, infantry, and American cruiser tanks, if your workshops are properly organised, besides a large number of miscellaneous light tanks and armoured cars.

4. This cannot be improved upon in the months of July and August, except by certain American arrivals and a few replacements from home. Even thereafter remember we have to be at concert pitch to resist invasion from September 1, and General Staff are naturally reluctant to send another substantial instalment of tanks round the Cape (now the only way), thus putting them out of action till early October at either end. After October American supplies should grow and our position here be easier, but much will have happened before then.

5. At present our Intelligence shows considerable Italian reinforcements of Libya, but little or no German. However, a Russian collapse might soon alter this to your detriment, without diminishing invasion menace here.

6. Scale of our air reinforcement has been laid before you. It seems probable that during July, August, and part of September you should have decided air superiority; but then, again, a Russian collapse would liberate considerable German air reinforcements for Africa, and if enemy do not attempt invasion, but merely pretend, they can obtain air superiority on your western front during September.

7. On top of this comes the question of Tobruk. We cannot judge from here what the offensive value of Tobruk will be in two months' time, or what may happen meanwhile. It would seem that reduction of complete penning-in of Tobruk by enemy is indispensable preliminary to [their] serious invasion of Egypt.

8. From all these points of view it is difficult to see how your situation is going to be better after the middle of September than it is now, and it may well be worsened. I have no doubt you will maturely but swiftly consider the whole problem. . . .

11. About the air. I feel that for all major operational purposes your plans must govern the employment of the whole air force throughout the Middle East, bearing in mind of course that the air force has its own dominant strategic rôle to play, and must not be frittered away in providing small umbrellas for the Army, as it seems to have been in the Sollum battle. In your telegram you speak of aircraft supporting the Army and aircraft supporting the Navy and aircraft employed on independent strategic tasks. The question is, what are the proportions? These will have to be arranged from time to time by the Commanders-in-Chief in consultation. But nothing in these arrangements should mar the integrity of the air force contribution to any major scheme you have in hand. One cannot help feeling that in the Sollum fight ["Battleaxe"] our air superiority was wasted and that our force in Tobruk stood idle while all available enemy tanks were sent to defeat our desert offensive.

To this message the General replied on July 15 that he proposed to reinforce Cyprus as soon as possible by one division; that he appreciated the need for regaining Cyrenaica, but that he could not be confident that Tobruk could be held after September. About the six regiments of trained armoured personnel, he said that the features and armament of the new American tanks introduced modifications in tactical handling, and time must be allowed for these lessons to be studied. He agreed that by the end of July he would have about five hundred cruiser, infantry, and American tanks. For any operation however fifty per cent reserves of tanks were required, thus permitting twenty-five per cent in the workshops and twenty-five per cent for immediate replacement of battle casualties. This was an almost prohibitive condition. Generals only enjoy such comforts in Heaven. And those who demand them do not always get there. Auchinleck stressed the importance of time both for individual and collective training, and the team spirit, which was essential for efficiency. He thought that the North (that is, a German attack through Turkey, Syria, and Palestine) might become the decisive front rather than the Desert.

It is clear from the foregoing telegrams that there were serious divergences of views and values between us. This caused me sharp disappointment. The General's early decisions were also perplexing. By long persistence I had at last succeeded in having the 50th British Division brought to Egypt. I was sensitive to the hostile propaganda which asserted that it was the British policy to fight with any other troops but our own and thus avoid the shedding of United Kingdom blood. British casualties in the Middle East, including Greece and Crete, had in fact been greater than those of all our other forces put together, but the nomenclature which was customary gave a false impression of the facts. The Indian divisions, of which one-third of the infantry and the whole of the artillery were British, were not described as British-Indian divisions. The armoured divisions, which had borne the brunt of the fighting, were entirely British, but this did not appear in their names. Repeated injunctions to add the word "British" did not overcome the practice which had become habitual. Many battalions of the 6th British Division had been heavily engaged, but it had not been possible in the stress of events to form the division as a united entity. This was not a trifle. The fact that "British" troops were rarely mentioned in any reports of the fighting gave colour to the enemy's taunts, and provoked unfavourable comment not only in the United States but in Australia. I had looked forward to the arrival of the 50th Division as an effective means of countering these disparaging currents. General Auchinleck's decision to pick this as the division to send to Cyprus certainly seemed unfortunate, and lent substance to the reproaches to which we were unjustly subjected. The Chiefs of Staff at home were equally astonished on military grounds that so strange a use should be made of this magnificent body of men. Indeed, it could not be reconciled with any strategic conception comprehensible to our thought.

A far more serious resolve by General Auchinleck was to delay all action against Rommel in the Western Desert, at first for three and eventually for more than four and a half months. The vindication of Wavell's action of June 15, "Battleaxe," is found in the fact that, although we were somewhat worsted and withdrew to our original position, the Germans were utterly unable to advance for the whole of this prolonged period. Their communications, threatened by Tobruk, were insufficient to bring them the necessary reinforcements of armour or even of artillery ammunition to enable Rommel to do more than hold on by his will-power and prestige. The feeding of his force imposed so heavy a strain upon him that its size could only grow gradually. In these circumstances he should have been engaged continuously by the British Army, which had ample road, rail, and sea communications, and was being continually strengthened at a much greater rate both in men and material.

Generals are often prone, if they have the chance, to choose a set-piece battle, when all is ready, at their own selected moment, rather than to wear down the enemy by continued unspectacular fighting. They naturally prefer certainty to hazard. They forget that war never stops, but burns on from day to day with ever-changing results not only in one theatre but in all. At this time the Russian armies were in the crisis of their agony.

A third misconception seemed to me to be a disproportionate concern for our northern flank. This indeed required the utmost vigilance and justified many defensive preparations and the construction of strong fortified lines in Palestine and Syria. The situation in this quarter however soon became vastly better than in June. Syria was conquered. The Iraq rebellion had been suppressed. All the key points in the Desert were held by our troops. Above all, the struggle between Germany and Russia gave new confidence to Turkey. While this hung in the balance there was no chance of a German demand for the passage of her armies through Turkish territory. Persia was soon to be brought into the Allied camp by British and Russian action. This would carry us beyond the winter. In the meanwhile the general situation favoured decisive action in the Western Desert.

*   *   *

On July 19 the Chiefs of Staff telegraphed to General Auchinleck:

Chiefs of Staff to General Auchinleck   19 July 41

You said that an offensive in the Western Desert could not be contemplated until you had at least two and preferably three properly trained armoured divisions. Until Germany attacked Russia it was impossible for us to contemplate sending any considerable reinforcement of cruiser tanks from here, since we had to regard invasion in August or September as a distinct probability. We cannot say this probability has now disappeared altogether, since Russia might crack quite soon, but we are prepared to take a chance if by doing so we can regain Cyrenaica, with all the benefits that this implies. . . . In your telegram of July 15 you expressed a doubt whether you can maintain Tobruk after September. We therefore assume that any offensive to regain Cyrenaica cannot be postponed beyond that month. In our estimation there is every chance of our relative air strengths improving up to September, and possibly even continuing to improve after that date, but this of course depends upon the outcome of the present Russian campaign.

Having regard to the above considerations, it looks from here that the best, if not the only, chance of retaking Cyrenaica is to launch an offensive by the end of September at the latest. Would you feel like doing this if we were to send you an additional one hundred and fifty cruiser tanks at once? We reckon they could reach Suez by September 13–20. We should also be prepared to send you up to forty thousand men in [Convoy] W.S.11, leaving it to you to decide what you most need from what we can make available. If, on the other hand, you do not feel that you can undertake the offensive in the Western Desert by the end of September, we would not feel justified in taking ships from food imports, breaking up the 1st Armoured Division, and sending you one hundred and fifty cruisers before it is practically certain that invasion cannot take place this year.

In full accord I also telegraphed personally:

Prime Minister to General Auchinleck   19 July 41

Prolonged consideration has been given both by the Chiefs of Staff and the Defence Committee of the War Cabinet to your telegram of July 15 in reply to mine of the 6th. The Chiefs of Staff now send you their view, with which we are in full agreement.

2. It would seem that if you had a substantial further consignment of tanks from here and the United States approaching during the middle of September, together with other large reinforcements, this might act as a reserve on which you could count either to press your offensive if successful or to defend Egypt if it failed.

3. The Defence Committee were concerned to see the 50th Division, your one complete, fresh British division, locked up in Cyprus in what appeared to be a purely defensive rôle, and wonder whether other troops might not have been found.

4. They did not see how a German offensive could develop upon Syria, Palestine, and Iraq from the north before the end of September at the earliest. The Defence Committee felt that Persia was in far greater danger of German infiltration and intrigue, and that strong action may have to be taken there. This however is in General Wavell's sphere, and his evident wish to act is receiving urgent and earnest attention here.

5. If we do not use the lull accorded us by the German entanglement in Russia to restore the situation in Cyrenaica, the opportunity may never recur. A month has passed since the failure at Sollum, and presumably another month may have to pass before a renewed effort is possible. This interval should certainly give plenty of time for training. It would seem justifiable to fight a hard and decisive battle in the Western Desert before the situation changes to our detriment, and to run those major risks without which victory has rarely been gained.

We still think that Wilson should have the command of the next offensive, if there is to be one, unless of course you propose to take personal command yourself.

On July 23 General Auchinleck answered my message. The decision, he said, to put the 50th Division into Cyprus was taken by him after the most careful consideration. "If you wish I can send you detailed reasons which actuated me and which appeared to me incontestable. I hope you will leave me complete discretion concerning dispositions of this kind." He thought that a German offensive against Syria through Anatolia might develop in the first half of September.

General Auchinleck to Prime Minister 23 July 41

I entirely agree as to the desirability of using present German preoccupation in Russia to hit enemy in Libya, but I must repeat that to launch an offensive with the inadequate means at present at our disposal is not, in my opinion, a justifiable operation of war, and is almost certain to result in a further lengthy postponement of the date on which we can assume offensive with reasonable chances of success. To gain results risks must be run, and I am ready to run them if they are reasonably justifiable.

Finally:

My immediate intentions are: First, to consolidate our positions in Cyprus and Syria as rapidly as possible, and to maintain our position in latter. Second, to press on with the sadly needed re-grouping, reorganisation,- and re-equipment of divisions and brigades, which have not only suffered casualties and losses of equipment in Greece, Crete, Libya, Eritrea, and Syria, but have had to be [used] in most instances not as formations but piecemeal. Third, with the Intendant-General, to expedite the reorganisation and modernisation of the rearward services of supply, movement, and repairs. Fourth, to safeguard the training and equipment of our armoured formations, without which no offensive is possible. Fifth, to reconnoitre and plan intensively for an offensive in Libya as foreshadowed in telegram of July 19 from Commanders-in-Chief to Chiefs of Staff. As a result of this planning, I shall, I am sure, be asking you in near future for further means necessary to success.

*   *   *

I could not help feeling at this time a stiffness in General Auchinleck's attitude, which would not be helpful to the interests we all served. Books written since the war have shown how subordinate but influential portions of the Cairo Operations Staff had deplored the decision to send the army to Greece. They did not know how fully and willingly General Wavell had accepted this policy, still less how searchingly the War Cabinet and Chiefs of Staff had put the issue to him, almost inviting a negative. Wavell, it was suggested, had been led astray by the politicians, and the whole chain of disasters had followed on his compliance with their wishes. Now as a reward for his good-nature he had been removed after all his victories in the moment of defeat. I cannot doubt that in these circles of the Staff there was a strong feeling that the new Commander should not let himself be pressed into hazardous adventures, but should take his time and work on certainties. Such a mood might well have been imparted to General Auchinleck. It was already clear that not much progress would be made by correspondence.

Prime Minister to General Auchinleck   23 July 41

All your telegrams to us and ours to you show that we should have a talk. Chiefs of Staff greatly desire this. Unless the immediate military situation prevents you leaving, hope you will come at once, bringing with you one or two Staff officers. In your absence, which should be kept secret, Blamey will act for you.

Auchinleck was willing to come. His brief visit to London was from many points of view helpful. He placed himself in harmonious relations with members of the War Cabinet, with the Chiefs of Staff, and with the War Office. He spent a long week-end with me at Chequers. As we got to know better this distinguished officer, upon whose qualities our fortunes were now so largely to depend, and as he became acquainted with the high circle of the British war machine and saw how easily and smoothly it worked, mutual confidence grew. On the other hand, we could not induce him to depart from his resolve to have a prolonged delay in order to prepare a set-piece offensive on November 1. This was to be called "Crusader," and would be the largest operation we had yet launched. He certainly shook my military advisers with all the detailed argument he produced. I was myself unconvinced. But General Auchinleck's unquestioned abilities, his powers of exposition, his high, dignified, and commanding personality, gave me the feeling that he might after all be right, and that even if wrong he was still the best man. I therefore yielded to the November date for the offensive, and turned my energies to making it a success. We were all very sorry that we could not persuade him to entrust the battle, when it should come, to General Maitland Wilson. He preferred instead General Alan Cunningham, whose reputation stood high on the morrow of the Abyssinian victories. We had to make the best of it, and that is never worth doing by halves. Thus we shared his responsibility by endorsing his decisions.

* * *

We now have a very full knowledge of what the German High Command thought of Rommel's situation. They greatly admired his audacity and the incredible success which had crowned it, but none the less they deemed him in great peril. They strictly forbade him to run any further risks until he could be strongly reinforced. Perhaps, with his prestige, he might bluff it out, in the precarious position in which he stood, until they could bring him the utmost aid in their power. His line of communications trailed back a thousand miles to Tripoli. Benghazi was a valuable short cut for a part at any rate of his supplies and fresh troops, but a toll of increasing severity had to be paid on the sea transport to both these bases. The British forces, already largely superior in numbers, were growing daily. The German tank superiority existed only in quality and organisation. They were weaker in the air. They were very short of artillery ammunition, and feared greatly to have to fire it off. Tobruk seemed a deadly threat in Rommel's rear, from which at any moment a sortie might be made, cutting his communications. They could not tell what offensive plans we had, either by sallying from Tobruk or by the advance of our main body. However, while we remained motionless they could be thankful for every day that passed.

On June 2, 1941, a conference had been held at the Brenner Pass, at which the military principals were Field-Marshal Keitel and General Cavallero. Keitel agreed that the offensive against Egypt could not begin before the autumn. It should be carried out, not with a mass of troops, but with a small number of well-equipped special troops. The strength of the attacking forces should be four Panzer divisions, two of them German, and three motorised divisions. *There could not be any superfluous consumers of food in North Africa, but only as many fighting men as could be supplied.* General Cavallero said that the Italian divisions serving under the Afrika Corps were worn out; they had lost forty to sixty per cent of their personnel and material. The vehicle situation was very bad, and *the Pavia division had only twenty-seven lorries.*

Keitel considered an even more pressing need to be the provision of flak and coastal artillery to afford better protection against enemy attacks on ports of supply and supply dumps. After this it was important that artillery reinforcements for the Afrika Corps should be brought over, for one of the first conditions for subsequent operations would be the capture of Tobruk. At present German and Italian troops could not reach it without heavy artillery. Apart from supplying the fighting troops, it was absolutely necessary to make large-scale provision of supplies and to prepare transport columns before the start of the offensive. Supplies required for the German Afrika Corps alone amounted to 40,000 to 50,000 tons per month; in addition there were supplies for the Italians. The Italians would get all the vehicles not required by the Afrika Corps. German air transport had very little space available. The Italians alone must protect sea and coastal transports, because the German air forces were being withdrawn from Sicily. Stronger Luftwaffe units were being posted to North Africa to protect the coast and coastal transport.

General Cavallero thanked the German chief for his statement. Both he and the Duce shared his opinions. Italy's most important task was to hold her present positions. Defence forces in North Africa were too small. The troops taking part in the siege of Tobruk must be relieved for a rest period. The situation at Sollum was one of constant danger.

In August the Luftwaffe Operations Staff reported:

The strain on the supply position of our forces in North Africa is well known. . . . So far full use has not been made of the harbour capacity at Benghazi. Since the recapture of Derna nothing has been done in the harbour area to repair the damage caused by the British. . . . Bardia Harbour must be repaired as well. We therefore urgently request that the Italians be informed that they should begin the necessary work immediately. It is absolutely necessary to make use of Benghazi, Derna, and Bardia for supplies; this will take some weight from the port of Tripoli and will reduce the dangerous coastal traffic from Tripoli to Benghazi. It is still more vital if we look at the very serious transport situation in Africa, which makes ever more difficult the use of the land route from Tripoli to Benghazi.

Reinforcement of the Luftwaffe in the Mediterranean area is impossible until after the cessation of operations in the East.

At the end of August, at a conference held at Hitler's Headquarters on the Russian front between Keitel and General Cavallero, Keitel said the position in North Africa could not be regarded as fixed until Tobruk had fallen. If all went well with regard to transport to Africa the German forces selected for the attack would be ready in the middle of September. General Cavallero replied that the Duce had ordered a speed-up in the preparations for the attack on Tobruk. It was certain that the Italians would not be ready for an offensive by the middle of September; they would probably not be ready until the end of the month.

They were not in fact ready at the end of September; nor were either Germans or Italians ready in October; nor in November. They could no doubt have offered a stiff resistance if attacked.

Agreement was reached between the German and Italian staffs on August 29 that—

In the near future there are no prospects of an offensive being staged from Libya against the Suez Canal. Even if Tobruk should be taken in the autumn, the balance of power would not allow of this. This applies equally to an attack with a limited goal, as every advance towards the east worsens our strained supply position and improves that of the British.

On September 9, 1941, the German Liaison Staff thus reviewed the situation:

Despite constant German and Italian air raids, there is no general change in the situation at Tobruk. So far we have not yet succeeded in putting an effective stop to the fortress's nightly provision by destroyers and small steamships. . . . According to statements made by Air Headquarters Africa, the anti-aircraft defences over Tobruk have become so strong that they are not far behind those of Malta. . . . The many thrusts, strong and weak, made by the British garrison appear to be made in order to discover the weak spots in the front of encirclement. This is to prepare for a break-out, which is to be expected at the same time as the coming offensive on the southern front. . . .

*   *   *

I have set out the military discussion about the delay in the offensive, and I must record my conviction that General Auchinleck's four and a half months' delay in engaging the enemy in the Desert was alike a mistake and a misfortune. This chapter must also include the account of differences with the Australian Government, whose brave troops played a vital part in the whole defence of Egypt.

*   *   *

Mr. Menzies, the Australian Prime Minister, left us in May. His prolonged visit to England had been most valuable. He had sat through two critical months with the War Cabinet, and had shared many of our most difficult decisions. He had not been satisfied either with the organisation of the Cabinet or with my exercise of such wide powers in the conduct of the war. He raised both points with me on several occasions, and I gave my reasons for not agreeing with him. He desired the formation of an Imperial War Cabinet containing representatives of each of the four self-governing Dominions. On his homeward journey through Canada Mr. Menzies formally submitted his proposals in writing to Mr. Mackenzie King, General Smuts, and Mr. Fraser. None of them was however in favour of the change, and Mr. Mackenzie King in particular deployed formidable constitutional arguments against Canada's being committed by her representative to the decisions of a council in London.

Prime Minister to Prime Minister of Australia   19 Aug. 41

I need not say that should you be able to pay us another visit as Prime Minister your presence at our councils for as long as you are able to stay would be most welcome. We shall welcome all Dominion Prime Ministers who will in this way share our responsibilities. It would not be possible for a Dominion Minister other than the Prime Minister to sit in the War Cabinet as representation of all four Dominions would then be involved resulting in too large a permanent addition to our members; this in turn would entail far-reaching structural changes which are not in contemplation. My inquiries suggest that there would be no chance of the other Dominions agreeing to a Minister from a single Dominion representing them in the War Cabinet. I hope you will bear these points in mind when making your plans. Kindest regards.

Soon however important changes took place in the Australian Government. As was natural, there were on the morrow of so many misfortunes differences of opinion in the Commonwealth Cabinet about the conduct of the war. The Labour Party in Australia opposed a vote approving Mr. Menzies' visit to London. In view of these political manifestations both within and outside the Government, he placed his resignation in the hands of his colleagues and offered to serve in an Australian National Cabinet. On August 25 the Australian Labour Party rejected this proposal and demanded the resignation of the Government. On the 28th Mr. Menzies resigned, and was succeeded by his deputy, Mr. Fadden. The Australian Government, weakened by the loss of its ablest figure, had a majority of only one, and were confronted in this grievous period by a party Opposition thirsting for local power. In spite of the differences which I have mentioned, it was with great regret that I learned of Mr. Menzies' fall. Although my disagreements with him were serious, our relations had been most friendly. I thought it was a great pity that all the knowledge he had acquired of our affairs and of the war while sitting for four months in the War Cabinet, and the many contacts we had all of us established with him, should be lost. I sent him the following telegram:

Prime Minister to Mr. Menzies   28 Aug. 41
While I scrupulously abstain from all interference in Australian politics, I cannot resist telling you with what sorrow I have learned of your resignation. You have been at the helm during these two terrible years of storm, and you were with us here during its most anxious time for Australia. We are all very grateful to you for the courage you showed and the help you gave. I am the gainer by our personal friendship. I went through a similar experience when I was removed from the Admiralty at a moment when I could have given the Anzacs a fair chance of victory at the Dardanelles. It is always a comfort in such circumstances to feel sure one has done one's duty and one's best. My wife and family send their regards.

I hastened to put myself in close personal relations with Mr. Fadden and to submit to him our arguments about the structure of the War Cabinet, and also about the Japanese danger.

Prime Minister to Prime Minister of Australia   29 Aug. 41

Now that you have taken up your great office, I send you my most cordial good wishes for success, and assure you that I and my colleagues will do everything in our power to work with you in the same spirit of comradeship and good-will as we worked with Mr. Menzies, who, we are so glad to see, is serving under you as Minister for the Co-ordination of Defence.

I then set forth as my colleagues saw it a full exposition of the Imperial and constitutional aspects of the issues which Mr. Menzies had raised. This will be found among the Appendices.[1]

Our relations with Mr. Fadden's Government, and afterwards with Mr. Curtin's Labour Administration, were not as easy as they had been with their predecessors, and one sharp divergence harmful to our war effort occurred. The new Government, under hard pressure from its opponents, was much concerned about the position of the Australian division in Tobruk. They desired to collect their troops in the Middle East into one force in order to give them an opportunity for refreshment, restoration of discipline and re-equipment, and to satisfy public opinion in Australia. They were also anxious about the "decline in health resistance" of their troops in the fortress and the danger of a catastrophe resulting from further decline and inability to withstand a determined attack. They therefore demanded their immediate relief by other forces. Auchinleck protested strongly against this change, pointing out the difficulties of the relief and the derangement of his plan for the new offensive. I tried to reassure the General.

Prime Minister to General Auchinleck   6 Sept. 41

I am pretty sure the Australians will play the game if the facts are put before them squarely. We do not want either your supply of Tobruk or your other combinations to be hampered. If meeting their demand would do this, let me have the facts to put to them. Australia would not tolerate anything shabby. Of course if it does not make any serious difference we ought to meet their wishes.

I thought it right to furnish the fullest explanations to our sister Government. These also will be found in the Appendices.[2]

* * *

Upon my representations General Auchinleck had managed to relieve one of the Australian infantry brigade groups in Tobruk and replace it by the Polish Brigade. Considerable

[1] Appendix B, Book Two, pages 725–727.
[2] *Ibid.*

naval risks were involved, as nearly all the ships were attacked by aircraft. The Commander-in-Chief gave at length his reasons for not completing this operation, declaring that it might entail "a further retardation of the offensive in the Western Desert." "I propose therefore," he said, "definitely to abandon the idea of a further large-scale relief of Australian personnel in Tobruk, and to reinforce the garrison at once with an 'I' tank battalion." I sent his telegram to Mr. Fadden, with the following appeal:

Prime Minister to Prime Minister of Australia   11 Sept. 41

I send you in its entirety General Auchinleck's private telegram to me about relieving the Australian troops in Tobruk. I do so in complete confidence in your discretion. General Auchinleck's telegram is the result of prolonged consultation with the Naval and Air Commanders in the Middle East.

2. You will see from his telegram that if you insist upon the relief of the Australians in Tobruk it is physically impossible for it to be completed in time for you to make the statement you desire to the Commonwealth Parliament by the middle of this month. In fact only half could be removed during the moonless period of September, and the other half would have to be removed during the latter half of October, which is the very time when all preparations for the offensive will be intense, and when the preparatory work of the air force will demand their complete concentration on the enemy's rear areas, dumps, and airfields. In no case [moreover] could you make any statement to the Commonwealth Parliament, because any suggestion in public that the reliefs were to take place might lead to heavy air attacks on Tobruk Harbour and along the coast at the time when your troops would be withdrawing. If however you insist that the Australian troops must be withdrawn, orders will be issued accordingly irrespective of the cost entailed and the injury to future prospects. I trust that you will weigh very carefully the immense responsibility which you would assume before history by depriving Australia of the glory of holding Tobruk till victory was won, which otherwise, by God's help, will be theirs for ever.

3. I feel bound again to impress upon you the vital importance of maintaining absolute secrecy about future operations or movements of troops which the question of relief of your forces has compelled the Commander-in-Chief to reveal to us.

This proved vain, and I had no choice but to reply:

Prime Minister to Mr. Fadden   15 Sept. 41

Orders will at once be given in accordance with your decision. The maintenance of secrecy for the present is of the highest consequence to all.

To Auchinleck I telegraphed:

Prime Minister to General Auchinleck   17 Sept. 41

I am grieved at Australian attitude, but I have long feared the dangerous reactions on Australian and world opinion of our seeming to fight all our battles in the Middle East only with Dominions troops. For this reason, apart from desire to reinforce you, I have constantly pressed sending out some British infantry divisions. Your decision to put 50th British Division in Cyprus was, as you know, painful to us. I know that when you put it there you thought Cyprus was a place of special danger, but the situation has been changed by Russian war, and I am sure you will continue to review employment of this British division in what looks like a safe defensive rôle. . . .

I trust the Australian withdrawal will not further delay [your] offensive. The situation has already worsened. The enemy are far better supplied with petrol. Afrikan Panzer Corps is now called Afrikan Panzer Gruppe. By waiting until you have an extra brigade you may well find you have to face an extra division. Your movements of transport and formation of dumps must be noted by the enemy. The whole future of the campaign of 1942 in the Middle East and our relations with Turkey and Russia are involved.

General Auchinleck for his part was so deeply affronted by the Fadden Government's persistence in their demand that he wished to tender his resignation, on the ground that he did not command the confidence of the Australian Government. This would at this moment have been harmful from every point of view.

I enlisted the good offices of Mr. Oliver Lyttelton, Minister of State, now installed in Cairo.

Prime Minister to Minister of State   18 Sept. 41

Impossible that Auchinleck should suppose we do not agree with him [about the Australians in Tobruk]. My whole series of telegrams, including especially mine of September 11 to Fadden, which was repeated to Auchinleck and is now repeated to you herewith, shows how strongly we deprecate Australian resolve to quit the line at this juncture. Moreover, I particularly stimulated Auchinleck when he was at home not to prejudice defence of Tobruk by making a needless relief.

2. I was astounded at Australian Government's decision, being sure it would be repudiated by Australia if the facts could be made known. Allowances must be made for a Government with a majority only of one faced by a bitter Opposition, parts of which at least are isolationist in outlook.

3. It is imperative that no public dispute should arise between Great Britain and Australia. All personal feelings must therefore be

subordinated to appearance of unity. Trouble has largely arisen through our not having any British infantry divisions in the various actions, thus leading the world and Australia to suppose that we are fighting our battles with Dominions troops only.

4. I am telegraphing to Auchinleck to assure him of Chiefs of Staff's full agreement with his military views.

Thus the personal difficulty was smoothed over for the moment, but the actual operation of removing the last of the Australians in October still hung over us.

Prime Minister to General Auchinleck   29 Sept. 41

All now depends upon the battle. It may well be that you will be granted by the enemy the time you have asked. But every day's delay is dearly purchased in the wider sphere. The prize is Turkey, whose action may well be determined by victory in Cyrenaica.

I hope to persuade the Australian Government not to hamper you by pulling out their last two brigades from Tobruk in the October moonless period.

I now reported the whole position to Mr. Fadden, making another strong appeal. The reply was obdurate, but at this moment Mr. Fadden's Government was defeated in a division on the Budget, and an Australian Labour Government with a similar majority of one was formed under Mr. Curtin. I hastened to put myself in friendly touch with the new Prime Minister, who had cabled me.

Prime Minister to Prime Minister of Australia   8 Oct. 41

I thank you for your telegram on assuming the direction of Commonwealth affairs, and cordially reciprocate the good wishes it contains. You may be sure we shall work with you on a basis of most intimate confidence and comradeship.

But the new Government was equally opposed to our request, and it will be well to complete the account of this unhappy episode. On October 5 I telegraphed to General Auchinleck:

Prime Minister to General Auchinleck   5 Oct. 41

I am sorry I could get no helpful response from the late Australian Government about avoiding a further "Supercharge" [relief of Australians in Tobruk], and I have not yet made any contact with the new Government. I trust however there will be no postponement of "Crusader."

*   *   *

After a suitable interval I addressed Mr. Curtin on the question of Tobruk.

352   WAR COMES TO AMERICA

Prime Minister to Prime Minister of Australia   14 Oct. 41

I feel it right to ask you to reconsider once again the issue raised in my telegram to your predecessor. I have heard again from General Auchinleck that he would be very greatly helped and convenienced if the remaining Australian [troops] could stay in Tobruk until the result of the approaching battle is decided. I will not repeat the arguments which I have already used, but I will only add that if you felt able to consent it would not expose your troops to any undue or invidious risks, and would at the same time be taken very kindly as an act of comradeship in the present struggle.

Prime Minister to General Auchinleck   14 Oct. 41

In view of your statement that it would be a great help to you if the relief of the remaining Australians could be postponed until after "Crusader," I sent this morning the attached [above] telegram to the Australian Government. It may be that the new Government will be willing to give you the easement you desire. I should be glad for the sake of Australia and history if they would do this. In a day or two I shall hear what they decide and will advise you.

2. The Russian news is increasingly grave. All now hinges on you.

Mr. Curtin's Government adhered to the decision of their predecessors, and I was forced to inform General Auchinleck that the relief must proceed.

*   *   *

Throughout its siege Tobruk was sustained by the Navy, despite a constant and increasing scale of air attack. Moreover, no fighter protection could be given over the harbour, as our airfields were now too far east. The route by sea from Egypt soon became impossible for ordinary merchant ships, and all had to be carried in destroyers and smaller vessels during moonless nights. From July onward this Tobruk Ferry was greatly aided by the addition of the two fast minelayers *Abdiel* and *Latona*. Apart from maintaining supplies of ammunition and stores, mass movements of troops to and from the beleaguered fortress had to be undertaken and new weapons of many kinds, including tanks, had to be brought in. In all the Navy delivered to the garrison thirty-four thousand men, seventy-two tanks, ninety-two guns, and thirty-four thousand tons of stores. In addition they evacuated almost as many troops, besides wounded and enemy prisoners of war. This severe but indispensable work cost the Navy one minelayer, two destroyers, and twenty-two other naval vessels sunk, besides eighteen seriously damaged. Nine merchant ships and two hospital ships were also sunk or damaged. These sacrifices enabled the Tobruk garrison to survive constant attack for two hundred and forty-two days. During all this period the fortress played an active and conspicuous part in the strategy of the whole campaign, and especially of the forthcoming offensive.

*   *   *

On the night of October 25 the operation so greatly desired by both Australian parties was attempted under conditions of great danger, and not without appreciable loss. I telegraphed the news to Mr. Curtin.

Prime Minister to Prime Minister of Australia   26 Oct. 41

Our new fast minelayer, *Latona*, was sunk and the destroyer *Hero* damaged by air attack last night in going to fetch the last twelve hundred Australians remaining in Tobruk. Providentially, your men were not on board. I do not yet know our casualties. Admiral Cunningham reports that it will not be possible to move these twelve hundred men till the next dark period, in November. Everything in human power has been done to comply with your wishes.

Prime Minister to Prime Minister of Australia   27 Oct. 41

Fortunately, H.M.S. *Latona* was only carrying thirty-eight other ranks to Tobruk; remainder, to number of about one thousand men, were in three accompanying destroyers. About fifteen low bombing attacks between 19.00 and 22.30. Casualties: H.M.S. *Latona*—Naval officers, four missing, one wounded; ratings, twenty-five missing, seventeen wounded. Army officers, six wounded; other ranks, seven missing, one wounded. H.M.S. *Hero*—No casualties. We must be thankful these air attacks did not start in the earlier stages of the relief.

*   *   *

It has given me pain to have to relate this incident. To suppress it indefinitely would be impossible. Besides, the Australian people have the right to know what happened and why. On the other hand, it must be remembered that, apart from the limitations of their rigid Party system, the Australian Governments had little reason to feel confidence at this time in British direction of the war, and that the risks their troops had run when the desert flank was broken, and also in the Greek campaign, weighed heavily upon them. We can never forget the noble impulse which had led Australia to send her only three complete divisions, the flower of her manhood, to fight in the Middle East, or the valiant part they played in all its battles.

3

My Meeting with Roosevelt

INVASION OF BRITAIN has often been discussed in this and
previous volumes, but in May, 1941, Sir John Dill, Chief
of the Imperial General Staff, presented it anew with formidable authority. On May 6 he submitted to me the following
serious paper, copies of which he sent to his Naval and Air
colleagues and to General Ismay. Compliance with this would
have meant a complete reversion to the defensive. There
could be no further reinforcements other than drafts for the
Middle East or the Far East. There would be nothing in hand
for taking the initiative. Indeed, as the armour in the Middle
East was merely to be maintained by supplying normal wastage of fifty tanks a month, General Auchinleck, so far from
being himself able to attack, might well have been overpowered.

The Relation of the Middle East to the Security
of the United Kingdom

6 May 1941

The probability of invasion may seem to have receded for the moment, but German land and air forces could be concentrated for invasion within six to eight weeks of their release from the Balkan theatre. As American aid grows, the enemy must be closely watching for a favourable opportunity to launch the campaign which might win him the war.

2. German successes both in the Balkans and Libya, two widely different types of terrain, prove once again the paramountcy of armoured forces supported by a powerful air force. Throughout the war this combination has dominated every battlefield. The defence, since the points of attack cannot be foretold, must suffer the disadvantage of dispersion, and must depend primarily for its success upon the maintenance of large reserves of counter-attacking tanks, anti-tank weapons, and aircraft.

3. The Chiefs of Staff, after exhaustive inquiry, recently calculated the scale of armoured attack on this country at six armoured divisions, a total of some 2400 tanks. In the opinion of the Commander-in-Chief Home Forces, with which I fully concur, a total of six armoured divisions and four army tank brigades (i.e., some 2600 tanks) are required to give security in Great Britain against this scale of attack. Of these, two armoured divisions and two army tank brigades would be disposed in each of the Eastern and Southeastern Commands for counter-attack against penetration through East Anglia and the Kent and Sussex coasts respectively. The other two armoured divisions would be in reserve, one being earmarked for use in the North.

He then set forth the state of the armoured formations at home by June 1941, showing that our total strength for home defence would be about 1250 tanks, including 150 light, and 490 tanks in schools, etc., of which about 360 would be fit for action at three weeks' notice. He dwelt upon the need for special training for armoured forces, and continued:

6. The infantry formations guarding our long and vulnerable coastline are disposed over wide frontages—a division covering forty-five miles can have little depth. Our beach obstacles are good, but divisions have less than half their full scale of anti-tank guns and are short of anti-tank mines. German armoured forces, carried in special craft, will certainly be able to land. The R.A.F. will have many tasks to fulfil, and we have no air forces designed and trained for close bombing co-operation with the Army. The Luftwaffe will risk everything for local air superiority over the lanes of advance. Our defence on land therefore will rest primarily on our ability to deliver strong and speedy armoured counter-attacks. Yet, taking into account the training factor, I calculate that the armoured

forces in this country in June will be the equivalent of three fully effective armoured divisions—this against the six armoured divisions of the enemy.

7. It is dangerous to discount the possibility of heavy armoured attack on the grounds that Germany has not command of the sea; that our own air force would destroy the expedition before it sailed and on the beaches, or would sweep its supporting air force out of the sky; or that the technical difficulties of landing on such a scale would be insuperable. It would take five to seven days for us to concentrate adequate naval forces in home waters. Our bombers cannot deal with more than six invasion ports effectively, and then only if the weather is favourable. Air attack cannot be relied on to break up a disembarkation, any more than it did our embarkation at Dunkirk. Our fighters will not neutralise completely the enemy's bombers if he is ready to face the heavy losses which he will certainly incur, and no doubt the German plan will include measures for smothering our fighters at their bases. As for technical difficulties of landing, the Germans have given many proofs of their skill and thoroughness in planning and in the preparation of special equipment; and they have had time to perfect their arrangements. Maintenance will not tax their resources as much as might be expected; the quantities of food and petrol required for armoured formations over a short period are comparatively small, and the enemy may find enough in the country for his needs.

8. We underestimated the Germans in Norway and in Belgium, and recent events in Libya and the Balkans have taught us once more their capacity for overcoming the most formidable difficulties.

9. The loss of Egypt would be a calamity which I do not regard as likely, and one which we would not accept without a most desperate fight; but it would not end the war. A successful invasion alone spells our final defeat. It is the United Kingdom therefore and not Egypt that is vital, and the defence of the United Kingdom must take first place. Egypt is not even second in order of priority, for it has been an accepted principle in our strategy that in the last resort the security of Singapore comes before that of Egypt. Yet the defences of Singapore are still considerably below standard.

10. Risks must of course be taken in war, but they must be calculated risks. We must not fall into the error of whittling away the security of vital points. If need be, we must cut our losses in places that are not vital before it is too late.

11. I believe that we have gone to the limit, if not beyond it, in respect of the security of Great Britain, with which the defence of Ireland and the seizure of the Atlantic islands are inextricably bound up. In my view it would be unjustifiable, during the next three months, to risk sending away from this country more than an adequate maintenance reserve for the tanks already in or on the way to the Middle East. Even this, at a wastage of ten per cent per month, will involve the monthly despatch of about fifty tanks.

I was astonished to receive this document, and replied a week later somewhat controversially as follows:

Prime Minister to C.I.G.S.   13 May 41

There is a great deal in your paper of May 6 with which I agree. There are also many statements which leave me unconvinced. I thoroughly agree with you in paragraph 8 that our military advisers underrated the Germans in Norway, in Belgium, and in Libya. Of these Belgium is the most remarkable. Yet I never remember hearing a single British soldier point to the weakness of the Sub-Maginot Line or deprecate our occupation of Belgium. I only mention this to show that even the most expert professional opinion may sometimes err amid the many uncertainties of war.

2. . . . I gather you would be prepared to face the loss of Egypt and the Nile Valley, together with the surrender or ruin of the army of half a million we have concentrated there, rather than lose Singapore. I do not take that view, nor do I think the alternative is likely to present itself. The defence of Singapore is an operation requiring only a very small fraction of the troops required to defend the Nile Valley against the Germans and Italians. I have already given you the political data upon which the military arrangements for the defence of Singapore should be based, namely, that should Japan enter the war the United States will in all probability come in on our side; and in any case Japan would not be likely to besiege Singapore at the outset, as this would be an operation far more dangerous to her and less harmful to us than spreading her cruisers and battle-cruisers on the Eastern trade routes.

At this time of course the Japanese were not established in Indo-China.

3. I wonder whether the German action in the Balkans can be cited as an example of "their capacity for overcoming the most formidable difficulties." As a mere exercise in historical perspective, I should have thought the opposite was true. They were allowed to accumulate unresisted overwhelming forces to attack Yugoslavia before it was mobilised, and when it had been betrayed by its pre-war Government; Greece was exhausted and held by the Italian Army, and we were left practically alone, with only one-fifth the armoured vehicles and practically no Air, to resist their overwhelming onslaught. The fact that with all these advantages, so cheaply gained, the Germans were unable to impede seriously the masterly extrication and re-embarkation of our forces inspires me with confidence and not with apprehension.

4. The truisms set forth in paragraph 10 depend entirely upon their application to circumstances. But I hope the last sentence is not intended to have any relevance to the present position in Egypt.

Many Governments I have seen would have wilted before so grave a pronouncement by the highest professional authority, but I had no difficulty in convincing my political colleagues, and I was of course supported by the Chiefs of the Navy and the Air. My views therefore prevailed and the flow of reinforcements to the Middle East continued unabated. It will be seen that I did not even think it necessary to repeat the arguments against the likelihood of a successful invasion of Britain. Sir John Dill must have been himself conscious of the consensus of opinion against him on this aspect, and having struck his note of warning he let the matter drop.

However, two months later the subject arose from another quarter. In the middle of July Mr. Harry Hopkins arrived in England on his second mission from the President. The first topic which he opened to me was the new situation created by Hitler's invasion of Russia and its reaction upon all the Lend-Lease supplies we were counting on from the United States. Secondly, an American general, after being given the fullest facilities for inspection, had made a report throwing doubt upon our ability to withstand an invasion. This had caused the President anxiety. Thirdly, and in consequence, the President's misgivings already mentioned about the wisdom of our trying to defend Egypt and the Middle East had been deepened. Might we not lose all through trying to do too much? Finally, there was the question of arranging a meeting between Roosevelt and me somehow, somewhere, soon.

This time Hopkins was not alone. There were in London a number of high United States officers of the Army and Navy, ostensibly concerned with Lend-Lease, and in particular Admiral Ghormley, who was working daily with the Admiralty on the Atlantic problem and the American share in its solution. I held a meeting with Hopkins's circle and the Chiefs of Staff on the night of July 24 at Number 10. Hopkins brought with him, besides Admiral Ghormley, Major General Chaney, who was called a "special observer," and Brigadier-General Lee, the American Military Attaché. Averell Harriman, who had just returned from his tour in Egypt, in which by my directions he had been shown everything, completed the party.

Hopkins said that the "men in the United States who held the principal places and took decisions on defence matters" were of the opinion that the Middle East was an indefensible position for the British Empire, and that great sacrifices were being made to maintain it. In their view the Battle of the Atlantic would be the final decisive battle of the war, and everything should be concentrated on it. The President, he said, was more inclined to support the struggle in the Middle East, because the enemy must be fought wherever he was found. General Chaney then placed the four problems of the British Empire in the following order: the defence of the United Kingdom and the Atlantic sea lanes; the defence of Singapore and the sea lanes to Australia and New Zealand; the defence of the ocean routes in general; and, fourth, the defence of the Middle East. All were important, but he placed them in that order. General Lee agreed with General Chaney. Admiral Ghormley was anxious about the supply line to the Middle East if American munitions were to go there in great volume. Might this not weaken the Atlantic battle?

I then asked the British Chiefs of Staff to express their views. The First Sea Lord explained why he felt even more confident of destroying an invading army this year than last. The Chief of the Air Staff showed how much stronger was the Royal Air Force compared with the German than in the previous September, and spoke of our newly increased power to batter the invasion ports. The Chief of the Imperial General Staff also spoke in a reassuring sense, and said that the Army was immeasurably stronger now than in the previous September. I interposed to explain the special measures we had taken for the defence of aerodromes after the lessons of Crete. I invited our visitors to visit any airfield in which they were interested. "The enemy may use gas, but if so it will be to his own disadvantage, since we have arranged for immediate retaliation and would have admirable concentrated targets in any lodgments he might make on the coast. Gas warfare would also be carried home to his own country." I then asked Dill to speak about the Middle East. Without expressing any opinion contrary to his paper of May, he gave a powerful exposition of some of the reasons which made it necessary for us to stay there.

My feeling at the end of our discussion was that our American friends were convinced by our statements and impressed by the solidarity among us.

*   *   *

Nevertheless, the confidence which we felt about Home Defence did not extend to the Far East should Japan make war upon us. These anxieties also disturbed Sir John Dill. I retained the impression that Singapore had priority in his mind over Cairo. This was indeed a tragic issue, like having to choose whether your son or your daughter should be killed. For my part I did not believe that anything that might happen in Malaya could amount to a fifth part of the loss of Egypt, the Suez Canal, and the Middle East. I would not tolerate the idea of abandoning the struggle for Egypt, and was resigned to pay whatever forfeits were exacted in Malaya. This view also was shared by my colleagues.

I felt the need for repeating in the Far East the institution of a Minister of State, who, in the closest touch with the War Cabinet, would relieve the Commanders-in-Chief and local Governors of some of their burdens and help them to solve the grave political problems which gathered swiftly. In Mr. Duff Cooper, then Minister of Information, I had a friend and colleague who from his central point of view knew the whole scene. His firmness of character which had led him to resign his office as First Lord of the Admiralty after the Munich Agreement in 1938, his personal gifts of speech and writing, his military record as an officer in the Grenadier Guards during the 1914–18 war, combined to give him the highest qualifications. On July 21 he was appointed Chancellor of the Duchy of Lancaster, and was succeeded as Minister of Information by Mr. Brendan Bracken. Early in August, accompanied by his wife, Lady Diana, he left for the Far East via the United States. It was not till the end of October that he submitted his report from Singapore, to which he had returned.

*   *   *

For several months the British and American Governments had been acting towards Japan in close accord. At the end of July the Japanese had completed their military occupation of Indo-China. By this naked act of aggression their forces were poised to strike at the British in Malaya, at the Americans in the Philippines, and at the Dutch in the East Indies. On July 24 President Roosevelt asked the Japanese Government that, as a prelude to a general settlement, Indo-China should be neutralised and the Japanese troops withdrawn. To add point to these proposals, an executive order was issued freezing all Japanese assets in the United States. This brought all trade to a standstill. The British Government took simultaneous action, and two days later the Dutch followed. The adherence of the Dutch meant that Japan was deprived at a stroke of her vital oil supplies.

*   *   *

One afternoon in late July Harry Hopkins came into the garden of Downing Street and we sat together in the sunshine. Presently he said that the President would like very much to have a meeting with me in some lonely bay or other. I replied at once that I was sure the Cabinet would give me leave. Thus all was soon arranged. Placentia Bay, in Newfoundland, was chosen, the date of August 9 was fixed, and our latest battleship, the *Prince of Wales*, was placed under orders accordingly. I had the keenest desire to meet Mr. Roosevelt, with whom I had now corresponded with increasing intimacy for nearly two years. Moreover, a conference between us would proclaim the ever closer association of Britain and the United States, would cause our enemies concern, make Japan ponder, and cheer our friends. There was also much business to be settled about American intervention in the Atlantic, aid to Russia, our own supplies, and above all the increasing menace of Japan.

Former Naval Person to President Roosevelt   25 July 41

Cabinet has approved my leaving. Am arranging, if convenient to you, to sail August 4, meeting you some time 8th-9th-10th. Actual secret rendezvous need not be settled till later. Admiralty will propose details through usual channels. Am bringing First Sea Lord Admiral Pound, C.I.C.S. Dill, and Vice-Chief Air Freeman. Am looking forward enormously to our talks, which may be of service to the future.

I said to Ismay: "You and Portal must stay behind and mind the shop."

I also took with me Sir Alexander Cadogan, of the Foreign Office; Lord Cherwell, Colonels Hollis and Jacob, of the Defence Office; and my personal staff. In addition there were a number of high officers of the technical and administrative branches and the Plans Division. The President said he would bring the chiefs of the United States fighting services with him, and Mr. Sumner Welles of the State Department. The utmost secrecy was necessary because of the large numbers of U-boats then in the North Atlantic. To ensure secrecy the President, who was ostensibly on a holiday cruise, transshipped at sea to the cruiser *Augusta*, and left his yacht behind him as a blind. Meanwhile Harry Hopkins, though far from well, obtained Roosevelt's authority to fly to Moscow, a long, tiring, and dangerous journey, by Norway, Sweden, and Finland, in order to obtain directly from Stalin the fullest knowledge of the Soviet position and needs. He was to join the *Prince of Wales* at Scapa Flow.

The long special train which carried our whole company, including a large ciphering staff, picked me up at the station near Chequers. We boarded the *Prince of Wales* from a destroyer at Scapa.

Before darkness fell on August 4 the *Prince of Wales* with her escort of destroyers steamed out into the broad waters of the Atlantic. I found Harry Hopkins much exhausted by his long air journeys and exacting conferences in Moscow. Indeed, he had arrived at Scapa two days before in such a condition that the Admiral had put him to bed at once and kept him there. Nevertheless, he was as gay as ever, gathered strength slowly during the voyage, and told me all about his mission.

Former Naval Person to President Roosevelt   4-5 Aug. 41

Harry returned dead-beat from Russia, but is lively again now. We shall get him in fine trim on the voyage. We are just off. It is twenty-seven years ago today that Huns began their last war. We must make a good job of it this time. Twice ought to be enough. Look forward so much to our meeting. Kindest regards.

The spacious quarters over the propellers, which are most comfortable in harbour, become almost uninhabitable through vibration in heavy weather at sea, so I moved to the Admiral's sea-cabin on the bridge for working and sleeping. I took a great liking to our captain, Leach, a charming and lovable man and all that a British sailor should be. Alas! within four months he and many of his comrades and his splendid ship were sunk for ever beneath the waves. On the second day the seas were so heavy that we had to choose between slowing down and dropping our destroyer escort. Admiral Pound, First Sea Lord, gave the decision. Thenceforward we went on at high speed alone. There were several U-boats reported, which we made zigzags and wide diversions to avoid. Absolute wireless silence was sought. We could receive messages, but for a while we could not speak except at intervals. Thus there was a lull in my daily routine and a strange sense of leisure which I had not known since the war began. For the first time for many months I could read a book for pleasure. Oliver Lyttelton, Minister of State in Cairo, had given me *Captain Hornblower, R.N.*[1], which I found vastly entertaining. When a chance came, I sent him the message, "I find *Hornblower* admirable." This caused perturbation in the Middle East Headquarters, where it was imagined that "Hornblower" was the code-word for some special operation of which they had not been told.

[1] A novel by C. S. Forester.

The sea was rough and the quarterdeck unusable, but I found plenty of exercise in making my way three or four times a day through all the compartments and up and down all the ladders to the bridge. In the evenings we had an excellent cinema, where the latest and best films were presented to our party and to those officers who were off duty. Cadogan in his diary notes: "Film *Lady Hamilton* after dinner. Excellent. P.M., seeing it for the fifth time, still deeply moved. At the close he addressed the company: 'Gentlemen, I thought this film would interest you, showing great events similar to those in which you have been taking part.'" The voyage was an agreeable interlude.

Resting in my small but comfortable sea-cabin and bed on the bridge, I brooded on the future battle in the Desert in the light of all the reports which I had studied of the spring fighting, and achieved a memorandum for the Chiefs of Staff, with the first sentence of which I was much pleased: "Renown awaits the Commander who first restores artillery to its proper place on the battlefield, from which it has been ousted by heavily armoured fighting vehicles." This will appear in its proper place in the narrative.

Mr. Attlee, who acted in my absence as Deputy Prime Minister, was concerned about my safety. He feared that the *Tirpitz* would be sent out to catch the *Prince of Wales* if the slightest leakage occurred.

Prime Minister to Lord Privy Seal   6 Aug. 41

I don't see much harm in leakage. If asked a direct question [in the House] questioner should be asked not to put his question; but if he persists the answer should be, "I cannot undertake to deal with rumour." About *Tirpitz*: I fear there will be no such luck. Have no doubt Roosevelt will see us out to sea on the return journey. We have now picked up new destroyer escort.

* * *

Before starting on my voyage I thought it would be best for Lord Beaverbrook to deal for us with the whole question of American supplies to Russia. I dreaded the loss of what we had expected and so direly needed. I had left behind me the following instructions:

Prime Minister to Sir Edward Bridges, General Ismay,   3 Aug. 41
and Private Office

On or about the 10th an aeroplane, possibly carrying Lord Beaverbrook, will come out to us. This must bring, apart from letters

and urgent papers, an assortment of the most important Foreign
Office telegrams, perhaps paraphrased. Competent people must be
put to make the assortments, and they must be put in a weighted
case, so that they will sink in the sea if anything happens to the
aeroplane.

Pray put this in train.

While at sea I signalled:

Prime Minister to Lord Beaverbrook   7 Aug. 41
    If you feel like coming, which I should greatly welcome, aim at
afternoon eleventh or morning twelfth, but please do not run needless risks. It may be advisable for you to stay longer on this
[American] side.

We arrived at our rendezvous in Placentia Bay, Newfoundland, at 9 A.M. on Saturday, August 9.

Prime Minister to His Majesty the King   9 Aug. 41
    With humble duty, I have arrived safely, and am visiting the
President this morning.

As soon as the customary naval courtesies had been exchanged, I went aboard the *Augusta* and greeted President
Roosevelt, who received me with all honours. He stood supported by the arm of his son Elliott while the national anthems
were played, and then gave me the warmest of welcomes. I
gave him a letter from the King and presented the members of
my party. Conversations were then begun between the President and myself, Mr. Sumner Welles and Sir Alexander Cadogan, and the Staff officers on both sides, which proceeded
more or less continuously for the remaining days of our visit,
sometimes man to man and sometimes in larger conferences.
    On Sunday morning, August 10, Mr. Roosevelt came
aboard H.M.S. *Prince of Wales* and, with his Staff officers
and several hundred representatives of all ranks of the United
States Navy and Marines, attended Divine Service on the
quarterdeck. This service was felt by us all to be a deeply
moving expression of the unity of faith of our two peoples,
and none who took part in it will forget the spectacle presented that sunlit morning on the crowded quarterdeck—the
symbolism of the Union Jack and the Stars and Stripes draped
side by side on the pulpit; the American and British chaplains
sharing in the reading of the prayers; the highest naval,
military, and air officers of Britain and the United States
grouped in one body behind the President and me; the close-

packed ranks of British and American sailors, completely intermingled, sharing the same books and joining fervently together in the prayers and hymns familiar to both.

I chose the hymns myself—"For Those in Peril on the Sea" and "Onward, Christian Soldiers." We ended with "O God, Our Help in Ages Past," which Macaulay reminds us the Ironsides had chanted as they bore John Hampden's body to the grave. Every word seemed to stir the heart. It was a great hour to live. Nearly half those who sang were soon to die.

4

The Atlantic Charter

My Original Draft of the Atlantic Charter—President Roosevelt's Proposed Alterations—Our Discussions of August 11—Need to Safeguard Imperial Preference—My Reports of August 11 to the Foreign Office and the Cabinet—The Cabinet's Prompt Reply— The Atlantic Islands—Our Agreement About Policy Towards Japan—Final Form of the Atlantic Charter—A Joint Anglo-American Message to Stalin—My Memorandum About American Supplies—Mr. Purvis Killed in a Plane Accident—Report of August 12 to the Cabinet—Congratulations from the King and Cabinet—Report to Australian Prime Minister—Voyage to Iceland—I Return to London, August 19.

PRESIDENT ROOSEVELT told me at one of our first conversations that he thought it would be well if we could draw up a joint declaration laying down certain broad principles which should guide our policies along the same road. Wishing to follow up this most helpful suggestion, I gave him the next day, August 10, a tentative outline of such a declaration. My text was as follows:

JOINT ANGLO-AMERICAN DECLARATION OF PRINCIPLES

The President of the United States of America and the Prime Minister, Mr. Churchill, representing His Majesty's Government in the United Kingdom, being met together to resolve and concert the means of providing for the safety of their respective countries in face of Nazi and German aggression and of the dangers to all peoples arising therefrom, deem it right to make known certain principles which they both accept for guidance in the framing of their policy and on which they base their hopes for a better future for the world.

First, their countries seek no aggrandisement, territorial or other.

Second, they desire to see no territorial changes that do not accord with the freely expressed wishes of the peoples concerned.

Third, they respect the right of all peoples to choose the form of government under which they will live. They are only concerned to defend the rights of freedom of speech and thought, without which such choice must be illusory.

Fourth, they will strive to bring about a fair and equitable distribution of essential produce, not only within their territorial boundaries, but between the nations of the world.

Fifth, they seek a peace which will not only cast down for ever the Nazi tyranny, but by effective international organisation will afford to all States and peoples the means of dwelling in security within their own bounds and of traversing the seas and oceans without fear of lawless assault or the need of maintaining burdensome armaments.

Considering all the tales of my reactionary, Old-World outlook, and the pain this is said to have caused the President, I am glad it should be on record that the substance and spirit of what came to be called the "Atlantic Charter" was in its first draft a British production cast in my own words.

August 11 promised to be a day of intense business.

Prime Minister to Admiralty　　　　　　　　　　　11 Aug. 41
Utmost strength to be put on deciphering telegrams from here during next twenty-four hours.

At our meeting in the morning the President gave me a revised draft, which we took as a basis for discussion. The only serious difference from what I had written was about the fourth point (access to raw materials). The President wished to insert the words, "without discrimination and on equal terms." The President also proposed two extra paragraphs.

Sixth, they desire such a peace to establish for all safety on the high seas and oceans.

Seventh, they believe that all the nations of the world must be guided in spirit to the abandonment of the use of force. Because no future peace can be maintained if land, sea, or air armaments continue to be employed by nations which threaten, or may threaten, to use force outside of their frontiers, they believe that the disarmament of such nations is essential. They will further the adoption of all other practicable measures which will lighten for peace-loving peoples the crushing burden of armaments.

Before we discussed this document, the President explained that his idea was that there should be issued simultaneously in Washington and London, perhaps on August 14, a short

Prime Minister's meeting with President Roosevelt — Aug. 9/41
Draft of Joint Declaration —

COPY NO: *1*

MOST SECRET

NOTE: This document should not be left lying about and, if it
is unnecessary to retain, should be returned to the
Private Office.

PROPOSED DECLARATION

The President of the United States of America and the
Prime Minister, Mr. Churchill, representing His Majesty's
Government in the United Kingdom, being met together, deem it
right to make known certain common principles in the national
policies of their respective countries on which they base their
hopes for a better future for the world.

First, their countries seek no aggrandisement,
territorial or other;

Second, they desire to see no territorial changes
that do not accord with the freely expressed wishes of the
peoples concerned.

Third, they respect the right of all peoples to choose
the form of government under which they will live; and they
wish to see self-government restored to those from whom it has
been forcibly removed

Fourth, they will endeavour, with due respect to their
existing obligations, to further the enjoyment by all peoples
of access, on equal terms, to the trade and to the raw
materials of the world which are needed for their economic
prosperity.

Fifth, they support fullest collaboration between all
Nations in Economic field with object of securing for all
peoples freedom from want, improved labour standards, economic
advancement and social security.

Sixth, they hope to see established a peace, after the
final destruction of the Nazi tyranny, which will afford to
all nations the means of dwelling in security within their own
boundaries, and which will afford assurance to all peoples
that they may live out their lives in freedom from fear.

Seventh, they desire such a peace to establish for all
on the high seas and oceans

Eighth, they believe that all of the nations of the
world must be guided in spirit to the abandonment of the use
of force. Because no future peace can be maintained if land,
sea or air armaments continue to be employed by nations which
threaten, or may threaten, aggression outside of their
frontiers, they believe that the disarmament of such nations
is essential pending the establishment of a wider and more
permanent system of general security. They will further the
adoption of all other practicable measures which will lighten
for peace-loving peoples the crushing burden of armaments.

Private Office,
August 12, 1941

The original draft of the Atlantic Charter showing Mr. Churchill's corrections.

statement to the effect that the President and the Prime
Minister had held conversations at sea; that they had been
accompanied by members of their respective staffs; that the
latter had discussed the working-out of aid to the democracies
under the Lend-Lease Act; and that these naval and military
conversations had in no way been concerned with future commitments other than as authorised by Act of Congress. The
statement would proceed to say that the Prime Minister and
the President had discussed certain principles relating to the
civilisation of the world and had agreed on a statement of
them. I deprecated the emphasis which a statement on these
lines would lay on the absence of commitments. This would be
seized on by Germany and would be a source of profound dis-
couragement to the neutrals and to the vanquished. We also
would not like it. I very much hoped therefore that the President could confine the statement to the positive portion which
dealt with the question of aid to the democracies, more
especially as he had guarded himself by the reference to the
Lend-Lease Act. The President accepted this.

There followed a detailed discussion of the revised text of
the declaration. Several minor alterations were easily agreed.
The chief difficulties were presented by Points 4 and 7, especially the former. With regard to this, I pointed out at once
that the words "without discrimination" might be held to call
in question the Ottawa Agreements, and I was in no position
to accept them. This text would certainly have to be referred
to the Government at home, and, if it was desired to maintain
the present wording, to the Governments in the Dominions.
I should have little hope that it would be accepted. Mr.
Sumner Welles indicated that this was the core of the matter,
and that this paragraph embodied the ideal for which the
State Department had striven for the past nine years. I could
not help mentioning the British experience in adhering to free
trade for eighty years in the face of ever-mounting American
tariffs. We had allowed the fullest importations into all our
colonies. Even our coastwise traffic around Great Britain was
open to the competition of the world. All we had got in
reciprocation was successive doses of American Protection.
Mr. Welles seemed to be a little taken aback. I then said that
if the words, "with due respect for their existing obligations,"
could be inserted, and if the words, "without discrimination,"
could disappear, and "trade" be substituted for "markets," I
should be able to refer the text to His Majesty's Government
with some hope that they would be able to accept it. The

President was obviously impressed. He never pressed the point again.

As regards the generalities of Point 7, I pointed out that while I accepted this text, opinion in England would be disappointed at the absence of any intention to establish an international organisation for keeping peace after the war. I promised to try to find a suitable modification, and later in the day I suggested to the President the addition to the second sentence of the words, "pending the establishment of a wider and more permanent system of general security."

*   *   *

Continuous conferences also took place between the naval and military chiefs, and a wide measure of agreement was reached between them. I had outlined to the President the dangers of a German incursion into the Iberian Peninsula, and explained our plans for occupying the Canary Islands—known as Operation "Pilgrim"—for countering such a move. I then sent to Mr. Eden a summary of this discussion.

Prime Minister to Foreign Office   11 Aug. 41

The President has received a letter from Doctor Salazar, in which it is made clear that he is looking to the Azores as a place of retreat for himself and his Government in the event of German aggression upon Portugal, and that his country's age-long alliance with England leads him to count on British protection during his enforced stay in these islands.

2. If however the British were too much occupied elsewhere, he would be willing to accept assistance from the United States instead. The President would be well disposed to respond to such an appeal, and would like the British in the circumstances foreseen to propose to Doctor Salazar the transference of responsibility. The above would also apply to the Cape Verdes.

3. I told the President that we contemplate the operation known as "Pilgrim"; that we might be forced to act before a German violation of the peninsula had occurred, and that while this was going on we should be very busy. I pointed out that "Pilgrim" would almost, though not absolutely certainly, provoke a crisis in the peninsula, and asked whether our having set events in train by "Pilgrim" would be any bar to his acceptance of the responsibility indicated in paragraph 1. He replied that as "Pilgrim" did not affect Portugal, it made no difference to his action.

4. He would feel justified in taking action if the Portuguese islands were endangered, and we agreed that they would certainly be endangered if "Pilgrim" were to take place, as the Germans would have all the more need to forestall us there.

5. In these circumstances he would none the less be ready to

come to the aid of Portugal in the Atlantic islands, and was holding strong forces available for that purpose.

I have shown foregoing to President, who agreed that it was a correct representation of the facts.

*   *   *

We then, on the same day, turned to the Far East. The imposition of the economic sanctions on July 26 had caused a shock in Tokyo. It had not perhaps been realised by any of us how powerful they were. Prince Konoye sought at once to renew diplomatic talks, and on August 6 Admiral Nomura, the Japanese Special Envoy in Washington, presented to the State Department a proposal for a general settlement. Japan would undertake not to advance farther into Southeast Asia, and offered to evacuate Indo-China on the settlement of "the China incident." (Such was the term by which they described their six-years war upon China.) In return the United States were to renew trade relations and help Japan to obtain all the raw materials she required from the Southwest Pacific. It was obvious that these were smoothly worded offers by which Japan would take all she could for the moment and give nothing for the future. No doubt they were the best Konoye could procure from his Cabinet. Around our conference table on the *Augusta* there was no need to argue the broad issues. My telegram sent from the meeting to Mr. Eden gives a full account of the matter:

Prime Minister to Foreign Secretary   11 Aug. 41

The position about Japan is as follows:

President proposed to Japan some time ago neutralisation of Indo-China and Siam under joint guarantee of United States, Japan, Britain, China, and others. Japanese reply, which will be cabled you fully as soon as more urgent messages have been dealt with, agrees to the principle of no encroachment upon Siam and military withdrawal from Indo-China, but adds a number of conditions fundamentally unacceptable. For instance, the withdrawal to take place after the China incident is settled, meaning thereby after Chiang Kai-shek is strangled, and further requiring recognition of Japan's preponderant position in these regions; also requiring United States to abstain from all further military preparations in these regions, and seeking lifting of the economic sanctions.

2. President's idea is to negotiate about these unacceptable conditions and thus procure a moratorium of, say, thirty days in which we may improve our position in Singapore area and the Japanese will have to stand still. But he will make it a condition that the Japanese meanwhile encroach no farther, and do not use Indo-China as a base for attack on China. He will also maintain in full

force the economic measures directed against Japan. These negotiations show little chance of succeeding, but President considers that a month gained will be valuable. I pointed out of course that the Japanese would double-cross him and would try to attack China or cut the Burma communications. However, you may take it that they consider it right to begin the negotiations on these lines, and in view of what has passed between United States and Japan it will be necessary to accept this fact.

3. In the course of these negotiations President would renew his proposals for neutralisation of Siam as well as Indo-China.

4. At the end of the Note which the President will hand to the Japanese Ambassador when he returns from his cruise in about a week's time he will add the following passage, which is taken from my draft: "Any further encroachment by Japan in the Southwest Pacific would produce a situation in which the United States Government would be compelled to take counter-measures, even though these might lead to war between the United States and Japan." He would also add something to the effect that it was obvious that, the Soviet being a friendly Power, United States Government would be similarly interested in any similar conflict in the Northwest Pacific.

5. I think this is entirely good, and that we should associate ourselves therewith and endeavour to get the Dutch to join in full agreement, because either the Japanese will refuse the conditions the President prescribes—namely, continuance of the economic sanctions and no movement on the Japanese part and no invasion of Siam—or alternatively they will go on with their military action while lying about it diplomatically.

In this case the conditions indicated by the final passage just quoted [in paragraph 4] would come into play with great force, and the full effect of parallel declarations could be realised. The Soviet Government should also be kept informed. It might be dangerous to tell the Chinese what we are doing for them, though they might be assured in general terms that we have had their security in mind in all that we have done.

6. On all these grounds I consider that we should endorse the proposed course of action, and that the Dominions should be told about it and made to see that it is a very great advance towards the gripping of Japanese aggression by united forces.

*   *   *

To Mr. Attlee I sent a comprehensive summary of all the main points under discussion.

Prime Minister to Lord Privy Seal   11 Aug. 41

Have reached satisfactory settlement about Naval Plan Number 4 [the United States Navy to take over the America-Iceland stretch of the Atlantic].

Secondly, President is prepared to take very helpful action corresponding with, or consequent upon, Operation "Pilgrim."

Thirdly, he intends to negotiate with Japan on the basis of a moratorium for, say, a month, during which no further military movements are to be made by Japan in Indo-China and no encroachment upon Siam. He has agreed to end his communication with a severe warning, which I drafted. . . .

Fourthly, the President wishes to issue at the moment of general release of meeting story, probably 14th or 15th, a Joint Declaration, signed by him and me on behalf of His Majesty's Government, of the broad principles which animate the United States and Great Britain at this favourable time. I send you herewith his draft of the statement, which you will see is not free from the difficulties attaching to all such declarations. The fourth condition would evidently have to be amended to safeguard our obligations contracted in Ottawa and not prejudice the future of Imperial Preference. This might fall into its place after the war in a general economic settlement, with decisive lowering of tariffs and trade barriers throughout the world. But we cannot settle it now. For the sake of speedy agreement I have little doubt he will accept our amendments.

The seventh paragraph is most remarkable for its realism. The President undoubtedly contemplates the disarmament of the guilty nations, coupled with the maintenance of strong united British and American armaments both by sea and air for a long indefinite period.

Having regard to our views about the League of Nations or other international organisations, I would suggest the following amendment after the word "essential": "pending the establishment of a wider and more permanent system of general security."

He will not like this very much, but he attaches so much importance to the Joint Declaration, which he believes will affect the whole movement of United States opinion, that I think he will agree.

It would be most imprudent on our part to raise unnecesary difficulties. We must regard this as an interim and partial statement of war aims designed to assure all countries of our righteous purpose, and not the complete structure which we should build after victory.

You should summon the full War Cabinet, with any others you may think necessary, to meet tonight, and please let me have your views without the slightest delay. Meanwhile full accounts are being sent you immediately on the other points, together with Cadogan's report of the conversation. I fear the President will be very much upset if no Joint Statement can be issued, and grave and vital interests might be affected.

I had purposed to leave afternoon 12th, but we have both now postponed departure twenty-four hours.

I had only finished dictating the telegrams about 2 P.M., and that I should have had in my hands within the next twelve hours the War Cabinet's most helpful reply reflects credit on all concerned. I subsequently learned that my telegrams had not reached London until after midnight, and that many of the Ministers had already gone to bed. Nevertheless, a War Cabinet meeting was summoned for 1.45 A.M., and there was a full attendance, including Mr. Peter Fraser, Prime Minister of New Zealand, who was in England at the time. As a result of a full discussion they sent me a telegram just after 4 A.M., welcoming the proposal and suggesting a further version of Point 4 (nondiscrimination in world trade) and the insertion of a new paragraph dealing with social security. Meanwhile I had heard that the President had accepted all the amendments I had suggested to him on August 11.

*   *   *

On August 12, about noon, I went to see the President to agree with him the final form of the Declaration. I put to the President the Cabinet's revised version of Point 4, but he preferred to adhere to the phrasing already agreed, and I did not press him further on this point. He readily accepted the insertion of the new paragraph about social security desired by the Cabinet. A number of verbal alterations were agreed, and the Declaration was then in its final shape.

JOINT DECLARATION BY THE PRESIDENT AND THE PRIME MINISTER

August 12, 1941

The President of the United States of America and the Prime Minister, Mr. Churchill, representing His Majesty's Government in the United Kingdom, being met together, deem it right to make known certain common principles in the national policies of their respective countries on which they base their hopes for a better future for the world.

First, their countries seek no aggrandisement, territorial or other.

Second, they desire to see no territorial changes that do not accord with the freely expressed wishes of the peoples concerned.

Third, they respect the right of all peoples to choose the form of government under which they will live; and they wish to see sovereign rights and self-government restored to those who have been forcibly deprived of them.

Fourth, they will endeavour, with due respect for their existing obligations, to further the enjoyment by all States, great or small, victor or vanquished, of access, on equal terms, to the trade and to the raw materials of the world which are needed for their economic prosperity.

Fifth, they desire to bring about the fullest collaboration between all nations in the economic field, with the object of securing for all improved labour standards, economic advancement, and social security.

Sixth, after the final destruction of the Nazi tyranny they hope to see established a peace which will afford to all nations the means of dwelling in safety within their own boundaries, and which will afford assurance that all the men in all the lands may live out their lives in freedom from fear and want.

Seventh, such a peace should enable all men to traverse the high seas and oceans without hindrance.

Eighth, they believe that all the nations of the world, for realistic as well as spiritual reasons, must come to the abandonment of the use of force. Since no future peace can be maintained if land, sea, or air armaments continue to be employed by nations which threaten, or may threaten, aggression outside of their frontiers, they believe, pending the establishment of a wider and permanent system of general security, that the disarmament of such nations is essential. They will likewise aid and encourage all other practicable measures which will lighten for peace-loving peoples the crushing burden of armaments.

It was only after this that I received the telegram giving the results of a further meeting of the Cabinet on the morning of August 12. This telegram made clear the reasons for the misgivings which the Cabinet felt on the subject of Point 4. But I felt that the final text with the words, "with due respect for their existing obligations," governing as they did the whole paragraph, sufficiently safeguarded our position.

The profound and far-reaching importance of this Joint Declaration was apparent. The fact alone of the United States, still technically neutral, joining with a belligerent Power in making such a declaration was astonishing. The inclusion in it of a reference to "the final destruction of the Nazi tyranny" (this was based on a phrase appearing in my original draft) amounted to a challenge which in ordinary times would have implied warlike action. Finally, not the least striking feature was the realism of the last paragraph, where there was a plain and bold intimation that after the war the United States would join with us in policing the world until the establishment of a better order.

* * *

The President and myself also drew up a joint message to Stalin:

12 Aug. 41

We have taken the opportunity afforded by the consideration of the report of Mr. Harry Hopkins on his return from Moscow to consult together as to how best our two countries can help your country in the splendid defence that you are making against the Nazi attack. We are at the moment co-operating to provide you with the very maximum of supplies that you most urgently need. Already many shiploads have left our shores, and more will leave in the immediate future.

We must now turn our minds to the consideration of a more long-term policy, since there is still a long and hard path to be traversed before there can be won that complete victory without which our efforts and sacrifices would be wasted.

The war goes on upon many fronts, and before it is over there may be yet further fighting fronts that will be developed. Our resources, though immense, are limited, and it must become a question as to where and when those resources can best be used to further to the greatest extent our common effort. This applies equally to manufactured war supplies and to raw materials.

The needs and demands of your and our armed services can only be determined in the light of the full knowledge of the many factors which must be taken into consideration in the decisions that we make. In order that all of us may be in a position to arrive at speedy decisions as to the apportionment of our joint resources, we suggest that we prepare for a meeting to be held at Moscow, to which we would send high representatives who could discuss these matters directly with you. If this conference appeals to you, we want you to know that, pending the decisions of that conference, we shall continue to send supplies and materials as rapidly as possible.

We realise fully how vitally important to the defeat of Hitlerism is the brave and steadfast resistance of the Soviet Union, and we feel therefore that we must not in any circumstances fail to act quickly and immediately in this matter of planning the programme for the future allocation of our joint resources.

❖   ❖   ❖

Lord Beaverbrook had been keen to accept my invitation, which I sent while on the outward voyage. At the same time I needed Mr. Purvis, who was in any case returning to Washington. I considered that the combination of Beaverbrook and Purvis, who in many ways represented Canada, would give us the best chance of coping with the painful splitting of supplies between Great Britain and Soviet Russia which was desirable and also inevitable. I also hoped that Beaverbrook would be able to spur and enlarge the whole scale of American production. In anticipation of their arrival I drafted a memorandum,

which will be found among the Appendices.[1] Beaverbrook and
Purvis started from Prestwick in different airplanes within a
few hours of one another. It was an even chance who went in
either plane. Beaverbrook arrived safely at the Newfoundland
airport, and joined me after a long train journey early on the
12th. Purvis and all with him were killed by one of those
sinister strokes of fortune which make a plane fly into a hill of
no great height within a few minutes of taking off. Purvis was
a grievous loss, as he held so many British, American, and
Canadian threads in his hands, and had hitherto been the
directing mind in their harmonious combination. When Max
arrived I told him this shocking news. He was silent for a
moment, but made no comment. It was wartime.

* * *

The following telegram summarises the result of our final
conference:

Prime Minister to Lord Privy Seal   12 Aug. 41
Please thank Cabinet for amazingly swift reply. I put your
alternative Clause 4 to President, but he preferred to stick to the
phrasing already agreed. I do not myself see any real difference.
Phrase about "respect for existing obligations" safeguards our
relations with Dominions. We could not see how competition of
cheap labour would come in, as all countries preserve the right
of retaining or imposing national tariffs as they think fit pending
better solutions.
2. The President cordially accepted your new paragraph 5, but
you will see that the reference to "want" comes in where the
President originally wished it—at the end of paragraph 6. A few
verbal flourishes not affecting substance have been added.
3. We have laid special stress on the warning to Japan which
constitutes the teeth of the President's communication. One would
always fear State Department trying to tone it down; but President has promised definitely to use the hard language.
4. Arrival of Russia as a welcome guest at hungry table and
need of large supplementary programmes both for ourselves and
the United States forces make review and expansion of United
States production imperative. President proposes shortly to ask
Congress for another five billion dollars Lend-Lease Bill. President
welcomes Beaverbrook's arrival at Washington, and I am convinced this is the needful practical step. See also the Roosevelt-
Churchill message to dear old Joe. I think they will send Harriman to represent them, and I should propose that Beaverbrook
should go for us to Moscow, or wherever Russian Government is.
We do not wish conference in Russia to start before latter part of

[1] Appendix C, Book Two.

September, by when it is hoped we shall know where the Russian front will lie for the winter.

5. They are sending us immediately 150,000 more rifles, and I look for improved allocations of heavy bombers and tanks. I hope they will take over whole ferry service and deliver both in England and in West Africa by American pilots, many of whom may stay for war-training purposes with us.

6. Your promptness has enabled me to start home today, 12th. President is sending American destroyers with us, who are not considered escort but will chip in if any trouble occurs. Franklin Junior is serving on one of them, and has been appointed Liaison Officer to me during my day in Iceland (C),[2] where there will be a joint review of British and American forces.

7. Lord Beaverbrook is now proceeding with Harriman by air to United States.

8. I trust my colleagues will feel that my mission has been fruitful. I am sure I have established warm and deep personal relations with our great friend.

Before sailing homeward I received a message of congratulation from the King. During the voyage I replied to this and other telegrams.

Prime Minister to His Majesty the King   13 Aug. 41

Most grateful to Your Majesty for good wishes. Lord Privy Seal will submit full text of all telegrams recording business. I have established with President most cordial personal relations, and trust Your Majesty will feel that results justify mission. President has given me personal letter, which I shall hope to deliver to you at luncheon on Tuesday, 19th.

And to Mr. Attlee, who telegraphed on behalf of the Cabinet:

Prime Minister to Lord Privy Seal   13 Aug. 41

Many thanks for your kind message. I am delighted you will broadcast statement and declaration yourself. Please make a definite break between the preliminary statement and the actual text by saying, "I will now read the actual text of the Joint Declaration." I do not consider any comment will be required from me, as announcement is itself sufficient to fill the newspapers. I might broadcast on the Sunday night following my return, when reaction in United States to our meeting and Joint Declaration will be apparent.

Any necessary guidance can be given to the press confidentially, but they will surely see that Joint Declaration proposing final destruction of Nazi power and disarmament of aggressive nations while Britain and United States remain armed is an event of first

---

[2] To avoid confusion with Ireland, I had directed that Iceland was always to be written by the British authorities as Iceland (C). This was indeed a necessary precaution.

magnitude. It would be well to let this soak in on its own merits on friend and foe.

2. For your secret information, President is remaining at sea until end of week in order to cover my return. I told him this was not necessary, but he insisted.

3. We shall be most interested to know how it is all taken.

4. I read with much pleasure your admirable war statement at end of session.

I sent the following message to Mr. Menzies, Prime Minister of Australia:

Prime Minister to Mr. Menzies   15 Aug. 41

You have no doubt seen the relevant cables about Atlantic meeting. I trust you approve of what was accomplished. President promised me to give the warning to Japan in the terms agreed. Once we know this has been done, we should range ourselves beside him and make it clear that if Japan becomes involved in war with United States she will also be at war with Britain and British Commonwealth. I am arranging this with Eden, and you will be advised through the regular channels. You should note that the President's warning covers an attack upon Russia, so that perhaps Stalin will line up too, and of course the Dutch. If this combined front can be established, including China, I feel confident that Japan will lie quiet for a while. It is however essential to use the firmest language and the strongest combination.

2. United States Navy is effectively taking over America-Iceland stretch of Atlantic, thus giving us relief equal to over fifty destroyers and corvettes, soon to be available for home waters and South Atlantic.

The voyage to Iceland was uneventful, although at one point it became necessary to alter course owing to the reported presence of U-boats near by. Our escort included two United States destroyers, in one of which was Ensign Franklin D. Roosevelt, Junior, the President's son. On the 15th we met a combined homeward-bound convoy of seventy-three ships, all in good order and perfect station after a fortunate passage across the Atlantic. It was a heartening sight, and the merchant ships too were glad to look at the *Prince of Wales*.

We reached the island on Saturday morning, August 16, and anchored at Hvals Fiord, from which we travelled to Reykjavik in a destroyer. On arrival at the port I received a remarkably warm and vociferous welcome from a large crowd, whose friendly greetings were repeated whenever our presence was recognised during our stay, culminating in scenes of great enthusiasm on our departure in the afternoon, to the accompaniment of such cheers and hand-clapping as have, I was assured, seldom been heard in the streets of Reykjavik.

After a short visit to the Althingishus, to pay respects to the Regent and the members of the Icelandic Cabinet, I proceeded to a joint review of the British and American forces. There was a long march past in threes, during which the tune "United States Marines" bit so deeply into my memory that I could not get it out of my head. I found time to see the new airfields we were making, and also to visit the wonderful hot springs and the glass-houses they are made to serve. I thought immediately that they should also be used to heat Reykjavik, and tried to further this plan even during the war. I am glad that it has now been carried out. I took the salute with the President's son standing beside me, and the parade provided another remarkable demonstration of Anglo-American solidarity.

On return to Hvals Fiord, I visited the *Ramillies*, and addressed representatives of the crews of the British and American ships in the anchorage, including the destroyers *Hecla* and *Churchill*.

As darkness fell after this long and very tiring ordeal we sailed for Scapa, where we arrived without further incident early on August 18, and I reached London on the following day.

5

Aid to Russia

*Russian Valour and the Approaching Winter—Lord Beaverbrook
Champions Aid to Russia—Our Sacrifices of Vital Munitions—
The Beaverbrook-Harriman Mission—My Letter to Stalin of
August 29—His Reply—Interview with Ambassador Maisky—An
Air of Menace—My Answer to Stalin—I Communicate My Anxi-
eties to President Roosevelt—Letter to Sir Stafford Cripps of
September 5—Further Message from Stalin—A Fantastic Sugges-
tion—My Response—Lord Beaverbrook Sails for Archangel in the
"London"—My Letter to Stalin of September 21—The Beaver-
brook Mission in Moscow—A Grim Reception—Cordial American
Contacts—Protocol for Supplies to Russia—Continuous Cycle of
Convoys to Archangel—Mr. Attlee Goes to Washington—Insistent
Demands in Moscow for the Second Front—The Crisis of the
Struggle in Russia—My Telegram to Sir Stafford Cripps of Octo-
ber 28—A Plain Statement—Winter Casts Its Shield Before the
Russian Armies—Mrs. Churchill's "Aid to Russia" Fund.*

Two MONTHS had now passed on the Russian front, and
terrific blows had been struck by the German armies. But
by now there was another side to the tale. Despite their fearful
losses Russian resistance remained tough and unbending. Their
soldiers fought to the death, and their armies gained in experience and skill. Partisans rose up behind the German fronts
and harassed the communications in a merciless warfare. The
captured Russian railway system was proving inadequate; the
roads were breaking up under the heavy traffic, and movement
off the roads after rain was often impossible. Transport vehicles
were showing many signs of wear. Barely three months remained before the dreaded Russian winter. Could Moscow be
taken in that time? And if it were, would that be enough?

Here then was the fateful question. Though Hitler was still elated by the victory at Kiev, the German generals might well feel that their early misgivings were justified. There had been four weeks of delay on what had now become the decisive front. The task of "annihilating the forces of the enemy in White Russia," which had been given to the Central Army Group, was still not done.

But as the autumn drew on and the supreme crisis on the Russian front impended, the Soviet demands upon us became more insistent.

*   *   *

Lord Beaverbrook returned from the United States having stimulated the already powerful forces making for a stupendous increase in production. He now became the champion in the War Cabinet of aid to Russia. In this he rendered valuable service. When we remember the pressures that lay upon us to prepare the battle in the Libyan Desert, and the deep anxieties about Japan which brooded over all our affairs in Malaya and the Far East, and that everything sent to Russia was subtracted from British vital needs, it was needful that the Russian claims should be so vehemently championed at the summit of our war thought. I tried to keep the main proportion evenly presented in my own mind, and shared my stresses with my colleagues. We endured the unpleasant process of exposing our own vital security and projects to failure for the sake of our new ally—surly, snarly, grasping, and so lately indifferent to our survival.

On the way home from Iceland I had felt that when Beaverbrook and Averell Harriman got back from Washington and we could survey all the prospects of munitions and supplies, they should go to Moscow and offer all we could spare and dare. Prolonged and painful discussions took place upon the details on the lines of our joint offer of August 12. The Service departments felt it was like flaying off pieces of their skin. However, we gathered together the utmost in our power, and consented to very large American diversions of all we longed for ourselves in order to make an effective contribution to the resistance of the Soviets. I brought the proposal to send Lord Beaverbrook to Moscow before my colleagues on August 28. The Cabinet were very willing that he should present the case to Stalin, and President Roosevelt felt himself well represented by Harriman.

I therefore informed Lord Beaverbrook:

Prime Minister to Lord Beaverbrook   30 Aug. 41

I wish you to go to Moscow with Mr. Harriman in order to arrange the long-term supply of the Russian armies. This can only be achieved almost entirely from American resources, though we have rubber, boots, etc. A large new installation must be made in the United States. Rate of supply is of course limited by the ports of entry and by the dearth of shipping. When the metre-gauge railway from Basra to the Caspian has been doubled in the spring, this will be an important channel. It is our duty and our interest to give the utmost possible aid to the Russians, even at serious sacrifices by ourselves. However, no large flow can begin till the middle or end of 1942, and the main planning will relate to 1943. Your function will be not only to aid in the forming of the plans to help Russia, but to make sure we are not bled white in the process; and even if you find yourself affected by the Russian atmosphere I shall be quite stiff about it here. I am sure however you are the man for the job, and the public instinct has already endorsed this.

The decision to send Harriman means that Hopkins does not feel well enough to go himself. There is no point in sending Eden at the present time.

As to the date, we are in the hands of the Americans, but we must act in a *bona-fide* spirit and not give occasion for anyone to say we have been fooling the Russians or playing for delay. It will be necessary to settle the date of the conference in the next few days. I do not think a fortnight one way or the other makes any difference, as ninety per cent of its work must relate to long-term projects.

As a preliminary to this mission I outlined the position in general terms in a letter to M. Stalin.

Prime Minister to Monsieur Stalin   29 Aug. 41

I have been searching for any way to give you help in your splendid resistance pending the long-term arrangements which we are discussing with the United States and which will form the subject of the Moscow Conference. Maisky has represented that fighter aircraft are much needed in view of heavy losses. We are expediting the two hundred Tomahawks about which I telegraphed in my last. Our two squadrons should reach Murmansk about September 6, comprising forty Hurricanes. You will, I am sure, realise that fighter aircraft are the foundation of our home defence, besides which we are trying to obtain air superiority in Libya, and also to provide for Turkey so as to bring her on our side. Nevertheless, I could send two hundred more Hurricanes, making four hundred and forty fighters in all, if your pilots could use them effectively. These would be eight- and twelve-gun Hurricanes, which we have found very deadly in action. We could send one hundred now and two batches of fifty soon afterwards, together with mechanics, instructors, spare parts, and equipment, to Archangel. Meanwhile arrangements could be made to begin accustoming your pilots and mechanics to the new type if you will send them to air squadrons at Murmansk. If you feel this would be useful orders will be given here accordingly, and a full technical memorandum is being telegraphed through our Military Air Mission.

2. The news that the Persians have decided to cease resistance is most welcome. Even more than safeguarding the oilfields, our object in entering Persia has been to get another through route to you which cannot be cut. For this purpose we must develop the railway from the Persian Gulf to the Caspian and make sure it runs smoothly with reinforced railway material from India. The Foreign Secretary has given to Maisky for you the kind of terms we should like to make with the Persian Government, so as to have a friendly people and not be compelled to waste a number of divisions merely guarding the railway line. Food is being sent from India, and if the Persians submit we shall resume payment of the oil royalties now due to the Shah. We are instructing our advance guards to push on and join hands with your forces at a point to be fixed by the military commanders somewhere between Hamadan and Kasvin. It would be a good thing to let the world know that British and Russian forces had actually joined hands. In our view it would be better at this moment for neither of us to enter Teheran in force, as all we want is the through route. We are making a large-scale base at Basra, and we hope to make this a well-equipped warm-water reception port for American supplies, which can thus surely reach the Caspian and the Volga region.

3. I must again express the admiration of the British nation for the wonderful fight the Russian armies and Russian people are making against the Nazi criminals. General Macfarlane was immensely impressed by all he saw at the front. A very hard time lies before us, but Hitler will not have a pleasant winter under our ever-increasing air bombardment. I was gratified by the very firm warning Your Excellency gave to Japan about supplies via Vladivostok. President Roosevelt seemed disposed, when I met him, to take a strong line against further Japanese aggression, whether in the South or in the Northwest Pacific, and I made haste to declare that we would range ourselves upon his side should war come. I am most anxious to do more for Chiang Kai-shek than we have hitherto felt strong enough to do. We do not want war with Japan, and I am sure the way to stop it is to confront those people, who are divided and far from sure of themselves, with the prospect of the heaviest combination.

On the evening of September 4, M. Maisky called to see me to deliver M. Stalin's reply. This was the first personal message since July.

Premier Stalin to Prime Minister   4 Sept. 41

Personal message of Premier Stalin to Premier Churchill.

I express thanks for promise *to sell* [1] to Soviet Union a further two hundred fighters in addition to the two hundred previously promised. I do not doubt that the Soviet aviators will succeed in mastering them and putting them into use.

I have however to say that these aeroplanes, which apparently cannot be put into use quickly and at once, but at different periods and in separate groups, will be incapable of effecting serious changes on the Eastern front. They will be unable to effect serious changes, not only because of the large scale on which the war is being waged, which necessitates the continuous supply of a large quantity of aeroplanes, but chiefly because the situation of the Soviet forces during the last three weeks has considerably deteriorated in such important areas as the Ukraine and Leningrad.

As a matter of fact, the relative stabilisation at the front which we succeeded in achieving about three weeks ago has broken down during the last week, owing to transfer to Eastern front of thirty to thirty-four fresh German infantry divisions and of an enormous quantity of tanks and aircraft as well as a large increase in activities of the twenty Finnish and twenty-six Rumanian divisions. Germans consider danger in the West a bluff, and are transferring all their forces to the East with impunity, being convinced that no second front exists in the West, and that none will exist. Germans consider it quite possible to smash their enemies singly: first Russia, then the English.

As a result we have lost more than one-half of the Ukraine, and in addition the enemy is at the gates of Leningrad.

These circumstances have resulted in our losing Krivoi Rog iron ore basin and a number of metallurgical works in the Ukraine; we have evacuated one aluminum works on Dnieper River and a further aluminum works at Tikhvin, one motor and two aircraft works in the Ukraine, two motor and two aircraft works at Leningrad; and these works cannot be put into operation in the new localities in less than from seven to eight months.

This has weakened our power of defence and faced the Soviet Union with a mortal menace. The question arises how to emerge from this more than unfavourable situation.

I think there is only one means of egress from this situation— to establish in the present year a second front somewhere in the Balkans or France, capable of drawing away from the Eastern front thirty to forty divisions, and at the same time of ensuring to the Soviet Union thirty thousand tons of aluminium by the beginning of October next and a *monthly* minimum of aid amounting to four hundred aircraft and five hundred tanks (of small or medium size).

Without these two forms of help the Soviet Union will either suffer defeat or be weakened to such an extent that it will lose for

[1] Author's italics.

a long period any capacity to render assistance to its allies by its actual operations on the fronts of the struggle against Hitlerism.

I realise that this present message will cause dismay to Your Excellency. But what is one to do? Experience has taught me to look facts in the face however unpleasant they are, and not to fear to express the truth however unwelcome it may be. The Persian affair has in fact turned out pretty well. The joint operations of the British and Soviet forces predetermined the issue. So it will be in future as long as our forces act jointly. But Persia is but an episode. The issue of the war will not of course be decided in Persia.

The Soviet Union, like England, does not desire war with Japan. The Soviet Union does not consider it possible to violate agreements, including its treaty of neutrality with Japan. But if Japan violates this agreement and attacks the Soviet Union, she will meet with a due rebuff on the part of the Soviet forces.

Finally, allow me to express thanks for the admiration you have expressed at the actions of the Soviet forces which are waging a bloody war with the robber hordes of Hitlerite bandits for our common cause of liberation.

*   *   *

The Soviet Ambassador, who was accompanied by Mr. Eden, stayed and talked with me for an hour and a half. He emphasised in bitter terms how for the last eleven weeks Russia had been bearing the brunt of the German onslaught virtually alone. The Russian armies were now enduring a weight of attack never equalled before. He said that he did not wish to use dramatic language, but this might be a turning-point in history. If Soviet Russia were defeated, how could we win the war? M. Maisky emphasised the extreme gravity of the crisis on the Russian front in poignant terms which commanded my sympathy. But when presently I sensed an underlying air of menace in his appeal, I was angered. I said to the Ambassador, whom I had known for many years, "Remember that only four months ago we in this Island did not know whether you were not coming in against us on the German side. Indeed, we thought it quite likely that you would. Even then we felt sure we should win in the end. We never thought our survival was dependent on your action either way. Whatever happens, and whatever you do, you of all people have no right to make reproaches to us." As I warmed to the topic the Ambassador exclaimed, "More calm, please, my dear Mr. Churchill," but thereafter his tone perceptibly changed.

The discussion went over the ground already covered in the interchange of telegrams. The Ambassador pleaded for an immediate landing on the coast of France or the Low Countries. I explained the military reasons which rendered this impossible, and that it could be no relief to Russia. I said that I had spent five hours that day examining with our experts the means for greatly increasing the capacity of the Trans-Persian Railway. I spoke of the Beaverbrook-Harriman Mission and of our resolve to give all the supplies we could spare or carry. Finally Mr. Eden and I told him that we should be ready for our part to make it plain to the Finns that we would declare war upon them if they advanced into Russia beyond their 1918 frontiers. M. Maisky could not of course abandon his appeal for an immediate second front, and it was useless to argue further.

* * *

I at once consulted the Cabinet upon the issues raised in this conversation and in Stalin's message, and that evening sent a reply.

Prime Minister to Monsieur Stalin   4 Sept. 41

I reply at once in the spirit of your message. Although we should shrink from no exertion, there is in fact no possibility of any British action in the West, except air action, which would draw the German forces from the East before the winter sets in. There is no chance whatever of a second front being formed in the Balkans without the help of Turkey. I will, if Your Excellency desires, give all the reasons which have led our Chiefs of Staff to these conclusions. They have already been discussed with your Ambassador in conference today with the Foreign Secretary and the Chiefs of Staff. Action, however well-meant, leading only to costly fiascos would be no help to anyone but Hitler.

2. The information at my disposal gives me the impression that the culminating violence of the German invasion is already over, and that winter will give your heroic armies a breathing-space. This however is a personal opinion.

3. About supplies. We are well aware of the grievous losses which Russian industry has sustained, and every effort has been and will be made by us to help you. I am cabling President Roosevelt to expedite the arrival here in London of Mr. Harriman's Mission, and we shall try even before the Moscow Conference to tell you the numbers of aircraft and tanks we can jointly promise to send each month, together with supplies of rubber, aluminium, cloth, etc. For our part we are now prepared to send you, *from British production,* one-half of the monthly total for which you ask in aircraft and tanks. We hope the United States will supply the other half of your requirements. We shall use every endeavour to start the flow of equipment to you immediately.

4. We have given already the orders for supplying the Persian Railway with rolling-stock to raise it from its present capacity of

two trains a day each way up to its full capacity, namely, twelve trains a day each way. This should be reached by the spring of 1942, and meanwhile will be steadily improving. Locomotives and rolling-stock have to be sent round the Cape from this country after being converted to oil-burners, and the water supply along the railway has to be developed. The first forty-eight locomotives and four hundred steel trucks are about to start.

5. We are ready to make joint plans with you now. Whether British armies will be strong enough to invade the mainland of Europe during 1942 must depend on unforeseeable events. It may be possible however to assist you in the extreme North when there is more darkness. We are hoping to raise our armies in the Middle East to a strength of three-quarters of a million before the end of the present year, and thereafter to a million by the summer of 1942. Once the German-Italian forces in Libya have been destroyed, all these forces will be available to come into line on your southern flank, and it is hoped to encourage Turkey to maintain at the least a faithful neutrality. Meanwhile we shall continue to batter Germany from the air with increasing severity and to keep the seas open and ourselves alive.

6. In your first paragraph you used the word "sell." We had not viewed the matter in such terms and have never thought of payment. Any assistance we can give you would better be upon the same basis of comradeship as the American Lend-Lease Bill, of which no formal account is kept in money.

7. We are willing to put any pressure upon Finland in our power, including immediate notification that we will declare war upon her should she continue beyond the old frontiers. We are asking the United States to take all possible steps to influence Finland.

I thought the whole matter so important that I sent simultaneously the following telegram to the President while the impression was fresh in my mind:

Former Naval Person to President Roosevelt   5 Sept. 41
The Soviet Ambassador brought the subjoined message to me and Eden last night, and used language of vague import about the gravity of the occasion and the turning-point character which would attach to our reply. Although nothing in his language warranted the assumption, we could not exclude the impression that they might be thinking of separate terms. The Cabinet have thought it right to send the attached reply. Hope you will not object to our references to possible American aid. I feel that the moment may be decisive. We can but do our best.
With kindest regards . . .

The Soviet appeal was very naturally supported by our Ambassador in Moscow in the strongest terms. To this also I sent what I deemed a reply which would arm him in future arguments.

Prime Minister to Sir Stafford Cripps   5 Sept. 41

If it were possible to make any successful diversion upon the French or Low Countries shore which would bring back German troops from Russia, we should order it even at the heaviest cost. All our generals are convinced that a bloody repulse is all that would be sustained, or, if small lodgments were effected, that they would have to be withdrawn after a few days. The French coast is fortified to the limit, and *the Germans still have more divisions in the West than we have in Great Britain,*[2] and formidable air support. The shipping available to transport a large army to the Continent does not exist, unless the process were spread over many months. The diversion of our flotillas to such an operation would entail paralysis of the support of the Middle Eastern armies and a breakdown of the whole Atlantic traffic. It might mean the loss of the Battle of the Atlantic and the starvation and ruin of the British Isles. Nothing that we could do or could have done would affect the struggle on the Eastern front. From the first day when Russia was attacked I have not ceased to press the Chiefs of Staff to examine every form of action. They are united in the views here expressed.

2. When Stalin speaks of a front in the Balkans you should remember that even with the shipping then available in the Mediterranean it took us seven weeks to place two divisions and one armoured brigade in Greece, and that since we were driven out the whole of the Greek and many of the island airfields have been occupied by the German and Italian Air Force and lie wholly outside the range of our fighter protection. I wonder that the losses sustained by our shipping and the Fleet in the evacuation of Greece and Crete have been forgotten. The conditions are far more adverse now than then, and our naval strength is reduced.

3. When you speak of "a superhuman effort" you mean, I presume, an effort rising superior to space, time, and geography. Unfortunately these attributes are denied us.

4. The situation in the West would be entirely different if the French front were in being, for then I have no doubt the invasion of Russia would have been impossible because of the enormous counter-attacks that could be immediately launched. No one wants to recriminate, but it is not our fault that Hitler was enabled to destroy Poland before turning his forces against France, or to destroy France before turning them against Russia.

5. The four hundred and forty fighter aircraft which we have taken from our seriously diminished reserve are no doubt petty compared with the losses sustained by the Russian Air Force. They constitute however a painful and dangerous sacrifice on our part. The attacks by the Royal Air Force both by day and by night are

[2] Author's italics.

maintained with our utmost strength, and the even character of the fighting above the French coast shows the high degree of air power still possessed by the Germans in the West.

6. Nothing that we could do or could have done can affect the terrible battle proceeding on the Russian front. Arrangements can still be made to provide for the campaign of 1942. The route established through Persia will be opened to the full, and whatever can be found and shipped from British resources, and from American resources which would otherwise have come to Britain, will be sent as fast as possible. I am pressing President Roosevelt to send Mr. Harriman here at the earliest moment in order that the Russians may know what aid they may expect in 1942 to compensate for the losses sustained by their munitions industry and make their plans accordingly. Meanwhile I am sending a reply to Stalin's telegram today, and this present message is solely for your own guidance. I sympathise keenly with your feelings as you watch the agony of Russia at close quarters, but neither sympathy nor emotion will overcome the kind of facts we have to face.

In response to one of Stalin's requests I sent on September 9 the following telegram to our Ambassador in Moscow:

Prime Minister to Sir Stafford Cripps (Moscow)   15 Sept. 41

Please inform M. Stalin from Prime Minister that we are arranging to supply five thousand tons of aluminium from Canada as soon as arrangements for shipment are completed, and two thousand tons monthly thereafter. First shipments will be via Vladivostok, unless Persian route would be preferable to Russian Government.

On September 15 I received another telegram from Stalin:

Premier Stalin to Prime Minister Churchill   15 Sept. 41

In my last message I stated the viewpoint of the Soviet Government that the establishment of a second front is the most fundamental remedy for improvement of the situation with regard to our common cause. In reply to your message, in which you stress once more the impossibility of a second front at the present moment, I can only reiterate that the absence of a second front simply favours the designs of our common enemy.

I have no doubt that the British Government desires to see the Soviet Union victorious and is looking for ways and means to attain this end. If, as they think, the establishment of a second front in the West is at present impossible, perhaps another method could be found to render to the Soviet Union an active military help?

It seems to me that Great Britain could without risk land in Archangel twenty-five to thirty divisions, or transport them across Iran to the southern regions of the U.S.S.R. In this way there could be established military collaboration between the Soviet and British troops on the territory of the U.S.S.R. A similar situation existed during the last war in France. The arrangement mentioned would constitute a great help. It would be a serious blow against the Hitler aggression.

It is almost incredible that the head of the Russian Government with all the advice of their military experts could have committed himself to such absurdities. It seemed hopeless to argue with a man thinking in terms of utter unreality. He continued:

I thank you very much for your promise to render us assistance by the monthly deliveries of aluminium, tanks, and aircraft.

I can only welcome the intention of the British Government to render this assistance in aluminium, tanks, and aircraft not on the usual commercial basis [but] of comradeship and collaboration. I hope the British Government will have ample opportunity of being convinced that the Soviet Government understands how to appreciate the help received from its ally.

One remark in connection with the memorandum delivered on September 12 to M. Molotov by the British Ambassador in Moscow, Sir Stafford Cripps. In this memorandum it is said: "If the Soviet Government were compelled to destroy its naval vessels at Leningrad in order to prevent their falling into the enemy hands, His Majesty's Government would recognise after the war claims of the Soviet Government to a certain compensation from His Majesty's Government for the restoration of the vessels destroyed."

The Soviet Government understands and appreciates the readiness of the British Government to make partial compensation for the damage sustained by the Soviet Union in case the Soviet vessels at Leningrad should actually be destroyed. There could be no doubt that such a course will be adopted should the necessity arise. However, the responsibility for this damage would not be Britain's, but Germany's. I think therefore that the damage after the war should be made good at the expense of Germany.

I sent the best answer I could to this message.

Prime Minister to Monsieur Stalin   17 Sept. 41

Many thanks for your message. The Harriman Mission has all arrived, and is working all day long with Beaverbrook and his colleagues. The object is to survey the whole field of resources so as to be able to work out with you a definite programme of monthly delivery by every possible route, and thus help repair as far as possible losses of your munitions industries. President Roosevelt's idea is that this plan should cover up till the end of June, but naturally we shall go on with you till victory. I hope the conference may open in Moscow on the 25th of this month, but no publicity should be given till all are safely gathered. The routes and method of travel will be signalled later.

2. I attach great importance to opening the through route from Persian Gulf to Caspian, not only by railway, but by a great motor road, and in the making of which we hope to enlist American energies and organisation. Lord Beaverbrook will be able to explain the whole scheme of supply and transportation; he is on the closest terms of friendship with Harriman.

3. All possible theatres in which we might effect military co-operation with you have been examined by the Staffs. The two flanks, north and south, certainly present the most favourable opportunities. If we could act successfully in Norway the attitude of Sweden would be powerfully affected, but at the moment we have neither the forces nor the shipping available for this project. Again, in the south the great prize is Turkey; if Turkey can be gained, another powerful army will be available. Turkey would like to come with us, but is afraid, not without reason. It may be that the promise of considerable British forces and supplies of technical material in which the Turks are deficient will exercise a decisive influence upon them. We will study with you any other form of useful aid, the sole object being to bring the maximum force against the common enemy.

4. I entirely agree that the first source from which the Russian Fleet should be replenished should be at the expense of Germany. Victory will certainly give us control of important German and Italian naval vessels, and in our view these would be most suitable for repairing losses to the Russian Fleet.

*   *   *

On October 25 I replied to the Ambassador about the fantastic proposals of twenty-five to thirty British divisions being landed at Archangel or Basra.

Prime Minister to Sir Stafford Cripps (Moscow)   25 Oct. 41

You were of course right to say that the idea of sending "twenty-five to thirty divisions to fight on the Russian front" is a physical absurdity. It took eight months to build up ten divisions in France, across the Channel, when shipping was plentiful and U-boats few. It is with the greatest difficulty that we have managed to send the 50th Division to the Middle East in the last six months. We are now sending the 18th Division by extraordinary measures. All our shipping is fully engaged, and any saving can only be made at the expense of our vital upkeep convoys to the Middle East or of ships engaged in carrying Russian supplies. The margin by which we live and make munitions of war has only narrowly been maintained. Any troops sent to Murmansk now would be frozen in darkness for the winter.

2. Position on the southern flank is as follows: Russians have

five divisions in Persia, which we are willing to relieve. Surely these divisions should defend their own country before we choke one of the only supply lines with the maintenance of our forces to the northward. To put two fully armed British divisions from here into the Caucasus or north of the Caspian would take at least three months. They would then only be a drop in the bucket.

*   *   *

Meanwhile the Beaverbrook-Harriman talks in London were completed, and on September 22 the Anglo-American Supply Mission set off in the cruiser *London* from Scapa Flow through the Arctic Sea to Archangel, and thence by air to Moscow. Much depended upon them. I furnished Lord Beaverbrook with general instructions, which were approved by my War Cabinet colleagues on the Defence Committee. This document, which is of importance, will be found among the Appendices.[3] In addition I gave Lord Beaverbrook the following letter to deliver personally to Stalin:

21 Sept. 1941

My dear Premier Stalin,

The British and American Missions have now started, and this letter will be presented to you by Lord Beaverbrook. Lord Beaverbrook has the fullest confidence of the Cabinet, and is one of my oldest and most intimate friends. He has established the closest relations with Mr. Harriman, who is a remarkable American, wholeheartedly devoted to the victory of the common cause. They will lay before you all that we have been able to arrange in much anxious consultation between Great Britain and the United States.

President Roosevelt has decided that our proposals shall, in the first instance, deal with the monthly quotas we shall send to you in the nine-months period from October, 1941, to June, 1942, inclusive. You have the right to know exactly what we can deliver month by month, in order that you may handle your reserves to the best advantage.

The American proposals have not yet gone beyond the end of June, 1942, but I have no doubt that considerably larger quotas can be furnished by both countries thereafter, and you may be sure we shall do our utmost to repair as far as possible the grievous curtailments which your war industries have suffered through the Nazi invasion. I will not anticipate what Lord Beaverbrook will have to say upon this subject.

You will realise that the quotas up to the end of June, 1942, are supplied almost entirely out of British production, or production which the United States would have given us under our own purchases or under the Lend-Lease Bill. The United States were resolved to give us virtually the whole of their exportable surplus,

[3] Appendix D, Book Two.

and it is not easy for them within that time to open out effectively new sources of supply. I am hopeful that a further great impulse will be given to the production of the United States, and that by 1943 the mighty industry of America will be in full war swing. For our part, we shall not only make substantially increased contributions from our own existing forecast production, but also try to obtain from our people an extra further effort to meet our common needs. You will understand however that our Army and its supply which has been planned is perhaps only one-fifth or one-sixth as large as yours or Germany's. Our first duty and need is to keep open the seas, and our second duty is to obtain decisive superiority in the air. These have the first claims upon the manpower of our forty-four million in the British Islands. We can never hope to have an army or army munitions industries comparable to those of the great Continental military Powers. None the less, we will do our utmost to aid you.

General Ismay, who is my personal representative on the Chiefs of Staff Committee, and is thoroughly acquainted with the whole field of our military policy, is authorised to study with your commanders any plans for practical co-operation which may suggest themselves.

If we can clear our western flank in Libya of the enemy we shall have considerable forces, both air and army, to co-operate upon the southern flank of the Russian front.

It seems to me that the most speedy and effective help would come if Turkey could be induced to resist a German demand for the passage of troops, or, better still, if she would enter the war on our side. You will, I am sure, attach due weight to this.

I have always shared your sympathy for the Chinese people in their struggle to defend their native land against Japanese aggression. Naturally we do not want to add Japan to the side of our foes, but the attitude of the United States, resulting from my conference with President Roosevelt, has already enforced a far more sober view upon the Japanese Government. I made haste to declare on behalf of His Majesty's Government that should the United States be involved in war with Japan Great Britain would immediately range herself on her side. I think that all our three countries should, as far as possible, continue to give aid to China, and that this may go to considerable lengths without provoking a Japanese declaration of war.

There is no doubt that a long period of struggle and suffering lies before our peoples, but I have great hopes that the United States will enter the war as a belligerent, and if so I cannot doubt that we have but to endure to conquer.

I am hopeful that as the war continues the great masses of the peoples of the British Empire, the Soviet Union, the United States, and China, which alone comprise two-thirds of the entire human race, may be found marching together against their persecutors; and I am sure the road they travel will lead to victory.

With heartfelt wishes for the success of the Russian armies and the ruin of the Nazi tyrants,

      Believe me,

              Yours sincerely,

                    WINSTON S. CHURCHILL

*   *   *

On September 28 our Mission arrived in Moscow. Their reception was bleak and discussions not at all friendly. It might almost have been thought that the plight in which the Soviets now found themselves was our fault. The Soviet generals and officials gave no information of any kind to their British and American colleagues. They did not even inform them of the basis on which Russian needs of our precious war materials had been estimated. The Mission was given no formal entertainment until almost the last night, when they were invited to dinner at the Kremlin. It must not be thought that such an occasion among men preoccupied with the gravest affairs may not be helpful to the progress of business. On the contrary, many of the private interchanges which occur bring about that atmosphere where agreements can be reached. But there was little of this mood now, and it might almost have been we who had come to ask for favours.

One incident preserved by General Ismay in an apocryphal and somewhat lively form may be allowed to lighten the narrative. His orderly, a Royal Marine, was shown the sights of Moscow by one of the Intourist guides. "This," said the Russian, "is the Eden Hotel, formerly Ribbentrop Hotel. Here is Churchill Street, formerly Hitler Street. Here is the Beaverbrook railway station, formerly Goering railway station. Will you have a cigarette, comrade?" The Marine replied, "Thank you, comrade, formerly bastard!" This tale, though jocular, illustrates none the less the strange atmosphere of these meetings.

*   *   *

In contrast with all this my American contacts were increasingly cordial.

Former Naval Person to President Roosevelt   22 Sept. 41
Your cheering cable [to Mr. Harriman] about tanks arrived when we were feeling very blue about all we have to give up to Russia. The prospect of nearly doubling the previous figures encouraged everyone. The Missions have started in great good-will and friendship.

    Kindest regards.

Prime Minister to Mr. Harry Hopkins   25 Sept. 41

Now that our Missions are on their way to Moscow, it may be profitable to survey the field covered by the discussions in London.

2. The offers which we both are making to Russia are necessary and worth while. There is no disguising the fact however that they make grievous inroads into what is required by you for expanding your forces and by us for intensifying our war effort. You know where the shoe will pinch most in the next nine months.

We must both bend our efforts to making good the gaps unavoidably created. We here are unlikely to be able to expand our programmes much above what is already planned. I earnestly hope that you will be able to raise the general level of yours by an immediate short-term effort.

3. You will have heard that good progress was made in the discussions on over-all requirements for victory. A joint memorandum giving estimated eventual requirements, as far as we can foresee them, was drawn up, and is being taken back to Washington by General Embick. Further work on this will have to be done in Washington, and an estimate of what is required to maintain Russian resistance will have to be added. Would it be possible to try to reach in the second half of 1942 the output now planned for the first half of 1943? If such an attempt were successful it would not only lay the foundations for the victory programme, but would help to meet more speedily than otherwise the short-term requirements of us both. It would also enable greater help to be given to the Russians in the second half of 1942.

On October 2 I heard from the President about American plans for future tank and aircraft production. From July, 1942, to January, 1943, the United States would allocate twelve hundred tanks a month to England and Russia together, and during the next six months two thousand a month. The American Mission in Moscow had been told to promise the Russians four hundred tanks a month as from July 1, and an increased number after that date after discussion with our representatives.

The United States would be able to fulfil this increased commitment as her tank production was being doubled, to reach a figure of over twenty-five hundred tanks a month.

The President also informed me that he had undertaken to supply Russia with thirty-six hundred front-line aircraft between July 1, 1942, and July 1, 1943, over and above those already agreed upon.

*   *   *

In the end a friendly agreement was reached in Moscow. A protocol was signed setting out the supplies which Great Britain and the United States could make available to Russia

within the period October, 1941, to June, 1942. This involved
much derangement of our military plans, already hampered by
the tormenting shortage of munitions. All fell upon us, because
we not only gave our own production, but had to forgo most
important munitions which the Americans would otherwise
have sent to us. Neither the Americans nor ourselves made any
promise about the transportation of these supplies across the
difficult and perilous ocean and Arctic routes. In view of the
insulting reproaches which Stalin uttered when we suggested
that the convoys should not sail till the ice had receded, it
should be noted that all we guaranteed was that the supplies
would "be made available at British and United States centres
of production." The preamble of the protocol ended with the
words, "Great Britain and the United States will give aid to the
transportation of these materials to the Soviet Union, and will
help with the delivery."

On October 4 Lord Beaverbrook telegraphed to me:

Lord Beaverbrook (at Moscow) to Prime Minister   4 Oct. 41

The effect of this agreement has been an immense strengthening
of the morale of Moscow. The maintenance of this morale will
depend on delivery. . . .

I do not regard the military situation here as safe for the winter
months. I do think that morale might make it safe.

We gave our treasures, and they were accepted by those
who were fighting for their lives.

Prime Minister to Lord Beaverbrook (at Moscow)   3 Oct. 41

Heartiest congratulations to you and all. The unity and success
proclaimed is of immense value. No one could have done it but
you. Now come home and make the (one group undecipherable)
stuff. Impossible to restrain the feeling of optimism here.

Prime Minister to Lord Beaverbrook (at sea)   6 Oct. 41

We have not lost an hour in making good your undertakings.
I have sent the following telegram to Stalin:

Prime Minister to Premier Stalin   6 Oct. 41

I am glad to learn from Lord Beaverbrook of the success of
the Tripartite Conference at Moscow. *Bis dat qui cito dat.* We
intend to run a continuous cycle of convoys, leaving every ten
days. Following are on the way and arrive Archangel October 12:
20 heavy tanks; 193 fighters (pre-October quota).

Following will sail October 12, arriving October 29: 140 heavy
tanks; 100 Hurricanes; 200 Bren carriers; 200 anti-tank rifles and
ammunition; 50 2-pounder guns and ammunition.

Following will sail October 22: 200 fighters; 120 heavy tanks.
Above shows the total of the October quota of aircraft, and 280
tanks will arrive Russia by November 6. The October quota of
Bren carriers, anti-tank rifles, and 2-pounder anti-tank guns will
all arrive in October. Twenty tanks have been shipped to go via
Persia, and fifteen are about to be shipped from Canada via Vladivostok. The total tanks shipped will therefore be 315, which is 19
short of our full quota. This number will be made up in November. The above programme does not take into account supplies
from United States.

2. In arranging this regular cycle of convoys we are counting
on Archangel to handle the main bulk of deliveries. I presume this
part of the job is in hand. Good wishes.

Although General Ismay was fully empowered and qualified
to discuss and explain the military situation in all its variants
to the Soviet leaders, Beaverbrook and Harriman decided not
to complicate their task by issues on which there could be no
agreement. This aspect was not therefore dealt with in Moscow. Informally the Russians continued to demand the immediate establishment of the Second Front, and seemed quite
impervious to any arguments showing its impossibility. Their
agony is their excuse. Our Ambassador had to bear the brunt.

It was already late autumn. On October 2 the Central Army
Group of von Bock renewed its advance on Moscow, with its
two armies moving direct on the capital from the southwest
and a Panzer group swinging wide on either flank. Orel on
October 8 and a week later Kalinin on the Moscow-Leningrad
road were taken. With his flanks thus endangered and under
strong pressure from the central German advance, Marshal
Timoshenko withdrew his forces to a line forty miles west of
Moscow, where he again stood to fight. The Russian position
at this moment was grave in the extreme. The Soviet Government, the Diplomatic Corps, and all industry that could be
removed were evacuated from the city over five hundred miles
farther east to Kuibyshev. On October 19 Stalin proclaimed a
state of siege in the capital and issued an Order of the Day,
"Moscow will be defended to the last." His commands were
faithfully obeyed. Although Guderian's armoured group from
Orel advanced as far as Tula, although Moscow was now three
parts surrounded and there was some air bombardment, the
end of October brought a marked stiffening in Russian resistance and a definite check to the German advance.

*   *   *

I continued to sustain our Ambassador in his many trials and hardships and his lonely, uphill task.

Prime Minister to Sir Stafford Cripps (Kuibyshev)   28 Oct. 41

I fully sympathise with you in your difficult position, and also with Russia in her agony. They certainly have no right to reproach us. They brought their own fate upon themselves when, by their pact with Ribbentrop, they let Hitler loose on Poland and so started the war. They cut themselves off from an effective second front when they let the French Army be destroyed. If prior to June 22 they had consulted with us beforehand, many arrangements could have been made to bring earlier the great help we are now sending them in munitions. We did not however know till Hitler attacked them whether they would fight, or what side they would be on. We were left alone for a whole year while every Communist in England, under orders from Moscow, did his best to hamper our war effort. If we had been invaded and destroyed in July or August, 1941, or starved out this year in the Battle of the Atlantic, they would have remained utterly indifferent. If they had moved when the Balkans were attacked, much might have been done, but they left it all to Hitler to choose his moment and his foes. That a Government with this record should accuse us of trying to make conquests in Africa or gain advantages in Persia at their expense or being willing to "fight to the last Russian soldier" leaves me quite cold. If they harbour suspicions of us, it is only because of the guilt and self-reproach in their own hearts.

2. We have acted with absolute honesty. We have done our very best to help them at the cost of deranging all our plans for rearmament and exposing ourselves to heavy risks when the spring invasion season comes. We will do anything more in our power that is sensible, but it would be silly to send two or three British or British-Indian divisions into the heart of Russia to be surrounded and cut to pieces as a symbolic sacrifice. Russia has never been short of man-power, and has now millions of trained soldiers for whom modern equipment is required. That modern equipment we are sending, and shall send to the utmost limit of the ports and communications.

3. Meanwhile we shall presently be fighting ourselves as the result of long-prepared plans, which it would be madness to upset. We have offered to relieve the five Russian divisions in Northern Persia which can be done with Indian troops fitted to maintain internal order but not equipped to face Germans. I am sorry that Molotov rejects the idea of our sending modest forces to the Caucasus. We are doing all we can to keep Turkey a friendly neutral and prevent her being tempted by German promises of territorial gain at Russia's expense. Naturally we do not expect gratitude from men undergoing such frightful bludgeonings and fighting so bravely, but neither need we be disturbed by their

400   WAR COMES TO AMERICA

reproaches. There is of course no need for you to rub all these
salt truths into the Russian wounds, but I count upon you to do
your utmost to convince Russians of the loyalty, integrity, and
courage of the British nation.

4. I do not think it would be any use for you and Macfarlane
[head of our military mission to Russia] to fly home now. I could
only repeat what I have said here, and I hope I shall never be
called upon to argue the case in public. I am sure your duty is to
remain with these people in their ordeal, from which it is by no
means certain that they will not emerge victorious. Any day now
Hitler may call a halt in the East and turn his forces against us.

Here we may for the present leave the unfolding of the
Hitler-Stalin drama. Winter now casts its shield before the
Russian armies.

*   *   *

My wife felt very deeply that our inability to give Russia
any military help disturbed and distressed the nation increasingly as the months went by and the German armies surged
across the steppes. I told her that a Second Front was out of
the question and that all that could be done for a long time
would be the sending of supplies of all kinds on a large scale.
Mr. Eden and I encouraged her to explore the possibility of
obtaining funds by voluntary subscription for medical aid. This
had already been begun by the British Red Cross and St.
John's, and my wife was invited by the joint organisation to
head the Appeal for "Aid to Russia." At the end of October,
under their auspices, she issued her first appeal:

There is no one in this country whose heart has not been deeply
stirred by the appalling drama now going on in Russia. We are
amazed at the power of the Russian defence and at the skill with
which it is conducted. We have been moved to profound admiration for the valour, the tenacity, and the patriotic self-sacrifice of
the Russian people. And above all, perhaps, we have been shaken
with horror and pity at the vast scale of human suffering.

.   .   .

Among the supplies we have already sent to Russia are 53
emergency operating outfits, 30 blood-transfusion sets, 70,000 surgical needles of various kinds, and 1,000,000 tablets of M. and B.
693. This drug is the wonderful new antiseptic which has revolutionised the treatment of many diseases caused by germs. In addition to these, we have sent half a ton of phenacetin and about
seven tons of absorbent cotton-wool. And this is of course only a
beginning.

.   .   .

We have declared our aim to be £1,000,000, and we have made a good start. Already the fund totals £370,000, and it is only twelve days old. Our gracious and beloved King and Queen, in sending a further £3000 to the Red Cross last week, expressed a wish that £1000 of their joint gift should be allocated to the Aid to Russia Fund. They have set a characteristic example.

Much depends upon employers, and I would like to say this: wherever the employer provides the facilities to get the fund started, the workers come gladly with their weekly pennies. Thus, from the King and Queen to the humblest wage-earner and cottage-dweller, we can all take part in this message of good-will and compassion. Between the cottage and the palace, between those who can spare only pennies and a great imaginative benefactor like Lord Nuffield—who can send a cheque for £50,000—there are millions of people who would like to share in this tribute to the Russian people.

A generous response was at once forthcoming. For the next four years she devoted herself to this task with enthusiasm and responsibility. In all nearly eight million pounds were collected by the contributions of rich and poor alike. Many wealthy people made munificent donations, but the bulk of the money came from the weekly subscriptions of the mass of the nation. Thus through the powerful organisation of the Red Cross and St. John's and in spite of heavy losses in the Arctic convoys, medical and surgical supplies and all kinds of comforts and special appliances found their way in unbroken flow through the icy and deadly seas to the valiant Russian armies and people.

6

Persia and the Middle East

Summer and Autumn, 1941

*Anglo-Soviet Requirements from Persia—Need for Joint Action—
General Wavell's Strong View—Mr. Eden's Minute of July 22
—My Caution and Inquiries—Report of the Lord President's
Committee—Decision to Act with Russia—Opposing Forces—
The Fighting Begins—The Shah Submits—Conditions Imposed
on the Persian Government—Abdication of the Shah and Accession of His Young Son—Anglo-Soviet Accords—Development of
the New Supply Route to Russia—Convoys to Malta—The German View of Mediterranean Fighting—Need for Surface Forces
at Malta—Birth of "Force K"—Design for a Mobile Reserve—I
Appeal to President Roosevelt—American Transports for Two
British Divisions—The President's Prompt Response—His Aid in
the Atlantic—Growing Strength of the Army of the Nile—Anxieties of the Chiefs of Staff—My Note of September 18—Priority
for the Desert Battle—My Telegram to General Smuts of September 20—My Note on Battle Tactics—Restoration of Artillery
—Guns versus Tanks—"Flak" Protection for Ground Troops—
Relations of Army and Air Commanders in Battle.*

THE NEED to pass munitions and supplies of all kinds to
the Soviet Government and the extreme difficulties of the
Arctic route, together with future strategic possibilities, made
it eminently desirable to open the fullest communication with
Russia through Persia. The Persian oilfields were a prime war
factor. An active and numerous German mission had installed
itself in Teheran, and German prestige stood high. The suppression of the revolt in Iraq and the Anglo-French occupation
of Syria, achieved as they were by narrow margins, blotted out

Hitler's Oriental plan. We welcomed the opportunity of joining hands with the Russians and proposed to them a joint campaign. I was not without some anxiety about embarking on a Persian war, but the arguments for it were compulsive. I was very glad that General Wavell should be in India to direct the military movements.

On July 11, 1941, the Chiefs of Staff were asked by a Cabinet Committee to consider the desirability of joint military action in conjunction with the Russians in Persia in the event of the Persian Government refusing to expel the German community at present employed in that country. On July 18 they recommended that we should adopt a firm attitude in dealing with the Persian Government. This view was also strongly held by General Wavell, who had telegraphed the War Office July 10 in the following terms:

General Wavell to War Office   10 July 41

The complaisant attitude it is proposed to adopt over Iran appears to me incomprehensible. It is essential to the defence of India that Germans should be cleared out of Iran now. Failure to do so will lead to a repetition of events which in Iraq were only just countered in time. It is essential we should join hands with Russia through Iran, and if the present Government is not willing to facilitate this it must be made to give way to one which will. To this end the strongest possible pressure should be applied forthwith while issue of German-Russian struggle is in doubt. . . .

On the 21st I replied to General Wavell:

Prime Minister to General Wavell   21 July 41

Cabinet will consider Persian situation tomorrow. I am in general agreement with your view, and would like to give Persians an ultimatum from Britain and Russia to clear out the Germans without delay or take the consequences. Question is what forces we have available in case of refusal.

The Chiefs of Staff advised that action should be confined to the South, and that we should need at least one division, supported by a small air component, to secure the oilfields. This force would have to come from Iraq, where we had already insufficient troops even for internal security. They concluded that if a force had to be sent into Persia during the next three months it would have to be replaced from the Middle East.

In a minute of July 22 the Foreign Secretary sent me his view of the situation:

Foreign Secretary to Prime Minister   22 July 41

I have been giving further consideration this morning to the problem of pressure upon Iran [Persia]. The more I examine the possibilities of doing this, the clearer it becomes that all depends upon our ability to concentrate a sufficient force in Iraq to protect the Iranian oilfields. It would be highly dangerous even to begin economic pressure until we were militarily in a position to do this, for the Shah is fully conscious of the value of the oilfields to us, and if he sees trouble with us brewing he is likely to take the first step.

Reports, apparently reliable, have reached us of Iranian concentrations on the Russian frontier, on the Iraqi frontier, and in the area of the oilfields. I hope that every effort will be made to strengthen our forces in Iraq at the earliest moment. If we can do this before the Russians suffer a severe reverse in the south there is a reasonable chance of imposing our will on the Iranians without resort to force. But we must not move diplomatically ahead of our military strength or we shall court disaster.

There is a further factor which increases the need for the early reinforcement of Iraq. Should Russia be defeated we shall have to be ready to occupy the Iranian oilfields ourselves; for in such an eventuality German pressure on the Iranians to attempt to turn us out would be irresistible.

*   *   *

I was not satisfied that this Persian operation had received the co-ordinated planning essential to its eventual success. On July 31 therefore on the eve of my voyage to Placentia I gave instructions that a special committee should be set up under the Lord President for this purpose.

I cannot feel that this operation, involving war with Persia in the event of non-compliance, has been studied with the attention which its far-reaching character requires. While agreeing to its necessity, I consider that the whole business requires exploring, concerting, and clamping together, as between the Foreign Office and the War Office, and between the Middle East Command and the Government of India. We must not take such grave steps without having clear-cut plans for the various eventualities. For instance, what happens if the Persian troops around and about the Ahwaz oilfields seize all Anglo-Persian Oil Company employees and hold them as hostages? What attitude is expected from the Bahktiari and the local inhabitants? What happens to British residents in Teheran? Is there any danger of the oilwells being destroyed rather than that they should fall into our possession? We must be very careful not to commit an atrocity by bombing Teheran. Are our available forces strong enough to occupy the Ahwaz oilfields in the face of local and official Persian opposition?

How far north do we propose to go? What aerodromes are available? How is the railway to be worked if the Persians refuse to help?

These and many other questions require to be thought out. It would be well if the Lord President with the Secretaries of State for Foreign Affairs, War, and India reviewed the whole matter and reported to the War Cabinet during the early part of next week. Meanwhile all necessary action of a preparatory character should proceed. I am in favour of the policy, but it is of a very serious character, and should not be undertaken until the possible consequences and alternative situations have been thoroughly surveyed and careful, detailed plans made and approved.

I was sure that the similarity of the names, Iran and Iraq, would lead to confusion.

Prime Minister to Foreign Secretary, Sir Edward   2 Aug. 41
Bridges and General Ismay

In all correspondence, it would be more convenient to use the word "Persia" instead of "Iran," as otherwise dangerous mistakes may easily occur through the similarity of Iran and Iraq. In any cases where convenient, the word "Iran" may follow in brackets after Persia.

Formal correspondence with the Persian Government should of course be conducted in the form they like.

And later:

Prime Minister to Minister of Information   29 Aug. 41

Do try to blend in without causing trouble the word Persia instead of Iran.

I am indeed glad to learn that the Persian Government have now (1949) adopted officially this change.

During my absence at sea this Committee reported to me by telegram the results of their work, which had meanwhile been approved by the War Cabinet. It was clear from their message of August 6 that the Persians would not meet our wishes regarding the expulsion of German agents and residents from their country, and that we should have to resort to force. The next stage was to co-ordinate our plans, diplomatic and military, with those of the Russians. On August 13 Mr. Eden received Mr. Maisky at the Foreign Office, and the terms of our respective Notes to Teheran were agreed. This diplomatic move was to be our final word. Mr. Maisky told the Foreign Secretary that "after the presentation of the memoranda the Soviet Government would be ready to take military action, but they would not take such action except in conjunction with us." On receiving this news I minuted (August 19), "I think the Russian view is reasonable, and we ought to move with them while there is time."

We were now committed to action. In the event of stronger Persian resistance than had been anticipated, we had to consider the possibility of further reinforcement of the Middle East area. On August 24, on the eve of our planned advance into Persia, I sent the following minute to the Chiefs of Staff:

Prime Minister to Chiefs of Staff   24 Aug. 41

It is essential that more reinforcements should be set in motion eastwards at once. Is it true that the 10th Indian Division has not got a British battalion to each brigade? If so, three battalions of British troops should be sent to join General Quinan by the fastest possible route. As General Auchinleck proposes to remain inactive in the Western Desert for many weeks, he should be directed to move larger forces eastwards than are at present arranged. At least the equivalent of one extra division, including the three British battalions aforesaid, should be set in motion now. If all goes well they can easily be countermanded. Let me know what forces are likely to be available in Egypt. Where is the last brigade of the 50th Division? Surely Cyprus is in no immediate danger.

In view of the recalcitrance of the Persian Government, General Quinan, who was commanding in Iraq, had been ordered on July 22 to be ready to occupy the oil refinery at Abadan and the oilfields, together with those two hundred and fifty miles farther north near Khanaqin. The joint Anglo-Soviet Note of August 17 met with an unsatisfactory reply, and the date for the entry of British and Russian forces into Persia was fixed for the 25th. The Imperial forces in the Abadan sector, under General Harvey, comprised the 8th Indian Infantry Division; in the Khanaqin sector, under General Slim, the 9th Armoured Brigade, one Indian regiment of tanks, four British battalions, and one regiment of British artillery. The supporting air forces consisted of one Army Co-operation, one fighter, and one bomber squadron. The first objective was the capture of the oilfields; the second, to advance into Persia and, with Russian co-operation, to control Persian communications, and secure a through route to the Caspian. Opposition on the southern front could be expected from two Persian divisions, with sixteen light tanks, and in the north from three divisions.

The capture of the Abadan refinery was made by an infantry brigade, which embarked in naval craft at Basra and landed at dawn on August 25. The majority of the Persian forces were surprised but escaped in lorries. Some street fighting took place and a few Persian naval craft were captured. At the same time other troops of the 8th Division captured the port of Khurramshahr from the landward side, and a force was sent north toward Ahwaz. As our troops were approaching Ahwaz news of the Shah's "Cease fire" order was received, and the Persian general ordered his troops back to barracks. In the north the oilfields were easily captured, and General Slim's force pushed thirty miles along the road toward Kermanshah. They were now faced however with the formidable Pai-tak Pass, which if held by determined troops would have been a definite obstacle. To deal with this a column was sent to turn the position from the south. After overcoming some opposition these troops reached Shahabad, behind the Persian defence, on August 27. This movement, combined with some bombing, proved too much for the defenders of the pass, who abandoned their positions hastily. The advance on Kermanshah was resumed, and on the 28th the enemy were found again to be drawn up on a position across the road. But just as the attack was about to be launched, a Persian officer arrived with a white flag and the campaign was over. Our casualties were twenty-two killed and forty-two wounded.

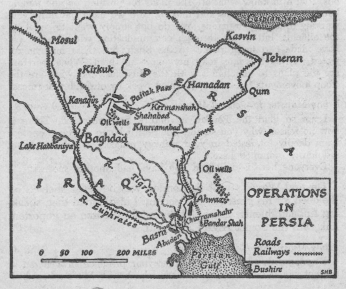

OPERATIONS IN PERSIA

Roads ———
Railways ∾∾∾∾∾

Thus ended this brief and fruitful exercise of overwhelming force against a weak and ancient state. Britain and Russia were fighting for their lives. *Inter arma silent leges.* We may be glad that in our victory the independence of Persia has been preserved.

*   *   *

Persian resistance had collapsed so swiftly that our contacts with the Kremlin became again almost entirely political. Our main object in proposing the joint Anglo-Russian campaign in Persia had been to open up the communications from the Persian Gulf to the Caspian Sea. We hoped also, by this direct co-operation of British and Soviet forces, to establish more intimate and friendly relations with our new ally. We were of course both agreed on the expulsion from Persia or capture of all Germans and the wiping-out of German influence and intrigues in Teheran and elsewhere. The deep and delicate questions about oil, Communism, and the post-war future of Persia lay in the background, but need not, it seemed to me, impede comradeship and good-will.

Prime Minister to General Ismay,   27 Aug. 41
for C.O.S. Committee

Now that it seems that the Persian opposition is not very serious, I wish to know what are the plans for pushing on and joining hands with the Russians and making sure we have the railway in working order in our hands. We do not simply want to squat on the oilfields, but to get through communication with Russia. We have made certain proposals to the Shah, but these may be rejected, or the Russians may not agree to them. What therefore are the plans to join hands with the Russians, and what are the troop movements foreseen in the next week by our different forces?

Prime Minister to General Wavell   30 Aug. 41

I am so glad the Persian adventure has prospered. There is now no reason why you should not return home as you proposed. I am deeply interested in your railway projects, which are being sedulously examined here.

Everyone here is delighted you have had another success.

General Wavell's visit to London was however shelved by the need for his presence in Teheran. I also hoped that, speaking Russian fluently as he did, he might became an important link with the Soviet High Command.

Prime Minister to General Wavell   1 Sept. 41

I agree with Chiefs of Staff that your presence in Teheran at present would be helpful to Bullard [the British Minister] in dealing with military requirements and for ensuring that Russian influence is kept within reasonable bounds.

Prime Minister to Sir R. Bullard (Teheran)   3 Sept. 41

We cannot tell how the war in these regions will develop, but the best possible through route from the Persian Gulf to the Caspian will be developed at the utmost speed and at all costs in order to supply Russia. It is very likely that large British forces will be operating in and from Persia in 1942, and certainly a powerful air force will be installed.

We hope it will not be necessary, in the present phase at any rate, to have an Anglo-Russian occupation of Teheran, but the Persian Government will have to give us loyal and faithful help and show all proper alacrity if they wish to avoid it. At the present time we have not turned against the Shah, but unless good results are forthcoming his misgovernment of his people will be brought into the account. Although we should like to get what we want by agreement with the Persian Government and do not wish to drive them into active hostility, our requirements must somehow be met, and it ought to be possible for you to obtain all the facilities we require, bit by bit, by using the leverage of a possible Russian occupation of Teheran. There is no need to fear undue Russian encroachments, as their one supreme wish will be to get the through route for American supplies.

Prime Minister to Premier Stalin   16 Sept. 41

I am most anxious to settle our alliance with Persia and to make an intimate efficient working arrangement with your forces in Persia. There are in Persia signs of serious disorder among tribesmen and of breakdown of Persian authority. Disorder, if it spreads, will mean wasting our divisions holding down these people, which again means burdening the road and railway communications with movements and supplies of aforesaid divisions, whereas we want to keep the lines clear and improved to the utmost in order to get supplies through to you. Our object should be to make the Persians keep each other quiet while we get on with the war. Your Excellency's decisive indications in this direction will speed forward the already favourable trend of our affairs in this minor theatre.

*   *   *

Prime Minister to Lord Beaverbrook   21 Sept. 41
(on Mission to Russia)

General Wavell proposes to go to Tiflis via Baghdad on his return to India. He speaks Russian, and I contemplate his directing, or possibly, if the forces grow large enough, commanding, the right hand we shall give to the Russians in and about the Caspian Basin in the forthcoming campaign. It is therefore important that he should confer with high Russian military authorities on the whole position of their southern flank and in Persia.

You may bring this into your discussions, and see that the most is made of it.

Prime Minister to Premier Stalin   12 Oct. 41

Our only interests in Persia are, first, as a barrier against German penetration eastward, and, secondly, as a through route for supplies to the Caspian Basin. If you wish to withdraw the five or six Russian divisions for use on the battle-front we will take over the whole responsibility of keeping order and maintaining and improving the supply route. I pledge the faith of Britain that we will not seek any advantage for ourselves at the expense of any rightful Russian interest during the war or at the end. In any case, the signing of the Tripartite Treaty is urgent to avoid internal disorders growing, with consequent danger of choking the supply route. General Wavell will be at Tiflis on October 18, and will discuss with your generals any questions which you may instruct them to settle with him.

Words are useless to express what we feel about your vast heroic struggle. We hope presently to testify by action.

*   *   *

All arrangements with the Russians were smoothly and swiftly agreed. The conditions imposed on the Persian Government were, principally, the cessation of all resistance, the ejection of Germans, neutrality in the war, and the Allied use of Persian communications for the transit of war supplies to Russia. The further occupation of Persia was peacefully accomplished. British and Russian forces met in amity, and Teheran was jointly occupied on September 17, the Shah having abdicated on the previous day in favour of his gifted twenty-two-year-old son. On September 20 the new Shah, under Allied advice, restored the Constitutional Monarchy, and his father shortly afterwards went into comfortable exile and died at Johannesburg in July, 1944. Most of our forces withdrew from the country, leaving only detachments to guard the communications, and Teheran was evacuated by both British and Russian troops on October 18. Thereafter our forces, under General Quinan, were engaged in preparing defences against the possible incursion of German armies from Turkey or the Caucasus, and in making administrative preparations for the large reinforcements which would arrive if that incursion seemed imminent.

The creation of a major supply route to Russia through the Persian Gulf became our prime objective. With a friendly Government in Teheran, ports were enlarged, river communications developed, roads built, and railways reconstructed.

Starting in September, 1941, this enterprise, begun and developed by the British Army, and presently to be adopted and completed by the United States, enabled us to send to Russia, over a period of four and a half years, five million tons of supplies.

*　　*　　*

We can now return to the dominant theatre of the Mediterranean.

Both sides used the summer to reinforce the armies in the Libyan Desert. For us the replenishment of Malta was vital. The loss of Crete deprived Admiral Cunningham's fleet of a fuelling base near enough to bring our protecting sea power into action. The possibilities of a seaborne assault on Malta from Italy or Sicily grew, though, as we now know, it was not until 1942 that Hitler and Mussolini approved such a plan. Enemy air bases both in Crete and Cyrenaica menaced the convoy route from Alexandria to Malta so seriously that we had to depend entirely on the West for the passage of supplies. In this task Admiral Somerville, with Force H from Gibraltar, rendered distinguished service. The route the Admiralty had judged the more dangerous became the only one open. Fortunately at this time the demands of his Russian invasion compelled Hitler to withdraw his air force from Sicily, which gave a respite to Malta and restored to us the mastery in the air over the Malta Channel. This not only helped the approach of convoys from the West, but enabled us to strike harder at the transports and supply ships reinforcing Rommel.

Two considerable convoys were fought through successfully. The passage of each was a heavy naval operation. In July a convoy of six supply ships reached Malta, and seven empty vessels were brought out. Two nights later the Italians delivered their only heavy attack upon Valetta Harbour, with about twenty E-boats and eight midget submarines. The harbour defences, manned largely by Maltese, destroyed almost the whole attacking force in spite of its daring. In September another convoy of nine transports came through, with the loss of only one, under a very strong escort, comprising the battleships *Prince of Wales* and *Rodney*, the *Ark Royal*, five cruisers, and eighteen destroyers. Besides these main convoys, a number of other supply ships reached the island. In all thirty-two ships out of thirty-four came in safely after much peril and gallant conduct. This nourishment enabled the fortress not only to live but to strike. During the three months ending with September

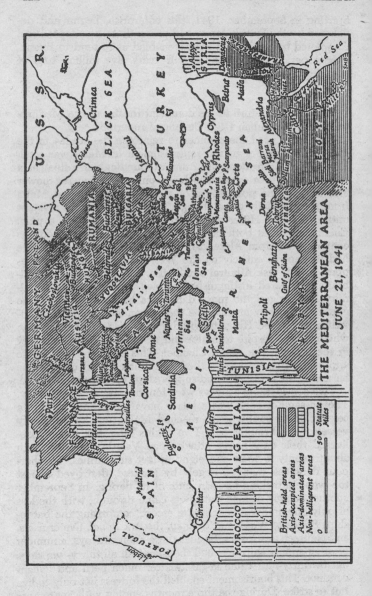

forty-three Axis ships, of 150,000 tons, besides sixty-four smaller craft, were sunk on the African route by British aircraft, submarines, and destroyers, acting from Malta. In October over sixty per cent of Rommel's supplies were sunk in passage. This may well have played a decisive part in the Desert struggle of 1941.

* * *

In September, as we now know, the German Admiral serving with the Italian High Command reported:

Now, as ever, the British Fleet dominates the Mediterranean. . . . The Italian Fleet has been unable to prevent operations by the enemy's naval forces, but, in co-operation with the Italian Air Force, it did prevent the Mediterranean route being used for regular British convoy traffic. . . .

The most dangerous British weapon is the submarine, especially those operating from Malta. In the period covered there were thirty-six submarine attacks; of these nineteen were successful. . . . Owing to the weakness of the Italian Air Force in Sicily, the threat from Malta to the German-Italian sea route to North Africa has increased in the last few weeks. . . . Moreover, almost daily attacks on Tripoli are made from Malta. Recently the Italian seaports in Sicily have been visited by British aircraft more frequently than before. . . . The formations of the Italian Air Force now stationed in Sicily and North Africa are insufficient to stop the British Air Force and naval operations. . . . I again issue an urgent warning against an underestimate of the dangers arising from the situation at sea in the Mediterranean.

* * *

My anxieties about the Desert delay and the reinforcements reaching Rommel were not allayed by the success of the measures described, and I urged even greater efforts upon the Admiralty. I desired specially that a new surface force should be based upon Malta.

Prime Minister to First Sea Lord (General Ismay to see) 22 Aug. 41

Will you please consider the sending of a flotilla, and, if possible, a cruiser or two, to Malta, as soon as possible?

2. We must look back to see how much our purpose has been deflected. There was the plan, considered vital by you, of blocking Tripoli Harbour, for which *Barham* was to be sacrificed. There was the alternative desperate proposal by the C.-in-C. Mediterranean to bombard it, which was afterwards effected without the loss of a man or a single ship being damaged. There was the arrival of Mountbatten's flotilla in Malta. All this took place several months ago. It would be well to get out the dates. How is it that the urgency of this matter has declined? How is it that we

are now content to watch what we formerly though unendurable, although it is going forward on a bigger scale against us?

3. The reason why Mountbatten's flotilla was withdrawn from Malta was less because of the danger there than for the needs of the Cretan affair, in which the flotilla was practically destroyed. We have thus lost sight of our purpose, on which there was such general agreement, and in which the Admiralty was so forward and strong.

4. Meanwhile three things have happened. First, the Malta defences have been markedly strengthened in the air and A.A. guns, and the German air forces have been drawn away to some extent to Russia. Secondly, the Battle of the Atlantic has turned sharply in our favour, we have more anti-U-boat craft, and we are to expect a substantial relief through American action west of the twenty-sixth meridian affecting our destroyers and corvettes. Thirdly, General Auchinleck is disinclined to move before November.

5. Are we then to wait and allow this ever-growing reinforcement, mainly of Italians and of supplies, to pile up in Libya? If so, General Auchinleck will be no better off, relatively to the enemy, when at last he considers himself perfectly ready than he is now.

6. I shall be glad to hear from you over the week-end, and we could discuss it at the Staff meeting on Monday night.

The policy was accepted, though time was needed to bring it into force. In October a striking force known as "Force K," comprising the cruisers *Aurora* and *Penelope* and the destroyers *Lance* and *Lively*, was formed at Malta. This presently rendered important and timely service.

* * *

I had at this time wider aims. In war it is always desirable, though not always possible, to plan ahead. The lull which followed Auchinleck's decision to delay his offensive and the successful Persian campaign offered an opportunity. From every point of view I desired at this time to reinforce the East to the utmost shipping limit. I could not tell what would happen in the impending Desert battle, nor how the Russian front in the Caucasus would hold. There was always, besides, the menace of Japan, with all its potential peril to Australia and New Zealand. I wished to have two more British divisions moving eastward. If these could be rounding the Cape about the end of the year, we should have something substantial in hand for unknowable contingencies. Here would be, in fact, that mobile reserve, that "mass of manoeuvre," which alone could give superior options in the hour of need. I had learnt about this in a hard school where lessons are often only given once.

It therefore became my ambition to make assurance doubly sure by throwing in another two divisions for the Desert Army, as well as to have a mobile reserve for other needs or chances in the Middle East. For this we had no shipping. All that could be spared from the Atlantic struggle was employed in convoys round the Cape or from Australia or India. Even Leathers could offer no solution. But I felt sure, from the increasing cordiality in my correspondence with President Roosevelt, that he would lend me some fast American transports. Nor, as will be seen, was I wrong. This could not of course operate for a good many months, but I longed to have something in hand moving through the Indian Ocean for one or other of the various disagreeable emergencies which might come upon us.

Prime Minister to C.I.G.S. and Minister of Shipping   22 Aug. 41

Let me have a scheme prepared that we could consider Monday night, for sending two more complete infantry divisions to the Middle East, at the earliest moment. Let me know what shipping will be required. Some of the lorries can surely go direct from the United States from the great numbers now being loaded. When these figures have been supplied, I will ask President Roosevelt for the loan of this shipping for this particular purpose, and I dare say I can get it.

As a modification of the above, the divisions could go to Halifax or New York, and re-embark there upon American ships. The Minister of Shipping should throw himself into this plan, and let me have a report from all angles. I am convinced that by the end of November we should have two more divisions in that theatre, though whether they would operate in Persia, Iraq, or the Middle East Command must depend upon circumstances. Let me also have the time-table of the movement of the 1st Armoured Division to the Middle East.

The intricate details were thrashed out with Lord Leathers and the Chiefs of Staff.

Prime Minister to General Ismay   26 Aug. 41

Pray make arrangements with Lord Leathers and the War Office Movements Branch to further this reinforcement in the light of our discussion last night. Ingenuity and contrivance must be used to minimise the demand I must make upon the President. The request will be for one round voyage of a certain number of ships from America to this country, to the Middle East, and back to the United States. They ought to have them at their disposal again in January or in February. If *Normandie* could be taken over, transshipment might be possible at Trinidad, which would release earlier some of the smaller liners. Arrangements for reception in the Middle East, involving transshipment to smaller vessels, must also in that case be considered.

Let me have the best plan possible, and focus the outstanding points of difficulty, so that I can myself preside over the final conference. Imports may be cut.

. I now appealed to President Roosevelt.

Former Naval Person to President Roosevelt					1 Sept. 41

The good results which have been so smoothly obtained in Persia puts us in touch with the Russians, and we propose to double, or at least greatly improve, the railway from the Persian Gulf to the Caspian, thus opening a sure route by which long-term supplies can reach the Russian reserve positions in the Volga Basin. Besides this there is the importance of encouraging Turkey to stand as a solid block against a German passage to Syria and Palestine. In view of both these important objectives, I wish to reinforce the Middle East armies with two regular British divisions, 40,000 men, in addition to the 150,000 drafts and units which we are carrying ourselves between now and Christmas. We cannot however manage to find the whole of the shipping by ourselves. Would it be possible for you to lend us twelve United States liners and twenty United States cargo ships manned by American crews from early October till February? These would come carrying cargo to United Kingdom ports under any flag arrangement convenient. If they could arrive here early in October we would send them forward as additions to our October and November convoys to the Middle East.

2. I know, Mr. President, from our talks that this will be difficult to do, but there is a great need for more British troops in the Middle East, and it will be an enormous advantage if we can hold Turkey and sustain Russia, and by so doing bar further advance eastward by Hitler. It is quite true that the loan of these liners would hamper any large dispatch of United States forces to Europe or Africa, but, as you know, I have never asked for this in any period we can reasonably foresee in the near future.

3. It is for you to say what you would require in replacements of ships sunk by enemy action. Hitherto we have lost hardly anything in our well-guarded troop convoys. I am sure this would be a wise and practical step to take at the present juncture, and I shall be very grateful if you can make it possible.

This produced a most helpful and generous response. "I am sure," said the President on the 6th, "we can help with your project to reinforce the Middle East army. At any rate I can now assure you that we can provide transport for twenty thousand men." He said that these ships would be United States naval transports manned by Navy crews, and that the American Neutrality Act permitted public ships of the Navy to go to any port. The United State Maritime Commission would besides this arrange to place ten or twelve additional ships in the North Atlantic to run between American ports and Great Britain, so that we could release ten or twelve of our British cargo ships for the voyage to the Middle East. "I am loaning you, he said, "our best transport ships. Incidentally I am delighted you are going to reinforce the Middle East."

Former Naval Person to President Roosevelt   7 Sept. 41

I am indeed grateful for your prompt response to my appeal about Middle East shipping, and very glad you like the policy. I am also planning to send seventeen more squadrons of fighter aircraft to the same theatre.

2. In my telegram about supply help for Russia, I meant to add: "If they keep fighting it is worth it; if they don't we don't have to send it." We are hitting ourselves very hard in tanks, but this argument decided me.

3. We all await with profound interest your promised statement for Monday. I am speaking Tuesday in the House.

At the same time the President brought into operation the agreements which he had made with me at Placentia to intervene more directly in the Atlantic.

* * *

I now proceeded to use the President's invaluable gift of transports to the best advantage.

Prime Minister to Colonel Hollis, for C.O.S. Committee 17 Sept. 41

All possible must be done to accelerate the movement and turn-round of the fast American transports in order to secure to us the benefits of a second trip. The sailing of these transports from America must not be delayed for the sake of carrying the Canadian armoured troops. To carry them is convenient, but not essential. The delay of reloading of these ships in U.K. ports from October 23 to November 15 cannot be accepted. An evolution should be made of putting Number 1 extra division on board in the shortest time. At least a fortnight should be saved on this if it can be reconciled with convoy movements.

2. The field state of the Army of the Nile is good. This is not surprising considering they are taking nearly five months' rest from all fighting. The 60 British battalions average 880, and the 45 artillery regiments are only short by 9 per cent. It is inconceivable that more than a quarter of this artillery can be heavily engaged in continuous bombardment during the next four months. Drafts for the artillery cannot therefore have high priority. The 6 Tank Transporter and 16 Standard M.T. companies deserve a high place. This applies also to the naval relief, to the Indian reinforcements and to the artillery, etc., for the two new Indian divisions in Iraq.

Ten thousand to twenty thousand drafts for the infantry can be worked in as convenient, and there may be some specialist items in the R.A.S.C. [Royal Army Service Corps] field which are urgently needed. Let us remember however that nothing can now get there before "Crusader." Malaya can wait, and West Africa can be fitted in or not as convenient. The problem we have to settle is one of priority.

3. The supreme object to be aimed at is to send British divisions Numbers 1 and 2 to the Middle East in accordance with the proposal made to President Roosevelt. Spreading the movements over another month or two, especially if we get the American second trip, will surely provide for all the desiderata. There is no question of saying that anything *never* goes.

4. I look to the Air Ministry to make the existing squadrons in Middle East go forward with their expansion to sixty-two and a half squadrons.

5. I should be grateful if these points could be woven into a revised programme of reinforcements for the Middle East, and I shall be very glad to discuss any difficulties outstanding with the C.O.S. Committee tonight or tomorrow night.

*   *   *

Although the Chiefs of Staff had agreed to the dispatch of the two additional divisions to the East, there were misgivings. Various dangers were pressed upon me. I still assigned priority to Auchinleck's offensive.

Prime Minister to Colonel Hollis, for C.O.S. Committee 18 Sept. 41

It is our duty to take a view about whether serious fighting will take place or not in the interval before all convoys arrive. It should not be assumed that the risk of this is evenly spread over the whole period, and that at any given moment we must provide the maximum addition of effective fighting strength. It would seem that the only serious fighting to be expected is our long-delayed offensive in the Western Desert, for which nothing more [*i.e.*, not yet dispatched] can now arrive in time. However, should this offensive succeed, very great strain will be thrown upon the transport (R.A.S.C.) services, including specialised units, either to hold the ground gained or to make an ambitious leap forward to the west. In these circumstances I am disposed to meet, if possible, the R.A.S.C. requirements, which at first I thought excessive. Thirteen thousand five hundred are provided in the C.O.S. minute; four thousand more could be obtained by delaying the five infantry battalions promised to India in the October convoy. There seems more urgency in the former than in the latter case. India is no doubt very thin, but on this new showing they will still receive seventy-nine hundred, namely, three battalions plus drafts for expansion. This is a considerable infusion of British troops. Therefore I wish the five battalions, four thousand, to be delayed till the

New Year, and the four thousand passages saved devoted to re-inforcement of the R.A.S.C. for Middle East. It should be explained to India at Headquarters that the delay is only a short one and that the expansion programme should proceed.

2. It is difficult to see from what quarter and by what line of advance other "serious fighting" will develop in the period covered by our convoys to the end of 1941 and their arrival by the end of February, 1942. In this five-month period it is not likely that Turkey will open the door to a German invasion of Syria, and still less likely that, if she refuses, a way through Asia Minor can be forced by the enemy. Unless there is a complete collapse of Russia, the Germans will be chary of embarking on a major war with Turkey, costing perhaps another million men. Therefore, I cannot see the risk of invasion of Syria, Palestine, etc., from the north as likely to be operative before the winter is over—say, March. This is also the view which has been taken in various C.O.S. papers.

3. The only other route by which serious attack can fall upon us is through the Caucasus and across the Caspian. This presupposes the mastery of the Black Sea, in which the Russians have at present an overwhelming naval superiority, involving the capture of Sebastopol and also of Novorossisk, the subsequent traversing of the Caucasus from Batum to Baku, or alternatively a movement north of the Black Sea and through the Caucasus from north to south. This would be a prohibitive winter operation. A third possibility would be a German march round the Caspian, forcing the line of the Volga and destroying the last reserve armies of Russia. This is plainly an operation impossible to complete within the next six months, unless we assume the surrender or collapse of Russia. Unless this happens, the Caspian, strongly held by Russian naval forces, must remain a great shield to the northward.

4. Therefore, in order to bring about the "serious fighting" suggested, Turkey and/or Russia must yield in the period mentioned, or the Germans must force their way from Anatolia or through the Caucasus or round the north of the Caspian. A sensible, practical view of the admitted uncertainties of war should exclude all these possibilities before the spring of 1942.

5. I cannot therefore accept the theory of continuous even risk from day to day, and I consider that we are justified in relying upon no "serious fighting" other than in the Western Desert in this theatre till March, 1942, unless of course we choose to take the offensive. In these circumstances I feel free to give proper weight to the major political-strategic issues involved in the broad decision to send two additional divisions in the van of the reinforcements.

6. What are these considerations? First, the moral need of our having a substantial, recognisable British stake and contribution in the Middle East, and freeing ourselves from the imputation,

however unjust, of always using other people's troops and blood. Secondly, the effect produced upon Turkey by our being able to add two divisions to the forces already mentioned in the Staff conversations, thus appreciably increasing the chances of influencing Turkish action. Thirdly, the basis of my appeal to the President, which I do not wish upset. Fourthly, the possibility that these two divisions may move in by Basra, in order to give an effective right hand to the Russian reserve forces to the north of the Caspian.

The various alternatives will remain open to us in the three months during which these divisions will be in transit. . . .

As usual I kept Smuts informed.

Prime Minister to General Smuts   20 Sept. 41

Am sending two divisions and about eighty thousand other reinforcements to Middle East between now and Christmas. To help in this I have had to beg loan of American transports from Roosevelt, which has been kindly given. If we can clear up Cyrenaica we shall have substantial forces to give right hand to Russia in Caspian region and/or influence action Turkey. This last regard as our most immediate prize. Hope at least to procure Turkish resistance to German demands for passage through Anatolia. Meanwhile Beaverbrook and Harriman are leaving for Moscow. We have had to make terrible sacrifices in tanks and aircraft and other munitions so sorely needed. If Russians stay in it is worth it. If they quit we don't have to send it. Hope to reach total of twenty-five divisions from Caspian to Nile during 1942. I doubt very much whether Russians would be wise to press us to cumber the Trans-Persian Railway, which we are rapidly developing, with movement and supply of the few divisions we could actually send into Russia. All these matters will be discussed at Moscow and studied by our Staffs. Will keep you informed.

*   *   *

All our minds were constantly turned to the Desert. I may recur to the note I had written on the voyage to Placentia in the first week of August about the impending Desert operations. I showed my draft to the Chief of the Imperial General Staff and to General Brooke, Commander-in-Chief of our Home Forces. They both expressed their full concurrence, subject to a few minor alterations not affecting the principles involved.

I circulated this paper to various high commanders as from October 7, 1941. The ruling given in paragraph 4 about the military and air commands was made operative by telegrams to General Auchinleck and Air Marshal Tedder, defining their relation and affirming the supremacy of the military commander over the use to be made of the air force, both during a battle and in its preparatory phase. This rule prevailed henceforward in the British Service, and was later independently developed by the United States.

A NOTE BY THE MINISTER OF DEFENCE

Renown awaits the Commander who first in this war restores artillery to its prime importance upon the battlefield, from which it has been ousted by heavily armoured tanks. For this purpose three rules are necessary:

(a) Every field gun or mobile A.A. gun should carry a plentiful supply of solid armour-piercing tracer shots; thus, every mobile gun will become an anti-tank gun, and every battery possess its own anti-tank protection.

(b) When guns are attacked by tanks they must welcome the occasion. The guns should be fought to the muzzle. Until the approaching tanks are within close range batteries should engage them at a rapid rate of fire with H.E. During this phase the tracks of the tanks are the most vulnerable target. At close quarters solid A.P. shot should be fired; this should be continued so long as any of the detachments survive. The last shot should be fired at not more than ten yards' range. It may be that some gun crews could affect to be out of action or withhold their fire, so as to have the superb opportunity of firing A.P. at the closest range.

(c) It may often happen as a result of the above tactics, especially when artillery is working with tanks, that guns may be overrun and lost. Provided they have been fought to the muzzle, this should not at all be considered a disaster, but on the contrary, the highest honour to the battery concerned. The destruction of tanks more than repays the loss of field guns or mobile A.A. guns. The Germans have no use for our captured guns, as they have a plethora of their own types, which they prefer. Our own supplies are sufficient to make good the deficiencies.

The principle must be established by the Royal Artillery that it is not good enough for tanks to attack a group of British batteries properly posted, and that these batteries will always await their attack in order to destroy a good proportion of tanks. Our guns must no more retreat on the approach of tanks than Wellington's squares at Waterloo on the approach of hostile cavalry.

2. The Germans made a practice from the beginning of their invasion of France, and have since developed it consistently, of taking what they call "flak" artillery with their most advanced parties and interspersing all their armoured and supply columns with it. We should do the same. The principle should be that all formations, whether in column or deployed, should be provided with a quota of A.A. guns for their protection. This principle is applicable to columns of all kinds, which should be freely supplied with machine guns, as well as with Bofors as the supply of these weapons becomes more plentiful.

3. Two hundred and fifty Bofors are now being sent to General Auchinleck for him to use in the best possible way with all his columns, and at all the assembly points of his troops or refuelling stations required in the course of offensive operations.

Nevermore must the Army rely solely on aircraft for its protection against attack from the air. Above all, the idea of keeping standing patrols of aircraft over moving columns should be abandoned. It is unsound to "distribute" aircraft in this way, and no air superiority will stand any large application of such a mischievous practice.

4. Upon the Military Commander-in-Chief in the Middle East announcing that a battle is in prospect, the Air Officer Commanding-in-Chief will give him all possible aid irrespective of other targets, however attractive. Victory in the battle makes amends for all, and creates new favourable situations of a decisive character. The Army Commander-in-Chief will specify to the Air Officer Commanding-in-Chief the targets and tasks which he requires to be performed, both in the preparatory attack on the rearward installations of the enemy and for air action during the progress of the battle. It will be for the Air Officer Commanding-in-Chief to use his maximum force for these objects in the manner most effective. This applies not only to any squadrons assigned to Army Co-operation permanently, but also to the whole air force available in the theatre.

5. Bombers may, if required, be used as transport or supply machines to far-ranging or outlying columns of troops, the sole object being the success of the military operation. As the interests of the two Commanders-in-Chief are identical, it is not thought that any difficulty should arise. The Air Officer Commanding-in-Chief would naturally lay aside all routine programmes and concentrate on bombing the rearward services of the enemy in the preparatory period. This he would do not only by night, but by day attacks with fighter protection. In this process he will bring about a trial of strength with the enemy fighters, and has the best chance of obtaining local command of the air. What is true of the preparatory period applies with even greater force during the battle. All assembly or refuelling points or marching columns of the enemy should be attacked by bombers during daylight with strong fighter protection, thus bringing about air conflicts not only of the highest importance in themselves, but directly contributing to the general result.

General Montgomery was not one of those to whom the paper was sent, and it was not till after I met him in Tripoli in 1943, after the victory of the Eighth Army at Alamein eighteen months later, that I chanced to show him a copy. "It is as true now," he wrote, "as when it was written." Renown by then had certainly attended his restoration of artillery to its position upon the battlefield.

7

The Mounting Strength of Britain

Autumn, 1941

Review of Our Military Position—My Minute of October 4—Need to Preserve the Military Efficiency of the Home Forces—Restrictions upon Air Defence of Great Britain—Immense Advance in Our Air Fighter Strength—Limitations on Our Bombing Offensive—Army Strength: My Directive of October 9—The Problem of Man-Power: My Memorandum of November 6—I Question the Invasion Menace—A Plan for the Home Guard—General Embick's Mission and Report—My Comments Thereupon—Our Atlantic Life-Line—President Roosevelt's "Shoot First" Order, September 11—Telegram to General Smuts—Greater Safety of the Convoys—Sinking of the "Reuben James," October 31—Our Air Offensive in the Bay of Biscay—A Submarine Surrenders to an Aeroplane—The Sea Routes to Russia—Our First Convoy to Russia, August 12—The Focke-Wulf Mastered—We Develop the Escort Carrier—Our Foremost U-Boat Killer—U-Boats in the Mediterranean—War on the German Surface Raiders—Table of Shipping Losses—British Power in the Autumn of 1941.

A S THE WINTER APPROACHED, the strength and organisation of the Army in 1942 had to be reviewed in a new light of circumstances. We could not be sure that Germany had not by now constructed many varieties of landing- and tank-landing-craft for invasion. We ourselves were doing this on an ever-increasing scale. Surely her need was even greater. We could not be certain in October that, having smitten and hurled back the Russian armies in the first phase of his onslaught, Hitler might not suddenly halt and take up a winter position as he was first advised to do by his host of generals. Having made preparations in good time, might he not switch back twenty or thirty divisions across his lateral roads for a spring invasion of Britain? It was not even known whether he had not sufficient good troops still remaining in the Western theatre. It also seemed possible that the German Air Force could very rapidly be made to shift its weight back again from the East to the West. At any rate, we must be ready for such a sudden change. Sir Alan Brooke, Commander-in-Chief of the Home Forces, was responsible for representing this vital need. He was quite right to set forth the claims of Home Defence, and this was certainly done by him and his powerful staff in a most vigorous fashion. They demanded large numbers of men and confronted us with grisly reductions of fighting units if these were not forthcoming. It fell on me as Minister of Defence with the Chiefs of Staff to decide the true apportionment of our already heavily strained man-power and woman-power.

Prime Minister to Secretary of State for War and   4 Oct. 41
C.I.G.S.

I was greatly disturbed by the statement of C.-in-C. Home Forces that he would have to reduce his standard divisional formations to eleven fully mobile divisions, apart from three in Ireland, by the spring. This destruction of more than half our Army would be intolerable, and the Cabinet should certainly have been warned by you before any such situation even approached the limits of discussion.

2. There is no sort of warrant or necessity for such mutilation of the Army. Apart from active operations, the impending losses in the winter through normal wastage cannot exceed sixty thousand men, and an intake of more than that number has been arranged. The twenty-six standard divisions and the nine county divisions and the seven armoured divisions, including the Guards (forming), are not on any account to be reduced. If new units are required, easement may be found in the four or five independent brigades and the twelve unbrigaded battalions.

3. Please investigate the Commander-in-Chief's statement at once, and give me your report upon it. In the meantime the following rule must be observed: No existing divisional formation is to be reduced in standard or converted to a different form without my express authority, obtained in each case beforehand in good time. I must also be informed of any new units you wish to create in substitution for existing units, and any important changes in the establishments, whether in personnel or equipment. Let me have a list of any that are now in progress or in prospect.

At the same time I did all in my power to uphold the efficiency of the Home Forces, and to ward off from them the many specious and plausible demands that were made upon them by the civil departments.

Prime Minister to Secretary of State for War   5 Oct. 41

I do not approve the idea of using the Army to dig land drains or for other work of this character during the winter. It is not the case that the air force have a similar scheme. Their proposal is to send eight thousand skilled technicians of the R.A.F., in uniform, on loan to the factories for about six months. Their case is entirely different from that of the Army, and I think their plan is a good one.

2. Military considerations should rule your thoughts, and you should not yield to the weak elements in the country who do not understand that quality, efficiency, smartness of bearing, high discipline, are the vital characteristics of an armed force that may have to meet the Germans.

3. In any emergency like heavy air raids or the harvest, the Army should of course give immediate and generous aid. But we shall want all our men in the spring, and every unit in the highest state of readiness. There may even be operational demands before the spring. Your responsibility is to have them all ready like fighting cocks, in accordance with the directions which I give as Minister of Defence. Parades, exercises, and manoeuvres, the detailed development of the individual qualities of sections, platoons, and companies, continual improvement and purging of the officers of middle rank, courses and competitions of all kinds, should occupy all ranks. There should be plenty of marching with bands through towns and industrial districts. The monotony should be relieved by more generous leave being granted both to officers and men. Facilities for transport to the towns for amusement should be elaborated, as a little fun is the counterpart of the hard training which must be exacted. We need regular units of the highest type, and not a mudstained militia that is supposed to turn out and take a hand in the invasion should it come. I pointed out to the House last week the dangers of yielding to soft, easy, and popular expedients, and the dark places into which we have been led thereby.

*   *   *

The main source from which our man-power for mobile fighting troops could be sustained was of course the anti-aircraft batteries and other air defence units under General Pile's command. The fear of renewed air attacks on an even larger scale had led to demands for actual increases in our Air Defence. I resisted these tendencies, and began again to argue the case against the invasion danger, which nevertheless always lurked in my mind.

Air Defence of Great Britain

Directive by the Prime Minister

Prime Minister to Colonel Hollis, for C.O.S. Committee 8 Oct. 41

We cannot state how severe the air raids will be this winter or what the danger of invasion will be in the spring. These two vultures will hang above us to the end of the war. We must be careful that our precautions against them do not unduly weaken our Mobile Field Army and other forms of our offensive effort.

2. It would seem reasonable to fix the total of Air Defence of Great Britain (A.D.G.B.) personnel at its present figure of 280,000, plus any additional recruitment of women that they can attract. This will give them at least 30,000 more than what we got through the air raids with last year. The proposed addition of 50,000, [making] a total of 330,000, cannot be supplied. Many more high- and low-ceiling guns are coming to hand now. Some of these might be mounted in additional batteries, but unless A.D.G.B. can contrive by praiseworthy thought and ingenuity to man them within the limits of the personnel mentioned, they will have to be kept in care and maintenance.

3. Having regard to the parity now existing between the British and German Air Forces, and the Russian factor, it is unlikely that the enemy will make heavy and continuous air attacks on Great Britain in combination with or as a prelude to invasion. He would need to save up for that. . . .

4. A.D.G.B. must therefore become as flexible as possible and keep static defence at a minimum. For this purpose as large a proportion as possible of A.D.G.B. should be in a mobile form. General Pile should prepare schemes for giving the utmost reinforcement of mobile flak to General Brooke's army. Sometimes they must take their guns from the site. In other cases a duplicate set of mobile guns may be made available. Thus we can shift the weight from one leg to the other as the need requires. . . .

5. Above all, we cannot go on adding gun to gun and battery to battery as the factories turn them out, and so get an ever larger proportion of our limited trained man-power anchored to static and passive defence.

6. General Pile should be assisted in every way to prepare schemes for increasing the mobile flak of the Army and reinforcing the coast batteries, while at the same time, without any addition (apart from women) to his numbers (280,000), maintaining the indispensable minimum which served us so well last year.

7. The Chiefs of Staff Committee is requested to advise, and consider what proposals should be made to give effect to the foregoing principles.

*   *   *

Our air fighter strength had now made an immense advance, and not only gave increased security against invasion but opened other prospects to strategic planning.

Prime Minister to C.A.S.   1 Sept. 41

I was delighted to see in the last return that we have practically one hundred fighter squadrons (ninety-nine and a half) in the Metropolitan Air Force. The vast changes in the war situation arising from the arrival of Russia as a combatant, and the improvement of our position in the Middle East, including Persia, make me inclined to a large further reinforcement of the Middle East to influence Turkey and/or sustain Russia on her southern flank. My thought is turning to the dispatch of as many as twenty fighter squadrons complete to the Iraq-Persia and Syrian theatre. It may be these squadrons would come into action against German bombers and dive-bombers while defending territories under our control or that of our allies, and that we should then reproduce the favourable conditions of fighting which enabled us to inflict such heavy losses upon the Germans when they made their air attack upon us last year in the Battle of Britain. This might be a more paying business than the very hard struggles in France, which of course we must continue as occasion serves. This force would have to go by long sea route round the Cape, and could not come into action till the end of the year. It should take with it the effective organisation of one or two control centres (like Number 11 Group), so that the full power of the fighter defence could be manifested. It would not leave the country till the invasion period is over. It is of course additional to all you have in hand for the East.

I shall be obliged if you will have this situation examined in all its bearings, and let me know about numbers of personnel required, what demands on shipping, and what you think of this important transference of war power. Such forces operating north and south of the Caspian would be a gigantic contribution to Russia's war effort, and allied with bomber forces might long dispute the eastward advance of the Germans. The Indian Air Force would come into action in the same areas.

I never ceased to do my utmost to increase and stimulate the production of bombers, which lagged far behind even the most moderate claims of their partisans.

Prime Minister to Lord President of the Council   7 Sept. 41

I have been deeply concerned at the slow expansion of the production of heavy and medium bombers. In order to achieve a first-line strength of four thousand medium and heavy bombers, the Royal Air Force require twenty-two thousand to be made between July, 1941, and July, 1943, of which 5500 may be expected to reach us from American production. The latest forecasts show that of the remaining 16,500 only 11,000 will be got from our own factories. If we are to win the war, we cannot accept this position, and, after discussion with the Minister of Aircraft Production and Sir Charles Craven, I have given directions for a plan to be prepared for the expansion of our effort to produce a total of 14,500 in the period instead of 11,000. This can only be done by a great concentration of effort and by making inroads on our other requirements. Materials and machine tools should not present an insuperable difficulty, and there will be enough pilots to fly the aircraft. The crux of the matter will be the provision of sufficient skilled labour to set up the machines and to train great numbers of fresh men and women. This skilled labour can only be found at the expense of other projects.

I have asked the Minister of Aircraft Production to draw up a plan for this new programme and to state the demands he must make for its fulfilment. I have also asked him to make suggestions as to how these demands could be met. I have asked the Secretary of State for Air to adjust his programme for the expansion of the Royal Air Force to fit the new production programme. This will give some easement in the preparation of airfields, the manufacture and filling of bombs, etc., since the full first-line strength will be achieved rather later than is at present planned.

I wish you to take the plan which the Minister of Aircraft Production will produce, to convene such Ministers as may be concerned, and to prepare for my consideration proposals for implementing the plan. It will be necessary to show what the effect on our other activities will be. It may be necessary to slow up the Admiralty programme or to reduce the flow of equipment for the Army. Above all, it will certainly be necessary drastically to curtail the building of the great number of new factories, which are now in the early stages of construction, or which are about to be started, and which absorb so much labour, not only in their erection but in the fabrication of the materials they require. You should call for a return of all such factories showing the object for which they are intended, the date when they were started and the state of their progress, and the year and month in which they are likely to come into operation. Other long-term projects must give way to the overriding need for more bomber aircraft.

I regard this subject as a major factor in the war at the present time, and I should like to receive your preliminary proposals in a fortnight. Thereafter you must watch over the progress of the scheme, and I will hold periodic conferences to stimulate action.

*   *   *

At the same time I was forced to cool down the claims which some of our most trusted officers put forward in their natural ardour. Coastal Command was particularly hard hit by the cuts which we were forced to make in its expected scale of expansion. My task at this time was to fight on all the administrative fronts at once, and amid conflicting needs to advise the Cabinet upon the right solution.

Prime Minister to C.A.S.   7 Oct. 41

We all hope that the air offensive against Germany will realise the expectations of the Air Staff. Everything is being done to create the bombing force desired on the largest possible scale, and there is no intention of changing this policy. I deprecate however placing unbounded confidence in this means of attack, and still more expressing that confidence in terms of arithmetic. It is the most potent method of impairing the enemy's morale we can use at the present time. If the United States enters the war, it would have to be supplemented in 1943 by simultaneous attacks by armoured forces in many of the conquered countries which were ripe for revolt. Only in this way could a decision certainly be achieved. Even if all the towns of Germany were rendered largely uninhabitable, it does not follow that the military control would be weakened or even that war industry could not be carried on.

2. The Air Staff would make a mistake to put their claim too high. Before the war we were greatly misled by the pictures they painted of the destruction that would be wrought by air raids. This is illustrated by the fact that two hundred and fifty thousand beds were actually provided for air-raid casualties, never more than six thousand being required. This picture of air destruction was so exaggerated that it depressed the statesmen responsible for the pre-war policy, and played a definite part in the desertion of Czechoslovakia in August, 1938. Again, the Air Staff, after the war had begun, taught us sedulously to believe that if the enemy acquired the Low Countries, to say nothing of France, our position would be impossible owing to the air attacks. However, by not paying too much attention to such ideas we have found quite a good means of keeping going.

3. It may well be that German morale will crack, and that our bombing will play a very important part in bringing the result about. But all things are always on the move simultaneously, and it is quite possible that the Nazi warmaking power in 1943 will be so widely spread throughout Europe as to be to a large extent independent of the actual buildings in the homeland.

4. A different picture would be presented if the enemy's Air Force were so far reduced as to enable heavy accurate daylight bombing of factories to take place. This however cannot be done outside the radius of fighter protection, according to what I am at present told. One has to do the best one can, but he is an unwise man who thinks there is any *certain* method of winning this war, or indeed any other war between equals in strength. The only plan is to persevere.

I shall be delighted to discuss these general topics with you whenever you will.

*   *   *

I now arrived at general conclusions about the strength and
character of the Army at which we should aim for 1942, as
well as upon the man-power measures necessary to sustain it.
I obtained the agreement of the authorities concerned to the
following programme and consequential measures which were
enforced.

ARMY STRENGTH

Directive by the Minister of Defence

9 Oct. 41

We have now in the United Kingdom (including Northern
Ireland) twenty-six standard motorised infantry divisions and the
Polish Division, total twenty-seven, well equipped with guns and
transport, with an average strength of about 15,500 men, with ten
corps organisations and corps troops (61,000). There are eight
county divisions for work on the beaches, averaging about 10,000,
without artillery other than coast artillery and with little transport.
We have five armoured divisions and four Army tank brigades; the
whole comprising fourteen armoured brigades (with five divisional
elements), four brigade groups with artillery and transport, seven
infantry brigades, and twelve un-brigaded battalions; furthermore,
eight aerodrome defence battalions and the 100,000 men in the
Home Defence and Young Soldiers battalions.

2. It is proposed to transform this organisation into twenty-seven
standardised divisions (hereinafter to be called Field Divisions),
plus the Polish Division (which will have an armoured element),
total twenty-eight; and to increase the armoured forces to seven
armoured divisions with eight Army tank brigades, the whole comprising twenty-two armoured brigades (with seven divisional elements). The four brigade groups are to remain. Instead of the
eight county divisions and other units mentioned above, there will
be thirteen brigades, plus the equivalent of two Ally brigades, and
eight "detached battalions"; the foregoing constituting the Home
Field Army, which can thus be reckoned the equivalent of forty-
five divisions. In addition, there will still be the eight aerodrome
battalions and the Home Defence and Young Soldiers battalions.

3. The object of these changes is to increase the war-power of
the Army, particularly in armoured troops, and to provide additional field, anti-tank, and flak artillery, including that required
for five additional Indian divisions, to be formed during 1942. For
this last purpose also it will be necessary to provide up to seventeen British battalions for the Indian Army.

4. No reduction in the force mentioned in paragraph 2 is compatible with our war needs. To maintain it during the next nine
months, i.e., to July 1, 1942, and also to maintain the drafts for
the Army of the Middle East, for India, and for our garrisons in
Iceland, Gibraltar, Malta, and Hong Kong, etc., with a normal

wastage of 50,000 a quarter, there must be provided an intake to the Army of 278,000 men. Measures are being taken to provide this. The Army also requires at least 142,000 more women above the 63,000 already recruited.

I then set forth in detail our forces at home and abroad. The conclusion shows the strength of our military resources and deployment before the supreme events which brought the United States into the war. The directive continues:

10. If we estimate our Army in divisions or their equivalent, the general layout for 1942 is as follows:

United Kingdom	45
Anti-aircraft divisions	12
Army of the Nile	16
Army of India in Iraq and Persia	9
Army of India at home	8
Fortress garrisons	7
Native African divisions	2
Grand total	99

11. It is our duty to develop, equip, and maintain all these units during 1942.

*   *   *

Besides manning the forces, heavier demands were now put forward on behalf of the expanding munitions factories and workshops. If the country's morale was to be sustained the civil population must also be well nourished. Mr. Bevin at the Ministry of National Service used all his knowledge and influence as an experienced trade-union leader to gather the numbers required. It was already obvious that man-power was the measure alike of our military and economic resources. Mr. Bevin, as the supplier of labour, and Sir John Anderson, Lord President of the Council, together devised a system which served us in good stead up to the end of the war, and enabled us to mobilise for war work at home or in the field a larger proportion of our men and women than any other country of the world in this or any previous war. At first the task was to transfer people from the less essential occupations. As the reservoir of man-power fell, all demands had to be cut. The Lord President and his Man-Power Committee adjudicated, not without friction, between competing claims. The results were submitted to me and the War Cabinet.

The first of these man-power surveys came before the War Cabinet in November. I put before my colleagues my own reflections on the main issues presented to us in the Lord

President's review. Obviously we must now cast a heavy burden on women.

MAN-POWER

Memorandum by the Prime Minister

6 Nov. 41

It may be a convenience to my colleagues if I set out the provisional views which I have formed on some of the major issues which we have to settle.

The age of compulsory military service for men should be raised by ten years, to include all men under fifty-one. While this might not make very many men available for an active fighting rôle, it would assist the Minister of Labour in finding men for non-combatant duties in the Services.

The possibility that the age should be raised again later on need not be excluded; but it would seem that an increase of ten years in the upper limit would be sufficient at the moment.

2. The case for calling up young men at eighteen and a half, instead of nineteen, seems fully established. Indeed, I would go further and call them up at eighteen if this would make any substantial contribution.

3. On the whole, I am not yet satisfied, in view of the marked dislike of the process by their Service menfolk, that a case has been established for conscripting women to join the Auxiliary Services at the present time. Voluntary recruitment for these Services should however be strongly encouraged.

4. Should the Cabinet decide in favour of compelling women to join the Auxiliary Services, it is for consideration whether the method employed should not be by individual selection rather than by calling up by age groups. The latter system would inevitably discourage women from joining up until their age group was called.

5. The campaign for directing women into the munitions industries should be pressed forward. The existing powers should be used with greater intensity. . . .

6. Employers might well be encouraged, in suitable cases, to make further use of the services of married women in industry. This would often have to be on a part-time basis, and means must be found to ease the burden on women who are prepared to perform a dual rôle.

*   *   *

It was inevitable that the whole question of an invasion would have to be argued out again, and I addressed myself to this task with increasing conviction that it would not happen. At the same time the process was healthy and led to important judicious dispositions of our available strength. Enormous requests were now made by the Home Command for armour, and tales of heavy German construction of tank-landing-craft received some credence. No one can understand without reading the papers written at the time how hard was the strain, and how easy it was to make decisions which might be tragically falsified by events. I was like a keeper in the Zoo distributing half-rations among magnificent animals. Luckily they knew I was an old and friendly keeper.

Prime Minister to C.I.G.S.   3 Nov. 41

All experience shows that all Commanders-in-Chief invariably ask for everything they can think of, and always represent their own forces at a minimum. . . . It is only a few months ago that I saw with pleasure that we might have a thousand tanks available to meet an autumn invasion. Now we have got two thousand or more, and at least another fifteen hundred should be available by the spring, making three thousand five hundred.

General Brooke should organise these in the best possible way, bearing in mind that for Home Defence against invasion the utmost possible should be put in the front line of formations, and that the reserve need not be on the scale required in the Middle East.

2. While I am calling for the most vigorous measures to resist invasion in the spring, I am of course very sceptical of the stories that are told about its scale. The evidence which supports the tale of the eight hundred flat-bottomed vessels, each carrying at eight knots ten tanks, rests on the flimsiest foundation—namely, an agent saw some of these vessels being made at one place, and he thought others were being made at other places to the number of eight hundred. If there is any other evidence behind this story, let me have it.

3. With the improvements in photography and the increased power in the air, very formidable resistance should be made to the assembly of large numbers of vessels in the river-mouths of the Low Countries. Now that we have the command of the air over the Pas de Calais, it is not seen how Dunkirk, Calais, and Boulogne can be used for the purposes of invasion. All shipping gathered in these harbours and the smaller ones could be bombed by daylight under fighter cover. This was not the case last year.

4. There can be no question of our going back on our promises to Russia. If of course Archangel freezes up, we must do our best by other routes. But it is far too soon to raise any such issues now, when the ink is hardly dry on our promise, and we have been unable to do anything else to help the Russians. . . .

I thought it necessary to have a scheme which would enable a selected proportion of the Home Guard to be used as military formations in the event of invasion.

Prime Minister to Secretary of State for War   23 Nov. 41

It is thought that the invasion danger will manifest itself gradually by the assembly in the ports and river-mouths of large numbers of ships and landing-craft, and also by troop movements on a great scale. At a certain stage in these proceedings, which may conceivably take months and after all may only be a blind, we should have to proclaim the "Alert." If this moment were rightly chosen, it should be about a fortnight before zero day. It is not intended that the whole of the Home Guard should thereupon cease their civilian occupations, but only that a special section of them should be called out and embodied, like the militia used to be.

2. The rest of the Home Guard would not be called out until a few days before zero hour, as far as we can tell, or perhaps only when the embarkation of the invaders had already begun. They would however increase their vigilance between the "Alert" and the alarm.

3. The special section I have in mind would of course consist, not of persons under eighteen and over sixty years, but of the great mass of hefty manhood now in reserved occupations who are not allowed to join the Army but have volunteered for the Home Guard. This class would attend additional drills, and would be paid for attendance at these drills. They would not come out whole-time till the "Alert." There is no need to make heavy weather of the proposal by forming brigades with the War Office standards of equipment. They would be armed with rifles, machine guns, and Bren carriers. They can be organised in battalions. They would not alter their characteristic civilian and voluntary status until the "Alert."

Pray let me have definite proposals on the scale of four battalions in each corps area.

*   *   *

I welcomed the keen interest which the United States military chiefs took in the defence of our Island, which they already regarded as the bastion of American security. We have seen how they feared lest in our efforts to hold the Middle East we should endanger our safety at home. In September and October an American officer, General Embick, was sent over by General Marshall, and I cordially invited him to go around all our home and beach defences and report fully the conclusions which he formed, both to me and to his own Government. General Embick was a most capable critic, and a good friend to Britain. I felt from the first however that he was unduly alarmist. Towards the end of November he produced his report, and I print my comment upon it as I wrote it at the time.

Prime Minister to General Ismay, for C.O.S. Committee
                                                    23 Nov. 41

This report by General Embick on the British defence system proceeds on the assumptions of the strength of invasion which has been adopted here as a basis for our preparations. These were no doubt imparted to General Embick, but I must make it clear that though these data may be accepted in order to keep our defence up to the mark, they do not rest on any solid basis other than that of prudent apprehension. . . .

The great fault of this paper, as of many studies about invasion, is that it ignores the time-sequence of events. An invasion on so vast a scale could not be prepared without detection. Not only eight hundred alleged landing-craft, but many other vessels and large ships, would have to be assembled in the river-mouths and harbours. Aerial photography would reveal this process, and the air force would subject them to the heaviest bombing during what might well be a fortnight or more. From Dunkirk to Dieppe our air strength is now sufficient to enable us to make daylight attacks under fighter air cover. When the difficulties of embarkation have been surmounted, it will still be necessary to marshal these ships and bring them across the sea. By that time it is reasonable to expect that naval resistance will be available in a very high form. General Embick assumes that there will be no warning, and that all our small craft will be engaged in the Battle of the Atlantic. But this is incorrect, once the scale of the invasion is raised above the level of heavy raids. Let me have a time-table (on one sheet of paper) of what the Navy will do on each day from the "Alert" on Day 1 to Day 20, and what forces will be in hand.

The whole of this preliminary but indispensable phase plays no part in General Embick's thought, yet in it is comprised the main and proved defence of the Island from invasion. Wishing to train our Army and keep it keen, we have, naturally, stressed what happens after the enemy lands, but the Royal Navy and Royal Air Force are responsible for shattering the assembly of the armada and for striking into it decisively in passage. There must be no lifting of this obligation off these two Services.

*   *   *

We could as the year 1941 drew to its end—and unforseeable climax—also survey the course of the mortal U-boat war with solid reassurance. The favourable tendencies which I had unfolded in secret session in Parliament at the end of June had become more plain with every week. Our resources were mounting. By July we had been able to institute continuous, if slender, escort for our convoys throughout the North Atlantic, and on the route to Freetown. While Germany was straining every nerve to multiply her U-boats, active co-operation by the United States was becoming a reality. Our new weapons, though still in their infancy, and the effective tactical combination of our sea and air forces in the task of killing U-boats, were improving. The seagoing radar equipment on which so much depended had been put into production, not without risk of failure, straight from the drawing-board. We still had to rely on evasion at sea as our principal means of defence. The day when we could court attack was still far ahead.

On September 4 the United States destroyer *Greer* was unsuccessfully attacked by a U-boat while proceeding independently to Iceland. A week later, on September 11, the President issued his "shoot first" order. In a broadcast he said: "From now on, if German or Italian vessels of war enter the waters the protection of which is necessary for American defence, they do so at their own peril. The orders I have given as Commander-in-Chief to the United States Army and Navy are to carry out that policy at once." On September 16, for the first time, direct protection was given to our Halifax convoys by American escorts. This brought instant relief to our hard-pressed flotillas. But two months elapsed before the President succeeded in freeing his hands from the neutrality laws, by which American ships could not carry goods to Britain nor even arm themselves in their own defence.

I kept General Smuts informed.

Prime Minister to General Smuts   14 Sept. 41

I am content with President's action, which can only be judged in relation to actual naval movements concerted at our meeting. His line runs from North Pole down tenth meridian to about Faroes, then trends away southwest to twenty-sixth meridian, which is followed to the equator. He will attack any Axis ship found in this vast area. Sixteen U-boats have cut up one of our convoys in last few days off the tip of Greenland, nearly a thousand miles inside the prohibited zone. When I asked that American destroyers should be sent from Iceland to help our escorts, they went yesterday at once, and, had the U-boats not vanished meanwhile, Anglo-American forces would have been in action together against them. United States assumption of responsibility for all fast British convoys other than troop convoys between America and Iceland should enable Admiralty to withdraw perhaps forty of the fifty-two destroyers and corvettes we now keep based on Halifax and concentrate them in home waters. This invaluable reinforcement should make killing by hunting groups other than escorts possible for the first time. Hitler will have to choose between losing the Battle of the Atlantic or coming into frequent collision with United States ships and warships. We know that he attaches more importance to starving us out than to invasion. American public have accepted the "shoot at sight" declaration without knowing the vast area to which it is to be applied, and in my opinion they will support the President in fuller and further application of this principle, out of which at any moment war may come. All the above is for your own most secret information.

* * *

Although five times as many U-boats were now operating as in 1940, our shipping losses were greatly reduced. No merchant ship in the fast Halifax convoys was sunk between July and November. The slow convoys sailing from Sydney, Cape Breton Island, for which British and Canadian escorts remained solely responsible throughout the voyage, were also free from attack in July and August. In September however there was the seven days' combat from Greenland to Iceland, mentioned in my cable to General Smuts, with a pack of over a dozen U-boats. Sixteen ships out of sixty-four in the convoy were sunk, and two U-boats. On October 31 the immunity of the Halifax convoys from attack was at last broken, and the American destroyer *Reuben James* was torpedoed and sunk with severe loss of life. This was the first loss suffered by the United States Navy in the still undeclared war. In August the limits on the number of ships sailing in any one convoy were removed. The fast and slow convoys were often combined for part of their voyage, and on August 9 a combined convoy comprising a hundred ships came safely in. For the three months up to the end of September the weekly average of imports was nearly a million tons, an increase of about eighty thousand tons a week.

Our air patrols watching the German cruisers in Brest noticed that the U-boats based on Biscay ports normally made the passage to and from these bases on the surface and along fairly well defined routes across the Bay of Biscay. Here was an opportunity for our Coastal Command, but to make full use of it, two needs had to be met. The first was the problem of identification. Although our airborne radar was now yielding modest results, we had no means of identifying targets at night until, a little later, the development of an aircraft searchlight solved the problem. The second need was an airborne weapon which would sink a U-boat. The bomb and the depth charge with which our aircraft were armed were not sufficiently accurate or deadly for the fleeting opportunities of attack which offered. Nevertheless, during the three months ending with November twenty-eighth attacks were made. By December the enemy was forced to cross the dangerous area of the bay either in darkness or under water. Thus the time during which a U-boat could hunt was reduced by about five days.

In August a Hudson aircraft of Coastal Command attacked a U-boat with depth charges in the western approaches. The U-boat was injured and unable to dive, and the crew attempted to man their gun; but the Hudson with her own machine guns drove them below, and for the first time in war a submarine hoisted the white flag and surrendered to an aeroplane. A heavy sea was running and no surface vessel was near, but the Hudson maintained relentless watch over her prize. Aid was summoned, and the next day the U-boat was towed by a trawler to Iceland. She was later commissioned into the Royal Navy. The incident is unique.

* * *

A new burden was now laid upon the British Navy. The need to aid Russia focused attention upon the sea routes to Archangel and Murmansk. Towards the end of July, Vian— now an Admiral—had been ordered to reconnoitre Spitzbergen. He landed a force to demolish the coal dumps and rescue the few Norwegians who had been pressed into German service. Three loaded German colliers were also captured in this neatly executed operation. About the same time fifty-six aircraft from the carriers *Furious* and *Victorious* gallantly attacked German shipping in the ports of Petsamo and Kirkenes at the top of the North Cape. Some damage was done, but sixteen of our planes were lost, and the operation was not repeated.

On August 12 the first "P.Q." convoy of six ships for Russia sailed from Liverpool by Iceland to Archangel. Henceforward convoys to North Russia ran regularly once or twice a month. They were strongly escorted and not yet interfered with by the enemy. When Archangel became icebound, Murmansk was used. There was too much jubilation and publicity about the successful passage of supplies to the Russian Army, and heavy forfeits were to follow in another year.

* * *

With the Russian entry into the war the German air attacks on shipping near our coasts somewhat lessened. The Focke-

Wulf ranged widely, but our fighter-catapult ships, devised for this very danger, were now coming out, and soon gained successes. The converging homeward routes from Gibraltar and Sierra Leone became the target of German air and U-boat attacks, costing us during August and September thirty-one ships and three escort vessels. Among these was the famous destroyer *Cossack* of *Altmark* and *Bismarck* fame. The first true escort carrier, H.M.S. *Audacity,* operating six aircraft from a flying deck, came into action in September, and immediately proved the value of her type. Not only could she destroy or drive off the Focke-Wulf, but by air reconnaissance in daylight she could keep the U-boats down and give timely warnings about them. The *Audacity* became the model on which in later years large numbers of vessels were built in the United States to play a vital part in the U-boat war and later in amphibious operations.

The *Audacity* herself had a short career. She was sunk by a U-boat on December 21 after a most gallant action while escorting a homeward-bound convoy from Gibraltar. Commander F. J. Walker, who commanded the convoy escort, greatly distinguished himself on this occasion in a combat lasting several days and nights, during which four U-boats were destroyed out of about nine, besides two Focke-Wulfs. One night his ship, the *Stork,* pursued and rammed a U-boat in the darkness. The two ships were side by side and so close together that the four-inch guns of the *Stork* could not be sufficiently depressed and the guns' crews were "reduced to fist-shaking and roaring curses," until depth charges did their work. Commander Walker was promoted and became our foremost U-boat killer. Before his untimely death from illness in 1944, he and the several groups he commanded had sunk twenty U-boats, six of them at one go.

Further relief was given to us in the Atlantic Ocean by the German decision to send U-boats into the Mediterranean. Five of these were destroyed in the Straits of Gibraltar, and six others damaged and forced to return, but twenty-four successfully made the passage, and, as will be seen in a later chapter, became a grievous factor there.

*   *   *

War on our ocean commerce was also maintained by the disguised German merchant ships. The Australian cruiser *Sydney* encountered "Raider G" off the west coast of Australia. The German, thanks to his disguise, succeeded in enticing his adversary to point-blank range before opening fire. Both ships were sunk. Twenty-five Germans were picked up later, and others eventually landed in Western Australia. Of the *Sydney's* crew of over seven hundred none survived. This was a sombre sacrifice in lonely waters.

A few days later "Raider C," which had destroyed twenty ships, of about 140,000 tons in all, was caught and sunk in the South Atlantic by the cruiser *Dorsetshire*. The losses inflicted by the disguised German surface raiders, of whom there were from first to last nine, were as follows:

	Ships Sunk	Gross Tons
1940	54	366,644
1941	44	226,527
1942	30	194,625
1943	6	49,482

We had therefore solid reasons, even in 1941, for satisfaction at the whole trend of the ocean war upon our commerce. In November, 1941, our losses from U-boats fell to the lowest figure since May, 1940. In spite of all Hitler's boasts and the multiplication of his U-boat and air strength and our ever-increasing convoys at sea, British and Allied shipping losses in 1941 were hardly greater than in 1940. Of course there were more targets on both sides, but the number of U-boats sunk by us (including Italian) rose from forty-two in 1940 to fifty-three in 1941. The table below showing total losses deserves careful study.

❊   ❊   ❊

Total Losses, in Gross Tons, of British, Allied, and Neutral Merchant Ships and Fishing Vessels by Enemy Action

(Numbers of ships in parentheses)

September 3 to December 31, 1939		
U-boat	423,769	(116)
Mine	262,697	(79)
Surface craft	61,337	(15)
Aircraft	2,949	(10)
Other and unknown causes	7,253	(4)
Total	758,005	(224)
1940		
U-boat	2,186,158	(471)
Mine	509,889	(201)
Surface craft	511,615	(94)
Aircraft	580,074	(192)
Other and unknown causes	202,806	(100)
Total	3,990,542	(1058)
1941		
U-boat	2,162,168	(429)
Mine	229,838	(108)
Surface craft	495,077	(113)
Aircraft	970,481	(324)
Other and unknown causes	332,717	(167)
Total	4,190,281	(1141)

Thus, on the eve of a supreme change in the war we had made formidable increases in our military power and were still steadily advancing both in actual strength and in the mastery of our many problems. We felt ourselves strong to defend our Island, and able to send troops abroad to the utmost limit of our shipping. We wondered about the future, but, after all we had surmounted, could not fear it. Invasion had no terrors, and at the same time our life-lines across the ocean grew safer, broader, more numerous and more fruitful. Our control of the approaches to the Island grew better every month. The threatened stranglehold of the German Air and U-boats had been broken, and the enemy was driven far from our shores. Food, munitions, and supplies arrived in an ever-expanding stream. The output of our own factories increased every month. The Mediterranean, the Desert, and the Middle East were still in peril, but in the closing days of November on land and sea and in the air we felt thankful with the way the war had so far gone.

8

Closer Contacts with Russia

Autumn and Winter, 1941

Anglo-Soviet Relations—Difficulties of Military Concert—Our Efforts to Help in the Caucasus—Question of Our Declaring War on Finland, Rumania, and Hungary—My Telegram to Stalin of November 4—His Reply, November 8—Mr. Eden's Conversation with the Soviet Ambassador, November 20—I Offer to Send Mr. Eden to Moscow—Stalin Accepts—I am Reluctant to Face the Breach with Finland, Rumania, and Hungary—My Appeal to Field-Marshal Mannerheim—Mr. Eden's Mission to Moscow—My Directive of December 6—The First Failure of a German Blitzkrieg.

TWO THEMES now dominated our relations with the Soviet Union. The first was the vague and unsatisfactory state of our consultations on military matters, and the second the Russian request that we should sever relations with the Axis satellites, Finland, Hungary, and Rumania. As we have seen, little progress had been made in the former direction during the recent meetings in Moscow. About the first, on November 1 I sent the following minute to the Foreign Secretary:

Prime Minister to Foreign Secretary   1 Nov. 41

I was not aware that we had ever taken the line that there should be no consultation on military matters. On the contrary, did we not tell them definitely we would consult on military matters? Certainly I wrote a paper for Lord Beaverbrook's guidance [1] which dealt entirely with the military situation apart from that of supply. General Ismay was sent to Russia for the purpose of embarking on the military discussion. It could have made no difference in fact, as there is no practical step of any serious importance which can

[1] See Appendix D, Book Two.

at present be taken. He might have explained by facts and figures how very foolish and physically impossible was the suggestion that we should send "twenty-five or thirty divisions" to the Russian front. He could have explained how even moving two or three divisions in at either end of the Russian front would choke the communications needed for Russian supplies. On the other hand, I do not see why these conversations did not take place at some time or other in the conference. Undoubtedly Lord Beaverbrook and Stalin touched upon the military issue.

General Wavell has already been to Tiflis without finding anyone in authority to speak to him. He speaks Russian well, and it might well be that he should undertake a journey to Moscow. It is only by the southern flank that we could enter for many months to come.

Anyhow, let us get the facts straightened out.

PS.—You should see Wavell's telegram just received, showing how even two divisions at or north of Tabriz will completely choke the Trans-Persian Railway.

I felt that if only a machinery of military consultation could be established the problem of joint operations could be discussed in a reasonable manner which would not lead to misunderstanding. The unsatisfactory nature of the existing position is clear from my following minute:

Prime Minister to General Ismay, for C.O.S. Committee   5 Nov. 41

We do not know when the Germans will arrive in the Caucasus, nor how long it will be before they come up against the mountain barrier. We do not know what the Russians will do, how many troops they will use, or how long they will resist. It is quite certain that if the Germans press hard neither the 50th nor the 18th British Division could be on the spot in time. We are held in a grip by the delay in "Crusader," and it is not possible to see beyond that at the present moment. I cannot feel any confidence that the Germans will be prevented from occupying the Baku oilfields, or that the Russians will effectively destroy these fields. The Russians tell us nothing, and view with great suspicion any inquiries we make on this subject.

2. The only thing we have it in our power to do is to base four or five heavy bombing squadrons in Northern Persia to aid the Russians in the defence of the Caucasus, if that be possible, and if the worst happens to bomb the Baku oilfields effectively and try to set the ground alight. These squadrons will of course require fighter protection. Neither the bombers nor the fighters can be provided till after "Crusader" and its consequences can be judged. A plan should however be made based on a large transference of air from Libya to Persia, so as to deny the oilfields to the enemy as long as possible. Pray let this be done during the next week, so that we can see what is involved. One cannot tell how long the Russians

will retain the command of the Black Sea, although with their forces it is inexcusable that they should lose it.

* * *

The question of our breaking off relations with Finland had first been raised, as we have seen, by M. Maisky in his interview with me on September 4. I knew this was a subject on which the Russians felt strongly. The Finns had taken the opportunity of the German attack on Russia to renew hostilities on the Karelian front in July, 1941. They hoped to regain those territories lost by the Treaty of Moscow the previous year. Their military operations in the autumn of 1941 represented a grave threat not only to Leningrad, but also to the supply lines from Murmansk and Archangel to the Russo-German front. Both the American Government and ourselves had since August been warning the Finns in severe terms of the possible consequences of the situation. Their attitude was that they needed the disputed province of Eastern Karelia for their own security against Russia, and the history of the previous two years lent strength to their view. But now that Russia was engaged in a life-and-death struggle with Germany it was clearly impossible for the Allies to allow the Finns, acting as a German satellite Power, to cut Russia's main northern lines of communication with the West.

The position of Rumania was similar to that of Finland. The Russians had occupied the Rumanian province of Bessarabia, and thereby gained control of the mouth of the Danube, in June, 1940. Now, under the leadership of Marshal Antonescu, and in alliance with Germany, the Rumanian armies had not only reoccupied Bessarabia, but had bitten deep into the Black Sea provinces of Russia, as the Finns were doing in Eastern Karelia. The Hungarians also, in a key position astride the communications of Central and Southeastern Europe, were of direct assistance to the German war effort.

But I was by no means certain that a declaration of war was the correct method of dealing with the situation. There was still a possibility that, under pressure from the United States and ourselves, Finland would agree to fair and reasonable peace terms. In the case of Rumania at least there was every reason to believe that the dictatorial régime of Antonescu would not last indefinitely. I decided therefore to address myself again to Marshal Stalin on both the question of military planning and co-operation, and that of avoiding a declaration of war against these Axis satellite Powers.

Prime Minister to Premier Stalin 4 Nov. 41

In order to clear things up and to plan for the future I am ready to send General Wavell, Commander-in-Chief in India, Persia, and Iraq, to meet you in Moscow, Kuibyshev, Tiflis, or wherever you will. Besides this, General Paget, our new Commander-in-Chief, secretly designated for the Far East, will come with General Wavell. General Paget has been in the centre of things here, and will have with him the latest and best opinions of our High Command. These two officers will be able to tell you exactly how we stand, what is possible and what we think is wise. They can reach you in about a fortnight. Do you want them?

2. We told you in my message of September 6 that we were willing to declare war on Finland. Will you however consider whether it is really good business that Great Britain should declare war on Finland, Hungary, and Rumania at this moment? It is only a formality, because our extreme blockade is already in force against them. My judgment is against it, because, first, Finland has many friends in the United States and it is prudent to take account of this fact. Secondly, Rumania and Hungary: these countries are full of our friends; they have been overpowered by Hitler and used as a cat's-paw, but if fortune turns against that ruffian they might easily come back to our side. A British declaration of war would only freeze them all and make it look as if Hitler were the head of a grand European alliance solid against us. Do not, pray, suppose it is any want of zeal or comradeship that makes us doubt the advantage of this step. Our Dominions, except Australia, are reluctant. Nevertheless, if you think it will be a real help to you and worth while, I will put it to the Cabinet again.

3. I hope our supplies are being cleared from Archangel as fast as they come in. A trickle is now beginning through Persia. We shall pump both ways to our utmost. Please make sure that our technicians who are going with the tanks and aircraft have full opportunity to hand these weapons over to your men under the best conditions. At present our Mission at Kuibyshev is out of touch with all these affairs. They only want to help. These weapons are sent at our peril, and we are anxious they shall have the best chance. An order from you is necessary.

4. I cannot tell you about our immediate military plans, any more than you can tell me about yours, but rest assured we are not going to be idle.

5. With the object of keeping Japan quiet we are sending our latest battleship, *Prince of Wales*, which can catch and kill any Japanese ship, into the Indian Ocean, and are building up a powerful battle squadron there. I am urging President Roosevelt to increase his pressure on the Japanese and keep them frightened so that the Vladivostok route will not be blocked.

6. I will not waste words in compliments, because you know already from Beaverbrook and Harriman what we feel about your splendid fight. Have confidence in our untiring support.

7. I should be glad to hear from you direct that you have received this telegram.

On November 11 M. Maisky brought to me Stalin's chilling and evasive reply to this message.

M. Stalin to the Prime Minister   8 Nov. 41

Your message received on November 7.

I fully agree with you that clarity should be established in the relations between the U.S.S.R. and Great Britain. Such a clarity does not exist at present. The lack of clarity is the consequence of two circumstances: (*a*) There is no definite understanding between our two countries on war aims and on plans for the post-war organisation of peace. (*b*) There is no agreement between the U.S.S.R. and Great Britain on mutual military assistance against Hitler in Europe. As long as there is no accord on both these questions there can be no clarity in the Anglo-Soviet relations. More than that: to be frank, as long as the present situation exists there will be difficulty in securing mutual confidence. Of course the agreement on military supplies to the U.S.S.R. has a great positive value, but it does not settle, neither does it exhaust, the whole problem of relations between our two countries. If the General Wavell and the General Paget whom you mention in your message will come to Moscow with a view to concluding agreement on the two fundamental questions referred to above, I naturally would be happy to meet them and to discuss with them these questions. If however the mission of the Generals is confined to the questions of information, and to the consideration of secondary matters, it would not be, I think, worth while to intrude upon the Generals. In such a case it would also be very difficult for me to find the time for the conversations.

2. It seems to me that an intolerable situation has been created in the question of the declaration of war by Great Britain on Finland, Hungary, and Rumania. The Soviet Government raised this question with the British Government through the secret diplomatic channels. Quite unexpectedly for the U.S.S.R., the whole problem, beginning with the request of the Soviet Government to the British Government and ending with the consideration of this question by the U.S.A. Government, received wide publicity. The whole problem is now being discussed at random in the press—friendly as well as enemy. And after all that the British Government informs us of its negative attitude to our proposal. Why is all this being done? To demonstrate the lack of unity between the U.S.S.R. and Great Britain?

3. You can rest assured that we are taking all the necessary measures for speedy transportation to the right place of all the arms coming from Great Britain to Archangel. The same will be done with regard to the route through Persia. In this connection may I call your attention to the fact (although this is a minor

matter) that tanks, planes, and artillery are arriving inefficiently packed, that sometimes parts of the same vehicle are loaded in different ships, [and] that planes, because of the imperfect packing, reach us broken?

* * *

Even Stalin seems after a while to have felt that he had gone too far in the tone of this communication, which I had not attempted to answer. The silence was expressive. On November 20 the Soviet Ambassador in London called on Mr. Eden at the Foreign Office. The following is Mr. Eden's record of the conversation as sent in a telegram to Sir Stafford Cripps, now at Kuibyshev:

Foreign Minister to Sir Stafford Cripps   20 Nov. 41

The Soviet Ambassador asked to see me this afternoon, when he said that he had received instructions from M. Stalin, who had asked him to convey to me that in sending his recent message to the Prime Minister he had only practical and businesslike questions in view. It had certainly not been M. Stalin's intention to cause any offence to any members of the Government, and least of all to the Prime Minister.

M. Stalin was very busy indeed with affairs at the front, and had had virtually no chance to think of anything else but affairs at the front. He had raised important practical issues about mutual military assistance in Europe against Hitler and the post-war organisation of peace. These questions were very important, and it was very undesirable to complicate them by any personal misunderstanding or feelings. M. Stalin had also overcome certain personal feelings in pursuing the line he had taken, because the Finnish business had greatly hurt him and the whole of the Soviet Union. "My Fatherland," said M. Stalin, "finds itself in a humiliating position. Our request was made secretly. Then the whole thing was published, and also the fact that His Majesty's Government did not consider it possible to accept the Soviet request. This has put my country in a humiliated position, and has had a depressing effect on the minds of my people." M. Stalin had felt himself hurt by this, but, in spite of this, he still pursued only one end: to reach an agreement on mutual military assistance against Hitler in Europe and the post-war organisation of peace.

Stalin's answer had made it clear that purely military talks would have little concrete result in the present state of mind of the Russian leaders. The almost hysterical note of Stalin's message about Finland showed the gap in understanding between our two countries. I proposed therefore to make a further attempt to smooth out relations between us by offering to send Mr. Eden himself on a mission to Russia. It was in this sense that I telegraphed to M. Stalin on November 21:

Prime Minister to Premier Stalin   21 Nov. 41

Many thanks for your message, just received. At the very beginning of the war I began a personal correspondence with President Roosevelt, which has led to a very solid understanding being established between us and has often helped in getting things done quickly. My only desire is to work on equal terms of comradeship and confidence with you.

2. About Finland. I was quite ready to advise the Cabinet to declare war upon Finland when I sent you my telegram of September 4. Later information has made me think that it will be more helpful to Russia and the common cause if the Finns can be got to stop fighting and stand still, or go home, than if we put them in the dock with the guilty Axis Powers by a formal declaration of war and make them fight it out to the end. However, if they do not stop in the next fortnight and you still wish us to declare war on them, we will certainly do so. I agree with you that it was very wrong that any publication should have been made. We certainly were not responsible.

3. Should our offensive in Libya result, as we hope, in the destruction of the German-Italian army there, it will be possible to take a broad survey of the war as a whole, with more freedom than has hitherto been opened to His Majesty's Government.

4. For this purpose we shall be willing in the near future to send the Foreign Secretary, Mr. Eden, whom you know, via the Mediterranean to meet you at Moscow or elsewhere. He would be accompanied by high military and other experts, and will be able to discuss every question relating to the war, including the sending of troops not only into the Caucasus but into the fighting line of your armies in the south. Neither our shipping resources nor the communications will allow large numbers to be employed, and even so you will have to choose between troops and supplies across Persia.

5. I notice that you wish also to discuss the post-war organisation of peace. Our intention is to fight the war in alliance with you and in constant consultation with you to the utmost of our strength, and however long it lasts, and when the war is won, as I am sure it will be, we expect that Soviet Russia, Great Britain, and the United States will meet at the council table of the victors as the three principal partners and agencies by which Nazism will have been destroyed. Naturally, the first object will be to prevent Germany, and particularly Prussia, breaking out upon us for the third time. The fact that Russia is a Communist State and Britain and the United States are not, and do not intend to be, is not any obstacle to our making a good plan for our mutual safety and rightful interests. The Foreign Secretary will be able to discuss the whole of this field with you.

6. It may well be that your defence of Moscow and Leningrad, as well as the splendid resistance to the invader along the whole Russian front, will inflict mortal injuries upon the internal structure of the Nazi régime. We must not count upon such good fortune, but simply keep on striking at them to the utmost with might and main.

M. Stalin replied two days later, and in a calmer tone:

Premier Stalin to Prime Minister   23 Nov. 41

Many thinks for your message. I sincerely welcome your wish as expressed in your message to collaborate with me by way of personal correspondence based on friendship and confidence. I hope this will contribute much to the success of our common cause.

2. On the question of Finland, the U.S.S.R. never proposed anything else—at least, in the first instance—but the cessation of the military operations and the *de facto* exit of Finland from the war. If however Finland refuses to comply with this in the course of the short period you indicated, then I believe the declaration of war by Great Britain would be reasonable and necessary. Otherwise an impression may be created that there is no unity between us on the question of war against Hitler and his most ardent accomplices, and that the accomplices of Hitler's aggression can do their base work with impunity. With regard to Hungary and Rumania, we can perhaps wait a little while.

3. I support by all means your proposal of an early visit to the U.S.S.R. by the Foreign Secretary, Mr. Eden. I believe our joint consideration and acceptance of an agreement concerning the common military operations of the Soviet and British forces at our front, as well as speedy realisation of such an agreement, would have a great positive value. It is right that consideration and acceptance of a plan concerning the post-war organisation of peace should be founded upon the general idea of preventing Germany, and in the first place Prussia, once more from violating peace and once more plunging peoples into terrible carnage.

4. I also fully agree with you that the difference of the State organisation between the U.S.S.R. on the one hand and Great Britain and the United States of America on the other hand should not, and could not, hinder us in achieving a successful solution of all the fundamental questions concerning our mutual security and our legitimate interests. If there are still some omissions and doubts on this score I hope they will be cleared away in the course of the negotiations with Mr. Eden.

5. I beg you to accept my congratulations on the successful beginning of the British offensive in Libya.

6. The struggle of the Soviet armies against Hitler's troops remains tense. In spite however of all the difficulties the resistance of our forces grows and will grow. Our will to victory over the enemy is unbending.

*   *   *

As a result of Stalin's pressing appeal it was decided to go ahead with arrangements to deliver an ultimatum with a time limit to the Finns, and also to Rumania and Hungary. I was most reluctant to be forced into this position, as the following minutes show:

Prime Minister to Foreign Secretary   28 Nov. 41

You seem to be taking it for granted that war will be declared on all three Powers [Finland, Rumania, and Hungary] on December 3. I did not wish this decision to be taken till we know what Finland will do. Moreover, the 3d is too soon. The 5th is a fortnight after my telegram to Stalin. I am only tonight sending my telegram to Mannerheim. We must leave reasonable time for a reply.

My opinion about the unwisdom of this measure remains unaltered, and I still have hopes that the Finns will withdraw. I was not aware that this step would be taken at this juncture.

Prime Minister to Foreign Secretary   29 Nov. 41

Finland and Company. I don't want to be pinched for time if there is a chance of Finland pulling out of the big war. See also my telegram to Stalin [of November 21], which says, "if they do not stop in the next fortnight *and you still wish us to declare war on them . . .*" Procedure therefore should be as follows. If we have not heard by the 5th that the Finns are not going to pull out, or have heard they are contumacious, we then telegraph to Stalin saying that "*if he still wishes it*" we will declare war forthwith. The Rumanian and Hungarian declarations will follow, also in accordance with whatever he may desire.

*   *   *

Meanwhile I thought it worth while, with the knowledge and agreement of the Soviet Government, to make a final and personal appeal to the Finnish leader, Field-Marshal Mannerheim.

Prime Minister to Field-Marshal Mannerheim   29 Nov. 41

I am deeply grieved at what I see coming, namely, that we shall be forced in a few days out of loyalty to our ally Russia to declare war upon Finland. If we do this, we shall make war also as opportunity serves. Surely your troops have advanced far enough for security during the war and could now halt and give leave. It is not necessary to make any public declaration, but simply leave off fighting and cease military operations, for which the severe winter affords every reason, and make a *de facto* exit from the war. I wish I could convince Your Excellency that we are going to beat the Nazis. I feel far more confident than in 1917 or 1918. It would be most painful to the many friends of your country in England

if Finland found herself in the dock with the guilty and defeated
Nazis. My recollections of our pleasant talks and correspondence
about the last war lead me to send this purely personal and private
message for your consideration before it is too late.

On December 2 I received Field-Marshal Mannerheim's
answer.

Field-Marshal Mannerheim to Prime Minister Churchill   2 Dec. 41

I had yesterday the honour to receive through the intermediary
of the American Minister at Helsinki your letter of November 29,
1941, and I thank you for your courtesy in sending me this private
message. I am sure you will realise that it is impossible for me to
cease my present military operations before my troops have reached
positions which in my opinion would give us the security required.
I would regret if these operations, carried out in order to safeguard
Finland, would bring my country into a conflict with England,
and I will be deeply grieved if you will consider yourself forced
to declare war upon Finland. It was very kind of you to send me a
personal message in these trying days, and I have fully appreciated
it.

This reply made it clear that Finland was not prepared to
withdraw her troops to her 1939 frontiers, and the British
Government therefore went ahead with the arrangements to
declare war. Similar action followed in regard to Rumania and
Hungary.

        *   *   *

It was against such a background that preparations were
made for Mr. Eden's mission to Moscow. He was to be accompanied by General Nye, Vice-Chief of the Imperial General Staff. A general review of the war in both its military and
general aspects was to be undertaken in these talks in Moscow,
and if possible the alliance was to be put on a formal and
written treaty basis.

On December 5 I drew up a general directive for the
Foreign Secretary, reviewing certain aspects of the military
situation as seen from our side. The battle in the Desert,
which will presently be described, was already at its height.

Prime Minister to Foreign Secretary   5 Dec. 41

The prolongation of the battle in Libya, which is drawing in so
many Axis resources, will probably require the use both of the
50th and 18th British Divisions, which we had hoped might be
available for the defence of the Caucasus or for action on the
Russian front. In the near future therefore these divisions cannot
be considered available. The best form which our aid can take
(apart from supplies) is the placing of a strong component of the

air force, say ten squadrons, on the southern flank of the Russian
armies, where, among other things, they can help protect the
Russian naval bases on the Black Sea. These squadrons will be
withdrawn from the Libyan battle at the earliest moment when
success has been gained. The movement of their ground personnel
and stores will not unduly choke the Trans-Persian communications, as would be the case if infantry divisions were sent. The
High Command in the Middle East has been ordered to make plans
for this movement, the completion of which will of course depend
upon the facilities afforded for detailed reconnaissance.

2. The attitude of Turkey becomes increasingly important, both
to Russia and to Great Britain. The Turkish army of fifty divisions
requires air support. We have promised a minimum of four and a
maximum of twelve fighter squadrons to Turkey in the event of
Turkey being attacked. In this event we might require to withdraw
some of the squadrons proposed to be sent into action on the Russian southern front. The best use of our aircraft on both shores of
the Black Sea and the types to be employed require to be decided
according to circumstances by consultation between the British and
Russian Governments and Staffs.

*   *   *

During these interchanges the urgency of the military crisis
on the Russian front had diminished. Hitler had determined
on one more great effort, and on November 13 he issued
orders for an "autumn campaign" to take Moscow before the
end of the year. The plan was opposed by Bock and Guderian, who suggested that the armies should dig in for the
winter. They were overruled. Some small progress was made
on the flanks during the latter part of November, but the
main attack in the centre, launched on December 4, broke
down completely, not only on account of the stubborn resistance of the garrison and of the inhabitants, but also because of the extreme cold which had now set in. Automatic
weapons failed to function; aircraft and tank motors could
not be started. With inadequate winter clothing the German
soldiers were half-frozen.

Like the supreme military genius who had trod this road a
century before him, Hitler now discovered what Russian
winter meant. He bowed to inexorable facts. Instructions were
given for the troops to withdraw to a better line in rear,
though they were to resist any Russian attacks in the meanwhile. These attacks were not lacking. For the rest of the
year they were continuous, and the German armour both north
and south of Moscow was forced back until by December 31
the front was stabilised on a line running north and south
sixty miles from the city, from which they had already been

within twenty miles. In the North the Germans had had no better fortune. Leningrad indeed had been completely cut off, and was closely invested in the south by the Germans and in the north by the Finns. But all assaults had been repulsed. There was more to show in the South. Rundstedt had once reached Rostov and rounded the corner to the Caucasus. Here he had overreached himself and was beaten back forty miles. Nevertheless, he had advanced five hundred miles. The southern industrial area of Russia and the rich wheatlands of the Ukraine were behind him. Only in the Crimea were there still Russians to dislodge or destroy.

Thus, in the six months' campaign the Germans had achieved formidable results and had inflicted losses on their enemy which no other nation could have survived. But the three main objectives which they had sought, Moscow, Leningrad, the lower Don, were still firmly in Russian hands. The Caucasus, the Volga, and Archangel were still far away. The Russian Army, far from being beaten, was fighting better than ever, and would certainly grow in strength in the coming year. The winter had fallen. The long war was certain.

All the anti-Nazi nations, great and small, rejoiced to see the first failure of a German Blitzkrieg. The threat of invasion to our Island was removed so long as the German armies were engaged in a life-and-death struggle in the East. How long that struggle might last no one could tell. Hitler at least was still confident of the future. The many arguments he had had with his generals during the autumn, and their failure to satisfy his far-reaching intentions, led to the removal of the Commander-in-Chief, Brauchitsch. Rundstedt went too. Henceforward Hitler took personal command of the armies in the East, confident in his generalship, and with high hopes of an early Russian collapse in 1942.

* * *

Our discussions with the Soviets, which seemed in their later stages to be progressing favourably, have anticipated the launching by General Auchinleck of his offensive in the Desert which has next to be described. Both discussions and offensive were alike relegated to a different plane by the Japanese attack upon the United States at Pearl Harbour on December 7. We shall return to them in due course amid a vastly different grouping of world forces.

9

The Path Ahead

British Plans for the Autumn of 1941—Hope of a Decisive Victory in the Western Desert—The Only Possible "Second Front"— Lord Louis Mountbatten Succeeds Sir Roger Keyes—Auchinleck Demands a Further Delay—Mr. Attlee's Visit to Washington— My Letter to the President of October 20—An Exposition of My War Thought—Suggestions for American Troops in Northern Ireland—Profound Effects of Gaining a Desert Victory—Tank-Landing Craft Indispensable for a Landing in Europe—My Telegram of October 25 to Minister of State, Middle East—Reactions of the Middle East Commanders-in-Chief—We Drop the Sicily Project—My Minute of October 28—German Plans if Russia Were Defeated—The Months of German Weakness in the Mediterranean—The U-Boats Arrive upon the Scene—A Message for the Desert Battle.

POLICY and inclination alike led me into the closest correspondence with President Roosevelt. Weekly and often almost daily I gave him the fullest tale of all I knew about our British thought and intentions and about the general war situation. There is no doubt that these interchanges commanded his closest attention, and excited his lively interest and sympathy. His replies were naturally more reserved, but by now I knew very well where he stood and what he wanted. I was in charge of a struggling country beset by deadly foes. He was aloft, august, at the head of a mighty neutral Power, whom he desired above all things to bring into the fight for freedom. But he could not as yet see how to do it. Meanwhile Britain had to plan her own scheme of war: how to fight Hitler, bringing all our forces to bear on the largest scale physically possible; how to help the Russians by supplies and by what could be only minor diversions; above all, how to keep alive!

Still, there was a plan for the rest of 1941 and for 1942 which had formed in my mind and obtained a great measure of fundamental acceptance from the Chiefs of Staff. This plan was of course at this date based upon the United States still staying out of the war while giving us all the aid that Congress would allow. I had become aware through my correspondence with the President that he was particularly alert about all naval affairs, and that he regarded French North Africa, including Dakar, and the Atlantic islands of Spain and Portugal, with special interest not only from American but from his personal ways of thought. These were also in harmony with my own views, and also, as I believe it will be judged, with a strategy which expressed the best we could possibly do alone, and also the best that we and the United States, should they become a belligerent, could do together.

My hopes were that we might win a decisive victory in the Western Desert and drive Rommel back through Libya and Tripolitania. If all went well this might bring about the rallying from Vichy of Tunis, Algeria, and Morocco, and perhaps even the accession of Vichy itself. This purpose was only a hope built on a hope. But we held ready in the United Kingdom one armoured and three field divisions, with sufficient naval power, while the German Air Force was absorbed in Russia, to carry them to any point in the Western Mediterranean. If we got Tripoli, and France would not move, our possession of Malta would enable us to descend upon Sicily, and thus open up the only possible "Second Front" in Europe within our power while we were alone in the West. I could not see anything else, except Norway, however good our fortune on the battlefield, which we could accomplish by ourselves in 1942. The plan for the invasion of Sicily had been carefully worked out by the Chiefs of Staff and the Planning Committee. We called it "Whipcord."

Once Rommel was beaten and his small, audacious army destroyed and Tripoli was ours, it was not thought impossible for four divisions of our best troops, about eighty thousand men, to land and conquer Sicily. The German Air Force, who had wrought us so much harm from the Sicilian airfields, had been called away to Russia, and there were now no German troops in the island. When our expedition was at sea and had entered the Mediterranean, it would of course be spotted. But the enemy could not know whether we were going to French North Africa—Bizerta, Algiers, Oran—or to Sicily or Sardinia. Such are the advantageous options open to naval power. What other plan of active offensive warfare was open to Britain and the Empire by themselves during 1942? How could we engage the Germans on a large scale? What schemes would offer to us so many choices, which are so desirable amid the uncertainties of war? It might be beyond our single-handed strength. It might go wrong. But at any rate it did not endanger our life-lines across the Atlantic or our power to defend ourselves from invasion at home.

It is one thing to see the forward path and another to be able to take it. But it is better to have an ambitious plan than none at all. All turned first on the success of General Auchinleck's long-prepared offensive in the Western Desert. All had to be reviewed in relation to the unknown dangers which would be opened upon us by a German penetration to the Caspian, or their possible movement through Turkey in the same direction, or into the Middle East—Syria, Palestine, Persia, and Iraq. But throughout I regarded all these as comparatively unlikely possibilities. In the event this proved the correct view. I carried with me in the pursuit of these conjectural schemes at every stage the convictions and support of the Chiefs of Staff, and of my Ministerial colleagues on the Defence Committee and in the War Cabinet. In the end all were fulfilled in the exact order designed, but not until 1942 and 1943, and in very different and more favourable circumstances than those we could foresee in October, 1941.

*   *   *

While all these speculations influenced opinion in our secret circles I was determined that the preparation of the apparatus and plans for the invasion of the Continent should not slacken. Sir Roger Keyes had now reached the age of seventy. He had performed invaluable service in building up the Commandos and in pressing forward the design and construction of invasion craft. His high rank as Admiral of the Fleet and strong personality had created a certain amount of friction in the Service departments, and I reached the conclusion with much regret on personal grounds that the appointment of a new and young figure at the head of the overseas organisation would be in the public interest. Lord Louis Mountbatten was only a captain in the Royal Navy, but his exploits and abilities seemed to me to fit him in a high degree for the vacant post. He was at this time on a special mission to the United States, where he was received with great consideration. He cruised with the Pacific Fleet, and on his return to

Washington had long discussions with the President, to whom he was authorised to disclose what we were doing in preparations for landings on the Continent and the plans I harboured. The President showed him the greatest confidence and invited him to stay at the White House. Before this visit could take place I had to summon him home.

Prime Minister to Lord Louis Mountbatten   10 Oct. 41

We want you home here at once for something which you will find of the highest interest.

Prime Minister to Mr. Harry Hopkins   10 Oct. 41

We want Mountbatten over here for a very active and urgent job. Please explain to the President how disappointed he was not to be able to fulfil the invitation to the White House with which he had been honoured. He will seek an audience before leaving.

* * *

I had been vexed by a final delay of nearly a fortnight which General Auchinleck demanded in order to perfect his arrangements.

Prime Minister to General Auchinleck   18 Oct. 41

Your telegram confirms my apprehensions. Date was mentioned by you to Defence Committee, and though we felt the delay most dangerous we accepted it and have worked towards it in our general plans. It is impossible to explain to Parliament and the nation how it is our Middle East armies have had to stand for four and a half months without engaging the enemy while all the time Russia is being battered to pieces. I have hitherto managed to prevent public discussion, but at any time it may break out. Moreover, the few precious weeks that remain to us for the exploitation of any success are passing. No warning has been given to me of your further delay, and no reasons. I must be able to inform War Cabinet on Monday number of days further delay you now demand.

Moreover, the Lord Privy Seal leaves Monday for United States, carrying with him a personal letter to the President. In this letter, which would be handed to Mr. Roosevelt for his eye alone and to be burnt or returned thereafter, I was proposing to state that in the moonlight of early November you intended to attack. It is necessary for me to take the President into our confidence, and thus stimulate his friendly action. In view of the plans we are preparing for "Whipcord," [1] I am in this letter asking him to send three or four United States divisions to relieve our troops in Northern Ireland, as a greater safeguard against invasion in the spring. I fixed the date of the Lord Privy Seal's mission in relation to the

[1] The invasion of Sicily.

date you had given us. Of course, if it is only a matter of two or three days the fact could be endured. It is not however possible for me to concert the general movement of the war if important changes are made in plans agreed upon without warning or reason. Pray therefore telegraph in time.

The date was finally fixed for November 18, as General Auchinleck desired.

*   *   *

Feeling the way the President's mind was probably moving, I determined, on the eve of Auchinleck's considerable venture in the Desert, to lay my whole thought before him. Mr. Attlee, now generally recognised as Deputy Prime Minister, was to visit Washington to attend the International Labour Conference, and I sent by his hand to the President the letter which follows. It will become evident that this fell in very closely with the march of Mr. Roosevelt's own thought.

Prime Minister to President Roosevelt   20 Oct. 1941

PART I

My dear Mr. President,

Some time this fall General Auchinleck will attack the German and Italian armies in Cyrenaica with his utmost available power.[2] We believe his forces will be stronger than the enemy's in troops, in artillery, in aircraft, and particularly in tanks. His object will be to destroy the enemy's armed and above all armoured forces, and to capture Benghazi as quickly as possible.

2. Should this operation prosper the plans which have been prepared for a further rapid advance upon Tripoli may be carried out. Should success attend this further effort important reactions may be expected which it is provident to study in advance.

3. General Weygand may be stirred into joining in the war, or the Germans may make demands upon him or Vichy for facilities in French North Africa which may force him into the war.

4. To profit by these contingencies we are holding a force equivalent to one armoured and three field divisions ready with shipping from about the middle of November. This force could either enter Morocco by Casablanca upon French invitation or otherwise help to exploit in the Mediterranean a victory in Libya.

5. In order to cover effectively these preparations we have prepared large-scale plans for a descent upon the Norwegian coast, and also for a reinforcement of the Russians in Murmansk. There is substance as well as shadow in these plans.

6. It seems therefore probable that we shall have to send away from Great Britain four or even five divisions, besides the 18th

[2] The actual date and the code-name "Crusader" were given in a separate note.

Division, which will arrive at Halifax on November 7 on its journey round the Cape to Suez. We must expect that as soon as Hitler stabilises the Russian front he will begin to gather perhaps fifty or sixty divisions in the West for the invasion of the British Isles. We have had reports, which may be exaggerated, of the building of perhaps eight hundred craft capable of carrying eight or ten tanks each across the North Sea, and of landing anywhere upon the beaches. Of course there will be parachute and airborne descents on a yet unmeasured scale. One may well suppose his programme to be: 1939, Poland; 1940, France; 1941, Russia; 1942, England; 1943—? At any rate, I feel that we must be prepared to meet a supreme onslaught from March onwards.

7. In moving four or five divisions, including one armoured division, out of the United Kingdom in these circumstances we are evidently taking risks. Should events happily take the course assumed in the earlier paragraphs of this letter, and should we in fact reduce our forces at home to the extent mentioned, it would be a very great reassurance and a military advantage of the highest order if you were able to place a United States Army Corps and Armoured Division, with all the air force possible, in the North of Ireland (of course at the invitation of that Government as well as of His Majesty's Government), thus enabling us to withdraw the three divisions we now have for the defence of Great Britain, besides the troops in Iceland, which are now being relieved.

8. We should feel very much freer to act with vigour in the manner I have outlined if we knew that such a step on your part was possible. Moreover, the arrival of American troops in Northern Ireland would exercise a powerful effect upon the whole of Eire, with favourable consequences that cannot be measured. It would also be a deterrent upon German invasion schemes. I hope this may find a favourable place in your thoughts. I do not suggest that any decision should be taken until we see the result of the approaching battle.

After some paragraphs dealing with questions of command and the relations of air and naval services to the Army, my letter continued:

PART II

13. All my information goes to show that a victory in Cyrenaica of the British over the Germans will alter the whole shape of the war in the Mediterranean. Spain may be heartened to fight for her neutrality. A profound effect may be produced upon the already demoralised Italy. Perhaps, most important of all, Turkey may be consolidated in her resistance to Hitler. We do not require Turkey to enter the war aggressively at the present moment, but only to maintain a stolid, unyielding front to German threats and blandishments. As long as Turkey is not violated or seduced, this great oblong pad of poorly developed territory is an impassable protection

for the eastern flank of our Nile Army. If Turkey were forced to
enter the war, we should of course have to give her a great deal
of support which might be better used elsewhere, either in French
North Africa or in the Caucasus. We are making promises of support to Turkey (contingent on the military situation) which amount
to between four and six divisions and twenty or thirty air squadrons, and we are actively preparing with them the necessary airfields in Anatolia. But what Turkey requires to keep her sound is
a British victory over Germans, making all promises real and
living.

14. These dispositions, as I have set them out, do not allow us
in the next six months to make any serious contribution to the
Russian defence of the Caucasus and Caspian Basin. The best help
we can give the Russians is to relieve the five Russian divisions
now crowded into Northern Persia. If these are brought home and
used in the battle, I have pledged the faith of Britain to Stalin
that no rightful Russian interest shall suffer and that we will take
no advantages in Persia at their expense. I do not however see
how, in the period mentioned, we can put more than a symbolic
force into the Caucasus and the Russians retain a similar representation in Persia. The Russians much disturb Persia by their presence, their theories, and their behaviour, and the outbreak of disorders would mean that we should have to spread three or four
British-Indian divisions to keep open the communications from the
Persian Gulf to the Caspian. These communications, which are a
vital part of our joint aid to Russia policy, would thus be largely
choked by the need of supplying the extra forces. I have been
trying to get the Russians to see this point.

15. In my telegram of July 25, 1941, which I sent you before
our Atlantic meeting, I spoke of the long-term project for 1943 of
the simultaneous landing of say fifteen thousand tanks from hundreds of specially fitted ocean-going ships on the beaches of three
or four countries ripe for revolt. I suggested that the necessary alterations could easily be made at this stage to a proportion of your
merchant ships now building on so vast a scale. I now send you
the drawings prepared by the Admiralty, which illustrate the kind
of treatment the vessels would require. You will see that it is estimated only to add about fifty thousand pounds to their cost, and I
suppose a proportionate delay. It seems to me that not less than
two hundred ships should be thus fitted. There is sufficient time, as
we cannot think of [executing] such a plan before 1943. But the
essential counterpart of the tank programme you have now embarked upon is the power to transport them across the oceans and
land them upon unfortified beaches along the immense coastline
Hitler is committed to defend. I trust therefore, Mr. President, that
this will commend itself to you.

16. I send you a short note which I have made upon the use of
artillery, both field and flak. This has its bearing upon the approaching offensive described in Part I, as well as upon the organi-

sation of our Home Army to meet invasion.[3] All the authorities are agreed upon the principles set forth, and you are very welcome to show this paper, should you think it worth while, to your officers.

17. I also send, for your own personal information, a note I have made on the structure, present and future, of the British and Imperial armies which we are endeavouring to organise in 1942.[4] Of course the figure of about one hundred divisions does not, as is fully explained, mean one hundred mobile standard field divisions. Some are garrison; some are anti-aircraft; and some are equivalents in brigade groups. Broadly speaking however it represents a much more considerable deployment of military strength than we had planned at the outbreak of the war. This has been rendered possible by the fact that we have not been engaged to any serious extent since the losses of Dunkirk, and that munitions and reserves have accumulated instead of being expended on a great scale.

18. I have not referred to the Japanese menace, which has seemed to grow so much sharper in the last few days, nor to the splendid help you are giving us in the Atlantic, because we discussed these great matters so fully at our meeting, and events are now telling their own tale in accordance with our anticipations. I still think however that the stronger the action of the United States towards Japan, the greater the chance of preserving peace. Should however peace be broken and the United States become at war with Japan, you may be sure that a British declaration of war upon Japan will follow within the hour. We hope to be able before Christmas to provide a considerable battle squadron for the Indian and Pacific Oceans.

10. Lastly, Mr. President, let me tell you how I envy the Lord Privy Seal in being able to fly over to the United States and have a good talk with you. My place is here, and therefore I have taken this opportunity of writing you so long a letter. Might I ask that all reference to the forthcoming operations shall be kept absolutely secret, and for yourself alone? For this purpose I have separated the first part of the letter [containing the actual date of our offensive] from the rest, in the hopes that after reading it you will speedily consign it to the flames.

With kindest regards and every good wish,

> Believe me, Mr. President,
> Your sincere friend,
> WINSTON S. CHURCHILL

*   *   *

I also exposed these designs fully to the Middle East Commanders-in-Chief through the Minister of State, in order that they might realise that "Crusader," the battle they were about to fight, might open to us a continuing path, and also to em-

[3] See Chapter VII, page 430.
[4] See Chapter VII, page 431.

phasise once again the urgency of their offensive. This paper, addressed to a different quarter, presents another aspect of the same conception as my letter which Mr. Attlee, in full accord, was bearing to the President.

Prime Minister to Minister of State   25 Oct. 41

No one can assume that Germany will continue to be inextricably engaged in Russia during the winter. It is far more probable that in a month or so the front in Russia, except in the South, will be stationary. Russia, through loss of munitions capacity, will have been reduced [temporarily] to a second-rate military Power, even if Moscow and Leningrad are held. At any time Hitler can leave, say, one-third of his armies opposite Russia and still have plenty to threaten Great Britain, to put pressure upon Spain, and to send reinforcements to discipline Italy, as well as pushing on in the East.

2. No one must suppose therefore that things will be better for us next year or in the spring. On the contrary, for "Whipcord" [Sicily] it is probably a case of "Now or never." In my view, by the end of December these prospects will be indefinitely closed.

3. Hitler's weakness is in the air. The British Air Force is already stronger than his, and, with American aid, increasing more rapidly. The Russian Air Force is perhaps two-thirds of the German, well organised in depth and quite good. Even when the Italian Air Force is counted for what it is worth, Hitler has not enough Air for the simultaneous support of the operations open to his armies. However, the main part of the British Air Force has to be kept at home against invasion, and is largely out of action.

4. It is therefore of importance to us to seek situations which enable us to engage the enemy's air force under favourable conditions in various theatres at the same time. Such an opportunity is presented in a high degree by "Whipcord."

5. If we can before January secure the combination of airfields —Tripoli, Malta, Sicily, and Sardinia—and can establish ourselves upon them, a heavy and possibly decisive attack can be made upon Italy, the weaker partner in the Axis, by bombers from home based on the above system of airfields. The lack of aerodromes in Italy north of Sicily should make this possible. All air fighting in this new theatre is a direct subtraction from the enemy's normal air effort against Great Britain, against the Nile Valley, and in support of his southeastward advance.

6. Other advantages would be gained from British air predominance in the Central Mediterranean. Subject to what is said in paragraph 9, the sea route from the Mediterranean would be opened to strongly escorted convoys, with all the savings in shipping accruing therefrom, as well as the stronger support of Eastern operations.

7. The reaction upon France and French North Africa following

such achievements, including the arrival of British forces on the Tunisian border, might bring Weygand into action, with all the benefits that would come from that.

8. The foundation of the above is of course a victorious "Crusader." You ought to welcome the very powerful diversion of enemy strengths, particularly air strengths, which "Whipcord" would bring, provided it runs concurrently with "Acrobat" [the British conquest of Tripolitania]. Nothing gives us greater safety or baffles the enemy more than the sudden simultaneous upspringing of a great variety of targets. This applies particularly in the few weeks which remain while the enemy is disentangling his surplus air forces from the Russian theatre and re-equipping them for action elsewhere. As I am sure you realise, a slow advance in Libya by gradual stages after full preparation, making everything sure as you go, while nothing else happens anywhere, ensures the maximum of opposition, and certainly gives the time for it to be brought to bear. Such a course would certainly give ample time for the strong German reinforcement of Sicily and for further domination of Italy by German troops. I hope you feel, as I do, the fleeting character of the opportunity presented and how short is the breathing-space which now remains before Germany, having tidied up her front against Russia, can redispose her forces in other theatres. It is, as you truly say, "a question of timing."

9. What will be the enemy's reaction to our attempt to gain a zone of air predominance in the Central Mediterranean and thus to open the passage? To bring superior air power to bear will take him time, in view of the disposition of the airfields which will remain to him in Italy. Therefore he will need to put pressure on Spain to procure the closing of the Straits of Gibraltar. We are led to believe that the Spaniards will resent and resist any invasion of their country by the Germans, who are hated by the morose and hungry Spanish people. A British victory in "Crusader" will powerfully affect the mood of the Spanish Government. Hitler no doubt can force his way through Spain, just as he can dominate Italy. His deterrent is found in the political sphere. His aim is to establish a United States of Europe under the German hegemony and the New Order. This depends not only upon the conquest, but even more upon the collaboration, of the peoples. Nothing will more effectively destroy such hopes than the continuance of the murders and reprisals, slaughter of hostages, etc., which is now going on in so many countries. It will be a very serious step for him to take to add Spain and Italy to the already vast subjugated and rebellious areas over which his troops are spread.

10. For all the above reasons the close synchronisation of "Crusader" and "Whipcord" and their intimate connection seem highly desirable. On the other hand, it must be realised that we shall not be able to remain inactive except for the advance in Libya. I am confronted with Russian demands for a British force to take its place in the line on the Russian left flank at the earliest moment.

It will not be possible in the rising temper of the British people against what they consider our inactivity to resist such demands indefinitely. If therefore it were decided to abandon "Whipcord" or alternative action in French North Africa at French invitation, as mentioned in Chiefs of Staff paper, it would be necessary to make preparations soon for moving a substantial force into Russia.

11. Your further comments should reach us by Monday night, when Defence Committee will meet.

*   *   *

The Commanders-in-Chief at Cairo took a different view. They looked to the defence of the Delta and the Canal, of Basra and the Caucasus, and the "bastion of the Taurus Range" as the first essentials. They did not consider Sicily either practicable or necessary. Their minds lay right-handed and to the East, and should it be decided to move westward and should our efforts prosper, they preferred the occupation of Bizerta to any attempt on Sicily. I fully understood their reasoning, which was strongly supported by General Wavell from India. They expressed their conclusions in a telegram on October 27 embodying the arguments I have set forth.

In consequence I abandoned the idea of an attack on Sicily ("Whipcord").

Prime Minister to General Ismay, for C.O.S. Committee 28 Oct. 41

In view of the Middle East latest telegram and of your own decisive abandonment of the project "Whipcord," which you advocated and which I espoused, I now consider that plan at an end.

2. A force equivalent to two divisions and one armoured division should however stand ready to exploit "Crusader" and "Acrobat" should they be successful. There is no reason, unless hope be a reason, to expect that General Weygand will invite us into Bizerta or Casablanca as the result of our impending operations. Should he do so, we must be ready to profit by so great a turn of fortune. The same Commanders should study this case forthwith, and it should be concerted with Middle East H.Q., and especially with Admiral Cunningham.

3. The situation might arise either through the effect of a British victory, if gained, on French morale, or, which is not to be excluded, by a German demand on Pétain for the use of this theatre in consequence of the loss of Tripoli, actual or probable.

4. The name of this operation will be "Gymnast."

5. It is important to know at once what orders should be issued to convert "Whipcord" into "Gymnast," so as to make the least possible inroads upon shipping, and, secondly, what the demands upon shipping would be and their full effect.

6. I have received advices from America that our friends there

are much attracted by the idea of American intervention in Morocco, and Colonel Knox talked to Lord Halifax about 150,000 United States troops being landed there. We must be ready, if possible, with a simultaneous offer, or anyhow a British offer, to General Weygand at any moment which seems timely after a success in "Crusader." This might turn the scale in our favour. The offer should therefore be couched in most effective terms. I will not myself address the President on the subject until after results of "Crusader" are apparent.

7. I have had a letter from him by Lord Louis Mountbatten, in which he expresses lively interest in Tangier. This should also be examined, but it evidently raises very great complications with the Spaniards and the French, and it would be wrong to sacrifice the chance of French co-operation for the sake of it.

Apart from dropping the Sicily project, we all held firmly to our estimate of values and chances, and I had no difficulty in procuring a united decision.

Prime Minister to General Ismay, for C.O.S. Committee   2 Nov. 41 and C.I.G.S.

While fully understanding General Wavell's point of view, we have definitely decided to play the sequence, "Crusader," "Acrobat," "Gymnast." There can be no going back on this.

Our plan, if everything prospered, was therefore: the clearance of Cyrenaica by the defeat of Rommel's army; the advance to Tripoli; and, with the French help and invitation, if forthcoming, the entry into French Northwest Africa. The Sicily project was dependent upon the favourable outcome of the first two, and would be an alternative to the third. All this was however so speculative that I did not wish to continue the strategic argument with the Middle East Command.

Prime Minister to Minister of State   11 Nov. 41

I could find no answer but silence to your and Auchinleck's telegrams about "Crusader." No view can be taken of the future until we know how this goes. A battle is a veil through which it is not wise to peer.

*   *   *

It may be well to see in the afterlight what was passing in the enemy's mind.

In July, 1941, the German Army Planning Staff had made a study of future operations, called Plan "Orient," to overthrow the British position in the Middle East. Their major assumption was that the Russian war would come to a successful end in the autumn. If so—a big "If"—a Panzer corps from the Caucasus would drive southward through Persia in the winter of 1941–42. From Bulgaria, if Turkey were acquiescent, a force of ten divisions, half of them armoured and motorised, would traverse Anatolia into Syria and Iraq. If Turkey resisted, double that strength would be needed, and in consequence the plan would have to wait till 1942. The German and Italian forces in Africa were given only the third place. Their rôle during the summer and autumn of 1941 was to be purely defensive, except that Tobruk was to be taken. By the winter their losses in men and equipment would be made up, and then, when the general assault was made on Persia and Iraq, and our attention and forces were distracted, the Axis army in Libya would advance on Cairo.

The African adventure had never been favoured by the German High Command. German forces had only been sent to stop the Italian rout. When this was checked, and we were driven back, the success did not lead to any change of heart. The sea voyage across the Mediterranean, with its perils from submarines and air attacks from Malta, was not to their liking. North Africa would always remain a minor theatre, owing to the "greater difficulties in reinforcement which would be experienced by the Axis as compared with the Allies." Nor was co-operation with Italians, on land, sea, or air, particularly attractive to German minds. It was only with grudging acquiescence that Rommel's shortages were made up. If the enemy had chosen, they could have spared and ferried, at an accepted cost, the forces necessary to make our position untenable. It will presently be seen how it was that Malta, their chief obstacle, was never assaulted. No doubt their heavy loss in Crete was a deterrent.

*   *   *

A letter sent at the beginning of August, 1941, from the German War Staff to the generals commanding the West, North, and South Groups outlined the objectives which would be pursued on the morrow of a Russian defeat.

(a) Strengthening of the armed forces in North Africa with a view to rendering possible the capture of Tobruk. In order to permit the passage of necessary transports, attacks by the German Air Force on Malta should be resumed.

Provided that weather conditions cause no delay and the service of transports is assured as planned, it can be assumed that the campaign against Tobruk will begin in mid-September.

(b) Plan "Felix" [i.e., the seizure of Gibraltar, with the active participation of Spain] must be executed in 1941.

(c) Should the campaign in the East be over, and Turkey comes to our side, an attack on Syria and Palestine in the direction of Egypt is contemplated, after a minimum period of eighty-five days for preparation. . . .

* * *

The autumn and winter months were therefore our opportunity. The German Air was gone from Sicily. The Russian front lapped up the fuel needed for the Italian Fleet. During August thirty-three per cent of the supplies and reinforcements to Rommel were lost. In October this important figure rose to sixty-three per cent. The Italians were pressed to organise an alternative route of supply by air. At the end of September Mussolini undertook to carry reinforcements by air to Tripoli at the rate of fifteen thousand men a month, but by the end of October only nine thousand had arrived. Sea transport to Tripoli was at the same time brought to a standstill, and only a few convoys ran our blockade and reached Benghazi. The October losses at last however forced the German High Command to send oil to the Italian Navy. A far more important step was also taken. Admiral Doenitz reluctantly agreed to move twenty-five German U-boats from the Atlantic struggle into the Mediterranean. Here was a real stroke, the consequences of which were not long to be delayed.

In the interval our control exercised from Malta was decisive, and the activities of "Force K," which the Admiralty, at my desire, had created there, yielded rich prizes. On the night of November 8, acting on an aircraft report, they pounced upon the first Italian convoy since the resumption of traffic, consisting of ten merchant ships, escorted by four destroyers with cruiser support. All the merchant ships were quickly annihilated. One destroyer was sunk and another damaged by our cruisers. The Italian cruisers took no part in the affair. I sent this good news to President Roosevelt.

Former Naval Person to President Roosevelt   9 Nov. 41

The destruction between Italy and Greece of the Axis convoy destined for Benghazi is highly important both in itself and in its consequences. It is also noteworthy that the two Italian heavy cruisers would not face our two six-inch light cruisers, nor their six [actually four] destroyers our two.

I have also an increasingly good impression of the Moscow front.

Once more the convoys were suspended, and Rommel had good reason to complain to the German High Command.

General Rommel to O.K.W.[5]   9 Nov. 41

The tempo of the transport of troops and supplies to North Africa has been reduced still more. To the end of October, 1941, of the sixty thousand tons of supplies promised by the Italians only 8093 tons have reached Benghazi. Of those troops originally intended for the attack on Tobruk about one-third of the artillery and various important communications units will not arrive from Europe even by November 20. Furthermore, it is uncertain when the twenty 15.5-cm. guns bought from France in Tunis will arrive. . . . Of the requested three Italian divisions for an attack in November only one will be available, and that below strength.

*   *   *

But now our interval of immunity and advantage came to its end. The U-boats arrived upon the scene. On November 12, while returning to Gibraltar after flying more aircraft into Malta, the *Ark Royal* was struck by a torpedo from a German U-boat. All attempts to save the ship failed, and this famous veteran, which had played such a distinguished part in so many of our affairs, sank when only twenty-five miles from Gibraltar. This was the beginning of a series of grievous losses to our Fleet in the Mediterranean and a weakness there which we had never known before. All was however now ready for our long-delayed offensive, and it is to the Western Desert that we must now turn.

*   *   *

On November 15 I sent General Auchinleck a message from the King for him to use "if, when, and as" he thought fit.

Prime Minister to General Auchinleck   15 Nov. 41

I have it in command from the King to express to all ranks of the Army and Royal Air Force in the Western Desert, and to the Mediterranean Fleet, His Majesty's confidence that they will do their duty with exemplary devotion in the supremely important battle which lies before them. For the first time British and Empire troops will meet the Germans with an ample equipment in modern weapons of all kinds. The battle itself will affect the whole course of the war. Now is the time to strike the hardest blow yet struck for final victory, home, and freedom. The Desert Army may add a page to history which will rank with Blenheim and with Waterloo. The eyes of all nations are upon you. All our hearts are with you. May God uphold the right!

[5] Oberkommando der Wehrmacht, Supreme Command of the German Army.

10

Operation "Crusader"

Ashore, Aloft, and Afloat

Sense of Drama Absent from Modern Battles—The Opposing Armies and Plans—The Eighth Army Attack—Surprise Achieved—The First Three Days—The XIIIth Corps Pierces the Frontier Line—General Auchinleck's Account of the Battle—Rommel's Daring Stroke—The Swaying Struggle—Auchinleck Flies to the Desert Headquarters—His Orders to General Cunningham Save the Battle—His Decision to Replace General Cunningham—My Letter to President Roosevelt of November 20—The Vichy Danger—Naval Attacks upon the Enemy Convoys—Resolute Advance of the New Zealand Division to Sidi Rezegh—Rommel Retreats, Abandoning His Frontier Garrisons—Tobruk Relieved—Losses in the Battle—Gloom in Rome—Naval Disasters "Ark Royal" and "Barham" Sunk—"Human Torpedoes" Attack in Alexandria Harbour—"Queen Elizabeth" and "Valiant" Heavily Damaged—"Force K" Stricken—Loss of the "Neptune"—Virtual Elimination of the British Eastern Mediterranean Fleet—Hitler Brings Back Air Power from Russia to Sicily—Our Nadir in the Mediterranean.

DESCRIPTIONS OF MODERN BATTLES are apt to lose the sense of drama because they are spread over wide spaces and often take weeks to decide, whereas on the famous fields of history the fate of nations and empires was decided on a few square miles of ground in a few hours. The conflicts of fast-moving armoured and motorised forces in the Desert present this contrast with the past in an extreme form.

Tanks had replaced the cavalry of former wars with a vastly more powerful and far-ranging weapon, and in many aspects their manoeuvres resembled naval warfare, with seas of sand

469

instead of salt water. The fighting quality of the armoured
column, like that of a cruiser squadron, rather than the position where they met the enemy, or the part of the horizon on
which he appeared, was the decisive feature. Tank divisions or
brigades, and still more smaller units, could form fronts in any
direction so swiftly that the perils of being outflanked or taken
in rear or cut off had a greatly lessened significance. On the
other hand, all depended from moment to moment upon fuel
and ammunition, and the supply of both was far more complicated for armoured forces than for the self-contained ships
and squadrons at sea. The principles on which the art of war
is founded expressed themselves therefore in novel terms, and
every encounter taught lessons of its own.

The magnitude of the war effort involved in these desert
struggles must not be underrated. Although only about ninety
or a hundred thousand fighting troops were engaged in each
of the armies, these needed masses of men and material two or
three times as large to sustain them in their trial of strength.
The fierce clash of Sidi Rezegh, which marked the opening of
General Auchinleck's offensive, when viewed as a whole, presents many of the most vivid features of war. The personal in-
terventions of the two Commanders-in-Chief were as dominant
and decisive and the stakes on both sides were as high as in
the olden times.

*   *   *

General Auchinleck's task was first to recapture Cyrenaica,
destroying in the process the enemy's armour, and, secondly, if
all went well, to capture Tripolitania. For these purposes General Cunningham, who was to command the newly-named
Eighth Army, was given the XIIIth and the XXXth Corps,
comprising, with the Tobruk garrison, about six divisions, and
three brigades in reserve.[1] The total British tank strength was
724, including 367 cruisers with another two hundred in reserve. The Royal Air Force was to intensify its action for a
month beforehand, so as to harry the hostile communications
and gain mastery in the air for the battle. Under Air Vice-
Marshal Coningham, the Western Desert Air Force consisted
of sixteen fighter squadrons, twelve medium bomber, five
heavy bomber, and three Army Co-operation squadrons. Out

[1] The following was the composition of the Eighth Army:
XIII Corps (Godwin-Austen): 4th Indian Division, New Zealand Division,
1st Army Tank Brigade.
XXX Corps (Norrie): 7th Armoured Division (7th Armoured Brigade, 22d
Armoured Brigade), 4th Armoured Brigade Group, 1st South African Division
(two brigades), 22d Guards Brigade Group.

of 1311 modern combat aircraft on the strength, 1072 were serviceable, in addition to ten squadrons operating from Malta.

Seventy miles behind Rommel's front lay the garrison of Tobruk, comprising five brigade groups and an armoured brigade. This fortress was his constant preoccupation, and had hitherto prevented by its strategic threat any advance upon Egypt. To eliminate Tobruk was the settled purpose of the German High Command, and all preparations possible had been made to begin the assault upon it on November 23. Rommel's army comprised the formidable Afrika Corps, consisting of the 15th and 21st Panzer Divisions and the 90th Light Division, and seven Italian divisions, of which one was armoured. The enemy tank strength was estimated at 388, but, as we now know from enemy records, was actually 558. Of the medium and heavy, two-thirds were German and carried heavier guns than the two-pounders of our tanks. The enemy were moreover markedly superior in anti-tank weapons. The Axis Air Force consisted of 190 German aircraft, of which only 120 were serviceable at the moment of attack, and over three hundred Italian aircraft, of which possibly two hundred were serviceable.

*   *   *

The Eighth Army, under General Cunningham, was to attack with its two corps and drive west and north towards Tobruk, whose garrison was at the same time to make a heavy and violent sortie towards them. For this purpose the XIIIth Corps was to engage and hold the enemy frontier defences from Halfaya to Sidi Omar, and outflank and surround them, thus cutting off all the troops who held them, and then march towards Tobruk. Meanwhile the XXXth Corps, which contained almost the whole of our armour, was to sweep widely on the desert flank, seeking to find and fight the mass of Rommel's armour, and at least to occupy them so that the XIIIth Corps should be shielded.

*   *   *

In spite of the immense preparations, complete tactical surprise was achieved. The Axis army was in process of taking up fresh positions for the attack on Tobruk due for November 23. Rommel himself was actually in Rome when the attack began. In order to strike at the brain and nerve-centre of the enemy's army at the critical moment, fifty men of the Scottish Commando, under Colonel Laycock, were carried by submarine to a point on the coast two hundred miles behind the enemy's line. The thirty who could be landed in the rough sea were formed into two parties, one to cut telephone and telegraph communications, and the other, under Lieutenant-Colonel Keyes, son of Admiral Keyes, to attack Rommel's Headquarters house. At midnight on the 17th, one of the Headquarters houses was broken into and a number of Germans were shot. In the close fighting of a pitch-dark room Keyes was killed. The award of a posthumous Victoria Cross was the tribute to his conduct.[2]

* * *

Early on November 18, in heavy rain, the Eighth Army leapt forward, and, according to their plan, the XIIIth Corps curled round the enemy positions on the frontier, while the XXXth Corps, meeting at first with no resistance, pressed upwards from the south to Sidi Rezegh. This ridge, about a hundred feet high, is almost a cliff on its northern side, dominating the Capuzzo track, Rommel's main line of communication from west to east. Near it lies a very large airfield. Southward, although not a conspicuous feature, it gives a good view over the undulating desert. It was judged by both sides to be the key to the whole battle area and the essential step to the relief of Tobruk.

For the first three days all went well. On the 19th what was thought to be the bulk of the German armour moved south from the coastal zone where they had been lying, and next day met our 4th and 22d Armoured Brigades fifteen miles west of Sidi Omar. The British 7th Armoured Division in its search for the enemy became widely dispersed. One of its brigades (the 7th) and the support group took Sidi Rezegh. These and other units were successfully attacked by the Afrika Corps, whose armour had been kept more concentrated. During the whole of the 21st and 22d a savage struggle raged, mainly around and upon the airfield. Into this arena virtually all the armour on both sides was drawn, and surged to and fro in violent struggles under the fire of rival batteries. The stronger armament of the German tanks and the larger numbers they brought to the points of collision gave them the advantage. In

[2] The sea was too rough for the re-embarkation of the survivors of the two raiding parties, and under fierce pursuit Colonel Laycock ordered them to scatter and hide in the broken country. Only Colonel Laycock and Sergeant Terry, who had been conspicuous in the attack on the German Headquarters, eventually regained our lines, after five weeks of privation and desperate adventures.

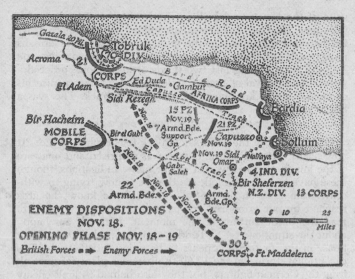

ENEMY DISPOSITIONS
NOV. 18.
OPENING PHASE NOV. 18–19
British Forces ▪▪▪➤ Enemy Forces ➤

FIRST BATTLE OF SIDI REZEGH
British Forces ▭▭▭➤ Enemy Forces ➤

0 5 10 15 20 25 30 MILES

spite of the heroic and brilliant leadership of Brigadier Jock Campbell, the Germans prevailed, and we suffered more heavily than they in tanks. On the night of the 22d the Germans recaptured Sidi Rezegh. General Norrie, commanding the XXXth Corps, having lost two-thirds of his armour, ordered a general withdrawal of twenty miles in order to reorganise his command in the area north of the El Abd track. This was a heavy setback.

*　　*　　*

On the night of the 19th Auchinleck telegraphed to me: "It now seems certain that the enemy was surprised and unaware of the imminence and weight of our blow. Indications, though these have to be confirmed, are that he is now trying to withdraw from area of Bardia-Sollum. Until we know the area reached by our armoured troops today, it is not possible to read the battle further at the moment. I myself am happy about the situation. . . ." Tedder also reported: "The present phase in the air battle appears to be going satisfactorily. The exceptional storms on the 17/18th upset our plans for neutralising the German fighters, but they also helped to limit enemy air action during the first two days. Another fourteen Ju. 87's were burnt on the ground yesterday. There were fifty-six heavy bomber sorties at night. Malta included Benghazi among its targets. Ten tons of ammunition were flown up to the 4th Armoured Brigade."

*　　*　　*

Meanwhile on November 21, the enemy armour being committed to battle, General Cunningham ordered the XIIIth Corps to advance. The 4th Indian Division had already curled round Sidi Omar. On its left the New Zealand Division, under General Freyberg, moved north, and reached the outskirts of Bardia, thus severing the communications of all the frontier garrisons. They captured the headquarters of the Afrika Corps, and on the 23d nearly regained Sidi Rezegh, from which their comrades of the 7th Armoured Division had just been driven. On November 24 Freyberg concentrated the bulk of the New Zealanders five miles to the east of the airfield. On this day therefore our armoured forces were reorganising after their repulse from Sidi Rezegh. The sortie from Tobruk had been launched, and was fighting hard against German infantry, but had not broken through. The New Zealand Division stood before Sidi Rezegh after a triumphant march. The enemy frontier garrisons had been cut off, and their armour, having

won its battle against the XXXth Corps, lay to the north of El
Gubi. Very heavy blows and severe losses had been exchanged, and the battle hung in the balance.

*   *   *

No better account can be given of this battle than is contained in General Auchinleck's final dispatch, which was published in the *Gazette* in 1948.

Since the Panzer divisions now seemed to be committed to battle
and were reported to be losing a considerable number of tanks,
General Cunningham allowed the signal to be given for the Tobruk
sorties to begin and for the XIIIth Corps to start operations. On
November 21 however our difficulties began. The enemy, as was to
be expected, reacted at once to the threat to Sidi Rezegh, and his
armoured divisions evaded the 4th and 22d Armoured Brigades.
The whole of the enemy armour then combined to drive us from
this vital area and to prevent help reaching the support group and
the 7th Armoured Brigade, which were isolated there. Neither of
these formations was designed to carry out a prolonged defence,
and it is greatly to their credit that they managed to do so, un-
aided, throughout the 21st. The 5th South African Infantry Brigade,
which was expected to reach the scene before the development of
the enemy attack, failed to do so, partly owing to the opposition of
the Ariete Armoured Division and partly because of inexperience in
handling the very large number of vehicles with which it took the
field.

Next day all three armoured brigades joined in the defence of
the area. But our tanks and anti-tank guns were no match for the
German, although they were fought with great gallantry, and on
the evening of November 22 the XXXth Corps was compelled to
retire, having lost two-thirds of its tanks and leaving the garrison
of Tobruk with a huge salient to defend.

The enemy rounded off his success in spectacular fashion. In a
night attack he surprised and completely disorganised the 4th
Armoured Brigade, whose hundred tanks represented two-thirds of
our remaining armoured strength. On the 23d he practically annihilated the 5th South African Infantry Brigade, one of the only
two infantry brigades General Norrie had under command—there
was no transport for any more—and then on the 24th with his
armoured divisions he made a powerful counter-stroke to the frontier. Before this it had become quite clear that the first reports
had grossly exaggerated enemy tank losses and that he had at least
as many tanks as we had and better, and was in a position to recover more from the battlefield, which remained in his hands.

This shifting of the balance of strength between the opposing
armoured forces produced a most critical situation. . . .

*   *   *

There was now a dramatic episode which recalls "Jeb" Stuart's ride round McClellan in 1862 on the Yorktown Peninsula in the American Civil War. It was however executed with an armoured force which was an army in itself, and whose destruction would have doomed the rest of the Axis army. Rommel resolved to seize the tactical initiative and to force his way eastward to the frontier with his armour in the hope of creating so much chaos and causing so much alarm as to prevail upon our command to give up the struggle and withdraw. He may well have had in his mind the fortune which had rewarded his armoured incursion in the preceding Desert battle of June 15 and led to General Messervy's retreat at the crucial moment. How nearly he succeeded this time will be apparent as the story proceeds.

He collected the greater part of the Afrika Corps, still the most formidable body in the field, and thrust down the El Abd road or track to Sheferzen, narrowly missing the headquarters of the XXXth Corps and two great dumps of supplies, without which we could not have continued the fight. On reaching the frontier he split his force into columns, some of which turned north and south, and others drove on twenty miles into Egyptian territory. He wrought havoc in our rearward areas and captured many prisoners. His columns however made no impression on the 4th Indian Division. They were pursued by de-

tachments hastily organised from the 7th Armoured Brigade, the support group, and the Guards Brigade. Above all our air force, which had now gained a high degree of mastery in the air above the contending armies, harried him all the time and all the way. Rommel's columns, virtually unsupported by their own air force, suffered the pangs our troops had known and endured when it was Germany who dominated the battle skies. On the 26th all the enemy's armour turned northward and sought haven in and near Bardia. Next day they hurried off to the west, back to Sidi Rezegh, whither they were urgently summoned. Rommel's daring stroke had failed, but, as will now be seen, only one man—the opposing Commander-inChief —stopped him.

* * *

It may be of interest to cite some extracts from the daily telegrams which reached me during this period from Auchinleck and Tedder. On the 21st Auchinleck sent favourable news. "With luck the earth is stopped and the hounds in full cry." And later in the day: "Engagements between the 22d Armoured Brigade and enemy armoured forces at El Gubi on November 18 heavier than earlier reports showed, and apparently resulted in our losing about forty cruiser tanks, of which many have since been repaired, against estimated enemy losses of fifty-five. Sidi Rezegh is held by the support group of the 7th Armoured Division and the 5th South African Infantry Brigade. Tobruk garrison made its sally this morning. . . . It is very difficult to arrive at a firm estimate of the enemy tank losses, as the battle has moved and is moving with such great speed. . . . A marked feature of operations to date has been our complete air supremacy and excellent co-operation between ground and air." On the 22d he summed up his report: "Prospects of achieving our immediate object, namely, the destruction of the German armoured forces, seem good." And later: "Spirit and dash shown by commanders and troops have been remarkable. In my opinion Cunningham has so far fought this extremely complicated battle with great skill and daring. . . . I think much depends on whether a substantial proportion of tanks of the 15th German Armoured Division took part with the 21st Armoured Division in the armoured battles of the last four days, or whether this division is still more or less intact. I hope for the first, but cannot yet be certain." On the 23d a somewhat darker impression was conveyed: "It looks as if the battle is moving to its climax. Some at any rate of the

German tanks north of El Gubi succeeded in breaking out.
Our troops at Sidi Rezegh were being strongly pressed yesterday from east and west by enemy reported to have a hundred
tanks in action. . . ."

These fragmentary quotations show the impressions prevailing almost from hour to hour at the Supreme Headquarters,
and are of course a very small part of the reports which they
sent.

*　　*　　*

The heavy blows we had received and the impression of disorder behind our front, caused by Rommel's raid, led General
Cunningham to represent to the Commander-in-Chief that a
continuation of our offensive might result in the annihilation of
our tank force, and so endanger the safety of Egypt. This
would mean acknowledged defeat and failure of the whole
operation. At this decisive moment General Auchinleck inter-
vened personally. At Cunningham's request he flew with Air
Marshal Tedder to the Desert Headquarters on November 23,
and, with full knowledge of all the dangers, ordered General
Cunningham "to continue to press the offensive against the
enemy." By his personal action Auchinleck thus saved the
battle and proved his outstanding qualities as a commander
in the field.

To me he telegraphed on the 24th from the Advanced Headquarters:

General Auchinleck to Prime Minister   24 Nov. 41

On arrival I found Cunningham perturbed at the situation,
owing to the very small number of our tanks reported still in running order. Apparently five days' continuous fighting and manoeuvring resulted in considerable disorganisation and losses from
enemy action and mechanical breakdowns in our armoured division. There are sure to be reasons for this, but they do not matter
now. . . . In his attack yesterday evening the enemy used Italian
tanks, which I take as evidence that he is running short of his own.
I am convinced that he is fully stretched and desperate, and that
we must go on pressing him relentlessly. We may immobilise temporarily at least practically all our tanks in the process, but that
does not matter if we destroy all his. The fact that he has abandoned Sidi Omar and Sollum garrisons to their fate and that we
have already taken over three thousand prisoners, including a thousand Germans, . . . is significant. I have accordingly ordered General Cunningham to attack with all available resources, regain Sidi
Rezegh, and join hands with Tobruk garrison, which is to co-operate by attacking the enemy on its front. Commanders and troops

in great heart, and New Zealand Division is concentrated in front of Sidi Rezegh with infantry tanks. The enemy is fighting desperately, but we always expected that.

I replied at once:

Prime Minister to General Auchinleck   25 Nov. 41

Yours of 24th. I cordially endorse your view and intentions, and His Majesty's Government wish to share your responsibility for fighting it out to the last inch, whatever may be the result. It is all or nothing, but I am sure you are the stronger and will win.

2. You have no doubt had my message about the rest of the 1st Armoured Division landing at Suez today. Ram it in if useful at earliest without regard for future. Close grip upon the enemy by all units will choke the life out of him.

3. Am immensely heartened by your magnificent spirit and will-power. Say "Bravo" to Tedder and R.A.F. on air mastery.

*   *   *

On Auchinleck's return to Cairo on the 25th he telegraphed to me:

General Auchinleck to Prime Minister   25 Nov. 41

I have decided to replace General Cunningham temporarily by General Ritchie, my present Deputy Chief of Staff. This is not on account of any misgiving as to the present situation in my mind, but because I have reluctantly concluded that Cunningham, admirable as he has been up to date, has now begun to think defensively, mainly because of our large tank losses. But before taking this drastic step I gave the matter prolonged and anxious consideration and consulted the Minister of State on my return this afternoon. I am convinced that I am right, though I realise the undesirability of such a step at present on general grounds. I will try and minimise publicity as much as possible.

In his dispatch of 1948, already quoted, General Auchinleck writes:

I most reluctantly decided that I must relieve General Cunningham of his command, as I had come to the conclusion that he was unduly influenced by the threat of an enemy counter-stroke against his communications.

The Minister of State, Oliver Lyttelton, explained and strongly supported the Commander-in-Chief's decision. To him I telegraphed at once.

Prime Minister to Minister of State   25 Nov. 41

General Auchinleck's authority over all commanders is supreme, and all his decisions during the battle will be confirmed by us.

Your action and attitude highly approved. Communicate [this] to General Auchinleck.

Here I shall leave this incident, so painful to the gallant officer concerned, to his brother the Naval Commander-in-Chief, and to General Auchinleck, who was a personal friend of both. I particularly admired General Auchinleck's conduct in rising superior to all personal considerations and to all temptations to compromise or delay action.

*   *   *

At this point in the battle I must turn aside to record some other closely related events. On November 20, while the news was still good, I sent an account to the President urging him to do all in his power to keep Vichy motionless in these cardinal days.

Former Naval Person to President Roosevelt   20 Nov. 41

The approach and deployment of our forces in Libya has been most successful, and the enemy was taken by surprise. Only now does he realise the large scale of our operations against him. Heavy fighting between the armoured forces seems probable today. Orders have been given to press what is now begun to a decision at all costs. The chances do not seem to be unfavourable.

2. It would be disastrous if Weygand were to be replaced by some pro-Hun officer just at the moment when we are likely to be in a position to influence events in North Africa both from the East and from home. I hope you will try your utmost to persuade Vichy to preserve Weygand in his command. If this cannot be achieved some friendly figure from retirement, like General Georges, might be agreed upon. I have not seen Georges since the collapse, but I have reason to believe his heart is sound. I knew him very well. Anyhow, Mr. President, Tunis and all French North Africa might open out to us if we gain a good victory in Libya, and we must be ready to exploit success. I am afraid, on the other hand, lest Hitler may demand to occupy Bizerta in view of possible danger to Tripoli. It is now or never with the Vichy French, and their last chance of redemption.

*   *   *

It was vital also at this moment to cut off Rommel's fuel supply, and I therefore telegraphed both to General Auchinleck and the Naval Commander-in-Chief urging that a blow should be struck at the enemy communications.

Prime Minister to General Auchinleck   23 Nov. 41

When one sees the invaluable cargoes of fuel now being directed upon Benghazi, and the enemy air concentration at Benina, it would seem that quite exceptional risk should be run to sterilise these places, even for three or four days. The enemy's fear of this operation is obviously well founded. The only time for such a venture is while he is in the throes of the battle. Chance of success will diminish as soon as he has been able to reinforce with troops withdrawing or escaping from the battle zone. There is a lot to be picked up cheap now, both at Benghazi and west of Agheila, which will rise in price enormously once the main battle is over. I am sure you will be considering this. Please remember how much they got by brass and bluff at the time of the French collapse. What is the mission of the Oasis force?

Prime Minister to Admiral Cunningham,   23 Nov. 41
Commander-in-Chief Mediterranean

I asked the First Sea Lord to wireless you today about the vital importance of intercepting surface ships bringing reinforcements, supplies, and above all fuel, to Benghazi. Our information here shows a number of vessels now approaching or starting. Request has been made by enemy for air protection, but this cannot be given owing to absorption in battle of his African air force. All this information has been repeated to you. I shall be glad to hear through Admiralty what action you propose to take. The stopping of these ships may save thousands of lives, apart from aiding a victory of cardinal importance.

The Admiral replied to me personally forthwith:

Admiral Cunningham to Prime Minister

Yours of the 23d. I am naturally very much alive to vital importance of Benghazi supply route, and First Sea Lord will by now have told you dispositions which were already in hand to deal with situation. Our first move was to hold up enemy convoys by means of threats from the forces at each end of Mediterranean, and this has had considerable success. Now that convoys are resuming sailings they will be attacked by surface air and submarine forces. Unfortunately the reported absorption of the German Air Force in land battles to which you refer has not been borne out in practice, and a very lively interest is being taken by the enemy in our movements. Conversely, our main weakness in reconnaissance forces is adding a heavy hazard to work of our light forces, who have of necessity to operate without close support if use is to be made of their speed.

He did his utmost, but it was from Malta that the most effective blow was struck. On the night of the 24th the cruisers and destroyers of "Force K" sallied forth and caught the two oil transports on which the enemy counted highly. To Auchinleck I was able to send this good news:

Prime Minister to General Auchinleck   25 Nov. 41

We sent *Aurora* and *Penelope* out from Malta last night, and duly sank the two vital oil transports *Procida* and *Maritza*. The Admiral is after the others.

*   *   *

While Rommel was engaged with the Afrika Corps on his audacious but costly excursion through the communications and rear of the British Eighth Army, Freyberg and his New Zealanders, supported by the 1st Army Tank Brigade, pressed hard upon Sidi Rezegh. After two days of severe fighting they recaptured it. Simultaneously the garrison of Tobruk resumed its sortie and captured Ed Duda. On the night of the 26th contact was established between the Tobruk garrison and the relieving force. Some units of the New Zealand Division and the XIIIth Corps Headquarters entered beleaguered Tobruk. This situation brought Rommel back from Bardia. He fought his way to Sidi Rezegh, attacked in flank by the reorganised 7th Armoured Division, now mustering a hundred and twenty tanks. He recaptured Sidi Rezegh. He drove back the 6th New Zealand Brigade with crippling loss. They and the 4th Brigade, except for two battalions which joined up with the Tobruk garrison, were withdrawn southward to the frontier, where the heroic division re-formed after losing more than three thousand men. The Tobruk garrison, again isolated, held on by a bold decision to all the ground gained.

General Ritchie now regrouped his army so as to bring the garrison of Tobruk under the XIIIth Corps and to pass the New Zealand Division into reserve. El Adem, in a valley fifteen miles west of Sidi Rezegh, lay also upon the main east-to-west communications of the enemy, and was now the objective. Both our corps were used. The XIIIth advanced from Ed Duda, and the XXXth came up from the south. During these preparations Rommel made a final thrust to rescue his frontier garrisons. It was repulsed. The general retreat of the Axis army to the Gazala line then began.

*   *   *

Our telegrams continued to flow. On the 26th Auchinleck said:

The news today is so far scanty, but good. Tobruk garrison was within sight of the New Zealanders this morning, and I have just heard that the latter recaptured Sidi Rezegh. Fierce fighting continues. Enemy armoured and motorised forces are still apparently milling around in our rear areas between Bardia, Sheferzen, and Halfaya, but with little result. It is now certain that this armoured and motorised thrust was a raid to divert our attention from Tobruk. It has failed signally.

About General Cunningham's replacement he added:

I am most grateful to you for your support. In this, as in everything else, I cannot tell you what it means to us, and it is not to be measured in terms of armoured divisions or anything else. Rommel is not done yet, but we have regained the initiative, I feel, and I trust we shall keep it.

Prime Minister to General Auchinleck 26 Nov. 41

You are no doubt constantly considering the movement forward of reserves towards the battle zone. I am well aware that this is conditioned by transport and how important it is for you to do the work with the minimum mouths to feed. I should be glad however to know what you have in reserve; suppose you need another division, or two or three brigades, where would you get them from? You could, I suppose, if necessary, bring a brigade of the 50th Division back from Baghdad.

Please let me know your resources and ideas.

Auchinleck replied that, on account of the difficulty of maintaining them in the Desert, it was more a question of being able to replace tired troops by fresh ones than of adding new formations, though he would of course be glad to have more troops forward to ensure momentum. He was bringing one infantry brigade group of the 50th Division into the G.H.Q. reserve, but did not think it necessary to recall the other two brigade groups, which were on their way to Iraq.

Although I cordially approved of what had been done in the High Command, I thought it a pity that Auchinleck did not take it over himself instead of entrusting it to one of his staff officers, as yet unproved in the field.

Prime Minister to General Auchinleck 27 Nov. 41

C.I.G.S. and I both wonder whether, as you saved the battle once, you should not go up again and win it now. Your presence on the spot will be an inspiration to all. However, this of course is entirely for you to judge.

He replied:

General Auchinleck to Prime Minister 30 Nov. 41

I considered very carefully whether I should not myself take Cunningham's place in command of the Eighth Army. I realise well what hangs on this battle, but concluded that I was more useful at

G.H.Q., where I could see the whole battle and retain a proper sense of proportion. . . . I shall go forward to visit [Ritchie] of course, as required.

Neither I nor the C.I.G.S. was convinced, but we did not press our point.

Auchinleck's message of the 30th concluded:

Our supply column reached Tobruk morning of 29th. The Commander of XIIIth Corps' [General Godwin-Austen] birthday message to you is, "Corridor to Tobruk clear and secure. Tobruk is as relieved as I am."

On December 1 Auchinleck went himself to the Advanced Headquarters, and remained for ten days with General Ritchie. He did not assume the command himself, but closely supervised his subordinate. This did not seem to me the best arrangement for either of them. However, the power of the Eighth Army was now predominant, and on December 10 the Commander-in-Chief could tell me:

Enemy is apparently in full retreat towards the west. El Adem is taken. South African and Indian troops joined hands there with British from Tobruk, and I think it now permissible to claim that the siege of Tobruk has been raised. We are pursuing vigorously in fullest co-operation with the Royal Air Force.

*   *   *

We now know from German records that the enemy losses in the "Crusader" battle, including the garrisons now cut off at Bardia, Sollum, and Halfaya and later made prisoners, were about thirteen thousand Germans and twenty thousand Italians, a total of thirty-three thousand, together with three hundred tanks. The comparable British and Imperial army losses in the same period (November 18 to mid-January) were: 2908 officers and men killed, 7339 wounded, and 7457 missing; total 17,704, together with 278 tanks. Nine-tenths of this loss occurred in the first month of the offensive.

*   *   *

Here then we reached a moment of relief, and indeed of rejoicing, about the Desert war. The German records show the gloom that descended on military circles in Rome.

2 Dec. 41

The situation in North Africa demands the utmost efforts to supply the German forces, to replenish the considerable losses and to bring up first-rate reinforcements. With the present position at sea air transport must be the main carrier across the Mediterranean.

And again on December 4:

The Duce speaks of freeing Bizerta as the only means of overcoming transport difficulties. The occupation of Malta is not possible. He does not believe that Libya can be held much longer without supply through Tunisia. The situation for the Axis in the Mediterranean and North Africa is critical because the supply routes were not kept open in time. Past decisions have been strongly influenced by the campaign against Russia.

The Fleet was at all times a vital factor in the Desert war. By destroying Axis supplies and sustaining the Eighth Army in its advance, the Royal Navy as well as the Royal Air Force had helped to bring Rommel's armies to the brink of ruin. But now at this crucial moment our naval power in the Eastern Mediterranean was virtually destroyed by a series of disasters.

*   *   *

The impact of the U-boats in the Mediterranean was heavy. The *Ark Royal* was gone. A fortnight later the *Barham* was struck by three torpedoes and capsized in as many minutes with the loss of over five hundred men. More was to follow. On the night of December 18 an Italian submarine approached Alexandria and launched three "human torpedoes," each controlled by two men. They penetrated the harbour while the boomgate was open for the passage of ships. They fixed time-bombs, which detonated early on the morning of the 19th under the battleships *Queen Elizabeth* and *Valiant.* Both ships were heavily damaged and became a useless burden for months. Thus in the course of a few weeks the whole of our Eastern battle fleet was eliminated as a fighting force. I have yet to tell of the loss in another theatre of the *Prince of Wales* and *Repulse.* We were successful in concealing the damage to the battle fleet for some time. In secret session a good deal later I said to the House of Commons: "In a few weeks we lost, or had put out of action for a long time, seven great ships, or more than a third of our battleships and battle-cruisers."

But "Force K" was also stricken. On the very day of the Alexandria disaster news reached Malta of an important enemy convoy heading for Tripoli. The cruisers *Neptune, Aurora,* and *Penelope,* with four destroyers, at once went out to catch them. Approaching Tripoli our ships ran into a new minefield. The *Neptune* was hard hit, and both the other cruisers were damaged, but were able to steam away. Presently the destroyer *Kandahar* entered the minefield to rescue the crew of the *Neptune,* but she too struck a mine and became helpless. The *Neptune,* drifting in the minefield, struck two more mines and sank. Only one man of her crew of over seven hundred survived—and he as a prisoner of war after four days on a raft, on which his captain, R. C. O'Connor, and thirteen others perished. The *Kandahar* remained afloat and eventually drifted clear of the minefield, and the next night the destroyer *Jaguar* found her, and saved most of her company.

The German Staff comment on this incident is instructive.

The sinking of the *Neptune* may be of decisive importance for holding Tripolitania. Without this the British force would probably have destroyed the Italian convoy. There is no doubt that the loss of these supplies at the peak of the crisis would have had the severest consequences.

Thus was extinguished the light of "Force K." The cruiser *Galatea* had also been sunk by a German U-boat. All that remained of the British Eastern Mediterranean Fleet was a few destroyers and the three cruisers of Admiral Vian's squadron.

Up to the end of November our combined efforts by land, sea, and air had prevailed in the Mediterranean. We had now suffered fearful naval losses. And now on December 5 Hitler, realising at last Rommel's mortal peril, ordered the transfer of a whole air corps from Russia to Sicily and North Africa. A new air offensive against Malta was launched under General Kesselring's direction. The attacks on the island reached a new peak, and Malta could do no more than struggle for life. By the end of the year it was the Luftwaffe who held the mastery over the sea routes to Tripoli, and thus made possible the refit of Rommel's armies after their defeat. Seldom has the interaction of sea, air, and land warfare been so strikingly illustrated as in the events of these few months.

But now all paled under the stroke of world events.

11

Japan

T HE MOMENT had come when in the long, romantic history of Japan the most fearful plunge was to be made. Not since 1592, when the war lord Hideyoshi resolved to embark on mortal conflict with China and used sea power to invade Korea, had any such fateful step been taken. A strong continuity of tradition and custom had guided the redoubtable is-

487

landers of the Far East across the centuries. Valour, discipline, and national spirit, never divorced from the mystic, had maintained the stamina of this stern and hardy Asiatic race. Europe had first heard of their existence from Marco Polo about A.D. 1300. The religion of the Japanese nation was a form of Buddhism. The later incursion of the Christian missionaries, the devotion of their converts, and their fierce-fought extermination had been an episode little noticed in Europe. The merciless slaughter of the Christian population, numbering over a quarter of a million, took twenty-four years, and was finished around the year 1638. After this deed Japan plunged into strict seclusion, and had remained almost unknown for many generations when the nineteenth century with its own strident challenges broke upon the world. There had been a spell of complete isolation. The arts, culture, and faith of the Japanese had supported a rigid structure of society. Science, machinery, and Western philosophies did not exist for them.

But the steam engine altered the proportions of the globe, and about a hundred years ago ships arrived from across the ocean spaces and knocked at the well-barred feudal doors of Japan with weapons and ideas. For some time after Commodore Perry's American squadron had paid its unwelcome visit in 1853 a British or American gunboat could enforce the will of a British or American Government upon the external behaviour of the Japanese State. With the foreign warships came the revelation of the wonderful tricks which the White Man had found out, and which he was prepared to teach or sell. The gaunt and grave civilisation of the thirteenth century was presented with that of the nineteenth, grinning, prosperous, and well armed.

* * *

Uncle Sam and Britannia were the godparents of the new Japan. In less than two generations, with no background but the remote past, the Japanese people advanced from the two-handed sword of the Samurai to the ironclad ship, the rifled cannon, the torpedo, and the Maxim gun; and a similar revolution took place in industry. The transition of Japan under British and American guidance from the Middle Ages to modern times was swift and violent. China was surpassed and smitten. It was with amazement that the world saw in 1905 the defeat of Czarist Russia, not only on the sea, but by great armies transported to the mainland and winning enormous battles in Manchuria. Japan now took her place among the Great

Powers. The Japanese were themselves astonished at the respect with which they were viewed. "When we sent you the beautiful products of our ancient arts and culture you despised and laughed at us; but since we have got a first-class Navy and Army with good weapons we are regarded as a highly civilised nation." But all they had added was the trappings and panoply of applied science. All was on the surface. Behind stood Old Japan. I remember how in my youth the British caricaturists were wont to depict Japan as a smart, spruce, uniformed messenger-boy. Once I saw an American cartoon in quite a different style. An aged priestly warrior towered up, august and formidable, with his hand upon his dagger.

I do not pretend to have studied Japan, ancient or modern, except as presented to me by the newspapers and a few books and in the official documents I saw in the many departments of State in which I have served. I was on her side in the Russo-Japanese War. I welcomed the Anglo-Japanese Treaty which had preceded it. At the Admiralty during the First World War I rejoiced in the Japanese accession to the Allies and at the extirpation of Germany from the Far East. It was with sorrow that in 1921 I became a party to the ending of the British alliance with Japan, from which we derived both strength and advantage. But as we had to choose between Japanese and American friendship I had no doubts what our course should be.

*　　*　　*

In war and policy one should always try to put oneself in the position of what Bismarck called "the Other Man." The more fully and sympathetically a Minister can do this, the better are his chances of being right. The more knowledge he possesses of the opposite point of view, the less puzzling it is to know what to do. But imagination without deep and full knowledge is a snare, and very few among our experts could form any true impression of the Japanese mind. It was indeed inscrutable. The old and new societies, with the chasm of the ages between them, were intermingled and reacted upon each other in ways that no foreigner could understand. Indeed, it is doubtful whether Japan knew her own mind, or what forces in her nature would predominate in the hour of decision.

The hierarchy of the Japanese Army formed a series of concentric circles united by the Samurai tradition, which inspired all its chiefs and their subordinates to die for the military honour of Japan and to face each man's court of ancestors with confidence. But as Japan emerged from long seclusion into the vast world which opened about her and blithely placed lethal weapons of hitherto unimagined power in the hands of her warriors, there also formed with cold, slow growth the design to master Asia, and perhaps thereafter lead that continent to the conquest of the world. There was even talk of "the Hundred Years' Plan," though this was but the impelling background to continually changing conditions and events.

The strongest check on the power and ambitions of the Army, in the period after the outbreak of the Second World War, came from the Navy. In the nineteenth century the Japanese Army was trained by German instructors, and the Navy by British. This left lasting differences of mentality, which were emphasised by the conditions of Service life. Army officers hardly ever went abroad—except to make war—and cultivated a more narrowly arrogant, nationalist spirit than naval officers, who frequently visited foreign ports and knew something of the world outside Japan. Whereas also the Army was conscious of its capacity to defeat or hold its own against any military forces existing in the Far East, or which could get there, the Navy was painfully aware of its inferiority in fleet strength to the British and American Navies, especially for action outside Japanese home waters. Thus the Navy tended to be more cautious and moderate in outlook than the Army.

The commercial classes had no official recognition or organisation like the Army or Navy, nor had they ever a single policy common to all the various financial, industrial, and trading interests by which they lived. Their influence was exerted partly through the political parties in the Diet, and partly through connections with Court circles. In general, the commercial interests were opposed to serious warlike adventures, but some of them, particularly those with investments in China, supported the Army in expansionist policies. The masses of the Japanese people tended in a crisis to support the Army rather than the liberal bourgeois leadership, because of the Army's traditional prestige and the popular belief that it was the custodian of the national interest against the aims of private capitalists.

*　　*　　*

By the Japanese Constitution of 1889 the making of treaties, the declaration of war, and conclusion of peace lay within the prerogative of the Emperor and were not subject to control by the Diet. The Emperor also had the supreme command of the

armed forces. He was however supposed to exercise his authority on the advice of the Army and Navy Chiefs of Staff
and to conduct foreign policy on the advice of the Cabinet.
The Cabinet under the Japanese Constitution was not responsible to the Diet, though it needed a majority in both Houses
in order to legislate. It was for the Emperor to choose and
appoint the Prime Minister. By custom he did so on the advice
of a body of "elder statesmen," or Genro. Early in the present
century there were several Genro, but they died without being
replaced, until in 1940 only Prince Saionji was left. After he
died at the end of that year the nomination was made by a
conference of all ex-Premiers, known as the "New Genro," of
whom in 1941 there were eight.

The Army and Navy Ministers of the Cabinet had to be
respectively a general and an admiral on the active list. If a
Prime Minister could not find a general or an admiral to hold
these offices he could not form or maintain a Cabinet, and
professional spirit was so strong that no general or admiral
would serve as Army or Navy Minister in a Cabinet whose
policy was strongly disapproved of by his Service. Thus the
Army and Navy Staffs were able to exert a continual, and at
times decisive, influence on policy by withdrawing, or threatening to withdraw, the Service Ministers from a Cabinet.

* * *

In 1936 Japan had concluded with Germany the Anti-
Comintern Pact, which was originally negotiated by the Japanese War Ministry, with Ribbentrop representing the Nazi
Party, behind the backs of both the then Foreign Ministers.
This was not yet an alliance, but it provided the basis for one.
In the spring of 1939 the Army Minister in the Cabinet,
headed by Baron Hiranuma, tried to conclude a full military
alliance with Germany. He failed owing to the opposition of the
Navy Minister, Admiral Yonai. In August, 1939, Japan was not
only engaged in the war in China which had begun in July,
1937, but was also involved in localised hostilities with Russia
about the boundary between the newly created State of Man-
chukuo and Outer Mongolia. Along and behind this smoulder-
ing front large armies lay. When, on the eve of the European
war, Germany made her Non-Aggression Pact with Russia
without consulting or informing Japan, her Anti-Comintern
partner, the Japanese felt with reason that they had been ill-
used. Their dispute with Russia fell into the background, and
Japanese resentment against Germany was strong. British sup-

port and sympathy for China had estranged us from our former ally, and during the first few months of the European war our relations with Japan were already by no means friendly. There was however in Japan little or no enthusiasm for Germany.

The Hiranuma Cabinet "lost face" on account of the German-Soviet Pact and had to resign. It was succeeded by a Cabinet under General Abe, who, although an Army man (retired), was reckoned a moderate, and he in January, 1940, was replaced by Admiral Yonai, who as Hiranuma's Navy Minister had opposed the alliance with Germany. Under the Abe and Yonai administrations Japan's policy was neutrality in Europe combined with the prosecution of Japan's own war in China. But soon supreme convulsions shook the world. With the fall of France and the Low Countries under Hitler's onslaught, and the prospect of the invasion and destruction of Britain in the autumn of 1940, long-cherished, glittering schemes sprang from dreamland into reality. Was Japan to gain nothing from the collapse of France, of Holland, and it might well be of Britain, with all their vast possessions in East Asia? Had not her historic moment come? Deep passions stirred in Army and Nationalist political circles. It was demanded that Japan should at once begin to move south and seize French Indo-China, Malaya, and the coveted Dutch East Indies. To force this policy the Army Minister, General Hata, withdrew from the Cabinet, and thus compelled Admiral Yonai to resign his Premiership.

The sober and prudent elements, which Japan has never lacked, were hard pressed to maintain their control. In Yonai's place the Genro nominated Prince Konoye, an aristocrat in the prime of life who had close connections with the Imperial Court, but was also on good terms with the leaders of the Army. Prince Konoye held office from July, 1940, to October, 1941. He was a highly respected and extremely subtle politician, whose method was to give the Army symbolic satisfactions without ever allowing it to drag the country into a major war. During the summer of 1940 Prince Konoye managed to restrain the Army from making any attack on British or Dutch possessions. On the other hand, he agreed to put pressure on Vichy France for air bases in Northern Indo-China, and in September he concluded the Tripartite Pact with Germany and Italy. This instrument bound Japan to enter the European war on the Axis side if America should enter it on behalf of Britain.

Meanwhile other great events became apparent. By the end of November, 1940, the result of the Battle of Britain and Hitler's recoil from his invasion boasts were recognised in Japan as facts of the first order. The successful British air attack on the Italian Fleet at Taranto, throwing modern first-class battleships out of action for many months, profoundly impressed the Japanese Navy with the power and possibilities of the new Air Arm, especially when combined with surprise. Japan became convinced that Britain was by no means finished. She was undoubtedly going on, and indeed growing stronger. There was a widespread feeling that the Tripartite Pact had been a mistake. Always there loomed the fear of united action by the British Empire and the United States, with its combination of the two strongest navies afloat and with resources, which once developed were measureless and incomparable. This danger seemed to draw ever nearer. In the spring of 1941 Konoye obtained the agreement of his Cabinet to open conversations with the United States for the settlement of outstanding issues between the two countries. It is worthy of note that on this occasion General Tojo, as Army Minister, supported the policy of Konoye against the Foreign Minister, Matsuoka, whose protests that such talks with America would be contrary to the German alliance were thus overruled.

* * *

Nevertheless, the ferment in Japanese minds grew constantly more intense. Beneath the normal modernised processes of their political life thousands of officers and persons occupying responsible, if minor, positions seemed to hear

Ancestral voices prophesying war.

Must they not be worthy of their fathers who had paid with interest the vengeance they owed to the Mongols of the thirteenth century, whom they had identified with the Russia of the Czars? This prodigious feat of the preceding generation incited their sons to the utmost daring. And here was the whole world in storm and flux. New forces and new Titans had appeared. There was to be a "New Order" in Europe. Was this not the time to have a "New Order" in Asia? Within all this framework lay plans evolved with minute and patient care and brought up to date with every change in the movement of world catastrophe. It was claimed by the Army leaders that *they* should be the authority to select the moment when the signal should be given. They could certainly assert that if Japan was to strike at all, the best opportunity—the fall of France—had already been missed by cautious or craven politicians.

The Emperor and the Imperial Princes, around whom gathered the highest aristocracy, were against an aggressive war. They had too much to lose in a violent era. Many of them had travelled and met their equals in foreign courts. They admired the life of Europe and feared its power and that of the United States. They admired the secure majesty of the English monarchy. They leaned continuously upon their skindeep parliamentarianism, and hoped they might continue to reign or rule in peace. But who should say what the Army would do? No patriarchate, no Emperor, no dynasty could separate themselves from it. The Emperor and the Princes were for peace and prudence, but had no wish to perish for such a cause.

* * *

The drastic application of economic sanctions in July, 1941, brought to a head the internal crisis in Japanese politics. Conservative elements were shocked and the moderate leaders scared. The domestic prestige of the Japanese Army as a constitutional factor in shaping Japanese policy was already involved. Hitherto the Navy had exerted its restraining force. But the embargoes which the United States, Britain, and Holland had enforced cut off from Japan all supplies of oil, on which the Navy, and indeed the whole war-power of Japan, depended. The Japanese Navy was at once forced to live on its oil reserves, and at the outbreak of the Pacific war had in fact consumed four out of eighteen months' supply. It was evident that this was a stranglehold, and that the choice before them was either for Japan to reach an agreement with the United States or go to war. The American requirements involved Japanese withdrawal, not only from their new aggression in Indo-China, but from China itself, where they had already been fighting at heavy expense for so long. This was a rightful but a hard demand. In these circumstances the Navy associated itself with the Army in the policy of war if an acceptable diplomatic agreement could not be obtained. The fact that the Navy had now developed its air arm to a high pitch of offensive capacity hardened them in this course of action.

The tense debate within the ruling circles in Japan was prolonged throughout the summer and autumn. The supreme question of facing war with the United States was, we now know, discussed on July 31, on the morrow of the embargoes. It was clear to all the Japanese leaders that the time for choice was short. Germany might win the war in Europe before Japan had realised any of her ambitions. The conversations between the Japanese and American Governments continued. The Japanese conservative politicians and the Imperial Court hoped to obtain terms which would enable them to control their war party at home. The State Department at Washington believed, as I did, that Japan would probably recoil before the ultimately overwhelming might of the United States.

*   *   *

The reader has seen how from the first day of the war our anxieties about Japan weighed relentlessly upon us. Her appetites and opportunity were alike obvious. We wondered why she had not struck at the moment of the French collapse. Afterwards we drew breath more freely, but all the time we were at our utmost stress and strain to defend the British Island from destruction and carry on the war in the Western Desert. I confess that in my mind the whole Japanese menace lay in a sinister twilight, compared with our other needs. My feeling was that if Japan attacked us the United States would come in. If the United States did not come in, we had no means of defending the Dutch East Indies, or indeed our own Empire in the East. If, on the other hand, Japanese aggression drew in America I would be content to have it. On this I rested. Our priorities during 1941 stood: first, the defence of the Island, including the threat of invasion and the U-boat war; secondly, the struggle in the Middle East and Mediterranean; thirdly, after June, supplies to Soviet Russia; and, last of all, resistance to a Japanese assault. It was however always understood that if Japan invaded Australia or New Zealand, the Middle East should be sacrificed to the defence of our kith and kin. This contingency we all regarded as remote and improbable because of the vast abundance of easier and more attractive conquests offered to Japan by Malaya, Siam, and above all the Dutch East Indies. I am sure that nothing we could have spared at this time, even at the cost of wrecking the Middle Eastern theatre or cutting off supplies to the Soviet, would have changed the march of fate in Malaya. On the other hand, the entry of the United States into the war would overwhelm all evils put together.

It must not be supposed that these broad decisions were

taken unconsciously or without profound and constant heart-searching by the War Cabinet and their military advisers.

* * *

As time passed and I realised the formidable effect of the embargoes which President Roosevelt had declared on July 26, and in which we and the Dutch had joined, I became increasingly anxious to confront Japan with the greatest possible display of British and American naval forces in the Pacific and Indian Oceans. Naval forces were all we could spare. Narrowly did we scan our resources.

On August 25 I sent a minute to the First Sea Lord about the formation of an Eastern Fleet and setting out my views regarding its composition. I felt strongly that it should be possible in the near future to place a deterrent squadron in the Indian Ocean, and that this should consist of the smallest number of the best ships. The First Sea Lord replied that the Admiralty plan was to build up a force in Ceylon by the beginning of 1942, comprising the battleships *Nelson* and *Rodney*, the battle-cruiser *Renown*, and the small aircraft-carrier *Hermes*. The *Ark Royal* would follow later, but not until April. Meanwhile the four "R" class battleships would be sent to the Indian Ocean as escorts for troop convoys. In his memorandum the First Sea Lord dwelt on the overriding importance of the Atlantic theatre, where he considered it essential to retain all three of our latest battleships of the *King George V* class to guard against a possible break-out by the *Tirpitz*.

I did not like these dispositions. The use of the old "R" class for convoy work was good against eight-inch cruisers, but if the enemy were prepared to detach a fast modern battleship for raiding purposes they and their convoys would become an easy prey. In their present state these old ships would be floating coffins. It would therefore be necessary to have one or two fast capital ships to deter the Japanese from detaching individual heavy raiders.

I ended my correspondence with the Admiralty as follows:

29 Aug. 41

. . . I must add that I cannot feel that Japan will face the combination now forming against her of the United States, Great Britain, and Russia, while already preoccupied in China. It is very likely she will negotiate with the United States for at least three months without making any further aggressive move or joining the Axis actively. Nothing would increase her hesitation more than the appearance of the force I mentioned, and above all a *K.G.V.* This might indeed be a decisive deterrent.[1]

* * *

It was decided to send as the first instalment of our Far Eastern Fleet both the *Prince of Wales* and the *Repulse*, with four destroyers, and as an essential element the modern armoured aircraft-carrier *Indomitable*. Unhappily, the *Indomitable* was temporarily disabled by an accident. It was decided in spite of this to let the two fast capital ships go forward, in the hope of steadying the Japanese political situation, and also to be in relation to the United States Pacific Fleet. Our general naval policy was to build up under the remote cover of the main American Fleet in the Pacific a British Eastern Fleet based on Singapore, which by the spring of 1942 would comprise seven capital ships of various quality, one first-class aircraft-carrier, ten cruisers, and twenty-four destroyers. Admiral Sir Tom Phillips, till now our trusted Vice-Chief of the Naval Staff, was selected for command, and hoisted his flag at Greenock on October 24.

* * *

At the end of October I telegraphed to the Prime Ministers of Australia and New Zealand, and gave them details of our proposed naval dispositions in the Far East.

Prime Minister to Prime Ministers Australia and New Zealand

I am still inclined to think that Japan will not run into war with A.B.C.D. [American-British-Chinese-Dutch] Powers unless or until Russia is decisively broken. Perhaps even then they will wait for the promised invasion of the British Isles in the spring. Russian resistance is still strong, especially in front of Moscow, and winter is now near.

2. Admiralty dispositions had been to build up towards the end of the year *Rodney, Nelson,* and four R's, based mainly on Singapore. This however was spoiled by recent injury to *Nelson,* which will take three or four months to repair.

3. In the interval, in order further to deter Japan, we are sending forthwith our newest battleship, *Prince of Wales*, to join *Repulse* in Indian Ocean. This is done in spite of protests from the Commander-in-Chief Home Fleet, and is a serious risk for us to run. *Prince of Wales* will be noticed at Cape Town quite soon. In addition the four "R" battleships are being moved as they become ready

[1] For those who wish to study this matter in more detail, the correspondence which passed between me and the First Sea Lord at this time is printed in Appendix E, Book Two, pages 735–740. For reasons which could not at this time be foreseen, the *Prince of Wales* and not the *Nelson* or *Rodney* was sent.

to Eastern waters. Later on *Repulse* will be relieved by *Renown*, which has greater radius.

4. In my view, *Prince of Wales* will be the best possible deterrent, and every effort will be made to spare her permanently. I must however make it clear that movements of *Prince of Wales* must be reviewed when she is at Capetown, because of danger of *Tirpitz* breaking out and other operational possibilities before *Duke of York* is ready in December.

*　　*　　*

In October Prince Konoye laid down his burden. He had asked for a personal meeting with President Roosevelt at Honolulu, to which he hoped to bring his military and naval chiefs, and thus bind them to what might be settled. But his proposal had been declined by the President, and Army opinion became increasingly critical of this wise statesman. His place was taken by General Tojo, who became Prime Minister, War Minister, and Home Minister at the same time. General Tojo, who after the war was hanged by the conquerors according to modern practice, said at his trial that he himself took over the Home Ministry because "he faced a fearful trend foreboding internal confusion if peace was decided upon instead of war." At the Emperor's behest he renewed diplomatic negotiations with the United States, but under a secret understanding with members of his Government that Japan would go to war if the Cabinet representations were rejected. When in November, 1941, Tojo and the Chiefs of the General Staff informed the Emperor that war might be necessary, the sovereign expressed the hope that still further efforts might be made to avert this calamity, but told Tojo that "if the state of affairs is as you have described it there will be no alternative but to proceed with the preparations for operations."

*　　*　　*

At the beginning of November I received an agitated warning of further Japanese action in China from General Chiang Kai-shek. He thought that the Japanese were determined upon an attack from Indo-China to take Kunming and cut the Burma Road. He appealed for British aid by air from Malaya. He concluded:

You might feel at a first glance that this would involve you in a war with Japan while you are fighting with such courage in Europe and the Middle East. I see things otherwise. I do not believe that Japan feels that she has the strength to attack so long as the resistance of China persists, but once she is rid of this she will attack you as and when it suits her. . . . China has reached the most critical phase of her war of resistance. Her ability to defend the land approaches to Singapore and Burma now depends primarily on British and American willingness to co-operate in the defence of Yunnan. If the Japanese can break our front here we shall be cut off from you, and the whole structure of your own air and naval coordination with America and the Netherlands East Indies will be gravely threatened in new ways and from a new direction. I should like to express with all the strength at my command the conviction that wisdom and foresight demand that China be given the help that I have indicated. Nothing else can ensure alike the defeat of Japan and success of countries now resisting aggression. I eagerly await your reply.

I could do little more than pass this to President Roosevelt.

Former Naval Person to President Roosevelt   5 Nov. 41

I have received Chiang Kai-shek's appeal addressed to us both for air assistance. You know how we are placed for air strength at Singapore. None the less, I should be prepared to send pilots and even some planes if they could arrive in time.

2. What we need now is a deterrent of the most general and formidable character. The Japanese have as yet taken no final decision, and the Emperor appears to be exercising restraint. When we talked about this at Placentia you spoke of gaining time, and this policy has been brilliantly successful so far. But our joint embargo is steadily forcing the Japanese to decisions for peace or war.

3. It now looks as if they would go into Yunnan, cutting the Burma Road, with disastrous consequences for Chiang Kai-shek. The collapse of his resistance would not only be a world tragedy in itself, but it would leave the Japanese with large forces to attack north or south.

4. The Chinese have appealed to us, as I believe they have to you, to warn the Japanese against an attack in Yunnan. I hope you might think fit to remind them that such an attack, aimed at China from a region in which we have never recognised that the Japanese have any right to maintain forces, would be in open disregard of the clearly indicated attitude of the United States Government. We should of course be ready to make a similar communication.

5. No independent action by ourselves will deter Japan, because we are so much tied up elsewhere. But of course we will stand with you and do our utmost to back you in whatever course you choose. I think myself that Japan is more likely to drift into war than to plunge in. Please let me know what you think.

The President replied on November 9 that, while it would be a serious error to underestimate the gravity of the threat, he doubted whether preparations for a Japanese land campaign against Kunming would warrant an immediate Japanese advance in the immediate future. He would do what he could by Lend-Lease aid to China and the building-up of the American Volunteer Air Force there. He felt that in Japan's mood any "new formalised verbal warning or remonstrance" might have at least an even chance of producing the opposite effect. "The whole problem will have our continuing and earnest attention, study, and effort."

I did my best to comfort the Generalissimo by repeating the substance of this guarded answer.

There was no course for us but to continue with our naval plans in the Far East and to leave the United States to attempt by diplomatic means to keep Japan as long as possible quiet in the Pacific.

*   *   *

I wrote to General Smuts, who had raised larger issues.

Prime Minister to General Smuts   9 Nov. 41

I do not think it would be any use for me to make a personal appeal to Roosevelt at this juncture to enter the war. At the Atlantic meeting I told his circle that I would rather have an American declaration of war now and no supplies for six months than double the supplies and no declaration. When this was repeated to him, he thought it a hard saying. We must not underrate his constitutional difficulties. He may take action as Chief Executive, but only Congress can declare war. He went so far as to say to me, "I may never declare war; I may make war. If I were to ask Congress to declare war, they might argue about it for three months." The Draft Bill without which the American Army would have gone to pieces passed by only one vote. He has now carried through the Senate by a small majority the virtual repeal of the Neutrality Act. This must mean, if endorsed by the other House, constant fighting in the Atlantic between German and American ships. Public opinion in the United States has advanced lately, but with Congress it is all a matter of counting heads. Naturally, if I saw any way of helping to lift this situation onto a higher plane I would do so. In the meanwhile we must have patience and trust to the tide which is flowing our way and to events.

*   *   *

On November 10 at the annual Guildhall banquet, which the Prime Minister by custom attends, I said:

I must admit that, having voted for the Japanese alliance nearly forty years ago, in 1902, and having always done my very best to promote good relations with the Island Empire of Japan, and always having been a sentimental well-wisher to the Japanese and an admirer of their many gifts and qualities, I should view with keen sorrow the opening of a conflict between Japan and the English-speaking world.

The United States' time-honoured interests in the Far East are well known. They are doing their utmost to find ways of preserving peace in the Pacific. We do not know whether their efforts will be successful, but should they fail and the United States become involved in war with Japan, it is my duty to say that the British declaration will follow within the hour.

Viewing the vast, sombre scene as dispassionately as possible, it would seem a very hazardous adventure for the Japanese people to plunge quite needlessly into a world struggle in which they may well find themselves opposed in the Pacific by States whose populations comprise nearly three-quarters of the human race. If steel is the basic foundation of modern war, it would be rather dangerous for a power like Japan, whose steel production is only about seven million tons a year, to provoke quite gratuitously a struggle with the United States, whose steel production is now about ninety millions; and this would take no account of the powerful contribution which the British Empire can make. I hope therefore that the peace of the Pacific will be preserved in accordance with the known wishes of Japan's wisest statesmen. But every preparation to defend British interests in the Far East, and to defend the common cause now at stake, has been and is being made.

On November 20 Japan forwarded to Washington her "final word." Although it was clear from these proposals that Japan was in effect attempting merely to obtain the fruits of victory without war, the United States Government felt obliged to make one last diplomatic offer. We were informed of the Japanese Note and were asked for our views. On November 23 I wrote in a minute to the Foreign Secretary:

Prime Minister to Foreign Secretary   23 Nov. 41

Our major interest is: no further encroachments and no war, as we have already enough of this latter. The United States will not throw over the Chinese cause, and we may safely follow them in this part of the subject. We could not of course agree to an arrangement whereby Japan was free to attack Russia in Siberia. I doubt myself whether this is likely at the present time. I remember that President Roosevelt at the Atlantic Conference himself wrote in, "There must be no further encroachment in the North." I should think this could be agreed [with the Americans]. The formal denunciation of the Axis Pact by Japan is not, in my opinion, necessary. Their stopping out of the war is in itself a great disappointment and injury to the Germans. We ought not to agree to any veto on American or British help to China. But we shall not be asked to by the United States.

502 WAR COMES TO AMERICA

Subject to the above, it would be worth while to ease up upon Japan economically sufficiently for them to live from hand to mouth —even if we only got another three months. These however are only first impressions.

I must say I should feel pleased if I read that an American-Japanese agreement had been made by which we were to be no worse off three months hence in the Far East than we are now.

* * *

On November 25 the President cabled to me an account of the negotiations. The Japanese Government had proposed to evacuate Southern Indo-China, pending a general settlement with China, or a general restoration of peace in the Pacific, when Japan would be prepared to withdraw altogether from Indo-China. In return the United States was to supply Japan with petroleum, to refrain from interfering with Japan's efforts to restore peace in China, to help Japan to obtain the products of the Netherlands East Indies, and to place commercial relations between Japan and the United States on a normal basis. Both sides were to agree to make no "armed advancement" in Northeast Asia and the Southern Pacific.

The American Government, in its turn, was proposing to make a counter-offer, accepting in general the terms of the Japanese Note, while outlining specific conditions to be attached to the Japanese withdrawal from Southern Indo-China and making no mention of the position in China. The United States was prepared to accept a limited economic arrangement modifying the original freezing order. For instance, petroleum could be shipped on a monthly basis for civilian needs only. This American proposal would be valid for three months on the understanding that during this period a general settlement covering the whole Pacific area would be discussed.

When I read the draft reply, which was, and is still, called the "modus vivendi," I thought it inadequate. This impression was shared by the Dutch and Australian Governments, and above all by Chiang Kai-shek, who sent a frantic protest to Washington. I was however deeply sensitive of the limits which we must observe in commenting on United States policy on an issue where decisive action lay with them alone. I understood the dangers attending the thought, "The British are trying to drag us into war." I therefore placed the issue where it belonged, namely, in the President's hands, and mentioning only the Chinese aspect, sent him the following cable:

Former Naval Person to President Roosevelt   26 Nov. 41

Your message about Japan received tonight. Also full accounts from Lord Halifax of discussions and your counter-project to Japan. . . . Of course it is for you to handle this business, and we certainly do not want an additional war. There is only one point that disquiets us. What about Chiang Kai-shek? Is he not having a very thin diet? Our anxiety is about China. If they collapse our joint dangers would enormously increase. We are sure that the regard of the United States for the Chinese cause will govern your action. We feel that the Japanese are most unsure of themselves.

This message of course arrived in Washington at dawn of the same day it was dated.

Mr. Hull says in his *Memoirs:*

During the night a cable came in for the President from Mr. Churchill commenting on our modus vivendi. Obviously influenced by Chiang Kai-shek's cable to him, the Prime Minister wondered whether the Generalissimo was not getting "rather meagre rations" under the modus vivendi. China, he said, was the cause of his being anxious, and the Chinese collapse would hugely augment our common danger. After talking this over again with the Far Eastern experts of the State Department I came to the conclusion that we should cancel out the modus vivendi. Instead we should present to the Japanese solely the ten-point proposal for a general settlement, to which originally the modus vivendi would have been in the nature of an introduction. Although the modus vivendi proposals contained only a little "chicken feed" in the shape of cotton, oil, and a few other commodities in very limited quantities as compared with the unlimited quantities the Japanese demanded, it was manifest that there would be widespread opposition from American public opinion to supplying Japan even limited quantities of oil. The Chinese were violently opposed, the other interested Governments either unfavourable or lukewarm. . . . The slight prospect of Japan's agreeing to the modus vivendi therefore did not warrant assuming the risks involved in proceeding with it, especially the risk of collapse of Chinese morale and resistance, and even of disintegration.[2]

*   *   *

We had not heard up to this moment of the "Ten-Point Note," which not only met our wishes and those of the associated Governments, but indeed went beyond anything for which we had ventured to ask. On this same 26th Mr. Hull received the Japanese envoys at the State Department. He did not even mention to them the modus vivendi about which the President had telegraphed to me on the 23d. On the con-

[2] *The Memoirs of Cordell Hull,* Volume II, page 1081.

trary, he handed them the "Ten-Point Note." Two points of this were as follows:

The Government of Japan will withdraw all military, naval, air, and police forces from China and Indo-China.

The Government of the United States and the Government of Japan will not support—militarily, politically, economically—any Government or régime in China other than the National Government of the Republic of China, with capital temporarily at Chungking.

The envoys were "dumbfounded," and retired in the greatest distress. This may well have been sincere. They had been chosen largely on account of their reputation as peace-seeking and moderate men who would lull the United States into a sense of security till all was decided and all was ready. They knew little of the whole mind of their Government. They did not dream that Mr. Hull was far better informed on this than they were. From the end of 1940 the Americans had pierced the vital Japanese ciphers, and were decoding large numbers of their military and diplomatic telegrams. In the secret American circles these were referred to as "Magics." The "Magics" were repeated to us, but there was an inevitable delay—sometimes of two or three days—before we got them. We did not know therefore at any given moment all that the President or Mr. Hull knew. I make no complaint of this.

That same afternoon the President sent the following message to the High Commissioner of the Philippines:

Preparations are becoming apparent . . . for an early aggressive movement of some character, although as yet there are no clear indications as to its strength or whether it will be directed against the Burma Road, Thailand, Malay Peninsula, Netherlands East Indies, or the Philippines. Advance against Thailand seems the most probable. I consider it possible that this next Japanese aggression might cause an outbreak of hostilities between the United States and Japan. . . .

*   *   *

When on November 29 our Ambassador, Lord Halifax, visited the State Department, Mr. Hull said to him that the danger from Japan "hung just over our heads."

The diplomatic part in our relations with Japan is now virtually over. The matter will now go to the officials of the Army and Navy, with whom I have talked. . . . Japan may move suddenly and with every possible element of surprise. . . . My theory is that the Japanese recognise that their course of unlimited conquest, now renewed all along the line, probably is a desperate gamble and requires the utmost boldness and risk. [He added:] When Churchill received Chiang's loud protest about the modus vivendi it would have been better if he had sent Chiang a strong cable to brace up and fight with the same zeal as the Japanese and Americans were displaying. Instead he passed the protest on to us without objection on his part. . . .

I did not know that the die had already been cast by Japan or how far the President's resolves had gone.

Former Naval Person to President Roosevelt   30 Nov. 41

It seems to me that one important method remains unused in averting war between Japan and our two countries, namely, a plain declaration, secret or public as may be thought best, that any further act of aggression by Japan will lead immediately to the gravest consequences. I realise your constitutional difficulties, but it would be tragic if Japan drifted into war by encroachment without having before her fairly and squarely the dire character of a further aggressive step. I beg you to consider whether, at the moment, which you judge right, which may be very near, you should not say that "any further Japanese aggression would compel you to place the gravest issues before Congress," or words to that effect. We would of course make a similar declaration or share in a joint declaration, and in any case arrangements are being made to synchronise our action with yours. Forgive me, my dear friend, for presuming to press such a course upon you, but I am convinced that it might make all the difference and prevent a melancholy extension of the war.

Both he and Tojo were already far ahead of this. So were events.

          *   *   *

On the 30th, shortly after noon (American time), Mr. Hull visited the President, who had on his desk my cable of the same date, sent overnight.[1] They did not think my proposal of a joint warning to Japan would be any good. Nor can we be surprised at this when they had already before them an intercept from Tokyo to Berlin, also dated November 30, telling the Japanese Ambassador in Berlin to address Hitler and Ribbentrop as follows:

Say very secretly to them that there is extreme danger that war may suddenly break out between the Anglo-Saxon nations and Japan through some clash of arms, and add that the time of the breaking-out of this war may come quicker than anyone dreams.

[1] The reader need not be puzzled by the datings of the telegrams, so long as they are in their proper sequence. I worked up till two or three in the morning (British time), and any message I sent took two or three hours to code and decode. Nevertheless, any message which I drafted before I went to bed would reach the President almost instantaneously for practical purposes —i.e., when he woke up, or was, if need be, awakened.

I received the decode of the telegrams on December 2. It required no special action from Britain. We must just wait. The Japanese carrier fleet had in fact sailed on the 25th with the whole naval air force which was to attack Pearl Harbour. Of course it was still subject to restraining orders from Tokyo.

* * *

At an Imperial Conference at Tokyo on December 1 the decision was taken to go to war with the United States. According to Tojo's testimony at his trial, the Emperor did not utter a word. For the following week a deadly hush settled in the Pacific. The possibilities of a diplomatic settlement had been exhausted. No act of military aggression had yet occurred. My deepest fear was that the Japanese would attack us or the Dutch, and that constitutional difficulties would prevent the United States from declaring war. After a long Cabinet on December 2 I sent a minute to the Foreign Secretary embodying our conclusions:

Prime Minister to Foreign Secretary   2 Dec. 41

Our settled policy is not to take forward action in advance of the United States. Except in the case of a Japanese attempt to seize the Kra Isthmus there will be time for the United States to be squarely confronted with a new act of Japanese aggression. If they move, we will move immediately in support. If they do not move, we must consider our position afresh. . . .

A Japanese attack on the Dutch possessions may be made at any time. This would be a direct affront to the United States, following upon their negotiations with Japan. We should tell the Dutch that we should do nothing to prevent the full impact of this Japanese aggression presenting itself to the United States as a direct issue between them and Japan. If the United States declares war on Japan, we follow within the hour. If, after a reasonable interval, the United States is found to be incapable of taking any decisive action, even with our immediate support, we will, nevertheless, although alone, make common cause with the Dutch.

Any attack on British possessions carries with it war with Great Britain as a matter of course.

* * *

British Intelligence and air reconnaissance, which were vigilant, soon perceived movements and activity showing that "Japan is about to attack Siam, and that this attack will include a seaborne expedition to seize strategic points in the Kra Isthmus." We reported this to Washington. A series of lengthy telegrams passed between us and our Commander-in-

Chief in the Far East, and also with the Australian and American Governments, about whether we should take forestalling action to protect the Kra Isthmus. It was rightly decided, both on military and political grounds, that we should not complicate the course of events by striking first in a secondary theatre. On December 6 it was known both in London and Washington that a Japanese fleet of about thirty-five transports, eight cruisers, and twenty destroyers was moving from Indo-China across the Gulf of Siam. Other Japanese fleets were also at sea on other tasks.

*   *   *

A prodigious Congressional Inquiry published its findings in 1946 in which every detail was exposed of the events leading up to the war between the United States and Japan and of the failure to send positive "Alert" orders through the military departments to their fleets and garrisons in exposed situations. Every detail, including the decoding of secret Japanese telegrams and their actual texts, has been exposed to the world in forty volumes. The strength of the United States was sufficient to enable them to sustain this hard ordeal required by the spirit of the American Constitution.

I do not intend in these pages to attempt to pronounce judgment upon this tremendous episode in American history. We know that all the great Americans round the President and in his confidence felt, as acutely as I did, the awful danger that Japan would attack British or Dutch possessions in the Far East, and would carefully avoid the United States, and that in consequence Congress would not sanction an American declaration of war. The American leaders understood that this might mean vast Japanese conquests, which, if combined with a German victory over Russia and thereafter an invasion of Great Britain, would leave America alone to face an overwhelming combination of triumphant aggressors. Not only the great moral causes which were at stake would be cast away, but the very life of the United States, and their people, as yet but half-awakened to their perils, might be broken. The President and his trusted friends had long realised the grave risks of United States neutrality in the war against Hitler and all that he stood for, and had writhed under the restraints of a Congress whose House of Representatives had a few months before passed by only a single vote the necessary renewal of compulsory military service, without which their Army would have been almost disbanded in the midst of the world convulsion. Roosevelt, Hull, Stimson, Knox, General Marshall, Admiral Stark, and, as a link between them all, Harry Hopkins, had but one mind. Future generations of Americans and free men in every land will thank God for their vision.

A Japanese attack upon the United States was a vast simplification of their problems and their duty. How can we wonder that they regarded the actual form of the attack, or even its scale, as incomparably less important than the fact that the whole American nation would be united for its own safety in a righteous cause as never before? To them, as to me, it seemed that for Japan to attack and make war upon the United States would be an act of suicide. Moreover, they knew, earlier than we in Britain could know, the full and immediate purpose of their enemy. We remember how Cromwell exclaimed when he watched the Scottish army descending from the heights over Dunbar, "The Lord hath delivered them into our hands."

Nor must we allow the account in detail of diplomatic interchanges to portray Japan as an injured innocent seeking only a reasonable measure of expansion or booty from the European war, and now confronted by the United States with propositions which her people, fanatically aroused and fully prepared, could not be expected to accept. For long years Japan had been torturing China by her wicked invasions and subjugations. Now by her seizure of Indo-China she had in fact, as well as formally by the Tripartite Pact, thrown in her lot with the Axis Powers. Let her do what she dared and take the consequences.

It had seemed impossible that Japan would court destruction by war with Britain and the United States, and probably Russia in the end. A declaration of war by Japan could not be reconciled with reason. I felt sure she would be ruined for a generation by such a plunge, and this proved true. But Governments and peoples do not always take rational decisions. Sometimes they take mad decisions, or one set of people get control who compel all others to obey and aid them in folly. I have not hesitated to record repeatedly my disbelief that Japan would go mad. However sincerely we try to put ourselves in another person's position, we cannot allow for processes of the human mind and imagination to which reason offers no key.

Madness is however an affliction which in war carries with it the advantage of *surprise*.

12

Pearl Harbour!

IT WAS SUNDAY EVENING, December 7, 1941. Winant and Averell Harriman were alone with me at the table at Chequers. I turned on my small wireless set shortly after the nine o'clock news had started. There were a number of items about the fighting on the Russian front and on the British front in Libya, at the end of which some few sentences were spoken regarding an attack by the Japanese on American shipping at Hawaii, and also Japanese attacks on British vessels in the Dutch East Indies. There followed a statement that after the news Mr. Somebody would make a commentary, and that the Brains Trust programme would then begin, or something like this. I did not personally sustain any direct impression, but Averell said there was something about the Japanese attacking the Americans, and, in spite of being tired and resting, we all sat up. By now the butler, Sawyers, who

509

had heard what had passed, came into the room, saying, "It's quite true. We heard it ourselves outside. The Japanese have attacked the Americans." There was a silence. At the Mansion House luncheon on November 11 I had said that if Japan attacked the United States a British declaration of war would follow "within the hour." I got up from the table and walked through the hall to the office, which was always at work. I asked for a call to the President. The Ambassador followed me out, and, imagining I was about to take some irrevocable step, said, "Don't you think you'd better get confirmation first?"

In two or three minutes Mr. Roosevelt came through. "Mr. President, what's this about Japan?" "It's quite true," he replied. "They have attacked us at Pearl Harbour. We are all in the same boat now." I put Winant onto the line and some interchanges took place, the Ambassador at first saying, "Good," "Good"—and then, apparently graver, "Ah!" I got on again and said, "This certainly simplifies things. God be with you," or words to that effect. We then went back into the hall and tried to adjust our thoughts to the supreme world event which had occurred, which was of so startling a nature as to make even those who were near the centre gasp. My two American friends took the shock with admirable fortitude. We had no idea that any serious losses had been inflicted on the United States Navy. They did not wail or lament that their country was at war. They wasted no words in reproach or sorrow. In fact, one might almost have thought they had been delivered from a long pain.

*   *   *

Parliament would not have met till Tuesday, and the Members were scattered about the Island, with all the existing difficulties of communication. I set the office to work to ring up the Speaker, the Whips, and others concerned, to call both Houses together next day. I rang the Foreign Office to prepare to implement without a moment's delay a declaration of war upon Japan, about which there were some formalities, in time for the meeting of the House, and to make sure all members of the War Cabinet were called up and informed, and also the Chiefs of Staff and the Service Ministers, who, I rightly assumed, had had the news.

This done, my thought turned at once to what has always lain near my heart. To Mr. de Valera I sent the following message:

8 Dec. 41

Now is your chance. Now or never! A nation once again! I will meet you wherever you wish.

I thought also of struggling China, and telegraphed to Chiang Kai-shek:

8 Dec. 41

The British Empire and United States have been attacked by Japan. Always we have been friends: now we face a common enemy.

We also sent the following:

Prime Minister to Mr. Harry Hopkins   8 Dec. 41
Thinking of you much at this historic moment.—WINSTON, AVERELL.

*   *   *

No American will think it wrong of me if I proclaim that to have the United States at our side was to me the greatest joy. I could not foretell the course of events. I do not pretend to have measured accurately the martial might of Japan, but now at this very moment I knew the United States was in the war, up to the neck and in to the death. So we had won after all! Yes, after Dunkirk; after the fall of France; after the horrible episode of Oran; after the threat of invasion, when, apart from the Air and the Navy, we were an almost unarmed people; after the deadly struggle of the U-boat war—the first Battle of the Atlantic, gained by a hand's-breadth; after seventeen months of lonely fighting and nineteen months of my responsibility in dire stress, we had won the war. England would live; Britain would live; the Commonwealth of Nations and the Empire would live. How long the war would last or in what fashion it would end, no man could tell, nor did I at this moment care. Once again in our long Island history we should emerge, however mauled or mutilated, safe and victorious. We should not be wiped out. Our history would not come to an end. We might not even have to die as individuals. Hitler's fate was sealed. Mussolini's fate was sealed. As for the Japanese, they would be ground to powder. All the rest was merely the proper application of overwhelming force. The British Empire, the Soviet Union, and now the United States, bound together with every scrap of their life and strength, were, according to my lights, twice or even thrice the force of their antagonists. No doubt it would take a long time. I expected terrible forfeits in the East; but all this would be merely a passing phase. United we could subdue everybody else in the world. Many disasters, immeasurable cost and tribulation lay ahead, but there was no more doubt about the end.

Silly people—and there were many, not only in enemy countries—might discount the force of the United States. Some said they were soft, others that they would never be united. They would fool around at a distance. They would never come to grips. They would never stand blood-letting. Their democracy and system of recurrent elections would paralyze their war effort. They would be just a vague blur on the horizon to friend or foe. Now we should see the weakness of this numerous but remote, wealthy, and talkative people. But I had studied the American Civil War, fought out to the last desperate inch. American blood flowed in my veins. I thought of a remark which Edward Grey had made to me more than thirty years before—that the United States is like "a gigantic boiler. Once the fire is lighted under it there is no limit to the power it can generate." Being saturated and satiated with emotion and sensation, I went to bed and slept the sleep of the saved and thankful.

*   *   *

As soon as I woke I decided to go over at once to see President Roosevelt. I put the matter to the Cabinet when we met at noon. On obtaining their approval I wrote to the King.

December 8, 1941

Sir,

I have formed the conviction that it is my duty to visit Washington without delay, provided such a course is agreeable to President Roosevelt, as I have little doubt it will be. The whole plan of the Anglo-American defence and attack has to be concerted in the light of reality. We have also to be careful that our share of munitions and other aid which we are receiving from the United States does not suffer more than is, I fear, inevitable. The fact that Mr. Eden will be in Moscow while I am at Washington will make the settlement of large-scale problems between the three great Allies easier.

These reasons were accepted by my colleagues in the Cabinet unanimously today, and I therefore ask Your Majesty's permission to leave the country. I should propose to start quite soon, in a warship, and to be absent altogether for about three weeks. I shall take with me a staff on the same scale as I took to the Atlantic meeting.

During my absence the Lord Privy Seal will act for me, assisted by the Lord President of the Council, the Chancellor of the Exchequer, and other members of the War Cabinet. I would propose that during this period the three Service Ministers should temporarily sit with the War Cabinet. While I am away the Foreign Office will report to the Lord President, and the Defence Committee to the Lord Privy Seal. I shall of course be constantly in touch by wireless with all that goes on, and can give decisions whenever necessary. I should propose to take with me the First Sea Lord and the Chief of the Air Staff, as the concert of all our arrangements with the Americans on a high level is all-important.

I hope I may receive Your Majesty's approval of this course. I am of course keeping my intention secret.

With my humble duty, I remain

Your Majesty's most devoted, faithful servant and subject,

WINSTON S. CHURCHILL

PS. I am expecting that Germany and Italy will both declare war on the United States, as they have bound themselves by treaty to do so. I shall defer proposing my visit to the President until this situation is more clear.

The King gave his assent.

Former Naval Person to President Roosevelt   9 Dec. 41

I am grateful for your telegram of December 8. Now that we are, as you say, "in the same boat," would it not be wise for us to have another conference? We could review the whole war plan in the light of reality and new facts, as well as the problems of production and distribution. I feel that all these matters, some of which are causing me concern, can best be settled on the highest executive level. It would also be a very great pleasure to me to meet you again, and the sooner the better.

2. I could, if desired, start from here in a day or two, and come by warship to Baltimore or Annapolis. Voyage would take about eight days, and I would arrange to stay a week, so that everything important could be settled between us. I would bring Pound, Portal, Dill, and Beaverbrook, with necessary staffs.

3. Please let me know at earliest what you feel about this.

The President feared that the return journey would be dangerous. I reassured him.

Former Naval Person to President Roosevelt   10 Dec. 41

We do not think there is any serious danger about the return journey. There is however great danger in our not having a full discussion on the highest level about the extreme gravity of the naval position, as well as upon all the production and allocation issues involved. I am quite ready to meet you at Bermuda, or to fly from Bermuda to Washington. I feel it would be disastrous to wait for another month before we settled common action in face of new adverse situation, particularly in Pacific. I had hoped to start tomorrow night, but will postpone my sailing till I have received

rendezvous from you. I never felt so sure about the final victory, but
only concerted action will achieve it. Kindest regards.

The next day I heard again from the President. He said
that he was delighted that I was coming to stay at the White
House. He felt that he could not leave the country himself.
Mobilisation was taking place, and the naval position in the
Pacific was uncertain. He felt sure that we could work out
all the difficulties connected with production and supply. He
emphasised again the personal risk of my journey, which he
thought should be carefully considered.

* * *

The War Cabinet authorised the immediate declaration of
war upon Japan, for which all formal arrangements had been
made. As Eden had already started on his journey to Moscow
and I was in charge of the Foreign Office, I sent the following
letter to the Japanese Ambassador:

Foreign Office, December 8

Sir,

On the evening of December 7th His Majesty's Government in
the United Kingdom learned that Japanese forces without previous
warning either in the form of a declaration of war or of an ultimatum with a conditional declaration of war had attempted a landing on the coast of Malaya and bombed Singapore and Hong Kong.

In view of these wanton acts of unprovoked aggression committed
in flagrant violation of International Law and particularly of Article
1 of the Third Hague Convention relative to the opening of hostilities, to which both Japan and the United Kingdom are parties, His
Majesty's Ambassador at Tokyo has been instructed to inform the
Imperial Japanese Government in the name of His Majesty's Government in the United Kingdom that a state of war exists between
our two countries.

I have the honour to be, with high consideration,

Sir,

Your obedient servant,

Winston S. Churchill

Some people did not like this ceremonial style. But after
all when you have to kill a man it costs nothing to be polite.

* * *

Parliament met at 3 p.m., and in spite of the shortness of
notice the House was full. Under the British Constitution the
Crown declares war on the advice of Ministers, and Parliament is confronted with the fact. We were therefore able to

be better than our word to the United States, and actually declared war upon Japan before Congress could act. The Royal Netherlands Government had also made their declaration. In my speech I said:

Mr. Churchill's Speech to Parliament, December 8, 1941

It is of the highest importance that there should be no underrating of the gravity of the new dangers we have to meet, either here or in the United States. The enemy has attacked with an audacity which may spring from recklessness, but which may also spring from a conviction of strength. The ordeal to which the English-speaking world and our heroic Russian Allies are being exposed will certainly be hard, especially at the outset, and will probably be long, yet, when we look around us over the sombre panorama of the world, we have no reason to doubt the justice of our cause or that our strength and will-power will be sufficient to sustain it.

We have at least four-fifths of the population of the globe upon our side. We are responsible for their safety and for their future. In the past we have had a light which flickered, in the present we have a light which flames, and in the future there will be a light which shines over all the land and sea.

Both Houses voted unanimously in favour of the decision.

* * *

I thought it necessary at this juncture that Mr. Duff Cooper, who had returned to Singapore, should be at once appointed Resident Minister for Far Eastern affairs.

Prime Minister to Mr. Duff Cooper   9 Dec. 41

You are appointed Resident Cabinet Minister at Singapore for Far Eastern affairs. You will serve under, and report directly to, the War Cabinet, through its Secretary. You are authorised to form a War Council, reporting first its composition and the geographical sphere it will cover. This will presumably coincide with the geographical sphere of the military Commander-in-Chief. Your principal task will be to assist the successful conduct of operations in the Far East (*a*) by relieving the Commanders-in-Chief as far as possible of those extraneous responsibilities with which they have hitherto been burdened; and (*b*) by giving them broad political guidance.

2. Your functions will also include the settlement of emergency matters on the spot, where time does not permit of reference home. You will develop a local clearing-house for prompt settlement of minor routine matters which would otherwise have to be referred to separate departments here. On all matters on which you require special guidance you will, provided there is time, refer the matter home. You will in any case report constantly to His Majesty's Government.

3. When Captain Oliver Lyttelton was appointed Minister of State at Cairo it was laid down that this did not affect the existing responsibilities of His Majesty's Representatives in the Middle East, or their official relationships with their respective departments at home. The same will apply in the Far East. The successful establishment of this machinery depends largely on your handling of it in these early critical days.

4. With your knowledge of the various public departments and of Cabinet procedure, it should be possible for you to exercise a powerful, immediately concerting influence upon Far Eastern affairs. Telegraph to me at once your concrete proposals and the form in which you would like your appointment and its scope to be defined and published. All good luck and kindest regards. We must fight this thing out everywhere to the end.

Duff Cooper addressed himself to these new duties with vigour and clarity of thought, but the arrangements we made at Washington with the United States for a Supreme Commander in the Far East to my regret made his office redundant, and a little more than a fortnight later I instructed him to return home. He was unlucky not to be allowed to go down fighting.

*   *   *

We were not told for some time any details of what had happened at Pearl Harbour, but the story has now been exhaustively recorded.

Until early in 1941 the Japanese naval plan for war against the United States was for their main fleet to give battle in the waters near the Philippines when the Americans, as might be expected, fought their way across the Pacific to relieve their garrison in this outpost. The idea of a surprise attack on Pearl Harbour originated in the brain of Admiral Yamamoto, the Japanese Commander-in-Chief. Preparation for this treacherous blow before any declaration of war went forward with the utmost secrecy, and by November 22 the striking force of six carriers, with a supporting force of battleships and cruisers, was concentrated in an unfrequented anchorage in the Kurile Islands, north of Japan proper. Already the date of the attack had been fixed for Sunday, December 7, and on November 26 (East longitude date) the force sailed under the command of Admiral Nagumo. Keeping far to the northward of Hawaii, amidst the fog and gales of these northern latitudes, Nagumo approached his goal undetected. Before sunrise on the fateful day the attack was launched from a position about two hundred and seventy-five miles to the north of Pearl Harbour.

Three hundred and sixty aircraft took part, comprising bombers of all types, escorted by fighters. At 7.55 A.M. the first bomb fell. Ninety-four ships of the United States Navy were present in the harbour. Among them the eight battle-ships of the Pacific Fleet were the prime targets. The carriers, with strong cruiser forces, were fortunately absent on missions elsewhere.

The story of this attack has often been vividly related. It is sufficient here to state the salient facts and to note the ruthless efficiency of the Japanese airmen. By 8.25 A.M. the first waves of torpedo and dive-bombers had struck their blow. By 10 A.M. the battle was over and the enemy withdrew. Behind them lay a shattered fleet hidden in a pall of fire and smoke, and the vengeance of the United States. The battleship *Arizona* had blown up, the *Oklahoma* had capsised, the *West Virginia* and *California* had sunk at their moorings, and every other battleship, except the *Pennsylvania*, which was in dry dock, had been heavily damaged. Over two thousand Americans had lost their lives, and nearly two thousand others were wounded. The mastery of the Pacific had passed into Japanese hands, and the strategic balance of the world was for the time being fundamentally changed.

*　*　*

Our American Allies had yet another set of misfortunes.

In the Philippines, where General MacArthur commanded, a warning indicating a grave turn in diplomatic relations had been received on November 20. Admiral Hart, commanding the modest United States Asiatic Fleet, had already been in consultation with the the adjacent British and Dutch naval authorities, and, in accordance with his war plan, had begun to disperse his forces to the southward, where he intended to assemble a striking force in Dutch waters in conjunction with his prospective allies. He had at his disposal only one heavy and two light cruisers, besides a dozen old destroyers and various auxiliary vessels. His strength lay almost entirely in his submarines, of which he had twenty-eight. At 3 A.M. on December 8 Admiral Hart intercepted a message giving the staggering news of the attack on Pearl Harbour. He at once warned all concerned that hostilities had begun, without wait-ing for confirmation from Washington. At dawn the Japanese dive-bombers struck and throughout the ensuing days the air attacks continued on an ever-increasing scale. On the 10th the naval base at Cavite was completely destroyed by fire, and on the same day the Japanese made their first landing in the north of Luzon. Disasters mounted swiftly. Most of the American air forces were destroyed in battle or on the ground, and by December 20 the remnants had been withdrawn to Port Darwin in Australia. Admiral Hart's ships had begun their southward dispersal some days before, and only the submarines remained to dispute the sea with the enemy. On December 21 the main Japanese invasion force landed in Lingayen Gulf, threatening Manila itself, and thereafter the march of events was not unlike that which was already in progress in Malaya; but the defence was more prolonged.

Thus the long-nurtured plans of Japan exploded in a blaze of triumph. But this was not the end.

*   *   *

The dispatch of the Japanese Ambassador to Berlin tells of his visit to Ribbentrop.

The day after Pearl Harbour at one o'clock I called on Foreign Minister Ribbentrop and told him our wish was to have Germany and Italy issue formal declarations of war on America at once. Ribbentrop replied that Hitler was then in the midst of a conference at General Headquarters [in East Prussia], discussing how the formalities of declaring war could be carried out so as to make a good impression on the German people, and that he would transmit your wish to him at once and do whatever he was able to have it carried out properly.

Both Hitler and his Staff were astonished. Jodl tells at his trial how Hitler "came in the middle of the night to my chart room in order to transmit this news to Field-Marshal Keitel and myself. He was completely surprised." On the morning of December 8 however he gave the German Navy orders to attack American ships wherever found. This was three days before the official declaration of war by Germany on the United States.

*   *   *

I convened a meeting, mostly Admiralty, in the Cabinet War Room at ten o'clock on the night of the 9th to review the naval position. We were about a dozen. We tried to measure the consequences of this fundamental change in our war position against Japan. We had lost the command of every ocean except the Atlantic. Australia and New Zealand and all the vital islands in their sphere were open to attack. We had only one key weapon in our hands. The *Prince of Wales* and the *Repulse* had arrived at Singapore. They had been sent to these waters to exercise that kind of vague menace which capital ships of the highest quality whose whereabouts is unknown can impose upon all hostile naval calculations. How should we use them now? Obviously they must go to sea and vanish among the innumerable islands. There was general agreement on that.

I thought myself they should go across the Pacific to join what was left of the American Fleet. It would be a proud gesture at this moment, and would knit the English-speaking world together. We had already cordially agreed to the American Navy Department withdrawing their capital ships from the Atlantic. Thus in a few months there might be a fleet in being on the west coast of America capable of fighting a decisive sea battle if need be. The existence of such a fleet and of such a fact would be the best possible shield to our brothers in Australasia. We were all much attracted by this line of thought. But as the hour was late we decided to sleep on it, and settle the next morning what to do with the *Prince of Wales* and the *Repulse*.

Within a couple of hours they were at the bottom of the sea.

* * *

The tragedy of these ships, in which Chance played so fatal a part, must now be told.

The *Prince of Wales* and *Repulse* had reached Singapore on December 2. On December 5 Admiral Tom Phillips arrived in Manila by air to discuss possible joint action with General MacArthur and Admiral Hart. Admiral Hart agreed that four American destroyers should join Phillips's flag. Both Admirals felt that neither Singapore nor Manila could at the moment be a suitable base for an Allied Fleet. Next day news came that a large Japanese seaborne expedition had entered the Gulf of Siam. It was clear that decisive events were at hand. Phillips got back to Singapore on the morning of the 7th. Soon after midnight on the 8th it was reported that a landing was actually in progress at Kota Bharu, and later that other landings were being made near Singora and also at Patani. A major invasion of Malaya had begun.[1]

---

[1] The Japanese attacks in Malaya and the Far East occurred within a few hours of that on Pearl Harbour. This is not readily apparent owing to the different times kept. The following table shows the sequence of events, related to Greenwich time:

	Local Time	Greenwich Time
First landing in Malaya	12.25 A.M., Dec. 8	4.55 P.M., Dec. 7
Attack on Pearl Harbour	8.00 A.M., Dec. 7	6.30 P.M., Dec. 7
First air raid in the Philippines	Dawn, Dec. 8	9.00 P.M., Dec. 7
First air raid in Hong Kong	8.00 A.M., Dec. 8	11.30 P.M., Dec. 7

Admiral Phillips judged it his duty to strike at the enemy
while they were disembarking. At a meeting of his senior
officers all agreed that it was impossible for the Navy to stand
out of the battle at this critical stage. He reported his intentions to the Admiralty. He requested the Singapore Air Command to move fighters to our northern airfields, and requested
the utmost help from our meagre air force—namely, reconnaissance a hundred miles north of his squadron on December 9, reconnaissance off Singora from daylight on December
10, and fighter protection over Singora on the morning of
December 10. This last all-important aid could not be given,
first, because of the expected attack on Singapore, and secondly, because the northern airfields were already untenable.
The Admiral had sailed at 5.35 p.m. on the 8th with the
Prince of Wales and *Repulse* and the destroyers *Electra, Express, Vampire,* and *Tenedos* when news of the landing
reached him. It added the warning that large Japanese
bomber forces were based in Southern Indo-China. As the
frequent rain squalls and low clouds were unfavourable for
air action, Phillips resolved to press on. On the evening of the
9th the weather cleared, and he soon had reason to believe
that he was being shadowed by enemy aircraft. The hope of
surprise was gone, and heavy air attacks must be expected the
next morning near Singora. At this Admiral Phillips reluctantly
abandoned his daring enterprise, and after dark turned homeward. He had certainly done his best, and all might have yet
been well. About midnight however by a hard mischance
another enemy landing was reported at Kuantan, more than
a hundred and fifty miles south of Kota Bharu. Admiral Phillips thought it unlikely that his force, last sighted by the
enemy on a northerly course, would be expected so far south
by daylight on the 10th. After all, he might achieve surprise.
He accepted the risk and turned his ships towards Kuantan.

Japanese records make no claim to have sighted the British
squadron from the air on the 9th, but a submarine reported
them steering north at 2 p.m. The Japanese 22d Air Flotilla,
based near Saigon, was loading bombs for an attack on Singapore. They immediately exchanged bombs for torpedoes and
decided to make a night attack on the British ships. They
found nothing, and returned to their base by midnight. Before
dawn on the 10th another Japanese submarine reported that
the British were steering south, and at 6 a.m. a searching
force of nine Japanese aircraft set forth, followed an hour
later by a powerful striking force of eighty-four bombers and

torpedo bombers, organised in waves of about nine aircraft each.

The report of the landing at Kuantan proved false, but as no amending message had been sent from Singapore the Admiral remained expectant, until soon after daylight the destroyer *Express* reached the harbour and found no sign of the enemy. Before resuming their southerly course the squadron spent some time in searching for a tug and other small craft which had been sighted earlier. But now the crisis came and fortune was hard. The Japanese air fleet had ranged as far south as Singapore without sighting anything. It was returning home on a northerly course, which by chance led them straight to their quarry.

At 10.20 A.M. a shadowing aircraft was sighted by the *Prince of Wales*, and soon after 11 A.M. the first wave of bombers appeared. The enemy attacked in successive waves. In the first the *Repulse* received one hit from a bomb which caused a fire, but this soon was under control and the ship's speed was not impaired. In the second the *Prince of Wales* was struck simultaneously by what seemed to be two torpedoes close together, which caused very severe damage and flooding. Both port propellors were put out of action, and the ship was never again under complete control. The *Repulse* was not hit in this attack. A few minutes later another wave closed in on the *Repulse*, and again she escaped damage. The ships by now had become somewhat separated, and Captain Tennant, having made an emergency signal to Singapore, "Enemy aircraft bombing," turned the *Repulse* towards the Admiral.

At 12.22 P.M. another attack proved fatal to both capital ships. After successfully avoiding a number of torpedoes the *Repulse* was struck amidships. Soon afterwards, in yet another attack, a torpedo wrecked her steering-gear, and then in quick succession three more torpedoes found their mark. Captain Tennant realised that his ship was doomed. He promptly ordered all hands on deck, and there is no doubt that this timely action saved many lives. At 12.33 P.M. the *Repulse* turned over and sank. The *Prince of Wales* had received two more torpedo hits at about 12.23 P.M., and another shortly afterwards. Her speed was reduced to eight knots, and she too was soon in a sinking condition. After another bombing attack, which scored one more hit, she capsized and sank at 1.20 P.M. The destroyers rescued two thousand officers and men out of nearly three thousand. The Commander-in-Chief,

Admiral Sir Tom Phillips, and his Flag-Captain, John Leach, were drowned.

*   *   *

In reply to certain questions of the Chiefs of Staff about why no fighter aircraft were sent from Singapore to aid the squadron, it was confirmed that Admiral Phillips did not signal his change of plan on the 9th, as he was keeping wireless silence. His position on the morning of the 10th was not therefore known in Singapore till Captain Tennant's emergency signal was received at noon. Fighters were then sent at once. They arrived only in time to witness the sinking of the *Prince of Wales*.

In judging the actions of Admiral Phillips during these calamitous days it should be emphasised that there were sound reasons for his belief that his intended attack at Kuantan would be outside the effective range of enemy shore-based torpedo bombers, which were his chief anxiety, and that he would only have to deal with hastily organised strikes by ordinary long-range bombers during his retirement. The distance from the Saigon airfields to Kuantan was four hundred miles, and at this date no attacks by torpedo bombers had been attempted at anything approaching this range. The efficiency of the Japanese in air warfare was at this time greatly underestimated both by ourselves and by the Americans.

*   *   *

I was opening my boxes on the 10th when the telephone at my bedside rang. It was the First Sea Lord. His voice sounded odd. He gave a sort of cough and gulp, and at first I could not hear quite clearly. "Prime Minister, I have to report to you that the *Prince of Wales* and the *Repulse* have both been sunk by the Japanese—we think by aircraft. Tom Phillips is drowned." "Are you sure it's true?" "There is no doubt at all." So I put the telephone down. I was thankful to be alone. In all the war I never received a more direct shock. The reader of these pages will realise how many efforts, hopes, and plans foundered with these two ships. As I turned over and twisted in bed the full horror of the news sank in upon me. There were no British or American capital ships in the Indian Ocean or the Pacific except the American survivors of Pearl Harbour, who were hastening back to California. Over all this vast expanse of waters Japan was supreme, and we everywhere weak and naked.

I went down to the House of Commons as soon as they met at eleven that morning to tell them myself what had happened.

Mr. Churchill's Speech to the House of Commons,
December 10, 1941

I have bad news for the House which I think I should pass on to them at the earliest moment. A report has been received from Singapore that H.M.S. *Prince of Wales* and H.M.S. *Repulse* have been sunk while carrying out operations against the Japanese in their attack on Malaya. No details are yet available except those contained in the Japanese official communiqué, which claims that both ships were sunk by air attack.

I may add that at the next sitting of the House I shall take occasion to make a short statement on the general war situation, which has from many points of view, both favourable and adverse, undergone important changes in the last few days.

*   *   *

All plans were now being made in secret for my starting for the United States on the 14th. The intervening ninety-six hours were crowded. On the 11th I had to make a full statement to the House upon the new situation. There was much anxiety and not a little discontent with the long-drawn battle in Libya, which evidently hung in the balance. I did not at all conceal the prospect that very severe punishment awaited us at the hands of Japan. On the other hand, the Russian victories had revealed the fatal error of Hitler's Eastern campaign, and winter was still to assert its power. The U-boat war was at the moment under control, and our losses greatly reduced. Finally, four-fifths of the world were now fighting on our side. Ultimate victory was certain. In this sense I spoke. I used the coolest form of factual narration, avoiding all promises of early success. I ended thus:

Naturally, I should not be prepared to discuss the resulting situation in the Far East and in the Pacific or the measures which must be taken to restore it. It may well be that we shall have to suffer considerable punishment, but we shall defend ourselves everywhere with the utmost vigour in close co-operation with the United States and the Netherlands. The naval power of Great Britain and the United States was very greatly superior—and is still largely superior—to the combined forces of the three Axis Powers. But no one must underrate the gravity of the loss which has been inflicted in Malaya and Hawaii, or the power of the new antagonist who has fallen upon us, or the length of time it will take to create,

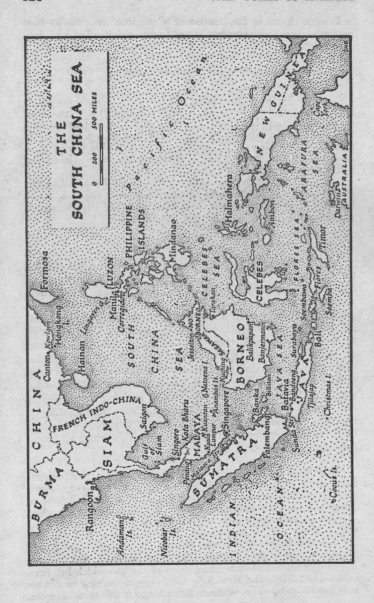

marshal, and mount the great force in the Far East which will be necessary to achieve absolute victory.

We have a very hard period to go through, and a new surge of impulse will be required, and will be forthcoming, from everybody. We must, as I have said, faithfully keep our engagements to Russia in supplies, and at the same time we must expect, at any rate for the next few months, that the volume of American supplies reaching Britain and the degree of help given by the United States Navy will be reduced. The gap must be filled, and only our own efforts will fill it. I cannot doubt however, now that the hundred and thirty million people in the United States have bound themselves to this war, that once they have settled down to it and have bent themselves to it—as they will—as their main purpose in life, then the flow of munitions and aid of every kind will vastly exceed anything that could have been expected on the peace-time basis that has ruled up to the present. Not only the British Empire now but the United States are fighting for life; Russia is fighting for life, and China is fighting for life. Behind these our great combatant communities are ranged all the spirit and hopes of all the conquered countries in Europe, prostrate under the cruel domination of the foe. I said the other day that four-fifths of the human race were on our side. It may well be an understatement. Just these gangs and cliques of wicked men and their military or party organisations have been able to bring these hideous evils upon mankind. It would indeed bring shame upon our generation if we did not teach them a lesson which will not be forgotten in the records of a thousand years.

The House was very silent, and seemed to hold its judgment in suspense. I did not seek or expect more.

* * *

During the night of December 7/8 Mr. Eden had sailed from Scapa Flow on his journey to Moscow while the news of Pearl Harbour was actually breaking upon us. There would have been time to turn him back, but I considered his mission was all the more important in consequence of the new explosion. The relations between Russia and Japan and the inevitable reshuffling of all American supplies of munitions both to Russia and Britain raised large issues, which were also delicate. The Cabinet took this view strongly. Eden continued his voyage, and I kept him well informed. There was plenty to tell.

Prime Minister to Mr. Eden (at sea)   10 Dec. 41

Since you left much has happened. United States have sustained a major disaster at Hawaii, and have now only two battleships effective in Pacific against ten Japanese. They are recalling all their battleships from the Atlantic. Secondly, according to American sources, we are going to be heavily attacked in Malaya and throughout Far East by Japanese forces enjoying command of the sea. Thirdly, it seems to me certain that Italy and Germany will declare war on United States. Fourthly, magnificent Russian successes at Leningrad, on whole Moscow front, at Kursk and in South; German armies largely on defensive or in retreat, under terrible winter conditions and ever-strengthening Russian counter-attacks. Fifthly, Auchinleck reports tide turned in Libya, but much heavy fighting lies ahead on this our second front. Sixthly, urgent necessity to reinforce Malaya with aircraft from Middle East.

2. In view of above you should not offer ten squadrons at present time. Everything is in flux with United States supplies, and I cannot tell where we are till I get there.

3. Hope you are better. We are having a jolly [sic] time here.

And further, as I embarked:

Prime Minister to Mr. Eden (at sea)   12 Dec. 41

The loss of the *Prince of Wales* and *Repulse*, together with United States losses at Pearl Harbour, gives Japanese full battle-fleet command of Pacific. They can attack with any force overseas at any point. Happily area is so vast that the use of their power can only be partial and limited. We think they will go for Philippines, Singapore, and the Burma Road. It will be many months before effective superiority can be regained through completion of British and American new battleships. The United States, under shock of Pacific disaster and war declarations, have embargoed everything for the present. I hope to loosen this up, but in present circumstances, with a Russian victory and our new dangers, we cannot make any promises beyond our agreed quota of supplies. You should point out what a grievous drain the airplanes are to us, with all these demands for fighters in the East. On the other hand, accession of United States makes amends for all, and with time and patience will give certain victory. . . .

Am just off.

13

A Voyage Amid World War

*Our Voyage in the "Duke of York"—My Party—Our Signals and
Contacts with Home—Should We Press the Soviets to Declare
War on Japan?—Mr. Eden's Conversations with Stalin and Molo-
tov, December 16/18—Stalin's Views on the Post-War Settlement
—Soviet Claim to the Baltic States—My Protests Are Supported
by the Cabinet—Further Moscow Conversations—Russia and
Japan—A Friendly Parting—Our Relations with Vichy: Blessing
or Cursing—The Japanese Attack on Hong Kong—Devoted Resist-
ance of the Garrison—Capitulation—Japanese Landings in Malaya
—My Telegram to Wavell, December 12—A Grave Strategic Issue
—Duff Cooper's Advice and My Convictions—Progress of the
Desert Offensive—Rommel Retreats to Agheila—The German Air
Force Returns to the Mediterranean—Anxieties About United
States Policy—Lord Beaverbrook's Optimism—Unfounded Fears.*

M ANY SERIOUS REASONS required my presence in London
at this moment when so much was molten. I never had
any doubt that a complete understanding between Britain and
the United States outweighed all else, and that I must go to
Washington at once with the strongest team of expert advisers who could be spared. It was thought too risky for us to
go by air at this season in an unfavourable direction. Accordingly we travelled on the 12th to the Clyde. The *Prince of
Wales* was no more. The *King George V* was watching the
Tirpitz. The newborn *Duke of York* could carry us, and work
herself up to full efficiency at the same time. The principals
of our party were Lord Beaverbrook, a member of the War
Cabinet; Admiral Pound, First Sea Lord; Air-Marshal Portal,
Chief of the Air Staff; and Field-Marshal Dill, who had now
been succeeded by General Brooke as Chief of the Imperial
General Staff. I was anxious that Brooke should remain in

London in order to grip the tremendous problems that awaited him. In his place I invited Dill, who was still in the centre of our affairs, trusted and respected by all, to come with me to Washington. Here a new sphere was to open to him.

With me also came Sir Charles Wilson, who had during 1941 become my constant medical adviser. This was his first voyage with me, but afterwards he came on all the journeys. To his unfailing care I probably owe my life. Although I could not persuade him to take my advice when he was ill, nor could he always count on my implicit obedience to all his instructions, we became devoted friends. Moreover, we both survived.

It was hoped to make the passage at an average of twenty knots in seven days, having regard to zigzags and détours to avoid the plotted U-boats. The Admiralty turned us down the Irish Channel into the Bay of Biscay. The weather was disagreeable. There was a heavy gale and a rough sea. The sky was covered with patchy clouds. We had to cross the out-and-home U-boat stream from the Western French ports to their Atlantic hunting grounds. There were so many of them about that our captain was ordered by the Admiralty not to leave our flotilla behind us; but the flotilla could not make more than six knots in the heavy seas, and we paddled along at this pace round the South of Ireland for forty-eight hours. We passed within four hundred miles of Brest, and I could not help remembering how the *Prince of Wales* and the *Repulse* had been destroyed by shore-based torpedo-aircraft attack the week before. The clouds had prevented all but an occasional plane of our air escort from joining us, but when I went on the bridge I saw a lot of unwelcome blue sky appearing. However, nothing happened, so all was well. The great ship with her attendant destroyers plodded on. But we became impatient with her slow speed. On the second night we approached the U-boat stream. Admiral Pound, who took the decision, said that we were more likely to ram a U-boat than to be torpedoed by one ourselves. The night was pitch-black. So we cast off our destroyers and ran through alone at the best speed possible in the continuing rough weather. We were battened down and great seas beat upon the decks. Lord Beaverbrook complained that he might as well have travelled in a submarine.

Our very large deciphering staff could of course receive by wireless a great deal of business. To a limited extent we could reply. When fresh escorts joined us from the Azores they could take in by daylight Morse signals from us in code, and then, dropping off a hundred miles or so, could transmit them without revealing our position. Still, there was a sense of radio claustrophobia—and we were in the midst of world war.

*   *   *

All our problems travelled with us, and my thoughts were with the Foreign Secretary, also at sea and hastening in the opposite direction. The most urgent question was our policy about asking the Soviet Government to declare war on Japan. I had already sent Mr. Eden the following telegram:

Prime Minister to Foreign Secretary   12 Dec. 41

Before you left you asked for views of Chiefs of Staff on the question whether it would be to our advantage for Russia to declare war on Japan. Chiefs of Staff considered views are as follows: Russian declaration of war on Japan would be greatly to our advantage, provided, but only provided, that the Russians are confident that it would not impair their Western front either now or next spring.

They then set forth in considerable detail the pros and cons. On the balance they emphasised the prime importance of avoiding a Russian breakdown in the West.

I continued to the Foreign Secretary:

2. If your discussions lead you to the opinion that the Russians would be prepared to declare war on Japan, it is for consideration whether the exercise of any pressure required should be by the Americans rather than ourselves.

As a postscript to him after his arrival in Moscow I added:

In view of evident strong wish of United States, China, and I expect Australia, that Russia should come in against Japan, you should not do anything to discourage a favourable movement if Stalin feels strong enough to do so. We should not put undue pressure upon him, considering how little we have been able to contribute.

And the next day:

It may well be that recent successes on the Russian front may make Stalin more willing to face a war with Japan. The situation is changing from day to day in our favour, and you must judge on the spot how far and how hard it is wise to press him.

During our voyage I received from Mr. Eden, soon at Moscow, a series of messages setting forth the Soviet ideas on other matters with which he had been confronted on arrival. The substance of these messages is summarised in his own words in the full dispatch, dated January 5, 1942, which he wrote on his return:

5 Jan. 42

. . . At my first conversation with M. Stalin and M. Molotov on December 16 M. Stalin set out in some detail what he considered should be the post-war territorial frontiers in Europe, and in particular his ideas regarding the treatment of Germany. He proposed the restoration of Austria as an independent state, the detachment of the Rhineland from Prussia as an independent state or a protectorate, and possibly the constitution of an independent State of Bavaria. He also proposed that East Prussia should be transferred to Poland and the Sudetenland returned to Czechoslovakia. He suggested that Yugoslavia should be restored, and even receive certain additional territories from Italy; that Albania should be reconstituted as an independent state, and that Turkey should receive the Dodecanese, with possible adjustments in favour of Greece as regards islands in the Aegean important to Greece. Turkey might also receive certain districts in Bulgaria, and possibly also in Northern Syria. In general the occupied countries, including Czechoslovakia and Greece, should be restored to their pre-war frontiers, and M. Stalin was prepared to support any special arrangements for securing bases, etc., for the United Kingdom in Western European countries—e.g., France, Belgium, the Netherlands, Norway, and Denmark. As regards the special interests of the Soviet Union, M. Stalin desired the restoration of the position in 1941, prior to the German attack, in respect of the Baltic States, Finland, and Bessarabia. The "Curzon Line" should form the basis for the future Soviet-Polish frontier, and Rumania should give special facilities for bases, etc., to the Soviet Union, receiving compensation from territory now occupied by Hungary.

In the course of this first conversation M. Stalin generally agreed with the principle of restitution in kind by Germany to the occupied countries, more particularly in regard to machine tools, etc., and ruled out money reparations as undesirable. He showed interest in a post-war military alliance between the "democratic countries," and stated that the Soviet Union had no objection to certain countries of Europe entering into a federal relationship, if they so desired.

In the second conversation, on December 17, M. Stalin pressed for the immediate recognition by His Majesty's Government of the future frontiers of the U.S.S.R., more particularly in regard to the inclusion within the U.S.S.R. of the Baltic States and the restoration of the 1941 Finnish-Soviet frontier. He made the conclusion of any Anglo-Soviet Agreement dependent on agreement on this point. I, for my part, explained to M. Stalin that in view of our prior undertakings to the United States Government it was quite impossible for His Majesty's Government to commit themselves at this stage to any post-war frontiers in Europe, although I undertook to consult His Majesty's Government in the United Kingdom, the United States Government, and His Majesty's Governments in the Dominions on my return. This question, to which M. Stalin attached fundamental importance, was further discussed at the third meeting on December 18.

In the forefront of the Russian claims was the request that the Baltic States, which Russia had subjugated at the beginning of the war, should be finally incorporated in the Soviet Union. There were many other conditions about Russian imperial expansion, coupled with fierce appeals for unlimited supplies and impossible military action. As soon as I read the telegrams I reacted violently against the absorption of the Baltic States.

Prime Minister to Lord Privy Seal   20 Dec. 41

Stalin's demand about Finland, Baltic States, and Rumania are directly contrary to the first, second, and third articles of the Atlantic Charter, to which Stalin has subscribed. There can be no question whatever of our making such an agreement, secret or public, direct or implied, without prior agreement with the U.S. The time has not yet come to settle frontier questions, which can only be resolved at the Peace Conference when we have won the war.

2. The mere desire to have an agreement which can be published should never lead us into making wrongful promises. Foreign Secretary has acquitted himself admirably, and should not be downhearted if he has to leave Moscow without any flourish of trumpets. The Russians have got to go on fighting for their lives anyway, and are dependent upon us for very large supplies, which we have most painfully gathered, and which we shall faithfully deliver.

3. I hope the Cabinet will agree to communicate the above to the Foreign Secretary. He will no doubt act with the necessary tact and discretion, but he should know decisively where we stand.

The Cabinet shared my view, and telegraphed accordingly. To Mr. Eden I replied as follows:

Prime Minister (at sea) to Foreign Secretary   20 Dec. 41
(at Moscow)

Naturally you will not be rough with Stalin. We are bound to United States not to enter into secret and special pacts. To approach President Roosevelt with these proposals would be to court a blank refusal, and might cause lasting trouble on both sides.

2. The strategic security of Russia on her western border will be one of the objects of Peace Conference. The position of Leningrad has been proved by events to be of particular danger. The first object will be the prevention of any new outbreak by Germany. The

separation of Prussia from South Germany, and actual definition of
Prussia itself, will be one of the greatest issues to be decided. But
all this lies in a future which is uncertain and probably remote.
We have now to win the war by a hard and prolonged struggle.
To raise such issues publicly now would only be to rally all Ger-
mans round Hitler.

3. Even to raise them informally with President Roosevelt at this
time would, in my opinion, be inexpedient. This is the sort of line
I should take, thus avoiding any abrupt or final closing of interviews. Do not be disappointed if you are not able to bring home
a joint public declaration on lines set forth in your Cabinet paper.
I am sure your visit has done utmost good and your attitude will
win general approval.

This voyage seems very long.

Mr. Eden's account gives in his own words the ending of his
talks with Stalin in Moscow:

We took leave of one another in a very friendly atmosphere.
After my explanations M. Stalin seemed fully to understand our
inability to create a second front in Europe at the present time. He
showed considerable interest in the progress of our Libyan offensive, and regarded it as most desirable to knock out Italy, on the
principle that the Axis would collapse with the destruction of its
weakest link.

He did not consider that he was yet strong enough to continue
the campaign against Germany and also to provoke hostilities with
Japan. He hoped by next spring to have restored his Far Eastern
army to the strength which it had before he had been obliged to
draw upon it for the West. He did not undertake to declare war
on Japan next spring, but only to reconsider the matter then, although he would prefer that hostilities should be opened by the
Japanese, as he seemed to expect might be the case.

*   *   *

The most acute issue however that lay in our minds in
foreign relations at this moment was France. What could be
the effect on Vichy France of the American declaration of war
between the United States and Germany? In Britain we had
our relations with de Gaulle. The United States Government
—and particularly the State Department—were in close and
helpful touch with Vichy. Pétain, held in the German grip, was
ailing. Some said he must undergo an operation for enlarged
prostate gland. Weygand had been recalled from North
Africa to Vichy and dismissed from his command. Admiral
Darlan was, it seemed, on the crest of the wave. Moreover,
Auchinleck's success in Libya and beyond opened on the
highest level all questions about French North Africa. Would

Hitler, rebuffed in the Desert and halted in Russia, insist upon sending German forces, not now through Spain, but by sea and air into Tunis, Algeria, Morocco, and Dakar? Would this, or some of it, be his rejoinder to the entry of America into the war?

There were indications that Admiral Darlan might succeed or supersede Pétain, and the Foreign Office had received surreptitious inquiries as to how he would stand with us and our great Ally. These baffling possibilities involved our whole naval position—the Toulon fleet, the two unfinished battleships at Casablanca and Dakar, the blockade, and much else. On our journey in the train from Chequers to the Clyde, I had sent a minute on the naval aspects to the First Sea Lord in his adjoining compartment.

Prime Minister to First Sea Lord   13 Dec. 41

I hope we may make together a joint offer of blessing or cursing to Vichy, or, failing Vichy, to French North Africa.

We cannot tell yet how France will have been affected by the American entry. There are also the hopes of favourable reactions from a Libyan victory. Above all, the growing disaster of the German armies in Russia will influence all minds. It may well be that an American offer to land an American Expeditionary Force at Casablanca, added to the aid we can give under "Gymnast," would decide the action of French North Africa (and incidentally Madagascar). At any rate, it is worth trying. I don't want any changes in our dispositions about "Gymnast" or "Truncheon" until we know what the reply of Vichy will be.

It must be borne in mind that the United States would be generally in favour of North and West Africa as a major theatre for Anglo-American operations.

To General Smuts I said:

Prime Minister to General Smuts   20 Dec. 41

I thought it my duty to cross the Atlantic again, and hope in a few days to confer with President Roosevelt on the whole conduct of the war. I hope of course to procure from him assistance in a forward policy in French North Africa and in West Africa. This is in accordance with American ideas, but they may well be too much preoccupied with the war with Japan. I will keep you informed.

* * *

Meanwhile the fighting proceeded in all the theatres, old and new. I had no illusions about the fate of Hong Kong under the overwhelming impact of Japanese power. But the finer the British resistance, the better for all. Hong Kong had been attacked by Japan at nearly the same moment of time as Pearl Harbour. The garrison, under Major-General Maltby, were faced with a task that from the outset was beyond their powers. The Japanese employed a force of three divisions, against which we could muster six battalions, of which two were Canadian. In addition there was a handful of mobile artillery, the Volunteer Defence Corps of civilians, two thousand strong, and the coast and anti-aircraft guns defending the port. Throughout the siege the Japanese enjoyed undisputed mastery of the air. An active fifth column among the native inhabitants was no small help to the enemy.

Three battalions of the garrison, with sixteen guns, were deployed on the mainland in order to delay the assailants until demolitions had been carried out in the port of Kowloon. They were soon heavily attacked, and on December 11 were ordered to withdraw to the island. This was skilfully accomplished during the ensuing two nights under conditions of much difficulty.

Prime Minister to Governor and Defenders of   12 Dec. 41
Hong Kong

We are all watching day by day and hour by hour your stubborn defence of the port and fortress of Hong Kong. You guard a link between the Far East and Europe long famous in world civilisation. We are sure that the defence of Hong Kong against barbarous and unprovoked attack will add a glorious page to British annals.

All our hearts are with you in your ordeal. Every day of your resistance brings nearer our certain final victory.

The enemy's preparations for crossing the mile-wide stretch of water between the mainland and the island took some days, during which they systematically shelled, bombed, and mortared our positions. On the night of December 18 they made their first landing, and successive reinforcements pushed actively inland. The defenders were forced back step by step by attacks of ever-growing strength, their own numbers diminished by heavy casualties. They had no hope of reinforcement or succour, but they fought on.

Prime Minister to Governor, Hong Kong   21 Dec. 41

We were greatly concerned to hear of the landings on Hong Kong Island which have been effected by the Japanese. We cannot judge from here the conditions which rendered these landings possible or prevented effective counter-attacks upon the intruders. There must however be no thought of surrender. Every part of the island must be fought and the enemy resisted with the utmost stubbornness.

The enemy should be compelled to expend the utmost life and equipment. There must be vigorous fighting in the inner defences, and, if the need be, from house to house. Every day that you are able to maintain your resistance you help the Allied cause all over the world, and by a prolonged resistance you and your men can win the lasting honour which we are sure will be your due.

These orders were obeyed in spirit and to the letter. Among many acts of devotion one may be recorded here. On December 19 the Canadian Brigadier Lawson reported that his headquarters were overrun; fighting was taking place at point-blank range; he was going outside to fight it out. He did so, and he and those with him were killed. For a week the garrison held out. Every man who could bear arms, including some from the Royal Navy and Royal Air Force, took part in a desperate resistance. Their tenacity was matched by the fortitude of the British civilian population. On Christmas Day the limit of endurance was reached and capitulation became inevitable. Under their resolute Governor, Sir Mark Young, the colony had fought a good fight. They had won indeed the "lasting honour" which is their due.

* * *

Another set of disasters loomed upon us in Malaya. The Japanese landings on the peninsula on December 8 were accompanied by damaging raids on our airfields which seriously crippled our already weak air forces and soon made the northerly aerodromes unusable. At Kota Bharu, where the beach defences were manned by an infantry brigade extended over a front of thirty miles, the Japanese succeeded in landing the greater part of a division, though not without heavy casualties inflicted both by our troops on shore and from the air. After three days of stiff fighting the enemy were firmly established on land, the near-by airfields were in their hands, and the brigade, which had lost heavily, was ordered to withdraw southward.

Farther north on that same December 8 the Japanese had made unopposed landings at Patani and Singora. Dutch submarines, boldly handled, sank several of their ships. There was no serious fighting until December 12, when the enemy with one of their finest divisions made a successful attack on the 11th Indian Division north of Alor Star, inflicting severe losses.

Before leaving I had telegraphed to General Wavell, Commander-in-Chief India:

Prime Minister to General Wavell   12 Dec. 41

You must now look east. Burma is placed under your command. You must resist the Japanese advance towards Burma and India and try to cut their communications down the Malay Peninsula. We are diverting the 18th Division, now rounding the Cape, to Bombay, together with four fighter squadrons of the R.A.F., now en route for Caucasus and Caspian theatre. We are also sending you a special hamper of A.A. and A.T. guns, some of which are already en route. You should retain 17th Indian Division for defence against the Japanese. Marry these forces as you think best and work them into the eastern fighting front to the highest advantage.

2. It is proposed, at a convenient moment in the near future by arrangement between you and Auchinleck, to transfer Iraq and Persia to the Cairo Command. The Russian victories and Auchinleck's Libyan advance have for the time being relieved danger of German irruption into the Syrian-Iraq-Persian theatre. The danger may revive, but we have other more urgent dangers to meet.

3. I hope these new dispositions arising from the vast changes in the world situation of the last four days will commend themselves to you. I shall endeavour to feed you with armour, aircraft, and British personnel to the utmost possible, having regard to the great strain we are under. Pray cable me fully your views and needs.

And also:

Prime Minister to Lord Privy Seal, and to General   13 Dec. 41
Ismay for C.O.S. Committee

Pray do all in your power to get men and materials moving into India, and reinforce with air from the Middle East as soon as the battle in Libya is decided in our favour. An effort should be made to send armoured vehicles at the earliest moment after a Libyan decision.

Prime Minister to Governor of Burma   13 Dec. 41

Wavell has been placed in charge of military and air defence of Burma. We have diverted 18th Division, four fighter squadrons, and A.A. and A.T. guns, which were rounding the Cape, to Bombay for him to use as he thinks best. The battle in Libya goes well, but I cannot move any air from there till decision [in the battle] is definitely reached. All preparations are being made to transfer four to six bomber squadrons to your theatre the moment battle is won.

Every good wish.

*   *   *

A grave strategic choice was involved in the tactical defence of the Malay Peninsula. I had clear convictions which I regret it was not my power to enforce from mid-ocean.

Prime Minister to General Ismay, for C.O.S. Committee 15 Dec. 41

Beware lest [that] troops required for ultimate defence Singapore Island and fortress are not used up or cut off in Malay Peninsula. Nothing compares in importance with the fortress. Are you sure we shall have enough troops for prolonged defence? Consider with Auchinleck and Commonwealth Government moving 1st Australian Division from Palestine to Singapore. Report action.

I was glad to find that our Minister of State, Mr. Duff Cooper, had independently reached the same conclusion.

Prime Minister to General Ismay, for C.O.S. Committee 19 Dec. 41

Duff Cooper expresses the same anxieties as I conveyed to you in my message beginning "Beware." Duff Cooper's proposal to concentrate on defence of Johore for the purpose of holding Singapore conforms exactly to view taken by Dill there.

2. After naval disasters to British and American sea power in Pacific and Indian Oceans we have no means of preventing continuous landings by Japanese in great strength in Siam and the Malay Peninsula. It is therefore impossible to defend, other than by demolitions and delaying action, anything north of the defensive line in Johore, and this line itself can only be defended as part of the final defence of Singapore Island fortress and the naval base.

3. The Commander-in-Chief should now be told to confine himself to defence of Johore and Singapore, and that nothing must compete with maximum defence of Singapore. This should not preclude his employing delaying tactics and demolitions on the way south and making an orderly retreat.

4. You do not say who is now Commander-in-Chief Far East. Has Pownall got there? If not, where is he? He should fly there at earliest moment.

5. It was always intended that all reinforcements diverted from the Cape to India should be used by Wavell for the defence of Burma or sent forward to Far East Command as situation requires. Your action in diverting the anti-aircraft guns and fighter squadrons is fully approved.

6. Eighteenth Division can similarly be used by Wavell either for his own needs or to help Far East Command. But why stop there? If 18th Division is sent eastward it would seem wise to get at least one Australian division moving into India to replace it.

7. Please say what you are doing and how you propose to overcome the growing difficulties of sending reinforcements into Singapore. Also what has been done about reducing number of useless mouths in Singapore Island? What was the reply about supplies?

*   *   *

It is not possible to pursue the story to its conclusion in this volume. The tragedy of Singapore must presently unfold itself.

Suffice it here to say that during the rest of the month the Indian Division fought a series of delaying actions against the enemy's main thrust down the west coast of the peninsula. On December 17 the enemy invaded Penang, where, despite demolitions, a considerable number of small craft were seized intact. These later enabled him to mount repeated flank attacks made by small amphibious forces. By the end of the month our troops, several times heavily engaged, were in action near Ipoh, a full hundred and fifty miles from the position they had first held, and by then the Japanese had landed on the peninsula at least three full divisions, including their Imperial Guard. In the air too the enemy had greatly increased his superiority. The quality of his aircraft, which he had speedily deployed on captured airfields, had exceeded all expectations. We had been thrown onto the defensive and our losses were severe. On December 16 the northern part of Borneo also was invaded, and soon overrun, but not before we had succeeded in demolishing the immense and valuable oil installations. In all this Dutch submarines took toll of the enemy ships.

*   *   *

While we sailed the seas General Auchinleck's battle in the Desert went well. The Axis army, skilfully evading various encircling manoeuvres, made good its retreat to a rearward line running southward from Gazala. On December 13 the attack on this position was launched by the Eighth Army. This now comprises the 7th Armoured Division, with the 4th Ar-

moured Brigade and support group, the 4th British Indian Division, the Guards Brigade (motorised), the 5th New Zealand Brigade, the Polish Brigade Group, and the 32d Army Tank Brigade. All these troops passed under the command of the XIIIth Corps Headquarters. The XXXth Corps had to deal with the enemy garrisons cut off and abandoned at Sollum, Halfaya, and Bardia, which were fighting stubbornly. The enemy fought well at Gazala, but their desert flank was turned by our armour, and Rommel began his withdrawal through Derna to Agedabia and Agheila. They were followed all the way by all the troops we could keep in motion and supplied over these large distances.

With the first week in December came a marked increase in the hostile air power. The 1st German Air Corps was withdrawn from the Russian theatre and arrived in the Mediterranean. The German records show that their strength rose from 400 (206 serviceable) on November 15 to 637 (339 serviceable) a month later. The bulk went to Sicily to protect the sea route to North Africa, but over the desert dive-bombers, escorted by the highly efficient Me. 109 fighters, began to appear in increasing numbers. The supremacy which the Royal Air Force had gained in the first week of the battle no longer ruled. We shall see later how the revival of the enemy air power in the Mediterranean during December and January and the virtual disappearance for several months of our sea command was to deprive Auchinleck of the fruits of the victory for which he had struggled so hard and waited too long.

*   *   *

Everyone in our party worked incessantly while the *Duke of York* plodded westward, and all our thoughts were focused on the new and vast problems we had to solve. We looked forward with eagerness, but also with some anxiety, to our first direct contact as allies with the President and his political and military advisers. We knew before we left that the outrage of Pearl Harbour had stirred the people of the United States to their depths. The official reports and the press summaries we had received gave the impression that the whole fury of the nation would be turned upon Japan. We feared lest the true proportion of the war as a whole might not be understood. We were conscious of a serious danger that the United States might pursue the war against Japan in the Pacific and leave us to fight Germany and Italy in Europe, Africa, and in the Middle East.

I have described in a previous chapter the enduring, and up to this point growing, strength of Britain. The first Battle of the Atlantic against the U-boats had turned markedly in our favour. We did not doubt our power to keep open our ocean paths. We felt sure we could defeat Hitler if he tried to invade the Island. We were encouraged by the strength of the Russian resistance. We were unduly hopeful about our Libyan campaign. But all our future plans depended upon a vast flow of American supplies of all kinds, such as were now streaming across the Atlantic. Especially we counted on planes and tanks, as well as on the stupendous American merchant-ship construction. Hitherto, as a non-belligerent, the President had been able and willing to divert large supplies of equipment from the American armed forces, since these were not engaged. This process was bound to be restricted now that the United States was at war with Germany, Italy, and above all Japan. Home needs would surely come first? Already, after Russia had been attacked, we had rightly sacrificed to aid the Soviet armies a large portion of the equipment and supplies now at last arriving from our factories. The United States had diverted to Russia even larger quantities of supplies that we otherwise would have received ourselves. We had fully approved of all this on account of the splendid resistance which Russia was offering to the Nazi invader.

It had been none the less hard to delay the equipment of our own forces, and especially to withhold vitally needed weapons from our army fiercely engaged in Libya. We must presume that "America First" would become the dominant principle with our Ally. We feared that there would be a long interval before American forces came into action on a great scale, and that during this period of preparation we should necessarily be greatly straitened. This would happen at a time when we ourselves had to face a new and terrible antagonist in Malaya, the Indian Ocean, Burma, and India. Evidently the partition of supplies would require profound attention and would be fraught with many difficulties and delicate aspects. Already we had been notified that all the schedules of deliveries under Lend-Lease had been stopped pending readjustment. Happily the output of the British munitions and aircraft factories was now acquiring scope and momentum, and would soon be very large indeed. But a long array of "bottlenecks" and possible denials of key items, which would affect the whole range of our production, loomed before our eyes as the *Duke of York* drove on through the incessant gales. Beaverbrook was, as usual in times of trouble, optimistic. He declared that the resources of the United States had so far not even been scratched; that they were immeasurable, and that once the whole force of the American people was diverted to the struggle results would be achieved far beyond anything that had been projected or imagined. Moreover, he thought the Americans did not yet realise their strength in the production field. All the present statistics would be surpassed and swept away by the American effort. There would be enough for all. In this his judgment was right.

All these considerations paled before the main strategic issue. Should we be able to persuade the President and the American Service chiefs that the defeat of Japan would not spell the defeat of Hitler, but that the defeat of Hitler made the finishing-off of Japan merely a matter of time and trouble? Many long hours did we spend revolving this grave issue. The two Chiefs of Staff and General Dill with Hollis and his officers prepared several papers dealing with the whole subject and emphasising the view that the war was all one. As will be seen, these labours and fears both proved needless.

14

Proposed Plan and Sequence of the War

*My Three Papers for the President—Part I, The Atlantic Front—
Hitler's Failure and Losses in Russia—My Ill-Founded Hopes of
General Auchinleck's Victory in Cyrenaica—Possible German
Thrust Through the Caucasus—Urgent Need to Win French
North Africa—British and American Reinforcements for North
Africa—Request for American Troops in Northern Ireland—Re-
quest for American Bomber Squadrons to Attack Germany from
Great Britain—Possible Refusal by Vichy to Cooperate in North
Africa—The Consequential Anglo-American Campaign of 1942—
Our Relations with General de Gaulle—The Spanish Problem—
The Main Objectives of 1942—Part II, The Pacific Front—Japa-
nese Naval Superiority—Their Resources a Wasting Factor—Our
Need to Regain Superiority at Sea—British Offer to America of
the "Nelson" and the "Rodney"—The Warfare of Aircraft-Car-
riers—Vital Need to Improvise—Danger of Creating Too Large an
American Army—My Assertion of the Need for Large-Scale Op-
erations on the Continent—Part III, The Campaign of 1943—
Possible Situation at the Beginning of 1943—West and North
Africa in Anglo-American Control—Turkey Effectively in the
Allied Front—A Footing Gained in Italy and Sicily—Need to
Prepare for Landings in Western and Southern Europe—Major
Assault in 1943—Largely an Amphibious Operation—Continuous
Preparation by Bombing of Germany and Italy—Hope of Ending
the War in 1943 or 1944—Staff Concurrence with My Views—
All the Objectives Ultimately Achieved—A Fortunate Delay in
the Final Assault.*

THE EIGHT DAYS' VOYAGE, with its enforced reduction of current business, with no Cabinet meetings to attend or
people to receive, enabled me to pass in review the whole war
as I saw and felt it in the light of its sudden vast expansion. I
recalled Napoleon's remark about the value of being able to

focus objects in the mind for a long time without being tired—
"*fixer les objets longtemps sans être fatigué.*" As usual I tried
to do this by setting forth my thought in typescript by dicta-
tion. In order to prepare myself for meeting the President and
for the American discussions and to make sure that I carried
with me the two Chiefs of Staff, Pound and Portal, and General Dill, and that the facts could be checked in good time by
General Hollis and the Secretariat, I produced three papers on
the future course of the war, as I conceived it should be
steered. Each paper took four or five hours, spread over two or
three days. As I had the whole picture in my mind it all came
forth easily, but very slowly. In fact, it could have been written
out two or three times in longhand in the same period. As each
document was completed after being checked, I sent it to my
professional colleagues as an expression of my personal convictions. They were at the same time preparing papers of their
own for the combined Staff conferences. I was glad to find
that, although my theme was more general and theirs more
technical, there was our usual harmony on principles and
values. No differences were expressed which led to argument,
and very few of the facts required correction. Thus, though
nobody was committed in a precise or rigid fashion, we all
arrived with a body of doctrine of a constructive character on
which we were broadly united.

The first paper assembled the reasons why our main objective for the campaign of 1942 in the European theatre should
be the occupation of the whole coastline of Africa and of the
Levant from Dakar to the Turkish frontier by British and
American forces. The second dealt with the measures which
should be taken to regain the command of the Pacific, and
specified May, 1942, as the month when this could be
achieved. It dwelt particularly upon the need to multiply aircraft-carriers by improvising them in large numbers. The third
declared as the ultimate objective the liberation of Europe by
the landing of large Anglo-American armies wherever was
thought best in the German-conquered territory, and fixed the
year 1943 as the date for this supreme stroke.

I gave these three papers to the President before Christmas.
I explained that while they were my own personal views, they
did not supersede any formal communications between the
Staffs. I couched them in the form of memoranda for the British Chiefs of Staff Committee. Moreover, I told him they were
not written expressly for his eye, but that I thought it important that he should know what was in my mind and what

I wanted to have done and, so far as Great Britain was concerned, would try to bring to action. He read them immediately after receiving them, and the next day asked whether he might keep copies of them. To this I gladly assented.

Although I had not had any formal reply to my letter of October 20 on these subjects [1] which Mr. Attlee had presented, and did not indeed expect one, I felt that the President was thinking very much along the same lines as I was about action in French Northwest Africa. In October I could only tell him what our British ideas and plans were while we remained alone. We were now Allies, and must act in common and on a greater scale. I felt confidence that he and I would find a large measure of agreement and that the ground had been well prepared. I was therefore in a hopeful mood.

PART I

THE ATLANTIC FRONT

December 16, 1941

Hitler's failure and losses in Russia are the prime fact in the war at this time. We cannot tell how great the disaster to the German Army and Nazi régime will be. This régime has hitherto lived upon easily and cheaply won successes. Instead of what was imagined to be a swift and easy victory, it has now to face the shock of a winter of slaughter and expenditure of fuel and equipment on the largest scale.

Neither Great Britain nor the United States have any part to play in this event, except to make sure that we send, without fail and punctually, the supplies we have promised. In this way alone shall we hold our influence over Stalin and be able to weave the mighty Russian effort into the general texture of the war.

2. In a lesser degree the impending victory of General Auchinleck in Cyrenaica is an injury to the German power. We may expect the total destruction of the enemy force in Libya to be apparent before the end of the year. This not only inflicts a heavy blow upon the Germans and Italians, but it frees our forces in the Nile Valley from the major threat of invasion from the west under which they have long dwelt. Naturally, General Auchinleck will press on as fast as possible with the operation called "Acrobat," which should give him possession of Tripoli, and so bring his armoured vanguard to the French frontier of Tunis. He may be able to supply a forecast before we separate at Washington.[2]

3. The German losses and defeat in Russia and their extirpation

---

[1] See Chapter IX, pages 458–461.
[2] This paragraph was to be falsified by General Auchinleck's later defeats. At this time we had good grounds for hope.

from Libya may of course impel them to a supreme effort in the spring to break the ring that is closing on them by a southeastward thrust either through the Caucasus or to Anatolia, or both. However, we should not assume that necessarily they will have the war energy for this task. The Russian armies, recuperated by the winter, will lie heavy upon them from Leningrad to the Crimea. They may easily be forced to evacuate the Crimea. There is no reason at this time to suppose that the Russian Navy will not command the Black Sea. Nor should it be assumed that the present life-strength of Germany is such as to make an attack upon Turkey and a march through Anatolia a business to be undertaken in present circumstances by the Nazi régime. The Turks have fifty divisions; their fighting quality and the physical obstacles of their country are well known. Although Turkey has played for safety throughout, the Russian command of the Black Sea and the British successes in the Levant and along the North African shore, together with the proved weakness of the Italian Fleet, would justify every effort on our part to bring Turkey into line, and are certainly sufficient to encourage her to resist a German inroad. *While it would be imprudent to regard the danger of a German southwest thrust against the Persian-Iraq-Syrian front as removed, it certainly now seems much less likely than heretofore.*

4. *We ought therefore to try hard to win over French North Africa, and now is the moment to use every inducement and form of pressure at our disposal upon the Government of Vichy and the French authorities in North Africa.* The German setback in Russia, the British successes in Libya, the moral and military collapse of Italy, above all the declarations of war exchanged between Germany and the United States, must strongly affect the mind of France and the French Empire. Now is the time to offer to Vichy and to French North Africa a blessing or a cursing. A blessing will consist in a promise by the United States and Great Britain to reestablish France as a Great Power with her territories undiminished. It should carry with it an offer of active aid by British and United States expeditionary forces, both from the Atlantic seaboard of Morocco and at convenient landing-points in Algeria and Tunis, as well as from General Auchinleck's forces advancing from the east. Ample supplies for the French and the loyal Moors should be made available. Vichy should be asked to send their fleet from Toulon to Oran and Bizerta and to bring France into the war again as a principal.

This would mean that the Germans would take over the whole of France and rule it as occupied territory. It does not seem that the conditions in the occupied and the hitherto unoccupied zones are widely different. Whatever happens, European France will inevitably be subjected to a complete blockade. There is of course always the chance that the Germans, tied up in Russia, may not care to take over unoccupied France, even though French North Africa is at war with them.

5. If we can obtain even the connivance of Vichy to French North Africa coming over to our side we must be ready to send considerable forces as soon as possible. *Apart from anything which General Auchinleck can bring in from the east, should he be successful in Tripolitania, we hold ready in Britain (Operation "Gymnast") about fifty-five thousand men, comprising two divisions and an armoured unit, together with the shipping. These forces could enter French North Africa by invitation on the twenty-third day after the order to embark them was given.* Leading elements and air forces from Malta could reach Bizerta at very short notice. *It is desired that the United States should at the same time promise to bring in, via Casablanca and other African Atlantic ports, not less than a hundred and fifty thousand men during the next six months.* It is essential that some American elements, say twenty-five thousand men, should go at the earliest moment after French agreement, either Vichy or North African, had been obtained.

6. It is also asked that the United States will send the equivalent of three divisions and one armoured division into Northern Ireland. These divisions could, if necessary, complete their training in Northern Ireland. The presence of American forces there would become known to the enemy, and they could be led to magnify their actual numbers. The presence of United States troops in the British Isles would be a powerful additional deterrent against an attempt at invasion by Germany. It would enable us to nourish the campaign in French North Africa by two more divisions and one complete armoured division. If forces of this order could be added to the French army already in North Africa, with proper air support, the Germans would have to make a very difficult and costly campaign across uncommanded waters to subdue North Africa. The Northwest African theatre is one most favourable for Anglo-American operations, our approaches being direct and convenient across the Atlantic, while the enemy's passage of the Mediterrnean would be severely obstructed, as is happening in their Libyan enterprise.

7. It may be mentioned here that we greatly desire American bomber squadrons to come into action from the British Isles against Germany. Our own bomber programme has fallen short of our hopes. It is formidable and is increasing, but its full development has been delayed. It must be remembered that we place great hopes of affecting German production and German morale by ever more severe and more accurate bombing of their cities and harbours, and that this, combined with their Russian defeats, may produce important effects upon the will to fight of the German people, with consequential internal reactions upon the German Government. The arrival in the United Kingdom of, say twenty American bomber squadrons would emphasise and accelerate the process, and would be the most direct and effective reply to the declarations of war by Germany upon the United States. Arrangements will be made in Great Britain to increase this process and develop the

Anglo-American bombing of Germany without any top limit from now on till the end of the war.

8. We must however reckon with a refusal by Vichy to act as we desire, and on the contrary they may rouse French North Africa to active resistance. They may help German troops to enter North Africa; the Germans may force their way or be granted passage through Spain; the French fleet at Toulon may pass under German control, and France and the French Empire may be made by Vichy to collaborate actively with Germany against us, although it is not likely that this would go through effectively. The overwhelming majority of the French are ranged with Great Britain, and now still more with the United States. It is by no means certain that Admiral Darlan can deliver the Toulon Fleet over intact to Germany. It is most improbable that French soldiers and sailors would fight effectively against the United States and Great Britain. Nevertheless, we must not exclude the possibility of a half-hearted association of the defeatist elements in France and North Africa with Germany. In this case our task in North Africa will become much harder.

A campaign must be fought in 1942 to gain possession of, or conquer, the whole of the North African shore, including the Atlantic ports of Morocco. Dakar and other French West African ports must be captured before the end of the year. Whereas however entry into French North Africa is urgent to prevent German penetration, a period of eight or nine months' preparation may well be afforded for the mastering of Dakar and the West African establishments. Plans should be set on foot forthwith. If sufficient time and preparation are allowed and the proper apparatus provided, these latter operations present no insuperable difficulty.

9. Our relations with General de Gaulle and the Free French movement will require to be reviewed. Hitherto the United States have entered into no undertakings similar to those comprised in my correspondence with him. Through no particular fault of his own his movement has created new antagonisms in French minds. Any action which the United States may now feel able to take in regard to him should have the effect, *inter alia,* of redefining our obligations to him and France so as to make these obligations more closely dependent upon the eventual effort by him and the French nation to rehabilitate themselves. If Vichy were to act as we desire about French North Africa, the United States and Great Britain must labour to bring about a reconciliation between the Free French (de Gaullists) and those other Frenchmen who will have taken up arms once more against Germany. If, on the other hand, Vichy persists in collaboration with Germany and we have to fight our way into French North and West Africa, then the de Gaullists' movement must be aided and used to the full.

10. We cannot tell what will happen in Spain. *It seems probable that the Spaniards will not give the Germans a free passage through Spain to attack Gibraltar and invade North Africa.* There

may be infiltration, but the formal demand for the passage of an army would be resisted. If so, the winter would be the worst time for the Germans to attempt to force their way through Spain. Moreover, Hitler, with nearly all Europe to hold down by armed force in the face of defeat and semi-starvation, may well be chary of taking over unoccupied France and involving himself in bitter guerrilla warfare with the morose, fierce, hungry people of the Iberian Peninsula. Everything possible must be done by Britain and the United States to strengthen their will to resist. The present policy of limited supplies should be pursued.

The value of Gibraltar Harbour and base to us is so great that no attempts should be made upon the Atlantic islands until either the peninsula is invaded or the Spaniards give passage to the Germans.

11. *To sum up, the war in the West in 1942 comprises, as its main offensive effort, the occupation and control by Great Britain and the United States of the whole of the North and West African possessions of France, and the further control by Britain of the whole North African shore from Tunis to Egypt, thus giving, if the naval situation allows, free passage through the Mediterranean to the Levant and the Suez Canal. These great objectives can only be achieved if British and American naval and air superiority in the Atlantic is maintained, if supply lines continue uninterrupted, and if the British Isles are effectively safeguarded against invasion.*

*   *   *

My second paper on the Pacific war was only completed after we had landed.

PART II

THE PACIFIC FRONT

December 20, 1941

The Japanese have naval superiority, which enables them to transport troops to almost any desired point, possess themselves of it, and establish it for an air-naval fuelling base. The Allies will not have for some time the power to fight a general fleet engagement. Their power of convoying troops depends upon the size of the seas, which reduces the chance of interception. Even without superior sea power we may descend by surprise here and there. But we could not carry on a sustained operation across the seas. We must expect therefore to be deprived one by one of our possessions and strong-points in the Pacific, and that the enemy will establish himself fairly easily in one after the other, mopping up the local garrisons.

2. In this interim period our duty is one of stubborn resistance at each point attacked, and to slip supplies and reinforcements

through as opportunity offers, taking all necessary risks. If our forces resist stubbornly and we reinforce them as much as possible, the enemy will be forced to make ever-larger overseas commitments far from home; his shipping resources will be strained, and his communications will provide vulnerable targets upon which all available naval and air forces, United States, British, and Dutch—especially submarines—should concentrate their effort. It is of the utmost importance that the enemy should not acquire large gains cheaply; that he should be compelled to nourish all his conquests and kept extended, and kept burning up his resources.

3. The resources of Japan are a wasting factor. The country has long been overstrained by its wasteful war in China. They were at their maximum strength on the day of the Pearl Harbour attack. If it is true, as Stalin asserts, that they have, in addition to their own air force fifteen hundred German airplanes (and he would have opportunities of knowing how they got there), they have now no means of replacing wastage other than by their small home production of three hundred to five hundred per month. Our policy should be to make them maintain the largest possible number of troops in their conquests overseas, and to keep them as busy as possible, so as to enforce well-filled lines of communication and a high rate of aircraft consumption. If we idle and leave them at ease they will be able to extend their conquests cheaply and easily, work with a minimum of overseas forces, make the largest gains and the smallest commitments, and thus inflict upon us an enormous amount of damage. It is therefore right and necessary to fight them at every point where we have a fair chance, so as to keep them burning and extended.

4. But we must steadily aim at regaining superiority at sea at the earliest moment. This can be gained in two ways: first, by the strengthening of our capital ships. The two new Japanese battleships built free from treaty limitations must be considered a formidable factor, influencing the whole Pacific theatre. It is understood that two new American battleships will be fit for action by May. Of course, all undertakings in war must be subject to the action of the enemy, accidents, and misfortune, but if our battleship strength should not be further reduced, nor any new unforeseen stress arise, we should hope to place the *Nelson* and the *Rodney* at the side of these two new American battleships, making four sixteen-inch-gun modern vessels of major strength. Behind such a squadron the older reconstructed battleships of the United States should be available in numbers sufficient to enable a fleet action, under favourable circumstances, to be contemplated at any time after the month of May. The recovery of our naval superiority in the Pacific, even if not brought to a trial of strength, would reassure the whole western seaboard of the American continent, and thus prevent a needless dissipation on a gigantic defensive effort of forces which have offensive parts to play. *We must therefore set before ourselves, as a main strategic object, the forming of a definitely superior battle*

fleet in the Pacific, and we must aim at May as the date when this will be achieved.

5. Not only then, but in the interval, the warfare of aircraft-carriers should be developed to the greatest possible extent. We are ourselves forming a squadron of three aircraft-carriers, suitably attended, to act in the waters between South Africa, India, and Australia. The United States have already seven regular carriers, compared with Japan's ten, but those of the United States are larger. *To this force of regular warship aircraft-carriers we must add a very large development of improvised carriers, both large and small. In this way alone can we increase our sea power rapidly. Even if the carriers can only fly a dozen machines, they may play their part in combination with other carriers. We ought to develop a floating air establishment sufficient to enable us to acquire and maintain for considerable periods local air superiority over shore-based aircraft and sufficient to cover the landing of troops in order to attack the enemy's new conquests. Unless or until this local air superiority is definitely acquired, even a somewhat superior fleet on our side would fight at a serious disadvantage. We cannot get more battleships than those now in sight for the year 1942, but we can and must get more aircraft-carriers. It takes five years to build a battleship, but it is possible to improvise a carrier in six months. Here then is a field for invention and ingenuity similar to that which called forth the extraordinary fleets and flotillas which fought on the Mississippi in the Civil War.* It must be accepted that the priority given to seaborne aircraft of a suitable type will involve a retardation in the full-scale bombing offensive against Germany which we have contemplated as a major method of waging war. This however is a matter of time and of degree. We cannot in 1942 hope to reach the levels of bomb discharge in Germany which we had prescribed for that year, but we shall surpass them in 1943. Our joint programme may be late, but it will all come along. And meanwhile the German cities and other targets will not disappear. While every effort must be made to speed up the rate of bomb discharge upon Germany until the great scales prescribed for 1943 and 1944 are reached, nevertheless, we may be forced by other needs to face a retardation in our schedules. The more important will it be therefore that in this interval a force, be it only symbolic, of United States bombing squadrons should operate from the British Isles against the German cities and seaports.

The paragraphs which follow, dealing with the acquisition of air bases, with Russian intervention, with convoy protection in the Pacific, and with the use to be made of Singapore, need not be reprinted here. Finally:

12. We need not fear that this war in the Pacific will, after the first shock is over, absorb an unduly large proportion of United States forces. The numbers of troops that we should wish them to

use in Europe in 1942 will not be so large as to be prevented by their Pacific operations, limited as these must be. *What will harm us is for a vast United States Army of ten millions to be created which for at least two years while it was training would absorb all the available supplies and stand idle defending the American continent.* The best way of preventing the creation of such a situation and obtaining the proper use of the large forces and ample supplies of munitions which will presently be forthcoming is to enable the Americans to regain their naval power in the Pacific and not to discourage them from the precise secondary overseas operations which they may perhaps contemplate.

* * *

So many tales have been published of my rooted aversion from large-scale operations on the Continent that it is important that the truth should be emphasised. I always considered that a decisive assault upon the German-occupied countries on the largest possible scale was the only way in which the war could be won, and that the summer of 1943 should be chosen as the target date. It will be seen that the scale of the operation contemplated by me was already before the end of 1941 set at forty armoured divisions and a million other troops as essential for the opening phase. When I notice the number of books which have been written on a false assumption of my attitude on this issue, I feel bound to direct the attention of the reader to the authentic and responsible documents written at the time, of which other instances will be given as the account proceeds.

PART III

THE CAMPAIGN OF 1943

December 18, 1941

If the operations outlined in Parts I and II should prosper during 1942 the situation at the beginning of 1943 might be as follows: (*a*) United States and Great Britain would have recovered effective naval superiority in the Pacific, and all Japanese overseas commitments would be endangered both from the assailing of their communications and from British and American expeditions sent to recover places lost. (*b*) The British Isles would remain intact and more strongly prepared against invasion than ever before. (*c*) The whole West and North African shores from Dakar to the Suez Canal and the Levant to the Turkish frontier would be in Anglo-American hands.

Turkey, though not necessarily at war, would be definitely incorporated in the American-British-Russian front. The Russian position would be strongly established, and the supplies of British and American material as promised would have in part compensated for the loss of Russian munitions-making capacity. It might be that a footing would already have been established in Sicily and Italy, with reactions inside Italy which might be highly favourable.

2. But all this would fall short of bringing the war to an end. The war cannot be ended by driving Japan back to her own bounds and defeating her overseas forces. The war can only be ended through the defeat in Europe of the German armies, or through internal convulsions in Germany produced by the un- favourable course of the war, economic privations, and the Allied bombing offensive. As the strength of the United States, Great Britain, and Russia develops and begins to be realised by the Ger- mans an internal collapse is always possible, but we must not count upon this. Our plans must proceed upon the assumption that the resistance of the German Army and Air Force will continue at its present level and that their U-boat warfare will be conducted by increasingly numerous flotillas.

3. We have therefore to prepare for the liberation of the captive countries of Western and Southern Europe by the landing at suit- able points, successively or simultaneously, of British and Ameri- can armies strong enough to enable the conquered populations to revolt. By themselves they will never be able to revolt, owing to the ruthless counter-measures that will be employed, but if ade- quate and suitably equipped forces were landed in several of the following countries, namely, Norway, Denmark, Holland, Belgium, the French Channel coasts and the French Atlantic coasts, as well as in Italy and possibly the Balkans, the German garrisons would prove insufficient to cope both with the strength of the liberating forces and the fury of the revolting peoples. It is impossible for the Germans, while we retain the sea power necessary to choose the place or places of attack, to have sufficient troops in each of these countries for effective resistance. In particular, they cannot move their armour about laterally from north to south or west to east; either they must divide it between the various conquered countries —in which case it will become hopelessly dispersed—or they must hold it back in a central position in Germany, in which case it will not arrive until large and important lodgments have been made by us from overseas.

4. We must face here the usual clash between short-term and long-term projects. War is a constant struggle and must be waged from day to day. It is only with some difficulty and within limits that provision can be made for the future. Experience shows that forecasts are usually falsified and preparations always in arrear. Nevertheless, there must be a design and theme for bringing the war to a victorious end in a reasonable period. All the more is this necessary when under modern conditions no large-scale offensive operation can be launched without the preparation of elaborate technical apparatus.

5. We should therefore face now the problems not only of driving Japan back to her homelands and regaining undisputed mastery in the Pacific, but also of liberating conquered Europe by the landing during the summer of 1943 of United States and British armies on their shores. Plans should be prepared for the landing in all of the countries mentioned above. The actual choice of which three or four to pick should be deferred as long as possible, so as to profit by the turn of events and make sure of secrecy.

6. In principle, the landings should be made by armoured and mechanised forces capable of disembarking not at ports but on beaches, either by landing-craft or from ocean-going ships specially adapted. The potential front of attack is thus made so wide that the German forces holding down these different countries cannot be strong enough at all points. An amphibious outfit must be prepared to enable these large-scale disembarkations to be made swiftly and surely. The vanguards of the various British and American expeditions should be marshalled by the spring of 1943 in Iceland, the British Isles, and, if possible, in French Morocco and Egypt. The main body would come direct across the ocean.

7. It need not be assumed that great numbers of men are required. If the incursion of the armoured formations is successful, the uprising of the local population, for whom weapons must be brought, will supply the corpus of the liberating offensive. Forty armoured divisions, at fifteen thousand men apiece, or their equivalent in tank brigades, of which Great Britain would try to produce nearly half, would amount to six hundred thousand men. Behind this armour another million men of all arms would suffice to wrest enormous territories from Hitler's domination. But these campaigns, once started, will require nourishing on a lavish scale. Our industries and training establishments should by the end of 1942 be running on a sufficient scale.

8. Apart from the command of the sea, without which nothing is possible, the essential for all these operations is superior air power, and for landing purposes a large development of carrier-borne aircraft will be necessary. This however is needed anyhow for the war in 1942. In order to wear down the enemy and hamper his counter-preparations, the bombing offensive of Germany from England and of Italy from Malta and, if possible, from Tripoli and Tunis must reach the highest possible scale of intensity. Considering that the British first-line air strength is already slightly superior to that of Germany, that the Russian Air Force has already established a superiority on a large part of the Russian front and may be considered to be three-fifths the first-line strength of Germany, and that the United States resources and future development are additional, there is no reason why a decisive mastery of the air should not be established even before the summer of 1943, and meanwhile heavy and continuous punishment [be] inflicted upon Germany. Having regard to the fact that the bombing offensive is necessarily a matter of degree and that the targets cannot be

moved away, it would be right to assign priority to the fighter and torpedo-carrying aircraft required for the numerous carriers and improvised carriers which are available or must be brought into existence.

9. If we set these tasks before us now, being careful that they do not trench too much upon current necessities, we might hope, even if no German collapse occurs beforehand, to win the war at the end of 1943 or 1944. There might be advantage in declaring now our intention of sending armies of liberation into Europe in 1943. This would give hope to the subjugated peoples and prevent any truck between them and the German invaders. The setting and keeping in movement along our courses of the minds of so many scores of millions of men is in itself a potent atmospheric influence.

I read this paper during our voyage to the Chiefs of Staff on the day it was written. The following is from the note of our conference:

The Prime Minister said he wished the Chiefs of Staff to examine the whole of this note, which he intended to use as the basis of his conversations with the President. He thought it important to put before the people of both the British Empire and the United States the mass invasion of the continent of Europe as the goal for 1943. In general the three phases of the war could be described as (1) Closing the ring. (2) Liberating the populations. (3) Final assault on the German citadel.

I found my professional colleagues in full agreement with these views, and generally with those set forth in the other papers, which indeed summed up the results of our joint study and discussion of the war problem as it had now shaped itself.

*   *   *

Reviewing these three documents, with which, in the afterlight, and taken as a whole, I am content, it will be seen that they bear a very close correspondence to what was actually done by Britain and the United States during the campaigns of 1942 and 1943. I eventually obtained the President's agreement to the expedition to Northwest Africa (Operation "Torch"), which constituted our first great joint amphibious offensive. It was my earnest desire that the crossing of the Channel and the liberation of France (the operation then called "Roundup," which was subsequently changed to "Overlord") should take place in the summer of 1943.

While however it is vital to plan the future, and sometimes possible to forecast it in certain respects, no one can help the time-table of such mighty events being deranged by the actions and counter-strokes of the enemy. All the objectives in these memoranda were achieved by the British and United States forces in the order here set forth. My hopes that General Auchinleck would clear Libya in February, 1942, were disappointed. He underwent a series of grievous reverses which will presently be described. Hitler, perhaps encouraged by this success, determined upon a large-scale effort to fight for Tunis, and presently moved about two hundred thousand fresh troops thither through Italy and across the Mediterranean. The British and American armies therefore became involved in a larger and longer campaign in North Africa than I had contemplated. A delay of four months was for this reason enforced upon the time-table. The Anglo-American Allies did not obtain control of "the whole of the North and West African possessions of France, and the further control by Britain of the whole North African shore from Tunis to Egypt," by the end of 1942.[3] We obtained these results only in May, 1943. The supreme plan of crossing the Channel to liberate France, for which I had earnestly hoped and worked, could not therefore be undertaken that summer, and was perforce postponed for one whole year, till the summer of 1944.

Subsequent reflection and the full knowledge we now possess have convinced me that we were fortunate in our disappointment. The year's delay in the expedition saved us from what would at that date have been at the best an enterprise of extreme hazard, with the probability of a world-shaking disaster. If Hitler had been wise he would have cut his losses in North Africa and would have met us in France with double the strength he had in 1944, before the newly raised American armies and staffs had reached their full professional maturity and excellence, and long before the enormous armadas of landing-craft and the floating harbours ("Mulberries") had been specially constructed. I am sure now that even if Operation "Torch" had ended as I hoped in 1942, or even if it had never been tried, the attempt to cross the Channel in 1943 would have led to a bloody defeat of the first magnitude, with measureless reactions upon the result of the war. I became increasingly conscious of this during the whole of 1943, and therefore accepted as inevitable the postponement of "Overlord" while fully understanding the vexation and anger of our Soviet Ally.

Once it became certain that we could not cross the Channel

[3] Part I, paragraph 11.

till 1944 the need of forcing the campaign in the Mediterranean was clear. Only by landing in Sicily and Italy could we engage the enemy on a large scale and tear down the weaker at least of the Axis partners. It was for the express purpose of securing this decision that I obtained the President's consent for General Marshall to come with me from Washington to Algiers in May, 1943. All this will be recounted in detail as the actual events occur.

15

Washington and Ottawa

Arrival at the White House—A Hearty Welcome—A Whirl of Business—Anglo-American Intervention in French North Africa—My Report to the War Cabinet of Our First Discussion—Design of the Grand Alliance—Mr. Hull and the Free French—Mr. Knox and Wake Island—Australian Anxieties—My Report to Mr. Curtin of December 25—Christmas at the White House—I Address Congress—An Impressive Experience on Boxing Day—The Southwest Pacific Command—General Wavell Appointed—An Unpromising Task—I Prolong My Stay—Journey to Ottawa—Address to the Canadian Parliament, December 30—Sir Harry Lauder—A Forecast of the War Future—New Year's Eve in the Train.

IT HAD BEEN INTENDED that we should steam up the Potomac and motor to the White House, but we were all impatient after nearly ten days at sea to end our journey. We therefore arranged to fly from Hampton Roads, and landed after dark on December 22 at the Washington airport. There was the President waiting in his car. I clasped his strong hand with comfort and pleasure. We soon reached the White House, which was to be in every sense our home for the next three weeks. Here we were welcomed by Mrs. Roosevelt, who thought of everything that could make our stay agreeable.

I must confess that my mind was so occupied with the whirl of events and the personal tasks I had to perform that my memory till refreshed had preserved but a vague impression of these days. The outstanding feature was of course my contacts with the President. We saw each other for several hours every day, and lunched always together, with Harry Hopkins as a third. We talked of nothing but business, and reached a great measure of agreement on many points, both large and small. Dinner was a more social occasion, but equally intimate and friendly. The President punctiliously made the preliminary cocktails himself, and I wheeled him in his chair from the drawing-room to the lift as a mark of respect, and thinking also of Sir Walter Raleigh spreading his cloak before Queen Elizabeth. I formed a very strong affection, which grew with our years of comradeship, for this formidable politician who had imposed his will for nearly ten years upon the American scene, and whose heart seemed to respond to many of the impulses that stirred my own. As we both, by need or habit, were forced to do much of our work in bed, he visited me in my room whenever he felt inclined, and encouraged me to do the same to him. Hopkins was just across the passage from my bedroom, and next door to him my travelling map room was soon installed. The President was much interested in this institution, which Captain Pim had perfected. He liked to come and study attentively the large maps of all the theatres of war which soon covered the walls, and on which the movement of fleets and armies was so accurately and swiftly recorded. It was not long before he established a map room of his own of the highest efficiency.

The days passed, counted in hours. Quite soon I realised that immediately after Christmas I must address the Congress of the United States, and a few days later the Canadian Parliament in Ottawa. These great occasions imposed heavy demands on my life and strength, and were additional to all the daily consultations and mass of current business. In fact, I do not know how I got through it all.

* * *

A record has been preserved of our first discussion on the night of the twenty-second. I immediately broached with the President and those he had invited to join us the scheme of Anglo-American intervention in French North Africa. The President had not of course at this time read the papers I had written on board ship, which I could not give him till the next day. But he had evidently thought much about my letter of October 20. Thus we all found ourselves pretty well on the same spot. My report home shows that we cut deeply into business on the night of our arrival.

Prime Minister to War Cabinet and C.O.S. Committee 23 Dec. 41

The President and I discussed the North African situation last night [December 22]. Mr. Hull, Mr. Welles, Mr. Hopkins, Lord Beaverbrook, and Lord Halifax also took part in the discussion.

560 War Comes to America

2. There was general agreement that if Hitler was held in Russia he must try something else, and that the most probable line was Spain and Portugal en route to North Africa. Our success in Libya and the prospect of joining hands with French North African territory was another reason to make Hitler want, if he could, to get hold of Morocco as quickly as possible. At the same time reports did not seem to suggest threat was imminent, perhaps because Hitler had enough on hand at the moment.

3. There was general agreement that it was vital to forestall the Germans in Northwest Africa and the Atlantic islands. In addition to all the other reasons, the two French battleships, *Jean Bart* and *Richelieu*, were a real prize for whoever got them. Accordingly, the discussion was not *whether*, but *how*.

4. Various suggestions were made:

(*a*) The United States Government might speak in very serious and resolute terms to Vichy, saying that this was final chance for them to reconsider their positions and come out on the side that was pledged to restoration of France. As a symbol of this Pétain might be invited to send Weygand to represent him at an Allied conference in Washington.

(*b*) An approach might be made to Weygand in the light of a North African situation fundamentally changed by British advance and by United States entering into war and their willingness to send a force to North Africa.

5. It was suggested, on the other hand, that the effect of such procedure might be to extract smooth promises from Pétain and Weygand, the Germans meanwhile being advised of our intentions, and that, accordingly, if these approaches were to be made, it would be desirable to have all plans made for going into North Africa, *with or without invitation*.[1] I emphasised immense psychological effect likely to be produced both in France and among French troops in North Africa by association of United States with the undertaking. Mr. Hull suggested that it might well be that a leader would emerge in North Africa as events developed.

The President said that he was anxious that American land forces should give their support as quickly as possible wherever they could be most helpful, and favoured the idea of a plan to move into North Africa being prepared for either event, i.e., with or without invitation.

6. It was agreed to remit the study of the project to Staffs on assumption that it was vital to forestall the Germans in that area and that the Libyan campaign had, as it was expected to do, achieved complete success. It was recognised that the question of shipping was plainly a most important factor.

7. I gave an account of the progress of fighting in Libya, by which the President and other Americans were clearly much impressed and cheered.

8. In the course of conversation the President mentioned that

[1] Author's italics.

he would propose at forthcoming conference that United States should relieve our troops in Northern Ireland, and spoke of sending three or four divisions there. I warmly welcomed this, and said I hoped that one of the divisions would be an armoured division. It was not thought that this need conflict with preparations for a United States force for North Africa.

* * *

The first major design which was presented to me a day or two later by the President was the drawing-up of a solemn Declaration to be signed by all the nations at war with Germany and Italy, or with Japan. The President and I, repeating our methods in framing the Atlantic Charter prepared drafts of the Declaration and blended them together. In principle, in sentiment, and indeed in language, we were in full accord. At home the War Cabinet was at once surprised and thrilled by the scale on which the Grand Alliance was planned. There was much rapid correspondence, and some difficult points arose about what Governments and authorities should sign the Declaration, and also on the order of precedence. We gladly accorded the first place to the United States. The War Cabinet very rightly did not wish to include India as a separate sovereign Power. Mr. Hull was opposed to the insertion of the word "authorities" by which I meant to cover the Free French, at that time in disgrace with the State Department.

This was the first time I had met Mr. Cordell Hull, with whom I had several conversations. He did not seem to me to have full access at the moment to the President. I was struck by the fact that, amid gigantic events, one small incident seemed to dominate his mind. Before I left England General de Gaulle had informed us that he wished to liberate the islands of St. Pierre and Miquelon, which were held by the Vichy Governor, Admiral Robert. The Free French naval forces were quite capable of doing this, and the Foreign Office saw no objection. However, as it appeared later on, the American State Department wished the occupation to be made by a Canadian expedition. We therefore asked de Gaulle to refrain, and he certainly said he would do so. Nevertheless, he ordered his Admiral Muselier to take the islands. The Free French sailors were received with enthusiasm by the people, and a plebiscite showed a ninety per cent majority against Vichy.

This made no impression on Mr. Hull. He considered that the policy of the State Department had been affronted. He issued a statement on Christmas Day, saying, "Our preliminary report shows that the action taken by the *so-called* [2] Free French ships at St. Pierre and Miquelon was an arbitrary action contrary to the agreement of all parties concerned, and certainly without the prior knowledge or consent in any sense of the United States Government." He wanted to turn the Free French out of the islands they had liberated from Vichy. But American opinion ran hard the other way. They were delighted in this grave hour that the islands had been liberated, and that an obnoxious radio station which was spreading Vichy lies and poison throughout the world, and might well give secret signals to U-boats now hunting United States ships, should be squelched. The phrase "so-called Free French" was almost universally resented.

Mr. Hull, whose sterling qualities I recognised, and for whom I entertained the highest respect, in my opinion pushed what was little more than a departmental point far beyond its proportions. The President in our daily talks seemed to me to shrug his shoulders over the whole affair. After all, quite a lot of other annoyances were on us or coming upon us. Strongly urged by our Foreign Office, I supported General de Gaulle and "so-called" Free France. Chapters have been written about this incident in various American and French books, but it did not at all affect our main discussions.

* * *

One afternoon Mr. Knox, Secretary for the Navy, came into my room in great distress. He said: "You have had plenty of disasters. I would like you to tell me how you feel about the following. We ordered our fleet to fight a battle with the Japanese to relieve Wake Island, and now within a few hours of steaming the Admiral has decided to turn back. What would you do with your Admiral in a case like this?" I replied: "It is dangerous to meddle with Admirals when they say they can't do things. They have always got the weather or fuel or something to argue about." Wake Island fell that day, having been desperately defended by a handful of United States Marines, who inflicted far heavier losses than their own numbers upon the Japanese before they were killed or captured.

* * *

Every allowance must be made for the state of mind into which the Australian Government were thrown by the hideous efficiency of the Japanese war machine. The command of the

[2] Author's italics.

Pacific was lost; their three best divisions were in Egypt and a fourth at Singapore. They realised that Singapore was in deadly peril, and they feared an actual invasion of Australia itself. All their great cities, containing more than half the whole population of the continent, were on the seacoast. A mass exodus into the interior and the organising of a guerrilla without arsenals or supplies stared them in the face. Help from the Mother Country was far away, and the power of the United States could only slowly be established in Australian waters. I did not myself believe that the Japanese would invade Australia across three thousand miles of ocean, when they had so much alluring prey in their clutch in the Dutch East Indies and Malaya. The Australian Cabinet saw the scene in a different light, and deep forebodings pressed upon them all. Even in these straits they maintained their party divisions rigidly. The Labour Government majority was only two. They were opposed to compulsory service even for Home Defence. Although the Opposition was admitted to the War Council no National Government was formed.

I cabled to Mr. Curtin as follows:

Prime Minister to Prime Minister of Australia   25 Dec. 41

On Japan coming into the war we diverted at once the 18th British Division, which was rounding the Cape in American transports, with President's permission, to Bombay and Ceylon, and Mr. Roosevelt has now agreed that the leading [British] brigade in the United States transport *Mount Vernon* should proceed direct to Singapore. We cancelled the move of the 17th Indian Division from India to Persia, and this division is now going to Malaya. A week ago I wirelessed from the ship to London to suggest that you recall one Australian division from Palestine either into India to replace other troops sent forward or to go direct, if it can be arranged, to Singapore. I have impressed upon the military authorities the importance of not using up the forces needed for the defence of Singapore and Johore approaches in attempting to defend the northern part of the Malay Peninsula. They will fall back slowly, fighting delaying actions and destroying communications.

2. The heavy naval losses which the United States and we have both sustained give the Japanese the power of landing large reinforcements, but we do not share the view expressed in your telegram to Mr. Casey of December 24 that there is the danger of early reduction of Singapore fortress, which we are determined to defend with the utmost tenacity.

3. You have been told of the air support which is already on the way. It would not be wise to loose our grip on Rommel and Libya by taking away forces from General Auchinleck against his

judgment just when victory is within our grasp. We have instructed Commanders-in-Chief Middle East to concert a plan for sending fighters and tanks to Singapore immediately the situation in Libya permits.

4. I and the Chiefs of Staff are in close consultation with the President and his advisers, and we have made encouraging progress. Not only are they impressed with the importance of maintaining Singapore, but they are anxious to move a continuous flow of troops and aircraft through Australia for the relief of the Philippine Islands, if that be possible. Should the Philippine Islands fall the President is agreeable to troops and aircraft being diverted to Singapore. He is also quite willing to send substantial United States forces to Australia, where Americans are anxious to establish important bases for the war against Japan. General Wavell has been placed in command of Burma as well as India, and instructed to feed reinforcements arriving in India to Malayan and Burmese fronts. He, like everyone else, recognises the paramount importance of Singapore. General Pownall has now arrived. He is a highly competent Army officer.

5. You may count on my doing everything possible to strengthen the whole front from Rangoon to Port Darwin. I am finding co-operation from our American allies. I shall wire more definitely in a day or two.

*   *   *

Simple festivities marked our Christmas. The traditional Christmas Tree was set up in the White House garden, and the President and I made brief speeches from the balcony to enormous crowds gathered in the gloom. I venture to reprint here the words that I used, as they seemed to rise so naturally in my mind on this occasion and in these surroundings.

*Mr. Churchill's Speech from the White House Balcony,
Washington, Christmas Eve, 1941*

I spend this anniversary and festival far from my country, far from my family, yet I cannot truthfully say that I feel far from home. Whether it be the ties of blood on my mother's side, or the friendships I have developed here over many years of active life, or the commanding sentiment of comradeship in the common cause of great peoples who speak the same language, who kneel at the same altars, and, to a very large extent, pursue the same ideals, I cannot feel myself a stranger here in the centre and at the summit of the United States. I feel a sense of unity and fraternal association which, added to the kindliness of your welcome, convinces me that I have a right to sit at your fireside and share your Christmas joys.

This is a strange Christmas Eve. Almost the whole world is locked in deadly struggle, and, with the most terrible weapons which science can devise, the nations advance upon each other. Ill would it be for us this Christmastide if we were not sure that no greed for the land or wealth of any other people, no vulgar ambition, no morbid lust for material gain at the expense of others, had led us to the field. Here, in the midst of war, raging and roaring over all the lands and seas, creeping nearer to our hearths and homes, here, amid all the tumult, we have tonight the peace of the spirit in each cottage home and in every generous heart. Therefore, we may cast aside for this night at least the cares and dangers which beset us, and make for the children an evening of happiness in a world of storm. Here, then, for one night only, each home throughout the English-speaking world should be a brightly lighted island of happiness and peace.

Let the children have their night of fun and laughter. Let the gifts of Father Christmas delight their play. Let us grown-ups share to the full in their unstinted pleasures before we turn again to the stern task and the formidable years that lie before us, resolved that, by our sacrifice and daring, these same children shall not be robbed of their inheritance or denied their right to live in a free and decent world.

And so, in God's mercy, a happy Christmas to you all.

The President and I went to church together on Christmas Day, and I found peace in the simple service and enjoyed singing the well-known hymns, and one, "O little town of Bethlehem," I had never heard before. Certainly there was much to fortify the faith of all who believe in the moral governance of the universe.

*   *   *

It was with heart-stirrings that I fulfilled the invitation to address the Congress of the United States. The occasion was important for what I was sure was the all-conquering alliance of the English-speaking peoples. I had never addressed a foreign Parliament before. Yet to me, who could trace unbroken male descent on my mother's side through five generations from a lieutenant who served in George Washington's army, it was possible to feel a blood-right to speak to the representatives of the great Republic in our common cause. It certainly was odd that it should all work out this way; and once again I had the feeling, for mentioning which I may be pardoned, of being used, however unworthy, in some appointed plan.

I spent a good part of Christmas Day preparing my speech. The President wished me good luck when on December 26 I set out in the charge of the leaders of the Senate and House of Representatives from the White House to the Capitol. There seemed to be great crowds along the broad approaches, but the security precautions, which in the United States go far beyond British custom, kept them a long way off, and two or three motor-cars filled with armed plainclothes policemen clustered around as escort. On getting out I wished to walk up to the cheering masses in a strong mood of brotherhood, but this was not allowed. Inside, the scene was impressive and formidable, and the great semicircular hall, visible to me through a grille of microphones, was thronged.

I must confess that I felt quite at home, and more sure of myself than I had sometimes been in the House of Commons. What I said was received with the utmost kindness and attention. I got my laughter and applause just where I expected them. The loudest response was when, speaking of the Japanese outrage, I asked, "What sort of people do they think we are?" The sense of the might and will-power of the American nation streamed up to me from the august assembly. Who could doubt that all would be well?

I ended thus:

Mr. Churchill's Speech to Congress, December 26, 1941

Members of the Senate and Members of the House of Representatives, I turn for one moment more from the turmoil and convulsions of the present to the broader basis of the future. Here we are together facing a group of mighty foes who seek our ruin; here we are together defending all that to free men is dear. Twice in a single generation the catastrophe of world war has fallen upon us; twice in our lifetime has the long arm of Fate reached across the ocean to bring the United States into the forefront of the battle. If we had kept together after the last war, if we had taken common measures for our safety, this renewal of the curse need never have fallen upon us.

Do we not owe it to ourselves, to our children, to mankind tormented, to make sure that these catastrophes shall not engulf us for the third time? It has been proved that pestilences may break out in the Old World which carry their destructive ravages into the New World, from which, once they are afoot, the New World cannot by any means escape. Duty and prudence alike command, first, that the germ-centres of hatred and revenge should be constantly and vigilantly surveyed and treated in good time, and, secondly, that an adequate organisation should be set up to make sure that the pestilence can be controlled at its earliest beginnings before it spreads and rages throughout the entire earth.

Five or six years ago it would have been easy, without shedding a drop of blood, for the United States and Great Britain to have insisted on fulfilment of the disarmament clauses of the treaties which Germany signed after the Great War; that also would have been the opportunity for assuring to Germany those raw materials which we declared in the Atlantic Charter should not be denied to any nation, victor or vanquished. That chance has passed. It is gone. Prodigious hammer-strokes have been needed to bring us together again, or, if you will allow me to use other language, I will say that he must indeed have a blind soul who cannot see that some great purpose and design is being worked out here below, of which we have the honour to be the faithful servants. It is not given to us to peer into the mysteries of the future. Still, I avow my hope and faith, sure and inviolate, that in the days to come the British and American peoples will for their own safety and for the good of all walk together side by side in majesty, in justice, and in peace.

Afterwards the leaders came along with me close up to the crowds which surrounded the building, so that I could give them an intimate greeting; and then the Secret Service men and their cars closed round and took me back to the White House, where the President, who had listened in, told me I had done quite well.

*   *   *

At Washington intense activity reigned. During these days of continuous contact and discussion I gathered that the President with his staff and his advisers was preparing an important proposal for me. In the military as in the commercial or production spheres the American mind runs naturally to broad, sweeping, logical conclusions on the largest scale. It is on these that they build their practical thought and action. They feel that once the foundation has been planned on true and comprehensive lines all other stages will follow naturally and almost inevitably. The British mind does not work quite in this way. We do not think that logic and clear-cut principles are necessarily the sole keys to what ought to be done in swiftly changing and indefinable situations. In war particularly we assign a larger importance to opportunism and improvisation, seeking rather to live and conquer in accordance with the unfolding event than to aspire to dominate it often by fundamental decisions. There is room for much argument about both views. The difference is one of emphasis, but it is deep-seated.

Harry Hopkins said to me, "Don't be in a hurry to turn down the proposal the President is going to make to you before you know who is the man we have in mind." From this I saw that the question of forming a Supreme Allied Command in Southeast Asia and drawing boundary lines was approaching.

The next day I was told that the Americans proposed that Wavell should be chosen. I was complimented by the choice of a British commander, but it seemed to me that the theatre in which he would act would soon be overrun and the forces which could be placed at his disposal would be destroyed by the Japanese onslaught. I found that the British Chiefs of Staff, when apprised, had the same reaction.

I am recorded as saying to them at a meeting on December 26 that I was not at all convinced that this arrangement was either workable or desirable. "The situation out there was that certain particular strategic points had to be held, and the commander in each locality was quite clear as to what he should do. The difficult question was the application of resources arriving in the area. This was a matter which could only be settled by the Governments concerned." Nevertheless, it was evident that we must meet the American view.

* * *

Mr. Attlee sent me his own and the Cabinet's congratulations on my speech to Congress, and in reply I opened to him the question of the Southwest Pacific Command.

Prime Minister to Lord Privy Seal   28 Dec. 41

Am so glad you were pleased. Welcome was extraordinary. Work here is most strenuous. Today for five hours President and I received representatives of all other Allied or friendly Powers and British Dominions, and made heartening statements to them. My talks with President increasingly intimate and friendly. Beaverbrook also had great success with him on the supply side.

2. Question of unity of command in Southwest Pacific has assumed urgent form. Last night President urged upon me appointment of a single officer to command Army, Navy, and Air Force of Britain, America, and Dutch, and this morning General Marshall visited me at my request and pleaded case with great conviction. American Navy authorities take opposite view, but it is certain that a new far-reaching arrangement will have to be made. The man President has in mind is General Wavell. Marshall has evidently gone far into detailed scheme and has draft letter of instructions. So far I have been critical of plan, and while admiring broadmindedness of offer have expressed anxiety about effects on American opinion. Chiefs of Staff have been studying matter all day, and tonight I will send you my considered advice after receiving their views.

3. I leave tomorrow afternoon for Ottawa, staying two clear days and addressing Canadian Parliament on Tuesday; then back here for another three or four days, as there is so much to settle. We are making great exertions to find shipping necessary for the various troop movements required. My kindest regards to all colleagues. It is a great comfort to act on such a sure foundation.

Before I could receive any considered advice from home it was necessary to meet the urgent wishes of the President and General Marshall. Events were moving too fast for lengthy discussions across the Atlantic. I passed the 28th in conference with the President and in drafting with my staff the series of telegrams which follow, and tell the tale in carefully weighed words.

Prime Minister to Lord Privy Seal   29 Dec. 41

I have agreed with President, subject to Cabinet approval, that we should accept his proposals, most strongly endorsed by General Marshall:

(*a*) That unity of command shall be established in Southwestern Pacific. Boundaries are not yet finally settled, but presume they would include Malay Peninsula, including Burmese front, to Philippine Islands, and southward to necessary supply bases, principally Fort Darwin, and supply line in Northern Australia.

(*b*) That General Wavell should be appointed Commander-in-Chief, or if preferred Supreme Commander, of all United States, British, British Empire, and Dutch forces of land, sea, and air who may be assigned by Governments concerned to that theatre.

(*c*) General Wavell, whose headquarters should in first instance be established at Surabaya, would have American officer as Deputy Commander-in-Chief. It seems probable General Brett would be chosen.

(*d*) That American, British, Australian, and Dutch naval forces in the theatre should be placed under the command of American admiral, in accordance with general principle set forth in paragraphs (*a*) and (*b*).

(*e*) It is intended General Wavell should have a Staff in the South Pacific portion, as Foch's High Control Staff was to the great Staffs of British and French Armies in France. He would receive his orders from an appropriate joint body, who will be responsible to me as Minister of Defence and to President of the United States, who is also Commander-in-Chief of all United States forces.

(*f*) Principal commanders comprised in General Wavell's sphere will be Commander-in-Chief Burma, Commander-in-Chief Singapore and Malaya, Commander-in-Chief Netherlands East Indies, Commander-in-Chief Philippines, and Commander-in-Chief of Southern Communications via South Pacific and North Australia.

(*g*) India, for which an acting Commander-in-Chief will have to be appointed, and Australia, who will have their own Commander-in-Chief, will be outside General Wavell's sphere, except as above mentioned, and are two great bases through which men and material from Great Britain and Middle East on the one hand and the United States on the other can be moved into the fighting zone.

(*h*) United States Navy will remain responsible for the whole

Pacific Ocean east of Philippine Islands and Australasia, including United States approaches to Australasia.

(*i*) A letter of instruction is being drafted for Supreme Commander safeguarding the necessary residuary interests of various Governments involved and prescribing in major outline his tasks. This draft will reach you shortly.

2. I have not attempted to argue case for and against our accepting this broadminded and selfless American proposal, of merits of which as a war-winner I have become convinced. Action is urgent, and may perhaps have to be taken even before my returning from Canada on January 1. Australia, New Zealand, and Dutch will of course have to be consulted, but this should not be done until I have been instructed by hearing views of War Cabinet. Meanwhile staff here will be working upon details on assumption that all consents will be obtained.

Prime Minister to Lord Privy Seal   29 Dec. 41

Things have moved very quickly. The President has obtained the agreement of the American War and Navy Departments to the arrangement proposed in my last telegram, and the Chiefs of Staff Committee have endorsed it. I therefore anxiously await your approval. The President will address the Dutch the moment I tell him you agree. Foreign Office should follow suit.

You should also dispatch the following telegram to General Wavell. Staffs here are working on details both by themselves and with Americans. Position of Duff Cooper's mission requires to be reviewed, and in any case must not complicate these larger solutions. Please give me your ideas.

I must rely on you to keep the King informed at every angle and obtain his approval.

The offer which I had to make to General Wavell was certainly one which only the highest sense of duty could induce him to accept. It was almost certain that he would have to bear a load of defeat in a scene of confusion.

Prime Minister to Lord Privy Seal   29 Dec. 41

Pray send following to General Wavell when Cabinet have approved general policy:

The President and his military and naval advisers have impressed upon me the urgent need for unified command in Southwest Pacific, and it is unanimously desired, pressed particularly by President and General Marshall, that you should become Supreme Commander of Allied forces by land, air, and sea assigned to that theatre. The letter of instructions referred to is being drafted, the terms of which will be issued shortly. While I hope these terms will set your mind at ease on the various unprecedented points involved, I should of course be ready to receive your observations upon them.

2. I feel sure you will value the confidence which is shown in you, and I request you to take up your task forthwith. Matters are so urgent that details which are being studied by the Chiefs of Staff Committee must not delay the public announcement, which must be made, at least, Thursday, January 1.

3. You are the only man who has the experience of handling so many different theatres at once, and you know we shall back you up and see you have fair play. Everyone knows how dark and difficult the situation is. President will announce that your appointment has been made by his desire.

4. Pray let me know your ideas as to Staff, which will be essentially a front Staff rather than an actual handling body. If you like to take Pownall as your Chief of Staff, Percival might discharge the duties of Singapore and Malaya Commander.

* * *

On December 27 I had sent the following telegram to Mr. Attlee:

Prime Minister to Lord Privy Seal   27 Dec. 41

Thank you so much for agreeing to lengthen my stay.

On Tuesday, December 30, I am addressing the Canadian House of Commons. Utterly impossible to lay another egg [i.e. deliver a speech in the House of Commons] so early as the New Year.

I travelled by the night train of December 28/29 to Ottawa, to stay with Lord Athlone, the Governor-General. On the 29th I attended a meeting of the Canadian War Cabinet. Thereafter Mr. Mackenzie King, the Prime Minister, introduced me to the leaders of the Conservative Opposition, and left me with them. These gentlemen were unsurpassed in loyalty and resolution, but at the same time they were rueful not to have the honour of waging the war themselves, and at having to listen to so many of the sentiments which they had championed all their lives expressed by their Liberal opponents.

On the 30th I spoke to the Canadian Parliament. The preparation of my two trans-Atlantic speeches, transmitted all over the world, amid all the flow of executive work, which never stopped, was an extremely hard exertion. Delivery is no serious burden to a hard-bitten politician, but choosing what to say and what not to say in such an electric atmosphere is anxious and harassing. I did my best. The most successful point in the Canadian speech was about the Vichy Government, with whom Canada was still in relations.

Mr. Churchill's Speech to the Canadian Parliament, Dec. 30, 1941

It was their duty [in 1940] and it was also their interest to go to North Africa, where they would have been at the head of the

French Empire. In Africa, with our aid, they would have had overwhelming sea power. They would have had the recognition of the United States, and the use of all the gold they had lodged beyond the seas. If they had done this, Italy might have been driven out of the war before the end of 1940, and France would have held her place as a nation in the councils of the Allies and at the conference table of the victors. But their generals misled them. When I warned them that Britain would fight on alone whatever they did, their generals told their Prime Minister and his divided Cabinet, "In three weeks England will have her neck wrung like a chicken." Some chicken! Some neck!

This went very well. I quoted, to introduce a retrospect, Sir Harry Lauder's song of the last war which began:

> If we all look back on the history of the past
> We can just tell where we are.

The words, "that grand old comedian," were on my notes. On the way down I thought of the word "minstrel." What an improvement! I rejoice to know that he was listening and was delighted at the reference. I am so glad I found the right word for one who, by his inspiring songs and valiant life, has rendered measureless service to the Scottish race and to the British Empire.

At the end of the speech I ventured to attempt a forecast of the war future:

We may observe three main periods or phases of the struggle that lies before us. First there is the period of consolidation, of combination, and of final preparation. In this period, which will certainly be marked by much heavy fighting, we shall still be gathering our strength, resisting the assaults of the enemy, and acquiring the necessary overwhelming air superiority and shipping tonnage to give our armies the power to traverse, in whatever numbers may be necessary, the seas and oceans which, except in the case of Russia, separate us from our foes. It is only when the vast shipbuilding programme on which the United States has already made so much progress, and which you are powerfully aiding, comes into full flood that we shall be able to bring the whole force of our manhood and of our modern scientific equipment to bear upon the enemy. How long this period will last depends upon the vehemence of the effort put into production in all our war industries and shipyards.

The second phase which will then open may be called the phase of liberation. During this phase we must look to the recovery of the territories which have been lost or which may yet be lost, and also we must look to the revolt of the conquered peoples from the moment that the rescuing and liberating armies and air forces appear in strength within their bounds. For this purpose it is imperative that no nation or region overrun, that no Government or State which has been conquered, should relax its moral and physical efforts and preparation for the day of deliverance. The invaders, be they German or Japanese, must everywhere be regarded as infected persons to be shunned and isolated as far as possible. Where active resistance is impossible passive resistance must be maintained. The invaders and tyrants must be made to feel that their fleeting triumphs will have a terrible reckoning, and that they are hunted men and that their cause is doomed. Particular punishment will be reserved for the Quislings and traitors who make themselves the tools of the enemy. They will be handed over to the judgment of their fellow-countrymen.

There is a third phase which must also be contemplated, namely, the assault upon the citadels and the home-lands of the guilty Powers both in Europe and in Asia.

Thus I endeavour in a few words to cast some forward light upon the dark, inscrutable mysteries of the future. But in thus forecasting the course along which we should seek to advance we must never forget that the power of the enemy, and the action of the enemy, may at every stage affect our fortunes. Moreover, you will notice that I have not attempted to assign any time-limits to the various phases. These time-limits depend upon our exertions, upon our achievements, and on the hazardous and uncertain course of the war.

I was lucky in the timing of these speeches in Washington and Ottawa. They came at the moment when we could all rejoice at the creation of the Grand Alliance with its overwhelming potential force, and before the cataract of ruin fell upon us from the long, marvellously prepared assault of Japan. Even while I spoke in confident tones I could feel in anticipation the lashes which were soon to score our naked flesh. Fearful forfeits had to be paid not only by Britain and Holland but by the United States, in the Pacific and Indian Oceans, and in all the Asiatic lands and islands they lap with their waves. An indefinite period of military disaster lay certainly before us. Many dark and weary months of defeat and loss must be endured before the light would come again. When I returned in the train to Washington on New Year's Eve I was asked to go into the carriage filled with many leading pressmen of the United States. It was with no illusions that I wished them all a glorious New Year. "Here's to 1942. Here's to a year of toil— a year of struggle and peril, and a long step forward towards victory. May we all come through safe and with honour!"

16

Anglo-American Accords

O<small>N MY RETURN</small> to the White House all was ready for the signature of the United Nations Pact. Many telegrams had passed between Washington, London, and Moscow, but now all was settled. The President had exerted his most fervent efforts to persuade Litvinov, the Soviet Ambassador, newly restored to favour by the turn of events, to accept the phrase "religious freedom." He was invited to luncheon with us in the President's room on purpose. After his hard experiences in his own country he had to be careful. Later on the President had a long talk with him alone about his soul and the dangers of hellfire. The accounts which Mr. Roosevelt gave us on several occasions of what he said to the Russian were impressive. Indeed, on one occasion I promised Mr. Roosevelt to recommend him for the position of Archbishop of Canterbury if he should lose the next Presidential election. I did not however make any official recommendation to the Cabinet or the Crown upon this point, and as he won the election in 1944 it did not arise. Litvinov reported the issue about "religious freedom" in evident fear and trembling to Stalin who accepted it as a matter of course. The War Cabinet also got their point in about "social security," with which, as the author of the first Unemployment Insurance Act, I cordially concurred. After a spate of telegrams had flowed about the world for a week, agreement was reached throughout the Grand Alliance.

The title of "United Nations" was substituted by the President for that of "Associated Powers." I thought this a great improvement. I showed my friend the lines from Byron's *Childe Harold:*

> Here, where the sword United Nations drew,
> Our countrymen were warring on that day!
> And this is much—and all—which will not pass away.

The President was wheeled-in to me on the morning of January 1. I got out of my bath, and agreed to the draft. The Declaration could not by itself win battles, but it set forth who we were and what we were fighting for. On New Year's Day President Roosevelt, I, Litvinov, and Soong, representing China, signed this majestic document in the President's study. It was left to the State Department to collect the signatures of the remaining twenty-two nations. The final text must be recorded here.

A Joint Declaration by the United States of America, the United Kingdom of Great Britain and Northern Ireland, the Union of Soviet Socialist Republics, China, Australia, Belgium, Canada, Costa Rica, Cuba, Czechoslovakia, the Dominican Republic, El Salvador, Greece, Guatemala, Haiti, Honduras, India, Luxemburg, the Netherlands, New Zealand, Nicaragua, Norway, Panama, Poland, South Africa, and Yugoslavia.

The Governments signatory hereto,

Having subscribed to a common programme of purposes and principles embodied in the Joint Declaration of the President of the United States of America and the Prime Minister of the United Kingdom of Great Britain and Northern Ireland, dated August 14, 1941, known as the Atlantic Charter,

Being convinced that complete victory over their enemies is essential to defend life, liberty, independence, and religious freedom, and to preserve human rights and justice in their own lands as well as in other lands, and that they are now engaged in a common struggle against savage and brutal forces seeking to subjugate the world, DECLARE:

(1) Each Government pledges itself to employ its full resources, military or economic, against those members of the Tripartite Pact and its adherents with which such Government is at war.

(2) Each Government pledges itself to co-operate with the Governments signatory hereto, and not to make a separate armistice or peace with the enemies.

The foregoing Declaration may be adhered to by other nations which are, or which may be, rendering material assistance and contributions in the struggle for victory over Hitlerism.

*   *   *

Among other requests which I had made to the President the movement of three or four United States divisions into Northern Ireland stood high. I felt that the arrival of sixty or seventy thousand American troops in Ulster would be an assertion of the United States resolve to intervene directly in Europe. These newly raised troops could just as well complete their training in Ulster as at home, and would at the same time become a strategic factor. The Germans would certainly consider the move as an additional deterrent against the invasion of the British Isles. I hoped they would exaggerate the numbers landed, and thus continue to pay attention to the West. Besides this, every American division which crossed the Atlantic gave us freedom to send one of our matured British divisions out of the country to the Middle East, or of course—and this was always in my mind—to North Africa. Though few, if any, saw it in this light, this was in fact the first step towards an Allied descent on Morocco, Algeria, or Tunis, on which my heart was set. The President was quite conscious of this, and while we did not give precise form to the idea I felt that our thoughts flowed in the same direction, although it was not yet necessary for either of us to discuss the particular method.

Mr. Stimson, the War Secretary, and his professional advisers also found this move to Ireland in harmony with their inclination to invade Europe at the earliest moment. Thus all went forward smoothly. We were anxious that the enemy should be aware of this strategic movement, and made the fact public, without of course specifying numbers. We hoped also that this would detain German troops in the West and thus be not unhelpful to the Russian struggle. The British public and newspapers could not be made privy to our reasons, and many unsound criticisms arose. "Why," for instance, it was asked, "should American troops be sent to Ulster? Would they not be much better employed at Singapore?" When later on I became conscious of this point of view I thought of Pope's lines:

> Ye gods, annihilate but space and time
> And make two lovers happy.

It was of course physically impossible to send an army all that way in time to be of any use.

* * *

I reported all these decisions to the War Cabinet.

Prime Minister to Lord Privy Seal   3 Jan. 42

You will have got my two telegrams about what we did yesterday. President has chosen the title "United Nations" for all the Powers now working together. This is much better than "Alliance," which places him in constitutional difficulties, or "Associated Powers," which is flat.

2. We could not get the words "or authorities" inserted in the last paragraph of the Declaration, as Litvinov is a mere automaton, evidently frightened out of his wits after what he has gone through. This can be covered by an exchange of letters making clear that the word "Nations" covers authorities such as the Free French, or insurgent organisations which may arise in Spain, in North Africa, or in Germany itself. Settlement was imperative because, with nearly thirty Powers already informed, leakage was certain. President was also very keen on January 1.

3. Speed was also essential in settling letter of instructions to Wavell. Here again it was necessary to defer to American views, observing we are no longer single, but married. I personally am in favour of Burma being included in Wavell's operational sphere; but of course the local Commander-in-Chief Burma will be based on India and will have a job of his own to do. He will have to get into friendly touch with Chiang Kai-shek, upon whom, it appears, Wavell and Brett made a none too good impression.

4. The heavy American troop and air force movements into Northern Ireland are to begin at once, and we are now beating about for the shipping necessary to mount "*Super*-Gymnast," if possible, during their currency.

5. We live here as a big family, in the greatest intimacy and informality, and I have formed the very highest regard and admiration for the President. His breadth of view, resolution, and his loyalty to the common cause are beyond all praise. There is not the slightest sign here of excitement or worry about the opening misfortunes, which are taken as a matter of course and to be retrieved by the marshalling of overwhelming forces of every kind. There will of course be a row in public presently.

6. Please thank the War Cabinet for their very kind New Year's message. I am so glad you like what I said in Canada. My reception there was moving.

* * *

It may well be thought by future historians that the most valuable and lasting result of our first Washington Conference

—"Arcadia," as it was code-named—was the setting up of the now famous "Combined Chiefs of Staff Committee." Its headquarters were in Washington, but since the British Chiefs of Staff had to live close to their own Government they were represented by high officers stationed there permanently. These representatives were in daily, indeed hourly, touch with London, and were thus able to state and explain the views of the British Chiefs of Staff to their United States colleagues on any and every war problem at any time of the day or night. The frequent conferences that were held in various parts of the world—Casablanca, Washington, Quebec, Teheran, Cairo, Malta, and the Crimea—brought the principals themselves together for sometimes as much as a fortnight. Of the two hundred formal meetings held by the Combined Chiefs of Staff Committee during the war no fewer than eighty-nine were at these conferences; and it was at these full-dress meetings that the majority of the most important decisions were taken.

The usual procedure was that in the early morning each Chiefs of Staff Committee met among themselves. Later in the day the two teams met and became one; and often they would have a further combined meeting in the evening. They considered the whole conduct of the war, and submitted agreed recommendations to the President and me. Our own direct discussions had of course gone on meanwhile by talks or telegrams, and we were in intimate contact with our own Staff. The proposals of the professional advisers were then considered in plenary meetings, and orders given accordingly to all commanders in the field. However sharp the conflict of views at the Combined Chiefs of Staff meetings, however frank and even heated the argument, sincere loyalty to the common cause prevailed over national or personal interests. Decisions once reached and approved by the heads of Governments were pursued by all with perfect loyalty, especially by those whose original opinions had been overruled. There was never a failure to reach effective agreement for action, or to send clear instructions to the commanders in every theatre. Every executive officer knew that the orders he received bore with them the combined conception and expert authority of both Governments. There never was a more serviceable war machinery established among allies, and I rejoice that in fact if not in form it continues to this day.

The Russians were not represented on the Combined Chiefs of Staff Committee. They had a far-distant, single, independent front, and there was neither need nor means of Staff integration. It was sufficient that we should know the general sweep and timing of their movements and that they should know ours. In these matters we kept in as close touch with them as they permitted. I shall in due course describe the personal visits which I paid to Moscow. And at Teheran, Yalta, and Potsdam the Chiefs of Staff of all three nations met round the table.

The enjoyment of a common language was of course a supreme advantage in all British and American discussions. The delays and often partial misunderstandings which occur when interpreters are used were avoided. There were however differences of expression, which in the early days led to an amusing incident. The British Staff prepared a paper which they wished to raise as a matter of urgency, and informed their American colleagues that they wished to "table it." To the American Staff "tabling" a paper meant putting it away in a drawer and forgetting it. A long and even acrimonious argument ensued before both parties realised that they were agreed on the merits and wanted the same thing.

* * *

I have described how Field-Marshall Dill, though no longer Chief of the Imperial General Staff, had come with us in the *Duke of York*. He had played his full part in all the discussions, not only afloat, but even more when we met the American leaders. I at once perceived that his prestige and influence with them was upon the highest level. No British officer we sent across the Atlantic during the war ever acquired American esteem and confidence in an equal degree. His personality, discretion, and tact gained him almost at once the confidence of the President. At the same time he established a true comradeship and private friendship with General Marshall.

* * *

Immense expansions were ordered in the production sphere. In all these Beaverbrook was a potent impulse. The official American history of their industrial mobilisation for war [1] bears generous testimony to this. Donald Nelson, the Executive Director of American War Production, had already made gigantic plans. "But," says the American account, "the need for boldness had been dramatically impressed upon Nelson by Lord

[1] *History of the War Production Board, 1940–1945.*

Beaverbrook on December 29. . . ." What happened is best
portrayed by Mr. Nelson's own words:

Lord Beaverbrook emphasised the fact that we must set our production sights much higher than for the year 1942, in order to
cope with a resourceful and determined enemy. He pointed out
that we had as yet no experience in the losses of material incidental
to a war of the kind we are now fighting. . . . He emphasised
over and over again the fact that we should set our sights higher in
planning for production of the necessary war material. For instance, he thinks we should plan for the production of forty-five
thousand tanks in 1942 against Mr. Knudsen's estimate of thirty
thousand.

The American account continues:

The ferment Lord Beaverbrook was instilling in the mind of
Nelson he was also imparting to the President. In a note to the
President Lord Beaverbrook set the expected 1942 production of
the United States, the United Kingdom, and Canada against British, Russian, and American requirements. The comparison exposed tremendous deficits in 1942 planned production. For tanks
these deficits were 10,500; for aircraft 26,730; for artillery 22,600;
and for rifles 1,600,000. Production targets had to be increased,
wrote Lord Beaverbrook, and he pinned his faith on their realisation in "the immense possibilities of American industry." Production goals for 1942 should include 45,000 tanks, 17,700 anti-tank
guns, 24,000 fighter planes, and double the quantity of anti-aircraft
guns then programmed, including all contemplated increases.

The outcome was a set of production objectives whose magnitude
exceeded even those Nelson had proposed. The President was
convinced that the concept of our industrial capacity must be completely overhauled. . . . He directed the fulfilment of a munitions
schedule calling for 45,000 combat aircraft, 45,000 tanks, 20,000
anti-aircraft guns, 14,900 anti-tank guns, and 500,000 machine-
guns in 1942.

I reported all this good news home.

Prime Minister to Lord Privy Seal   4 Jan. 42
A series of meetings has been held on supply issues. These were
presided over by the President himself and the Vice-President.
Negotiations were carried forward and discussions of details took
place every day. Then on Friday there was a meeting presided
over by the President and myself. There were two meetings on
Saturday. Final conclusions were:
It was decided to raise United States output of merchant shipping in 1942 to 8,000,000 tons deadweight and in 1943 to 10,000-
000 tons deadweight. New 1942 programme is increase in production of one-third.

War weapons programmes for 1942 and 1943 were determined as follows:

Weapons	1942	1943
Operational aircraft	45,000	100,000
Tanks	45,000	75,000
Anti-aircraft guns	20,000	35,000
Anti-tank guns	14,900	Not fixed
Ground and tank machine guns	500,000	Not fixed

New 1942 programme represents increase on programme for 1942, which has been fixed *after* United States entry into the war as follows:

Operational aircraft	31,250
Tanks	29,550
Anti-aircraft guns	8,900
Anti-tank guns	11,700
Ground and tank machine guns	238,000

Directives have been issued to all the departments concerned [Presidential]. Message to Congress this week will give abridged account of programme. Budget will contain necessary financial provisions.

Max has been magnificent and Hopkins a Godsend. Hope you will be pleased with immense resultant increase in programme.

These remarkable figures were achieved or surpassed by the end of 1943. In shipping for example the new tonnage built in the United States was as follows:

1942	5,339,000 tons
1943	12,384,000 tons

*   *   *

Continued concentration of mind upon the war as a whole, my constant discussions with the President and his principal advisers and with my own, my two speeches and my journey to Canada, together with the heavy flow of urgent business requiring decision and all the telegrams interchanged with my colleagues at home, made this period in Washington not only intense and laborious but even exhausting. My American friends thought I was looking tired and ought to have a rest. Accordingly Mr. Stettinius very kindly placed his small villa in a seaside solitude near Palm Beach at my disposal, and on January 4 I flew down. The night before I started, the air-conditioning of my room in the White House failed temporarily, the heat became oppressive, and in trying to open the window I strained my heart slightly, causing unpleasant sensations which continued for some days. Sir Charles Wilson, my medical adviser, however decided that the journey South should not be put off. General Marshall came with us in the

plane all the way, and I had some very good talks with him.
Five days we passed in the Stettinius villa, lying about in the
shade or the sun, bathing in the pleasant waves, in spite of the
appearance on one occasion of quite a large shark. They said it
was only a "ground shark"; but I was not wholly reassured. It
is as bad to be eaten by a ground shark as by any other. So I
stayed in the shallows from then on.

My movements were kept strictly secret, and a notification
was given from the White House to the press that all movements by the President or by me were to be regarded as if they
were the movements of American battleships. Consequently
no word ever appeared. On the other hand, numbers of people
greeted me in Florida, and many pressmen and photographers,
with whom I had pleasant interchanges, waited outside the
entrance to our retreat; but not a trickle ever leaked into print.

Prime Minister to Lord Privy Seal   5 Jan. 42

I am going South for a few days, hoping to remain in complete
privacy, and President will go to Hyde Park. Meanwhile the Staffs
are working hard, and on our return we shall deal with results.
There are many difficulties to be overcome in making offensive
plans, but we must persevere. The big movement of United States
troops into Ireland is all arranged at this end. You must make sure
that everything is getting prepared on our side. Please see that a
fine job is done over this, and their special food, etc., studied.

2. I suppose you realise we are trying not only to meet the immediate needs, but to make a plan for the effective application of
the American armies to the enemy's fronts wherever possible. Shipping is the limiting factor.

3. I shall be glad to have everything necessary sent forward, as
I shall be in constant telegraphic touch. They are trying here to
keep my whereabouts secret. It would be well to discourage speculation in our press about my return or movements.

Prime Minister to Lord Privy Seal   7 Jan. 42

Am resting in the South on Charles Wilson's [2] advice for a few
days after rather a strenuous time. President is stopping all mention in the United States press. Please make sure no notice is issued
in England, otherwise American press will be vexed, and I shall be
overrun with them and tourists.

*   *   *

While I was reclining in the mellow sunlight of Palm Beach
and dictating all these telegrams and memoranda, the news
reached me of the Italian "human-torpedo" attack in Alexan-

[2] Sir Charles Wilson, now Lord Moran.

dria Harbour which had disabled the *Queen Elizabeth* and *Valiant*. This has already been described in an earlier chapter. This misfortune, following upon all our other naval losses at this time, was most untimely and disturbing. I saw its gravity at once. The Mediterranean battle fleet was for the time being non-existent, and our naval power to guard Egypt from direct overseas invasion in abeyance. It seemed necessary in the emergency to send whatever torpedo planes could be gathered from the south coast of England. This had, as will presently be seen, an unpleasant sequel.

* * *

Prime Minister to General Ismay, for C.O.S. Committee, 7 Jan. 42
and Secretary of State for Air

In view of naval position Mediterranean it is evidently urgent and important to send strong air reinforcements, especially torpedo planes, from Coastal or Bomber Command. Proportionate relaxation of bomber offensive against Germany, etc., and shipping must be accepted. General Arnold[3] tells me he is sending as soon as possible two bomber groups, i.e., eighty bombers, as well as some fighter squadrons for Ulster. Pray tell me what you are doing and whether Admiral Cunningham is comforted.

I was also concerned lest the Italian exploit should be repeated at Scapa Flow.

Prime Minister to First Sea Lord   9 Jan. 42

The incident at Alexandria, which was so unpleasant, has raised in my mind the question of the security of Scapa Flow against this form of attack. Are we in fact patrolling the entrances with depth-charges every twenty minutes? No doubt the strong currents would give far greater protection than the calm water of Alexandria.

How does the matter stand?

It was above all things important that the true condition of our two great battleships, which rested upon even keels in Alexandria Harbour, should not become known to the enemy.

* * *

I now found time to deal with several difficult questions which pursued me. There was of course a recurrence, both by the Viceroy and the Cabinet, to the idea of making a new constitution for India under which the Congress Party would rally to the common cause and their own security. We shall see in a later volume that this was a vain illusion.

[3] Head of the United States Army Air Force.

Prime Minister to Lord Privy Seal   7 Jan. 42

I hope my colleagues will realise the danger of raising constitutional issue, still more of making constitutional changes, in India at a moment when enemy is upon the frontier. The idea that we should "get more out of India" by putting the Congress in charge at this juncture seems ill-founded. Yet that is what it would come to if any electoral or parliamentary foundation is chosen. Bringing hostile political elements into the defence machine will paralyse action. Merely picking and choosing friendly Indians will do no serious harm, but will not in any way meet the political demands. The Indian Liberals, though plausible, have never been able to deliver the goods. The Indian troops are fighting splendidly, but it must be remembered that their allegiance is to the King Emperor, and that the rule of the Congress and Hindu priesthood machine would never be tolerated by a fighting race.

2. I do not think you will have any trouble with American opinion. All press comments on India I have seen have been singularly restrained, especially since they entered the war. Thought here is concentrated on winning the war as soon as possible. The first duty of Congress nominees who have secured control of provincial government is to resume their responsible duties as ministers, and show that they can make a success of the enormous jobs confided to them in this time of emergency. Pray communicate these views to the Cabinet. I trust we shall not depart from the position we have deliberately taken up.

*   *   *

I was much disturbed by the reports which Mr. Eden had brought back with him from Moscow of Soviet territorial ambitions, especially in the Baltic States. These were the conquests of Peter the Great, and had been for two hundred years under the Czars. Since the Russian Revolution they had been the outpost of Europe against Bolshevism. They were what are now called "social democracies," but very lively and truculent. Hitler had cast them away like pawns in his deal with the Soviets before the outbreak of war in 1939. There had been a severe Russian and Communist purge. All the dominant personalities and elements had been liquidated in one way or another. The life of these strong peoples was henceforward underground. Presently, as we shall see, Hitler came back with a Nazi counter-purge. Finally, in the general victory the Soviets had control again. Thus the deadly comb ran back and forth, and back again, through Estonia, Latvia, and Lithuania. There was no doubt however where the right lay. The Baltic States should be sovereign independent peoples.

Prime Minister to Foreign Secretary   8 Jan. 42

We have never recognised the 1941 frontiers of Russia except *de facto*. They were acquired by acts of aggression in shameful collusion with Hitler. The transfer of the peoples of the Baltic States to Soviet Russia against their will would be contrary to all the principles for which we are fighting this war and would dishonour our cause. This also applies to Bessarabia and to Northern Bukhovina, and in a lesser degree to Finland, which I gather it is not intended wholly to subjugate and absorb.

2. Russia could, upon strategical grounds, make a case for the approaches to Leningrad, which the Finns have utilised to attack her. There are islands in the Baltic which may be essential to the safety of Russia. Strategical security may be invoked at certain points on the frontiers of Bukhovina or Bessarabia. In these cases the population would have to be offered evacuation and compensation if they desired it. In all other cases transference of territory must be regulated after the war is over by freely and fairly conducted plebiscites, very differently from what is suggested. In any case there can be no question of settling frontiers until the Peace Conference. I know President Roosevelt holds this view as strongly as I do, and he has several times expressed his pleasure to me at the firm line we took at Moscow. I could not be an advocate for a British Cabinet bent on such a course.

3. I regard our sincerity to be involved in the maintenance of the principles of the Atlantic Charter, to which Stalin has subscribed. On this also we depend for our association with the United States. . . .

5. About the effect on Russia of our refusal to prejudice the peace negotiations at this stage in the war, or to depart from the principles of the Atlantic Charter, it must be observed that they entered the war only when attacked by Germany, having previously shown themselves utterly indifferent to our fate, and indeed they added to our burdens in our worst danger. Their armies have fought very bravely and have shown immense unsuspected strength in the defence of their native soil. They are fighting for self-preservation and have never had a thought for us. We, on the contrary, are helping them to the utmost of our ability because we admire their defence of their own country and because they are ranged against Hitler.

6. No one can foresee how the balance of power will lie or where the winning armies will stand at the end of the war. It seems probable however that the United States and the British Empire, far from being exhausted, will be the most powerfully armed and economic *bloc* the world has ever seen, and that the Soviet Union will need our aid for reconstruction far more than we shall then need theirs.

7. You have promised that we will examine these claims of Russia in common with the United States and the Dominions. That promise we must keep. But there must be no mistake about the

opinion of any British Government of which I am the head, namely that it adheres to those principles of freedom and democracy set forth in the Atlantic Charter, and that these principles must become especially active whenever any question of transferring territory is raised. I conceive therefore that our answer should be that all questions of territorial frontiers must be left to the decision of the Peace Conference.

Juridically this is how the matter stands now.

*   *   *

While at Palm Beach I was of course in constant touch by telephone with the President and the British Staffs in Washington, and also when necessary I could speak to London. An amusing, though at the moment disconcerting, incident occurred. Mr. Wendell Willkie had asked to see me. At this time there was tension between him and the President. Roosevelt had not seemed at all keen about my meeting prominent members of the Opposition, and I had consequently so far not done so. Having regard however to Wendell Willkie's visit to England a year before in January, 1941, and to the cordial relations I had established with him, I felt that I ought not to leave American shores without seeing him. This was also our Ambassador's advice. I therefore put a call through to him on the evening of the 5th. After some delay I was told, "Your call is through." I said in effect, "I am so glad to speak to you. I hope we may meet. I am travelling back by train tomorrow night. Can you not join the train at some point and travel with me for a few hours? Where will you be on Saturday next?" A voice came back: "Why, just where I am now, at my desk." To this I replied, "I do not understand." "Whom do you think you are speaking to?" I replied, "To Mr. Wendell Willkie, am I not?" "No," was the answer, "you are speaking to the President." I did not hear this very well, and asked, "Who?" "You are speaking to me," came the answer, "Franklin Roosevelt." I said, "I did not mean to trouble you at this moment. I was trying to speak to Wendell Willkie, but your telephone exchange seems to have made a mistake." "I hope you are getting on all right down there and enjoying yourself," said the President. Some pleasant conversation followed about personal movements and plans, at the end of which I asked, "I presume you do not mind my having wished to speak to Wendell Willkie?" To this Roosevelt said, "No." And this was the end of our talk.

It must be remembered that this was in the early days of

our friendship, and when I got back to Washington I thought it right to find out from Harry Hopkins whether any offence had been given. I therefore wrote to him:

> I rely on you to let me know if this action of mine in wishing to speak to the person named is in any way considered inappropriate, because I certainly thought I was acting in accordance with my duty to be civil to a public personage of importance, and unless you advise me to the contrary I still propose to do so.

Hopkins said that no harm had been done.

* * *

It was now time to come home.

Prime Minister to Lord Privy Seal   9 Jan. 42

You will have seen by the telegrams which have passed that I have not been idle here. Indeed, the seclusion in which I have lived has enabled me to focus things more clearly than was possible in the stir of Washington. I am in the midst of preparing a considerable paper on Anglo-American co-operation, which I shall discuss with the Staffs and then with the President as soon as I get back.

I am so glad the debate of the 8th passed off peacefully, and that the House was willing to postpone the discussion on the main issue. Of course the naggings and snarlings have been fully reported over here, and one would think that they represented the opinion of the House. Several remarks have been reported which are not very helpful to American opinion, and I am pointing out to the President that we can no more control the expression of freak opinion by individual members than he can those of Congress backwoodsmen. Try to let me have a gist of what you and Anthony said.

It might be convenient if I made my statement on Tuesday as a statement, and the adjournment was moved by somebody else immediately after. This would enable the usual criticisms to be made without my having exhausted my right to reply. Perhaps however you will not think this necessary. I cannot help feeling we have a good tale to tell, even though we cannot tell the best part of it.

I set out by train to return to Washington on the night of the 9th, and reached the White House on the 11th. Business kept me company.

17

Return to Storm

Some Further Notes on the War After Anglo-American Discussions—Expansion of the United States Army—And of the Air Force—Growing Output of Munitions and Shipping—Importance of Sending an American Army to Northern Ireland—Rommel's Stubborn Resistance and Retardation of North African Plans—Need to Wear Down the German Air Power by Continuous Engagement—Relief Afforded by the Successful Russian Resistance in the South—Potential Dangers to the Caucasus—The War Against Japan—Our Need to Regain the Initiative—Mobile Striking Force to Attack Japanese Conquests—Final Conference at the White House on January 12—Complete Anglo-American Agreement—General Marshall's Question—We Start for Home—The President's Apprehensions—The Boeing Clipper—My Wish to Use Her—Expert Advice of Portal and Pound—I Address the Bermuda Assembly—The Decision to go by Air Instead of in the "Duke of York"—A Very Long Flight—A Critical Moment at Dawn—Arrival at Plymouth, January 17.

DURING MY REST in Florida I prepared a fourth memorandum in two parts addressed to the Chiefs of Staff Committee and for the Defence Committee of the War Cabinet. This was written also for American eyes. It differed from the three previous papers in that it was composed after the opening discussions in Washington between me and the President and his advisers and between the Combined Chiefs of Staff. Subsequently on my return to London I circulated all these papers to the War Cabinet for information. A very large measure of agreement had already been reached between our two countries, and the War Cabinet accorded in effect a very wide degree of approval to the direction which had been given to our affairs. I present only the more general aspects here.[1]

[1] Paragraphs 9, 10, 14, 15, and 16 are omitted for reasons of space.

*Prime Minister to General Ismay, for C.O.S. Committee   10 Jan. 42
and Defence Committee*

I have availed myself of a few days' quiet and seclusion to review the salients of the war as they appear after my discussions here.

The United States has been attacked and become at war with the three Axis Powers, and desires to engage her trained troops as soon and as effectively as possible on fighting fronts. Owing to the shipping stringency this will not be possible on any very large scale during 1942. Meanwhile the United States Army is being raised from a strength of a little over thirty divisions and five armoured divisions to a total strength of about sixty divisions and ten armoured divisions. About 3,750,000 men are at present held or about to be called up for the Army and Air Force (over a million). Reserves of man-power are practically unlimited, but it would be a misdirection of war effort to call larger numbers to the armed forces in the present phase.

2. It does not seem likely that more than between a quarter and a third of the above American forces can be transported to actual fighting fronts during the year 1942. In 1943 however the great increases in shipping tonnage resulting from former and recent shipping programmes should enable much larger bodies to be moved across the oceans, and the summer of 1943 may be marked by large offensive operations, which should be carefully studied meanwhile.

3. The United States Air Force, already powerful and rapidly increasing, can be brought into heavy action during 1942. Already it is proposed that strong bomber forces, based on the British Isles, should attack Germany and the invasion ports. American fighter squadrons can participate in the defence of Great Britain and the domination of such parts of the French shore as are within fighter reach.

4. The declaration by the President to Congress of the enormous increases in United States output of munitions and shipping to proceed during 1942, and reach full flow in 1943, makes it more than ever necessary for Hitler to bring the war to a decision in 1942, before the power of the United States can be fully brought to bear.

5. Hitler has had the time to prepare, perhaps in very great numbers, tank-transporting vehicles capable of landing on any beach. He has no doubt developed airborne attack by parachutes, and still more by gliders, to an extent which cannot easily be measured. The President, expressing views shared by the leading American strategists, has declared Great Britain an essential fortress of the United Nations. It is indeed the only place where the war can be lost in the critical campaign of 1942 about to open. It would be most imprudent to allow the successful defence of the British Isles to be hazarded. . . .

6. The sending of four United States divisions (one armoured) into Northern Ireland is therefore a most necessary war measure,

which nothing should be allowed to prevent. The replacing of the British troops in Iceland (C) liberates an additional British division. It is suggested however that the United States authorities should be asked to consider the training in Iceland (C) of as many troops as possible to work on mountains and under snow conditions, as only the possession of such trained mountain and ski troops in considerable numbers can enable a liberating operation in Scandinavia to be prepared for the future. . . .

7. The stubborn resistance of the enemy in Cyrenaica, the possibilities of General Rommel withdrawing, or of being able to escape with a portion of his troops, the reinforcements which have probably reached Tripoli, and others which must be expected during the delay, and above all the difficulties of supply for our advancing troops—all will retard, or may even prevent, the full completion of "Acrobat" [the clearance of Tripoli]. We are therefore in a position to study "Super-Gymnast" [the Anglo-American occupation of French North Africa], more thoroughly, and to proceed with "Magnet" [the movement of American troops to Northern Ireland], with the utmost speed.

8. . . . The German front-line air force is already less strong numerically than the British. A considerable portion of it must now be left opposite Russia. But the bulk of the British Air Force has to be tied up at home, facing, at the present time, a much smaller concentration of German bombers and fighters, and yet not able to be moved because of the good interior communications possessed by the enemy and his power of rapid transference. In addition, there is the Italian Air Force to consider.

11. The object we should set before ourselves is the wearing-down by continuous engagement of the German air power. This is being done on the Russian front. On the British front it can only be done to a limited extent, unless the enemy resumes his bombing or daylight offensive. But in the Mediterranean the enemy shows an inclination to develop a front, and we should meet him there with the superior strength which the arrival of American air forces can alone give. It is of the utmost importance to make the German Air Force fight continuously on every possible occasion, and at every point of attack. We can afford the drain far better than they can. Indeed, like General Grant in his last campaign, we can almost afford to lose two for one, having regard to the immense supplies now coming forward in the future. Every German aircraft or pilot put out of action in 1942 is worth two of them in 1943. It is only by the strain of constant air battle that we shall be able to force his consumption of air power to levels which are beyond the capacity of his air plants and air schools. In this way the initiative may be regained by us, as the enemy will be fully occupied, as we have been hitherto, in meeting day-to-day needs and keeping his head above water.

12. We must acclaim the very great deliverance afforded to us by the successful Russian resistance along the Don and in the

Crimea, carrying with it the continued Russian command of the Black Sea. Three months ago we were forced to expect a German advance through the Caucasus to the Caspian and the Baku oilfields. That danger is almost certainly staved off for perhaps four or five months till the winter is over, and of course continued successful Russian resistance in the South would give complete protection to us.

13. The danger may however recur in the late spring. The oil stringency, which is already serious in Germany and the German-conquered countries, makes the seizure of the Baku and Persian oilfields objects of vital consequence to Germany, second only to the need of successfully invading the British Isles. . . . The enormous power of the German Army may be able to reassert itself as soon as weather conditions improve. In this case they might well be content to adopt a defensive attitude along the northern and central sectors of the Russo-German front, and thrust an offensive spearhead southeast through the Caucasus to the oilfields which lie beyond.

The War Against Japan

17. It is generally agreed that the defeat of Germany, entailing a collapse, will leave Japan exposed to overwhelming force, whereas the defeat of Japan would not by any means bring the World War to an end. Moreover, the vast distances in the Pacific and the advantageous forward key points already seized or likely to be seized by the Japanese will make the serious invasion of the homelands of Japan a very lengthy business. Not less lengthy will be the piecemeal recovery, by armies based mainly on Australia and India, of the islands, airfields, and naval bases in the Southwest Pacific area now confided to General Wavell. It seems indeed more probable that a decision can be reached sooner against Germany than against Japan. In any case, we cannot expect to develop adequate naval, air, and military superiority in the aforesaid area for a considerable time, having regard to other calls made upon us and the limitation of shipping.

18. While therefore it is right to assign primacy to the war against Germany, it would be wrong to speak of our "standing on the defensive" against Japan; on the contrary, the only way in which we can live through the intervening period in the Far East before Germany is defeated is by regaining the initiative, albeit on a minor scale.

19. In a theatre of a thousand islands, many capable of being converted into makeshift air and naval bases, insoluble problems are set to purely passive defence. The Japanese having obtained temporary command of the sea, and air predominance over considerable areas, it is within their power to take almost any point they wish, apart, it is hoped, from the fortress of Singapore. They can go round with a circus force and clean up any local garrisons

we or the Dutch have been able so far to hold. They will seek to secure their hold by a well-conceived network of air bases, and they no doubt hope to secure, in a certain number of months, the possession of the fortress of Singapore. Once in possession of this as well as Manila, with their air bases established at focal points, they will have built up a system of air and naval defence capable of prolonged resistance. . . . The naval superiority of the United States, to which Great Britain will contribute to the best of her ability, ought to be regained by the summer of 1942.

20. Thereupon, or at least as soon as possible, raids should be organised upon islands or seaports which the Japanese have seized. The President has, I understand, ordered the formation of a force on the west coast of America akin to the commandos. Such a force, on account of its individual qualities, will be exceptionally valuable by gaining key points and lodgments in amphibious operations. It would require to be supported by a number of small brigade groups, whose mobility and equipment would be exactly fitted to the particular task foreseen, each task being a study in itself. It is not necessary, unless required on strategic grounds, to stay in the captured or recaptured islands. It will be sufficient to destroy or make prisoners of the garrison, demolish any useful installations, and depart. The exact composition of the forces for each undertaking and enterprise is a matter for separate study. According to our experiences, it would seem essential that there should be adequate cover by seaborne aircraft and detachments of tanks and tank-landing craft. The enemy cannot possibly be prepared, and must be highly vulnerable at many points. After even a few successful enterprises of this character, all of which are extremely valuable experiences to the troops and commanders for instructional purposes, he will be terrorised out of holding places weakly, and will be forced to concentrate on a certain number of strong points. It may then be possible for us to secure very easily suitable islands, provided we do not try to hold too many, in which air and refuelling bases of a temporary or permanent character can be improvised. The establishment of a reign of terror among the enemy's detached garrisons would seem to be an extremely valuable preliminary to the larger operations for reconquest and the building-up of strong bases as stepping-stones from Australia northward.

This paper I gave to the President.

*   *   *

When I got back to the White House I found that great progress had been made by the Combined Chiefs of Staff, and that it was mostly in harmony with my views. The President convened a meeting on January 12, when there was complete agreement upon the broad principles and targets of the war.

The differences were confined to priorities and emphasis, and all was ruled by that harsh and despotic factor, shipping. "The President," says the British record, "set great store on organising a 'Super-Gymnast'—i.e., a combined United States-British expedition to North Africa. A tentative time-table had been worked out for putting ninety thousand United States and ninety thousand British troops, together with a considerable air force, into North Africa." It was settled to send two divisions of American troops to Northern Ireland, with the objects which have been described. The President had told me privately that he would, if necessary as quickly as possible, send fifty thousand United States troops to Australia and the islands covering its approach by the Japanese. Twenty-five thousand were to go as soon as possible to occupy New Caledonia, and other stepping-stones between America and Australasia. On "Grand Strategy" the Staffs agreed that "only the minimum of forces necessary for the safeguarding of vital interests in other theatres should be diverted from operations against Germany." No one had more to do with obtaining this cardinal decision than General Marshall.

One evening the General came to see me and put a hard question. He had agreed to send nearly thirty thousand American soldiers to Northern Ireland. We had of course placed the two "Queens"—the only two 80,000-ton ships in the world—at his disposal for this purpose. General Marshall asked me how many men we ought to put on board, observing that boats, rafts, and other means of flotation could only be provided for about eight thousand. If this were disregarded, they could carry sixteen thousand men. I gave the following answer: "I can only tell you what *we* should do. You must judge for yourself the risks you will run. If it were a direct part of an actual operation, we should put all on board they could carry. If it were only a question of moving troops in a reasonable time, we should not go beyond the limits of lifeboats, rafts, etc. It is for you to decide." He received this in silence and our conversation turned to other matters. In their first voyages these ships carried only the lesser numbers, but later on they were filled to the brim. As it happened, Fortune stood our friend.

*   *   *

The time had now come when I must leave the hospitable and exhilarating atmosphere of the White House and of the American Nation, erect and infuriate against tyrants and ag-

gressors. It was to no sunlit prospect that I must return.
Eager though I was to be back in London, and sure of ultimate victory, I felt continually the approaching impact of a
period of immense disasters which must last for many months.
My hopes of a victory in the Western Desert, in which Rommel
would be destroyed, had faded. Rommel had escaped. The
results of Auchinleck's successes at Sidi Rezegh and at Gazala
had not been decisive. The prestige which these had given us
in the making of all our plans for the Anglo-American descent
on French North Africa was definitely weakened, and this operation was obviously set back for months.

*   *   *

Prime Minister to Lord Privy Seal   12 Jan. 42
   As I shall soon be silent for a while, though I trust not for ever,
pray cable tonight any outstanding points which require decision
here before I leave.

   On the 14th I took leave of the President. He seemed concerned about the dangers of the voyage. Our presence in
Washington had been for many days public to the world, and
the charts showed more than twenty U-boats on our homeward
courses. We flew in beautiful weather from Norfolk to Bermuda, where the *Duke of York*, with escorting destroyers,
awaited us inside the coral reefs. I travelled in an enormous
Boeing flying-boat, which made a most favourable impression
upon me. During the three hours' trip I made friends with
the chief pilot, Captain Kelly Rogers, who seemed a man of
high quality and experience. I took the controls for a bit, to
feel this ponderous machine of thirty or more tons in the air.
I got more and more attached to the flying-boat. Presently
I asked the Captain, "What about flying from Bermuda to
England? Can she carry enough petrol?" Under his stolid
exterior he became visibly excited. "Of course we can do it.
The present weather forecast would give a forty miles an hour
wind behind us. We could do it in twenty hours." I asked
how far it was, and he said, "About thirty-five hundred miles."
At this I became thoughtful.

   However, when we landed I opened the matter to Portal
and Pound. Formidable events were happening in Malaya; we
ought all to be back at the earliest moment. The Chief of the
Air Staff said at once that he thought the risk wholly unjustifiable, and he could not take the responsibility for it. The
First Sea Lord supported his colleague. There was the *Duke*

of York, with her destroyers, all ready for us, offering comfort
and a certainty. I said, "What about the U-boats you have been
pointing out to me?" The Admiral made a disdainful gesture
about them, which showed his real opinion of such a menace
to a properly escorted and fast battleship. It occurred to me
that both these officers thought my plan was to fly myself and
leave them to come back in the *Duke of York*, so I said, "Of
course there would be room for all of us." They both visibly
changed countenance at this. After a considerable pause Portal
said that the matter might be looked into, and that he would
discuss it at length with the Captain of the flying-boat and go
into weather prospects with the meteorological authorities. I
left it at that.

Two hours later they both returned, and Portal said that he
thought it might be done. The aircraft could certainly accomplish the task under reasonable conditions; the weather
outlook was exceptionally favourable on account of the strong
following wind. No doubt it was very important to get home
quickly. Pound said he had formed a very high opinion of the
aircraft skipper, who certainly had unrivalled experience. Of
course there was a risk, but on the other hand there were the
U-boats to consider. So we settled to go unless the weather
deteriorated. The starting time was 2 P.M. the next day. It was
thought necessary to reduce our baggage to a few boxes of
vital papers. Dill was to remain behind in Washington as my
personal military representative with the President. Our party
would consist only of myself, the two Chiefs of Staff, and Max
Beaverbrook, Charles Wilson, and Hollis. All the rest would go
by the *Duke of York*.

That afternoon I addressed the Bermuda Assembly, which
is the oldest Parliamentary institution in the Western Hemisphere. I pleaded with them to give their assent and all their
aid to the establishment of the United States naval and air
bases in the island, about which they were in some distress.
The life of the whole Empire was at stake. The smooth working of our alliance with the United States made final victory
certain, however long the journey might be. They did not
demur. The Governor, Lord Knollys, gave a banquet that
night to the island notables and their fleeting guests. We were
all in high spirits. Only Tommy,[2] my Flag Commander as I
called him, was in terror that there would be no room for him.
He explained how deeply wounded he was at the idea of
going home by sea. I reminded him of his devotion to the

[2] Commander Thompson, R.N.

naval service, and of the pleasures to a hardy sailor of a life on the ocean wave. I dwelt upon the undeniable hazards from the U-boats. He was quite inconsolable. However, he had a plan. He had persuaded one of the stewards of the flying-boat to let him take his place; he would do the washing up himself. But what, I asked, would the Captain say? Tommy thought that if at the last moment the Captain were confronted with the arrangement he would make no objection. He had ascertained that he weighed less than the steward. I shrugged my shoulders, and on this we went to bed in the small hours of the morning.

I woke up unconscionably early with the conviction that I should certainly not go to sleep again. I must confess that I felt rather frightened. I thought of the ocean spaces, and that we should never be within a thousand miles of land until we approached the British Isles. I thought perhaps I had done a rash thing that there were too many eggs in one basket. I had always regarded an Atlantic flight with awe. But the die was cast. Still, I must admit that if at breakfast, or even before luncheon, they had come to me to report that the weather had changed and we must go by sea, I should have easily reconciled myself to a voyage in the splendid ship which had come all this way to fetch us.

Divine sunlight lapped the island, and the favourable weather prospects were confirmed. At noon we reached the flying-boat by launch. We were delayed for an hour on the quay because a picket-boat which had gone to the *Duke of York* for items of baggage had taken longer than expected. Tommy stood disconsolate. The Captain had brushed his project aside in a way that captains have. The steward was a trained member of the crew; he could not take one single person more; every tank was filled to the brim with petrol. It would be quite a task getting off the water even as it was. So we taxied out to the far end of the harbour, leaving Tommy lamenting as bitterly as Lord Ullin in the poem,[3] but for different reasons. Never before and never afterwards were we separated in these excursions.

It was, as the Captain had predicted, quite a job to get off the water. Indeed, I thought that we should hardly clear the low hills which closed the harbour. There was really no danger; we were in sure hands. The flying-boat lifted ponderously a quarter of a mile from the reef, and we had several hundred feet of height to spare. There is no doubt about the

[3] Thomas Campbell's *Lord Ullin's Daughter*.

comfort of these great flying-boats. I had a good broad bed in the bridal suite at the stern with large windows on either side. It was quite a long walk, thirty or forty feet, downhill through the various compartments to the saloon and dining-room, where nothing was lacking in food or drink. The motion was smooth, the vibration not unpleasant, and we passed an agreeable afternoon and had a merry dinner. These boats have two storeys, and one walks up a regular staircase to the control room. Darkness had fallen, and all the reports were good. We were now flying through dense mist at about seven thousand feet. One could see the leading edge of the wings, with their great flaming exhausts pouring back over the wing surfaces. In these machines at this time a large rubber tube which expanded and contracted at intervals was used to prevent icing. The Captain explained to me how it worked, and we saw from time to time the ice splintered off as it expanded. I went to bed and slept soundly for several hours.

* * *

I woke just before the dawn, and went forward to the controls. The daylight grew. Beneath us was an almost unbroken floor of clouds.

After sitting for an hour or so in the co-pilot's seat, I sensed a feeling of anxiety around me We were supposed to be approaching England from the southwest and we ought already to have passed the Scilly Islands, but they had not been seen through any of the gaps in the cloud floor. As we had flown for more than ten hours through mist and had had only one sight of a star in that time, we might well be slightly off our course after such a lengthy flight. Wireless communication was of course limited by the normal wartime rules. It was evident from the discussions which were going on that we did not know where we were. Presently Portal, who had been studying the position, had a word with the Captain, and then said to me, "We are going to turn north at once." This was done, and after another half-hour in and out of the clouds we sighted England, and soon arrived over Plymouth, where, avoiding the balloons, which were all shining, we landed comfortably.

As I left the aircraft the Captain remarked, "I never felt so much relieved in my life as when I landed you safely in the harbour." I did not appreciate the significance of his remark at the moment. Later on I learnt that if we had held on our course for another five or six minutes before turning north-

ward we should have been over the German batteries in
Brest. We had slanted too much to the southward during the
night. Moreover, the decisive correction which had been made
brought us in, not from the southwest, but from just east of
south—that is to say, from the enemy's direction rather than
from that from which we were expected. This had the result,
as I was told some weeks later, that we were reported as a
hostile bomber coming in from Brest, and six Hurricanes from
Fighter Command were ordered out to shoot us down. However, they failed in their mission.

To President Roosevelt I cabled, "We got here with a good
hop from Bermuda and a thirty-mile wind."

END OF BOOK TWO

You have just finished THE GRAND ALLIANCE,
one volume in the most important historical
work of our century. If you learned from it,
or if you were moved by it, may we suggest
that you share your experience and
recommend it to a friend?

APPENDICES

Contents

Contents

Appendix A, Book One

LIST OF ABBREVIATIONS

A.A. GUNS	Anti-aircraft guns, or ack-ack guns
A.D.G.B.	Air Defence of Great Britain
A.F.V.s	Armoured fighting vehicles
A.G.R.M.	Adjutant General Royal Marines
A.P.	Armour-piercing
A.R.P.	Air Raid Precautions
A.T. RIFLES	Anti-tank rifles
A.T.S.	(Women's) Auxiliary Territorial Service
C.A.S.	Chief of the Air Staff
C.I.G.S.	Chief of the Imperial General Staff
C.-in-C.	Commander-in-Chief
CONTROLLER	Third Sea Lord and Chief of Material
C.O.S.	Chiefs of Staff
D.N.C.	Director of Naval Construction
F.O.	Foreign Office
G.H.Q.	General Headquarters
G.O.C.	General Officer Commanding
H.E.	High Explosive
H.F.	Home Forces
H.M.G.	His Majesty's Government
M.A.P.	Ministry of Aircraft Production
M.E.W.	Ministry of Economic Warfare
M.O.I.	Ministry of Information
M. OF L.	Ministry of Labour
M. OF S.	Ministry of Supply
M.T.	Motor Transport
P.M.	Prime Minister
U.P.	Unrotated projectiles—i.e., code name for rockets
V.C.A.S.	Vice-Chief of the Air Staff
V.C.I.G.S.	Vice-Chief of the Imperial General Staff
V.C.N.S.	Vice-Chief of the Naval Staff
W.A.A.F.	Women's Auxiliary Air Force
W.R.N.S.	Women's Royal Naval Service ("Wrens")

Appendix B, Book One

LIST OF OPERATIONAL CODE NAMES

ACROBAT: Advance from Cyrenaica into Tripoli.

ARCADIA: First Washington Conference, December, 1941.

BARBAROSSA: German plan for invasion of Russia.

BATTLEAXE: Offensive operations in Sollum, Tobruk, and Capuzzo area, June, 1941.

CANVAS: Attack on Kismayu.

COLORADO: Crete.

CRUSADER: Operations in Western Desert, November, 1941.

EXPORTER: Operations in Syria.

FELIX: German plan for seizure of Gibraltar.

GYMNAST: British occupation of French North Africa.

INFLUX: Occupation of Sicily.

JAGUAR: Reinforcements to Malta, 1941.

LUSTRE: Aid to Greece.

MAGNET: Movement of American troops to Northern Ireland.

MANDIBLES: Operations against Dodecanese.

MARIE: Operation against Jibouti.

MARITA: German plan for invasion of Greece.

MULBERRY: Artificial harbour.

ORIENT: German plan to overthrow British positions in Middle East.

OVERLORD: Liberation of France, 1944.

PILGRIM: Occupation of Canary Islands.

PUNISHMENT: German bombing of Belgrade.

ROUND-UP: Liberation of France, 1943 (subsequently changed to OVERLORD).

SCORCHER: Defence of Crete.

SEA LION: German plan for invasion of Britain.

SUPERCHARGE: Relief of Australians in Tobruk.

SUPER-GYMNAST: Anglo-American occupation of French North Africa.

TIGER: Passage of part of convoy W.S.8 through the Mediterranean.

TORCH: Anglo-American operations against French North Africa.

TRUNCHEON: Combined raid on Leghorn.

WHIPCORD: Plan for invasion of Sicily.

WORKSHOP: Capture of Pantelleria.

Appendix C, Book One

PRIME MINISTER'S PERSONAL MINUTES
AND TELEGRAMS

January—June, 1941

JANUARY

Prime Minister to Sir Edward Bridges, General Ismay,   1.1.41.
and Mr. Seal

With the beginning of the New Year a new intense drive must be
made to secure greater secrecy in all matters relating to the conduct
of the war, and the following points should have your attention.
You should consider them together and report to me.

Renewal of the cautions issued a year ago against gossip and talk
about Service matters. Probably a new set of posters is required to
attract attention.

2. Renewal of the orders which were then issued to all departments.

3. Severe further restrictions on the circulation of secret papers,
especially those relating to operations, strength of the armed forces,
foreign policy, etc. Every department should be asked to submit
proposals for restricting the circulation of papers. This is all the
more important on account of the ever-increasing elaboration of
Government departments and the Whitehall population.

4. The use of boxes with snap locks is to be enforced for all
documents of a secret character. Ministers and their private secretaries should have snap-lock boxes on their desks, and should never
leave confidential documents in trays when they are out of the
room.

5. Boxes should always be snapped to when not immediately in
use. Access to rooms in which confidential secretaries and Ministers
are working should be restricted wherever possible, and anterooms
provided into which visitors can be shown.

6. A small red star label should be devised to be placed on most
secret papers—i.e., those dealing with operations and the strength
of the armed forces. It is not necessary for all the private secretaries
in the office to read these starred documents. They should always
be circulated in locked boxes, and transferred immediately to
other locked boxes for my use and for the use of Ministers.

7. A restriction of telegrams relating to future operations is to be
made. Sometimes lately I have received an account of future

605

operations where the name of the place is mentioned as well as its future code word. This happened in the case of "Influx" yesterday. All such documents which contain the name of the place and the code word should be collected and either destroyed by fire or put in a safe.

8. Ministers should be requested to restrict as far as possible the circle within which it is necessary to discuss secret matters. It is not necessary for Parliamentary Private Secretaries (unless Privy Councillors) to be informed more than is necessary for the discharge of their Parliamentary and political duties.

9. We are having trouble through the activities of foreign correspondents of both sexes. The disclosures of Engel published in today's papers are a capital example. Proposals should be made for restricting the facilities accorded to them in obtaining confidential information. It must be remembered that everything said to the American press is instantly communicated to Germany, and that we have no redress.

10. The wide circulation of Intelligence Reports and the general tendency to multiply reports of all kinds must be curtailed. Each department connected with the war should be asked to submit a report showing what further restrictions and curtailments they propose to introduce in the New Year. Some time ago the late Cabinet decided that Ministers not in the War Cabinet should submit beforehand speeches on the war, or references in speeches to the war, to the Minister of Information. This has apparently fallen into disuse. Let me have a report as to what is happening. A more convenient method might be that Ministers wishing to refer to these subjects should consult General Ismay, as representing the Minister of Defence, beforehand. No officials who have, for instance, been on missions abroad should make public statements concerning their work without previous Ministerial approval.

11. I have already dealt with the circulation of secret information to friendly attachés, and we have restricted the character of the information. This process should continue—the bulk of the documents circulated being made up by interesting padding such as might well appear in the newspapers.

12. The newspapers repeatedly publish—mostly with innocent intentions—facts about the war and policy which are detrimental. Where these have not been censored beforehand a complaint should be made afterwards in every case. The Ministry of Information should report what they are doing.

Pray consider all these matters and let me know of any others that occur to you, and advise me on how these points are to be made, and through what channels, to the various authorities affected.

Prime Minister to Colonel Jacob   3.1.41.

I presume that this [German] corps will be most carefully scrubbed and rescrubbed to make sure no Nazi cells develop in it.

I am very much in favour of recruiting friendly Germans and keeping them under strict discipline, instead of remaining useless in concentration camps, but we must be doubly careful we do not get any of the wrong breed.

Prime Minister to First Lord and First Sea Lord   3.I.41.
(Copies sent to Minister of Supply and Minister of Shipping.)

I was greatly distressed at the loss of the cargo of the *City of Bedford*. It is the heaviest munition loss we have sustained. Seven and a half million cartridges is a grievous blow. It would be better to disperse these cargoes among more ships.

2. I presume you have inquired into the causes of this collision, and of the two incoming, outgoing convoys being routed so close together. I must again emphasise the gravity of the loss.

Prime Minister to Sir Edward Bridges   4.I.41.

Let me have a list of all committees of a Ministerial character forming part of the Central Government, with any offshoots there may be.

2. Ask each department to furnish a list of all the committees of a departmental nature which exist at the present time.

3. This information is the prelude to a New Year's effort to cut down the number of such committees.

Prime Minister to Sir Edward Bridges   4.I.41.

The Committee on War Aims has largely completed its work in the draft statement which it has drawn up, and which should now be circulated to the Cabinet. In any case, war aims is quite a different matter from the reconstruction of this country, which is entrusted to the Minister without portfolio. . . . We must be very careful not to allow these remote post-war problems to absorb energy which is required, maybe for several years, for the prosecution of the war.

(Action this day.)
Prime Minister to General Ismay, for General Loch   4.I.41
and others concerned

In the Photo-Electric [P.E.[1]] fuze the greatest interest attaches to high-altitude work against machines flying over ten thousand feet which are not dive-bombing but trying to hit H.M. ships or land targets, perhaps with improved bomb-sights. It is desired to be able to burst salvoes of eight or more in close proximity to the enemy aircraft with fatal results. Even if this could be achieved only in clear, good weather, it would be of the highest advantage, as important operations would be arranged to seek that weather.

2. Is this high-altitude work being pressed to the full, both in the manufacture and in the Research-Training sphere? Are the officers concerned fully apprised? Defence against dive-bombing was the

[1] P.E.: An early type of proximity fuze.

original purpose, and this may well be achieved both by P.E. and A.D.,[2] but the emphasis must now be placed upon high-altitude work.

3. This also applies to the A.D. fuze firing and aerial mines at the highest altitudes of all. It is in this direction that the highest tactical and operational results will be achieved.

Prime Minister to Home Secretary and Minister of Health   4.I.41.

What happens in the case where a shelter is not safe, but is nevertheless occupied, as many are? The ruling should be, I think, that every shelter that is occupied, whether safe or not, must be under the responsibility of the Minister of Health for its internal arrangements, and that there should be no distinction between approved and unapproved shelters. The Minister of Health must *act* wherever the shelter is used. On the other hand, as shelter accommodation increases and improves, the Minister of Home Security would naturally be closing down the most unsafe ones.

Pray let me know that this view is correct.

Prime Minister to S. of S. for Foreign Affairs and   5.I.41.
Minister for Economic Warfare

My message to Italy was deliberately designed to separate the Italian people from the Fascist régime and from Mussolini; and now that France is out of the war I certainly intend to talk rather more about the Nazis and rather less about the Germans. We must not let our vision be darkened by hatred or obscured by sentiment.

A much more fruitful line is to try to separate the Prussians from the South Germans. I do not remember that the word "Prussia" has been used much lately. The expressions to which I attach importance and intend to give emphasis are "Nazi tyranny" and "Prussian militarism."

(Action this day.)
Prime Minister to Minister for Works and Buildings   6.I.41.
(Minister of Health to see.)

The great increase in the destruction and damage to house property makes it all the more necessary that you should regard emergency first-aid work to buildings slightly damaged as the most important task. Please let me have a weekly report of what you are doing in this respect. I continue to see great numbers of houses where the walls and roofs are all right, but the windows have not been repaired, and which are consequently uninhabitable. At present I regard this as your Number 1 war task. Do not let spacious plans for a new world divert your energies from saving what it left of the old.

Prime Minister to Secretary of State for Foreign Affairs   11.I.41.

You spoke to me the other day about the length of telegrams. I feel that this is an evil which ought to be checked. Ministers and

---

[2] A.D.: A rocket and parachute device for use against aircraft.

Ambassadors aboard seem to think that the bigger the volume of their reports home, the better is their task discharged. All kinds of gossip and rumours are sent, regardless of credibility. The idea seems to be to keep up a continued chat which no one ever tries to shorten. I suggest that you should issue a general injunction, but that in addition telegrams which are unduly verbose or trivial should be criticised as such, and their authors told "this telegram was needlessly long." It is sheer laziness not compressing thought into a reasonable space. I try to read all these telegrams, and I think the volume grows from day to day.

Please let me know what can be done.

Prime Minister to Secretary of State for War and   12.I.41.
C.I.G.S.

The mechanisation of the Cavalry Division in Palestine is a distressing story. These troops have been carried out with their horses and maintained at great expense in the Middle East since the early months of the war. Several months ago it was decided by the War Office that they should be mechanised. I gladly approved. Now I learn, as the result of one of my own inquiries, that nothing has been done about this, that the whole division is to be carted back again home—presumably without their horses—and that this is not to begin until June 1. After that there will be a further seven or eight months before they will be of any use. Thus eight thousand five hundred officers and men, including some of our finest Regular and Yeomanry regiments, will, except for security work, have been kept out of action at immense expense for two years and five months of war.

2. Let me have a calculation of the cost involved in: (*a*) Sending these troops to the Middle East. (*b*) Maintaining them with rations, pay, and allowances from the beginning of the war to the beginning of March, 1942. (*c*) Transporting them home again.

3. There must be many better uses to which these troops could be put in the Middle East. Having regard to their high intrinsic quality, they should very quickly acquire new additional training. It is not necessary that the organisation and establishment should follow exactly the same patterns approved for mechanised or armoured formations at home. The establishments of the independent motorised brigade groups here might be more suitable than those of a division. The Household Cavalry in the spring of 1918 or autumn of 1917 were very rapidly converted into a machine-gun regiment, and achieved their training in a couple of months at Etaples. I cannot understand why the Cavalry Division should not train in Palestine, where at any rate they count as local security troops. One would have thought it was the very country.

4. Some of the captured Italian tank equipment might be taken

over by these highly competent Regular or quasi-Regular units. Alternatively, or in partial substitute, we have a good supply of Bren-gun carriers, two hundred of which could certainly be sent out.

5. There are various other solutions. They might be converted into an infantry division, as several cavalry divisions were in the last war, or formed, perhaps, into independent brigade groups. In this case they would be drafted up to full strength as infantry battalions. If this is not acceptable, they could be sent to India to liberate an equal number of Regulars in battalions serving there—say, eight battalions. Or, again, they might form the kernel of a force to dominate Iraq. One thing is certain: now that we are starving ourselves to send men to the East with ever-dwindling shipping, there can be no question of bringing this large body of men and these invaluable cadres home, especially perhaps at the very moment when the fighting in the Middle East is at its height.

Prime Minister to Secretary of State for Air and C.A.S.   12.I.41.

Must the operational reports from the Middle East be of their present inordinate length and detail? It surely is not necessary to describe minutely what happened in every individual raid of a dozen aircraft over the enemy's lines and encipher and decipher all this at each end, and cable it, thus congesting the lines.

I suggest that the average weekly wordage of these routine telegrams should be calculated for the last two months and Air Marshal Longmore asked to reduce them to, say, one-third their present length.

The Foreign Office are also asking for condensation of their messages.

Prime Minister to Home Secretary   12.I.41.

This kind of propaganda [3] ought not to be allowed, as it is directly contrary to the will of Parliament, and hampers the maintenance of resistance to the enemy. I do not see why, if Mosley is confined, subversives and Communists should not be equally confined. The law and the regulations ought to be enforced against those who hamper our war effort, whether from the extreme Right or the extreme Left. That is the position which the Conservative Party adopt, and I think it is a very strong one, and one of which the country as a whole would approve. I know it is your wish to enforce an even justice, and if you bring the matter before the Cabinet I am sure you will receive full support. "Sauce for the goose is sauce for the gander!"

Prime Minister to General Ismay, for C.O.S. Committee   13.I.41.

I do not think it would be wise to attack these smaller islands of the Dodecanese. They are no use in themselves; they are not

[3] A Communist circular addressed to all active working men and women.

necessary for the attack upon the larger islands now that we hold Crete. Stirring up this quarter will put the enemy on their guard, and will bring about the disagreement between Greece and Turkey, which has become only too apparent as we have explored tentatively this subject. The Defence Committee have not approved these operations.

Prime Minister to Dominions Secretary   17.I.41.

I have read these two documents, which do not seem to me to add very much to what we already know or what is obvious in the existing Southern Irish situation. The strategic position has been repeatedly examined, and the Admiralty have a paper on the urgent need for the Irish bases, as well as for airfields on the south and west coasts. I am asking General Ismay to see that this information is placed before you.

I do not consider that it is at present true to say that possession of these bases is vital to our survival. The lack of them is a grievous injury and impediment to us. More than that it would not at present be true to say. I could not, however, give the assurance suggested by Mr. Dillon that in no circumstances should we "violate Irish neutrality." I do not personally recognise Irish neutrality as a legal act. Southern Ireland having repudiated the Treaty, and we not having recognised Southern Ireland as a Sovereign State, that country is now in an anomalous position. Should the danger to our war effort through the denial of the Irish bases threaten to become mortal, which is not the case at present, we should have to act in accordance with our own self-preservation and that of our Cause. Meanwhile the policy which we recently decided on should be carried out as you are doing, and the influence of the United States must be invoked by every means open to us. It is possible that Mr. Hopkins, with whom I have had long talks, will himself visit Ireland, and I am of opinion that his visit might be useful. I do not think the time is ripe yet for you to visit Ireland, unless you receive a direct invitation from Mr. de Valera. It would be better to see how the economic and shipping pressures work. At any time the slow movements of events in Ireland may be violently interrupted by a German descent, in which case with or without an invitation we should have to go to turn out the invaders. For the present therefore I see no policy other than the one we have recently adopted.

Prime Minister to Foreign Secretary   18.I.41.

If you approve I should like Livorno to be called in the English—Leghorn; and Istanbul in English—Constantinople. Of course, when speaking or writing Turkish we can use the Turkish name; and if at any time you are conversing agreeably with Mussolini in Italian, Livorno would be correct.

And why is Siam buried under the name of Thailand?

(*Action this day.*)
Prime Minister to General Ismay, for C.O.S. Committee   19.I.41.
and Home Secretary

Many and increasing indications point to the early use of gas against us. The Armed Forces have been kept fully abreast of these possibilities, and are accustomed to use their masks and eye-shields. It would be well however to issue renewed instructions to all Commands, and also to consider whether any new filter is required for possible new toxic gases.

Let me have a report on this (one page).

2. But what is the condition of the gas masks in the hands of the civil population? Have they been overhauled regularly? Very few people carry masks nowadays. Is there any active system of gas training? It appears that the whole of this has become extremely urgent. Let me have an early report of the present position, and what is being done to bring it up to full efficiency. This report should also cover the decontamination system, and staffs.

3. Finally, it is important that nothing should appear in the newspapers, or be spoken on the B.B.C., which suggests that we are making a fuss about anti-gas arrangements, because the enemy will only use this as part of his excuse, saying that we are about to use it on him. I am of opinion nevertheless that a nation-wide effort must be made.

Prime Minister to Commander-in-Chief, Home Forces   20.I.41.

How would you propose to deal with a limited number of large amphibian tanks which got ashore and roamed about? Am I right in supposing that your light forces would surround them and follow them about at the closest quarters, preventing the crews from refueling or getting food and sleep, or from ever leaving the armour of their vehicles? If, say, not more than forty of these tanks came ashore, would they be followed and hunted to death in this manner, apart from anything that artillery, mines, and tank traps could do?

Anyhow, please let me know what would be your plan.

Prime Minister to Lord President of the Council   21.I.41.

I see that deliveries of coal to London during recent weeks have been running at 250,000 tons per week. It appears, if the Mines Department's estimates of requirements are correct, that there will be a shortage unless 410,000 tons a week are delivered from now until the end of March.

I should be glad to know whether you agree with the estimates of the Mines Department, and, if so, what steps you propose to take to increase deliveries by the required amount. I find it hard to understand why deliveries by rail during the last three months should have fallen to only three-fifths of last year's figure.

Prime Minister to Minister of Health   21.I.41.

Is it not possible to reduce more rapidly the number of homeless people in the London rest centres? I am hoping that this week will show that they have practically all been dispersed. One cannot tell when another heavy attack may not be made upon us, and a quiet week should be a precious gain.

Prime Minister to General Ismay, for C.O.S. Committee   22.I.41

I should like to feel sure that the Chiefs of Staff have carefully considered whether this operation against the Lofoten Islands [4] is likely to stir up the Norwegian coast and lead to reinforcements of the German forces in the peninsula. It seems to me that as the attack is on islands, and obviously connected with blockade measures, this danger is obviated. There would be no need to go on to the mainland, as I understand the operation.

Pray advise me.

Prime Minister to C.A.S., First Sea Lord, and Fifth Sea   23.I.41.
Lord
(Copy sent to First Lord and Secretary of State for Air.)

I wish to draw your attention to the prime importance of arranging as speedily as possible for a dozen or more Grumman Martletts or converted Brewsters being embarked upon aircraft-carriers operating in the Mediterranean. I have pressed for this for some time, and now the C.-in-C. Mediterranean, 824, says quite definitely that "Fulmars are really not fast enough." It is absolutely necessary to have a comparatively small number of really fast fighter aircraft on our carriers. Without these the entire movement of our ships is hampered. I am well aware of the difficulties of non-folding wings, absence of arresting hooks, etc., but I cannot easily believe that they cannot be solved before April.

I beg that you will give your earnest consideration to antedating this. Even if only a small number could be supplied you would gain an important relief and advantage. Surely a few dozen could be converted to folding wings by hand-labour as a special job.

I am not satisfied that the urgency and significance of this comparatively small change is realised.

Prime Minister to Minister of Supply   23.I.41.

Rifles, New. Since August the production of rifles has fallen off as follows: August, 9586; September, 8320; October, 7545; November, 4363; December, 4743 (mainly from existing stocks of component parts).

I understand that this fall is due to raids on Small Health, Birm-

---

[4] A highly successful raid was carried out in the Lofoten Islands in northern Norway on March 4, 1941, by two Commandos. Important enemy supplies and much shipping were destroyed, two hundred German prisoners taken and 314 Norwegian volunteers brought safely out.

In a second raid, carried out December 26, the port was again occupied temporarily by our forces.

ingham, which completely stopped production. Pray inform me
what progress has been made towards resuming production.

2. *A.A. Mountings*, 3.7-inch. Production of 3.7-inch A.A. mountings, which control the assembly of equipment, was at the rate of
about eighty per month in September, October, and November. In
December however it was down to 67 per cent, which I am informed is a repercussion of the raids on Birmingham and Coventry.
How will the forecasts of deliveries be affected?

Prime Minister to General Ismay, for C.O.S. Committee   26.I.41.

I was much concerned when I visited Dover on Friday to find
the slow and halting progress in the installation of the latest and
best batteries.

(*a*) Some guns which are ready mounted cannot be brought into
action because ancillary material, such as sights and control instru-
ments, has not been delivered. A suggestion of the Controller indicated that these guns could be brought into action quickly by the
intelligent improvisation of simple means of control, workable, although not so technically satisfying as those to be supplied eventually.

(*b*) Some guns cannot be completed for action owing to delay
in the work involved in anchoring the mountings, reasons given for
this being lack of shuttering timbers for concreting, inefficient labour, and the weather.

As regards (*a*), the attached Progress Report shows the situation,
and it is difficult to escape the conclusion that there is a lack of initiative on the spot when such a bald statement as "no dates given
for delivery" is accepted.

As regards (*b*), the lack of the necessary facilities for progress
seems to demand some immediate action, while the labour position
might be referred to the Ministry of Labour.

I was informed that all the causes of delay had been reported
through the "usual channels," but as far as those on the spot were
aware nothing very much seems to have happened. It would seem
best therefore to start from the other end of the "usual channels"
and sound backwards to find where the delay in dealing with the
matter has occurred.

I gathered from Admiral Ramsay that in his opinion the lack of
drive behind this work was due to the fact that no one senior officer
seemed to regard the whole matter as his personal interest, although
several, somewhat less senior, were active in their own particular
spheres.

The Controller said that he could deal with the two points raised
about deficiencies in ammunition—i.e., shortage of 5.5-inch fuzes
and 6-inch cartridges—but the report of this too seems to be
grounded in mid-"usual channels."

The completion of these batteries is of the utmost urgency, and
I request the Chiefs of Staff to give all the necessary instructions
and to call for a weekly report to be forwarded to me.

Prime Minister to Dominions Secretary   31.I.41.

I agree with the general line of your talk [with Mr. Dulanty]. I could in no circumstances give the guarantee asked for, and for the reasons you state.

About arms. If we were assured that it was Southern Ireland's intention to enter the war, we would of course, if possible beforehand, share our anti-aircraft weapons with them, and make secretly with them all possible necessary arrangements for their defence. Until we are so satisfied we do not wish them to have further arms, and certainly will not give them ourselves.

The concession about Lough Swilly is important and shows the way things are moving. No attempt should be made to conceal from Mr. de Valera the depth and intensity of feeling against the policy of Irish neutrality. We have tolerated and acquiesced in it, but juridically we have never recognised that Southern Ireland is an independent Sovereign State, and she herself has repudiated Dominion status. Her international status is undefined and anomalous. Should the present situation last till the end of the war, which is unlikely, a gulf will have opened between Northern and Southern Ireland which it will be impossible to bridge in this generation.

FEBRUARY

Prime Minister to Minister of Economic Warfare   1.II.41.
(Copies to Chancellor of the Exchequer, Minister of Supply.)

You have no doubt been considering what we can do to prevent Germany obtaining supplies of copper, in view of the fact that although she may be able to substitute aluminium, she may well become subject to a severe stringency in the two metals taken together.

I understand that considerable excess capacity exists in the South American copper mines. I am told that we have no evidence that copper has proceeded from South America to Germany, but that last year South America exported about 70,000 tons to Russia and 150,000 tons to Japan, whose stocks are estimated at a year's consumption. As soon as Germany exhausts her stocks, it is obvious that she will make every effort to obtain South American copper, and it is vital to take measures in advance to prevent Japan and Russia building stocks and to prevent Germany obtaining access to the surplus capacity which exists in Chile.

Apparently we are importing about 600,000 tons of copper from Canada, Rhodesia, South Africa, and the Belgian Congo. As these sources are under our control we should be able to divert purchases to South America without danger that Germany would obtain supplies from the sources we gave up.

I understand that you have been giving consideration to this problem, and that the Treasury is doubtful if the expenditure of dollars on preemptive purchase is justifiable. Will you let me have a report on your plans?

Prime Minister to General Ismay, for C.O.S. Committee   2.II.41.

"Marie" [Jibouti] might be an operation of the greatest value. The Senegalese should not be sent into Abyssinia, but should be kept till the Foreign Legion battalion arrives. Where would they be kept, and how?

One must consider that at any moment Weygand might move our way, in which case the Free French troops could go into Jibouti to animate the converted garrison, and even begin operations against the Italians.

Another favourable situation might be reached if, as a consequence of our advance in Eritrea, the British forces were able to get into touch with the French colony at Jibouti. Anyhow, with these favourable possibilities in the wind it would be a great pity not to keep our Free French force in hand. As for the political consequences, they can only be judged a few days before launching operations.

Prime Minister to Secretary of State for War   4.II.41.

Please see the *Times* of February 4. Is it really true that a seven-mile cross-country run is enforced upon all in this division, from generals to privates? Does the Army Council think this a good idea? It looks to me rather excessive. A colonel or a general ought not to exhaust himself in trying to compete with young boys running across country seven miles at a time. The duty of officers is no doubt to keep themselves fit, but still more to think for their men, and to take decisions affecting their safety or comfort. Who is the general of this division, and does he run the seven miles himself? If so, he may be more useful for football than war. Could Napoleon have run seven miles across country at Austerlitz? Perhaps it was the other fellow he made run. In my experience, based on many years' observation, officers with high athletic qualifications are not usually successful in the higher ranks.

Prime Minister to General Ismay, for Secretary of   4.II.41.
State for War and C.I.G.S.
(Copy to C.-in-C. Home Forces.)

The statement that one division could not be transferred from Great Britain to Ireland in less than eleven days, no matter how great the emergency nor how careful the previous preparations, is one which deserves your earnest attention. When we remember the enormous numbers which were moved from Dunkirk to Dover and the Thames last May under continued enemy attack, it is clear that the movement of personnel cannot be the limiting factor. The problem is therefore one of the movement of the artillery and vehicles. This surely deserves special study. Let me see the exact programme which occupies the eleven days, showing the order in which men, guns, and vehicles will embark. This would show perhaps that, say, nine-tenths of the division might come into action in much less than eleven days. Or, again, a portion of the mechanical transport, stores, and even some of the artillery, including Bren-gun carriers, might be found from reserves in this country and sent to Ireland in advance, where they would be none the less a reserve for us, assuming no need in Ireland arose. Surely now that we have the time some ingenuity might be shown in shortening this period of eleven days to move fifteen thousand fighting men from one well-equipped port to another—the voyage taking only a few hours. If necessary some revision of the scale of approved establishments might be made in order to achieve the high tactical object of a more rapid transference and deployment.

We must remember that in the recent training exercise "Victor" five German divisions, two of which were armoured and one motorised, were [supposed to be] landed in about forty-eight hours in the teeth of strenuous opposition, not at a port with quays and cranes, but on the open beaches. If we assume that the Germans can do this, or even half of it, we must contrast this with the statement of the eleven days required to shift one division from the Clyde to Belfast. We have also the statement of the Chiefs of Staff Committee that it would take thirty days to land one British division unopposed alongside the quays and piers of Tangier. Perhaps the officers who worked out the landings of the Germans under "Victor" could make some suggestion for moving this division into Ireland via Belfast without taking eleven days about it. Who are the officers who worked out the details that this move will take eleven days? Would it not be wise to bring them into contact with the other officers who landed these vast numbers of Germans on our beaches so swiftly and enabled whole armoured divisions and motorized troops to come into full action in forty-eight hours?

Evidently it would be wiser to keep open the option of moving this division as long as possible, and in order to do this we must have the best plan worked out to bring the largest possible portion of the division into action in Ireland in the shortest possible time. I am not prepared to approve the transfer of the division until this inquiry has been made. There must be an effort to reconcile the evident discrepancies as between what we assume the enemy can do and what in fact we can do ourselves.

Prime Minister to Home Secretary   5.II.41.

I think it would be wrong to use soldiers or men of military age for smoke-protection purposes. You ought to try to do your best with overage volunteers, or women or young persons. Pressure upon effective manpower will be very heavy in the near future. I could not support your claim to the War Office as at present advised.

(Action this day.)
Prime Minister to First Lord and First Sea Lord   5.II.41.

A number of convoys with most important munition cargoes are now approaching. I know what your stresses are, and I feel sure you will make every effort possible.

2. We have now the gift announced of 250,000 more rifles and 50,000,000 rounds—.300. To get this here quickly and safely is a prime object. Pray go into the matter with others concerned and let me know what is possible. I cannot bear to see more than 50,000 rifles or 10,000,000 rounds in any one ship. Less if possible.

Prime Minister to Minister of Agriculture   6.II.41.

I observe that you fear that anything up to 500,000 tons of Northern Ireland potatoes may have to be destroyed as unsaleable, the heavy decline in pig population having limited the stock-feeding outlet.

I notice that you held out hopes to the fifth meeting of the Food Policy Committee, but only gave definite proposals in regard to 200,000 tons, which only goes halfway to meet the problem.

It seems a great pity that there should have been this great reduction in the number of pigs owing to the fear of shortage of feeding stuffs, if there really is this large surplus. I trust that some way will be found of utilising it. We cannot afford in these days to throw away hundreds of thousands of tons of edible material.

Prime Minister to C.A.S.   6.II.41.

Some time ago we asked Greece to prepare airfields for fourteen squadrons, and this work is still going on. Then, after various interchanges, you proposed sending ten squadrons to Turkey, which the Turks have not yet accepted, but which they may accept. The President has cut short his journey on my message. Suppose they do accept, and after that Greece demands further aid beyond the five squadrons allotted, what are you going to do? I am afraid you have got to look at this very seriously. I am in it with you up to the neck. But have we not in fact promised to sell the same pig to two customers? We might have a legal quibble about the word "promise," but I think we have got to look into this matter rather more deeply than that. Let me know what you feel about it and what you think can be done.

Nothing was said about time or priority, so we have that to veer and haul on.

(Action this day.)
Prime Minister to Minister of Shipping   11.II.41.

Is it true that the steamship *New Toronto*, which arrived at Liverpool, was ordered to proceed north-about to London, and is it true that this order was only cancelled as a result of the protest of the captain, who pointed out the enormous value of the cargo, which contained, *inter alia*, 19,677 sub-machine guns and 2,456,000 cartridges? The arrival of these ships with large consignments of invaluable munitions ought to receive your personal attention in every case.

Pray give me a report. I attach my copy of the expected arrivals, on which I always follow the movements of these important cargoes. The ship referred to is on page 5.

Prime Minister to First Lord and First Sea Lord   12.II.41.

I should be glad to have a report every three days on the state of the *Furious*. Night and day work is required to fit her for her duties, which are of the highest urgency.

Prime Minister to Foreign Office   12.II.41.

We have made Weygand great offers, to which we have had no reply. It is clear that he will be actuated only by forces set in motion by pressure of Nazis on Vichy. Our attitude at the present time should not be one of appeal to him. Until he has answered through some channel or other the telegram I sent him, he ought not to be given supplies. Not one scrap of nobility or courage has been shown by these people so far, and they had better go on short commons till they come to their senses.

The policy of occasional blockade should be enforced as naval means are available.

(*Action this day.*)
Prime Minister to General Ismay and Sir E. Bridges   12.II.41.

I see a new marking [on telegrams] "Officers Only." I do not think this is suitable, considering how many people who are not officers must be privy to the most secret matters. I should like to know the reasons which have led up to starting this, but at present I am entirely unconvinced that it should continue.

Prime Minister to Lord President of the Council   12.II.41.

There is too much truth in what Doctor Burgin says [in his letter of complaint about the State as an employer] for him to be put off by the usual official grimace. I suggest that you see him and deal with his proposition. I hear a great many cases where the Government absolutely fail to pay individuals what is admittedly their due. It seems to me that Doctor Burgin's letter might prove a very good peg for you to hang a real stirring-up of these departments upon. When one is in office one has no idea how damnable things can feel to the ordinary rank and file of the public. Doctor Burgin is a very able man and has experience. Could you not draw him out and see what suggestions he has to make, and also what examples he has to give of the shortcomings which I fear with too much justice he alleges?

Prime Minister to Minister of Supply, for Import Executive 14.II.41.

I am very anxious to send a complete infantry division, with their guns and essential vehicles, to the Middle East in Convoy W.S.7. The men can be fitted in by displacing others, but the guns and vehicles will require extra ships. I am told that eight mechanical transport ships will be wanted over and above those required to carry the four hundred and fifty vehicles which the War Office already wish to send in the convoy.

I understand that loading would have to start about February 21 if these ships are to arrive in Egypt at the same time or shortly after the convoy. Pray consider how these eight ships could be found, and let me have a report of what can be done and at what cost in imports, but take no action in the meanwhile.

Prime Minister to A.C.I.G.S.   15.II.41.

From your account one would think that everything was going on splendidly, and that no ground for complaint existed [about the Dover defences]. But this was certainly not the opinion of the responsible officers I met on the spot. I was distressed by the vigour of their complaints, and the evident feeling behind them. Let me have a report each week from the Commander of the Corps Coast Artillery, and let it pass through your office, with any comments you may wish to make.

Prime Minister to Sir Edward Bridges   15.II.41.
(Circulate to War Cabinet and Service Ministers only, by my special directions.)

We went through all this [vulnerability of Whitehall to air attack] last September, and came to the conclusion that we could fight it out in London. Meanwhile, many improvements have been made, although the buildings are far from secure. The difficulties of moving are very great indeed, but certainly the alternative citadels should be brought to a live state of readiness by March 1. I have been concerned that there is no kind of protection for G.H.Q. Home Forces except that afforded by the fairly strong structure of the building in which they live.

How many bombs have been thrown within a thousand yards of the Central War Room? I do not myself agree that no serious attempt has been made, but we should certainly be prepared for a new assault with two thousand- and even five thousand-pound bombs.

More speed and energy should be put into covering G.H.Q.

Prime Minister to Minister of Economic Warfare   16.II.41.
(Minister of Information to see.)

I agree about co-ordinated leaflets [for propaganda in France and Belgium], but all depends upon an intimate liaison between you and the Ministry of Information on the one hand and de Gaulle on the other. We must not tie de Gaulle up too tightly. We have never received the slightest good treatment or even courtesy from Vichy, and the Free French movement remains our dominant policy. I am sure if you consult with de Gaulle or his people all will be satisfactory. I think he is much the best Frenchman now in the arena, and I want him taken care of as much as possible.

(Action this day.)
Prime Minister to Secretary of State for War   17.II.41.
and V.C.I.G.S.

I do not think it is desirable to move this division [to Northern Ireland], especially in view of the possibilities of our sending the 50th away.

2. Meanwhile, plans should be worked out to procure the necessary acceleration should a move become indispensable. These plans should include: (*a*) A reconsideration of the Admiralty objections to using the Mersey as well as the Clyde. Are there no smaller ports from which embarkation could be made? (*b*) Would it not be possible to arrange the move on the basis of a precautionary period of four days in which additional M.T. ships could be assembled? (*c*) The objections about moving part of the vehicles deserve further study. For instance, the troops might have issued to them an additional quantity of transport while in England to break it in, and then either this or the old could be sent to Ireland. I cannot believe that there is no floating reserve of transport capable of providing for such a small need as this. A little combing-out and tightening-up of the Mechanical Transport depots, Slough, etc., would certainly yield what is required.

3. We must not be content with anything less than a saving of five days out of the eleven during which the division will be out of action on both sides of the Channel. This period must be shortened to six days, but a reasonable precautionary notice might be expected.

Prime Minister to Secretary of State for War   17.II.41.

I deeply regret the whole story of this fine body of men [the Cavalry Division in Palestine], and that the War Office can devise nothing better than to bring them all home in June to begin a training which will keep them so long out of effective action.

What exactly does the C.I.G.S. mean by "late autumn"?

Meanwhile, the division will have to render whatever service is necessary in guarding the Suez Canal, maintaining order, etc., or, if necessary, escorting prisoners, so as to liberate British battalions for active service.

The 1st Cavalry Division was redesignated 10th Armoured Division on July 23, 1941, but it did not appear in the field for a long time. Its tanks were taken from it during the spring of 1942 to replace the battle losses of the 1st and 7th Armoured Divisions. In August, 1942, its Headquarters and one brigade (8th) went up to the front and took part in the battle of Alam Halfa. The other brigade (9th) came up later and was attached to the New Zealand Division, taking part in the Alamein battle.

Prime Minister to General Ismay   17.II.41.

What are the arrangements in British Columbia for dealing with the Japanese colony there should Japan attack? The matter is of course for the Canadian Government, but it would be interesting to know whether adequate forces are available in that part of the Dominion. About thirty years ago, when there were anti-Japanese riots, the Japanese showed themselves so strong and so well organised as to be able to take complete control.

Prime Minister to Foreign Office   17.II.41.

I regard these developments [about appointment of Admiral Darlan as successor to Marshal Pétain] with misgiving and distrust. We have received nothing but ill-treatment from Vichy. It would have been better to have had Laval, from our point of view, than Darlan, who is a dangerous, bitter, ambitious man, without the odium which attaches to Laval. I think it is important at the moment to be stiff with these people, and to assert the blockade whenever our ships are available. In the meantime an end should be put to the cold-shouldering of General de Gaulle and the Free French movement, who are the only people who have done anything for us, and to whom we have made very solemn engagements. The emphasis should be somewhat shifted.

Please also see in this connection my telegram to the President.

Prime Minister to Sir Alexander Cadogan   17.II.41.

Please draw attention again to Mr. Eden's injunction against the length of telegrams sent to the Foreign Office by their representative abroad.

The zeal and efficiency of a diplomatic representative is measured by the quality and not by the quantity of the information he supplies. He is expected to do a good deal of filtering for himself, and not simply to pour out upon us over these congested wires all the contradictory gossip which he hears. So much is sent that no true picture can be obtained. One cannot see the wood for the trees. There is no harm in sending "background" on by bag.

Prime Minister to C.O.S. Committee, Secretary of State   17.II.41.
for War, and V.C.I.G.S.

The term "division" must not become a stumbling-block. A division is a tactical unit of all arms for use in its integrity against the enemy. Divisions are joined together to form corps, armies, and groups of armies, with appropriate troops for the larger formations. These characteristics do not arise where there is no prospect of using a division in its integrity, or as a part of a larger formation. Although for administrative purposes a divisional command may be bestowed upon a number of troops equal to a division, who have special duties assigned to them, this should not mislead us.

2. We speak, for instance, of a "division" in Iceland, but it would be absurd to treat this division as similar to those which would operate against the Germans. We now know what this division has got to do, and how it is distributed. It is divided into the garrisons of several posts at landing-places in a considerable country, and no

doubt should have a number of mobile columns which can rapidly proceed to any threatened spot. Its artillery and extra divisional troops and lines of communication services should be organised and accounted for on a scale suited to the actual task of these troops in Iceland. It should properly be called "the Iceland Force," and would in no way resemble the conventional establishment of a division. It might want more of one thing and less of another.

3. The African Colonial divisions ought not surely to be called divisions at all. No one contemplates them standing in the line against a European army. They comprise a large body of West and East African riflemen organised in battalions, and here and there, largely for administrative purposes, in brigades. We can now expect that the Italians will in a few months be liquidated in Northeast Africa. What enemy then will oppose these three African Colonial divisions? Anyone who knows these vast countries can see that these African "divisions" will be distributed in small posts and garrisons, with a number of mobile columns comprising armoured cars, etc. The idea of their being supplied with divisional and corps artillery, together with a share of the lines of communication troops on the British scale, is not sensible. They cannot be used so far north as Libya on account of the cold. We cannot contemplate holding down Abyssinia once it has been "liberated." Indeed, one imagines the whole of Northeast Africa returning very rapidly to peacetime conditions. Therefore, I cannot accept these three African Colonial divisions as such. They are, indeed, only miscellaneous units of the African Defence Force.

Prime Minister to Minister of Transport   18.II.41.

I am shocked to learn that those who had to take the decision to unload or divert the *New Toronto* were ignorant of the cargo which she carried. I always keep check myself personally of the approaching ships which are carrying large consignments of munitions. Do you not get these lists in good time, and do you not yourself personally watch over the fate of these vitally important cargoes? If not, please make arrangements to do so, and report to me when these arrangements are made and what they are.

Prime Minister to V.C.I.G.S. and Director of   17.II.41.
Military Operations

General Wavell has thirty-one British Regular battalions, of which, as far as I can make out, only about fifteen are incorporated in divisional formations. Pray correct me if I am wrong. It is indeed astonishing that he should be put to these straits to find a few battalions for Crete and Malta. If the West African Brigade were transferred from Kenya to Freetown, two British battalions now degenerating there could come forward to the Nile Army.

The use of three battalions to escort prisoners to India, the whole Yeomanry and Regular Cavalry Division unemployed in Palestine, large numbers of Australian troops for which we are told there is no equipment on the Regular scale of establishment, the Polish Brigade, the drafts awaiting incorporation in units which have not yet suffered any casualties—all these are large resources if ingeniously and economically used.

Are there any British battalions in East Africa?

Please give me your aid in the study of these aspects.

Prime Minister to Minister of Labour and National Service 20.II.41. *(Copy to Minister of Supply.)*

We are very short of ammunition. Production is held up entirely on account of filling, which in turn is held up on account of labour. With our present factories we could increase the ammunition output two-and-a-half-fold by mid-May if we could provide the labour to run them.

The additional labour required is:

	By March 31	By Mid-May
Skilled males	340	940
Other males	9,100	20,100
Females	22,500	40,900
Total (say)	32,000	62,000

Please inform me what difficulties stand in the way of providing this labour and what measures are being taken to overcome them.

Prime Minister to Minister of Supply   20.II.41.

It is satisfactory that arrangements have now been made to link the shipping figures more closely to those on which plans for consumption will be based.

Meanwhile, it appears that the rate of delivery of steel to consumers during the first five weeks of the current quarter has been no higher than during the last three quarters, despite the greater need.

I understand that imports of steel during the last seven months have been equivalent to 2.3 million finished tons and output to 5.1 million finished tons, while deliveries to consumers have been only 6.1 million finished tons. Would not the position be greatly relieved if some of this apparent excess of 1.3 million tons could be made available for consumption?

I see that imports of iron ore continue ahead of programme, while steel and other commodities lag behind. This seems strange in view of the shipping situation.

Prime Minister to Secretary for Petroleum   21.II.41.

The very low imports of oil previously reported for the week ended January 11 have remained low, amounting to only half what they were in January last year, and covering only half the consumption.

I trust steps are being taken to draw as much oil as possible from America, thus avoiding the long pull from the Persian Gulf round the Cape. It should be possible to arrange with the American producers for their customers in the East to be supplied from the Persian Gulf, Burma, and the Netherlands East Indies in return for a corresponding amount of oil being delivered to us, some arrangement being made to retain good-will.

Prime Minister to Prime Minister of Canada   21.II.41.

I was delighted to read your speech in the Canadian House of Commons on February 17. You are quite right to prepare men's minds for a coming shock of extreme severity. It is a comfort to think how much better prepared we are than in the autumn.

Let me also tell you how encouraged everyone here was by the strong array of facts which you brought together when broadcasting on February 2. Your ships and planes are doing great work here. The air-training scheme is one of the major factors, and possibly the decisive factor, in the war. Your plans for the Army are of enormous help. I lunched with McNaughton last week, and had very good talks with him and his principal officers about the Canadian Corps. They lie in the key positions of our National Defence. The Secretary of State for War, who is with me now, wishes to endorse all this, and sends his kindest regards.

What a pleasure it is to see the whole Empire pulling as one man, and believe me, my friend, I understand the reasons for your success in marshalling the great war effort of Canada.

Prime Minister to Secretary of State for War   22.II.41.

The approved scale of the Army is fifty-five divisions plus one additional South African division, and minus, in my opinion, three African Colonial divisions; total tactical divisional units, fifty-three, of which eleven are to be armoured. I see no reason to alter this target at the present time.

2. During the next six months only 130,000 men are required by the Army, and the Minister of Labour is ready to supply 150,000. Would it not be prudent to take a decision governing the six months only, and review the position in four months' time, when we shall know more of the scale and character of the fighting?

3. Will you kindly give me your views upon the Minister of Labour's paper, and also some notes prepared for me by Professor Lindemann, which are to be treated as private. I am very much inclined to a greater development of armoured divisions than we have now, but it is not necessary to take a decision at the present time, as tanks and tank guns, not personnel, are the bottleneck.

4. You may count on me to sustain the Army in every possible way, provided I am convinced that it will comb itself.

Prime Minister to Sir A. Cadogan   23.II.41.

All this goes to show that we should continue to give increasing support to General de Gaulle. I cannot believe that the French nation will give their loyalty to anyone who reaches the head of the State because he is thought well of by the Germans. We should reason patiently with Washington against giving any food to un-occupied France or North Africa. For this purpose all the unsatis-factory feeling about the Vichy-Weygand scene should be in the hands of our Ambassador in Washington. I am sure Darlan is an ambitious crook. His exposure and Weygand's weakness will both, as they become apparent, enure to the credit of de Gaulle.

Prime Minister to V.C.I.G.S.   25.II.41.

Let me know what older guns they have in India now, and how many of each nature. I should like the new regiments which are forming out there to train on the twenty-five-pounders, but actually to have available for local purposes enough of the older unconverted eighteen-pounders. I presume also that the old regiments of artil-lery in India not to be included in the artillery of the four divisions have also got their regular complements of guns.

Are there any reserves of guns of the older natures in India?

Prime Minister to General Ismay   26.II.41.

Let me know the field state and ration strength of the troops in Malaya and of the garrison at Singapore, showing what military formations there are.

(Action this day.)
Prime Minister to First Lord and First Sea Lord   28.II.41.

City of Calcutta, due Lock Ewe March 2, is reported to be going to Hull, arriving March 9. This ship must on no account be sent to the East Coast. It contains 1700 machine guns, forty-four aeroplane engines, and no fewer than 14,000,000 cartridges. These cartridges are absolutely vital to the defence of Great Britain, which has been so largely confided by the Navy to the Army and the Air. That it should be proposed to send such a ship round to the East Coast, with all the additional risk, is abominable. I am sending a copy of this minute to the Minister of Transport.

Another ship now of great importance is the *Euriades,* due Liver-pool March 3. She has over 9,000,000 cartridges.

I shall be glad to receive special reports as to what will be done about both these ships.

MARCH

Prime Minister to Secretary of State for War   1.III.41.

I am relieved to hear that the 250,000 rifles and the 50,000,000 rounds of ammunition have arrived safely with the Canadian troop convoy. When I raised the point of getting the Admiralty to give up the .303 rifles and take the American .300 in exchange, it was pro-posed to me on other papers that a very much larger and better change was possible by giving the newly arrived American rifles to the static troops in Great Britain, thus liberating 250,000 .303's for the Regular Army. I presume this will now be done. On the last occasion when we got the American rifles across we made a regular evolution of it, and had special trains waiting, and the like. I now hope you will make a rapid evolution of this new windfall, so that the weapons are in the hands of those who need them at the earliest moment.

Perhaps you will let me know what arrangements are being made.

Prime Minister to Secretary of State for the Colonies   1.III.41.

General Wavell, like most British military officers, is strongly pro-Arab. At the time of the licences to the shipwrecked illegal immigrants being permitted, he sent a telegram not less strong than this, predicting widespread disaster in the Arab world, together with the loss of the Basra-Bagdad-Haifa route. The telegram should be looked up, and also my·answer, in which I overruled the General and explained to him the reasons for the Cabinet decision. All went well, and not a dog barked.

It follows from the above that I am not in the least convinced by all this stuff. The Arabs, under the impression of recent victories, would not make any trouble now. However, in view of the "Lustre" [Greek] policy I do not wish General Wavell to be worried now by lengthy arguments about matters of no military consequence to the immediate situation. Therefore, Doctor Weizmann should be told that the Jewish Army project must be put off for six months, but may be reconsidered again in four months. The sole reason given should be lack of equipment.

Prime Minister to Minister of Home Security, Minister of   7.III.41.
Information, and Secretary of State for Air

For the last two months there has been a great decline in air raids, and I do not see why the carefully considered method by which we got through the period July-November, inclusive, should be now cast aside. I am not aware of any "depressing effect" produced upon the public morale, and as a matter of fact I thought they were settling down very well to the job. I should therefore, as at present advised, strongly deprecate change in the practice which has carried us through a very severe (and now perhaps discarded) indiscriminate attack upon the civil population. Still more should I regret precise signals being given of the hits the enemy make on specific military targets. These are however my personal views, and I am quite agreeable to the whole matter being discussed again in Cabinet, should you think this necessary.[5]

Prime Minister to General Ismay   9.III.41.

I am thoroughly mystified about this operation [against Castelorizzo], and I think it is the duty of the Chiefs of Staff to have it probed properly. How was it that the Navy allowed these large reinforcements to be landed, when in an affair of this kind every-

[5] This is a reply to a minute from the Minister of Home Security, the Secretary of State for Air, and the Minister of Information about measures to check the spread of harmful rumours about air-raid casualties and damage.

thing depended upon the Navy isolating the island? It is necessary to clear this up, on account of impending and more important operations. One does not want to worry people who are doing so well for us in many ways and are at full extension, and yet it is indispensable for our success that muddles of this kind should not be repeated.[6]

Prime Minister to General Ismay   10.III.41.

Low-flying attack should only be a real danger on days of low cloud or mist, when our fighters cannot find the enemy. The use of aerial mines hung from small balloons should be considered for the defence of factories. Only twenty-pound lift is required, so that quite a small balloon should be sufficient. When this proposal was put forward for defending estuaries it was decided that a considerably greater altitude was required, so as to have a double-purpose defence, which has entailed the production of much larger balloons, which in turn require power winches, etc. We must be content with defence up to heights of one thousand or fifteen hundred feet by smaller, simpler balloons without power winches. On windy days they could be replaced by kites.

This method of defence is not desirable for aerodromes, since the balloons would all have to be hauled down when our own machines were taking off or landing. For the defence of aerodromes therefore rockets carrying mines into the air seem particularly suited.

(Action this day.)
Prime Minister to Minister of Information   10.III.41.

Obviously there are two conditions, districts where fighting is going on and districts where it is not. The words "stay put" are wholly inapplicable to the second class, which is by far the more numerous, probably ninety-nine one-hundredths of the country. For these districts the order should be "Carry on."

Neither is the expression "Stay put" really applicable to the districts where fighting is going on. First of all, it is American slang; secondly, it does not express the fact. The people have not been "put" anywhere. What is the matter with "Stand fast," or "Stand firm"? Of the two I prefer the latter. This is an English expression, and it says exactly what is meant by paragraph 3.

The paragraphs about destroying maps, etc., clearly apply only to the fighting areas. In the present context you might have a wholesale massacre of maps, motor-cars, and bicycles throughout the country.

You might begin like this: "If this Island is seriously invaded,

---

[6] Castelorizzo Island lies midway between Rhodes and Cyprus and forms a link in the chain reaching out from the Dodecanese towards Syria. A British Commando occupied this island on February 25 after slight opposition. The naval forces then withdrew to Cyprus without watching events. Later heavy air attacks developed and the enemy landed reinforcements, unopposed by our naval forces. It was necessary to abandon the island.

everyone in it will immediately receive orders either to 'Carry on' or to 'Stand firm.' In the vast majority of cases the order will be 'Carry on' as is set out in the first three paragraphs of the following paper. The order 'Stand firm' applies only to those districts where fighting is actually going on, and is intended to make sure that there will be no fugitives blocking the roads, and that everyone who has decided to stay in a likely area of attack, as, for instance, on the East and South Coasts, will 'Stand firm' in his dwelling or shelter till the enemy in the neighbourhood have been destroyed or driven out."

Prime Minister to Minister of Food   10.III.41.

Yours of March 8. Would you kindly let me know what will be the objects and duties of the Food Mission you propose to send to the United States. I am at this time actively considering sending Sir Arthur Salter there to expedite and animate the whole business of merchant shipbuilding. This is a process which requires continued effort and attention, as an enormous scheme of shipbuilding has to be set on foot in American yards. What has been done up to the present is less than half of what we need.

I do not however see food problems in the same plane as this. There is plenty of food in the United States, and with our dollar allocations we should be able to select wisely what to use in our tonnage. Why does this require a special mission?

I have been trying as much as possible to keep the missions to the United States as few as possible. However, I shall be very glad to hear what your reasons are.

Prime Minister to Secretary of State for War and others   10.III.41.

It is of the utmost importance that a clear and consistent picture of our requirements should be presented to the United States Administration, and that their efforts on our behalf should not be hampered by any doubts as to our vital needs and their order of priority.

I had occasion to deal with one aspect of this matter recently, when I directed that all statistical statements relating to our war effort intended for the United States Government should be co-ordinated centrally here and despatched through our Ambassador at Washington.

Another aspect of the same question has now been brought to my notice. Mr. Hopkins has reported that the Service attachés at the American Embassy in London are in the habit of sending messages, based on contacts with subordinate officers in the Service and Supply Departments in London, which may well differ from the case which is being put to the Navy and Army Departments in Washington. He quoted a case in which the Navy Department were being pressed to allot destroyers to us, and found themselves confronted with an expression of opinion of some anonymous officer in one of the Service Departments in London, conveyed through a

Service attaché of the United States Embassy in London, to the effect that it was no good hoping to cope with submarines by destroyers until we had more long-range fighters.

I should be glad if you would be good enough to take the necessary steps to ensure that officers in your department who are brought into contact with the staff of the American Embassy, and particularly with the Service attachés, do not express opinions which are likely to conflict with the views which are being urged on our behalf in Washington. These officers may not perhaps be aware that the views which they happen to express casually are liable to be reported to Washington. It would also seem important that officers who are in contact with the United States Service attachés should be acquainted in general terms with the nature of the requests which are being put from time to time to the United States Government in Washington, so that they may be on their guard against making remarks which would be inconsistent with those requests.

Prime Minister to Professor Lindemann   11.III.41.

I am expecting you to have ready for me tonight the general layout of the imports programme under different heads, so that I can see where I can scrape off with a pencil another half-million tons for food.

Prime Minister to C.A.S.   12.III.41.

I see accounts of Germans increasing their aerodrome accommodation in Northern France. I suppose our aerodromes in the southeast of the Island which we planned some time ago will now be coming steadily into use? Let me have a note on the augmentation which is in progress or has been achieved.

(Action this day.)
Prime Minister to C.A.S.   14.III.41.

The egg-layer pulled off another success last night. Only one was up, but it got its prey. I cannot understand how there has been this frightful delay in devising and making the release gear. More than three months seem to have been consumed upon a task so incomparably easier than many which are being solved. Failing any mechanical solution, why cannot a hole be cut in the floor of the aeroplane and a man lying on his stomach push by hand the eggs, which are about the size of a Stilton cheese, one after another through the hole? The spacing would not be absolutely regular, but it might be just as lucky. At any rate, I want to see this hold-up and hitch for myself. I could come to Northolt Aerodrome at four o'clock this afternoon, Friday, if you can arrange to have the people concerned on the spot. It would be very nice if you would come too, and spend the night at Chequers.

There is a new danger. Now that the Admiralty balloon barrage people have exposed the idea of the aerial mine and its wire, parachute, etc., the cutter may soon be coming along, and when we are at last ready we may be too late.

Surely now, when they seem to be turning onto the Mersey and the Clyde and will have to be working up to those fixed points, *now* is the time of all others for the egg-layers to reap their harvest.

Prime Minister to Secretary of State for Air   14.III.41.

Your programme [of R.A.F. expansion] assumed for these four months a loss [in pilots] of 1550, whereas actually 1229 was the figure. You have therefore saved 321 pilots, and your original estimate was 26 per cent on the safe side. This is satisfactory.

2. I always expected and repeatedly told you that there would be a marked falling-off in war activity during the winter months. This has always been so. Let me know what are your forecasts for the next four or six months, including March. The "postulates," as you like to call them, though "forecasts" seem more natural, are in any case only of academic interest, because we are making every pilot we can as fast as we can, and our programme is based on capacity, not assignment. None the less, one may just as well see what the possibilities are.

Prime Minister to General Ismay   15.III.41.

I agree that the 50th Division should go with W.S.8, and that that convoy should have additional ships provided to make sure that none of the essentials, apart from the 50th Division, which is to go in its integrity, are cut out. Let me know what this will involve, in extra drain on shipping.

(Action this day.)
Prime Minister to Controller, Admiralty   15.III.41.

Give me a report on the progress of the ships to carry and disgorge tanks. How many are there? What is their tonnage? How many tanks can they take in a flight? When will each one be ready? Where are they being built? What mark of tank can they carry?

Prime Minister to Foreign Office   15.III.41.

Being a strong monarchist, I am in principle in favour of constitutional monarchies as a barrier against dictatorships, and for many other reasons. It would be a mistake for Great Britain to try to force her systems on other countries, and this would only create prejudice and opposition. The main policy of the Foreign Office should however be to view with a benevolent eye natural movements among the populations of different countries towards monarchies. Certainly we should not hinder them, if we cannot help.

Prime Minister to Minister of Food   21.III.41.

I hope the term "Communal Feeding Centres" is not going to be adopted. It is an odious expression, suggestive of Communism and the workhouse. I suggest you call them "British Restaurants."

Everybody associates the word "restaurant" with a good meal, and they may as well have the name if they cannot get anything else.

(Action this day.)
Prime Minister to First Lord and First Sea Lord   21.III.41.

When I was at the Admiralty I repeatedly asked that more attention should be paid to the development of fuelling at sea. Now we find the German battle-cruisers are able to remain out for many weeks at a time without going into any base or harbour to replenish. If they can refuel at sea, it is a scandal that we cannot do so. Again and again our ships have to be called off promising hunts in order to go back to fuel, six or seven hundred miles away. The argument that the Germans can send their tankers where they know they will find them, when we never know what is going to happen, being on the defensive and not having the initiative, does not appeal to me. Arrangements should be made to have a few tankers in suitable positions off the usual routes, so that if our ships are operating as they are now they could call one of these up and make a rendezvous. The neglect of this principle of fuelling at sea is a grievous drag on the power of the Fleet. It is the duty of the Admiralty to solve the problem.

2. Even more painful is the fact that we are not apparently able to fuel our destroyers in the comparatively calm waters off the African coast. The spectacle of this big convoy now coming up from Sierra Leone having one or two ships sunk every day by a trailing U-boat, and now the battleship escort herself also being torpedoed, is most painful. Nothing can be more like "asking for it" than to have a battleship escort waddling along with a six-and-a-half-knot convoy without any effective anti-submarine escort (other than the three corvettes). The Sierra Leone convoys will have to have destroyers with them. Ships sunk in these waters are just as great a loss to us, and just as much a part of the Battle of the Atlantic, as if they are on the northwestern approaches. I am told that destroyers cannot go the distance. Why can they not be refuelled at sea, as has now been done, under pressure of events, for the corvettes? I am glad to hear about the air reinforcements. But destroyers are needed too. They must go all the way and be refuelled by the escort.

3. The whole question of the Cape Verde Islands being used as a German U-boat fuelling base must now be reviewed with a view to action being taken. I shall be glad to hear from you on all these points.

Prime Minister to First Lord of the Admiralty and   21.III.41.
Secretary of State for Air

The use of aeroplanes, not only to attack our ships, but also to direct the U-boats onto them, is largely responsible for our losses in the northwestern approaches. No effort to destroy the Focke-Wulfs should be spared. If we could employ radar methods to find their positions and to direct long-range fighters or shipborne aircraft to the attack we ought to be able to inflict serious casualties. Might it not be feasible to place a radar station on Rockall? However inconvenient and unpleasant, the geographical position appears to be so good that it would be worth making a great effort to maintain a station there, at any rate during the summer months. The hills south of Lough Erne would also offer a valuable site. It might be even better if we could find ways and means of establishing stations on Tory Island or on one of the islands off the Kerry coast. These islands might be leased privately by some wealthy American friends. Please let me have a report from the technical point of view on the military results which could be expected if any of these things could be done, and upon any other possibilities that have been, or might be, examined.

We should also study methods of disturbing the aircraft's communications with U-boats. I understand that the system is that the Focke-Wulf signals to Brest, whence directions are sent to the U-boat, the process taking about an hour and a half. Is it not practicable either to jam these communications or to confuse all concerned by a series of spurious messages? Presumably apparatus of the usual type for interfering with the Focke-Wulf's radio methods of navigation, which must be vital over the sea in bad weather, has not been neglected.

I assume that we D.F.[7] the signals he uses. If he uses A.S.V.[8] it should be practicable to locate and home on him with suitable apparatus.

(*Action this day.*)
Prime Minister to First Lord and First Sea Lord   22.III.41.

If the presence of the enemy battle-cruisers in a Biscayan port is confirmed, every effort by the Navy and the Air Force should be made to destroy them there, and for this purpose serious risks and sacrifices must be faced. If however unhappily they escape and resume their depredations, then action on the following lines would seem to be necessary, and should be considered even now:

In order to regain the initiative in the Atlantic, three hunting groups should be formed at earliest, namely: *Renown* and *Ark Royal, Hood* and *Furious, Repulse* and *Argus.* Each of these groups must have one or two tankers, and every device is to be used to enable them to refuel at sea. The tankers need not necessarily accompany the groups, but should be in positions where the groups could rendezvous with them.

2. The sea-front from Iceland to Cape Verde will be roughly divided into three sectors, in each of which one hunting group will normally be working. Although working independently of the convoys, they will give an additional measure of protection to convoys passing in their neighbourhood. These dispositions should be com-

[7] *D.F.*: Direction-finding equipment used to determine the direction of the source of a wireless signal.
[8] *A.S.V.*: Airborne radar.

pleted by the end of April, and will come into operation in instalments at earliest.

3. A plan will be made to replace *Furious* at earliest, by converting one or more ships as aircraft transports. At the same time the Air Ministry will arrange for increased crating to Takoradi.

4. Considering how far we have carried the dispersal of the Fleet on escort duty, no objection could be taken to using *Nelson* in place of *Hood*.

5. A flotilla must be found for the Freetown convoys. This can be achieved out of the remaining twenty-five American destroyers which will have to work up in this Southern area. Arrangements must be made to fuel the destroyers from the escort cruiser or battleships.

6. The evidences of German infiltration into the Cape Verde Islands, and the probability that they are being used to refuel U-boats, make it necessary to carry out Operation "Brisk" at the earliest date. Once we have got possession we must make a good refuelling base there, and expel the enemy's U-boat tenders from these islands. I will discuss separately the political pros and cons of this.

As many flying-boats as can be spared, up to six, should be employed in the Freetown area, and will also work from the islands when captured.

7. Pray let me have your thought on the above, together with all possible means of carrying it out.

Prime Minister to Professor Lindemann   22.III.41.

On the assumption that an [import] programme of thirty-five million tons is maintained, you should consider transferring in the least harmful manner 2 million tons from Ministry of Supply to Ministry of Food. If the thirty-five million tons is not realised, this transference must be reduced *pro rata*, but in any case the existing minimum requirements of food should be met. Make a sketch plan for me to discuss with Sir Andrew Duncan tomorrow night.

(*Action this day.*)
Prime Minister to General Ismay   23.III.41.

War Office and Middle East should be called upon for an exact account of all refrigerated meat ships they have requisitioned, and where and how these are at present employed. I have been told that some are used in the Middle East as depots for stores. Let me have a full list, distinguishing between vessels which have been heavily converted to troop carriers and those which could easily return to their normal duties.

Prime Minister to General Ismay, for C.O.S. Committee 23.III.41.
and Admiralty

Is it true that the War Office demand provision for eight gallons of water a day per man on a troopship, and that this has become a factor greatly reducing the numbers which can be taken? Has there been any impartial investigation of the War Office standards? I was much surprised to learn that only about three thousand five hundred men were taken in the *Queen Elizabeth* and the *Queen Mary* each. This is hardly more than the numbers they carry when engaged in luxury passenger service. If I remember rightly, over eight thousand men were sent in the *Aquitania* or *Mauretania* to the Dardanelles in May, 1915.

2. Could any saving in shipping be effected by transhipping personnel from the transports into the giant liners at Capetown? Now that the Red Sea will soon be clear of enemy submarines and aircraft, it would seem attractive to organise a fast service from Capetown. The matter should at any rate be examined.

Prime Minister to General Ismay   23.III.41.

Most of this is mere talk. What is the use, for instance, of saying that no demand has been made for cranes at the smaller ports when these smaller ports have not been used and so do not feel the pinch? Surely we ought to have facilities prepared both for unloading into lighters and coasters and for removing traffic from the small ports by improved land communications by road or rail. Let me have a list of the ports which could so be used, and let me have proposals for a minute, which I will thereafter draft, to procure effective action as a vital insurance. We have far too much at stake in the Clyde and Mersey.

For the purposes of this use any help you may require.

Prime Minister to the Maharaja Jam Sahib of Nawanagar 24.III.41

My colleagues and I are moved by the terms of the resolution passed by the Chamber of Princes of March 17, and I am specially touched by the generous reference to myself. His Majesty's Government in the United Kingdom gratefully recognise the valiant contribution which Indian troops have made to the Imperial victories in North Africa, and they well know that this contribution will increase still further in size and in scope as the months roll on. On behalf of my colleagues I ask Your Highness to express to the Chamber of Princes our appreciation of the resolute spirit with which the Princes and the peoples of India have shown themselves to be inspired.

Prime Minister to Dominions Secretary   25.III.41.

What is the point of worrying the Dominions with all this questionable stuff [about the likelihood of invasion]? Have they asked for such an appreciation? Surely the other side should be stated too, namely:

(1) That even if they make their original landings the communications to these lodgments will be interrupted by the Fleet inside a week.

(2) That we have every reason to believe that we can maintain

the superiority in the British daylight air, and that our bomber force will therefore "Namsos" all the landings by day as well as by night.

(3) That, apart from the beaches, we have the equivalent of nearly thirty divisions with one thousand tanks at April 1, held in reserve to be hurled at the different invasion points.

(4) That we have 1,600,000 men in the Home Guard, of whom a million possess rifles or machine guns to deal with sporadic descents of parachutists, etc.

Frankly however I do not see the object of spouting all this stuff—some of it injurious if it leaked—unless it is thought the Dominions require to be frightened into doing their duty.

Prime Minister to Foreign Office   28.III.41.

Monsieur Stoyadinovitch should be treated with formal courtesy, but kept under constant surveillance. The Governor should be informed that he is a bad man, and was at this juncture undoubtedly a potential Serbian Quisling. It is not desirable that relations other than formal should spring up between him and the Governor or his household, or between him and people in Mauritius. Food and comfort should be appropriate to the scale of a colonel.

Prime Minister to General Ismay, for C.O.S. Committee 30.III.41. *and Commander-in-Chief, Home Forces*

In the invasion exercise "Victor" two armoured, one motorised, and two infantry divisions were assumed to be landed by the enemy on the Norfolk coast in the teeth of heavy opposition. They fought their way ashore, and were all assumed to be in action at the end of forty-eight hours.

2. I presume the details of this remarkable feat have been worked out by the staff concerned. Let me see them. For instance, how many ships and transports carried these five divisions? How many armoured vehicles did they comprise? How many motor lorries, how many guns, how much ammunition, how many men, how many tons of stores, how far did they advance in the first forty-eight hours, how many men and vehicles were assumed to have landed in the first twelve hours, what percentage of loss were they debited with? What happened to the transports and storeships while the first forty-eight hours of fighting was going on? Had they completed emptying their cargoes, or were they still lying inshore off the beaches? What naval escort did they have? Was the landing at this point protected by superior enemy daylight fighter formations? How many fighter aeroplanes did the enemy have to employ, if so, to cover the landing-places?

All these data would be most valuable for our future offensive operations. I should be very glad if the same officers would work out a scheme for our landing an exactly similar force on the French coast at the same extreme range of our fighter protection, and assuming that the Germans have naval superiority in the Channel.

Such an enterprise as this accomplished in forty-eight hours would make history, and if the staffs will commit themselves definitely to the adventure and can show how it is worked out in detail, I should very much like to bring it before the Defense Committee for action at the earliest moment.

April

Prime Minister to Sir Andrew Duncan and Imports Executive

1.IV.41.

At the last meeting of the "Battle of the Atlantic" Committee the impression was conveyed that the great improvement in the turn-round of tankers was mainly due to improved methods of pumping. This is not so. The time has been reduced from 11.3 days to 3.3 days. The main proportion of this time saved was due to good and improved organisation. This is shown in the subjoined table. Improved discharge accounts for less than a third of the total saving. Two-thirds of it is in more able organisation.

You and your committee should look into this and see how far the Ministry of Shipping can adopt the methods of the Petroleum Department.

Prime Minister to Home Secretary

2.IV.41.

I see a note in the *Daily Telegraph* that you are shortly going to make a statement to Parliament on the future of horse-racing. Will you kindly let me know beforehand what you think of saying? If anything were done which threatened to terminate horse-racing in time of war or ruin the bloodstock, it would be necessary that the whole matter should be thrashed out in Cabinet first.

Prime Minister to First Lord and First Sea Lord

4.IV.41.

Fuelling at sea. Considering that the *Malaya* was escorting an eight-knot convoy, or perhaps even a six-knot convoy, I do not see why the danger of her oiling a destroyer at twelve knots should be stressed. It is quite true that during the period of oiling the destroyer, the battleship could not manoeuvre to avoid a torpedo. On the other hand, the advantages of having destroyers along with the convoy far more than repay this temporary disability. If four destroyers were taken along with the convoys, one would be oiling while the other three would be protecting. Anyhow, nothing could be worse than to have a battleship tethered to a six- or eight-knot convoy without any anti-U-boat craft to protect her. This is what was done on the convoy in question.

Prime Minister to C.A.S.

5.IV.41.

Two things [about the air force in the Middle East] are to me incredible:

(1) That with a total personnel strength of 26,600 and a pilot

strength of 1175 and 1044 aircraft on charge we can only fight 292 aircraft against the enemy.

(2) That with this immense personnel and mass of obsolete machines the C.-in-C. Air cannot find the necessary servicing staff for the new aeroplanes as they arrive, but that large numbers have to be sent round the Cape, with resultant destructive delays.

Prime Minister to First Lord and First Sea Lord   5.VI.41.

See attached eminently satisfactory answer to our requests. If seven cutters are available at New York within a week, why not make an evolution of getting them manned and into action from Iceland a fortnight later? Anyhow, let me be assured that all is in train for manning and bringing into action these vessels at the earliest moment.

Prime Minister to Sir Edward Bridges   8.IV.41.

It is very important not to have a serious break in the work at Easter. The normal Monday meeting should be at 5 P.M. Ministers are responsible for being available on the telephone at the shortest notice. It is much better for Ministers to take their holidays in rotation.

Let me have a list of who will go and who will stay. I am told that Easter is a very good time for invasion.

Prime Minister to General Ismay   8.IV.41.

We must have the fullest information about Tobruk. Let a large-scale plan be prepared, and as soon as possible a model, comprising not only Tobruk but the El Adem area. Let me have meanwhile the best photographs available, both from the air and from the ground.

Prime Minister to Minister of Supply   8.IV.41.

I observe with some concern from the census of machine tools that there was a reduction in the average hours worked by production machine tools from sixty-six to fifty-eight hours per week between June and November, 1940. It is of course not possible to reach such perfect balance between different machines that all machines are fully exploited. But the hours actually worked seemed lower than might have been hoped. A small loss (one and a half hours per week) is attributed directly to air raids. Some further loss is presumably due to the tendency to close factories during hours of darkness. Perhaps you would let me know the number of shifts that are being worked in factories.

It will be extremely difficult to make a case for the urgent delivery of machine tools from America if we cannot employ those we have to better advantage.

I am addressing similar minutes to the Minister of Aircraft Production and the First Lord.

(Action this day.)
Prime Minister to Secretary of State for India   10.IV.41.

Thank you very much for prompt and efficient action which you took yesterday. I shall be greatly interested to see the plan you will make in the next few days for making Basra a great American assembly point. Naturally you will plan your scheme in stages so that we can have the use of it as it develops progressively. A wide-spread defence scheme against air attack must also be prepared. The necessary radar stations to enable our fighters to get into the air in good time must be provided. Ask the military for plenty of photographs of the place, and send them forward with your report. Try to keep the report very short.

Prime Minister to C.I.G.S.   15.IV.41.

By this return, which I study every week, you will see that you have 1169 heavy tanks in this country in the hands of troops. The monthly production of over two hundred is going to increase in the near future. If the training of the men has not kept pace with the already much-retarded deliveries of the tanks, that is the responsibility of the War Office. I do not wonder that difficulties are encountered in training when two hundred and thirty-eight cruiser tanks are given to one armoured division and only thirty-eight to another. Perhaps if the 11th Armoured Division had a few more "I" tanks it would come along quicker.

Personally, I am not convinced that it is right to make each division entirely homogeneous. A judicious mixture of weapons, albeit of varied speeds, should be possible in the division. Moreover, some of these armoured vehicles ought to carry field artillery, and even one or two large guns or mortars. Let me have a report on what the Germans do.

Prime Minister to First Lord   15.IV.41.

I have heard that the use of long Actaeon nets or similar devices for towing behind escort vessels on either side of convoys is being investigated by the Admiralty. I should be glad to have a report on progress made.

If something of this sort could be developed, it might go a long way to solving our problems.[9]

Prime Minister to Secretary of State for Air   15.IV.41.

I remain far from satisfied with the state of our preparations for offensive chemical warfare, should this be forced upon us by the actions of the enemy.

I have before me a report on this matter by the Inter-Service Committee on Chemical Warfare, together with a commentary thereon by the Ministry of Supply. From these two documents the following special points emerge:

[9] The Actaeon net defence against torpedoes was being developed for use in merchant ships. It could not be towed by escort vessels without seriously hampering their freedom of movement. See Volume I, page 653.

(1) The deficiency of gas shell is still serious. Although the production of 6-inch and 5.5-inch gas shell was due to start in February, none has yet been produced. I understand that the shortage of 25-pounder gas-filled shell is due to the lack of empty shell cases.

(2) The production of 30-pound L.C. bomb, Mark I, will not keep pace with the production of the 5-inch U.P. weapon, the new mobile projector for use with the Army. Indeed, supplies will be insufficient even for training purposes.

(3) The production of phosgene gas is inadequate. The output from the plant is now about 65 per cent of capacity, having previously been only 50 per cent over a period of some months.

I propose to examine the whole position at an early meeting of the Defence Committee (Supply).

In order that this examination may be as complete as possible, I shall be glad to receive from the Minister of Aircraft Production and the Minister of Supply, for circulation in advance of the meeting, brief comprehensive statements of the position so far as each is concerned, showing in respect of each of the main gas weapons and components (including gases): (1) Total requirements notified to them, with dates; (2) stocks of components in the custody of each on April 1; (3) supplies delivered by April 1 to R.A.F. or Army authorities; (4) estimated output during each of the next six months.

I shall be glad if these statements can be submitted within a week. They should be addressed to Sir Edward Bridges.

I am addressing similar minutes to the Secretary of State for War, the Minister of Supply, and the Minister of Aircraft Production.

Prime Minister to Colonel Jacob 16.IV.41.

Let me have on one sheet of paper lists showing present time and in September last the strength of British Home Forces in (*a*) rifles and S.A.A.; (*b*) artillery—including all types of field and medium guns under one head, and also coast-defence batteries, and also A.A., both heavy and light; (*c*) number of "I" tanks and cruiser tanks in the hands of the troops; (*d*) ration and rifle strength of the fighting formations; (*e*) number of divisions and brigade groups; (*i*) on the beaches, (*ii*) behind the beaches in Army or G.H.Q. Reserve or otherwise; (*f*) strength of fighter aircraft available for action at the two dates; (*g*) strength and weight of discharge of bomber aircraft at the two dates; (*h*) strength of flotillas in home waters at the two dates. Very general and round figures will do. Don't go too much into details.

(*Action this day.*)
Prime Minister to C.A.S. 17.IV.41.

It must be recognised that the inability of Bomber Command to hit the enemy cruisers in Brest constitutes a very definite failure of this arm. No serious low-level daylight attack has been attempted.

The policy of the Air Ministry in neglecting the dive-bomber type of aircraft is shown by all experience to have been a very grievous error, and one for which we are paying dearly both in lack of offensive power and by the fear of injury which is so prevalent afloat.

2. The German battle-cruisers are two of the most important vessels in the war, as we have nothing that can both catch and kill them. I have never asked that you should try to fight weather at the same time as the enemy, but good weather may increasingly be expected. I do not think this target ought to be abandoned. On the contrary, efforts ought to be made to overcome the causes of failure. Let the following be examined with the Admiralty: Take *Victorious* in her unworked-up condition and let her mount twenty Hurricane fighters on her upper deck. Would this degree of fighter protection suffice to enable a dawn attack to be made by daylight by, say, a dozen bombers with the best-aiming bomb-sight we have been able to develop? Let this be studied forthwith and a report made to me.

3. Naturally, I sympathise with the desire to attack Germany, to use the heaviest bombs and to give Berlin a severe dose, and I agree that the bulk of Bomber Command should be used against German targets; but photographs should be taken every day of the battle-cruisers and frequent attacks made upon them, by smaller numbers when weather is suitable or by larger forces when any movement is observable, during dark hours, apart altogether from the special daylight operations suggested above.[10]

(*Action this day.*)
Prime Minister to C.I.G.S.   18.IV.41.

After the capture of Benghazi on February 6, the 7th Armoured Division, which had done so much good hard service, was ordered back to Cairo to refit. This involved a journey of over four hundred miles, and must have completed the wearing-out of the tracks of many of the tanks. It was an act of improvidence to send the whole division all this way back, in view of the fact that German elements were already reported in Tripoli. The whole of the tanks in this division could not have been all simultaneously in a condition of needing prolonged heavy repairs. Workshops should have been improvised at the front for lighter repairs, and servicing personnel sent forward. Thus, besides the 3d Armoured Brigade, there would have been a considerable proportion of the armoured brigades in the 7th Division. General Wavell and his officers seem

[10] The *Gneisenau* had in fact been torpedoed in Brest Harbour on April 6 by an aircraft of Coastal Command. In this gallant attack the aircraft and all the crew were lost. The pilot was awarded a posthumous V.C. A few days later Bomber Command aircraft scored four hits on the same ship with bombs. These successes were not known to us at the time.

In July the *Scharnhorst* moved from Brest to La Pallice, in the Bay of Biscay, for trials and sea training, but three days later she was successfully bombed in harbour there and severely damaged. She returned to Brest for further extensive repairs.

however to have thought that no trouble could arise before the end of May. This was a very serious miscalculation, from which vexatious consequences have flowed.

2. After their journey back, at least 114 cruisers and 48 infantry tanks, total 162, entered the workshops in Egypt, and are still there, and are not expected to come out faster than 40 by May 15 and 41 by May 30. It seems incredible that machines that could have made their journey back under their own power should all have taken this enormous time, and that only the handful of tanks in Tobruk have emerged from the workshops. Let me have a return showing exactly on what dates the cruiser and infantry tanks entered the Egyptian workshops, and on which dates any came out and the rest are expected to come out. There seems to be a degree of slackness and mismanagement about this repair work which is serious.

3. What exactly are the sixty cruisers M.3, said to be arriving from the United States by the end of April? We have not heard about these so far.

Prime Minister to Secretary of State for War   20.IV.41.

In Libya some German tanks are now in our possession. Even if these were damaged, we should take all possible steps to get them examined by a skilful designer of British tanks or some other suitable engineering expert.

If circumstances permit, a German tank, or suitable parts of one, could be sent home in due course. Meanwhile, if there is no adequate expert already in the Middle East, one should be sent out immediately to conduct an examination on the spot.

I am sending a similar minute to the Minister of Supply.

Prime Minister to General Ismay   21.IV.41.

I wish to have a conference on tank questions and future developments, to which the commanders of the tank divisions should be invited, as well as representatives of the Ministry of Supply. This conference should be fixed for Monday week—i.e., May 5.

The officers of the tank forces should be encouraged to prepare papers of suggestions, and are to be free to express their views. An agenda should be prepared in the same way as is done for the conferences of Commanders-in-Chief.

Pray put this all in train, and let me have a minute in a suitable form to send to the War Office.

(*Action this day.*)
Prime Minister to C.I.G.S.   22.IV.41.

I have examined the tank situation with General Crawford. After the sixty-seven cruiser tanks and their spares have gone, deliveries in the next three months should be over 288. Deliveries of "I" tanks may reach five hundred, and we shall almost certainly have in May and June a good delivery of the A.22's. It appears that the spare parts of the Mark IV's and the Mark VI's are largely identical, except for the steering gear and one or two minor points. The engines are identical, and there is a good supply of spares already in the Middle East on which the Mark VI can draw. Therefore, we only have to send the parts which are not identical.

Your trouble in the next three months is going to be finding properly trained units for the tanks which will reach you.

2. I should be very glad if you would yourself look into the question of not wearing out too rapidly in training the eleven hundred tanks now in the hands of troops. We do not want to be told all of a sudden that the tanks of a whole division on which we are counting have to go in for a long refit, like those of the 7th Armoured Division, just at the moment we need them most. It seems to me that training should be divided into two parts: (a) training in the use of the tank, for which, even in divisions not yet fully supplied, model tanks must be provided; and (b) tactical training. In this field everything possible should be done to spare the movement of masses of tanks. A great number of exercises can surely be carried out with Bren-gun carriers driven at the corresponding speed of the tanks, and only now and again should the tanks themselves be made to wear out their tracks. The principle of the "cover hack" being ridden till you get to the meet should commend itself to cavalry officers.

Pray give me a report on this.

Prime Minister to C.I.G.S.   23.IV.41.

I fancy your trouble in the near future is going to be a plethora of tanks [at home]. You speak of the speed and range of these vehicles. In practice things do not work out like that. It is only very rarely that a large homogeneous force has to make a prolonged advance or manoeuvre. Most times there are many hours wasted in each action when everyone is standing about and only a few can get on. Thus there is far more to be said for a mixed grill, and I cannot think of anything more foolish than stripping five divisions of cruiser tanks in order to have one all of a kind. This is one of the matters which must be discussed at the Tank Parliament about which I am sending you a note. A meeting must be held in the near future. In England there are very short distances and enclosed country, and the differences between cruiser and "I" tanks will tend to diminish almost to vanishing point. Uniform organisations ought not to be higher than a brigade. The tanks ought to be more evenly distributed between the units in this lull.

Prime Minister to Secretary of State for War   23.IV.41.

All the lessons of this war emphasise the necessity for good anti-tank weapons and plenty of them. The number of anti-tank guns that can be produced is necessarily limited; all the more need therefore to press forward with whatever substitutes can do the trick.

I thought that the bombard was distinctly hopeful, and I was told that you had decided to order two thousand of these, with three hundred thousand anti-tank projectiles and six hundred thousand anti-personnel projectiles. When can we expect these weapons to be in the hands of the troops? And at what rate? Pray let me have a programme.

Prime Minister to Secretary of State for War   23.IV.41.

There are persistent rumours that the Germans are constructing tanks with very thick armour—figures of four to six inches are mentioned. Such armour would be impervious to any existing anti-tank gun, or indeed any mobile gun; the tracks and other vulnerable parts are very small targets.

Tests have shown that plastic explosive applied to armour plate, as, for instance, in the bombard developed by Colonel Blacker and Colonel Jefferis, has very great cutting power, and this may be a solution to the problem. In any event, we must not be caught napping. I feel sure that the War Office are alive to the threat of the very thick-skinned tank, and have an antidote in mind. Pray let me have a report.

Prime Minister to General Wavell   24.IV.41.

Would not smoke-screens used from different directions, according to wind, give considerable immunity to ships in Tobruk Harbour? Have you the necessary materials and appliances?

2. We should be glad to have details about the German tanks recently captured by the Tobruk garrison. In particular, are they tropicalised, desert-worthy, and fitted for use in the very hot weather?

Prime Minister to Secretary of State for War and   24.IV.41.
Minister of Supply

I propose to hold periodical meetings to consider tank and anti-tank questions, the first of which will be at 10 Downing Street on Monday, May 5, at 11 A.M. These meetings would be attended by yourselves, accompanied by appropriate officers. From the War Office I would propose that the C.I.G.S., A.C.I.G.S. and General Pope should come, and General Martel and his Armoured Divisional Commanders should also be invited. On the Supply side I should like Mr. Burton, Admiral Brown, and General Crawford to be present.

2. I am particularly anxious that all officers attending the meeting should be encouraged to send in their suggestions as to the points which should be discussed, and to express their individual views with complete freedom. I contemplate, in fact, a "Tank Parliament."

3. An agenda will be prepared for each meeting by my Defence Office, and it will include any points which you wish to place upon it, and any suggestions or questions which the Tank Commanders

wish to put forward. I myself should like to discuss the organisation of armoured divisions, and the present state of their mechanical efficiency, as well as the larger questions which govern 1943.

Prime Minister to Viscount Halifax   28.IV.41.

Do not discourage the President from posing his questions direct to me or allow any of the Naval Staff to do so. My personal relations with him are of importance, and it would be a pity if they were superseded by ordinary staff routine.

Prime Minister to General Ismay   28.IV.41.

Let me have this day the minute [11] which I wrote in the summer of last year directing that five thousand parachute troops were to be prepared, together with all the minutes of the departments concerned which led to my afterwards agreeing to reduce this number to five hundred. I shall expect to receive the office files before midnight.

2. Let me have all the present proposals for increasing the parachute and glider force, together with a time-table of expected results.

Prime Minister to C.I.G.S.   28.IV.41.

The Director of Military Operations yesterday spoke of plans which had been prepared in certain eventualities for the evacuation of Egypt.

Let me see these plans, and any material bearing upon them.

Prime Minister to First Lord and First Sea Lord   28.IV.41.

The C.-in-C. Mediterranean has been fully occupied in the successful conduct of the evacuation, but now he must resume his efforts to blockade Cyrenaican ports and to catch these ships or as many of them as possible. It ought to be far easier to blockade Cyrenaican ports than Tripoli. Both must be attempted, but failure to achieve the second would be specially lamentable.

Prime Minister to General Ismay, for C.O.S. Committee   29.IV.41.

Is it not rather strange that, when we announced that the port of Benghazi while in our occupation was of no use, and, secondly that on our evacuation we had completely blocked it, the enemy are using it freely?

Prime Minister to General Ismay   29.IV.41.

I noticed that the parachutists who landed on Saturday several times had their knuckles terribly cut. Has the question of protecting their hands and [also giving them] knee-caps been considered?

[11] *General Ismay, for C.O.S. Committee*   1.IX.40.

Of course, if the glider scheme is better than parachutes, we should pursue it, but is it being seriously taken up? Are we not in danger of being fobbed off with one doubtful and experimental policy and losing the other which has already been proved? Let me have a full report of what has been done about the gliders.

MAY

Prime Minister to General Ismay   4.V.41.

Let me have a report on the efficiency of the gunners and personnel managing the fifteen-inch batteries and searchlights at Singapore. Are they fitted with radar?

Prime Minister to Secretary of State for Air   4.V.41.

This [draft telegram to President Roosevelt about expansion of bomber production in U.S.A.] should surely be put forward through the regular channels. I do not like to send telegrams to the President about the general programme, which ought to be thrashed out by the very elaborate machinery provided for the purpose.

Prime Minister to Chancellor of the Exchequer   4.V.41.

Is it true that the widow of a Service man killed by enemy action on leave gets only half the pension she would if her husband were killed on duty?

Prime Minister to Chancellor of the Exchequer   10.V.41.

Do you think this distinction is justifiable? Is there much money in it? I was told of a case of a sailor who was drunk on duty and drowned in consequence, his widow getting full pension; while another sailor on well-earned leave, killed by enemy action, was far worse treated in respect of his wife. I doubt very much whether treating leave earned by service as equivalent to service for these purposes would cost you much, and it would remove what seems to be a well-founded grievance.

Prime Minister to Chancellor of the Exchequer   16.V.41

I draw a clear distinction between deaths arising from the fire of the enemy and ordinary accidents. This is the line of demarcation which we have successfully maintained in the Bill dealing with compensation for war injuries. The air attack on this country is novel and sporadic, and can also quite safely be kept in a compartment by itself. Therefore, I reject the arguments about the concessions spreading to ordinary accidents, and from the armed forces to persons in employ on a part-time system, such as air-raid wardens and the like. I consider that in a Regular service persons bound by discipline on permanent engagement have a right to be considered when on leave as enjoying the same privileges in regard to pensions for their widows, etc., as when they are with their units. Here again is a frontier which can be effectively maintained.

In a Regular disciplined force leave is regarded as earned, and is part of the normal system of the force, and it breeds contempt of the governing machinery when one man's widow is left with half the pension of the other merely because he was hit by the enemy's fire while on leave.

Let me know what would be the expense if the regulations were amended as I have here suggested.

Prime Minister to C.I.G.S.   6.V.41.

Inquiries should be made whether the troops in Crete have a sufficiency of good maps. Otherwise we shall soon find that any German arrivals will be better informed about the island than our men.

Prime Minister to First Sea Lord   6.V.41.

How was it [the Mobile Naval Base Defence Organisation] took twelve weeks on passage, and why was the equipment packed without any relation to its employment? One would have thought a mobile naval base plant would above all other things have been stowed so that it could have been taken out and employed.

It seems to me an inquiry should be held into this lapse of staff work.

Prime Minister to Foreign Secretary   7.V.41.

Will you consider whether it would not be a good thing to publish my letter to Matsuoka. I think it is important that the people of Japan generally and a circle wider than the Matsuoka military circle should be apprised of the direction in which they are moving.

Prime Minister to General Ismay   8.V.41.

Now that we have taken Bardia, Tobruk, Massawa, Assab, Kismayu, and other Italian African ports, pray let me have a report of the exact armament of coastal and aerial defence found there, and compare this with our Intelligence estimates beforehand. A fortnight may be allowed for the preparation of this paper. I want, in the first instance, the facts, and the Intelligence must not realise that a comparison will be made with their figures.

Prime Minister to General Smuts   8.V.41.

I wonder if you would care for me to suggest to the King your appointment as an Honorary Field-Marshal of the British Army. It seems to me that [*sic*] the great part you are playing in our military affairs and the importance of the South African Army that this would be appropriate in every way, and I need not say how pleasing it would be to your old friend and comrade to pay you this compliment.

Prime Minister to the Belgian Prime Minister   10.V.41.

On the anniversary of the day when, in violation of the utmost solemn undertakings, the German Government, without cause or provocation, launched their armed forces against the territory of Belgium, I wish to acknowledge in the name of His Majesty's Government the effective help which the Belgian Government, the

Belgian Empire, and the Belgian armed forces and merchant
marine have given to the Allied cause throughout the past year.
We remember also your soldiers who resisted the invader in the
Battle of Belgium, and who now in their homes oppose the will
of the invader. The sympathy and admiration of His Majesty's
Government and of the British people go out in especial measure
to the Belgian people now under the hateful Nazi tyranny, who,
by their courage and endurance, daily contribute to the defence of
freedom.

(*Action this day.*)
Prime Minister to C.A.S.   10.V.41.

The result of the Battle of Egypt now depends more upon the
air reinforcements than upon the tanks. From every quarter and
by every route, including repeated "Jaguars," fighter aircraft must
be sent. The Takoradi bottleneck must be opened up and the congestion relieved. I have asked on other papers for a further large
despatch of Wellingtons, half a dozen additional squadrons at the
least. A regular flying-boat service should be established to bring
back pilots who are accumulating in Egypt surplus to machines.
Advantage should be taken of the presence of Air Chief Marshal
Longmore in England to make a comprehensive plan of reinforcements. Speed is essential, as from every side one gets information
of the efforts the enemy are making.

Prime Minister to Mr. Mackenzie King   11.V.41.

I am delighted to hear that Mr. Menzies' visit was so successful.
He was with us here through times of peculiar stress, and we
found him a staunch comrade. A meeting of the Imperial Conference about July or August for a month or six weeks would be
most desirable if it could be arranged. I hope we shall give a good
account of ourselves in the Middle East. It will not be for the want
of trying. Every good wish. It is splendid the way you have carried
Canada forward in such perfect unity.

Former Naval Person to President Roosevelt   10.V.41.

I expect you are now acquainted with the splendid offer which
General Arnold made to us of one-third of the rapidly expanding
capacity for pilot training in the United States to be filled with
pupils from here. We have made active preparations, and the first
five hundred and fifty of our young men are now ready to leave,
as training was to have begun early next month. A second batch
of five hundred and fifty will follow on their heels. I now understand there are legal difficulties. I hope, Mr. President, that these
are not serious, as it would be very disappointing to us and would
offset our arrangements if there were now to be delay. General
Arnold's offer was an unexpected and very welcome addition to
our training facilities. Such ready-made capacity of aircraft, airfields, and instructors all in balance we could not obtain to the

same extent and in the same time by any other means. It will greatly accelerate our effort in the air.

Prime Minister to General Arnold 11.V.41.

I am much obliged for the information reported by your observer in Egypt. The Air Ministry tell me that we have recently sent out to Takoradi the best officers we can find, but they are necessarily less familiar with American than with British types of aircraft and engines and welcome your offer of American experts. Details of numbers and grades desired will be sent to you by the Air Ministry as soon as possible.

2. In the climate of tropical West Africa no man can work as hard or as long as at home. We should like to work three shifts, and are planning to use ships for additional living quarters.

3. We are sending to Africa one of our most energetic and competent senior technical officers, who will be responsible to Commander-in-Chief for repair and maintenance in Egypt and for general control of Takoradi reinforcement route, sole responsibility for which lies with Air Ministry. Some decentralisation of local control is necessary on a route which begins in British or American factories and ends in Egypt.

4. Criticism of technical inexperience of certain drafts to Takoradi is justified, but there is now great dilution throughout R.A.F. We are now sending picked men. We gratefully accept your offer of loan of experts, and M.A.P. is being pressed to provide tools and equipment.

5. We agree about importance of B.P.C. inspection, and I am passing your criticism to the M.A.P.

6. I am much obliged for the help already given and for your offer of skilled men. Assembly of aircraft is not sole bottleneck of deliveries from Takoradi. Any acceleration must be matched by corresponding increase in transport aircraft for ferry pilots. Can your promised deliveries of American transport aircraft to Africa be accelerated? Thank you so much for cabling direct to me.

(*Action this day.*)
Prime Minister to First Lord and First Sea Lord 14.V.41.

Further to my "Tiger" Number 2, one would hope that it could be fitted in during the moonless period after about the middle of June. In order to give greater security it might be well to send *Victorious* right through, and thus give the C.-in-C. Mediterranean what he longs for, namely, two armoured aircraft-carriers. For this purpose however it is most desirable that *Victorious*, and if possible the other aircraft-carriers who would be accompanying her, should have a proportion of the best and fastest fighters which can be thrown off a float. What happened to those American Martlett aircraft? I have not heard of them for some months, yet we were told they were so promising on account of their high speed. How is the unloading of "Tiger" going on?

Prime Minister to General Ismay   16.V.41.

What is the situation at Martinique? Are the fifty million pounds
of gold still there? What French forces are there? What French
vessels are in harbour? I have it in mind that the United States
might take over Martinique to safeguard it from being used as a
base for U-boats in view of Vichy collaboration.

Prime Minister to C.I.G.S.   16.V.41.

Your minute of May 15. You tell me that the total number of
cruiser tanks in a brigade of the 7th Armoured Division is 210
(including 20 per cent reserves), and that of the "I" Tank Brigade
200 "I" tanks—say, 400 heavy tanks in the 7th Armoured Division.
We must try to compare like with like. I am told that the German
principle is two light tanks to every heavy; thus there would be in
a German armoured division about 135 heavy tanks. In other
words, it would have fewer heavy tanks than one of our tank
brigades. What is the additional outfit of our armoured brigades in
light tanks or armoured cars? Surely they have an adequate outfit
of these ancillaries. It would be enormously helpful and simplify
our work if you would kindly let me have in two columns the
standard outfit of the 7th Armoured Division on the basis you
indicate, and the outfit of a German full armoured division, and
add a third column for a German colonial division.

Have you noticed the reports from various sources that the Germans are using only one brigade in their divisions identified by
contact?

Prime Minister to First Lord and First Sea Lord   17.V.41.

At the end of February the Admiralty seemed to have had forty
ships of ten thousand tons and over employed as armed merchant
cruisers, since when I believe about three have been sunk. We
are so short of troop-carriers now that I must ask for some of these
ships to be surrendered. I suggest you hand over any you have
left in excess of thirty—i.e., about seven—leaving them with their
armaments, but with reduced naval crews, and choosing those
which will carry the largest number of troops. They will thus be
able to defend themselves and the convoy of which they form a
part.

Prime Minister to First Lord   17.V.41.

This chart of the immense work of the Salvage Department
makes me anxious that you should convey to those in charge of
that branch a very high and express measure of commendation.
Perhaps you will let me see a draft of what you propose.

Prime Minister to General Ismay   26.V.41.

It is interesting to see how very much exaggerated were the
estimates formed by our Intelligence Service of the coastal defences
of the various Italian ports that have now come into our hands.

I have long suspected that the Italians, and probably the French also, like to have it thought that their seaward defences are on a very heavy scale. We were told, for instance, that Massawa was defended by four eight-inch, ten large calibre, and sixteen six-inch, total thirty high-powered guns. Not one existed. In the light of this exposure the Intelligence branches of the different departments should carefully re-examine their scale of foreign coastal fortifications, which otherwise may prove to be a deterrent upon action.[12]

Prime Minister to General Ismay, for C.O.S. Committee   27.V.41.

This is a sad story [about parachute troops and gliders], and I feel myself greatly to blame for allowing myself to be overborne by the resistances which were offered. One can see how wrongly based these resistances were when we read the Air Staff paper in the light of what is happening in Crete, and may soon be happening in Cyprus and in Syria.

2. See also my minute on gliders of September 1, 1940.[13] This is exactly what has happened. The gliders have been produced on the smallest possible scale, and so we have practically now neither the parachutists nor the gliders, except these 500.

3. Thus we are always found behindhand by the enemy. We ought to have five thousand parachutists and an airborne division on the German model, with any improvements which might suggest themselves from experience. We ought also to have a number of carrier aircraft [i.e., transport aircraft]. These will all be necessary in the Mediterranean fighting of 1942, or earlier if possible. We shall have to try to retake some of these islands which are being so easily occupied by the enemy. We may be forced to fight in the wide countries of the East, in Persia or Northern Iraq. A whole year has been lost, and I now invite the Chiefs of Staff to make proposals for trying, so far as is possible, to repair the misfortune.

The whole file is to be brought before the Chiefs of Staff this evening.

Prime Minister to General Ismay, for C.O.S. Committee   27.V.41.

I am in general agreement with the appreciation of C.I.G.S.; but it is clear that priority and emphasis of the operations must be prescribed from here.

I should be glad if the Chiefs of Staff would consider forthwith the following proposed directive:

[12] Port	Total Intelligence Estimate	Total reported after capture
Tobruk	26	15
Benghazi	37	12
Bardia	7 to 9	5
Massawa	64	29
Kismayu	10 to 11	23
Grand Total	144 to 147	84

[13] See footnote at page 645.

In view of General Wavell's latest messages, he should be ordered to evacuate Crete forthwith, saving as many men as possible without regard to material, and taking whatever measures, whether by reinforcement or otherwise, are best.

2. With the capture of Suda Bay or Kastelli on the south side the enemy will be most eager to land a seaborne force. The Navy must not open their sea guard yet, and should try, in any case, to take the heaviest toll, thus getting some of our own back.

3. The defence of Egypt from the west and from the north under the increased weight of the air attack from Crete presents the standard military problem of a central force resisting two attacks from opposite quarters. In this case the choice seems clearly dictated by the facts.

4. The attack through Turkey and/or through Syria cannot develop in great strength for a good many weeks, during which events may make it impossible.

5. In the Western Desert alone the opportunity for a decisive military success presents itself. Here the object must not be the pushing-back of the enemy to any particular line or region, but the destruction of his armed force, or the bulk of it, in a decisive battle fought with our whole strength. It should be possible in the next fortnight to inflict a crushing defeat upon the Germans in Cyrenaica. General Wavell has upwards of four hundred heavy tanks, against one hundred and thirty enemy heavy tanks, plus their nine-tonners, as well as light armoured forces upon both sides. He has a large plurality of other arms, particularly artillery. He has sure communications, ample supplies, and much help from the sea. He should therefore strike with the utmost strength in the Western Desert against an enemy already in great difficulties for supplies and ammunition. Here is the only chance of producing a major military success, and nothing should stand in its way.

6. There is no objection meanwhile to the advance he proposes with the forces specified into Syria, and he may get the aerodromes there before the Germans have recovered from the immense drain upon their air power which the unexpectedly vigorous resistance of Freyberg's army has produced.

7. Forces should not be frittered away on Cyprus at this juncture. We cannot attempt to hold Cyprus unless we have the aerodromes in Syria. When we have these, and if we have gained a decisive victory in Cyrenaica, an advance under adequate air cover into Cyprus may become possible. We must not repeat in Cyprus the hard conditions of our fight in Crete.

8. For the above purposes "Jaguar" must immediately be resumed and expanded. *Victorious* is now at liberty. The movement of all troops and transport from Abyssinia northward must be pressed to the utmost, observing that the 50th Division from England less one brigade is also already approaching, together with other reinforcements.

9. To sum up, the orders should be: (*a*) Evacuate Crete. (*b*)

Destroy the German force in Cyrenaica, thus disengaging Tobruk and securing the airfields to the westward. (c) Endeavour to peg out claims in Syria for reinforcement after a Cyrenaican victory as in (b).

All these operations should be capable of completion before the middle of June.

Prime Minister to Prime Minister of Australia   29.V.41.
(Mr. Menzies)

Sincere congratulations on the powerful, moving addresses you have delivered in Canada, the United States, and above all on your return home. These have been fully reported in England, and have confirmed all the good-will you gathered from our people. I thank you also for your very kindly references to me. Reading the Australian dispatches, I often think of Chatham's famous invocation: "Be one people!" Best of luck.

Prime Minister to Minister of Agriculture and   30.V.41.
Secretary of State for Scotland

I have been considering the minutes you sent me early in April concerning the production of sugar-beet in Scotland. It seems to me agreed that it is desirable that in order to save shipping space the production of sugar-beet should be maintained. I am also informed that the starch equivalent of beet products per acre is two-thirds greater than that of potatoes. But I infer from what you say that for financial reasons farmers prefer to produce potatoes, of which there is no shortage.

It seems clear therefore that measures should be taken to ensure that sufficient beet is produced, if necessary at the expense of potatoes. It ought to be possible to settle between the Ministries concerned whether the increase is to be made in Scotland or in Northern England, but it certainly appears that it would be most convenient to produce the additional quantity for the Cupar factory in Scotland.

If it is too late to obtain this extra output this year, steps should be taken to make sure that the shortage is not repeated in 1942. Indeed, since beet is apparently a very valuable crop in present circumstances, it should be considered whether a much larger acreage should not in future be devoted to it. Please report to me further on this at a later date.

JUNE

Prime Minister to General Ismay, for C.O.S. Committee   1.VI.41.

Although I hold most strongly that we should not fritter away our forces in defence of Cyprus [at this moment], I do not wish to exclude the possibility of air defence, even before we are masters of the Syrian airfields. If as a result of a successful outcome of "Tiger Cubs" it should be found possible to spare two or three fighter squadrons, these should be sent; and anyhow meanwhile preparations should be made to receive them at short notice in Cyprus. I do not know what is the position and state of the existing aerodromes.

I should be glad if the whole subject could be reviewed by the Staffs.

(Action this day.)
Prime Minister to General Ismay, for Chiefs of Staff   1.VI.41.
Committee

Adverting to my wish that the West African Brigade should be returned from East Africa to Freetown forthwith, and that the captured Italian arms should be used to equip the Shadow Brigade now forming at Freetown or thereabouts, I have had a talk with General Giffard. He says that the West African battalions require an average of eighty British officer and non-commissioned officer personnel, and that these will be lacking for the Shadow Brigade, and that even if supplied they would be better employed on handling any modern equipment we can find. It has been suggested to me that the great plethora of Polish officers in Polish divisions, amounting to several thousands, might be married up to this West African Shadow Brigade. I am sure that General Sikorski could easily be persuaded to find two or three hundred, and they would be very good.

Pray let this be examined and a plan made. General Giffard should be consulted, and I should like to have a report before he leaves the country, the object being the transfer of the West African Brigade from east to west, and the development of the Shadow Brigade on Italian equipment and Polish white infusion.[14]

Prime Minister to Minister of Information   1.VI.41.

It is most dangerous to inform the enemy that Parliament is sitting on any particular day while there is time for an attack to be made. I do not admit the assumption that the enemy knows all that is attributed to him.

(Action this day.)
Prime Minister to C.A.S.   2.VI.41.

I am glad you are pressing on with this vital business [of lengthening the range of fighters]. Anyone can see you will have to pay in gunfire and manoeuvrability for the advantage of range, but this may be well worth while.

I do not regard your last sentence as exhaustive. Machines must be modified so as to enable us to fight at particular points in daylight, both by bombers and fighters. This is particularly true of the Aegean Archipelago, where we ought to be able to bomb the Cretan and Dodecanese aerodromes *by daylight* under fighter protection. We have got to adapt machines to the distances which

[14] About four hundred Polish officers were sent as proposed to the West African Division and served with high credit.

have to be traversed. Again, now that so much of the German Air Force is moving East, and France is largely weakened, we ought to attempt daylight raids into Germany for bombing on a severe scale. For this the range of our fighters must be extended. If this is not done, you will be helpless in the West and beaten in the East.

Prime Minister to Governor of Malta   6.VI.41.

I am entirely in agreement with your general outlook. The War Office will deal in detail with all your points. It does not seem that an attack on Malta is likely within the next two or three weeks. Meanwhile, other events of importance will be decided, enabling or compelling a new view to be taken. You may be sure we regard Malta as one of the master-keys of the British Empire. We are sure that you are the man to hold it, and we will do everything in human power to give you the means.

(*Action this day.*)
Prime Minister to Professor Lindemann   7.VI.41.

I have several times asked you to check up on German and British air strengths as we left it at the end of Mr. Justice Singleton's investigations. Pray let me have this return by Monday at latest.

I should imagine that the enemy have lost a great many more aircraft than we have, but what is the new rate of construction which he has achieved? How do matters stand? It is over two months ago since I had a thorough check made.

Prime Minister to Prime Minister of Australia   9.VI.41.

It is not possible to hold Cyprus without having control of the Syrian airfields. We therefore thought it better to try to gain these, when we should be in a position to support Cyprus more effectively. In the meanwhile there is one Australian divisional mechanised cavalry regiment and one British battalion with local troops and six Hurricanes. They are a deterrent on anything but a fairly substantial hostile scale of attack. If the enemy comes in force before we have got hold of Syria, the fifteen hundred men in Cyprus will have to take to the mountains, which are rugged and high, and there maintain a guerrilla as long as possible. If we cannot get control of Syria or if the Germans defeat the guerrilla in the mountains, we shall probably get a good many away. Chiefs of Staff do not think this is an unfair task to set troops. There are many worse in war. No other course is open except immediate evacuation, inviting unopposed landing. I am anxious to help you in your difficulties, and, if you wish it, I will see that Australian troops are withdrawn from Cyprus with or without relief.

Prime Minister to Colonial Secretary and General Ismay   11.VI.41.

Our policy is the strictest possible blockade of Jibuti. The fairest terms have been offered to these people. Nothing must be done to mitigate the severity of the blockade. It might however be possible to arrange that if a return were furnished of the number of new-born babies and young children a very limited amount of nourishment might be allowed to pass into the town under the most strict restrictions and surveillance.

On no account must the Governor of Aden take any action which will weaken the blockade, and no supplies of any kind are to move into the town without my approving the arrangements first.

Prime Minister to Lord President   14.VI.41.

I learn that under the scheme for reducing the basic civilian ration of petrol by half once every three months the reduction is to be made for the first time this August.

Could not this be avoided? We have to think of Bank Holiday and of the fact that many people may be getting leave this August for the first time since the war. They are no doubt counting on having their cars full at the end of July, and having also at their disposal the full ration for August.

Could you not arrange to begin the experiment in October? To make good the loss an extra half-ration month could be intercalated during the winter.

(Action this day.)
Prime Minister to Lord Woolton and Minister of   14.VI.41.
Agriculture

I was very glad to hear from you that the twelve hens scheme would be abandoned in favour of "No official food for more than twelve hens unless you come into the public pool." "Public chicken-food for public eggs."

2. Have you done justice to rabbit production? Although rabbits are not by themselves nourishing, they are a pretty good mitigation of vegetarianism. They eat mainly grass and greenstuffs, so what is the harm in encouraging their multiplication in captivity?

3. I welcome your increase of the meat ration, but it would be a pity to cut this down in the winter, just when fresh vegetables will also drop. Can you not get in additional supplies of American corned beef, pork, and bacon to bridge the winter gap? The more bread you force people to eat, the greater the demands on tonnage will be. Reliance on bread is an evil which exaggerates itself. It would seem that you should make further efforts to open out your meat supplies.

4. I view with great concern any massacre of sheep and oxen. The reserve on the hoof is our main standby.

Prime Minister to Secretary of State for Air and C.A.S.   15.VI.41.

I suggested to you some time ago that Sir Hugh Dowding should be asked to write a dispatch about the Battle of Britain, which was fought under his command during July, August, and September last. I understood from the C.A.S., and I think also from you, that there was no objection to this.

Will you kindly have the necessary official action taken?

Prime Minister to General Ismay   18.VI.41.

Please have a glossary drawn up today of the places in Syria and Libya which are most frequently mentioned. Choose in each case the simplest spelling and well-known form. This will then be telegraphed to the Middle East and circulated with supplements to all concerned.

Prime Minister to Secretary of State for Air and C.A.S.   18.VI.41.

I saw a statement in the papers the other day that the air force were calling for several thousand volunteers to defend their aerodromes. What is the meaning of this? It was represented that this was a part of the application of the lessons of Crete. But many people have wondered why such a petty measure should have been paraded. Perhaps however it is all nonsense.

2. This gives me the opportunity to say that all air force ground personnel at aerodromes have got to undergo sharp, effective, and severe military training in the use of their weapons, and in all manoeuvres necessary for the defence of the aerodromes. Every single man must be accounted for in the defence, and every effort should be made to reach a high standard of nimbleness and efficiency.

Will you kindly let me have a report on this?

Prime Minister to General de Gaulle   19.VI.41.

Thank you for your message to me of June 13. I value your views highly. They have been specially helpful in the light of most recent events in Syria. You may be sure that I always cherish the interests of the Free French Movement, so vital to the rebirth of France. Best wishes.

Prime Minister to General Ismay   20.VI.41.

Please focus clearly in writing: (*a*) The arrangements now proposed for more intimate association of the Army and the co-operating air force squadrons; and (*b*) the responsibility for airfields in the United Kingdom in the event of invasion.

Prime Minister to General Ismay, for C.O.S. Committee   23.VI.41.

The success which has attended the admirable offensive of the R.A.F. over the Pas de Calais should encourage this to be pressed day after day as long as it proves profitable. The number of bombers going by day should be increased as much as possible, so as to take full advantage by daylight of the various targets presented. For this purpose the Cabinet should be asked to agree to the bombing of any important factories which are being used on a large scale for the repair or manufacture of enemy aircraft, and any important objectives in the area dominated should be subjected to the heaviest daylight bombing and effectively destroyed. The French workmen should at the right moment be warned to keep away from the factories, though this should not prevent our beginning before they have notice.

2. On the assumption that our domination of the air over this area will be successfully established, the Staffs should consider whether a serious operation in the form of a large raid should not be launched under full air protection. I have in mind something on the scale of twenty-five thousand to thirty-thousand men—perhaps the Commandos plus one of the Canadian divisions. It would be necessary to create a force exactly adapted to the tactical plan rather than to adhere to the conventional establishments of divisions. As long as we can keep air domination over the Channel and the Pas de Calais, it ought to be possible to achieve a considerable result.

3. Among the other objectives, the destruction of the guns and batteries, of all shipping (though there is not much there now), of all stores, and the killing and capturing of a large number of Germans present themselves. The blocking of the harbours of Calais and Boulogne might also be attempted.

4. I should like to have a preliminary discussion this evening at 9.45 P.M., and if the principle is approved the plans should be perfected as soon as possible, in case the air domination should be achieved. Now the enemy is busy in Russia is the time to "Make hell while the sun shines."

Prime Minister to General Ismay, for C.O.S. Committee   27.VI.41.
Controller, Admiralty, and others concerned

British amphibious attacks overseas are begun usually in the dark hours, during which it is hoped to get a certain number of Bofors guns ashore, but these will be quite inadequate to cover the landing-places from the dive-bomber attack, which must be expected almost anywhere at dawn or shortly after. The guns will have taken up positions in the dark, and cannot possibly have their predictors and combined control effective in so short a time.

2. To bridge the gap between the first landing and the seizure of airfields, with consequent establishment of British fighter squadrons and air protection, it is necessary that effective A.A. artillery support, at least in low-ceiling fire, should be provided. How is this to be done? It can only be done by the provision of floating barriers which can take their stations in the dark hours of the first attack and be ready to protect the landing-places from daylight onward.

3. One hundred and seventy tank-landing-craft are now rapidly coming out month by month. At least one dozen of these should be fitted as floating batteries. They should be armed either with Bofors or with multiple U.P. projectors with A.D. or P.E. fuze. The large-size Tank Landing Craft are well suited to this. Let a plan be made of the best possible arrangement of the guns or projectors, or both mixed. The best forms of fire-control and the principle of the four-cornered ship, so as to fire at attacks from various quarters simultaneously, should be developed. This is a task for gunnery and U.P. experts, who should be given the dimensions of the deck

space available, and should work out a full scheme in technical appliances and personnel required. The Controller should report what alterations would be necessary in the ships. One ship should be so fitted at once, and a nucleus of officers trained in the fighting of a floating battery under these conditions. It would not be necessary to arm more than one ship at the present time, and it could be used for training and experimental purposes, but the remaining eleven should be got ready, with any improvements which may suggest themselves, to receive their guns or projectors. All the base fittings should be made and built in so that the weapons can be rapidly mounted. Meanwhile, the guns and projectors can continue to play their part in A.D.G.B., the necessary number being earmarked for a speedy transfer should an amphibious operation become imminent.

Pray let me have a report in one week, showing the proposed action and the time-table.[15]

Prime Minister to General Ismay   27.VI.41.

Let me have a note of the number of Commanders-in-Chief, and the names, who have visited the room at the Ministry of Defence for the purpose of reading the files each week, so that I can see who take advantage of it. Let me also see the first specimen file available for their scrutiny.

(*Action this day.*)
Prime Minister to Secretary of State for War and C.I.G.S. 27.VI.41.

Some time ago I formed the opinion that it would be far better to give names to the various marks of tanks. These could be kept readily in mind, and would avoid the confusing titles by marks and numbers. This idea did not find favour at the time, but it is evident that a real need for it exists, because the "I" tank, Mark II, is widely known as "Matilda," and one of the other infantry tanks is called "Valentine." Moreover, the existing denominations are changed and varied. A.22 has an alias, I think. Pray therefore set out a list of existing official titles of all the tanks by types and marks now existing or under construction or design in our service and in the American service, together with suggested names for them, in order that these may be considered and discussed.

(*Action this day.*)
Prime Minister to Foreign Secretary, First Lord, and First 28.VI.41.
Sea Lord

Who has been responsible for starting this idea among the Americans that we should like their destroyer forces to operate on their own side of the Atlantic rather than upon ours? Whoever

[15] This minute shows the genesis of the landing-craft flak (L.C.F.) which was a converted tank-landing-craft carrying a powerful battery of light and anti-aircraft guns. It was used to provide close air defence to landing-craft during an assault. Six of these were in service by May, 1942, and thereafter the numbers greatly increased.

has put this about has done great disservice, and should be immediately removed from all American contacts. I am in entire agreement with Mr. Stimson. May I ask that this should be accepted at once as a decision of policy, and that it should be referred, if necessary, to the Cabinet on Monday?

Prime Minister to Secretary of State for Air   28.VI.41.

I understand that little or no provision is made for the defence of aerodromes between the date at which they are fit for operational use and the date at which they are actually taken over, and that this interval is often a long one, especially if some minor adjustments have to be made after the main work is completed. This appears to be a serious gap in our defences. Pray let me know what the position is.

Prime Minister to Secretary of State for Air and   29.VI.41.
Chief of the Air Staff

Further to my minute of June 20, about the responsibility of the air force for the local and static defence of aerodromes. Every man in air force uniform ought to be armed with something—a rifle, a tommy-gun, a pistol, a pike, or a mace; and everyone, without exception, should do at least one hour's drill and practice every day. Every airman should have his place in the defence scheme. At least once a week an alarm should be given as an exercise (stated clearly beforehand in the signal that it is an exercise), and every man should be at his post. Ninety per cent should be at their fighting stations in five minutes at the most. It must be understood by all ranks that they are expected to fight and die in the defence of their airfields. Every building which fits in with the scheme of defence should be prepared, so that each has to be conquered one by one by the enemy's parachute or glider troops. Each of these posts should have its leader appointed. In two or three hours the troops will arrive; meanwhile, every post should resist and must be maintained—be it only a cottage or a mess—so that the enemy has to master each one. This is a slow and expensive process for him.

2. The enormous mass of non-combatant personnel who look after the very few heroic pilots, who alone in ordinary circumstances do all the fighting, is an inherent difficulty in the organisation of the air force. Here is the chance for this great mass to add a fighting quality to the necessary services they perform. Every airfield should be a stronghold of fighting air-groundmen, and not the abode of uniformed civilians in the prime of life protected by detachments of soldiers.

3. In order that I may study this matter in detail, let me have the exact field state of Northolt Aerodrome, showing every class of airman, the work he does, the weapons he has, and his part in the scheme of defence. We simply cannot afford to have the best part of half a million uniformed men, with all the prestige of the Royal Air Force attaching to them, who have not got a definite fighting

value quite apart from the indispensable services they perform for the pilots.

Prime Minister to Secretary of State for War and C.I.G.S. 29.VI.41.

We have to contemplate the descent from the air of perhaps a quarter of a million parachutists, glider-borne or crash-landed aeroplane troops. Everyone in uniform, and anyone else who likes, must fall upon these wherever they find them and attack them with the utmost alacrity—

> "Let every one
> Kill a Hun."

This spirit must be inculcated ceaselessly into all ranks of H.M. forces—in particular military schools, training establishments, depots. All the rearward services must develop a quality of stern, individual resistance. No building occupied by troops should be surrendered without having to be stormed. Every man must have a weapon of some kind, be it only a mace or a pike. The spirit of intense individual resistance to this new form of sporadic invasion is a fundamental necessity. I have no doubt a great deal is being done.

Please let me know exactly how many uniformed men you have on ration strength in this Island, and how they are armed.

I should like Sir Alan Brooke to see this minute and enclosure, and to give me his views about it. Let me also see some patterns of maces and pikes.

Prime Minister to General Ismay, for C.O.S. Committee 30.VI.41.

Although we take a heavy toll, very large enemy reinforcements are crossing to Africa continually. The Navy seem unable to do anything. The air force only stop perhaps a fifth. You are no doubt impressed with the full gravity of the situation.

(*Action this day.*)
Prime Minister to Minister of Supply   30.VI.41.

In the secret session on Sir Andrew Duncan's vote questions were asked by Mr. Shinwell and others about how we stood in "heavy tanks." We have hitherto regarded A.22 as the heaviest we should make, though a great deal of work has been done, I think by Stern, on a still larger type. I believe there is even a pilot model. Of course, our problem is different from the Russian or great Continental Powers because of shipment, although that is no final bar.

However, it now appears, on the highest authority, that the Russians have produced a very large tank, said to be over seventy tons, against which the German A/T six-pounder has proved useless. It seems to me that the question of a much heavier tank has now come sharply to the front. The whole position must be reviewed, and we must know where we are—and that soon.

Appendix D, Book One

ESTIMATED BRITISH AND GERMAN AIR STRENGTHS, 9 DECEMBER, 1940

NOTE BY PRIME MINISTER AND MINISTER OF DEFENCE [16]

Since the war began fifteen months ago the German Air Force is believed to have received 22,000 aircraft of all types, and the British Air Force 18,000 of all types for use in all theatres and for all purposes. In the last eight months of hard fighting the German Air Force has received from April to November inclusive 12,000 new machines, and the British Air Force 11,000, exclusive of 1000 from overseas. In these eight battle months, when both air forces have been at full extension, the intake has been about equal, averaging 1400 to 1500 machines a month.

2. During these eight months the front-line strength of the British Air Force of about 2100 machines has scarcely changed. Thus a monthly output of 1400 machines has just sufficed in a period of active warfare to keep up a front-line strength of 2100 machines.

If we reckon that of the 1400 machines 500 were trainers, and another 200 were operational machines devoted to training—a very generous allowance in the heat of the battle—this implies that 700 operational machines, i.e., one-third of our front-line establishment, was written off every month. Actually the number is probably greater than this, at any rate in the bomber squadrons, where a number of bombers equal to two-fifths of the front-line establishment is lost monthly.

3. The German losses have certainly not been less *pro rata*. Their battle losses between May and August were estimated by the Air Ministry as about 3000, and from August to the end of October as 2800 machines—i.e., 5800 in all. Our battle losses in the equivalent period were less than half of this.

4. Information leads the Air Intelligence Branch at the Air Ministry to believe that the German front-line Air Force on May 1 was about three times as great as ours—say, 6000 machines. If this were so, and their *pro rata* losses were not higher than ours, their monthly wastage must have been at least 2000 machines (on the two-fifths figure even higher). If our figures for their average output, i.e., 1500 machines, are correct, and if the statement that

[16] See Book One, Chapter 3, page 32 *et seq.*

1100 of these were operational is accepted, the German Air Force must diminish at the rate of 2000 minus 100, i.e., at least 900 machines in the first month. As the front line decreased, of course the losses and the rate of drop would fall, but the strength would be well below 4000 at the end of four months.

The only way of escaping this conclusion is to assume that the Germans carried an immense reserve of machines stored for such an eventuality. The pre-war output does not justify such an assumption. In any event, it would be an uneconomical proceeding, as the machines would rapidly become out of date. Any well-arranged air force reckons to have a reserve at the outbreak of war to tide it over the first two or three months while the war machine begins to operate, and to run on production thereafter.

An investigation should be made showing exactly what proportion of our front-line establishment was written off each month, and what were the causes. It should be possible to make a fairly accurate estimate of our battle losses and the German battle losses, and the calculation should be made assuming that their other losses are *pro rata* the same as ours. It should be borne in mind that the Germans must send to the training establishments and write off therein an equivalent number of those which we have to devote to this purpose, O.T.U.'s counting as training establishments.

5. According to our information, only four hundred German trainers are produced each month. This number seems most inadequate to replace the pilot wastage in such a huge air force as the Air Intelligence attributes to the Germans. We use considerably more, without counting those delivered direct to the training schools in Canada.

We are told that Germany had a huge reserve of pilots trained before the war, and that few pilots trained since have been found amongst the prisoners. If this were so, and if the huge reserve of machines also had really been in existence, it seems inconceivable that they should not have been brought together and the operational strength correspondingly increased for the duration of the great air battles.

6. Every effort must be made to clear up the present contradiction. The M.E.W. estimate for the output is incompatible with a front-line strength much higher than three thousand machines. This figure is consonant with the weight of the German effort at Dunkirk and in the Battle of Britain (taking account of the favourable geographical factors). The Air Intelligence estimate is nearly twice as great.

At present the only possible explanations seem to be:

(*a*) That M.E.W. is wildly wrong, and that the German output is nearly twice as great as they believe. Further, that the Germans did not make any very great effort in the Battle of Britain or at Dunkirk. (*b*) That, on the contrary, our German Section have been misled, possibly intentionally, by the Germans, and are pinning —

their faith to an estimate far in excess of the real figure. (c) That the units identified by the German Intelligence Section are not all of them what we should call front-line units, but that a considerable proportion of them (at least one-third) are non-operational, perhaps corresponding to O.T.U.'s.

MONTHLY SUMMARY OF LOSSES [17] OF BRITISH, ALLIED, AND NEUTRAL MERCHANT SHIPS AND FISHING VESSELS BY ENEMY ACTION

(Figures corrected to May 1, 1949)

1941	BRITISH		ALLIED		NEUTRAL		TOTAL	
	No. of Ships	Gross Tons	No. of Ships	Gross Tons	No. of Ships	Gross Tons	No. of Ships	Gross Tons
Jan.	44	209,394	30	107,692	1	2,962	75	320,048
Feb.	79	316,349	20	82,222	1	3,197	100	401,768
March	98	366,847	32	138,307	9	32,339	139	537,493
April	79	362,471	67	256,612	8	34,877	154	653,960
May	96	387,303	24	98,559	6	14,201	126	500,063
June	63	268,634	35	142,887	10	19,516	108	431,037
July	36	95,465	6	23,994	1	1,516	43	120,975
Aug.	31	96,989	9	32,010	1	1,700	41	130,699
Sept.	61	215,207	13	47,950	9	22,595	83	285,752
Oct.	32	151,777	14	53,434	5	13,078	51	218,289
Nov.	29	91,352	4	6,260	1	55,308	34	104,212
Dec.	124	271,401	44	159,276	19	6,600	187	485,985
Totals	772	2,833,189	298	1,149,203	71	207,889	1,141	4,190,281

Far East. Of this 194,000 tons was British.

[17] The losses in December include about 270,000 tons lost in the

665

Appendix F, Book One

MILITARY DIRECTIVES AND MINUTES

January—June, 1941

Prime Minister to Secretary of State for War and C. I. G. S. 6.I.41.

W.S.5A has already started and B starts immediately. There is therefore no question about them. They contain together 55,000 men, of whom 12,000 are for India, etc., and 43,000 for M.E. Of the 43,000 M.E., about 22,000 are for fighting units and drafts, and 21,000 technical, L. of C., base, etc., of which about 4000 are Navy and R.A.F. Thus the Army in M.E. receives 22,000 fighting and 17,000 other men.

2. The present composition of the Army in the Middle East (excluding Kenya and Aden, nearly 70,000) reveals 150,000 fighting troops. Behind this are 40,000 L. of C. and 20,000 base establishments and details—i.e., 150,000 to 60,000. To this will now be added by W.S.5A and B 22,000 fighting and 17,000 L. of C., base, etc., making a total of 172,000 fighting and 77,000 rearward services.

3. Convoy W.S.6, now being loaded, contains 8500 fighting troops, plus fighting share of 4000 drafts—say 2500—equals total fighting troops 11,000; excluding the mobile naval base, 5300 (of which later); and the R.A.F. (including training school to Cape Town) and R.N. 7000, 2000 Free French, and about 9000 base and other details. Upon the arrival of this convoy the total figure for the Middle East will stand at fighting troops 183,000 and 86,000 rearward units—i.e., 15 to 7. The progressive deterioration in the proportion between fighting troops and rearward services must be noted.

4. But the category "fighting troops" requires further searching analysis. We are told, for example, that the 7th Australian Division, 14,800, is untrained and largely unequipped, and there is the cavalry division, 8500, whose mechanisation has not yet made progress, and who cannot really be called fighting troops except for local order. There are several other units I could specify which are similarly not fighting troops in the effective mobile sense—say, 6000. Thus 29,000 should properly be subtracted from the fighting total, reducing it from 183,000, to 154,000, and added to the rearward services and non-effective, raising them from 86,000 to 115,000. The condition of the Army of the Middle East (excluding the

70,000 in Kenya and Aden) is therefore represented by 154,000 fighting troops and 115,000 rearward and non-effective (except for immediate local security). The proportion of non-effectives seems much too high. It must be remembered that further great reductions could be made from the effective fighting troops, since every division or brigade group has its own first-line transport and is supposed to be a self-contained military unit. Further, it should not be forgotten that in order to supply all this rearward and un-organised or non-effective strength the rations of the British people have had to be severely reduced, and further cuts are in prospect, and that every man and every ton of stores has to be carried and transported at heavy risk from enemy U-boat, air, and raider at-tacks round the Cape of Good Hope by ships whose there-and-back voyage occupies, with turn-round, not less than four months. It is therefore incumbent upon all loyal persons, whether at home or in M.E., to try to increase the fighting troops and to keep at the lowest possible the rearward and non-effective services. In this lies a great opportunity for brilliant administrative exertion which might produce results in war economy equal to those gained by a considerable victory in the field.

5. If I could be assured that the plethora of rearward services contained in the aforesaid convoys W.S.5A and B and W.S.6 would animate and render effective the 29,000 non-effective figthing men mentioned in paragraph 4 above, I should be content. For instance, will the 7th Australian Division gain the ancillary services neces-sary to fit it for other than local action? Will the 8500 cavalry divi-sion become a mechanised unit capable of acting in brigades, or at least regiments, against the enemy? Then, although the propor-tions of non-fighting troops now crowding our convoys would still be a very hard measure, at any rate the Army in the M.E. would grow markedly in fighting strength, and the delay in sending the 50th Division would be tolerable. It may be that some consoling information will be forthcoming about this.

The question of whether it would be better to send the 1st Brigade of the 50th Division instead of the mobile naval base in W.S.6 is nicely balanced, but preparations may have advanced too far for a convenient change of plan. This must be considered to-morrow (7th) by C.O.S. Committee, observing that it will be out of action for nearly three months.

6. It is otherwise necessary to approve the despatch of W.S.6 (reduced to 34,000 or less) as now proposed. I deeply regret the resultant composition of the Army in the M.E. When all these convoys have arrived, its total will amount to 240,000, plus 43,000, plus 20,000—total over 300,000, to which must be added 70,000 in Aden and Kenya—total 370,000 men, on pay and ration strength. From this enormous force the only recognisable fighting military units are the following: 6th Australian Division, one New Zealand division, comprising two brigade groups, 4th Indian Division, 5th Indian Division, 16th Infantry Brigade, 2d Armoured Division, 7th

Armoured Division (incomplete), 6th British Division (incomplete). And such fighting units as have been formed from the 70,000 men in Kenya and Aden—e.g., two South African brigades, two West African brigades, and local East African forces. It is hoped that to these will soon be added (a) the completion of the above incomplete units, (b) a seventh British division formed out of the unclassified and by combing the rearward services, the 7th Australian Division, and a mechanised cavalry division.

This will amount to about ten divisions, infantry, armoured, and cavalry, plus, say, one division from Kenya—total eleven divisions. Even this would be a very small crop to gather from so vast a field.

Prime Minister to General Ismay, for C.O.S. Committee   21.I.41.

The following decisions arise from our discussion last night:

Three Glen ships, with full complement of landing craft and with the Commandos assigned to those ships on board, less one Commando (which General Wavell already has), should sail at earliest round the Cape to Suez.

2. There will remain behind: (a) The Commando redundant through one being already in Egypt. (b) The Commando troops embarked on *Karanja*. (c) The rest of the Commando force in this country. This should be made up immediately to the full strength of five thousand and be fully equipped, and should continue their training at full speed. If this is not done we shall have lost an essential weapon of offence needed to man and use the new landing-craft, which are coming out steadily now from the builders. It will be necessary for D.C.O. to remain at home to reorganise and rebuild this force up to its full five thousand.

Pray let me have a plan to implement paragraphs 1 and 2 during the day (21st).

3. General Wavell should be told that his plans for advancing to Benghazi are approved. Unless this presents altogether unexpected difficulties he should at the same time be able to prepare in the Delta a force sufficient to take the principal "Mandibles" [Rhodes] when the landing-craft and the Commandos arrive. In the meanwhile he is to make all preparations in order that the attack may be delivered at the earliest moment. He should be asked to report on the above assumption when he could do this, and what main units he would use. It is hoped that the attack would be delivered not later than March 1.

4. General Wavell should also begin immediately to build up in the Delta a strategic reserve to be used in Greece or Turkey as occasion may require. Having established himself strongly at Benghazi with a field force and an armoured division based on that port, he could drop the overland line of communication and thus save both men and transport.

Benghazi, if captured [by us], should be made a strongly defended naval and air base, guns, etc., being drawn as may be necessary both from Alexandria and intermediate ports or posts on the lines of communication. He ought therefore to be able to create a strategic striking force (of which the troops for "Mandibles" will form a first instalment) in the next two months. It is hoped that this force may soon attain the equivalent of four divisions, though probably brigade group organisation would be preferable.

5. The air disposition must conform to the above, subject to the commitments we have already made to Greece. The first duty of the A.O.C.-in-C. M.E. is none the less to sustain the resistance of Malta by a proper flow of fighter reinforcements. To enable these tasks to be performed, *Furious* will make another voyage with a third consignment of forty Hurricanes.

6. An expeditionary force of two divisions, plus certain corps units and the Commandos when reorganised, should be prepared for action in the Western Mediterranean, whether for "Influx" or "Yorker" to aid General Wavell as circumstances may suggest. Both these plans are to be studied and perfected, "Yorker" being the more probable. A commander should be appointed and an attempt made to be ready to act after March 1. The impingement of the above on later convoys to M.E. must be examined and reported.

Prime Minister to Secretary of State for War   29.I.41.

I am very much obliged to you for the considerable effort you have made to meet my views and reduce Army demands upon the man-power of Great Britain.

2. I still do not understand how a division supposed to be complete with 15,000 men of all arms requires 35,000 men, or 20,000 extra. Perhaps it will be simpler to take a corps of three divisions, which on your calculations would require 105,000 men, of which 45,000 only would be included in field units. Let me have a table showing how the remaining 60,000 are divided between (*a*) corps troops, (*b*) share of Army troops, (*c*) lines of communication troops.

3. Neither do I understand the scale on which the lines of communication troops is calculated. The troops in Great Britain lie in the midst of their base of supplies and of the most highly developed railway network in the world. They have roads innumerable and of high quality. In the event of invasion the advances they would have to make are in the nature of seventy to one hundred miles at the outside, although of course a larger lateral movement by rail from south to north, or vice versa, might be required. Such conditions are not comparable at all with those prevailing in France, where, owing to our choosing to base ourselves on St. Nazaire, etc., we had a five-hundred-mile line of communication, mainly by road, to maintain. What are the differences in the scale of L. of C. troops provided for the first ten divisions in France this time last year and those you now propose for the troops retained in Great Britain for defence?

4. The problem will not be solved without taking a view forward of what is likely to happen in the next twelve months. We shall certainly have to keep not less than fifteen British divisions behind the beaches to guard against invasion. For the bulk of these a scale much less than the French scale (B.E.F.) should suffice. The forces in the Middle East, now that the Mediterranean is closed, can only be built up at a reduced rate. But we ought to assume that by July there will be in the Delta or up [along] the Nile four Australian, one New Zealand, one + one South African,[18] six out of eight Indian, and three British divisions, or their equivalents in brigade groups. In addition, there will be in Africa the four African Colonial divisions. These last, surely, are not divisions in the ordinary sense—i.e., capable of being used as integral tactical units in the field? Are they not, in fact, the garrisons of East and West Africa and the Sudan, requiring only small complements of artillery and technical troops, and with lines of communication provided locally? Let me know what scale of corps troops, share of Army troops and L. of C. troops you contemplate for these four sedentary or localised so-called "divisions." Is it not a mistake to call them divisions in any sense?

5. Returning to the Army of the Nile, with its sixteen divisions, it must be observed that, once Benghazi has been taken and strongly fortified with a field force based upon it, the conditions in Egypt should be such as to enable internal order to be maintained by Indian divisions, who will in fact be living very close to the possible centres of disturbance, and who will not have to take the field like a British division acting in France or Flanders, or even a British division at home. What scale of L. of C. troops are you providing for these? Do you think it necessary to organise them in corps, and supply them with the European quota of medium and heavy artillery, etc.?

6. We must however contemplate as our main objective in this theatre the bringing into heavy action of the largest possible force from the Army of the Nile to fight in aid of Greece or Turkey or both. How many divisions, or their equivalent, do you contemplate being available by July for action in Southeast Europe? I should have thought that the four Australian, one New Zealand, one of the two South Africans, the three British, and three of the six Indian divisions, should be available—total twelve. These troops must be equipped on the highest scale, for it is Germans they will have to fight. On the other hand, they will come into action only gradually —probably four divisions by the end of March, and the rest as shipping and equipment becomes available. The problem therefore is for a first-class scale for twelve divisions against the Germans, a very much reduced second-class scale against the disorders in Egypt or to take charge of conquered Italian territory, and a still lower scale for the so-called African Colonial Division. I hope that with this picture, which the General Staff should consider carefully,

18 Extra to original 57.

your problem may be more precisely defined—viz., five British divisions at home at highest mobility; ten at secondary, working up to twelve in the Middle East in action against the Germans in Greece or Turkey on the highest scale; four in Egypt, Sudan, etc., on a moderate scale; and four African Colonials, according to local conditions—total thirty-five, to which must be added two Indian divisions, for service in Malaya, total thirty-seven, leaving from your total of fifty-eight [19] twenty-one divisions. Of these nine are armoured divisions, leaving twelve British infantry divisions to be accounted for.

7. What is the picture and forecast for these twelve British divisions? Up to six they have to go at very short notice to French North Africa, or alternatively perhaps to work with a friendly Spain. We cannot do both. These six divisions will come into operation in 2 corps of three divisions each, but owing to shipping exigencies they can only come gradually into operation. In so far as they come into action at all, it will be against the Germans. Therefore, whatever is thought to be the most appropriate scale must be provided. It must however be observed that neither of these theatres offers opportunities for the use of heavy or much medium artillery, and that in the Spanish alternative the war might well take a guerrilla form.

8. We cannot hope to arm the remaining six divisions to the full scale for many months to come, but if they were brought to the anti-German scale for overseas operations by the end of August it would be satisfactory.

9. Nine armoured divisions are comprised in the total number of fifty-eight. What is the distribution contemplated for these? At first sight four at home, two available for amphibious action in the West, and three in the Middle East or Balkan theatre would seem appropriate. It is clear that the rearward and repair services of any of these divisions sent abroad require to be on a larger scale than those which lie handy to all the great workshops of Great Britain. Have these differentiations been allowed for?

10. Battle wastage at 8500 a month is not excessive as a theoretical forecast. In practice however it does not seem likely that, apart from invasion, action on this scale will begin for several months. It might be safe as a working arrangement to bring this monthly figure of 8500 into account only from July 1, 1941. This would save 60,000 men [from the calculation].

11. The wastage from normal causes of 18,750 a month, or 243,750 a year, appears a high figure, and one wonders whether it may not be reduced as better accommodation and more settled conditions are established in Great Britain, and as the men themselves become more seasoned. . . . I should like to know how many of these men discharged from the Army are unfit for any other form of war work. What is the number of deaths per month, the total incapacitated, those fit for lighter duties, and those fit for munitions

[19] One South African division extra to original 57.

work? I should expect that at least ten thousand a month would be capable of some other form of employment. This point is important for the War Office, as in stating the man-power demand which is to be made upon the nation the Army should credit itself with any men who are yielded up who are still capable of civilian service. This of course does not affect the problem, but only the statement of the problem; none the less it is important.

12. I regard A.D.G.B. as a source which may well at some future date yield economies because of new methods and our increasing ascendancy in the air. It is astonishing how great are the numbers of men required per gun. Careful study should make it possible to reduce the numbers in many localities, and to accept a slightly lower scale of immediate preparedness. Even a small percentage of saving under these heads would enable the additional guns and searchlights now coming into action to be manned with a smaller demand upon man-power.

13. I hope I am not to infer from the expression "beach battalions" that any body of young, physically fit, efficiently trained men would be relegated to a particular function. It is indispensable that a continuous rotation should take place, all brigades taking their place on the beaches in turn, or coming into the back areas for service in the mobile divisions.

14. Generally speaking, I do not consider that a demand by the Army for 900,000 men, less 60,000, less 150,000 (paragraphs 10 and 11) = 690,000 net up to October 1, 1942, is excessive. The training process must be maintained; wastage must be made good. [When] once the Army is heavily engaged it would be more natural to draw large numbers from the public and to comb the munitions and A.R.P. services. It is the demand in the next six months, while military operations are at a minimum, that I am anxious to keep within limits.

15. I await the further information which I ask for in this paper, but meanwhile I should greatly regret to see twenty medium regiments or 480 guns retrenched for a mere saving of 18,000 men out of the enormous totals presented, and similarly, seven field regiments of 168 guns for the sake of saving 5600 men. It is essential to strengthen the Army in fighting troops, and it is better to take some risks in theoretical calculations of wastage, even if these should be falsified at a later date, than to fail at this moment to produce the proper quota of artillery.

ARMY SCALES

Directive by the Minister of Defence

6 March 41

When in September, 1939, the Cabinet approved the formation of a Field Army of fifty-five divisions it was not realised that a division as contemplated by the War Office, with its share of corps,

Army, G.H.Q., and L. of C. formations, would require 42,000 men, exclusive of all training establishments and of all garrisons, depots, or troops not included in the Field Army. At that time also it was assumed that the bulk of our Army would stand in the line with the French under conditions comparable to those of the last war, whereas the bulk of our Army now has to stay at home and defend the Island against invasion. Thirdly, the shipping stringency makes it impossible to transport and maintain very large forces overseas, especially on the high scales which the War Office regard as necessary.

2. Out of the fifty-five divisions (now become fifty-seven), thirty-six are British and twenty-one overseas troops. Of the thirty-six British divisions, one (so-called) division is in Iceland, and one (the 6th) is forming in Egypt, together with two armoured divisions there, total British divisions now overseas, four.

3. Twenty-five British infantry divisions and the equivalent of seven armoured divisions in process of formation, total thirty-two, are now included in the Home Forces Army. At 19,500 men apiece, these twenty-five British infantry divisions aggregate 487,500 men, and the seven armoured divisions at 14,000 apiece aggregate 98,-000, total 575,500. In addition to the divisional organisation, C.-in-C. Home Forces has ten independent brigades, including the Guards brigades, twenty-seven beach brigades, and fourteen unbrigaded battalions, all British. At an average of 3500 men apiece, these forty-two brigades or equivalents account for about 150,000 men. Therefore, the total number of British in tactical formations at home amounts to 735,500 men.

4. There are on our ration strength at home 1,800,000 British soldiers; 735,500 are accounted for in the above formations, leaving 1,064,500 to be explained as corps, Army, and G.H.Q. troops and A.D.G.B., or as training establishments, depots, etc., and as part of the rearward services of the forces overseas.

5. It is upon this pool of 1,064,500 that the Army must live. By wise economies, by thrifty and ingenious use of man-power, by altering establishments to fit resources, it should be possible to make a very great improvement in the fighting strength. Apart from this capital fund of man-power, the Army can count each year upon its eighteens and nineteens. It is only in the event of heavy casualties being sustained through many divisions being simultaneously and continuously in action, which, except in the case of invasion, is extremely unlikely, that any further inroad can be allowed upon the man-power resources of Great Britain. In other words, the Army can rely on being kept up to something like their present figure of about two million British, and they will be judged by the effective fighting use they make of it.

6. At the same time, it will be well to plan an eventual increase of armoured formations to the equivalent of fourteen armoured divisions (or fifteen if the Australian armoured division materialises), in which would be included the Army Tank Brigades. A reduction

of several infantry divisions would be required, and the British Army would then be composed of fourteen armoured divisions (or their equivalent) and about twenty-two infantry divisions. The War Office and Ministry of Supply should work out proposals on these lines.

7. The three East African divisions and the West African division should not be organised in formations higher than brigades or small mobile groups adapted to the duties they have to perform.

8. It will be impossible for us to maintain from Great Britain any large addition to our Army in the Middle East, because we have to go round the Cape. The main accretion of this Army must come from India, Australasia, and South Africa, with later on munitions from the United States. Three or four more British divisions is the most we can hope to send and keep there. One must consider that General Weygand's silence has released us from any offer of helping him up to six divisions, although of course we might act on our own volition. An amphibious striking force of eight or ten divisions, mostly armoured, is the utmost that need be envisaged in the West. There can be no question of an advance in force against the German armies on the mainland of Europe.

9. The above considerations and the situation as a whole make it impossible for the Army, except in resisting invasion, to play a primary rôle in the defeat of the enemy. That task can only be done by the staying power of the Navy, and above all by the effect of Air predominance. Very valuable and important services may be rendered overseas by the Army in operations of a secondary order, and it is for these special operations that its organisation and character should be adapted.

10. The reactions of the foregoing directive on man-power accommodation, ammunition, stores, etc., should be worked out.

Prime Minister to General Wavell   4.VI.41.

I have for some time been considering means by which I could lighten the burden of administration which falls on your shoulders while you have four different campaigns to conduct and so much quasi-political and diplomatic business.

2. During the last nine months we have sent you close on 50 per cent of our whole output here, excepting tanks and less India's subshare. You have at the present moment 530,000 soldiers on your ration strength, 500 field guns, 350 A.A. guns, 450 heavy tanks, and 350 anti-tank guns. In the months of January to May upward of 7000 mechanical vehicles have reached you. In drafts alone, apart from units, we have sent since the beginning of the year 13,000. The fighting in the South has for two month past enabled a northward movement to begin, yet you are evidently hard put to find a brigade, or even a battalion, and in continual telegrams you complain of your shortage of transport, which you declare limits all your operations.

3. In order to help you to produce the best results, I wish to re-

lieve you as much as possible of administration, and thus leave you free to give your fullest thought to policy and operations. Here at home General Brooke has a very large army to handle and train, but he has behind him the departments of the War Office and of the Ministry of Supply. Something like this separation of functions must be established in the Middle East, although in this case your ultimate authority as Commander-in-Chief will reign over the whole theatre.

4. What has been said above applies also, *mutatis mutandis*, to the air force and Fleet Air Arm.

5. The shipping stringency has prevented the reinforcement of the Middle East to the scale which I had hoped for some months ago, and the undoubted threat of invasion in the late summer and autumn had made the General Staff and the Home Forces Command most close-fisted. Nevertheless, it is hoped, depending on the situation, to send you in the next four months—that is to say, June, July, August, and September—an additional infantry division, besides the 50th, as well as a full supply of drafts, details, and equipment of all kinds. Thus it should be possible to organise for the autumn and winter campaigns, which may well be very severe, the following mobile field forces: Four Australian divisions, one New Zealand division, two British Indian divisions (4th and 5th), two South African divisions, the 6th British Infantry Division—to be organised on the spot, the 50th British Infantry Division, and the new division (total British divisions three).

You have now ready or in process of construction the 7th and the 2d Armoured Divisions, and you have got to make the best you can of the trained Cavalry Division, which is being reconstituted as an armoured force. Total, fifteen divisions. This represents about 600,000 men, from which, without prejudice to the mobile divisions, internal security forces and rearward services must also be provided.

6. All future British Indian divisions will go in at Basra, and I hope that Eritrea, Abyssinia, Kenya, and the Somalilands can be left to native African forces (less one West African brigade to be returned to West Africa) and armed white police.

7. The development and maintenance of the Army of the Nile, operating in Cyrenaica and in Syria, would require organisation and workshops on a far larger scale than you have yet enjoyed. Not only must the Egyptian workshops be raised in strength and efficiency, but further bases, with adequate port facilities, will have to be built up, say, at Port Sudan and Massawa, using perhaps the town of Asmara, which has fine buildings, and also Jibuti, when we get it. At the same time developments on a great scale will be set on foot by the Government of India, with our active aid, it being hoped that at least six or seven divisions, with apparatus, may presently operate thence.

8. I therefore propose to set up under your general authority an organisation under an officer of high rank, who will be styled "In-

tendant-General of the Army of the Middle East." This officer will be equipped with an ample staff, drawn largely from your existing administrative staff and with a powerful and growing civilian element, to discharge for you, as mentioned above, many of the services rendered by the War Office and Ministry of Supply to General Brooke. His duties will include the supervision and control of rearward administrative services, including the military man-power not embodied in the tactical units or employed in the active military zone.

9. President Roosevelt is now sending, in addition to the thirty ships under the American flag, another forty-four vessels, which carry, among other things, two hundred additional light tanks from the United States Army Production, and many other important items, of which I will furnish you a list. It seems to me probable, and I am trying to arrange, that a great part of the supply of your armies shall come direct from the United States, both by the eastern and western routes.

10. Accordingly, we are sending out by air General Haining and Mr. T. C. L. Westbrook, of the Ministry of Aircraft Production. General Haining will be appointed Intendant-General. The War Office is telegraphing to you separately instructions which are being issued to him. Under him Mr. Westbrook will take charge of the development of ports and transportation facilities and the reception, maintenance, and repair of the whole of the armoured vehicles and mechanical transport. He will be accompanied by a number of consultants on specialised subjects, such as transportation, port development, and workshops. He will collaborate with Air Marshal Dawson, who is in charge of the cognate activities of the Royal Air Force and Fleet Air Arm, with a view to pooling resources.

11. General Haining's duties in the first place will be to examine on the spot and to discuss with you the implementing and precise definition of the general directive and policy set forth in the preceding paragraphs, which must be accepted as a decision of His Majesty's Government. After not more than a fortnight from the date of his arrival the report must be telegraphed home. I hope it may be agreed, but any points of difference will be settled promptly by me. Moreover, I shall not allow the scheme to lose any of its force and scope in the detailed application which must now be given to it.

12. Because of the great mass and importance of the American supplies, and the fact that the war in the Middle East cannot be conducted at its needful scale without them, I have asked President Roosevelt to allow his envoy here, Mr. Harriman, to proceed forthwith to the Middle East with the other members of the mission. Mr. Harriman enjoys my complete confidence, and is in the most intimate relations with the President and with Mr. Harry Hopkins. No one can do more for you. Mr. Harriman will be accompanied by one or two of his own assistants, who have shown great aptitude and ardour over here. It would be disastrous if large accumulations

of American supplies arrived without efficient measures for their reception and without large-scale planning for the future. Besides this it will be necessary that considerable numbers of American engineers and mechanics should come for the servicing and repair of their own types of aircraft, tanks, and M.T. I commend Mr. Harriman to your most attentive consideration. He will report both to his own Government and to me as Minister of Defence.

Appendix A, Book Two

PRIME MINISTER'S PERSONAL MINUTES
AND TELEGRAMS

July—December, 1941

July

Prime Minister to King of Greece   1.VII.41.

I have been thinking a great deal about Your Majesty in these
months of stress, danger, and sorrow, and I wish to tell you how
much your bearing amid these vicissitudes has been admired by
your many friends in England, as well as by the nation at large.
The warmest welcome awaits you here, where all are resolved to
conquer or to perish. It is my confident hope that when the good
days come the glory which Greece has won will help to heal the
memory of her present suffering.

Prime Minister to General Ismay   1.VII.41.

The Germans are making a good deal of use of flame-throwers.
How does this matter stand?

(Action this day.)
Prime Minister to First Lord and First Sea Lord   1.VII.41.

I presume that effective arrangements have been made to prevent
reinforcement of the Vichy forces in Syria by sea. How does this
stand?

Prime Minister to Secretary of State for Air   1.VII.41.

I note that your actual expenditure of bombs in May, 2920 tons,
was less than half the monthly estimated expenditure for the second
quarter of this year, and that at this rate of expenditure your stock
represents thirty months' supply.

The last thing we wish of course is to have any shortage of
bombs if and when you are ready to drop them in quantity. But in
the light of these figures you might perhaps wish to review your
requirements, which seem to be largely attributable to your desire
for a six months' reserve.

Unless you are really assured that you will be in a position to
make full use of these great quantities, we should consider whether
some filling capacity should be transferred to other uses.

Prime Minister to Minister of Food   2.VII.41.

I am glad that the egg scheme attributed to you was not actually the scheme you had in mind. It is always difficult to hold the balance between the need for increasing total food supplies and the need to maintain a fair distribution. We should not be too hard on the private individual who increases his supplies by his own [productive] efforts.

It is satisfactory that the meat prospects are improving, and I hope that pressure on the United States to increase her pork output will soon enable us to raise the ration without risk of having subsequently to reduce it.

We do not wish to create a grievance amongst farmers by compelling them to slaughter beasts which they can fatten without imported feeding stuffs; on the other hand, of course the country cannot go hungry because farmers do not choose to bring their beasts to market. It will no doubt be possible to arrange with the Minister of Agriculture, perhaps by a carefully worked-out price policy, a scheme which will keep the meat supply as constant as possible having regard to seasonal factors.

As to wheat, the point I had in mind was not so much our stock as the danger of getting into a vicious circle: people eat more bread owing to a shortage of meat, and thereby compel you to import more wheat, thus reducing the shipping space available for bringing in other foods. I do not believe there is great danger of the harvest being destroyed by the enemy this year. We have found it very hard to burn crops, and if you will ask the Air Ministry they will explain to you why the dew conditions in this country make it even harder here than on the Continent.

Prime Minister to Secretary of State for War and C.I.G.S. 3.VII.41.

In forming a very large armoured force such as we contemplate, while at the same time carrying on the war, a large element of improvisation is necessary, and this applies especially to the more backward formations. It is highly questionable whether the divisional organisation is right for armoured troops. A system of self-contained brigade groups forming part of the Royal Tank Corps would be operationally and administratively better. One can see how ill-adapted the divisional system is when the 7th Armoured Division, one of our most highly trained and armoured units, goes into action "less one brigade," it having in fact only two, with certain additional elements. However, where divisional formations have grown up and have been clothed with armed reality, the conditions of war do not permit the disturbance of a change. With the more backward formations the case is different. They should be brought into coherent existence as brigade groups, armed with the best weapons available at the moment, and worked up gradually by increasing the proportion of the latest armoured vehicles. Care should be taken that in every phase of their working-up they should have a definite fighting value. It may not be possible to give all the armoured brigade groups the same equipment at the same time. They must take what is going, and make the best of it. For instance, in forming a new or backward armoured brigade group in this country, it should first of all receive a full complement of armoured cars or Bren gun carriers, and should immediately become "brigade conscious." They should be trained in regimental and brigade exercises just as if they were a fully equipped armoured formation. This is specially true in all wireless telegraphy services. In an emergency they would act as a motor machine-gun unit. As proper tanks become available, these should be infused into the regiments as a growing core, until finally the men are well used to looking after motor vehicles and well-trained in the manoeuvres of an armoured brigade formation. They would then eventually receive their full equipment of whatever tanks are available, these tanks themselves being replaced by later models as they come to hand or are transferred to them from the more fully equipped formations. Thus, at every stage there would be weeded out the non-tank-minded personnel, there would be an expansion of instruction in tank tactics, and a practical value in the event of emergency would be maintained.

2. Different conditions present themselves in the case of the cavalry division, which has so long been in Palestine ineffective as a military factor. This cavalry division should be reorganised, as fast as emergency conditions of war permit, in two brigade groups, each of which should consist of three tank regiments, twelve motorised field guns, one motorised machine-gun regiment, and ancillary services. The formation of these two armoured brigade groups should have a high priority, certainly one in advance of any more backward British armoured units. It would be a great convenience if these two brigades could in the first instance be ripened from mere motor machine-gun units into tank units by receiving the flow of light medium tanks from the United States which has now begun. President Roosevelt has informed me that he has allocated (apart from the sixty already approaching and other orders) two hundred light cruiser tanks for shipment in American vessels to Suez in the next few months. Surely these additional two hundred should form the main equipment of the two ex-cavalry amoured brigade groups. The balance of the various regiments would continue to use *pro tem.* the armoured cars or Bren gun carriers which they had begun to work with. The marrying of these good troops to the windfall of two hundred extra American light cruiser tanks would bring into being two effective armoured brigade units extremely well adapted for Palestinian, Syrian, and Iraqian warfare at a far earlier date than any equal fighting value could be [otherwise] achieved.

Prime Minister to Major Morton   6.VII.41.

Please make sure that a list is kept of young Frenchmen who are sentenced by the Vichy courts to imprisonment for de Gaullist sympathies in France or in Morocco, so that they may be looked after later on.

(*Action this day.*)
Prime Minister to C.I.G.S. 6.VII.41.

It is nearly six months since you and Mr. Eden went to Cairo, charged *inter alia*, with the task of reporting on the interior economy of the Army in the Middle East. Yet today the condition is deplorable, and our detailed knowledge most defective. The War Office ought to have a full picture of the development of the fighting formations, and I certainly cannot discharge my responsibilities without it.

2. It is not much to ask a division or brigade group to send in a monthly return of their major items of equipment. I cannot imagine a competent divisional general who would not know where he was in this matter from week to week—indeed, almost from day to day.

3. We should have a monthly return, considering the immense daily flow, including Air Force trivialities.

General Haining's organisation ought to know the whole position, and there ought to be no difficulty in their telling us.

You are wrong in supposing that this return is needed for statistical purposes only. Without a clear up-to-date picture of the state of Middle East formations no view or major decisions can be taken by the Defence Committee or the War Cabinet. The alternative is to continue in the state of ignorance and confusion which is leading us towards disaster.

While I should be ready to agree to some small simplification of details, if you will propose it to me, I must insist upon knowing all the essential facts.[20]

(*Action this day.*)
Prime Minister to Secretary of State for War 6.VII.41.

Why have we not yet been told that the Blues, Life Guards, and Essex Yeomanry took part in the capture of Palmyra? These units have long ago been identified by contact, and there cannot be any military reasons for not disclosing this interesting piece of information to the British public.

It is this kind of abuse of censorship, in the name of operational secrecy, that rightly irritates the House as well as the press, and makes the more important positions more difficult to hold.

Prime Minister to Minister of Food 7.VII.41.

I am glad that you are preparing for the American authorities an estimate of our full requirements of pork and dairy products, and that you have asked them for a greatly increased programme for eggs. The total figure of the food imports to be obtained from

[20] C.I.G.S.'s Minute of 5.VII.41, referring to the Prime Minister's request for a detailed distribution list of equipment, by formations, in the Middle East.

America will, I trust, be much bigger than the one and a third million tons at present envisaged. With due notice I feel sure that the Americans, without rationing themselves, could produce much more food for export to us. (Pork production in the United States frequently fluctuates by nearly half a million tons from year to year.)

I trust that every effort is made to get our meat from the nearest sources. With due warning and a guarantee perhaps the Argentine could also expand their meat production.

Oil and oil-seeds are no doubt obtained so far as possible from Africa and imported on ships returning from the Middle East. We can ill afford to send ships to India or the Pacific for this purpose now.

Prime Minister to Foreign Secretary   9.VII.41.

Something like the following should be sent to the Minister of State for his information:

Following from Prime Minister. Personal and secret. Begins. An agent who we think is sure came a fortnight ago to establish a liaison between us and Vichy. Our talks with him were on the dead level. He now sends us the following, dated July 5:

"(1) The French Government has given the following general instructions to General Dentz: When Syria is occupied by the British, the French civil servants must remain at their posts and carry on with their duties in collaboration with the Free French forces.

"(2) I am requested to beg of you most earnestly to take these instructions into account. Good-will on your part on this occasion will make the best impression.

"(3) Failure to meet this, the first wish expressed by my Government so soon after my return, would have an unfortunate influence on my future actions."

This must be considered in relation to the formal request for armistice with which you have already been acquainted. We propose replying to the agent for Pétain and Huntziger to the effect that:

(1) England has no interest in Syria except to win the war.

(2) Arab independence is a first essential and nothing must conflict with that.

(3) De Gaulle must naturally in the circumstances represent French interests in Syria in the interim. He will thus keep alive the fact that, without prejudice to Arab independence, France will have the dominant privileged position in Syria among all European nations.

(4) Everything must be done to soften (*adoucir*) the relations between the de Gaulle and French adherents in the meanwhile. We are all committed to Arab independence, but we think that France could aim at having in Syria after the war the same sort of position as we had established between the wars in Iraq.

(5) Don't forget that when we win, as we shall, we shall not tolerate any separation of Alsace-Lorraine or of any French colony

from France. So try your best to feel your way through the detestable difficulties by which we are both at present afflicted.

Prime Minister to General Ismay   10.VII.41.

In future the expression "landing" will be applied exclusively to landings from the sea. All arrivals from the air will be described as "descents," and this terminology will rule throughout official correspondence.

PARACHUTE EXERCISE

Prime Minister to Commander-in-Chief Home Forces,   10.VII.41.
and to General Ismay for C.O.S. Committee

It is said that the attack will be made at dawn. This cannot however imply that all the parachute and glider troops will arrive simultaneously at dawn. To move as many as one thousand troop-carrying planes, or their equivalent, from French, Belgian, and Dutch bases would occupy several hours—at least four or five, i.e., almost all the present hours of darkness. Therefore, as the journey is short, they would either be arriving in instalments during the night (in which case zero hour would probably be 1 A.M.), or if the first ones arrived at dawn the rest would straggle out during the remaining hours of daylight. In the latter case they would be cut to pieces by our fighters. There can be no question of parachutists arriving in instalments by daylight. It is noticeable that the Germans have never yet tried these descents by night. There are very great difficulties in finding exact points in which to make low-altitude descents at night.

The Air Staff must be consulted upon all these vital problems. It is no good starting staff exercises or studies of this kind, involving so much dislocation, upon a basis which is unreal and could not possibly occur. It is quite easy to say, "Twelve thousand parachutists land at dawn. What would you do?" but this statement is meaningless without a detailed analysis of the movements which I have indicated.

2. A smaller-scale attack might well be more dangerous. Five hundred desperadoes, coming out of the blue without the slightest preliminary indication, might descend by day, or at any rate in the half-light of dawn, at or near the centre of government. These however would first be picked up by the R.D.F., and would run serious risk of interception by night and almost certain destruction by day. Nevertheless, surprise has such sovereign virtues in war that the proposition should be attentively examined. The centres of government and executive control should at any rate be made reasonably secure against a sudden rush of this kind if upon examination any probability can be attached to it. The first hour is the only hour that matters, and the first ten minutes are the minutes that matter most.

3. I shall be glad if Home Forces will consult with the Air Staff,

and hack me out clear-cut answers to the above queries and suggestions. Two or three days should suffice for the study.

Prime Minister to Commander-in-Chief Home Forces,   10.VII.41.
and to General Ismay for C.O.S. Committee

How do we stand at present on the strategic and tactical camouflaging of defences against enemy attacks on airfields? What body is studying the lessons of Maleme and the batteries thereabouts?

Obviously action proceeds on two lines, namely: (*a*) The concealment of the real guns and deceitful presentation of the dummy guns. There might well be two or three dummy guns, or even more, for every real gun. (*b*) The best of all camouflage is a confusing variety of positions made in which no one can tell the real from the sham.

The tactics of holding fire from particular batteries during the early phases of an attack are no doubt also being studied.

Pray let me have a report by Saturday next.

Prime Minister to Sir Edward Bridges   11.VII.41.

Take the Hansards of the two days' production debate, and have all the passages which affect particular departments extracted and sent to the departments concerned with a request for their answers by July 19.

Also pick out any passages which affect the central direction of the war and let me have them.

It seems to me there were a lot of very good points made.

Prime Minister to Secretary of State for Air   11.VII.41.

Although radio beam bombing was neutralised last winter by our interference, it seems that the enemy is re-equipping his whole bomber force with improved radio receivers, and hopes to overwhelm our counter-measures next winter by the multiplicity of his beam stations.

No radio methods can of course prevent his finding and bombing targets like Coventry and Birmingham on fine moonlight nights. But it is on these that our normal night defence should be most effective. It is the dark, cloudy nights that will be our main danger, and we should make every preparation to deal with the enemy beams, whose positions and wave-lengths we now know.

I am informed that the equipment needed is not very remote from that used in ordinary commercial practice, so that it should be possible to obtain it from America even if it cannot be manufactured here. Everything should be ready by the autumn. Pray let me know what the position is and what measures are in hand to counter enemy developments.

Prime Minister to Minister of Food   12.VII.41.

I am pleased to learn that the amount of food "requisitioned" in U.S.A. is now far above the figure quoted in your May report. I understand that the programme of our full requirements is much higher than the amount "requisitioned" so far. I am sure that, given sufficient warning, America can and will produce or in some way provide a very large quantity of the foodstuffs we need so badly. If we can import them on the short haul, shipping for almost all we require should be available.

The only point in doubt is whether you have asked for sufficient pork. America would find it difficult to provide us with beef or mutton, but pork supplies can be rapidly expanded, and if necessary imported in non-refrigerated tonnage.

(Action this day.)
Prime Minister to Ministry of Aircraft Production, Sir   12.VII.41.
Charles Craven, Secretary of State for Air, C.A.S.
(General Ismay to implement or report progress in one week), and Lord Cherwell

I was deeply concerned at the new programmes of M.A.P., which show a static condition for the next twelve or eighteen months in the numbers of aircraft. No doubt new production would be bent on in the later phase. I asked that these figures should be subjected to the test of man-hours involved in each type of machine. This certainly shows an improvement of about fifty per cent in the British field by the twelfth month from now. The American figures improve the calculation both from the number of aircraft and the man-hours standpoint, and one might almost say that the output for July, 1942, would be to the present output as 1 to 1.75.

2. I cannot feel that this is enough. Our estimate of German monthly production by numbers is twenty-one hundred, which is the numerical level at which we stand up till July, 1942, and indeed thereafter, apart from new projects. We must assume that the Germans also would derive comfort from translating their numbers of aircraft into the man-hours. They may or they may not be making a similar expansion in size and quality. Broadly, from the figures put before me, the impression would be one of equality for the next twelve months, so far as British and German construction is concerned, leaving any increase to be supplied by our share of United States production. Moreover, this takes no count of M.A.P.'s caveat that their estimates may be reduced by fifteen per cent.

3. We cannot be content with the above situation, which excludes all possibility of decisive predominance indispensable for victory. I wish therefore these programmes to be re-examined, and the following three methods of expansion, together with any others suggested, to be explored by the highest authorities concerned. The three methods are: (a) An improvement in the existing figures by speeding up and working the machine tools longer, or by any other measures taken in the sphere of M.A.P. production. (b) By the construction of new factories and assembling plants, or by the re-occupation or full occupation of plants vacated for the sake of dispersion. This may well be justified in view of our increasing com-

mand of the British air by day and the improvement in night-fighting devices. (c) By a reclassification of the bomber programme so as to secure a larger delivery from well-tried types in that period.

Fighter aircraft must continually strive for mastery, and rapid changes of design may be imperative. But a large proportion of the bomber force will in the next twelve months be employed under steady conditions and within ranges which are moderate. While all bombers required for long-distance or great heights or daylight action must be the subject of intensive improvement, a large proportion of the bombing force will be carrying their nightly load to, say, the Ruhr or other near-by targets. It would seem that the Air Staff could divide their activities into near and far, and that on this basis some good lines of production, which have not yet reached their maximum, could be given a longer run at the peak, with very definite addition to numbers. This would, for instance, seem to apply to the Blackpool Wellington, which is a new supply, reaching its peak in November, but only running for six months at that level. If it were allowed a twelve-month run at the peak, it may be that a larger delivery would be possible from November on.

4. The criterion of bomber strength is the weight of bombs deliverable per month on the reasonably foreseeable targets in Germany and Italy. Have the Air Staff plans been applied to the figures of production with this end in view? It may be that a heavier load carried by a new machine would give better results. But a machine which is good enough to carry two tons to the Ruhr ought to have a long run in continuous production before it is discarded. There are no doubt other instances. I have asked the M.A.P. to review their programmes accordingly, having regard to the grievous loss on too hasty change-overs.

5. The new programme is substantially less than the March figures, and far below the October [1940] figures. However, many materials have been accumulated on the October basis. A substantial expansion should therefore be possible if all factors are fitted to the optimum. The Air Ministry should show how this latest programme, apart from any expansion, fits in with their pilot production for the next twelve months, having regard, on the one hand, to the reduced scale of losses which has been found operative by experience, and, on the other, to the much more lavish pilot establishment now said to be necessary in proportion to machines. Bombs, explosives, guns, and all accessories must be measured in relation both to the existing programme and the necessary expansion. *In principle however we must aim at nothing less than having an Air Force twice as strong as the German Air Force by the end of 1942. This ought not to be impossible if a renewed vast effort is made now. It is the very least that can be contemplated, since no other way of winning the war has yet been proposed.*

Prime Minister to Secretary of State for Air   16.VII.41.
Investigations by the Ministry of Home Security into the effect

of German high-explosive bombs has shown that a far greater amount of damage is done by blast, which destroys buildings, etc., than by splinters, which find very few useful targets, especially at night, when most people are under cover.

The higher the proportion of high explosive to bomb-case the greater the blast. If the weight of the metal case is increased, we get more splinters.

Our general purpose bombs have a charge-weight ratio of about 30 to 70. The Germans work with a larger ratio, about 50–50. These are not only more efficient for destroying cities; they are also cheaper.

In these circumstances the charge-weight ratio of our bombs ought to be reconsidered, especially now that the Air Ministry have asked for such a large expansion in output.

Prime Minister to Secretary of State for Air 16.VII.41.

I should be glad if you could send me a brief report on the blind-landing position, showing how far the R.A.F. is equipped with this aid.

Prime Minister to Sir Edward Bridges 17.VII.41.

I have a feeling that Parliament does not at all understand the very great advance made in the refinement of priority questions through the development of the allocation principle. Let me have a note on this not exceeding one page. In fact, I think we hear very little about priorities now. Here and there there may be a focal point, but, speaking generally, am I not right in supposing that all is running smoothly? See, for instance, how well the giving of first priority to the production of tanks on psychological grounds has been adjusted. Priorities now resolve themselves into the opening-out of bottlenecks. No one has an absolute priority to the exclusion of all others. There have been no recent clashes. Comment freely on this by Friday.

Prime Minister to General Ismay, for departments concerned 17.VII.41.

What is the cause of the failure to produce containers in June? A fall from fifteen hundred to five hundred tons is shocking, and absolutely contrary to the express instructions of the Cabinet over many months. Who is responsible? The absolute maximum effort must be used, with superpriority to make, store, and fill into containers the largest possible quantities of gas.

Let me know exactly who is responsible for this failure.

At any moment this peril may be upon us. Papers must be prepared for Cabinet discussion next week.

Prime Minister to Home Secretary 19.VII.41.

I should like to have my opinion put on record that this sentence [of five years' penal servitude on Miss Elsie Orrin for saying to two

soldiers that Hitler was a good ruler, a better man than Mr.
Churchill] is far too heavy for expressions of opinion, however
pernicious, which are not accompanied by conspiracy. Nothing in
the internal state of the country justifies such unreasonable and un-
natural severity. I consider such excessive action defeats its own
ends.

(Action this day.)
Prime Minister to First Sea Lord and General Ismay for   20.VII.41.
C.O.S. Committee

I strongly deprecate bringing this [Glen] ship home. We sent
these three ships all round the Cape with much heart-burning in
the hopes of "Mandibles" and for other island attacks. Commandos
have been fritted away, and are now disbanded. The late régime
in the Middle East showed no aptitude for combined operations.
There was no D.C.O. [Director of Combined Operations], but only
a lukewarm and uninfluential committee. Nevertheless, we cannot
exclude the need of landing operations in the future. The other two
Glen ships are being mended, and it would be altogether wrong to
take this one away. I hope therefore the Chiefs of Staff will consider the matter in all its bearings.

(Action this day.)
Prime Minister to C.A.S.   21.VII.41.

Under the directions given at the time when the Battle of the
Atlantic was declared in March, the Coastal Command received a
special flow of reinforcements. I understand that in pursuance of
this all the Flying Fortresses, B.24's, that have come from the
United States recently have been sent to Coastal Command. In the
United States these machines are considered the ideal bombers for
Berlin, etc. Mr. Hopkins has been asking me about their use, and
seemed to be recording an American impression that they were
lying idle because we had no crews wherewith to man them. I am
correcting this impression, but I think on the widest grounds it
would be a very good thing if these bombers were used against
Germany in bombing raids. Furthermore, Coastal Command have
been reinforced by sixty-five Catalinas and many Sunderlands, and
the Battle of the Atlantic is very much eased by recent results, as
well as by the impending developments following upon the United
States occupation of Iceland, of which the First Sea Lord will tell
you.

Pray let me have your views.

C.-in-C. Bomber Command says he is very short and not expanding.

Prime Minister to General Ismay, for C.O.S. Committee   23.VII.41.

I wish the Commandos in the Middle East to be reconstituted as
soon as possible. Instead of being governed by a committee of

officers without much authority, Brigadier Laycock should be appointed Director of Combined Operations. The three Glen ships and the D.C.O., with his forces, should be placed directly under Admiral Cunningham, who should be charged with all combined operations involving sea transport and not exceeding one brigade. The Middle East Command have indeed maltreated and thrown away this invaluable force.

Prime Minister to General Ismay   25.VII.41.

Let me have on one sheet of paper the exact strength and details of the reinforcements and stores which got into Malta, and also the previous strength of the Malta garrison.

Prime Minister to Colonel Jacob   25.VII.41.

Let me have a short account of what has happened to our rifle production. What were the forecasts in September, 1939? What have been the results? What loss was attributed to the bombing? What are the new forecasts up to the end of the year 1941?

Former Naval Person to President Roosevelt   25.VII.41.

I am most grateful for your message about the tank programme. This addition to our tank resources in the coming critical months is splendid. As to the longer-term policy, all our experience goes to show that more heavily armed and armoured vehicles are required for modern battle, and we should therefore plan to increase the output of medium tanks at the expense of light tanks, but not of course at the expense of your air programme.

2. I am much interested in your suggestion that men for our Tank Corps should be trained in the United States. We are examining it here, and will let you know our views as soon as possible.

3. We have been considering here our war plans, not only for the fighting of 1942, but also for 1943. After providing for the security of essential bases, it is necessary to plan on the largest scale the forces needed for victory. In broad outline, we must aim first at intensifying the blockade and propaganda. Then we must subject Germany and Italy to a ceaseless and ever-growing air bombardment. These measures may themselves produce an internal convulsion or collapse. But plans ought also to be made for coming to the aid of the conquered populations by landing armies of liberation when opportunity is ripe. For this purpose it will be necessary not only to have great numbers of tanks, but also of vessels capable of carrying them and landing them direct onto beaches. It ought not to be difficult for you to make the necessary adaptation in some of the vast numbers of merchant vessels you are building so as to fit them for tank-landing fast ships.

4. If you agree with this broad conception of bringing Germany to her knees, we should not lose a moment in: (*a*) Framing an agreed estimate as to our joint requirements of the primary

weapons of war, e.g., aircraft, tanks, etc. (b) Thereafter considering how these requirements are to be met by our joint production.

5. Meanwhile I suggest that our combined staffs in London should set to work as soon as possible on (a), and that thereafter our technical experts should proceed with (b).

Prime Minister to General Ismay and Colonel Hollis, for   26.VII.41.
C.O.S. Committee

Great importance should be attached to furnishing C.-in-C. Home Forces with a much larger number of mobile anti-aircraft batteries, particularly of low-ceiling guns, to work with the field divisions and accompany the troops and armoured columns.

The Germans are quite right in always keeping their flak to the fore. No large body of troops should be assembled or be on the line of march without mobile Bofors batteries, to give them protection.

Do I understand that the two hundred and eighteen guns will be employed in this way? If so, I think the arrangement is very sound. If not, I should like the Chiefs of Staff to consider this point.

Otherwise I am in full agreement with the redeployment proposed.

Prime Minister to Minister of Food   27.VII.41.

I understand that you have under consideration a flexible coupon system, should it become necessary to ration the secondary foodstuffs, which would make the coupons available for the purchase of a variety of alternative goods and dispense with registration at particular shops. Though rigid rationing might be easier to administer, some system which left the consumer a reasonable feedom of choice would seem much better. Individual tastes have a wonderful way of cancelling out. Besides, your power of varying the prices of the different commodities both in money and coupons would enable you to exercise great control over demand.

Should you decide that the extension of rationing is inevitable, it would seem therefore that the flexible coupon system has much to commend it. I look forward to hearing your views about this in due course.

Prime Minister to Lord President of the Council,   27.VII.41.
Minister of Labour and National Service, and
Secretary of State for War

Evidence is accumulating that the figure of 2,195,000 men is too small for Army needs, and that the number ought to be increased as soon as possible; and the Secretary of State for War is now engaged on a detailed examination of his additional requirements.

2. Accordingly, the comprehensive review by the Man-Power Committee which has already been ordered by the War Cabinet

must be pressed forward with all speed. As soon as the main facts have been assembled, and without waiting for the full report, I should be glad if the Lord President of the Council, in consultation with the Ministers concerned, would give consideration, as a matter of urgency, to the additional requirements of the Army in the light of the general man-power position, and report on the measures that will be necessary to meet these requirements.

Prime Minister to Minister of Aircraft Production   30.VII.41.

I shall look forward with interest to hearing of the success or otherwise of the trials of the Whittle engine in the fortnight's time. I hope they will be favourable, but I gathered from you that the present turbine blades were working. We must not allow the designer's desire for fresh improvements to cause loss of time. Every nerve should be strained to get these aircraft into squadrons next summer, when the enemy will very likely start high-altitude bombing.

Prime Minister to General Ismay   31.VII.41.

I shall want plenty of photographs of Port Sudan, Massawa, the new port which is being developed in the Red Sea, Asmara, Basra, Tobruk, etc.

AUGUST

Prime Minister to Lord President   9.VIII.41.

I understand there is a proposal to make it a penal offence for any motorist who gets a supplementary ration of petrol not to keep a logbook in which every journey is entered.

To create and multiply offences which are not condemned by public opinion, which are difficult to detect and can only be punished in a capricious manner, is impolitic. To make it a penal offence not to keep a logbook might come under this heading, especially as only one-twenty-fifth of our oil consumption is involved.

I understand there is an alternative proposal to tell motorists that unless they can produce a logbook they will risk having their supplementary ration refused or reduced. Might not this be sufficient?

Prime Minister to Chairman of the Import Executive   9.VIII.41.

I understand that the Import Executive will shortly consider the arrangements made to provide cargoes for the additional ships to be put at our disposal by the U.S.A. in the near future. It is of the first importance that all the shipping space that becomes available to us, whether from United States sources or from an improvement in the shipping position, is fully utilised to bring in cargoes which will increase our war effort and give the people a healthy and varied diet.

2. Cargoes must be readily available for shipment as opportunity

offers, and a report should be prepared at once, showing the steps taken to this end by increasing our orders and by building up reserve stocks close to ports overseas.

3. I see that it is proposed to import 748,000 tons of softwood and 422,000 tons of hardwood in the second half of the year. This is far more than the figures mentioned at a recent Battle of the Atlantic meeting. Is this large import of timber being brought in because no more useful cargoes are available? Has the Minister of Agriculture been given the chance of suggesting any alternatives? For example, half a million tons of maize (which should be obtainable in the United States) would be of great value in keeping our chicken population going.

Prime Minister to First Lord of the Admiralty,   16.VIII.41.
Secretary of State for Air, and Minister of Aircraft
Production

This is a melancholy story. You will see from reading the minutes that we were promised Grummans, with folding wings, at twenty a month, beginning in April. We still have none, and are only promised the schedule set out in the First Lord's minute of July 26.[21]

2. I regard the supply of from six to twelve Grummans to *Victorious* and *Ark Royal* as of first importance. Especially is this the case with any carrier operating in the Mediterranean. The surprise which will be effected upon the enemy when these fast fighters rise to engage them may give considerable easement, almost at once.

The cutting-down of enemy bomber aircraft attack at sea far exceeds in importance and urgency any other duty which can be performed by a carrier in the Mediterranean. Even if they can only work within forty to fifty miles of the parent ship they can do all that is necessary. The enemy must be made to feel that to go near a ship convoyed by an aircraft-carrier is to incur heavy losses from aircraft almost equal to shore-based fighters.

3. We have now no aircraft-carriers in the Eastern Mediterranean. Therefore, there is no point in sending folding-wing Grummans there at present. The August, September, and October quotas for Grummans now assigned to the United Kingdom (total twenty-two), and the twenty-four now assigned to the Middle East in the September and October quotas—total forty-six—should all be made available in the United Kingdom for the equipping of our aircraft-carriers. Deliveries to the Middle East after October should be considered later.

Let me have a monthly report of the equipment of the aircraft-carriers with Grummans.

4. When do we get our next new aircraft-carrier, *Indomitable*?

5. Unless there is some reason to the contrary of which I am not aware, the following orders should be given now: "The September

21 About deliveries of Martlet II aircraft.

and October batches of twelve Grummans with folding wings should be sent to the United Kingdom and *not* [repeat *not*] to the Middle East."

COMMANDOS

Prime Minister to General Ismay   16.VIII.41.

I settled with General Auchinleck that the three Glen ships were all to remain in the Middle East and be refitted for amphibious operations as soon as possible.

2. That the Commandos should be reconstituted, as far as possible, by volunteers, by restoring to them any of their former members who may wish to return from the units in which they have been dispersed, and that Brigadier Laycock should have the command and should be appointed Director of Combined Operations.

3. The D.C.O. and the Commandos will be under the direct command of General Auchinleck. This cancels the former arrangement which I proposed of their being under the Naval Commander-in-Chief.

(Action this day.)
Prime Minister to C.I.G.S., and General Ismay, for   19.VIII.41.
C.O.S. Committee

The important thing is not so much to reduce our troops in Iceland as to make it a training ground for Alpine units. Can you not give some mountain guns to the artillery, instead of withdrawing them? Let me have a scheme for providing skis, snowshoes, etc., for the largest number that can be trained in mountain fighting under glacial conditions. The fact that a few more Americans have come should make the training all the easier. I regard the creation of these Alpine units as a vital feature in our organisation. I ask that this may be taken up with the utmost vigour.

Prime Minister to C.A.S.   19.VIII.41.

Thank you very much for your full explanation.[22] Even if the airmen had been in error they would not have been to blame, because it is the system that is at fault. The lack of effective and intimate contact between the air and the ground forces calls for a drastic reform. The needs of the Army should be met in a helpful spirit by the Air Ministry. It is the responsibility of the air force to satisfy the Army now that the resources are growing. I hope I may have your assurance that you are striving night and day to end this lamentable breakdown in the war machine. We need not go into the past, but if the Army is not well treated in the future the Air Ministry will have failed in an essential part of its duties.

[22] About the action of the 2d Armoured Division during the withdrawal from Cyrenaica, in March and April, 1941.

(*Action this day.*)
Prime Minister to Minister of Supply   20.VIII.41.

Pray see the attached statement [on gas and gas weapons] prepared at my direction by Lord Cherwell. We must expect gas warfare on a tremendous scale. It may break out at any moment. Please see the alarming restriction which has had to be imposed on the production of mustard gas; and also the explanation of this. What do the Air Ministry mean by stopping the charging of two-hundred-and-fifty-pound bombs? This seems most improvident, and is contrary to a number of Cabinet decisions, which are to the effect that the maximum possible gas is to be produced and charged into suitable containers, or otherwise stored.

I invite you to give your personal attention to this new aspect. The whole matter is dangerous and urgent in the last degree.

Prime Minister to Lord President   20.VIII.41.

I am by no means convinced that there are sufficient reasons for imposing this additional obligation [of keeping a logbook by motorists] on the public. There is a growing and justifiable impatience of multiplying the filling-up of forms and providing a new foundation upon which further layers of officials may build their homes. If you feel there is no other means of securing your objects it would be better to bring the matter before the Cabinet.

Prime Minister to Secretary of State for India   20.VIII.41

Certainly let an invitation be sent, provided that in general you see U Saw.[23]

Prime Minister to First Sea Lord   25.VIII.41.

Will you please let me have on one sheet of paper a list of the effective Japanese Fleet and flotillas, with dates of construction, and the ships which are ready now.

(*Action this day.*)
Prime Minister to Minister of Agriculture   26.VIII.41.

I hear bad tales about the harvest. What is the position today? We are clear of Saint Swithin's forty days now. If we get fine weather what sort of estimate can you make? Alas, we spoke too soon!

Prime Minister to Production Executive   26.VIII.41.

I am concerned at the great amount of man-power and raw materials which are still being directed to constructional work. The works and building programme is using two and one-fourth million tons of imported materials a year (iron, steel, and timber) and three-quarters of a million men.

Has not the time come to disallow all new projects of factory construction, save in very exceptional cases? Can we justify fur-

[23] This refers to a Minute from Mr. Amery about conditions in Burma and a proposed visit to this country by the Burmese Premier, U Saw.

ther expenditure when so much existing plant is only half-employed? Could not building resources be better used in providing hostels and amenities for the labour needed to man extra shifts in the existing plant?

The utmost economy should also be sought in Service requirements, which are apt to be on a more lavish scale than the needs of the moment or the available resources justify.

I trust that there is some machinery for preventing designs being accepted which are wasteful of imported material.

Please inform me what safeguards you have to ensure: (a) That new factories or building undertakings are really essential. (b) That the plans and designs for such undertakings are of the most economical character. (c) That building labour is used to the best advantage.

Prime Minister to C.A.S. 27.VIII.41.

I have certainly sustained the impression that the Air Ministry in the past has been most hard and unhelpful both to the Army and to the Navy in meeting their special requirements. The Navy succeeded in breaking away before the war, but the Army lies under a sense of having been denied its proper air assistance. To some extent this can be excused by the plea that the need of increasing the R.A.F. was paramount. Now that that need is no longer so overwhelming I trust the Army's grievances and complaints will be met.

There is a widespread belief that we have not developed dive-bombers because of the fear of the Air Ministry that a weapon of this kind specially associated with the Army might lead to a formation of a separate Army wing.

All these things happened before your time, but their consequences are with us today.

Prime Minister to Foreign Office 27.VIII.41.

Give me in a few lines the reasons which led to Siam calling itself Thailand. What are the historic merits of these two names?

Prime Minister to General Ismay, for C.O.S. Committee 27.VIII.41.

In several quarters there are indications of a German move against Murmansk. It appears that, though there were no transports found when we made our abortive attack, considerable numbers are on the move now. What are we going to do about it now? Is it settled that we can do nothing more in the North? When do our two squadrons reach Murmansk? Can nothing naval be done to obstruct the movement of German transports?

Prime Minister to Chancellor of the Exchequer 28.VIII.41.

How much gold have we actually got left in this island or under our control in South Africa? Don't be alarmed: I am not going to ask you for anything.

Prime Minister to Sir E. Bridges   28.VIII.41.

Mr. Harcourt Johnstone will preside over an interdepartmental committee containing representatives of the offices concerned for the purpose of devising the best possible plan for relaxation of the black-out restrictions during the present comparative lull in the enemy's air attack: (*a*) on vehicles required for vital war services; and (*b*) for factories and ports. The object is to secure the maximum of production for war purposes.

2. The committee should consider, *inter alia:* (*a*) the categories of vehicles permitted to relax; (*b*) the subdued character of the lighting enabling them to proceed at a reasonable speed; (*c*) the particular routes over which and areas in which these relaxations may be especially required by the Ministry of Supply, Ministry of Aircraft Production, and the Admiralty; and finally, (*d*) the means of speedy return to present style if and when this is rendered necessary by enemy action in any district or throughout the country.

3. The committee is to report in one week to the Prime Minister. All departments are expected to co-operate in the public interest to the utmost. The preparation of the best possible plan must be considered a technical study, and does not necessarily commit the Ministerial heads of the departments concerned to its adoption. This may be remitted to a committee of War Cabinet Ministers on grounds of general policy.

(*Action this day.*)
Prime Minister to Secretary of State for War   29.VIII.41.

I must draw your attention to the state of the cruiser tanks [in Britain]. This week, out of four hundred and eight, there are actually more unfit for service than fit. This figure and the system on which it rests require evidently strong handling. The proportion of unfit is getting worse each week.

Let me know who is responsible, and what you are going to do about it.

(*Action this day.*)
Prime Minister to C.A.S.   29.VIII.41.

The loss of seven Blenheims out of seventeen in the daylight attack on merchant shipping and docks at Rotterdam is most severe. Such losses might be accepted in attacking *Scharnhorst, Gneisenau,* or *Tirpitz,* or a south-bound Tripoli convoy, because, apart from the damage done, a first-class strategic object is served. But they seem disproportionate to an attack on merchant shipping not engaged in vital supply work. The losses in our bombers have been very heavy this month, and Bomber Command is not expanding as was hoped. While I greatly admire the bravery of the pilots, I do not want them pressed too hard. Easier targets giving a high damage return compared with casualties may more often be selected.

Let me have a return showing all bombers written off in August for any cause, including crashes on landing, and also the number of bombers received from M.A.P., and the number manufactured and imported.

(Action this day.)
Prime Minister to C.A.S. 30.VIII.41.

What is being done about increasing the night-fighter defence in the Middle East? I gather they are by no means up to date with our devices, yet Alexandria, Suez, and the Suez Canal are places of the highest consequence.

Pray let me have a short report. General Pile might be helpful in drawing up a list of an advanced echelon of night-fighting devices, organization, and supplies. All this is very important. Speed is vital.

Prime Minister to C.A.S. 30.VIII.41.

This estimate of seventeen hundred German aircraft knocked out in the Russian fighting should now be brought into relation to the results of the second Singleton survey of the relative British and German air strength in all theatres.

Let me know the result at your convenience.

Prime Minister to V.C.A.S. 30.VIII.41.

Good.

"The devotion and gallantry of the attacks on Rotterdam and other objectives are beyond all praise. The charge of the Light Brigade at Balaclava is eclipsed in brightness by these almost daily deeds of fame."

Tell the squadrons and publish if you think well.[24]

Prime Minister to General Ismay, for C.O.S. Committee 30.VIII.41.

Although personally I am quite content with the existing explosives, I feel we must not stand in the path of improvement, and I therefore think that action should be taken in the sense proposed by Lord Cherwell, and that the Cabinet Minister responsible should be Sir John Anderson.[25]

I shall be glad to know what the Chiefs of Staff Committee think.

Prime Minister to First Sea Lord 31.VIII.41.

If you think fit, and the ships are safely in port, please convey to the Admiralty War Staff, Trade Division, C.-in-C. Western Approaches, Coastal Command, and others concerned my compliments upon the vigilance, ingenuity, and flexible organisation which has in the last week enabled so great a number of ships to pass through the exceptionally heavy U-boat concentration.

[24] This refers to a minute about Blenheim attacks on shipping in Rotterdam.
[25] This refers to early plans for atom-bomb research for which we used the code-word "Tube Alloys."

Prime Minister to Minister of Information   31.VIII.41.

How is our big broadcasting station, which is to override foreign broadcasts, getting on? There was a long delay in setting about it, but I understand the fullest priorities have been given. Please give me a short report—half a page.

2. I think it very important that the German films of the invasion of Russia should be shown in England, and also that they should be sent to the United States. Mr. Winant fully concurs with this last. I sent you a message last week that I thought ten minutes of these German atrocities would be the best possible prelude to the Atlantic meeting and Iceland films. What has been done about this?

3. Have the Icelanders got a copy of the film about themselves?

SEPTEMBER

Prime Minister to C.I.G.S.   8.IX.41.

Please let me have a short report on the present position of delayed-action fuzes.

At the end of the last war the Germans used these on a great scale for rendering impossible the use of railway lines, and also for booby-traps, when they retreated in France.

The periods of delay should be varied from a few days to several months, so that uncertainty is never absent and breakdowns on the lines are continual. I understand the method was a small metal box, not much bigger than a cigar-case, in which an acid gradually ate through a metal wire, thus establishing a contact or opening an orifice. No doubt many improvements have taken place.

The whole aspect of our layout in the East leads me to think that provision of these devices on a very considerable scale should be undertaken. We are making airfields in Anatolia, Syria, Persia, Cyprus, etc., and railways and roads are being improved and pushed forward. We ought to have the means of making them unusable by the enemy for a considerable time should we have to fall back. The best way of doing this would be to build in the mines beforehand, leaving a small sealed passage through which the appropriate fuze could be passed, should it become necessary to arm these mines. Every airfield should have twenty or thirty mines built into it. Should it be necessary to evacuate, the fuzes could be put in and the surface smoothed over. The danger period must certainly last at least six months, and railroads (at any rate in their forward sections) should have at least three or four mines to the mile, and all bridges and tunnels should be mined. The uncertainty of when a line or road would be out of order is more baffling than even widespread destruction, which is over once and for all.

Pray let me have your thought on this.

Prime Minister to Minister of Labour   8.IX.41.

Is there any truth in the allegations made in the newspapers that many of the so-called Jehovah's Witnesses are strong young healthy fellows, who do not take part in the war effort?

Prime Minister to Minister of Supply   10.IX.41.
(*Copy to the Secretary of State for Air.*)

In your minute of August 29 you tell me that the order for fifty thousand Jefferis bombs (puff balls) cannot be produced and that you can offer ten thousand only.

I take it that this is due to the shortage of the explosive. I am informed that the contents of nine sticky bombs will fill two puff-balls. We could thus obtain the remaining forty thousand puff-balls by postponing the filling of 180,000 stickies. This, I understand, is only about six weeks' output at the present rate, and I therefore agree that we should postpone filling in this way.

The bombard should continue in production unaffected.

(*Action this day.*)
Prime Minister to C.I.G.S.   10.IX.41.

Please see attached from Lord Beaverbrook [about the Trans-Persian Railway]. In view of the danger to Murmansk and the masses of stuff we are planning to send to Russia and the difficulties of developing the railway through Persia and carrying at the same time, it seems most urgent to explore the full possibilities of road transport. I could cable Mr. Hopkins asking for the necessary lorries, drivers, and mechanics, if these are necessary, and I have little doubt the United States would ship them to Basra pretty quickly. I know nothing about the roads, but the whole matter must be examined, together with a plan for improving the roads while the vehicles are coming from America.

Let me have your views on this, if possible by tomorrow, so that I can act.

Prime Minister to General Ismay, for C.O.S. Committee 12.IX.41.

It will not be possible for the whole British Army (other than those in the Middle East) to remain indefinitely inert and passive as a garrison of this Island against invasion. Such a course, apart altogether from military considerations, would bring the Army into disrepute. I do not need to elaborate this.

2. An expeditionary force equivalent to six divisions should be organised for action oversea.

3. Unless unexpected developments open a new theatre in Spain or Morocco, or invasion becomes imminent, we should attempt the liberation of Norway at the earliest suitable moment.

4. A plan should be prepared to act in whatever is thought to be the best place. This plan should be brought before the Defence Committee before the end of the present month.

Prime Minister to Sir Edward Bridges and   13.IX.41.
General Ismay

It is certain that confusion will arise between Bandar Shahpur and Bandar Shah at either end of the Trans-Persian Railway. Therefore, for all British official purposes the two places should be called Bandar Caspian and Bandar Gulf. Pray let directions be given in this sense.

Prime Minister to General Ismay   13.IX.41.

It is certainly necessary that this appreciation [on general strategy for the Dominions Prime Ministers] should be brought up to date. It does not take any account of our occupation of Persia, and of the importance of the through route to Russia, with whom we have joined hands. It will be much easier at the end of September or in mid-October to take a view about Russian prospects. No reference is made to a possible attack or pressure upon Turkey, and its consequences.

What is the hurry about this paper? In its present form it will only hustle and worry the Dominions. Take, for instance, the suggestion that one of the reasons for holding Egypt is to prevent the Italian fleet from charging through the Canal to hunt the British Navy out of the Indian Ocean. I should be very sorry to base our case for holding Egypt on such an argument.

Prime Minister to General Ismay, for C.O.S.   13.IX.41.
Committee

I have never asked for a second voyage [of American ships for convoying Middle East reinforcements], though I hoped it would come. But it would be a great help in working off the masses of troops overdue for the Middle East. All this is most gratifying. I should be glad presently of details to express thanks. Please report on facilities opened up by second trip.

Prime Minister to Minister of Information   13.IX.41.

Surely more stir ought to be made about Hitler shooting the Norwegian trade-unionists, and sending others for long periods of penal servitude. Ought not the Trade Union Congress to pass resolutions of sympathy? Why don't you get into touch with Citrine and work up a steady outcry? The names of the two victims should be publicised as martyrs.

Prime Minister to Sir Andrew Duncan   13.IX.41.

At my request Lord Cherwell has prepared a short note upon the import forecast. You are now considering the programmes at the Import Executive. I work in calendar years, and the import budget which I wish to make must be for the year 1942. I should like to settle this budget at latest during November. Meanwhile, comparisons between the first and second years of the war, and forecasts of the third year, are useful.

You must always bear in mind that I may have to make a large further demand for shipping, in case an expeditionary force has to be dispatched. Perhaps you will let me have your preliminary ideas, for which the Professor's paper forms a convenient peg.

Prime Minister to Lord Cherwell   13.IX.41.

It will be necessary to prevent any diminution in the strength of the Army in 1942, and very special measures will have to be adopted to secure this. There can be no question of switching off Army munitions for some time to come. I have asked that an expeditionary force of six divisions, in addition to the two going East, should be prepared. Where it will go must depend on events. What is left will be barely sufficient to give security at home.

The provision of the necessary men will cause great difficulties. I hope, however, that A.D.G.B., A.R.P., Coastal Defence, and the heavy artillery, together with some of the rearward services, may yield two or three hundred thousand men. We shall draw sharply upon reserved occupations. At the present time there is grave danger of several divisions having to be broken up.

Please take the above for your guidance.

(Action this day.)
Prime Minister to General Ismay, for C.O.S. Committee   14.IX.41.

The air force demand shows the unbridled use of ground personnel. We are planning to place eighty squadrons in the Middle East by the spring of 1942. There are already forty-five thousand air-groundsmen there, and it is now proposed to add forty thousand more, making a total of well over one thousand men to every squadron of sixteen aircraft first-line strength. It is evident that a searching inquiry must be held into these establishments, which on their present scale will ruin our war effort.

In the meanwhile only twenty thousand air force personnel can be included in the convoys up to the end of December.

It should be noted that only thirteen air squadrons are being sent from here, not seventeen, as stated in these papers.

2. The additional divisions should go intact, in accordance with my request to the President. He would never have given me the extra shipping but for the attraction of placing two strong additional divisions in the Middle East. I cannot face him with a demand to use his ships for details and drafts.

3. The above makes a total of sixty thousand. The troops for India would seem to come next, in view of the four extra divisions we are to get as a result of them. The A.T. and A.A. artillery would naturally have precedence over the field and medium, with which the Middle East is already so heavily supplied. Eighteen thousand additional Army Service Corps is a requirement very hard to justify. What particular task is this force, almost equivalent to a division in numbers, needed for?

4. With regard to drafts. The Army of the Nile has not fought

lately, and although there is the usual wastage for sickness I cannot feel that drafts to complete the first reinforcements—i.e., ten per cent drafts at the base over and above full strength with the units, or drafts to cover estimated additional wastage—should take precedence over organised fighting troops. They should fit in as convenient.

5. Meanwhile, let me have a table showing the present strength of each of the battalions or artillery regiments (British) for which these thirty-one thousand additional drafts are now said to be required. Infantry drafts should receive priority over other branches.

6. Some time ago I had some figures showing the ratio of fighting troops to the rearward services in the Middle East. Could these be brought up to date, on the assumption that it was possible to carry the whole 142,000 now asked for?

Prime Minister to Foreign Secretary   20.IX.41.
(Copy to Secretary of State for Air.)

I think that great value might be obtained at the present time by dropping leaflets on Italy referring particularly to the fact that hundreds of thousands of Italians have been sent from sunny homes to die in the frozen mud of the Ukraine. Pray have this matter considered by the Political Warfare Executive.

I am sending a copy of this minute to the Secretary of State for Air, in order that the operational aspect also may be considered.

(Action this day.)
Prime Minister to Colonel Hollis   21.IX.41.

Many bombards are now being delivered. What has been done about their tactical employment? An experimental bombard battery or regiment should be set up at once to develop the use of the weapon and to further its distribution to troops. Let me have proposals how this can be achieved.

Prime Minister to C.A.S.   21.IX.41.

Do our fighter pilots over France carry a sufficient supply of French money? I am told they are only given fifty francs. In my view at least three thousand francs should be carried as part of a pilot's equipment, and passed from hand to hand.

Prime Minister to C.I.G.S.   21.IX.41.

I am not prepared to let this lapse or be slurred over, or fall into oblivion. More than admonitions are required when six hundred German Legionnaires are allowed to go back to Vichy France for further use by Germany against us. It might take six hundred British lives to deal with these men so casually and incontinently allowed to slip through our fingers. A formal letter should be written by the War Office to the Commander-in-Chief Middle East, asking for the action taken by him, and pointing out the gravity of the injury to British interests involved in this supine conduct of the Command in Syria. If a sergeant or a corporal makes a slip, he is punished or reprimanded. The Staff Officers around General Wilson are to blame for not having raised the point and understood what was going on. If General Wilson takes the blame himself, it can be written off against his good services in other directions, but he ought to be left in no doubt of the harm that has been done. The fullest detailed explanation should be provided.[26]

Prime Minister to C.I.G.S.   21.IX.41.

Thank you. I am glad to see by later telegrams that it is proposed to reorganise the forward area, so that any similar movement of the enemy can be struck at offensively by the forward troops. I understand this readjustment is to be completed about twenty-third instant. If this is right now, I still do not see why it was not right earlier. The losses of ten tanks, etc., that the enemy suffered at the hands only of armoured cars without tanks shows that a pretty good "cop" could have been staged. However, perhaps we shall get a second chance. P'raps not. Fortune is a jade.

Prime Minister to Chiefs of Staff   25.IX.41.

I attach a summary of the official correspondence which has passed in the last fifteen months in regard to offensive and defensive measures in chemical warfare, together with a table showing the stock position of the more important gas-filled weapons. Please report whether you are satisfied with the present position and our means of retaliating on the Germans if necessary.

There may be a difficulty in maintaining stocks owing to chemical deterioration. Normally, if there were a consumption stocks could be replaced. Please let me have your views on this aspect of the matter as well.

Prime Minister to Foreign Secretary   25.IX.41.

We now know that the Grand Mufti is in the Japanese Legation at Teheran. It seems of the utmost importance to obtain his surrender, and meanwhile I presume all measures are being taken to prevent his getting away. Will you please do whatever is possible?

Prime Minister to Secretary of State for War   25.IX.41.

Many plans are being made for the amusement of troops during the winter. They are allowed to use Government transport, within limits, to get to the nearest sizeable town. Officers are not allowed to have this privilege. It might be possible to arrange for officers to have reasonable use of available Government transport on paying for the petrol. Many of them are too poor to hire any other form of transport, but this would be fair and acceptable. The use might be controlled by the Corps Divisional Staff.

[26] The explanation divided the responsibility to an extent which was difficult to follow by disciplinary action.

Pray let me have your views on this.

Prime Minister to First Lord and First Sea Lord   25.IX.41.

Why not give the *Graph* U-boat, when she is repaired, to the Yugoslav Navy? They have a submarine crew which has arrived at Alexandria, but their vessel was in too bad a condition for the Admiral to allow it to go to sea. I rather like the idea of the Yugoslavs working a captured German U-boat.[27]

Prime Minister to Minister of Works and Buildings   27.IX.41.

I doubt very much whether it will ever be possible for me to live at Walmer Castle, or indeed whether anybody will be able to live in such fine houses after the war. I mentioned this to the King when accepting the Lord Wardenship of the Cinque Ports, which I regard as a compliment. Clearly I cannot attempt to reside there at the present time, as it is well within range of the enemy's batteries on the French coast, and the mere report of my residing there would be sufficient to get the whole place knocked down. In these circumstances I think it would be perfectly proper for the Office of Works to take it over during the war in whatever way they think most conducive to the public interest. I should hope therefore that, as long as I do not use the castle at all or derive any benefit from it, it and the gardens could be taken care of by the State. After the war the position could be reviewed.

Perhaps you will let me know what you think can be done.

(*Action this day.*)
Prime Minister to Colonel Hollis, for C.O.S. Committee   30.IX.41.

When I visited *Indomitable* last week I was astonished to learn that the handful of Hurricanes to be allotted to this vital war unit were only of the lower type, Hurricane 1's. I trust it may be arranged that only the finest aeroplanes that can do the work go into all aircraft-carriers. All this year it has been apparent that the power to launch the highest class fighters from aircraft-carriers may reopen to the Fleet great strategic doors which have been closed against them. The aircraft-carrier should have supreme priority in the quality and character of suitable types.[28]

OCTOBER

(*Action this day.*)
Prime Minister to Secretary of State for War and C.I.G.S.   1.X.41.

The danger of our forces being organised on a basis so cumbrous that they will be incapable of effective overseas or amphibious action has now grown very great. The condition of the armoured

---

[27] This was the U-boat captured by a Hudson aircraft in the western approaches in August 1941. See Book Two, Chapter 7, "The Mounting Strength of Britain," page 438.
[28] Later types of British fighters could not at this time be spared by the R.A.F. for the use of the Navy. (See also minute of 16.VIII.41, pages 692–693.)

divisions has recently attracted attention. As new ideas and new requirements come along, the tendency to growth is continual. In order to preserve the efficiency of the Army a continued process of pruning is indispensable.

2. The dire need of finding men to maintain the fighting units at proper strength makes ceaseless economy in the rearward services imperative. I am doing my utmost to sustain the strength of the Army against the growing volume of criticism about its reputed size and obvious enforced passivity. I feel therefore bound to press for assistance from the War Office, and I hope I may count upon you to help me.

3. For this purpose a committee of officers acquainted with the establishments should be set up, with orders to make a plan for a twenty-five per cent reduction in the rearward services and non-fighting troops, showing how this can be done with the least possible injury. This work should be completed by the fifteenth instant, and the Defence Committee will then be able to see what is entailed in the particular cuts proposed. I wish to be consulted about the personnel of this committee. If it fails, I shall have to ask for an outside committee, as I know how hard it is for a department to reform itself.

Prime Minister to Minister of War Transport   3.X.41.

I should be glad if you would submit a report for consideration at the next meeting of the Battle of the Atlantic Committee, showing the progress which has been made with the provision of alternative port facilities for use if any of the major ports on which we now rely should be put out of action.

(*Action this day.*)
Prime Minister to Colonel Hollis, for C.O.S. Committee   4.X.41.

I attach the utmost importance to tanks and aircraft reaching Archangel early in October. It is vital that delivery should begin at once. Pray let proposals and preparation for this be made forthwith and let me have a report on Monday evening. A special convoy will probably be necessary.

I cannot too strongly emphasise the vital importance and extreme urgency of this transaction.

(*Action this day.*)
Prime Minister to Secretary of State for War   6.X.41.

I feel some anxiety regarding the scheme conducted by the new Army Bureau of Current Affairs. The test must be whether discussions of such matters conducted by regimental officers will weaken or strengthen that tempered discipline without which our armies can be no match for the highly trained forces of Germany. The qualities required for conducting discussions of the nature indicated are not necessarily those which fit for command in the field. Will not such discussions only provide opportunities for the professional grouser and agitator with a glib tongue? They seem to be in a different category from educative lectures by trained teachers or experts.

Pray consider this matter and let me have your personal views. Meanwhile please suspend action.

Former Naval Person to President Roosevelt   8.X.41.

After discussion with Ambassador Winant I send you this note setting out the result of our Cabinet discussion on the matter which has been causing us some difficulty.

We have been considering carefully what should be the next step regarding the conference upon wheat which is due to resume its deliberations next week. I feel a certain amount of concern as to the repercussions on the war situation of the proposed wheat agreement in its present form. The draft seems to give the impression that it is contemplated to force on the wheat-importing countries of Europe, as a condition of immediate post-war relief, a series of obligations, including a drastic restriction of their wheat production, which would vitally affect their agricultural systems. This is to touch a tender spot in the policy of many countries. Any wheat agreement capable of this construction would, in our view, be dangerous in the extreme. It would supply Nazi propaganda with a weapon which it would not be slow to use. It would arouse widespread suspicions as to the spirit in which the United States and the United Kingdom mean to use their power when the war is over, and would confuse and dishearten the elements in Europe now hoping and working for the defeat of Germany. We regard it as essential therefore to remove from the draft agreement all provisions implying Anglo-American interference in European agricultural policy.

The relation of Russia to any agreement also raises a difficulty. Russia was still a neutral at the time when the arrangements for the wheat conference were made. But, as things are now, it appears to us virtually out of the question either to conclude an agreement which may seriously affect her interests without consulting her, or to approach her on such a matter at a time when she is engaged in a life-and-death struggle, and when her richest wheatfields are in the battle area.

We have been considering what instructions we can give to our delegates, who are now on their way to Washington, with a view to meeting these difficulties, but we have not been able to find a really satisfactory solution consistent with the present framework of the draft agreement. Considerable revision would certainly be required; and we are alive to the danger, which we are anxious to avoid, of protracted negotiations which might lead to a breakdown. For our part, we welcome the proposals for establishing a pool of wheat for post-war relief. There are other important features of the agreement which do not prejudice, or which could easily be given a form which would not prejudice, the interests of unrepresented countries—e.g., the agreement of the four exporting countries represented as to the ratios of their respective export quotas, and the provisions for an "ever-normal" granary.

The other issues of policy might usefully be explored by the conference with a view to preparing the ground for later decisions; but it seems to me that we should be ill-advised to attempt to reach definite conclusions about these now. Apart from the fact that important countries not represented at the conference are affected, there seems to be advantage in trying to fit these questions into the larger discussions on Anglo-American collaboration in regard to post-war economic problems generally which, as Lord Halifax will be able to explain more fully, we hope to be able to begin at an early date.

If you agree generally with my view I will instruct our delegation accordingly.

Prime Minister to Secretary of State for War and   8.X.41.
Secretary of State for Air
(*Copy to Secretary of State for Dominion Affairs.*)

I think now the time is ripe to form an Irish Brigade, also an Irish Wing or Squadron of the R.A.F. If these were taken in hand they would have to be made a great success of. The pilot Finucane might be a great figure.[29]

Pray let me have proposals. The movement might have important political reactions later on.

(*Action this day.*)
Prime Minister to Secretary of State for War and C.I.G.S   9.X.41.

Pray let me have your views, and if possible your plans, for the forming of an Irish Brigade.

Prime Minister to Secretary of State for War   10.X.41.

I see some odd court-martial cases mentioned in the papers. First a sergeant who told a Home Guard lieutenant, "So what?" and "Put a sock in it," in the presence of troops, but who was merely reprimanded. He should have surely been reduced to the ranks. Second, some soldiers who were heard calling the sergeants "Bastards with three stripes," but who apparently were honourably acquitted on the grounds that this was a word of common use in

---

[29] Wing-Commander "Paddy" Finucane, D.F.C. and two bars, was killed at the age of twenty-two in July, 1942, when after continuous exploits, he was leading a fighter wing in a mass attack on enemy targets in France. It was always said that the Luftwaffe would never get him, and it was actually a ground shot from an unusual single machine-gun post which hit his Spitfire. He flew slowly out to sea, talking calmly to his comrades. Finally, when ten miles from the French coast, he sent his last message, spoken probably as his engine stopped: "This is it, chaps." He crashed from about ten feet above the sea, and his machine sank at once.

Finucane had always vowed not to be taken prisoner, and it was probably this that made him fly out to sea rather than inland, where he would have had a good chance of survival.

the Army. The major giving evidence said he had often turned a deaf ear to it when used about himself.

In sharp contrast, two Canadians who deserted in Canada, and made their way over here after great adventure in order to fight, received sixty days.

All this seems to require very clear guidance from you and the Army authorities.

(*Action this day.*)
Prime Minister to Secretary of State for Air, Minister   11.X.41.
of Supply, and M.A.P.

I have re-read the report of the Select Committee on the Albemarles, and I think it requires a far more definite and categorical reply than those which have hitherto been presented to me. I should be glad to know what is the evidence which the two Supply Ministers will give, especially on the financial side; and from the Secretary of State for Air I desire to learn (*a*) what real use this machine will be when the first five hundred are completed. Can he tell me that it will be a *bona-fide* useful machine in the summer of next year? What parts of Germany could it bomb, or is it only of use on the French invasion ports? (*b*) What are the reasons, shortly, for refusing to publish the report? What information in particular is contained in it which would be of value to the enemy?

As this matter will be debated on Wednesday and I shall have to watch over it myself in all probability, I want to be sure of my ground. The matter is urgent.

Prime Minister to Minister of Supply   12.X.41.

During your absence I have considered the questions you raised with me about the U.P.[30] weapon and its subsidiary variants of the proximity fuze, namely, P.E. and radio. The great need is the manufacture of A.D. ammunition for the fifty batteries which are already deployed. P.E. and radio are in the sphere of research and experiment, but these researches should be pressed to the utmost because of the immense strategic advantages to the Navy which would flow from their effective solution.

Up to the present time I take full responsibility for all that has been done. You wish as Minister of Supply to have full control of both the manufacture and research, and I shall be very glad if you will assume it as from the date of this minute. As the three Services are concerned, you will no doubt arrange for the necessary consultations.

Prime Minister to Secretary of State for India   15.X.41.

Kindly let me know how many words His Majesty's representative at Kabul has telegraphed since the day when the question of turning the Germans out of Afghanistan was first mentioned to him.

[30] Unrotated Projectile. Disguised name for rocket. See footnote to minute of 6.XII.41, page 720.

Prime Minister to Sir Edward Bridges 16.X.41.

An inquiry should be held into the question of who was responsible for the various messages sent over the radio to the Germans about the exchange of prisoners. These messages contained expressions of thanks and were couched in the form of direct communications with the enemy. The inquiry is to be formal and a report is to be made to me as Minister of Defence.

Pray suggest the composition of the inquiry.

(*Action this day.*)
Prime Minister to Lord President of the Council 17.X.41.

The Shelter Programme has had a pretty good run since March, and although it may not be completed according to the target plan it must be far better than last year. Having regard to the air-raid and air-raid defence situation, they must expect to have to make a definite contribution to the man-power stringency, including particularly the Army. De-reservation should play over this area. Before I send any minute to the Home Secretary and others on the subject, I should like you to take this into the scope of your general scheme and report to me.

Prime Minister to Secretary of State for War 17.X.41.

I do not approve of this system of encouraging political discussion in the Army among soldiers as such. The material provided for the guidance of the officers in the short notes is hopelessly below the level of that available in the daily press. Discussions in which no controversy is desired are a farce. There cannot be controversy without prejudice to discipline. The only sound principle is "No politics in the Army."

I hope you will wind up this business as quickly and as decently as possible and set the persons concerned in it to useful work.

(*Action this day.*)
Prime Minister to Secretary of State for War 18.X.41.

During my visit to the Richmond Anti-Aircraft Mixed Battery I learned, with much surprise, that the present policy of the [Women's] Auxiliary Territorial Service is that A.T.S. personnel in mixed batteries should not consider themselves part of the battery, and that no "battery *esprit de corps*" was to be allowed. This is very wounding to the A.T.S. personnel, who have been deprived of badges, lanyards, etc., of which they were proud. Considering that they share the risks and the work of the battery in fact, there can be no justification for denying them incorporation in form.

2. In present circumstances it is possible also that the whole efficiency of a battery could be upset by an order from the War Office, A.T.S. Headquarters, moving one of a predictor team to another unit. The A.A. Command has no say in such matters. Obviously this cannot continue when we are relying upon these mixed batteries as an integral part of our defence.

3. I found a universal desire among all ranks that the women who serve their country by manning guns should be called "Gunners" and "Members of the Royal Regiment of Artillery." There would be no objection to the letters "A.T.S." being retained.

Prime Minister to Chief Whip   18.X.41.

If the House wishes to divide in secret session it must itself organise the division, and provide not only the ordinary tellers, but also Members who would act as clerks, and mark the lists accordingly. These division lists would remain privileged documents in the custody of Mr. Speaker.

2. Should however the House by a majority, whether on the motion of the Government or otherwise, decide that it was in the public interest, or necessary because of constitutional reaction following the division, that the division list and the questions put should be published, the House would also have to decide by conference among the party leaders upon such version of what had taken place in secret session as might be in accord with public interest being made public at the same time. The consultations between the party leaders or members chosen by the House would follow the lines of the consultations which take place when it is necessary to express differences with the House of Lords, or perhaps of the conferences contemplated under the Parliament Act. In this case however it would be necessary that the version of the debate in secret which was to be published should be debated and approved by the House word by word as if it were a Bill, and with full right of amendment.

3. Thus the House, which is the only authority, would in every stage be master of its own proceedings and express its will by majority. I am of opinion that they would endorse this procedure.

Prime Minister to President of the Board of Trade   19.X.41.

I am very much obliged to you for the clear and full account you have given me of the forecast for 1942 in accordance with my minute of September 13. You seem to me to be sufficiently insured in wheat and steel, and we have also a very good account of oil from the Petroleum Executive. I approve the principle of a 33,000,-000-ton import, which we should by all means in our power try to achieve. I should be very glad if the meat ration could be improved. I am assuming that the impact of the Russian liabilities will be met outside the 33,000,000 limit, which limit we should regard as our minimum in all our discussions with the United States.

You should now prepare a statement for the War Cabinet, which, after examination by the Lord President's Committee, can be discussed during November.

Prime Minister to His Majesty's Representative at Kabul   19.X.41.

I have been much pleased with the way in which you have handled the question of turning out the Germans and Italians, but I think you ought to know that from September 11, when this task was entrusted to you, to October 17, you have sent 6639 cipher groups. The labour and cost of this profuse telegraphing and the choking effect of such lengthy messages upon the higher administration ought never to be forgotten. Clarity and cogency can, I am sure, be reconciled with a greater brevity.

(Action this day.)
Prime Minister to Minister of Labour 20.X.41.

In my Army Strength paper, which you have seen, the total [intake] for the Army was given as 278,000, including 50,000 casualties. This covers the nine months from now till the end of June, 1942. How do these figures square with your 355,000 for the twelve months so ending?

2. The Royal Air Force demands cannot be accepted as they stand. They are queueing up more and more air-groundmen behind the pilot. Have you subjected them to any cutting or analysis, or do you have to face the figures as they put them? I should think 50,000 could be got off here.

3. *Prima facie* I am not prepared to recognise the need for any additions to Civil Defence. How was this figure arrived at? Has it been subjected to any scrutiny? Far from adding to Civil Defence personnel, I am hoping that 1942 will see them increasingly combed.

Prime Minister to C.A.S. 24.X.41.

I am not content with the arrangements made for the two squadrons in Murmansk. I thought they were to take their aircraft and move to the south of the front, where they might have come into action with the Russian Air Force. Instead of this, the personnel only is being sent. When is it expected that these two squadrons will again come into action, and where? The most serious mistake we have made about the Russians was in not sending eight air force fighter squadrons, which would have gained great fame, destroyed many German aircraft, and given immense encouragement all along the front. This is the only criticism, among the many that have been made, which I feel strikes home.

Prime Minister to Director of Military Intelligence 24.X.41.

My general impression is that the scale of the fighting [in Russia] has diminished on both sides, and that many fewer divisions are engaged each day than a month ago. What do you say to this?

What date is the winter expected to set in earnest in the Moscow region?

Is there any sign of digging in on any part of the front?

What, in your opinion, are the chances of Moscow being taken before the winter? I should be inclined to put it evens.

Prime Minister to Secretary of State for War   29.X.41.

All this seems to make many difficulties out of fairly simple things. Women should be enlisted in the A.T.S. and should always wear that badge. This ensures that their special needs in treatment, accommodation, etc., are kept up to a minimum standard wherever they may be by the women influences organising the A.T.S. When however they are posted to a combatant unit and share in practice with the men the unavoidable dangers and hardships of that unit, they should become in every respect members of it. They should wear, in addition to the A.T.S. badge, all regimental insignia appropriate to their rank. Although their well-being is still supervised by the A.T.S. authorities, they should be considered as detached from the A.T.S. and incorporated in the combatant unit. This does not imply any alteration in their legal status, nor need it involve any Parliamentary discussion (although Parliamentary authority could easily be obtained were it necessary).

2. Considering the immense importance of having a large number of women in A.A. batteries and that the efficiency of the batteries depends upon carefully organised gun teams, it is imperative that these women should not be moved without reference to the Battery Command. The idea that there is an army of A.T.S. under its own Commander-in-Chief, part of which lives alongside particular batteries and gives them a helping hand from time to time, is contrary to our main interest, namely, the maintenance of a larger number of A.A. batteries with a smaller number of men.

3. You are good enough to say that I have been misinformed on various points. I should like to go further into this. I shall be glad to have a meeting at 5 P.M. on Tuesday, November 4, at which General Pile and other officers of the A.D.G.B., as well as representatives of the A.T.S., are present, and I trust you and the Adjutant-General will also come.

(Action this day.)
Prime Minister to C.I.G.S.   31.X.41.

I am very glad to see the 50th Division moving out of Cyprus, and am glad that it can be relieved by elements of the 5th Indian Division. No decision has however yet been taken about moving the 50th Division to the Caucasus. Where will it wait in the interval?

2. Nothing in these moves is on any account to interfere with "Crusader." Pray reassure me on this.

NOVEMBER

Prime Minister to First Lord and First Sea Lord   5.XI.41.

I much regret that the number of U-boat prisoners taken by us should have been published. I commented unfavourably upon this publication six months ago. The figure is so small that it advertises to the world the failure of all our efforts against them. There was absolutely no need to make such a disclosure gratuitously encouraging the enemy and discouraging our friends.

Were you aware beforehand that this was going to be done?

Prime Minister to Secretary of State for Air   5.XI.41.

Your reply to my minute.

I do not think you should dismiss a matter like this [whereby mechanics and fitters worked for certificates of competence in each different make of engine] so lightly. I am told it is the explanation of the far higher economy reached by the Germans in maintaining their air force.

I must beg you to have the matter more searchingly examined.

Prime Minister to First Lord   7.XI.41.

The twenty assault landing-craft, the twenty heavy support craft, and one hundred and twenty-seven tank-landing-craft seem to me insufficient. This programme must be carefully concerted with the Army. Very large operations may be required in 1943. . . .[31]

3. If a small floating dock is constructed in India, how long will it take and what alternative construction will it displace?

4. In view of the sad tale of the *King George V* class, it would be wrong to proceed with the construction of the *Lion*, let alone the later ones, without the whole design being examined by a conference of sea officers who have either commanded or used these ships. I favour the principle of three triple sixteen-inch-gun turrets. What are your armour demands for 1942? If the question of design were satisfactorily settled I would support making a beginning upon the turrets and mountings, provided of course that the tank programme is not interfered with.

5. Let me have the legend of the one hundred convoy escort vessels to be built in the United States.

6. Let me have the list of the eleven new or modernised capital ships attributed to Germany, Italy, and Japan at the end of 1943,

---

[31] These comments refer to the Admiralty programme of new naval construction for 1942. Many changes were made in it at later dates. The following notes indicate the size of our effort:

(1) *Convoy escort vessels.* Over one hundred frigates, ordered about this time and built in American yards, were delivered to us by the middle of 1944.

(2) The aircraft-carrier *Eagle* is referred to here for the first time. She was laid down late in 1942, and was expected to take nearly four years to build. In fact this ship has not yet been completed.

(3) *6-inch-gun cruisers.* Two of the ships mentioned became H.M. ships *Defence* and *Superb.* The eight-inch-gun cruiser was never built.

(4) *Destroyers.* The following were on order or in various stages of construction:

Type	On order	Rate of completion per annum
Fleet destroyers	74	8, rising to 15
Destroyers classed as frigates	50	30
Canadian	4	All by late 1943
Ex-foreign	2	Early 1942

(5) *Landing-craft.* Very large increases in all types of landing-craft construction were made in later years.

and the list of our eleven. It seems probable that the war will be finished before any new capital ships can be built—i.e., 1947. If we win the war, we shall disarm the enemy. If we lose it, he will disarm us.

7. The new aircraft-carrier must be weighed against other demands for armour and shipbuilding labour. How long will she take to make?

8. I agree to the three six-inch cruisers and to the triple eight-inch turrets of one eight-inch-gun cruiser.

9. Let me have the brief legend for the "heavy support craft."

10. You do not mention destroyers in your programme. I suppose this is because all the yards are fully booked up with them. Let me have a return showing what you have got building, dividing them into three classes and showing the rates at which each class can be built.

(Action this day.)
Prime Minister to General Ismay, for C.O.S. Committee,   9.XI.41.
and C.A.S.

Let us hurry up the arrangements for sending volunteer pilots and aeroplanes to join Chennault's party [International Air Force in China]. Let me know what is proposed.

(Action this day.)
Prime Minister to Secretary of State for Air and C.A.S.   11.XI.41.

The losses sustained both by the night bombers and day fighters have lately been very heavy. There is no need to press unduly the offensive by the figures over France; about two sweeps a month instead of four should be sufficient, combined with a continuance of the attacks on shipping. While the degree of attack may be lightened, the impression of its continuance should be sustained.

2. I have several times in Cabinet deprecated forcing the night bombing of Germany without due regard to weather conditions. There is no particular point at this time in bombing Berlin. The losses sustained last week were most grievous. We cannot afford losses on that scale in view of the short fall of the American bomber programme. Losses which are acceptable in a battle or for some decisive military objective ought not to be incurred merely as a matter of routine. There is no need to fight the weather and the enemy at the same time.

3. It is now the duty of both Fighter and Bomber Command to regather their strength for the spring.

4. Let me have a full report about the heavy losses of bombers on the night of the last heavy raid on Berlin.

(Action this day.)
Prime Minister to C.A.S.   11.XI.41.

The continued wastage of aircraft in relation to production is very serious. Let me have each week a precise return by types of all aircraft stationed in the United Kingdom written off either by enemy action or other causes. Let me also have, though this is not so urgent, a list of aircraft damaged each week, repairs of which cannot be executed by the squadrons.

Prime Minister to C.A.S. 11.XI.41.

Is it true that for the first fortnight in October Bomber Command were withdrawn from attacks on shipping to take part in Army manoeuvres, and that consequently there were no losses to the enemy in that period?

When was this decision to abandon operations for manoeuvres taken, and by whom?

Prime Minister to Viceroy of India 12.XI.41.

I was startled to learn how far you had gone about the release of the remaining Satyagrahi prisoners. As you know, I have always felt that a man like Nehru should be treated as a political *détenu* and not as a criminal, and have welcomed every mitigation of his lot. But my general impression of this wholesale release is one of a surrender at the moment of success. Undoubtedly the release of these prisoners as an act of clemency will be proclaimed as a victory for Gandhi's party. Nehru and others will commit fresh offences, requiring the whole process of trial and conviction to be gone through again. You will get no thanks from any quarter. The objections of Hope and Hallett should not be lightly turned aside.

2. The Cabinet, to whom I mentioned it this evening, felt they must have more time to consider the matter after they have received your official advice. It will not be possible for us to send an answer before Monday at earliest, so I asked the Secretary of State to desire you to postpone the motion on the 17th for a few days. We often do this in the House of Commons when replies from other Governments have to be awaited.

3. Kindest regards.

(Action this day.)
Prime Minister to Secretary of State for War 13.XI.41.

Pray see the attached epitome of the Beveridge report on skilled men in the Services and the letter of the Minister of Labour. Evidently the report is most damaging to the War Office, and before it can be published it is imperative that good, clear proposals for mending the evil should be formulated by the War Office and published at the same time as the report.

No one would expect the Army, which is expanding twentyfold, to have the same efficiency of organisation as the Navy, which is hardly doubled. But you ought to be up to the standard of the air force, which is also growing very rapidly.

I should advise you to set up a small committee, with perhaps the Financial Secretary in the chair, to hack out a good scheme.

This scheme should be ready in a fortnight, and after I have approved it the whole publication can be brought before the Cabinet.

(Action this day.)
Prime Minister to First Lord and First Sea Lord   14.XI.41.

I am much disquieted by these facts. We are sinking less than two U-boats a month.[32] They are increasing by nearly twenty. The failure of our methods, about which so much was proclaimed by the Admiralty before the war, is painfully apparent. I presume we have lost a far higher proportion of British submarines placed in service since the beginning of the war than the enemy.

Let me have the actual figures.

2. I regard the whole position as so serious that I wish to have a special meeting in the near future to survey the whole problem and consider whether anything can be done beyond the present measures.

Let me know what increases are to be expected month by month in our anti-U-boat hunting-craft. Let all the considerations about the German difficulty of training crews and other aspects be assembled and reviewed. Let me know when you will be ready.

Prime Minister to Home Secretary   15.XI.41.

I shall be glad to know what action you have taken about enabling the twelve couples of married internees to be confined together. Now that order has been restored in the Isle of Man there should be no particular reason against their going there. If not there must surely be some prisons in England in which arrangements could be made for reasonable association of husband and wife.

Is it true that when aliens are interned husband and wife are interned in one place? If so it seems invidious to discriminate against those of British nationality.

Feeling against 18B is very strong, and I should not be prepared to support the regulation indefinitely if it is administered in such a very onerous manner. Internment rather than imprisonment is what was contemplated.

Sir Oswald Mosley's wife has now been eighteen months in prison without the slightest vestige of any charge against her, and separated from her husband.

Has the question of releasing a number of these internees on parole been considered, or on condition of their finding sureties for good behaviour, etc.?

I should be glad if you would make proposals to the Cabinet before the debate in the House takes place.

Prime Minister to Secretary of State for War and C.I.G.S. 17.XI.41.

It seems a pity that the nine beach or county divisions should be rated at a lower level than the field divisions. All they lack are two

---

[32] Post-war analysis shows that German U-boat losses at this period were as follows: September, 2; October, 2; November, 5; December, 9. British submarine losses during the same period were three.

Royal Engineer companies and one regiment of artillery each, together with transport on the higher scale. Pray let me have a plan to raise these divisions to the field division scale by March 31, or, if that is impossible by the end of June, 1942, and let me know what additional man-power would be required and whether the equipment is forthcoming.

At the rate at which lorries, etc., are coming out, the extra transport should soon be available, especially if reasonable tail-combing is used on the main corpus of the Army.

Prime Minister to Lord Cherwell, Sir Edward Bridges,   17.XI.41.
and General Ismay

It is my wish before the end of the year to have fully planned the War Production Budget of 1942 and to submit this for approval to the Cabinet. For this purpose the programmes of the Navy, Army, and air force, which are already far advanced, must be settled and the resulting tasks of the Supply Department set forth.

At the same time the import programme, already completed on a basis of thirty-three million tons, and the home production should be surveyed. I should propose that of the extra two million tons import available half a million tons should go to food or feeding-stuffs and the other one and a half million tons to munitions in order to make up for their heavy cut this year. But this does not mean that needless imports, like timber, should be allowed undue expansion. The emphasis must be placed on a sharper war effort.

The third major element is man-power, now under Cabinet discussion but far advanced towards settlement.

It should be possible to state the above in broad outlines in a directive to be circulated about December 15. Perhaps you will let me have a preliminary study. The directive should not exceed one of my white square double sheets and should follow the model of last year.

Prime Minister to President of the Board of Education   22.XI.41.

Let me have a short note showing the number of boys who leave the public elementary schools at fifteen years and over, under the war conditions of 1941.

How many of these go into any form of industry and employment? How many are there in munitions between the ages of fifteen and eighteen and one-half years? How many go into cadet corps of various kinds? How many pursue their education in secondary schools or go to the universities?

I am anxious that the educational and disciplinary aspects of these boys' lives shall rank as prominently in our minds as the need to find considerable numbers for A.R.P., A.A. batteries, etc.

Prime Minister to First Sea Lord   23.XI.41,

What is the present plan about the distribution of the aircraft-carriers? Since these telegrams were received we have lost the *Ark*

Royal, but we still have four good new ones. I do not want to waste any one of them by sending it all round the Cape, unless such a voyage coincided with an inevitable working-up period. At present I am waiting to see what will happen in the Mediterranean. Of course, if Admiral Cunningham is going to take station in the Central Mediterranean, or if we get Tripoli or perhaps French North Africa comes out, it would be worth putting at least two aircraft-carriers there. We cannot see ahead clearly enough at present. I suppose you will give one of the older ones to the Indian Ocean and Pacific.

Please let me have a short note.

Prime Minister to Commander, "Force K"   27.XI.41.

Many congratulations on your fine work since you arrived at Malta, and will you please tell all ranks and ratings from me that the two exploits in which they have been engaged, namely, the annihilation of the enemy's convoys on November 8 and of the two oil ships on Monday last, have played a very definite part in the great battle now raging in Libya. The work of the force has been most fruitful, and all concerned may be proud to have been a real help to Britain and our cause.

Prime Minister to General Ismay, for C.O.S. Committee   28.XI.41.
and C.A.S.

Everything in human power should be done [to help the guerrilla fighters in Yugoslavia]. Please report what is possible.

Prime Minister to First Sea Lord   28.XI.41.

I cannot help feeling that the estimate of thirty-six U-boats operating in the North Atlantic by December 15 is worse than it will be.[33] I hope you will consider the possibility of reinforcing the Mediterranean with at least a dozen destroyers. They need not necessarily be there very long, as the situation may change with the decision in Libya. Numbers are however the essence of successful hunting, and we ought to get good results.

Pray let me know whether anything more can be done.

Let me have U-boat sinkings for November.

Prime Minister to General Ismay   29.XI.41.

I am dissatisfied with the way in which this project for Polish officers in West Africa, in which I took a personal interest, has been followed up. It was evidently necessary that a proper outfit allowance should be paid to the Polish officers proceeding to these tropical regions. Yet all these months have passed haggling about it. First five pounds is offered, then finally fifteen pounds. I expect this is typical of the way in which the experiment has been handled.

[33] Post-war figures show that the average daily number of U-boats operating in the North Atlantic during December, 1941, was eight. In addition, on any given day many others were on outward or homeward passages.

The shipping losses by U-boats during November, 1941, were 61,700 tons, the lowest figure recorded for any month since May, 1940.

On other papers I have directed that two hundred more Polish officers are to be invited to present themselves for examination. A weekly report is to be supplied to me personally of the progress made both in West Africa and at home. Please report to me any signs of obstructionism, and pursue the matter yourself from the Defence Office. Let me know who is the officer responsible in the War Office for dealing with this, and make sure you keep him up to the mark by constant inquiries.

Prime Minister to Foreign Secretary 30.XI.41.

I think it most important that the United States should continue their relations with Vichy and their supplies to North Africa and any other contacts unostentatiously for the present. It would be a great mistake to lose any contacts before we know the result of the battle in Libya and its reactions. There is always time to break, but it is more difficult to renew contacts.

DECEMBER

Prime Minister to C.A.S. and Commander in Chief 6.XII.41.
Fighter Command

The following are the main conclusions which we reached in our talk last night:

"Gee" [34] is to be started on February 1, 1942, unless examination shows that the weather conditions over the last ten or twelve years prove that March is likely to be for more favourable than February. In that event the matter should be referred to me again for decision.

2. Every effort is to be made to broaden the front of the fighter force. To this end reserves of pilots and machines should be disposed in squadrons, and thus allow *roulement* to be extended in the event of protracted fighting.

3. As an experiment a night-fighter wing is to be issued with day-fighting machines with a view to introducing a system of dual-purpose fighter squadrons, if the experiment proves successful.

Prime Minister to Minister of Food 6.XII.41.

Amid your many successes in your difficult field, the egg distribution scheme seems to be an exception. I hear complaints from many quarters, and the scarcity of eggs is palpable.

I send you a note which the Minister of Agriculture has furnished on his side of the problem.

Will you please give me a very short statement of your plans and policy.

Prime Minister to Minister of Supply 6.XII.41.

I hope to be able to go to Shoeburyness on the afternoon of Thursday, December 11, and would be grateful if you would ar-

[34] "Gee" was the name given to a radio device by means of which our bombers could fix their positions when operating over Germany.

range for a demonstration of the following types of U.P. weapons: [35] (1) Type K; (2) Apparatus A.D., Type L; (3) Apparatus A.D., Type J; (4) Rocket U, 5-inch; (5) Rocket U, 3-inch.

Before coming to a decision on the priority proposals set out in your minute of December 2, it is desirable, I think, to see these various weapons and decide their relative merits. I hope therefore that you will be able to accompany me.

Of course, if cloudy it must be cancelled.

Prime Minister to General Ismay   7.XII.41.

What has been done with the Italian rifles which have been captured in Abyssinia, Gondar, and elsewhere? How many of them were there, and how much ammunition?

Prime Minister to Secretary of State for War (Personal) 9.XII.41.

I have considered carefully your minute to me about the A.T.S., and I am willing that the principles you propose should have a trial. It is up to you to make these batteries attractive to the best elements in the A.T.S. and those who are now being compelled to join the A.T.S. I fear there is a complex against women being connected with lethal work. We must get rid of this. Also there is an idea prevalent among the ladies managing the A.T.S. that nothing must conflict with loyalty to the A.T.S. and that battery *esprit de corps* is counter to their interest or theme. No tolerance can be shown to this. The prime sphere of the women commanders is welfare, and this should occupy their main endeavours.

The conditions are very bad and rough, and I expect will get worse now that large numbers are being brought into the War Office grip by compulsion or the shadow of compulsion. A great responsibility rests upon you as Secretary of State to see that all these young women are not treated roughly. Mrs. Knox and her assistants should be admirable in all this, but do not let them get in the way of the happy active life of the batteries or deprive women of their incentives to join the batteries and to care as much about the batteries as they do about the A.T.S.

I shall be very glad to have a further report from you on how the principles enunciated in your minute are in fact being applied. Every kind of minor compliment and ornament should be accorded to those who render good service in the batteries.

Prime Minister to Chairman of the Forestry Commission 9.XII.41.

I see reports in the papers that timber-felling companies are ruthlessly denuding for profit many of our woodlands. What arrangements have you got to make sure that some of the finest trees are left and that due consideration is given to the appearance of the

[35] Type K—Anti-aircraft rocket.

Apparatus A.D., Type L, Apparatus A.D., Type J—Rockets for defence of aerodromes and similar places against low flying aircraft.

Rocket U, 5 inch—Original design was for delivering chemical warfare charge, but subsequently became area barrage weapon.

Rocket U, 3 inch—Anti-aircraft barrage weapon.

countryside? I know we have got to cut down very severely, but there is no reason why a certain number of trees should not be left.

Let me know in a few lines what you are doing to replant. Surely you are replanting two or three trees for every large one you cut down.

Prime Minister to Minister of Food   9.XII.41.

You say that you would have preferred to bring sweets and chocolates within the points scheme, and hope to do so subsequently. Would it not be better to postpone rationing of them until you are able to do so? If you introduce a sweets ration now all the forces of conservatism and arguments of administrative economy will be arrayed against any subsequent proposal to alter matters.

I gather that it was admitted in the Lord President's Committee that a sweets ration would lend itself to irregularities more easily than our other rations. Anything which diminishes respect for the rationing regulations is objectionable. If we create artificial illegalities that are neither enforceable nor condemned by public opinion the habit of evasion may spread to cases where it would be injurious.

We have done without a sweets and chocolate ration for so long that a small further delay may be tolerated. We should avoid allowing exceptions to the principle that any rationing of the secondary foods which you feel compelled to introduce should be incorporated in the points system.

(Action this day.)
Prime Minister to Minister of Labour   10.XII.41.

I see it reported that you say Members of Parliament are liable to be called up equally with others. The rule I have made, which was followed in the last war and must be followed in this, was that service in the House of Commons ranks with the highest service in the State. Any Member of Parliament or Peer of Parliament has a right to decide at his discretion whether he will fulfil that service or give some other form. Members of either House are free, if at any time they consider their political duties require it, and reasonable notice is given, to withdraw from the armed forces or any other form of service in order to attend Parliament.

I could not possibly agree to any smirching of this principle.

Prime Minister to Lord Privy Seal and Minister of Food 12.XII.41.

It would be a mistake, in my opinion, to announce these restrictions of rations now. It would savour of panic. Our position has immeasurably improved by the full involvement of the United States. The reserves are good. We are all in it together, and they are eating better meals than we are.

I trust no announcements of this character will be made in the immediate future, and I hope I may be consulted before any final decision is taken by the War Cabinet.

Prime Minister to C.I.G.S. (Sir Alan Brooke)   18.XII.41.

[Your minute about the possibility of forming a Polish Armoured Division.]

I do not consider that the issue of tanks to the Poles should be delayed until all the British armoured divisions have not only been completed but have a large reserve of tanks standing behind them. I thought it was agreed that in the first place the divisions were to be given their initial equipment, and the reserve built up afterwards as more tanks come to hand. The Poles should be treated on this footing equally with the British divisions. I do not see how the date of April 1, 1943, could possibly be accepted as a fair treatment of the problem by General Sikorski. I hope therefore you will let me have proposals on the basis I have indicated.

2. It should surely be possible to give a good outfit of tanks to the Poles and yet enable them to work together as a corps. It is convenient, but not indispensable, that every unit in the Army should have exactly the same organisation. It is not necessary that the Poles should have the identical equipment, i.e., the whole thirty-five hundred vehicles to which the British armoured divisions have been expanded. A practical solution would be to let them have a couple of hundred more tanks during the next six months, and work up to the full usual formation later. It should surely be possible to use the Polish force together, and not to separate the tank component from the rest.

I hope you will let me have further proposals.

Prime Minister to Secretary of State for War   21.XII.41.

Your minute about the Beveridge report.

The memorandum to be published by the War Office at the same time as the Beveridge report on the use of skilled men in the Services must be both more effective and more precise than that at present proposed.

2. The War Office should also take their stand on the grounds that it is their duty to make an efficient fighting machine rather than a well-conducted industrial establishment. Nothing must therefore be done seriously to break the cohesion of section, platoon, and company, and no general disturbance of the Army system in home ports can be tolerated in view of the danger of invasion.

3. It must however be clearly shown how skilled men in units, as they at present exist, are being used, and how still better use will be made of them. The memorandum should thus firmly rebut those suggestions in the Beveridge report which would affect the cohesion and military efficiency of the Army.

4. This does not mean that the War Office can use the excuse of military efficiency to cover over the grave defects brought to light by the report. The memorandum should not appear merely to be a white-washing document, but should show that a really serious effort is being made to rectify shortcomings. Parliament and the

public will only be reassured if the War Office can state in concrete, rather than in abstract, how amendment is being made. The memorandum should therefore deal specifically and in a manner readily understood by the layman with the main points in the report.

5. These are: (a) That the reservoir of unused skill in the Army is sufficient to cover all future demands for skilled men, except armament artificers. (b) That economy in skilled men could be secured by review of the establishment of many field units. (c) That more effective steps could be taken to utilise the skill of those men whose units will be required at the front but which at present are not engaged. (d) That great improvements are possible in the machinery for testing, remuster, and transfer of skilled men. (e) That a special corps of mechanised engineers should be formed to put an end to present duplication. (f) That men should be enlisted into the Army as a whole and not into specific corps or units.

6. The War Office reply will have to be carefully drafted if it is to be effective. You should set up a small committee, which I suggest might consist of the Financial Secretary, Sir James Grigg, and the Adjutant-General, to prepare it. I should like the reply to be submitted to me about January 10, so that the matter can, if necessary, be brought before the Cabinet in good time.

Prime Minister to Commander-in-Chief Home Forces   22.XII.41.
(General Paget)

This is a most admirable paper [on the training of infantry by General Utterson-Kelso], and I agree with every word of it. I am glad to think that in your new great sphere you will have an opportunity of putting into force the many wise and stimulating principles it contains. You may count on my assistance in every way. I have already done all in my power to prevent sections and platoons from being disturbed needlessly, or the infantry used for civil purposes other than in emergencies or the harvest. While I greatly admire the conception of a well-armed infantry battalion working with the *élan* and combined individualism of a pack of hounds, I am also anxious about the smart side of things. I hope there are going to be no fussy changes in the manual exercises and that "spit and polish" will not be incompatible with effective field training.

2. Pray let me have a further note to show how you are applying the ideas of this paper, and return it to me. I have been very much pleased by it.

Prime Minister to Minister of Food   22.XII.41.

Your minute about the egg distribution scheme.

The fact that 370,000 small producers have enough gumption to keep chickens is a matter for congratulation; under this head the only complaint I have heard is that this practice is not sufficiently encouraged. After all, the backyard fowls use up a lot of scrap, and so save cereals.

I quite recognize your difficulties, with your imports cut to one-third, but I hope that you will get in the quantity which you had planned, so that this important animal protein which is so essential in the kitchen should not be deficient.

Prime Minister to C.I.G.S. (Sir Alan Brooke)   22.XII.41.

Surely it was a very odd thing to create these outlandish numbered regiments of Dragoons, Hussars, and Lancers, none of which has carbines, swords, or lances, when there exist already telescoped up the 18th, 20th, and 19th Hussars, 5th Lancers and 21st Lancers. Surely all these should have been revived before creating these new unreal and artificial titles. I wish you would explain to me what was moving in the minds of the War Office when they did this.

Appendix B, Book Two

PRIME MINISTER'S TELEGRAMS TO THE GOVERNMENT OF AUSTRALIA

Prime Minister to Prime Minister of Australia[36]   29.VIII.41.

Now that you have taken up your great office, I send you my most cordial good wishes for success, and assure you that I and my colleagues will do everything in our power to work with you in the same spirit of comradeship and good-will as we worked with Mr. Menzies, who, we are so glad to see, is serving under you as Minister for the Co-ordination of Defence.

2. We have followed attentively the difficulties which have arisen in Australia about your representation over here, and perhaps it will be a help if I let you see our side of the question and how we are situated.

3. Since the declarations of the Imperial Conference of 1926, embodied in the Statute of Westminster, all Dominion Governments are equal in status to that of the Mother Country, and all have direct access to the Crown. The Cabinet of His Majesty's Government of Great Britain and Northern Ireland, of which at present I have the honour to be the head, is responsible to our own Parliament, and is appointed by the King because they possess a majority in the House of Commons. It would not be possible, therefore, without organic changes, about which all the Dominions would have to be consulted, to make an Australian Minister who is responsible to the Commonwealth legislature a member of our body. The precedent of General Smuts in the last war does not apply, because he was an integral member of the War Cabinet of those days, appointed by the King because of his personal aptitudes, and not because he represented the South African or Dominions point of view.

4. In practice however whenever a Dominion Prime Minister visits this country—and they cannot visit it too often or too long—he is always invited to sit with us and take a full part in our deliberations. This is because he is the head of the Government of one of our sister Dominions, engaged with us in the common struggle, and has presumably the power to speak with the authority of the Dominion concerned, not only on instructions from home, but upon many issues which may arise in the course of discussion. This is a great advantage to us, and speeds up business.

[36] See Book Two, Chapter 2, page 348.

5. The position of a Dominions Minister other than the Prime Minister would be very different, as he would not be a principal, but only an envoy. Many Dominions Ministers other than Prime Ministers have visited us from Australia, Canada, New Zealand, and South Africa during the present war, and I am always ready to confer with them or put them in the closest touch with the Ministers of the various departments with which they are concerned. In the normal course the Secretary of State for the Dominions and the High Commissioner for the Dominion concerned look after them, and secure them every facility for doing any work they may have to do. This arrangement has given satisfaction, so far as I am aware, to all concerned.

6. I have considered the suggestion that each of the Dominions should have a Minister other than the Prime Minister sitting with us in the Cabinet of the United Kingdom during this time of war. I have learnt from the Prime Ministers of the Dominions of Canada, South Africa, and New Zealand that they do not desire such representation and are well content with our present arrangements. Some of the Dominions Prime Ministers have indeed taken a very strongly adverse view, holding that no one but the Prime Minister can speak for their Governments except as specifically instructed, and that they might find their own liberty of action prejudiced by any decisions, some of which have to be made very quickly in wartime, to which their Minister became a party.

7. From our domestic point of view, as His Majesty's servants in the United Kingdom, there are many difficulties. We number at present eight, and there has been considerable argument that we should not be more than five. The addition of four Dominions representatives would involve the retirement from the War Cabinet of at least an equal number of British Ministers. Dwelling within a Parliamentary and democratic system, we rest, like you do, upon a political basis. I should not myself feel able, as at present advised, to recommend to His Majesty either the addition of four Dominions Ministers to the Cabinet of the United Kingdom, which would make our numbers too large for business, or the exclusion of a number of my present colleagues, who are the leading men in the political parties to which they belong.

8. If you desire to send anyone from Australia as a special envoy to discuss any particular aspect of our common war effort, we should of course welcome him with the utmost consideration and honour, but he would not be, and could not be, a responsible partner in the daily work of our Government.

9. His relationship with the existing High Commissioner for Australia and with the Secretary of State for the Dominions would be for you to decide. It would seem however if such an envoy remained here as a regular institution that the existing functions of the High Commissioner would to some extent be duplicated, and the relations of the Secretary of State with the High Commissioners generally might be affected. Such difficulties are not insuperable,

but they may as well be faced. The whole system of the work of the High Commissioners in daily contact with the Secretary of State for the Dominions has worked well, and I am assured that the three other Dominions would be opposed to any change.

10. We should of course welcome a meeting of Dominions Prime Ministers if that could be arranged, but the difficulties of distance and occasion are, as you know, very great. We are also quite ready to consider, if you desire it, the question of the formation of an Imperial War Cabinet. So far-reaching a change could not however be brought about piecemeal, but only by the general wish of all the Governments now serving His Majesty.

Prime Minister to Prime Minister of Australia   7.IX.41.

Our position in Syria and Iraq may be threatened by a German advance: (*a*) on Syria through Anatolia; (*b*) on Iraq through the Caucasus and Persia (Iran); (*c*) a combination of (*a*) and (*b*).

Through Anatolia.—If Turkey does not grant passage to German forces the large land and air forces necessary for conquering Turkey could hardly be withdrawn from Russia, refitted and reconcentrated, in less than six to eight weeks. Weather conditions in Anatolia virtually preclude operations from December 1 to the end of March. We therefore feel that the concentration by the Germans of sufficient forces on the Turkish frontier to overcome that country is now improbable until a date so late that an attack on Syria through Anatolia is not likely before the spring.

If however, contrary to expectations, Turkey were to give passage to German forces, three or four German divisions might arrive on the Syrian frontier before the end of the year, and be reinforced at the rate of one division a month. This force might be supplemented if sea routes through Turkish territorial waters were available. A great deal therefore depends on what help the Turks may expect from us. As to this we have instructed our Attachés at Ankara to speak on the following lines: (*a*) If Turkey resists we will come to her aid at once with substantial forces. Our essential object in the Middle East is the destruction of the German Afrika Corps and the reconquest of Cyrenaica, but we expect that at latest by December 1 we could send to Turkey four divisions and at least one armoured brigade. Air support will be on a considerable scale, and preparations should be made to receive a force of eight fighter, one Army co-operation, two heavy, and six medium bomber squadrons. (*b*) We shall provide a strong force of anti-aircraft artillery for the defence of our own troops and of those aerodromes allotted to us, and in addition we are sending to the Turks an immediate and special consignment of one hundred 3.7-inch anti-aircraft guns. These are in addition to the normal allocation of six equipments per month.

Through the Caucasus and Persia.—Even in the event of an early Russian collapse, a full-scale drive through the Caucasus on Persia and Iraq would not be possible this year. The control we have gained in Persia adds greatly to the security of our right flank in these regions.

Turning now to our own action to meet a German advance, whichever way it may come, our first requirement is facilities to operate air forces both offensively and defensively. Steps are accordingly being taken to improve and increase aerodrome facilities throughout this area, and by consent of the Turks in Anatolia. These will give flexibility to our air forces in the Middle East.

The second requirement is to improve communications, both rail and road, throughout the areas under our control. This is being pushed forward with all despatch.

In addition, steps are being taken to develop as rapidly as possible our maintenance arrangements in the Basra area, including construction of additional ports, so that the proposed increased forces in the Persian Gulf area can be maintained.

Western Desert.—We must clear Eastern Cyrenaica at the earliest possible moment, not only for the defence of our base in Egypt, but also to retain control of the Eastern Mediterranean. Position is as follows:

It is estimated that the enemy has at present in Cyrenaica two German divisions (one armoured and one light motorised) and six Italian (including one motorised and one armoured). We do not think that with these forces he could undertake a major offensive against the Delta. He is in considerable difficulties with his supply and is short of mechanical transport. In addition, we are sinking a good proportion of his reinforcements of men and material from Italy. If however he were able to establish a firm base on the Halfaya-Capuzzo-Bardia line and to build up the necessary mechanical transport and supplies, it is possible that a limited offensive might be carried out against Sidi Barrani.

Our aim is to take the offensive as soon as a favourable opportunity presents itself, but Comander-in-Chief does not wish to risk another setback, such as "Battleaxe," or to move until he feels he can go right forward. He estimates that for this offensive his armoured force must not be less than two armoured divisions. These will not be ready for action until November 1, but this would not preclude him from attacking sooner if favourable opportunity were presented to him. The importance of holding Tobruk has been clearly demonstrated.

Appendix C, Book Two

THE BRITISH PURCHASING COMMISSION

August 11, 1941

A great mass of orders has already been placed in the United States for British war munitions, etc. These have been harmonised both as between British departments and between British home production and British orders placed in America. Mr. Purvis has been made finally responsible, and any discordances should be reported to him for settlement in the office of the Minister of Defence. However, it is now necessary to make further large provision, particularly in respect of shipping, bomber aircraft, and tanks, both for the British account and for the United States' armed forces. Moreover, the arrival of Russia as an active partner against Hitler will require not only certain readjustments of British orders, original and supplementary, but also a very considerable expansion of plants and installations for the longer-term policy.

2. So far as the British supplementary programme is concerned, there need be no trouble about priorities as between heavy bomber aircraft and tanks. We no longer consider priorities as dominated by the time factor, but prefer to deal in simultaneous quantitative al locations.

On this basis, if our American colleagues will state what are the prospects, whether through improved production from existing plants or the preparation of new ones, of greatly increasing production, and will let us know their views about how it is to be divided between British and United States needs, we will do the share-out between our British departments. For instance, we do not think that our need for a supplemental programme of heavy bomber aircraft should exclude all simultaneous expansion in tanks. The ratio for the whole programme as between heavy bomber aircraft and tanks would be, say 6 to 4, or 6½ to 3½, both types of production proceeding simultaneously as fast as possible. This method of approach is suggested as the most convenient.

3. We greatly welcome a further assignment of 150,000 rifles. Although ammunition is very short, these are absolutely needed to arm the personnel defending the fighter airfields. At least 150,000 of them have at present to rely on pikes, maces, and grenades. Even although .300 ammunition in Great Britain is very short and does not amount to above eighty rounds per rifle, production is now flowing in the United States for our benefit, which will this month

be clear of the paying off of the overdrawn fifty million rounds, and should amount to twenty to twenty-five million rounds per month. Even if only ten rounds could be handed out to the men at certain airfields with their rifles, this would be far better than the makeshifts we now have to employ, and would enable the strictest instructions to be given to all uniformed personnel to fight to the death, which instructions can hardly be given very confidently when no weapon can be placed in the hands of soldiers and airmen concerned.

We hope therefore that the most rapid deliveries possible of 150,000 rifles will be made, as the invasion season is fully operative after September 15. In the event of our reporting to the President that great and active preparations are being made by the enemy in the Dutch, Belgian, and French ports for invasion, of which there is no sign at present, we would ask as a matter of emergency that a further consignment of .300 ammunition should be rushed across, this being recovered later from our monthly quotas of production.

4. It would seem indispensable that the re-equipment of the Russian armies should be studied at once upon the grand scale. After preliminary conferences between the British and United States supply departments, it would seem advisable, and indeed inevitable, that a further conference should be held in Moscow. Both for this purpose and in any preliminary conference that may be necessary the Prime Minister would nominate Lord Beaverbrook, Minister of Supply, who should arrive here today, as the British representative, with power to act for all British departments.[37]

[37] See Book Two, Chapter 4, page 377.

Appendix D, Book Two

ANGLO-AMERICAN-RUSSIAN CONFERENCE

General Directive by the Prime Minister and Minister of Defence

22.IX.41.

The position reached as the result of the Beaverbrook-Harriman conversations is set out in Lord Beaverbrook's report of today's date. We must consider ourselves pledged to fulfil our share of the tanks and aircraft which have been promised to Russia, and Lord Beaverbrook must have a considerable measure of discretion as to what quantities of other equipment and of material should be offered at the conversations in Moscow.

2. Assurance must be given to Russia of increased quotas from July 1, 1942, to June 30, 1943. During this period British war production will be at its height, and American ditto in its third year of development. It would be wiser not to be committed to precise figures based on optimistic forecasts of Anglo-American production. There are dangers also in promising the Russians a percentage of British and American output, which they may immediately ask should be increased. We should not disclose speculative figures of our joint production when none are given of theirs by the Russians. They should however be invited to set forth their remaining resources in accordance with the various rearward lines they may hope to hold. Lord Beaverbrook should be free to encourage the prolonged resistance of Russia by taking a justifiably hopeful view of these more distant prospects.

3. Russian attention should be directed to the limitations of shipping, and still more of transportation from the various ports of access. The rapid destruction of world shipping, the effort required to make it good, and the vital needs of this country, now cut to the bone, should be stressed.

4. Encouragement should be offered, with American approval, to the keeping open of the Vladivostok route and overawing Japan for that purpose. Special emphasis should be laid upon the development on the largest scale and with the utmost energy of the route from the Persian Gulf to the Caspian, both by rail and road. The practical limitations which time enforces both upon working up the traffic on the Trans-Persian Railway and upon the motor-

road construction should be explained. The conflict between the movement of supplies and of troops and their maintenance at any given period along this route must be pointed out. The Russians will no doubt give their own estimate of the capacity and facilities of Archangel and of its railway connections with Central Russia, having regard both to winter ice and probable enemy action.

5. The Conference must proceed upon the basis that the United States is not a belligerent. The burden upon British man-power is already heavy, and the strain will be intense during 1942 and onwards. Apart from the help we get from the Dominions, India, and the Colonies, our man-power is fully engaged. We have to feed ourselves and keep alive by maintaining vast merchant fleets in constant movement. We have to defend the British Isles from invasion, for which the Germans can at any time gather a superior army, and also from the most dangerous forms of air attack by the main strength of the enemy air force, which can rapidly be transferred from East to West at the enemy's convenience. We have to maintain our armies in the Middle East and hold a line from the Caspian to the Western Desert. We hope to develop on this front during 1942 approximately twenty-five divisions. British, Indian, and Dominion, comprising, with all the exceptional rearward services needed in these undeveloped regions and strong proportionable air force, about a million men. The strain on shipping in supplying these forces largely round the Cape, and the time taken in the turn-round of available ships, should be explained, if necessary, in detail.

6. For the defence of the British Isles we have an army of slightly over 2,000,000 men, backed by about 1,500,000 Home Guard. We possess only about 3,500,000 rifles, and can only get 100,000 more or so in the next year. Of this army of 2,000,000 men, 900,000 constitute the field force, comprising twenty mobile infantry divisions, nine less mobile county or beach divisions, and six armoured divisions, three of which are only partly formed, together with five Army tank brigades, of which only one is as yet complete. Nearly 1,000,000 men will be required for the enormous air force we are creating; 750,000 are already enrolled. The Navy already absorbs half a million sailors and Marines. When to this is added the shipbuilding, aircraft production, and munitions industries, and the need of food production at home and other domestic civilian industries, all cut to a minimum, it will be seen that the man-power and available woman-power of a population of 44,000,000 is, or will soon be, engaged to the limit.

7. Out of the 1,100,000 men behind the field army at home, the air defence of Great Britain, the coastal defence, the garrison of Northern Ireland, the draft-producing units and training schools, the defence of aerodromes and vulnerable points, leave only a small margin.

8. It will not be possible to increase the field army at home beyond the number of divisions—less than forty—already men-

tioned, and great efforts will be needed to maintain the existing strength at home while supplying the drafts for the Middle East, India, and other garrisons abroad—e.g., Iceland, Gibraltar, Malta, Aden, Singapore, Hong Kong.

9. We could not allow the force needed in Great Britain to repel invasion to fall below twenty-five infantry and four or five armoured divisions. It must be noted that troops can be transferred by the enemy across the main lateral railways of Europe incomparably quicker than any of our divisions could be recalled from abroad. The number of divisions available for offensive oversea action is therefore small.

10. Apart from the twenty-five British and Imperial divisions proposed to be built up in the Middle East during 1942, an expeditionary force of six or seven divisions, including two armoured divisions, is the maximum that can be conceived. This is being prepared. Even if more were available the shipping does not exist to carry larger forces and maintain them overseas. All ideas of twenty or thirty divisions being launched by Great Britain against the western shores of the Continent or sent round by sea for service in Russia have no foundation of reality on which to rest. This should be made clear.

11. We have every intention of intervening on land next spring, if it can be done. All the possibilities are being studied, including action on the northern and southern flanks of the Russian front. In the North an expedition into Norway would raise a serious revolt, and might, if it succeeded, win the Swedish Government, with its good army, to our cause. This has been studied in detail. It is not however seen how the Russian forces could help; in fact, their intervention would antagonise Sweden beyond all hope. The hostility of Finland is already declared.

12. At any moment we may be called upon to face the hostility of Spain and the penetration of the Germans into Morocco, Algeria, and West Africa. Should the French resist in Africa our available force might be sent to help them there. In both these cases the sea routes are short and not comparable with the vast distances round the Cape.

13. In the Middle East, on the southern flank of Russia, we shall deploy the strong forces mentioned above. Once the Western Desert and Cyrenaica have been cleared of the German and Italian armies now active there, our Middle Eastern forces would have a choice of action. If they increasingly give their right hand to the Russians, either in the Caucasus or east of the Caspian, it must be realised that their supply will choke the rail and road connection from the Persian Gulf. On the other hand, Turkey, if she could be gained, is the great prize. Not only would the German road to Syria and Egypt be barred by powerful Turkish armies, but the Black Sea naval defence could be maintained with great advantages, thus helping the defence of the Caucasus. The action of Turkey one way or the other may be determined in the

near future by the promises, should she become involved, of help in troops and modern equipment, including especially aerodromes, tanks, anti-tank and anti-aircraft artillery, etc. It should be made clear to the Russians that much of this equipment and the greater part of the troops would of course be withdrawn from the contributions available for Russia, which are all we can give. In order however to induce Turkey to come in on our side, especially in the near future, it would be well worth Great Britain and Russia revising their arrangements.

14. We are much interested in the development of the Polish and Czech armies in Russia, the latter being only small, and we should be glad to help in their equipment. It should be pointed out that the Poles and Czechs have influential communities in the United States. If a proportion of our equipment could be earmarked for the Poles and Czechs it would have a good effect.

15. The Russians will no doubt ask how you propose to win the war, to which our answer should be, "By going on fighting till the Nazi system breaks up, as the Kaiser's system broke up last time." For this purpose we shall fight the enemy wherever we can meet them on favourable terms. We shall undermine them by propaganda, depress them with the blockade, and, above all, bomb their homelands ceaselessly, ruthlessly, and with ever-increasing weight of bombs. We could not tell last time how and when we should win the war, but by not giving in and not wearying we came through all right. We did not hesitate to face Germany and Italy alone all last year, and the determination of the British masses to destroy the Nazi power is inflexible. The phrases "Nazi tyranny" and "Prussian militarism" are used by us as targets rather than as any implacable general condemnation of the German people. We agree with the Russian Government in hoping to split the Germans and to isolate the criminal Nazi régime.

16. Of course we cannot predict what action the United States will take. The measures already sanctioned by President Roosevelt and his Government may at any time in the near future involve the United States in full war, whether declared or undeclared. In that case we might look forward to a general offensive upon Germany in 1943. If German morale and unity were seriously weakened and their hold upon the conquered European countries relaxed, it might be possible to land large numbers of armoured forces simultaneously on the shores of several of the conquered countries and raise widespread revolts. Plans for this are now being studied by the British Staffs.

Appendix E, Book Two

FLEET DISPOSITIONS IN THE INDIAN OCEAN

Prime Minister to First Lord and First Sea Lord   25.VIII.41.

It should be possible in the near future to place a deterrent squadron in the Indian Ocean. Such a force should consist of the smallest number of the best ships. We have only to remember all the preoccupations which are caused us by the *Tirpitz*—the only capital ship left to Germany against our fifteen or sixteen battleships and battle-cruisers—to see what an effect would be produced upon the Japanese Admiralty by the presence of a small but very powerful and fast force in Eastern waters. It may be taken as virtually certain that *Tirpitz* will not sally forth from the Baltic while the Russian Fleet is in being, as she is the only unit which prevents Russian superiority there. Nevertheless, in making dispositions which take some time to alter we must provide for two *K.G.V.'s* [*King George V's*] and one *Nelson* with the C.-in-C. This allows for accidents, refits, and leave. One aircraft-carrier, preferably [one of the] unarmoured, should also be provided for the broad waters.

2. The most economical disposition would be to send *Duke of York*, as soon as she is clear of constructional defects, via Trinidad and Simonstown to the East. She could be joined by *Repulse* or *Renown* and one aircraft-carrier of high speed. This powerful force might show itself in the triangle Aden-Singapore-Simonstown. It would exert a paralysing effect upon Japanese naval action. The *Duke of York* could work up on her long, safe voyage to the East, leaving the C.-in-C. Home Fleet with two *K.G.V.'s*, which are thoroughly efficient. It would be, in my opinion, a more thrifty and fruitful use of our resources than to send *Prince of Wales* from regions where she might, though it is unlikely, meet *Tirpitz*.

3. I do not like the idea of sending at this stage the old "R" class battleships to the East. The manning problem is greatly increased by maintaining numerically large fleets in remote waters, owing to the greater number of men in transit. Besides this, the old ships are easy prey to the modern Japanese vessels, and can neither fight nor run. They might however be useful for convoy should we reach that stage, which is not yet by any means certain, or even, in my opinion, probable.

4. I am however in principle in favour of placing a formidable, fast, high-class squadron in the aforesaid triangle by the end of

October, and telling both the Americans and Australians that we will do so. It seems probable that the American negotiations with Japan will linger on for some time. The Americans talk now of ninety days, and the Japanese may find it convenient to wait and see how things go in Russia.

5. It would always be an advantage, if possible, to change the armoured [aircraft-carrier] *Victorious* for the *Ark Royal* for service in the narrow waters of the Mediterranean, and I suppose you will wish to strengthen "Force H" with one of the *Nelsons* as well as either *Repulse* or *Renown*.

6. Naturally, C.-in-C. Home Fleet will require a first call upon an aircraft-carrier, preferably *Ark Royal*. *Furious* will have to do some more work on ferrying aircraft to Takoradi. *Victorious* would be well placed in "Force H." This would leave *Illustrious, Formidable,* and *Indomitable,* as they come to hand, together with *Eagle* and *Argus,* for the needs of the Eastern triangle and the Mediterranean. You ought to be very well off by the end of the year.

Pray let me have your thoughts on the above.

First Sea Lord to Prime Minister   28.VIII.41.

Please see attached proposed disposition of capital ships and aircraft-carriers:

1. This question had been under review before receipt of your minute, and was again reviewed after its receipt.

2. The chief difference between your suggestion and the proposed disposition is in the allocation of *King George V* class and *Nelson* class. I fully appreciate the attractiveness of sending one of the *King George V* class to the Indian Ocean when fully worked up, but after considering this most carefully I cannot recommend it, for the reasons given in this memorandum.

3. I do not consider that any of the *King George V* class should be sent abroad until fully worked up, for the following reasons: (*a*) A ship cannot work up unless she has all the necessary targets at her disposal. (*b*) If a ship does not get an uninterrupted working-up period she never really recovers from it. (*c*) With a combination of the intricate machinery and electrical installations, and sixty per cent of the crew being men under twenty-one who have never been to sea before, it is inevitable that mishandling of material should occur at first. It is therefore essential that the working-up should be carried out in proximity to a dockyard or contractor's yard.

4. It is unfortunate that we cannot achieve the redistribution of capital ships earlier, but the number of ships under repair or refitting prevents this. As long as both *Bismarck* and *Tirpitz* were afloat we had to postpone refits.

5. The situation as regards aircraft-carriers is also unsatisfactory, but this is due to action damage to *Illustrious* and *Formidable* and essential refits to *Furious* and *Ark Royal*.

CAPITAL SHIP AND AIRCRAFT-CARRIER DISPOSITIONS

The date in parentheses against the name of a ship is the date on which she will arrive on her station.

Final Dispositions to be Worked to

	Capital Ships	Aircraft-Carriers
Home Fleet	Two *King George V* (Sept. 3)	*Victorious* (now)
	Malaya (Sept. 21)	*Furious* (Feb.)
Force H	One *King George V* (early Dec.?)	*Indomitable* (Nov.)
Mediterranean	*Queen Elizabeth* (now)	*Illustrious* (Jan.)
	Valiant (now)	*Formidable* (Feb.)
	Barham (now)	
	Warspite (late Jan.)	
Trincomalee	*Nelson* (end Nov.)	*Hermes* (now)
	Rodney (end Jan.)	*Ark Royal* (Apr. '42)
	Renown (mid-Jan.)	*Indomitable* (in emergency)
Indian Ocean Troop Convoy Escort	*Revenge* (mid-Sept.)	
	Royal Sovereign (mid-Nov.?)	
	Ramillies (mid-Dec.)	
	Resolution (early Jan.)	
Spare Ship	*Repulse*	

Reasons for the Proposed "Final Dispositions"

Home Fleet and Force H

(1) The Atlantic is the vital area, as it is in that ocean and that alone in which we can lose the war at sea.

(2) As long as *Tirpitz* is in being it is essential to have two ships of *King George V* class available to work in company.

(3) A combination of a *King George V* and a *Nelson* is not a satisfactory one, owing to their difference in speed.

(4) In order to have two *King George V's* available at all times it is necessary to have three of that class in home waters, to allow for one being damaged by torpedo, bomb, or mine or refitting.

(5) It is considered that the third ship can be in "Force H" at Gibraltar and that all three ships need not be at Scapa.

(6) If the *Tirpitz* did manage to break out, she could paralyse our North Atlantic trade to such an extent that it would be essential to bring her to action at the earliest possible moment, and we could not afford to have one of the *King George V's* absent from the scene of operations.

(7) The capital ship in "Force H" should not only be able to resist air attack, but should also be fast. This combination is only obtained in the *King George V* class.

(8) *Malaya* is allocated to Home Fleet, as it is necessary to have one capital ship in the Atlantic in addition to *King George V* class for the following duties: (*a*) Escorting important troop convoys. (*b*) Giving cover to convoys east of 26° W. in emergency. (*c*) To back up "Force H" for operations in Western Mediterranean when necessary.

(9) (*a*) *Ark Royal* is not shown in the dispositions, as she has to refit on relief by *Indomitable* and will not be available until April '42. (*b*) *Eagle* is not shown in the dispositions, as she is being kept available in home waters for "Pilgrim" [occupation of the Canary Islands].

Trincomalee

(10) It is proposed to send *Nelson, Rodney,* and *Renown* to Trincomalee or Singapore, for the following reasons: (*a*) *Nelson* and *Rodney* will eventually form part of the Eastern Fleet, when it is possible to form one, which is dependent on the availability of cruisers and particularly of destroyers. (*b*) *Nelson* and *Rodney* will give the best backing to the "R" class when the Eastern Fleet is formed, and the combination will form the most homogeneous fleet we can provide as regards speed. (*c*) Until we can form a fleet in the Far East which is capable of meeting a Japanese force of the strength they are likely to send south, it is necessary to deter Japanese action in the Indian Ocean. By sending capital ships to escort our convoys in the Indian Ocean we hope to deter the Japanese from sending any of their battleships to this area. By sending a battle-cruiser and aircraft-carrier to the Indian Ocean we hope to deter the Japanese from sending their eight-inch cruisers to attack our trade in this area. It is not considered that the substitution of one of the *King George V* class for one of the above would give sufficient added security to justify the disadvantages which her absence from the home area would involve, as her speed is inadequate to run down a Japanese eight-inch cruiser. (*d*) Depending on the situation at the time, and if war with Japan has not broken out, it may be found desirable to send *Nelson, Rodney, Renown,* and the aircraft-carrier to Singapore in the first instance, as they would thus form a greater deterrent. If war eventuated they would have to retire to Trincomalee. (*e*) Owing to the necessity to refit *Ark Royal* it will not be possible to send a large carrier to join this force until April, '42, unless we take *Indomitable* away from "Force H."

Indian Ocean Troop Convoy Escorts

It is proposed to send the four "R" class to the Indian Ocean now, for the following reasons: (*a*) They are no longer required for North Atlantic convoy escort. (*b*) They will eventually form part of the Eastern Fleet, and until this time it is desirable to keep them in waters where they will be free from air and U-boat attack.

(*c*) By employing them for escorting troop convoys they will relieve the cruiser situation. (*d*) Their presence in the Indian Ocean, together with *Nelson, Rodney,* and *Renown,* will go some way to meet the wishes of Australia and New Zealand for the Far East to be reinforced.

Interim Dispositions to Strengthen Indian Ocean

It is necessary to retain the *Repulse* in home waters until *King George V* is again available on September 3. *Repulse* will escort W.S. 11, and subsequently arrive at Trincomalee on October 7.

Prime Minister to First Sea Lord   29.VIII.41.

It is surely a faulty disposition to create in the Indian Ocean a fleet considerable in numbers, costly in maintenance and man-power, but consisting entirely of slow, obsolescent, or unmodernised ships which can neither fight a fleet action with the main Japanese force nor act as a deterrent upon his modern fast, heavy ships, if used singly or in pairs as raiders. Such dispositions might be forced upon us by circumstances, but they are inherently unsound in themselves.

2. The use of the 4 "R's" for convoy work is good as against enemy eight-inch cruisers. But if the general arrangements are such that the enemy is not afraid to detach an individual fast, modern battleship for raiding purposes, all these old ships and the convoys they guard are easy prey. The "R's", in their present state, would be floating coffins. In order to justify the use of "R's" for convoy work in the Indian and Pacific Oceans it would be necessary to have one or two fast heavy units, which would prevent the enemy from detaching individual heavy raiders without fear of punishment. We should inculcate the true principles of naval strategy, one of which is certainly to cope with a superior force by using a small number of the best fast ships.

3. The potency of the dispositions I ventured to suggest in my minute is illustrated by the Admiralty's own extraordinary concern about the *Tirpitz. Tirpitz* is doing to us exactly what a K.G.V. in the Indian Ocean would do to the Japanese Navy. It exercises a vague general fear and menaces all points at once. It appears, and disappears, causing immediate reactions and perturbations on the other side.

4. The fact that the Admiralty consider that three *K.G.V.'s* must be used to contain *Tirpitz* is a serious reflection upon the design of our latest ships, which, through being under-gunned and weakened by hangars in the middle of their citadels, are evidently judged unfit to fight their opposite number in a single-ship action. But, after making allowances for this, I cannot feel convinced that the proposal to retain three *K.G.V.'s* in the Atlantic is sound, having regard (*a*) to the American dispositions which may now be counted upon, and (*b*) to the proved power of aircraft-carriers

to slow down a ship like *Tirpitz* if she were loose. It also seems unlikely that *Tirpitz* will be withdrawn from the Baltic while the Russian Fleet remains in being; and, further, the fate of *Bismarck* and all her supply ships must surely be present in the German mind. How foolish they would be to send her out, when by staying where she is she contains the three strongest and newest battleships we have, and rules the Baltic as well! I feel therefore that an excessive provision is being made in the Atlantic, and one which is certainly incomparably more lavish than anything we have been able to indulge in so far in this war.

5. The best use that could be made of the "R's" would be even at this late date to have them rearmoured against aircraft attack and used as a slow-moving squadron, which could regain for us the power to move through the Mediterranean and defend Malta indefinitely.

6. I must add that I cannot feel that Japan will face the combination now forming against her of the United States, Great Britain, and Russia, while already preoccupied in China. It is very likely she will negotiate with the United States for at least three months without making any further aggressive move or joining the Axis actively. Nothing would increase her hesitation more than the appearance of the force I mentioned, and above all a *K.G.V.* This might indeed be a decisive deterrent.

Appendix F, Book Two

TANKS FOR THE MIDDLE EAST

Prime Minister to Secretary of State for War and   11.VIII.41.
Minister of Supply

Out of 1441 infantry and cruiser tanks with the troops [at home] 391 are "unfit for action." This is far too high, and I am sure it is capable of reduction if something like the arrangements for repair introduced into the air force last year could be provided.

Will you please consult together and make me a proposal for the more prompt handling of these repairs. The number of tanks out of action ought never to exceed ten per cent of those in this country. More especially is this the case in view of the period of maximum preparedness which is now approaching.

Prime Minister to Secretary of State for War   19.VIII.41.

Your minute of July 15, 1941 [about repair of tanks at home], states a number of requirements which, if they could all be met, would make life too easy. Everything practicable should be done to meet the various desiderata, but the main contribution must be a genuine effort and good management. I am shocked to see that a month later we still have twenty-five per cent of infantry tanks out of order, and that out of 400 cruiser tanks no fewer than 157 are unfit for action. I have no doubt there can be made plenty of explanations for such a failure, but failure it remains none the less.

Pray do not let it be thought that you are satisfied with such a result. If you simply take up the attitude of defending it there will be no hope of improvement.

Prime Minister to Secretary of State for Air   27.VIII.41.

Your minute of August 6 shows that the most promising weapon at present in sight for aerial attack on tanks is the Jefferis bomb, and I am pleased to note that you have ordered fifty thousand of these.

As I understand these weapons go into the ordinary light bomb container, it should be possible to put them into use at once, and I should favour postponing further manufacture of the sticky bomb and a part of the bombard ammunition in order to obtain immediately an adequate supply of these aerial bombs. It seems likely that when the tactics have been worked out and the pilots have had some practice, considerable improvement in the chance of hitting, as shown in the first trials, may be expected. We should get immediately a large supply of dummy bombs and give a selected group of pilots plenty of practice against ground targets. If the expected improvement is achieved, we should investigate at once the possibility of sending through the Mediterranean at an early date in a warship an adequate supply with the pilots who have practised with the dummy bombs.

It might also be well to consider whether the Russians might be able to improvise these bombs rapidly, in which case they should be given full details.

* * *

(*Action this day.*)
Prime Minister to Minister of Supply and C.I.G.S.   27.VIII.41.

We ought to try sometimes to look ahead. The Germans turned up in Libya with six-pounder guns in their tanks, yet I suppose it would have been reasonable for us to have imagined they would do something to break up the ordinary "I" tank. This had baffled the Italians at Bardia, etc. The Germans had specimens of it in their possession taken at Dunkirk, also some cruiser tanks, so it was not difficult for them to prepare weapons which would defeat our tanks.

2. I now try to look ahead for our side, to have Alpine troops formed for Norway, and to have the power to spring a surprise in tanks on the enemy in Libya. Instantly everyone tries to make difficulties, so that in three or four months, should it be desired to take action, we shall be confronted with the usual helpless negation. We ought to have it in our power to place at least one hundred A. 22's in a desert-worthy condition in the field by January or February at latest. To do this it is necessary to get over all the minor modifications for desert warfare. Why should this not go forward at the same time as the final improvements are being made in the tank itself? The people in Egypt will never believe the tank is desert-worthy unless they have it tried on the spot. The various improvements made at home can be flown out or explained by telegram. Instead of this, we are to wait till the beginning of 1942, and then send two tanks out, which are to be then sniffed at and experimented with, and a whole new lot of faults found by the Nile authorities.

3. What I have asked is this: That two of these tanks shall go out now with a certain number of skilled men and spare parts; that these men shall be kept in close touch with the improvements made here, and shall at the same time deal with the "desert-worthy" aspect, imparting to us the result of any improvements they make. I would have been willing to have allowed the double

process to go on at home, but if it is going to take till 1942 anyhow at home, and then have to be gone over all again in the Middle East, I feel that my original thought was right.

Pray let me have some help in this matter.

Where is it supposed these tanks will fight in the spring of 1942, except in the Middle East?

[These two Churchill tanks were shipped to the Middle East at the end of September, and arrived on December 12. General Auchinleck had promised to give his personal attention to their tests in the Desert, and I was therefore shocked to receive the following telegram from him on the 25th:]

"These vehicles were stowed on forward well-deck, unsheeted and unlocked. In consequence vehicles were exposed to sea-water, and when received both tanks had water on floors and showed rust markings nine inches up the walls.

"Considerable damage to electrical and wireless gear, requiring fourteen days' expert attention before tanks can run. Method of dispatch and stowage most unsatisfactory. All American tanks are dispatched with all crevices and doors pasted up with masking tape. . . ."

I immediately asked Mr. Justice Singleton to conduct an inquiry. He reported on March 10, 1942: "The case discloses mismanagement to an amazing degree." The tanks had been loaded on the open deck, ungreased, their doors unlocked, and not even covered with waterproof sheets. "The damage," he said, "was caused through their not having been prepared for shipment in the normal way. Much of it could and would have been avoided if the two fitters had accompanied the tanks." This of course was precisely what Lord Beaverbrook and I had asked should be done and what the War Office had ordered. Mr. Justice Singleton said that it was difficult to tell who was responsible, as the General concerned in the War Office was dead. He continued as follows: "The arrangement which had been made was altered under somewhat strange circumstances which it is not easy to follow. The managing director of the firm of manufacturers and the Major-General met at a luncheon party at the Savoy on September 15, when the former asked if it was not possible for his fitters to be sent to the Middle East by air, as they could be usefully employed here and could keep in touch with improvements. The General then instructed the Ministry of Supply to arrange for the two men to be flown to the Middle East rather than that they should waste several weeks on board ship."

No one from the firm of manufacturers even saw the tanks loaded on board. The Ordnance Officer at the port did not go inside either of them and knew nothing of their condition. His staff sergeant entered one and noticed that it was not properly "greased up," but reported the fact to nobody.

[By the time however that the investigation had been finished, the war had swept on, and on June 1, 1942, I minuted to General

Ismay: "Alas I am too busy to chase these rabbits as they deserve, and no one else will do anything."]

* * *

(Action this day.)
Prime Minister to General Ismay   21.X.41.

Please check and point this up for me in time for tonight's meeting:

Clarification is needed about the telegrams from Middle East. General Auchinleck says that the one hundred and fifty tanks which he had expected in September only *arrived* October 4 to 14. Actually they arrived on October 2, or only one day later than he had expected. Twelve days were taken in unloading the whole of these tanks. What happened to them then? We are told they had to be stripped down to be made desert-worthy and have their front axles strengthened. We now know this was not necessary so far as the axles were concerned, and that the desert-worthy additions could all have been executed at the unit in a day or two. We do not know however what Middle East has done. Have they in fact already pulled these tanks to pieces and begun splicing the axles? If so the three weeks' delay of which they speak may be unavoidable, even though the process was unnecessary. How was it no one went out with the tanks to tell the people out there about them?

2. By other telegrams and discussions it is known that an armoured brigade or division requires to be a month with its new vehicles to fire the guns and perform combined exercises. How far does this apply to the 22d Armoured Brigade, who were fully trained with these very tanks when they went out? I suppose they would say they must have some additional *desert* practice, which seems reasonable.

3. But if these one hundred and fifty tanks only cleared arrival on October 14 and then there is a three weeks' period to make them desert-worthy, this would carry us to November 7. What then happens to the necessary month, or perhaps somewhat shorter period, for them to be practised in the hands of troops and work in the Desert with their commanders? The story we have been told, as now pieced together, does not hold water, even on the revised programme. We have got to find out (1) what has been or is being done mechanically and what is the existing state of each of the hundred and fifty tanks; (2) what changes will be made in their treatment as a result of the War Office telegram about the axles, and will any shortening-up of the date be possible; (3) what about the desert training period of the 22d Armoured Brigade?

Have this all cleaned up and the necessary telegram drafted for my consideration tonight.

Prime Minister to General Ismay   24.XI.41.

Let me have your full report about the remainder of the 1st Armoured Division. When did they arrive, and what is the condition of their tanks? How far are they desert-worthy? What about their axles? How far are they trained? Can anything be done to speed them up or to speed up their unloading?

❋   ❋   ❋

[I print these details to show how difficult it is to get things done even with much power, realised need, and willing helpers.]

Appendix G, Book Two

NAVAL DIRECTIVES AND MINUTES
March—December, 1941

NAVAL BUILDING PROGRAMMES

The gun-power of our new battleships had always interested me deeply. In Volume I, I have summarised my discussions with the Admiralty in 1937, when the design of the *King George V* class was under review.[38] These five ships were in my view gravely undergunned. The four ships of the *Lion* class which were to follow them were intended to mount the sixteen-inch gun, and the first two had been actually laid down before the outbreak of war, but all work on them had been stopped in October, 1939. I reverted to this subject in my directive of March 27, 1941, where I stated my general views on our future naval building programme, in the light of the many other pressing commitments which clamoured for attention.

NAVAL PROGRAMME, 1941
Directive by the Minister of Defence

27.III.41.

Naval programmes have been continuous throughout the war, all slips being filled as vacated. It is nevertheless convenient at this time of year that the Admiralty should present their present needs of new construction in a general list and obtain Cabinet sanction for their policy.

2. No one can doubt that the construction of small craft for anti-U-boat warfare, for minesweeping, for combating the E-boats, and for assault landings should proceed to the full extent of our resources. It is essential however that simplicity of design, speed of construction, and the largest possible numbers should govern the whole of this small-craft programme. The construction of destroyers should in no case exceed fifteen months. I understand from the Controller that, apart from enemy action or strikes, he can guarantee this in respect of the forty now projected.

3. We cannot at the present time contemplate any construction of heavy ships that cannot be completed in 1942. This rules out further progress upon the *Lion* and *Temeraire* and the laying-

[38] See Volume I, Book One, Chapter 9.

down of *Conqueror* and *Thunderer*. It also makes it impossible to begin the four heavy cruisers contemplated in the programme of 1940. Work will therefore be limited to completing the three remaining battleships of the *King George V* class and to building the three light cruisers of the 1941 programme, all of which, it is understood, can be completed before the end of 1942. An additional monitor, for which the guns are already available, can also be completed before the end of 1942.

4. The need of concentrating labour on merchant repairs and on repairs to the fighting fleet makes it impossible to begin any new aircraft-carriers after *Victorious, Indomitable,* and *Indefatigable* have been completed. Such new aircraft-carriers could not in any case be ready until 1944.

5. The requirements of the Navy in armour-plate can on the above basis be adjusted to meet the needs of the Army tank programme, and can be limited to 16,500 tons in 1941 and 25,000 tons in 1942. No new armour-plate plant need be erected at present.

6. The one exception to the above principles is the *Vanguard,* which can be completed in 1943 and is the only capital ship we can by any means obtain before 1945. As we have the guns and turrets for the *Vanguard,* it is eminently desirable that this vessel should be pressed forward, provided that this can be done within the limits of the armour-plate provision in paragraph 5.

7. Nothing in the above should hinder the work on the drawings and designs of any of the postponed vessels, including especially the new aircraft-carrier.

8. In view of the need to concentrate on repairs, the output of new merchant ships may be reduced from 1,250,000 tons, which is the present target, to 1,100,000 tons in 1942, and we should not at the present time proceed with any merchant vessels which cannot be completed by the end of 1941. It is to the United States building that we must look for relief in 1942.

9. The whole of our heavy ship construction will be reviewed on September 1, 1941, in the light of (*a*) the Battle of the Atlantic, and (*b*) the relation of the United States to the war.

Prime Minister to First Lord, First Sea Lord and   16.VIII.41.
Controller

I am greatly interested in the proposed design of the *Lion* and *Temeraire.* Let me know the exact point which has been reached in the general construction and in the drawings.

2. It is most important not to reproduce in these two ships the faults which are apparent in the five *K.G.V.'s;* namely: (*a*) The retrogression to the fourteen-inch gun from our well-tried fifteen-inch type; and (*b*) the marring of the structure by the provision of the aerodrome amidships. Merely for the sake of having a couple of low quality aircraft, the whole principle of the citadel so well exemplified in the *Nelson* and the *Rodney* has been cast aside.

The space of about forty feet amidships entails a degree of heavy armouring in this vital area, which is improvident having regard to the needs for carrying a lesser protection as far forward and aft as possible. It may well be that one thousand or fifteen hundred tons of armour are misplaced through the opening of this hiatus in the citadel of the ship.

3. I understand, and hope, that the *Lion* and *Temeraire* will carry nine sixteen-inch guns in three triple turrets, with six guns firing directly ahead, and the rear turret on the most forward bearing possible. These three turrets should be grouped together as closely as possible to form the central citadel, comprising funnels and director tower, and covering with the turret and heaviest armour the magazines and vital machinery spaces. If this were done it should be possible to give a six-inch turtle [underwater] deck carried very far forward, if possible to the bow, thus protecting the speed of the ship from bow damage.

4. Although it looked very progressive to be able to fly two aeroplanes off a battleship, the price paid in the rest of the design was altogether excessive. It might however be possible in a ship with a citadel outlined above to arrange to flip off one or two aircraft from the quarterdeck, but no serious sacrifice of design must be made for this. A capital ship of the consequence of the *Lion* or *Temeraire* must depend upon having an aircraft-carrier working with her, or at the very least a cruiser capable of flying off an aircraft. She should on no account be spoiled for the sake of carrying aircraft.

5. I should very much like to see these two ships pressed forward beyond what is at present approved. Before however any final decision is taken upon the design there ought to be a conference of a number of sea officers, including the late and present Commanders-in-Chief, who have served in the *King George V* or *Prince of Wales*. The successful design of the *Arethusa* was evolved from a conference of Admirals convened, at my direction, in the winter of 1911.

Pray let me have your views.

The First Sea Lord confirmed that these ships would mount nine sixteen-inch guns in three triple turrets and that the Commanders-in-Chief had been consulted about the design. He maintained that the aircraft hangars in the *King George V* class did not weaken the citadel. This had to include protection for the machinery spaces, which were enormously increased in these ships as compared with the *Nelsons*.

[The resumption of work on the *Lion* and *Temeraire* was closely considered, but we decided against it for the following reasons: (*a*) The building of turrets would interfere with the production of A.A. equipment and coast-defence gun mountings. (*b*) The requirements for armour would conflict with tank production. (*c*) The demands which these ships would make on our shipyard labour force.

What finally clinched the matter was the fact that there could be no reasonable chance of completing these vessels during the war. They were therefore cancelled.

I was anxious to know how our *King George V* class compared with contemporary American ships.]

Prime Minister to First Sea Lord   1.IX.41.

I cannot help grieving that we have not got the three triple sixteen-inch turrets for the five *K.G.V.'s*. The matter is academic and irretrievable. None the less, as my thought has dwelt on these matters for the last thirty years, I should like to know what is known at the Admiralty about the American ships contemporary to *K.G.V.* Admiral Stark told me that they were three triple turrets of sixteen-inch. When I asked him whether he had not overrun the 35,000-ton limit he said, "No, but they had given up the five hundred tons they used to keep to veer and haul upon."

Please let me have the legend of these American ships as far as you have knowledge of them at the Admiralty.

Let me also know what they do about the hangar, and any advantages in strength and structure possessed by *K.G.V.* to compensate for the loss of gun-power.

[The First Sea Lord replied that the equivalent American ship (U.S.S. *North Carolina*) had a heavier main armament but somewhat lighter secondary armament. The British ship had heavier protection and slightly higher speed. He preferred the British method of carrying two aircraft in hangars amidships as compared with the American practice of providing two exposed catapults on the quarterdeck. The discussion continued with my minute of September 22 and his reply dated October 2:]

COMPARISON BETWEEN U.S.S. "NORTH CAROLINA" AND H.M.S. "KING GEORGE V"

Prime Minister to First Sea Lord, Controller and D.N.C.   22.IX.41.

Naturally, being all for stiff ships, I am very glad we have 1370 tons more armour, and another 790 tons of weight in the hull. The deeper armour belt and hard nose are good. It is very satisfactory to be able to combine this with superior speed, as has been done. I am still not convinced however that the lengthening of the citadel area caused by interpolating the aerodrome amidships instead of aft has not used up a lot of this fine armour without advantage to the "citadel" principle, on which fighting and flotation alike depend. I should like to go further into this on other papers.

2. Our ship is longer, narrower, and deeper than the American. I presume this makes for speed.

3. We have exceeded the treaty limit by 1750 tons, while the Americans with the sixteen-inch guns are either within it or only two hundred tons over it. Can this be true?

4. There is as much to be said for twenty five-inch guns for A.A. and secondary armament as for sixteen 5.25-inch guns; in fact,

some people would prefer more numerous gun positions to deal with multiplied air attacks.

5. It is when we come to compare nine sixteen-inch guns with ten fourteen-inch guns that sorrow rises in the heart, or ought to. Nine sixteen-inch at 2700 pounds per round equals 24,300 pounds. Ten fourteen-inch guns at 1590 pounds equals 15,900 pounds. Difference, 8400 on the broadside.

6. It is interesting to note that the Germans in the *Bismarck* chose four turrets of two fifteen-inch, whereas we went to the other extreme of three turrets, of which two were four-gun, but a smaller gun. The Americans, coming in between the two, may have hit the happy medium, and have as well the biggest punch.

First Sea Lord to Prime Minister   2.X.41.

I attach some further remarks referring paragraph by paragraph to the points you have raised:

The *King George V* arrangement of space amidships for aircraft has been repeated in *Lion* and *Temeraire*. This space, fifty-five feet long gives the impression of a hiatus, but actually involves no hiatus in the citadel below the armoured deck. The space from the fore end of "A" turret to the after end of "Y" turret is completely occupied by magazines, shell-rooms, and propelling machinery, which must be protected by heavy armour. Were the aircraft removed, no armour would become available to be fitted elsewhere.

2. This is confirmed.

3. In *King George V* we set out to build a ship of 35,000 tons standard displacement, but additions were made during construction and some of the estimated weights (principally armament) were not realised. Hence the ship came out 1750 tons heavy.

The American ship may also have come out heavy. But if we were prepared to accept the hull scantling reported and the protection of the American ship, we estimate we could build her to a standard displacement of 35,200 tons.

4. The number of five-inch guns mounted in the American ship are got in at the expense of close-range A.A. weapons.

5. I agree generally. The *King George V* was designed for twelve fourteen-inch guns, but two guns were given up for increased armour protection. It is probable that the rate of fire of the fourteen-inch is slightly greater.

6. *Bismarck's* standard displacement is estimated to be 41,150 tons. It would appear that as soon as the Americans could design a ship they really liked with sixteen-inch guns they went to 45,000 tons in the *Iowa* class.

Appendix H, Book Two

MINISTERIAL APPOINTMENTS FOR YEAR 1941

(Members of the War Cabinet are shown in italics)

Prime Minister and First Lord of the Treasury, Minister of Defence	*Mr. Winston S. Churchill*
Admiralty, First Lord of the	Mr. A. V. Alexander
Agriculture and Fisheries, Minister of	Mr. R. S. Hudson
Air, Secretary of State for	Sir Archibald Sinclair
Aircraft Production, Minister of	(*a*) *Lord Beaverbrook*
	(*b*) Lieut.-Colonel J. T. C. Moore Brabazon (appointed May 1)
Burma, Secretary of State for	Mr. L. S. Amery
Colonies, Secretary of State for the	(*a*) Lord Lloyd (till Feb. 4)
	(*b*) Lord Moyne (appointed Feb. 8)
Dominion Affairs, Secretary of State for	Viscount Cranborne
Economic Warfare, Minister of	Mr. Hugh Dalton
Education, President of the Board of	(*a*) Mr. Herwald Ramsbotham
	(*b*) Mr. R. A. Butler (appointed July 20)
Exchequer, Chancellor of the	*Sir H. Kingsley Wood*
Food, Minister of	Lord Woolton
Foreign Affairs, Secretary of State for	*Mr. Anthony Eden*
Health, Minister of	(*a*) Mr. Malcolm J. MacDonald
	(*b*) Mr. A. E. Brown (appointed Feb. 8)
Home Department, Secretary of State for the; and Home Security, Minister of	Mr. Herbert S. Morrison
India, Secretary of State for	Mr. L. S. Amery
Information, Minister of	(*a*) Mr. A. Duff Cooper
	(*b*) Mr. Brendan Bracken (appointed July 20)
Labour and National Service, Minister of	*Mr. Ernest Bevin*

751

Lancaster, Chancellor of the Duchy of	(a) Lord Hankey (b) Mr. A. Duff Cooper (appointed July 20)

Law Officers:
  Attorney-General
  Lord Advocate
	Sir Donald Somervell
	(a) Mr. T. M. Cooper
	(b) Mr. J. S. C. Reid (appointed June 6)

Solicitor-General Solicitor-General for Scotland	Sir William Jowitt (a) Mr. J. S. C. Reid (b) Sir David King Murray (appointed June 6)
Lord Chancellor	Viscount Simon
Lord President of the Council	*Sir John Anderson*
Lord Privy Seal	*Mr. Clement R. Attlee*
Middle East, Minister of State Resident in the	*Mr. Oliver Lyttelton* (appointed July 1)
Minister of State	*Lord Beaverbrook* (May 1–June 29)
Minister without Portfolio	*Mr. Arthur Greenwood*
Paymaster-General	(a) Viscount Cranborne (b) Lord Hankey (appointed July 20)
Pensions, Minister of	Sir Walter Womersley
Postmaster-General	Mr. W. S. Morrison
Scotland, Secretary of State for	(a) Mr. A. E. Brown (b) Mr. Thomas Johnston (appointed February 8)
Shipping, Minister of [39]	Mr. R. H. Cross (resigned May 1)
Supply, Minister of	(a) Sir Andrew Duncan (b) *Lord Beaverbrook* (appointed June 29)
Trade, President of the Board of	(a) Mr. Oliver Lyttelton (b) Sir Andrew Duncan (appointed June 29)
Transport, Minister of [39]	Lieutenant-Colonel J. T. C. Moore-Brabazon (resigned May 1)
War, Secretary of State for	Captain H. D. R. Margesson
War Transport, Minister of [39]	Lord Leathers (appointed May 1)
Works and Buildings, Minister of	Lord Reith

[39] The office of Minister of Transport was united with that of the Minister of Shipping, and a new office of Minister of War Transport created May 1, 1941.

Index

BOOKS BEHIND THE LINES:

The side of war you will never read about in the history books

Bantam Book Catalog

Here's your up-to-the-minute listing of every book currently available from Bantam.

This easy-to-use catalog is divided into categories and contains over 1400 titles by your favorite authors.

So don't delay—take advantage of this special opportunity to increase your reading pleasure.

Just send us your name and address and 25¢ (to help defray postage and handling costs).

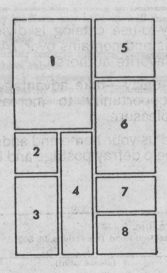

1 President Franklin Delano Roosevelt declaring war on Japan after the surprise attack on Pearl Harbor, December 7, 1941.

2 Winston Churchill during his December 1941 visit to Washington for the historic "war effort" conferences with Roosevelt.

3 Somewhere on the Russo-German war front in 1941 German soldiers march past the burnt-out ruins of homes in a Russian town.

4 General George Marshall during the Roosevelt-Churchill meeting at sea on board the British battleship, *Prince of Wales*.

5 A group of German troops are shown about to make a river crossing in Russia in a photograph passed by the German censor.

6 This photograph shows American ships going up in smoke and flame after the attack on Pearl Harbor on December 7, 1941.

7 Japanese Ambassador Kichisaburo and Secretary of State Cordell Hull leave for a meeting with Roosevelt at the White House.

8 Taken at very close range, this photograph shows a British tanker about to sink after a successful German torpedo attack.